D1189702

SPEAK, SILENCE

BY THE SAME AUTHOR

Jean Rhys (Lives of Modern Women)
Jean Rhys: Life and Work
The Double Bond: Primo Levi, a Biography
Life Writing (with Sally Cline)

The Story of My Life: refugees writing in Oxford (ed.)
Lyla and Majnon: Poems of Hasan Bamyani (transl. and ed.)
See How I Land: Oxford poets and exiled writers (ed., et al.)
Writers' and Artists' Companions (ed., with Sally Cline)
Echoes of a Lost Voice: Encounters with Primo Levi (ed.)
by Gabriella Poli and Giorgio Calcagno

SPEAK, SILENCE

In Search of W. G. Sebald

CAROLE ANGIER

BLOOMSBURY CIRCUS
LONDON · OXFORD · NEW YORK · NEW DELHI · SYDNEY

Bloomsbury Circus
Bloomsbury Publishing Plc
50 Bedford Square, London, WC1B 3DP, UK
29 Earlsfort Terrace, Dublin 2, Ireland

BLOOMSBURY, BLOOMSBURY CIRCUS and the Bloomsbury Circus logo are trademarks
of Bloomsbury Publishing Plc

First published in Great Britain 2021

Copyright © Carole Angier, 2021

Carole Angier has asserted her right under the Copyright, Designs and Patents Act, 1988,
to be identified as Author of this work

For legal purposes the Acknowledgements on p. 451
constitute an extension of this copyright page

All rights reserved. No part of this publication may be reproduced or transmitted in any form or by
any means, electronic or mechanical, including photocopying, recording, or any information storage or
retrieval system, without prior permission in writing from the publishers

Bloomsbury Publishing Plc does not have any control over, or responsibility for, any third-party websites
referred to in this book. All internet addresses given in this book were correct at the time of going to
press. The author and publisher regret any inconvenience caused if addresses have changed or sites have
ceased to exist, but can accept no responsibility for any such changes

A catalogue record for this book is available from the British Library

ISBN: HB: 978-1-5266-3479-5; EBOOK: 978-1-5266-3478-8; EPDF: 978-1-5266-4535-7

2 4 6 8 10 9 7 5 3 1

Typeset by Newgen KnowledgeWorks Pvt. Ltd., Chennai, India
Printed and bound in Great Britain by CPI Group (UK) Ltd, Croydon CRO 4YY

To find out more about our authors and books visit www.bloomsbury.com
and sign up for our newsletters

Contents

Preface

Biography is always a matter of joining holes together, like a net, for reasons that W. G. Sebald's own work explores: the fallibility of memory, the death or disappearance of witnesses, the dubious role of the narrator. All these reasons must exercise any biographer. But Sebald's biographer more than most. For the holes in the net of this story are many.

The central absence is his family life, because his widow wishes to keep this private. Without her permission, his words from privately held sources, such as certain letters, cannot be quoted, only paraphrased. Even his published words, in books and interviews, can be quoted only within the limits laid down by the law.

There are other gaps as well. For instance, I shall write about Sebald's four great prose books, but less about his academic writing and his poetry. There are excellent books on both by the scholar Uwe Schütte;[1] so far they are available only in German, but I hope one day we will have them in English.

There are gaps too about an important friendship and about Sebald's work with his last English editor, because both the friend and the editor preferred not to speak to me.[2] I regret these, but not as much as the last and greatest silence, which takes us back to the first. It is the question why, despite a long and loyal marriage, despite devotion to his daughter, he was always alone. His books are so full of this aloneness that some critics scoff at it – why is every street, every landscape, so improbably empty? But really it was no laughing matter. Like his pessimism – which critics with more fortunate dispositions also question – his essential solitude was with him for most of his life. It co-existed with his charm, his humour, his deep empathy, but it could leap out at any moment and fix him in its icy grip. When he was young it leapt out rarely, with the closest friends and relatives of his youth not at all, but as time went on it took him over more and more. So that he felt for many years – the years of his writing – deeply alone, and the people he loved must have felt alone as well.

Why on earth, with these limitations, did I persist? I persisted because W. G. Sebald is the most exquisite writer I know; because I accept his widow's right to protect her privacy and his, but not to stop any enquiry whatsoever into the roots of his writing; because I am as stubborn as the next person. But the main reason I would not give up writing this book is a limitation of my own.

Readers of Sebald increasingly agree that it is wrong to see the Jewish and German tragedy of the Holocaust as the sole focus of his work: the darkness of his vision extends much further, to the whole of human history, to nature itself. That is true. But here is my limitation: I am the daughter of Jewish refugees from Nazism. It was the fact that Sebald was the German writer who most deeply took on the burden of German responsibility for the Holocaust that first drew me to him; and it is still one of the things that most amaze and move me about his work. He didn't want to be labelled a 'Holocaust writer' and I don't call him one here. But though the Holocaust was far from the only tragedy he perceived, it was *his* tragedy, as a German, the son of a father who had fought in Hitler's army without question. It was also my tragedy, as the daughter of Viennese Jews who had barely escaped with their lives. I think it is right to see the Holocaust as central to his work. But if I make it too central, that is why.

W. G. Sebald is famous for many things apart from the sheer quality of his prose, and for identifying more powerfully with Germany's victims than any other German writer. What he is most famous for is that his books are uncategorisable. Are they fiction or non-fiction? Are they travel writing, essays, books of history or natural history, biography, autobiography, encyclopaedias of arcane facts? His first British publisher, Christopher MacLehose, was so unsure that he listed *The Rings of Saturn* and *Vertigo* under three genres: fiction, travel and history. (He would really have liked to list them under four, but three was the maximum allowed.[3]) And no one has been sure ever since. Eventually, scholars and critics – and even publishers and booksellers – accepted something surprising but true: he had invented a new genre, balanced somewhere between fiction and non-fiction. And many younger writers have followed his lead, from Robert Macfarlane in Britain to Teju Cole in the United States and Stephan Wackwitz in Germany, and many more besides. Every great writer creates a new genre, said Walter Benjamin. The twentieth-century writer who best passes that crazy test is W. G. Sebald.[4]

The second most famous thing about him is the main way he achieved this balance between fiction and non-fiction: by placing photographs and documents throughout his work. When you first open a Sebald book it looks like a biography: there are not only photographs of Edward Fitzgerald and Roger Casement, but also of Paul Bereyter and Ambros Adelwarth, and of Jacques Austerlitz on his cover. Or else it looks like autobiography, with photographs of Sebald leaning against a tree in *The Rings of Saturn*, or with his face struck through in a cancelled passport picture in *Vertigo*. And it reads like autobiography too, with the narrator following almost exactly W. G. Sebald's path through life, from birth in a south German village to living in Norfolk and teaching at an English university.

There is no problem with Fitzgerald or Casement, or – as far as the photographs go – with Sebald. And at first there seems no problem about Bereyter or Adelwarth or Austerlitz either. Their photographs bring us closer to them than words – even Sebald's words – can do. The encounter with their flesh-and-blood presence adds something immeasurable to their stories. It is as though we can look, if we can bear it, straight into their eyes.

But then we read the next story, and the next, and we begin to wonder. The stories are so doomed, so fatal, with their obsessive portrayal of suffering, mental and physical: this is beyond mere observation; it is a vision of life, or rather of death. Then you notice too how literary they are, with constant echoes of other writers; and how *Vertigo* is held together by a motif from Kafka, *The Emigrants* by the image of Nabokov.

Those two works, then, are fiction, and so are all the others. There were models for all the characters, from Dr Henry Selwyn to Austerlitz, but they were changed and combined by Sebald into fictional creations. And at this point something strange happens. Those photographs and documents that made them all so real to us – what are we to make of them now? If the characters are fictions, *who are the photographs of*? And suddenly they flip. Where first they created an extraordinary closeness, now they create distance; instead of feeling intensely with the people pictured, we're asking, *Who are you?* Precisely the technique Sebald adopted to make his creations real to us now makes us more aware they're *not* real than if we had simply been left to imagine them, as in a normal novel. This is a circle he cannot escape from, like several others in his life. And my book traps him in it. If you read him without questioning, and are moved – that is his main aim. I remind you of the truth. That is the job of the biographer. It's why writers don't want biographers, and I know Sebald wouldn't want me. But I would say to him, *You're wrong*. You always wanted people to believe your stories. But they will believe them more, not less, when they know the truth.

It is not only the relationship of the subjects and their photos that is a game of smoke and mirrors. It is also the relationship of Sebald and his narrator – and even the relationship of Sebald to his interviewers.

I interviewed him soon after *The Emigrants* was published in Britain. He was kind, gloomy and funny; he told me many things in his excellent English, slowly and seriously, and I believed every word. But doing the research for this book, I saw that I'd been wrong. He had been honest about himself, and shockingly honest about his parents, but about his work he had spun me a tale.[5] Which I published in my interview, and which has been repeated as a fact ever since. So I've made one of the holes in the biographical net myself. That would amuse him, at least.

Note to Readers

W. G. Sebald wrote all his books in German. But as I write in English, and most of my readers will have read Sebald in English, I concentrate on the English versions. I hope this is excusable. He lived and taught in English for nearly forty years, and worked so intensively on his English translations that he effectively created the final versions himself.

Though he hated modern technology, he used the technology of his day: photographs, photocopies, reproductions of art. There are two media as important to him as photography and art, which can't be printed on a page: music and film. Some references to these will be marked by a dagger (†). This symbol leads readers to the companion page to this book on the Bloomsbury website, where they can listen or watch. I have also included links to a few of his key interviews, in case people would like to read them in full. The link is www.bloomsbury. com/speak-silence.

PART I

Beginnings

W. G. Sebald

How far must one go back, Sebald asked in *After Nature*, to find the beginning? And answered: perhaps to the morning of 9 January 1905, when his grandparents drove in an open landau to the nearest town to be married.

That was the beginning of the social being W. G. Sebald – and more, since the grandfather in the poem was his mother's father, Josef Egelhofer, the person he loved most throughout his childhood, perhaps throughout his life. But the origins of the writer may lie elsewhere: not in a source of security and happiness – even a lost one – but in the opposite. As Sebald's sister Gertrud says, 'You only write if you have to.'[1] Sebald had to write. Why? If we could answer that, we might find the beginning.

He grew up, he wrote, with the feeling that there was 'some sort of emptiness somewhere'.[2] Already as a child he thought, *There's something wrong here*. It was connected to his name, Winfried: even as a small boy he felt it wasn't right. (And surely all this makes us think of Austerlitz.) Often he imagined 'a silent catastrophe'.[3] But what was it? No one would tell him.

In fact, there were two silent catastrophes, both of which had happened around the time of his birth: the genocide of the Jews and the bombing of the German cities. These were the silences that demanded to be filled, the secrets he would be driven to explore.

The silence was so complete that for the first eight years of his life in the village of Wertach, and for several more in the small town of Sonthofen, he had no conscious knowledge of either. No one ever spoke of Jews, either at home or at school. Not of the Jews of Europe, or of

Germany, or of Sonthofen itself, where, despite its remoteness on the southern edge of Bavaria, there had been several before the war. Georg Goldberg, for instance, an engineer in the ironworks, whose daughter had left Germany when she was barred from finishing her training as a dentist. And Dr Kurt Weigert, the director of the Sonthofen Hospital, who had been dismissed on racial grounds in 1935. He survived the war, and in 1945 returned to Sonthofen and took up his post in the hospital again. After his death thirty years later, the council erected an official memorial to him in the cemetery. Thus Sonthofen attempted, belatedly, to make amends.[4]

Oberstdorf, where Sebald went to school, was much smaller than Sonthofen, but still had a few Jews. Most were rich retirees who could keep a low profile. For the one working person, however – the dentist, Julius Löwin – there was no hiding. In 1938 the Nazis of Oberstdorf enthusiastically expelled Löwin, together with his wife and son.[5]

Ein Jude weniger! Am 1. August verläßt der Jude L ö w i n , der hier Dentist war, endlich unser schönes Oberstdorf. Die Bevölkerung ist froh, ihn hier nicht mehr sehen zu müssen. Löwin wandert nach Amerika aus und er wird es so machen, wie seine Rassengenossen alle, die draußen über das neue Deutschland jammern. Dabei konnte er jahrelang hier seine Geschäfte machen und wir lassen ihn sogar noch völlig unge= schoren zu seinen Brüdern reisen. Wir sind herzlich froh, daß endlich wieder einer vom „Auserwählten Volke" uns verläßt. Nur ganz wenige Juden wohnen nun noch im Kreis Sonthofen. Ihnen möge Löwins Auszug ein leuchtendes Vorbild sein.

'**One Jew fewer!**' *The* Allgäuer Anzeigeblatt *reports the departure of Julius Löwin and his family from Oberstdorf in August 1938. 'We are sincerely happy that another of the "Chosen People" has finally left us,' it ends. 'There are very few Jews left now in the Sonthofen area. May the Löwins' departure be a shining example to them.*'[6]

The Löwins emigrated to the United States, and so, like Dr Weigert, survived the war. The 'few Jews left' – like the playwright Carl Zuckmayer's mother, for instance – didn't, in fact, follow their example. As it turned out, the wartime mayor of Oberstdorf, and also the *Kreisleiter* (head) of the Sonthofen area, as we'll see, were among the more humane Nazi officials, so they too survived. But the anti-Jewish propaganda was unrelenting, and like all Jews who remained in

Germany, they will have lived the twelve years of the Thousand-Year Reich in fear.

All this, in both Sebald's towns, was buried and forgotten as though it had never existed. He was never even told that his beloved schoolteacher had been dismissed from his post for being a quarter Jewish – which became the story 'Paul Bereyter' in *The Emigrants*. And it wasn't only that Jews were never mentioned. Apart from Dr Weigert, and the few elderly ladies in Oberstdorf, there weren't any left, for obvious reasons; so that Winfried grew up without ever meeting a single Jewish person.[7] So did his sister: 'I never even knew what a Jew was,' she says.

That began to change when he was seventeen, and a film about the concentration camps was shown at his school (as it was at Gertrud's school as well).[8] The plan must have been to have a sober discussion on the subject afterwards, but for Sebald this sudden eruption of death into the classroom, without preparation and after a lifetime of silence, was too much to take in. It was a nice spring afternoon, with a football match afterwards, and he 'didn't know what to do with it', he said.[9] He wasn't the only one: the school friends I spoke to had only vague recollections of the film, if any at all. This breaking of a taboo through the surface of their young lives was too horrifying to assimilate, as anyone who has seen that film can testify, even if they are neither Jewish nor German. For Sebald and his friends it was an early example of something his later work was largely about: a trauma that cannot be registered at the time or remembered afterwards.

But by now it was the early 1960s, and the atmosphere was changing. He and his friends began to talk worriedly together: *What had their fathers done in the war?* And from sixteen or seventeen on Winfried himself began to change. He had always been notably intelligent, but now he began to pull away from his classmates. He became a wide, unorthodox reader, and more and more critical of accepted opinions – beginning with the Catholic religion, the unquestioned authority both at home and at school.

It was probably because of his wide reading, Gertrud thinks, that he began to challenge the conspiracy of silence in the family before she did, though she was three years older. It didn't work. He was too direct, too critical; his father would stubbornly repeat, 'I don't remember,' and it would end in a blazing row. It never did work; Sebald could never get either of his parents to talk about the past.[10] Perhaps if they had, he wouldn't have had to write his books. That is what they come out of, despite the public efforts at 'overcoming the past': the private silence of German families.

And then there was the other secret, about the Germans' own suffering at the end of the war. He would write about this too – again breaking a taboo, since Germans were not supposed to complain, given how much more serious their own crimes had been. But Sebald would speak out against any crime, whoever had committed it.

This silence was even deeper than the first: at least they were shown the film about the camps towards the end of their school years. The devastation of the Allied bombing that fell on Germany between 1942 and 1945 was never mentioned at all. Not only was the suffering too close, still worse was the shame. They were the master race; their land would be cleansed of vermin – and suddenly they were the vermin themselves,[11] living in cellars with rats, scavenging for the same filthy scraps. How could people survive this, how could they bear to remember it? They couldn't. They wiped it out of their memories, and concentrated on making themselves the richest and cleanest country in Europe in record time. Because of what they covered up in Germany, extreme richness and cleanness were suspect to Sebald for the rest of his life.

Wertach was a tiny village in the Alps, and even the nearby towns were too unimportant to target (though a few bombs did fall on Sonthofen in early 1945). Munich, however, was badly hit, and for several years after the war its streets remained littered with rubble. In 1947 Georg Sebald, newly returned from a prisoner-of-war camp in France, took his children to Plattling on the Danube to see his parents. Their journey took them through Munich.[12] Little Winfried had never seen a city before, and he gazed in awe at the tall buildings and the huge piles of rubble between them. At both equally, because his father did not explain, and he knew he shouldn't ask. For a long time afterwards, Sebald said, 'It seemed to me the natural condition of cities: houses between mountains of rubble.'[13] But the memory of that strange city was surely part of the silent catastrophe, which, since no one explained it, he had to imagine.

One of Sebald's best-loved books, Nabokov's *Speak, Memory*,[14] begins: 'The cradle rocks above an abyss, and common sense tells us that our existence is but a brief crack of light between two eternities of darkness.'[15] It continues: 'I know... of a young chronophobiac who experienced something like panic when looking for the first time at homemade movies that had been taken a few weeks before his birth' – in which, of course, he is as absent as if he had already died.

Sebald echoed Nabokov in a letter to his friend Marie, when he sent her a photo of his sister Gertrud and his friend Sepp Willers taken six months or so before he was born. It's outrageous, he told her, they clearly don't miss me.[16] And in *After Nature* he records a more serious glimpse into the eternity of darkness before his birth: an extreme collapse of time.

On 28 August 1943, he wrote, his mother was on her way home from Bamberg, where she had been staying with his father on leave. But during that night hundreds of aircraft flew in to attack Nürnberg. 'Mother,' he went on,

> got no further than
> Fürth. From there she
> saw Nürnberg in flames,
> but cannot recall now
> what the burning town looked like
> or what her feelings were
> at this sight.[17]

He does not explain – he never explains – but this is plainly another case of trauma, unable to be registered or recalled. The first trauma of his own life. For on the same day his mother realised that she was with child, and the child was himself. And years later, in Vienna, when he saw Altdorfer's painting of the city of Sodom on fire,

> I had the strange feeling
> of having seen all of it
> before, and a little later,
> crossing to Floridsdorf
> on the Bridge of Peace,
> I nearly went out of my mind.[18]

Perhaps, like so much in Sebald, this is pure quotation, an echo of Nabokov and no more? But his mother, Rosa, did travel through Nürnberg on 27 (not 28) August, and stay in Fürth; and during the night of 27/28 there *was* a huge air raid on Nürnberg: 1,500 tons of bombs were dropped and thousands of civilians died. It was a cloudless night, and very dark, because there was a new moon, but the firestorms blazed so fiercely that a scarlet light lit up the sky as high as the bombers dropping their loads.[19] Rosa told the story many times to her children, and it was certainly true. The only detail that Sebald changed was the fact that he and his mother were not alone, since Gertrud, aged three, was with them. She doesn't remember the scene, only her mother's story of it; and, rationally, the same was true of her unborn brother. Except that he was W. G. Sebald, and his imagination would be soaked in the blood of that war. Whatever was true of the handful of cells he was in August 1943, it *would* nearly drive him out of his mind.

Fire starts for Sebald in Nürnberg, the city whose patron saint is St Sebaldus. From there it will rage through many of his books – through *Vertigo*, which ends with the Great Fire of London, to *The Rings of Saturn* and the book after it, which he would never publish. And through many of his interviews as well, in which he said that fire was the most terrifying thing.[20] This goes back to his childhood in a village in which many of the buildings were still made of wood, and which had burned to the ground several times. But it goes back even more to the two horrors that he was driven to write about. For they are united by silence afterwards, but at the time by fire: the furnaces of the extermination camps, the firestorms of the cities.

After Nature records a moment even earlier than the Nabokovian one: on the day before, 26 August. Rosa and Georg Sebald are still in Bamberg, visiting the botanical gardens. The poet possesses a photograph of them, standing beside a pond on which a swan and its reflection calmly sail. It's astonishing, he says, how relaxed his parents seem, as he would never see them in his own lifetime.

In 2001 he gave another photograph taken on that visit to an interviewer. We see the parents' light-heartedness, even though Georg will soon be sent to France and may not survive. But we don't see the pond or the swan. Or many other things. We don't see the past in Bamberg, in which there was a sizeable Jewish population, we don't see the present in the extermination camps or the burning cities, and we don't see the poet. But they are all there.[21]

Finally there was the normal beginning: his birth, on Ascension Day, 18 May 1944. The date runs through his work like a thread through a maze. Near the end of *The Emigrants*, for instance, in the Jewish cemetery of Bad Kissingen, we see the grave of Meier Stern, who died on 18 May 1889; in Sebald's imagination he morphs into Max Stern, who on the last page of *Austerlitz* has scratched his name on the wall of Fort IX near Kaunas, where more than 30,000 deportees died: *Max Stern, Paris, 18.5.44*. A main model for Jacques Austerlitz was born on 17 May, the day before; so was the mother of a main model for Max Ferber in *The Emigrants*, and Sebald gave the date to Ferber's mother Luisa for her birthday. And so it goes on.

Sebald knew perfectly well that such coincidences mean nothing in sober reality, or can't be shown to. [22] But what matters about an idea, he said, is its beauty of form and its power to move; and also its mystery, which as E. M. Forster said, was the most important ingredient in a novel.[23] In other words, coincidence worked in art, which is what mattered most to him. But coincidences were important to him in life as well, and later became almost an obsession. They show that things hang together in ways we don't understand, he said, and we should pay attention to them; at the very least they answer our need to make 'some sort of sense, which there isn't, as we all know'.[24]

The coincidence of events is one of the main movers of Sebald's imagination; and his birth on 18 May 1944 is the most important and appalling example, because of what was happening in the German Reich at the same time. If there is one thing that drove W. G. Sebald to write – even more than the silences, even more than the insane memory of seeing Nürnberg on fire from the womb – it was this. He said it over and over again, in different ways: just as he was born in a remote corner of the Alps untouched by the war, and was being pushed in his pram through the flowery fields, Kafka's sister was being deported to Auschwitz, along with hundreds of thousands of people from Hungary, from Corfu, from the whole of the Mediterranean.[25] 'It is the simultaneity of a blissful childhood and these horrific events that now strikes me as quite incomprehensible,' he said. 'I know now that these things cast a very long shadow over my life.'[26] And, 'It seems to me … unjust, so to speak, that I was allowed to grow up in this peaceful valley; and I don't really know how I deserved it.'[27]

When I hear these words I think that that is how all Germans should feel; indeed, how all people should feel who live through a terrible time, and could have done something, or couldn't have done anything, like the infant Winfried in his pram. But he is the only one, or the only one I know, who suffered from survivor's guilt, though he had nothing to do with it at all.

For his first few years Winfried lived in a stable, secure little family. It consisted of his grandparents, his mother and his sister, and it suited him perfectly. Then in early 1947 came a shock: a stranger turned up 'and claimed to be my father'.[28]

He spoke about this shock often. He was not brought up by his father, he would say,[29] who returned when he was three, and came home only on Sundays for another three years. For the first six years of his life his grandfather was his father, and so he remained until he died, six years later.

This key early story of the writer's life is already partly fiction: in fact, for the first year after Georg's return he worked at his old metal-working trade in Wertach, before finding a better-paid job in Sonthofen.[30] But the emotional meaning of the tale – as usual with Sebald – is entirely true. He never accepted his father. In his teens and twenties he would add militarism and Nazism to his charges. But that was later and more complicated. From the day Georg came home, he was an old-fashioned, authoritarian father, and Winfried would have none of him. The celebratory photograph taken a few months after his return makes this almost comically plain. The parents are decked out in their Sunday best, sent by Rosa's sisters all the way from America, the children in the prettiest things their mother had made. Gertrud is happy to have a father, but just look at little Winfried.

He was not alone. Many late-returned fathers had difficulty with their children, which played its part in the rebellion of the second generation. It is a sad truth, says Gertrud, that the families who did best after the war were often the ones in which the fathers did not come home.

Then there was the other side of the coin: Winfried's relationship with his grandfather. Sebald spoke about this almost as often as about coincidence. He spent his childhood in the care of his grandfather, he said: 'I learned everything from him and still think of him every day.'[31] His grandfather taught him to read and to love stories. Two of his greatest passions, for nature and for walking, came from his grandfather; he preserved his grandfather in his swinging walk, in his care for plants and animals, in the moustache he grew from the age of nineteen, in the way he checked the sky when he stepped outside. And perhaps he preserved him in his humour too, because Josef Egelhofer loved to tell his grandchildren tall tales with a straight face: that a lorry was coming to bring the holes for the Emmentaler, that they should go and buy him ten pfennigs' worth of seeds for pins.

His grandfather was 'an exceptionally kind man', Sebald said. 'As a boy I felt protected. His death when I was twelve wasn't something I ever quite got over.'[32] His interest in death and the dead came from 'that moment of losing someone you couldn't really afford to lose'. A great deal changed for him then, including his health: 'I broke out in a skin disease right after his death, which lasted for years.' In fact, it lasted on and off for his whole life. To the journalist Maria Alvarez he said that when his grandfather died, 'This huge hole entered my universe. It's now forty-five years hence, and I still miss the man.'[33] His voice, Alvarez noted, had 'thickened just a little'. Even though he was fifty-seven years old, and had lost his grandfather forty-five years before.

There is something extraordinary here. Their grandfather was the most important person in their childhood, Gertrud agrees. His gentleness stood in sharp contrast to Georg's strictness. But many boys have strict fathers; and Gertrud is certain that Georg's discipline never went beyond the shouts and slaps that were normal for the time. Sebald himself, despite his tendency to tell dramatic tales, never told any about his father, and despite his tendency to gloom, said there was nothing 'evidently terrible' in his childhood: 'I'm a perfectly normal case.'[34] I think we can believe him. All it takes for things to go wrong, someone once told me, is for a sensitive child to be born into a simple family.[35] This was the last beginning: that Winfried was a sensitive boy. And his grandfather knew it. He called his small grandson 'Mändle', 'little man', and teased him about his thinness: 'If you go on like this,' he said, 'you'll be able to get changed behind a broom handle.'[36]

Winfried with his grandfather, 1947/8.

I called this the last beginning, because Josef Egelhofer died when Winfried was twelve. But in fact there was one more, which had happened seven years before. I place it last in this dubious list (I admit it's dubious, for who can really tell where anything began, most of all the mind of a writer, even though it's the one thing I want to know?) because it is the most mysterious. Sebald spoke of it to the journalist Arthur Lubow in August 2001, four months before his car veered across a road and smashed against a lorry. They were looking through a family album from 1933, when he pointed to a photograph his father had taken of a dead young man lying on a bier, his unseeing eyes staring upward. The young man was a fellow soldier of Georg's, Gertrud remembers, and he was very pale and beautiful. Seeing this picture for the first time at five years old, Sebald said, he 'had a hunch that this is where it all began – a great disaster that had occurred, which I knew nothing about'.[37] Was this the silent catastrophe he felt around him, hidden not in the past, but the future? For the young man had died, his father told them, in a car accident.

2

Dr Henry Selwyn

The first book by W. G. Sebald to reach readers in English was *The Emigrants*.

The two earlier ones, *After Nature* and *Vertigo*, had had only a secret fame¹ among the literati in Germany. *Die Ausgewanderten* was the first to break through to a wider audience there, and the first to be translated.

This was a great piece of luck for us, and for its author. For *The Emigrants* is the Sebald book *par excellence*. First, in its subject: three of its four stories are about Jews or part-Jews who have been driven from their countries, two of them from Germany. And second, in its inclusion of photos and documents in fictional stories. For the main characters of the two books before and the one after are almost all genuine historical figures. It is *The Emigrants* at the start of our encounter with Sebald and *Austerlitz* at the end that document fictions. *Austerlitz*, however, is sparsely documented: there are only two pictures of Jacques Austerlitz, as a small child and a teenage boy, and no diaries or other records of his passage through the world. By contrast *The Emigrants* is packed with photographs of at least two of its subjects, Paul Bereyter and Ambros Adelwarth; Adelwarth also has his diary and farewell note (*Gone to Ithaca*) and Bereyter a notebook, all of which we see. And though there are no photos of Dr Henry Selwyn, there are many of his garden, and though none of Max Ferber, many of his murdered parents. With *The Emigrants* W. G. Sebald burst upon us complete, so to speak, as he wouldn't have done with any of his other books, as extraordinary as they also are.

Because Sebald's fame had been so secret, no other critic grabbed *The Emigrants*, and the *Spectator* sent it to me to review. I opened it with mild interest: who *was* W. G. Sebald? And before I knew what had happened I was at the end of the first story, rubbing my eyes like someone waking from a dream.

I rushed through the others without stopping, as though they might escape if I put the book down. Each was as strange and beautiful as the first. When I closed the cover on the last story late that night I was like someone in love – elated, longing to tell the world about this marvellous writer only I knew. Over the next few weeks and months I discovered that readers all over the English-speaking world felt the same.

Later I found in *Austerlitz* two ideals of art: the rapid watercolour sketch, like Turner's *Funeral at Lausanne*, and the account by Austerlitz's teacher André Hilary of the final day of the battle of Austerlitz, which, though it went on for hours, was still too short, because 'it would take an endless length of time to describe the events of such a day properly, in some inconceivably complex form recording who had perished, who survived, and exactly where and how'.[2] 'Dr Henry Selwyn' is like Turner's watercolour sketch. After it, each story in *The Emigrants* is longer than the last, and *The Rings of Saturn* longer again, until in *Austerlitz* itself we arrive at the 'inconceivably complex form' of Hilary's ideal. All are supreme works of art, but 'Dr Henry Selwyn' still astounds me the most, for the way it distils in its twenty short pages the essence of Sebald's vision.

From the beginning, mystery is at its heart. The windows of Dr Selwyn's house are like dark mirrors through which no one could see in or out; it reminds the narrator of a chateau he'd once seen in France, in front of which 'two crazy brothers' had built a false façade of the palace of Versailles. In other words, this is not a normal house, or even perhaps a real one. And so it continues. The garden is a neglected wilderness, the bathroom of the flat the narrator and his wife will live in is an extraordinary contraption 'on cast-iron columns and accessible only via a footbridge'.[3] The flat itself is reached via a dark stairwell from which hidden passageways once ran behind the walls, so that the owners of the house did not have to see the servants carrying their burdens up and down. We are in a dream or nightmare world, in which the peace and beauty that attract the narrator shimmer with something else behind them.

Then we meet Dr Selwyn, who is lying on the ground, counting blades of grass. He too – he especially – is mysterious. He is clearly the owner of Prior's Gate but says that his wife Elli owns it now. He is tall and broad-shouldered, but seems short; his thoughts, he tells the narrator, grow vaguer every day and at the same time more precise. Clearly there is as much behind Dr Selwyn as behind his house.

It is Elli who shows the narrator and his wife the flat and handles their tenancy. She is a far more down-to-earth person – a factory owner's daughter from Switzerland, who inherited a fortune and is a good businesswoman herself. Yet she too is given to strange comments, remarking that ever since her last tenants painted the bathroom white it has reminded her of a dovecote. On which the narrator makes an even stranger comment: that this observation 'has stuck in my mind to this day as an annihilating verdict on the way we lead our life, though I have not been able to make any change in it'. These sudden glimpses of an abyss – in Dr Selwyn's thoughts, in the narrator's – are almost the most striking strangeness in this story; and they remain so in all the books. This is one of the things that immediately divide Sebald lovers from Sebald sceptics. If something in the hyper-vigilant anxiety of his work strikes a chord with you, you are ready to accept those vertiginous glimpses, and to be moved by the beauty of their expression. If not, probably not.

There is one more inhabitant of Prior's Gate, who is the oddest of all: the maid Elaine, with her shorn hair, whinnying laugh and long grey apron, her alarming collection of dolls and her mysterious activity, since she has never been seen to cook a meal. Nonetheless, she must sometimes do so, since on the one occasion that Dr Selwyn has a guest and invites the narrator and his wife to join them, she wheels in on a serving trolley a supper prepared from the neglected garden. It is during this meal that Dr Selwyn first reveals part of his history: his friendship as a young man with an elderly Alpine guide called Johannes Naegeli, in whose company he felt better than with anyone before or since, including Elli, but which ended with Naegeli's death, when he fell into a crevasse in the Aare glacier in 1914. The news, Dr Selwyn says, plunged him into a deep depression. It was as if he was buried under snow and ice himself.

These images – snow and ice as death and depression, the precious friendship with an elderly man, even Elli's dovecote and Elaine's grey apron – will all recur in other Sebald books. But they make their first appearance here in 'Dr Henry Selwyn', like the appointment in the past that Austerlitz will imagine.

When the four people – Dr Selwyn, his naturalist friend Edwin
Elliott, the narrator and his wife – have finished their meal, served on
a great oak table 'at which thirty people could have been seated', they
adjourn to the drawing room. Now Elaine pushes in another trolley
with a slide projector on it. (These trolleys, and the picture of four
people at a table for thirty, make you laugh out loud on a third or
fourth reading.) And Dr Selwyn shows his tenants slides of his and
Edwin's trip to Crete ten years before. Now the narrator remarks that
one of the shots of Dr Selwyn, with his knee-length shorts and butterfly
net, 'resembled, even in detail, a photograph of Nabokov' he had
clipped from a Swiss magazine: thus laying down the subtle trace that
will connect this story to the others. And further traces too, that will
connect the book to the other books: the view of the Lasithi Plateau,
for instance, is studded with the white sails of wind pumps, which will
return in *The Rings of Saturn*.

After the Cretan slide show, the story moves swiftly to its conclusion.
The narrator's wife buys a house 'on the spur of the moment' and they
move out of Prior's Gate. Dr Selwyn calls on them regularly, bringing
vegetables and herbs from his garden. And one day he asks the narrator
if he is ever homesick. The narrator doesn't know what to reply, but
it doesn't matter. Despite his tweed jacket, despite his perfect English
manners, Dr Selwyn himself, it turns out, is far from home. And he
wants to tell the narrator his story.

In sum it is this: that he was born near Grodno in Lithuania, and
came as a small boy of seven with his family to England. He never
explains why, and never mentions the word *Jewish*, but it is clear from
his real name and his sisters' why they left pogrom-ridden Lithuania in
1899 and ended up in Whitechapel. He tells the narrator of his youth,
of his friendship with Naegeli, of his declining marriage to Elli. The
years of the Second World War and after were a bad time for him, he
says, and in 1960 he gave up his practice and his last ties with 'what they
call the real world'. As he leaves, most unusually he gives the narrator
his hand.

Though he explains so little, we understand. Dr Selwyn has lost his
past and his home, just as Bereyter, Ferber and Austerlitz will do, and
for the same reason. But in his case there is something else as well.
The others remain outsiders and alone. Dr Selwyn married and melted
into English society; for a long time he kept his secret from his wife

and from everyone. His suffering, therefore, is not only about loss, but about betrayal: of his wife, of his Jewish family ('I have never been able to bring myself to sell anything, except perhaps, at one point, my soul'). His house is indeed not real; the façade of which it reminded the narrator so apparently fancifully was instead quite precise. This double loss – both emigration and assimilation – is what shimmers behind the peace and beauty of Prior's Gate, behind the sadness of Dr Selwyn.

Later that summer, when the narrator and his wife come home from a holiday in France, they learn that the doctor has taken his own life with the hunting rifle he never used. When he first heard the news, the narrator says, he got over the shock without great difficulty, but 'certain things … have a way of returning', as he is increasingly aware. This is Sebald's most recurring theme of all in *The Emigrants* and *Austerlitz*: that trauma is unregistered and repressed, but will eventually emerge. And at the end we see it emerge, in the extraordinary, ambivalent image of the release of Johannes Naegeli's body from the ice, seventy-two years after his death. '*And so they are ever returning to us, the dead,*' Sebald wrote: both consolation and renewed desolation, both return and reminder.

*

In late 2014 I walked down the crescent-shaped drive to the front door of Prior's Gate, forty-four years after the narrator and his wife. It wasn't called Prior's Gate and it wasn't in Hingham, as Sebald had written. It's called Abbotsford, and it's in a beautiful small town ten miles from Norwich called Wymondham (pronounced 'Wyndham'). Both names for the house, real and fictional, come from the fact that it is very near the grand, half-ruined Wymondham Abbey, where in 1970 'Dr Henry Selwyn' was churchwarden, and a pillar of the congregation, hosting the annual Abbey fête in Abbotsford's large garden.

The door was opened by Christine, Dr Selwyn's daughter-in-law. It was particularly kind of her to agree to see me, because at first she'd been reluctant; in fact, she had avoided talking about Sebald as much as possible for many years. Eventually she would introduce me to other members of the family, all of whom felt the same. But for today we stayed on safer ground. All I wanted was to see the house and garden.

Christine led me into a large, light hall. In the middle was a vast oak table (yes, Christine said, *the* oak table, from Dr Selwyn's time). On our right a wide staircase curved upwards, and through an open door in front of us I glimpsed the green of the garden. Now I knew why Sebald had loved Abbotsford: it is one of those quiet places he would write about, where time seems to stand still.

We entered the open door, which led to a drawing room – the drawing room of the Cretan slide show long ago, with its great fireplace and the tall mirror above it. Then we went out and walked around, past the kitchen garden, the tennis court, the great cedar tree on the southwest side. All, I said, as Sebald had described! 'Yes,' Christine said, 'apart from two things. First of all, it wasn't at all a wilderness, nature "collapsing beneath the burden we placed upon it". My parents-in-law had always had gardeners, and it was a perfectly civilised place.' She said these last words rather sharply.

The other difference, Christine said, was that none of the photographs was of the Abbotsford garden. Really? I asked. Nothing much had changed, Christine said, I could see for myself. We went back to the kitchen garden and the tennis court, and I peered at the pictures in *The Emigrants*. She was right. Probably Sebald simply hadn't taken photos at the time, or hadn't kept them, so had to find others that were close to what he remembered. As a result, all the photographs of Prior's Gate were as fake as the first one, and not the 'authentic' documents Sebald claimed that most of his photos were.[4] The mystery of the story remained.

Back inside, Christine unlocked a door and led me into a bright, white corridor. 'It used to be incredibly dim and dark in here,' she said, 'with just one light at each end, and yellow vinyl wallpaper, and dark blue lino on the floor. I left the old servants' bells on the wall, I didn't have the heart to get rid of those.'

I looked where she pointed, and there were the bells, just as Sebald had recounted. 'So this was—?' I began. 'Eileen's corridor,' Christine said. '*Eileen?*' I asked. 'That's right,' Christine replied. 'My parents-in-law's maid, whom Sebald called Elaine. This is where she would push her trolley, from the kitchen in the east wing right through to the dining room in the west. It used to take her ages. By the time she got the food to the table it was always cold.'

Christine couldn't show me the Sebalds' flat, which was occupied. So we sat down to talk over a cup of coffee.

'Yes,' Christine said, 'Eileen was almost exactly as Sebald described her; he barely even changed her name.[5] She was a strange, silent creature, perhaps a bit simple. But she was very loyal to my parents-in-law, and they to her.'

'Sebald was always interested in odd, eccentric people,' I said, 'he felt they brought an element of fantasy into life.'

'And made good subjects for satire,' Christine said, very sharply this time. 'Saying her hair was cut like a lunatic's, and she mumbled to herself…'

'Did she?' I asked.

'Sometimes,' Christine replied. 'But he didn't have to say so.' She pushed her chair firmly back from the table and stood up. 'I'll show you where they used to come in,' she said.

We went back out the front door and along the gravelled driveway. 'The Sebalds would turn in here,' Christine said, 'into a small courtyard. Those windows up there were theirs.'

I looked up, almost afraid I might see them looking out. But the windows were blind in the late-afternoon sunshine, like the ones in the story. 'That's where the outside staircase used to be,' Christine said, pointing. 'So there was one?' I asked.

'Yes,' she said, 'we took it down recently, along with the bathroom.'

I looked at her. 'The crazy bathroom Sebald described, on cast-iron columns – surely that was a fantasy?'

'Oh no,' Christine said. 'He exaggerated, as usual – there was no footbridge, only a small landing. But otherwise the bathroom was exactly as he said. It was added when the flat was first built, because there was no indoor bathroom near. It *was* a crazy structure, but it lasted nearly seventy years. You've only just missed it.'

The bathroom was the first surprise. And it was the opposite of what Sebald told us, that it was the minor details he invented. It was a minor detail, but it wasn't invented. What about his other claim, that the main things in the stories were real?[6] How did that fit with 'Dr Henry Selwyn'?

It didn't. Sebald's landlord and friend in Abbotsford *was* a doctor, a naturalist, and a reserved man of old-fashioned courtesy. He was also married to a Swiss wife who was more practical and socially ambitious than himself; he was tall and broad-shouldered but stooped, and he often lay on the grass of his lawn to examine an insect, a plant, perhaps even a blade of grass. And he did, a few years after the Sebalds left Abbotsford, take his own life with a hunting rifle. In other words, he was almost exactly like Dr Henry Selwyn, except in the most important respect. For he not only seemed English; he *was* English, through and through. He was born in Cheshire, not Lithuania, and he didn't have a Jewish bone in his body.

Not long after my visit to Abbotsford, I met two more of his close family, his daughter Esther and her daughter Tessa. And though they, too, were reluctant, they filled in the story of the real Dr Henry Selwyn.[7]

His name was Philip Rhoades Buckton, always known as Rhoades. His father was a clergyman; his mother, Janey Edwards, came from a family who began as farmers and ended as owners of the largest English dairy company, Unigate. There was, accordingly, a good deal of money on that side of the family. Rhoades was born in 1901, which made him nine years younger than Dr Henry Selwyn, and in his late sixties, not seventies, when Sebald knew him. He'd been too young to serve in the First World War like Dr Selwyn, and began his career straight out of medical school. In the meantime, one of Janey's sisters had married a German, who had a niece called Mädi (short for *Mädchen*, girl). Through this family connection Rhoades met Mädi, and Dr Selwyn acquired his Swiss wife.

In 1946, together with his Edwards aunts, Dr Buckton bought Abbotsford, and for over twenty years practised as a humane and much-loved doctor there. He and Mädi didn't live the grand life Sebald gave the Selwyns, but a civilised one. They held musical evenings, at which Mädi played the piano and Rhoades sang in his deep bass voice. He directed Shakespeare in the garden and mystery plays in the Abbey; when he staged Molière's *Le Malade imaginaire*, he translated it himself. He didn't really fit in with the stolid Norfolk gentry. Nonetheless, with his beautiful house, his courtly manner and his Norfolk tweeds, he could seem the local squire. Mädi would have liked that. She hunted, and aspired to join the county set, but Rhoades wasn't interested.

None of his family saw in him the melancholy that Sebald describes in Dr Selwyn. He loved his practice, they say, his children, the church, birds and insects and wildflowers. By the time the Sebalds arrived in 1970 he had retired and his children were grown up and gone. But he still had the rest, especially the birds and insects and wildflowers, which he shared with his friend Ted Ellis, a well-known Norfolk character whom Sebald turned into Edwin Elliott very faithfully. Ted *was* a small, slight man with a scrawny neck and eyes shining with life, and a vast knowledge of the natural world. He and Rhoades made two botanising and entomologising trips together to Crete, on one of which they nearly missed their plane in Athens because Ted had disappeared. He was found just in time on a nearby hillside, collecting flowers.

What the family do recall is that Dr Buckton and his wife, like Dr Selwyn and his, slowly drifted apart. They, too, were very different: Rhoades the dreamer, Mädi the doer. Her mother liked parties, Esther says, her father liked interesting people. Mädi was an extravagantly talented person – a concert-level pianist, a great skater in her youth, a rider, sailor and tennis player. Christine calls her 'a firework'; Esther says she was 'bubbly and exhausting'. Tessa says she was bossy and a good businesswoman, like Elli Selwyn. She was too much for her children, Esther says; and too much, it's clear, for her quiet husband.

No one knows why Rhoades Buckton shot himself. He left no note, and never complained to anyone. But perhaps he did become a bit morose towards the end, Tessa says. The arthritis in his knees had got so bad he could no longer walk around his garden but had to ride round it on his big black bicycle. Mädi was pressing him to leave Abbotsford to their son Stephen. But Rhoades didn't want to lose his home. Christine, who is a doctor herself, adds another reason. Doctors have a different idea of death, she says. We see so much of it, it just seems part of things.

Rhoades Buckton in Crete, 1970, looking like Nabokov with his net
(see The Emigrants, *p. 16).*

Esther, who is now in her eighties, was very close to her father. 'I was devastated by his death,' she told me, 'and I still am.' I remember what Sebald said about talking to people about the past for his books: you can't be certain whether you might not cause some damage.[8] I hope I didn't cause damage to Esther, but I can't be sure. Like her father, she wouldn't complain.

In fact, the whole Buckton family was reluctant to talk to me: not so much because it might cause them damage, but because Sebald already had. This was the first time I came across what I would discover again and again about the models for his fictions: they were all furious. People who find themselves used for art almost always are. But the power of Sebald's stories, their fidelity to their models, and above all the claim to reality implicit in their photographs, made this worse than usual.

Tessa remembered the experience very clearly. A friend rang up and said, Have you seen this new book? It's about your grandfather! Tessa rushed out and bought *The Emigrants*, and was, she told me, 'taken aback', by which she meant appalled. Her grandfather, Mädi, Eileen, were all unmistakeable – but described, it seemed to her, in a horrible way. Her grandfather's marriage was falling apart, he'd had a most peculiar relationship with an older man in his youth… 'He was portrayed as a miserable old git and his wife as a bitch,' Tessa said, their beautiful garden as a derelict wilderness, their house as a symbol of exploitation. Her grandfather was the kindest, most generous man she'd ever known, Sebald was a guest in his house, and what did he do? Snooped around taking notes, and never said a word.

So I started carefully, and asked about Eileen. 'She *was* a bit alarming at first,' Tessa said, 'with her strange laugh, which shook her whole body. But she wasn't really simple, just completely uneducated.' Was she a good cook? I asked. 'Absolutely terrible,' Tessa said. 'We all got food poisoning several times.'

After that she embarked with a will to set the record straight. Rhoades was witty and funny, unlike gloomy Dr Selwyn, with comical names for things, like 'Moloch' for Abbotsford's hopeless old boiler. As for Mädi – Tessa had clashed with her in life, but she was cross on her behalf too. She wasn't the daughter of a factory owner, she said. It was an uncle who ran the family factory; Mädi's father was an academic. As a result she never inherited a fortune, and in fact Rhoades' family was considerably richer. The picture of a hermit married to a materialist was Sebald's invention. Mädi didn't share Rhoades' values, but she was intelligent and educated, his intellectual equal. You wouldn't guess that from Elli Selwyn.

Curiously, Sebald's main invention, the element of Jewishness, had more to do with Mädi than Rhoades as well: one of her grandmothers was half Jewish, which made Mädi herself an eighth. She never mentioned this, and when Tessa once asked her about it, she pretended not to hear. She would have laughed heartily at the idea of anyone thinking her husband a Jew from Grodno. She was still alive when *The Emigrants* was published in 1996, and Tessa showed it to her one day on the terrace at Abbotsford. Mädi leafed through the book for a while, then handed it back with a dismissive wave. 'That's not me,' she said.

None of the Bucktons minded the Jewish part of the story. I still hear Esther's sad voice when we spoke of this. 'We have many close Jewish friends,' she said, 'and I don't mind Sebald's using my father for a Jewish character. What I do mind is that he used his suicide.'

It wasn't only in fiction that Sebald made Rhoades Buckton into a Jewish character. It was also outside it, especially in our interview. 'Dr Selwyn,' he'd said,

> …. told me about Grodno sooner than I say in the story, but very cursorily. The first time I thought, *This is not a straight English gentleman*, was at a Christmas party they gave. There was this huge living room and a blazing fire, and one very incongruous lady.
> Dr Selwyn introduced her as his sister from Tel Aviv. And of course then I knew.[9]

I believed him implicitly, and so did other people. One of them was the writer Will Self, who gave the annual W. G. Sebald lecture in 2010. Tessa went to it, and was astonished to hear Self say that Dr Selwyn was based on a 'real Jewish émigré'. She asked him where he'd got this information from, since she happened to know it wasn't true. And Self referred her to my interview.

That was my first encounter with a question that would haunt my research: *what was Sebald doing in his interviews?* He had claimed that the model for Dr Selwyn was a real Jewish emigré, who had really told him about coming from Grodno ('sooner than I say in the story' – now that was a convincing touch!). But could he really have forgotten the true inhabitants of Abbotsford, whom he had described in such accurate detail? And who was that other person, with the sister in Tel Aviv? Had Sebald imported him from some other encounter, or just made him up? Well, it didn't matter. Real or invented, he was another element stirred into the mix, and the mix was fiction. Perhaps Sebald could forget that sometimes. But I couldn't believe he had forgotten Rhoades Buckton. So what on earth was he up to?

I can see only one answer: that he wanted readers to believe his story, and used me to confirm it. He wanted us to believe that he had known a mysteriously suffering Englishman who turned out to be a Jew. If he wasn't a Jew, it would be a quite different story.

After our interview Tessa's husband Jonathan joined us, and we went out for lunch together. They teased me about the way Sebald had tricked me into convincing people that his suffering Jewish character was real. Then Tessa looked serious.

'But you're going to tell everyone he wasn't,' she said.

'Yes,' I said. 'So I'll upset the point of the story.'

'But the real problem,' Jonathan said, 'is the photographs. They're all fakes, aren't they? They can't be of the people they say they are. That's the last thing anyone should suggest about the Holocaust, isn't it – that anything about it could be fake?'

'He did it,' I said, 'for the opposite reason – to make readers feel these people were real.'

'But it doesn't work in the end, does it?' Tessa said.

'No,' I replied. 'I suppose it doesn't.'

That was the first time I had to admit to this doubt, because other people had confirmed it. No one had wanted to make us face the reality of what had happened more than Sebald. Yet here I was, planning to show how in his very eagerness he had almost provided a foothold for Holocaust deniers. How had he achieved this? How had I? I felt his vertigo swirl around me, as it would often do over the next few years. I would either find a solution, or I would have to live with it. I already guessed which it would be.

PART II
Winfried

3

Wertach, 1944–52

In the lean days after the war, nothing was ever thrown away. Rosa Sebald cut down her father's old uniforms to make her children's clothes; every scrap of material that was left she tied into bunches, to be turned into rag rugs for the floor. And when packages began to arrive from her sisters and brother in America, she would never cut the string or tear the wrapping paper. She would smooth out the paper, untie the string and add it to the ball she'd already made, and carefully store both away in a drawer.

Every morning, two-year-old Winfried would fetch the ball from the drawer, crawl under the kitchen table, and wind the string around the legs to make a nest. Every evening Rosa would patiently unwind the string and put it back in the drawer; and every morning Winfried would take it out and build his nest again.[1]

As long as they lived with his grandparents, Winfried was too small to go anywhere by himself. He and his sister would walk by their mother's side, but when they passed near the Gypsy encampment on the edge of the village, Rosa would clasp Gertrud's hand more tightly and pick Winfried up and carry him. She was often fearful in face of the unknown; later Sebald would say that he probably inherited his anxiety from his mother.[2]

In the safety of her parents' home, however, Rosa was strong and competent, leading her little family through the deprivations of wartime and after. Her mother Theresia was often ill and unable to help, but her father Josef was the rock on whom she depended. He gathered mushrooms and berries from the woods, and caught frogs to cook their legs; he made the rounds of the farmers and came home with milk, eggs, sometimes even a scrawny old chicken. When the children were ill, Rosa needed no doctor: Josef's knowledge of plants and herbs saw them through. 'Our grandfather was the central person of our childhood,' Gertrud says. Much of this feeling surely came down to them from their mother.

But now came the first big shock of Winfried's life: the return of his father from prisoner-of-war camp in early 1947. Gertrud, who was old enough to understand, shared her mother's excitement when the day finally came. But when their father stepped off the train at Kempten station and came towards them, she was disappointed. Was this small, thin, hollow-faced man really their long-awaited papa? After two years as a POW in starving France, Georg Sebald weighed under fifty kilos – little more than a hundred pounds – and was ill with gastric trouble. Little Winfried noticed something else too, though he wasn't yet three. The only languages he knew were the Allgäu dialect and his grandfather's soft south Swabian accent, but this man spoke quite differently. He seemed to know Rosa and Gertrud, and they seemed to know him. But Winfried had never seen him before, and he didn't even speak their language. From that first moment on Kempten station, Winfried set his face against his father.

Once again, some of this feeling may have come to him from his mother. For after the first joy of having her husband home again, Georg's return was hard for her too. In the years he'd been away she had learned to do without him, and now she lost control overnight. Georg's set ideas included the obedience of his wife, while she in turn had strict notions of bourgeois decorum, which she was determined to impose on him. These battles would continue throughout their lives. But the first and worst clashes happened now, as they jostled to establish their positions, with Josef trying to keep the peace and little Winfried doing his best to undermine it.

One of Georg's new middle-class habits was taking his wife and children on weekly strolls after church, decked out in their Sunday best. The farmers of Wertach found this ridiculous, the grown-up Max Sebald (as he would call himself) would write, and his childhood self had agreed. He hated it all – his parents' pretentious clothes, his own lederhosen that itched unbearably; and already at three, he said, he was as he would remain – rebellious, intractable, with his own ideas about these awful bourgeois affectations. And he expressed his dissent clearly. He would trail along as far behind his parents as he dared, until finally they would stop and wait for him. They would turn around and open their arms wide, but instead of running to them Winfried would stop dead, and not move again until they'd given up and walked on.[3]

Winfried on a hated Sunday walk, aged three.
Georg took the photo.

Soon after Georg's return came another big change: the move from the grandparents' rooms in Number 3 Grüntenseestrasse to a flat at Number 9, above one of Wertach's several inns, the Weinstube Steinlehner.

For Rosa and Georg this was a big step up. They'd had their own home in Bamberg when they were first married, but when war broke out Rosa went home to her parents in Wertach. Now at last she could reclaim her Bamberg possessions, which, as her son would write, included 'living room furniture befitting their station':[4] a sideboard and ornate dresser, a bone-china tea service, which was too precious ever to be used, and a set of expensively bound books that Georg had bought in a moment of aspiration but never read.[5] But they couldn't yet afford a proper bourgeois home, and the flat at Steinlehner's was a makeshift affair. The kitchen had been squeezed in as an afterthought, there was no running water, and the toilet was an earth closet – a seat with a pit beneath. Still, it was a first step, and to some of Winfried's schoolmates it even seemed luxurious.[6]

The two houses were only a short distance apart: from the back door of No. 9 – the one the Sebalds used – you could see No. 3, perhaps a hundred child-steps away. So despite the move, Winfried did not lose his beloved grandfather. Then, after a year, his father found his job with the Sonthofen police, and was no longer at home during the week. For those days, at least, Winfried's life returned to what it had been before.

Gertrud remembers endless games in the living room at Steinlehner's during the long winter afternoons when they were small. She sat at one end of the sofa playing with her dolls' house, her brother at the other end with his model farm, both made by their father; Winfried would bring his animals to visit her dolls and the dolls would repay the compliment. Rosa kept both children immaculately dressed, and now Georg took charge of Winfried's hair. Once a month he took him to the barber to have it cut as short as possible; when he was at home he combed it in the conventional style of the time, sharply parted and slicked down to one side. Winfried resisted as much as he could during these operations, but for as long as he was small, Georg's heavy hand kept him still.

Perfect children, 1947/8.

When Winfried was five and Gertrud not quite eight, death came close for the first time. Rosa's mother Theresia had suffered from heart disease for many years; now her body was filling up with water. One morning in early June of 1949 Gertrud set out on the hundred steps from her back door to the grandparents' house and halfway there saw Josef coming towards her. 'Your grandmother is dead,' he said. She was only sixty-eight. It was a great blow to Rosa, who loved and admired her pious, upright mother, and a blow to Gertrud, who had been close to her when she was less gravely ill. Winfried hardly knew her. Nonetheless, her burial in Wertach's churchyard was a solemn occasion, and that first death must have been an intimation. People could suddenly appear out of nowhere, like his father, and now he knew that they could disappear into nowhere as well.

Soon after this, however, his world started to expand – and like all good things, this came from his grandfather.[7] As Wertach's policeman, Josef Egelhofer had walked for miles around the village every day, checking the papers of vagrants on the roads, breaking up drunken brawls in the inns and chatting with the villagers, all of whom he knew. Now that he was retired, he continued to walk for three or four hours every day, and often he took his grandchildren with him. Sometimes he pulled them around in a special wagon he'd made for them out of a barrel, but mostly he just walked, especially with his small grandson. Now Winfried began to see not just the whole of Wertach, but the fields and hamlets all around – distances of five miles and more, often up steep mountainsides, and double to come home. Perhaps Josef thought of strengthening his skinny little *Mändle*; certainly Winfried would grow into a strong boy, and Max would be an indefatigable walker.

The next great step for Winfried was the same as for all children: he started school. He was away from home all morning – primary school in Germany went from 8 a.m. to 1 p.m. in those days – and in a small village like Wertach he could soon walk the whole way alone. Perhaps it was this prospect of independence, or more likely just a lucky moment, but the six-year-old boy caught by the camera on his first day of school looks happy, even jaunty.

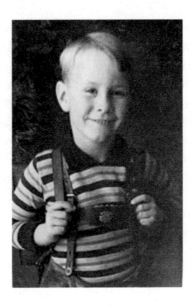

He would spend the next two years in the *Volksschule* in Wertach. The classmates I met more than six decades later kindly gave me a photograph of the first year – very kindly, as the memories they had of Winfried Sebald the author were not happy ones, as we'll see. The teacher, they said, was Master Schorer. And Winfried is the boy with the long thin legs larking about in the front row.

First-year class, Wertach Primary School, 1950–1.

This is the Wertach childhood Max Sebald later described to many interviewers:[8] a happy one, indeed an idyll, a life lived in security and silence, before the invasion of modernity. It's how Gertrud remembers Wertach too. The sun always shone, she says, there was always snow, and it was always Christmas. Max's rosy memories were just as partial, or even more so. But there was also his other side, the one inscribed in *Vertigo:* the dark side that feared the gigantic figures painted on the walls, that was terrified by the barber (or was it his father?), that felt some silent catastrophe had occurred. Gertrud did not see any of this in their early years. But the deep darkness of his later nature cannot have sprung from nowhere halfway through his life, she agrees. 'I think he always suffered,' she says, 'but when he was young he thought that everyone did. It was when he realised, perhaps in his early teens, that most people took life more easily that he began to feel alone with his dark thoughts.'

In Wertach in the late 1940s and early 1950s there was plenty of darkness to be noticed, if you were that way inclined. There was the *Beinhaus*, for instance, the ossuary, where the bones of the long-dead were piled up in the dark. And when the family went to Mass on Sunday morning they would pass the statue of St George on the wall by the church gate. St George, the patron saint of Wertach, stamps on the dragon and plunges his sword into its open mouth. Beneath this gruesome scene two stone plaques list the endless catastrophes that befell Wertach for more than 400 years: plague, fire, war, always fire. Sebald put the whole list into *Vertigo,*[9] with the greatest fire of all happening in the nineteenth century: on 16 April 1893 the entire village burned to the ground, and most of its inhabitants fled. The inscriptions end by noting, as *Vertigo* says, that sixty-eight of Wertach's sons gave their lives for the fatherland in the First World War and 125 in the Second.

Between the two lists of disasters is another plaque, which sums up the world view to which this baleful history naturally led:

> Don't be proud, O Child of Man
> to Death you're only chaff in the wind
> and though your head may wear a crown
> the sand runs out, the hour sounds
> and before a breeze can move a leaf
> your own hour will come to grief.

The punishment, the cutting down to size, the certain doom are all very Allgäu, and very Catholic. It's easy to imagine young Winfried glancing defiantly at this threat as his parents hurry him to Mass, and every word sinking in.

He often recalled another thing: that the Wertach winters were so hard the ground froze, and the dead had to be kept in the woodshed until they could be buried in the spring. So, he said, he grew up with the notion that the dead 'aren't really gone, they just hover somewhere at the perimeter of our lives'.[10] By the time he said this in 1997 it had become a consolatory idea, a redemption of all those he mourned, from his grandfather to the victims of the Holocaust. But it was also the opposite, revenge rather than redemption. 'Where I grew up,' he said in 2001, 'the old still thought the dead needed attending to … If you didn't, they might exact revenge upon the living.'[11] Or, as he also said, 'There were always bodies in the woodshed.'[12] He certainly intended this little English joke. A 'body in the woodshed' is a shameful secret, and to Winfried after the death of his grandfather and the concentration-camps film, to Max always, death was precisely that – a shameful, unjust thing that people didn't talk about.

Even in those early days his nature was becoming clear. For years before, his grandfather had read Grimms' fairy tales to him and his sister out of an old book. Winfried loved these tales and knew every word. By the time he went to school, he had taken over the precious book himself and regularly read the stories to his proud mother. One day, however, Rosa met her friend Fräulein Winter, who taught at the school. 'You know, Rosa,' Fräulein Winter said, 'Winfried can't read.' 'That's not possible!' Rosa cried. 'He reads at home perfectly!' 'That's because he knows those fairy tales by heart,' her friend said. 'Test him and you'll see.'

Rosa tested him, and it was true: presented with a story he didn't know, her son couldn't read. Of course, he learned quickly and easily soon after. But as long as he could seem a perfect reader by using his infallible memory, rather than make mistakes like all the other children, he did so. His mother wanted him to look perfect; he wanted to be perfect. It would make his life hard, but it would never change.

Half a century later he told Marie a similar story from his days in kindergarten. There was a big chest, he said, containing 200 or more tiny wooden animals. There were several models of most kinds, but only one bull. Every morning the children would reach in and take out an animal to play with – and every morning Winfried Sebald would get the bull. This seemed like magic; no one could understand how he did it. Until he had to confess to his mother: each afternoon when the toys were put away he kept the bull hidden in his hand. At the last minute he put it in a particular corner, where the next morning, of course, he instantly found it. This is so unflattering a tale, it's surely true. So is another he told Marie. Later, in his teens, he was a decent skier, like everyone brought up in the Allgäu. But many of his friends were much better than decent; much better, in other words, than he was. So he went off secretly and practised, until he could hold up his head on the slopes with the best of them.

Finally, when he was in his thirties, Gertrud asked him why he didn't write anything other than academic articles, when she knew from his letters that he was a wonderful writer. Because I don't want to write simple things, he said. I only admire writing that can be read on many levels, like Kafka's. If I could ever write like Kafka… Miraculously, he could. But if he wasn't ready to try until he was forty, it was for the old reason. He needed to practise in secret; he needed to bury the treasure himself, so he would know where to find it.

In the years after the war few people could afford to travel. So apart from that one glimpse of Munich when he was three, Winfried's knowledge of the world beyond Wertach wasn't Germany. It was America. For as long as he could remember, everything exciting had come from there: the birthday cards from Aunt Anny with five-dollar bills taped inside, American clothes and toys and chewing gum from all his aunts and uncles, and best of all, tins of sweet pineapple.

In the summer of 1951, when he was seven, four of these exotic American beings descended on Wertach: his Aunt Fanny, his cousins Suzanne and Les, and his great-uncle William. The village was agog; for weeks Winfried's family was the subject of every conversation. The outside world had come in.

Winfried and Les are the two small boys at the front. On the right, in his usual hat and suit, is Josef Egelhofer. Suzanne is the tall girl in the middle, with Gertrud beside her in a matching American outfit. Rosa looks out between them. Behind Suzanne is her mother, Rosa's older sister, Fanny Stehmer. On Suzanne's other side is Grandma Babette, matriarch of the Stehmer clan and sister of Great-Uncle William. The rest are other Stehmers from Kempten and the US.[13]

Max didn't record Winfried's impressions of his Aunt Fanny, who probably spent most of her time in grown-up conversation with Rosa. Suzanne was nine, and a girl, and spent most of *her* time with Gertrud. The two Americans who interested Winfried were his cousin Les and his Great-Uncle William.

Les was a year and a half younger than Winfried. But Fanny's children had been reared on American plenty, unlike their German cousins. Though Winfried was tall like all the Egelhofers, at seven he was much the same size as his five-year-old cousin. The two boys looked startlingly alike, and this made them more alike still – so much so that the family called them twins.

Sixty-five years later we had Facebook, and Les Stehmer was on it. I stared at his picture. The same long face and white moustache, like their grandfather's, a big black dog by his side – he was still Max's twin. Then I found a phone number for him and rang. And the feeling was even stronger, even odder. It was Sebald's voice I heard – the same rich, deep timbre, but rough at the edges, and American.[14]

Les didn't recall being with his cousin Winfried during that long-ago summer in Wertach. He mostly remembered playing on the muck heap on Willers' farm next door and getting into trouble with his mother. This was nothing new, he said: 'I was a bad kid, always in trouble for some damn thing.' We laughed – I often laughed with Les – but I didn't believe he'd done it alone. Winfried was constantly in trouble with his own mother for coming home covered in muck; surely he had introduced his younger cousin to this mother-baiting game. Les had dropped Winfried from his memory. Max had remembered Les, but turned him into a character in a story (and then cut him out again). That was alike too: two ways of being alone.

During our FaceTime conversations it became clear that Les was not a happy man. He and Max were alike in that too. But while Max hid his unhappiness in irony, Les paraded his in a bitter, sardonic humour. Nothing had ever gone right for him, he said. Not Vietnam, where he spent nine months as a medic, because he had 'MBA' after his name – Master of Business Administration – and nobody knew the difference. Not his business, providing technical support to lawyers, 'which meant screwing them as much as they screwed their clients'. Not his marriage, or the girlfriend for whom he left New York after a lifetime ('the last big mistake of my life'), or even his son, to whom he hadn't spoken for years. Not any of the places he'd been to, which were either too hot ('Don't go to India') or too cold ('Don't go to Leeds').

His vicissitudes had reduced him to a pretty rackety level, and he seemed to be living in a beach hut somewhere in Florida. His only pleasures were his dogs, deep-sea fishing and drink. All he told me about a visit he paid to Max in England was that they drank a whole bottle of Jack Daniel's in a single night. When he described his father Joe and great-uncle William to me, he drew their characters in terms of their favourite tipples: Joe, Scotch and beer; William, Scotch and martinis – proper martinis with an olive, *never* Gibsons with a pickled onion – Les did Uncle William's shiver of distaste. That was like Max too; they were both good mimics.

Drink was probably behind Les's failures and bitterness, and not only them. A few months after our last conversation, I rang him again several times, but he never answered. Gertrud confirmed my fears: Les had died of cirrhosis of the liver. He'd made it to seventy-one, fourteen years longer than his cousin and twin. But both small boys in that 1951 photo were now dead. That was the sort of hidden fate in photographs that would fascinate and distress W. G. Sebald.

Les †2017 – Winfried †2001.

The most important visitor that year for Winfried was Great-Uncle William. Winfried called him Uncle William, as everyone did, but he wasn't a blood relation.[15] William was a brother of Fanny's mother-in-law, Babette Stehmer, née Schindele. William was thus William Schindele, born in Gopprechts, a tiny hamlet halfway between Kempten and Sonthofen, in 1880. This made him seventy-one in 1951, just eight years younger than Josef Egelhofer. Perhaps that was a factor in Winfried's interest too, or at any rate no barrier, as it would have been for most seven-year-old boys. But the real reason was different, and once again shows the link between this boy and Max: what most impressed Winfried was Uncle William's language.

In his story about William, 'Ambros Adelwarth', Sebald recorded this deep impression. Uncle Adelwarth had an air of distinction, he wrote, that made all the other adults seem ordinary. And then he began to speak. 'I do not remember what Uncle Adelwarth said,' the narrator says, but he remembers how he said it: in perfect, proper German, without a trace of dialect, and using 'words and turns of phrase the meanings of which I could only guess at'.[16] The elegance of this man's language, its mysteriousness, its effortless ease – these are what impressed the narrator, what certainly impressed Winfried, and what probably gave him the first hint of what he himself wanted to do. *This* was the real world outside Wertach for him: not the rest of Germany, not even America, but words. Beautiful, mysterious words. They were what he wanted, and he wouldn't find them at home.

There's something else we don't see in the family photo of 1951: Rosa was pregnant. This brought the next big change into Winfried's life.

There was a family story among the Egelhofers that would be important for him later on, but for the moment was most important for his mother. It was that grandfather Josef, despite walking for several hours every day, had a congenital heart defect, probably an arrhythmia, which he might well have passed on to his children. And grandmother Theresia had had heart disease too. Rosa always thought she would die young because her mother had, and all four of the Egelhofer children worried about inheriting Josef's arrhythmia. In fact, both Fanny and Rosa did have heart problems, but Josef's, if he had it, didn't kill him, and theirs wouldn't kill them. When it came to delivering this third baby, however, Rosa's heart was not strong enough. She went into the village clinic to receive better care, but the birth was long and difficult, and after it she was ill. For the first six months of Beate's life Rosa spent much of the time in bed, and from then on she had angina pectoris, for which she took digitalis for the rest of her life.

For the older children, and for Georg, this meant a hard time. Rosa was the perfect *Hausfrau* who did everything for the family, and now suddenly she couldn't. And Beate too had suffered from her struggle to be born: she cried for weeks without stopping. Gertrud remembers their father walking the crying baby around for hours on end, their mother appearing in her dressing gown and begging to help, until Josef made her lie down again.

There was a photograph, Gertrud said, that would show me how it was. She hunted through the albums until she found it. She is ten and Winfried is seven; they are sitting in the kitchen at Steinlehner's, and Gertrud is holding baby Beate on her lap. And surely it wasn't just that she'd told me the story: the strain was clear on their young faces.

By now Winfried was living the outdoor life of a country child. 'You went out to the stable and looked after the cows,' Max told his colleague Christopher Bigsby, who interviewed him in 2001.[17] In the summer you went down to the river; in the winter you were out skiing or tobogganing. There was no library or bookshop in Wertach and few books at home, apart from those expensive, unread ones, so 'you grew up without reading', he said. This was patently an exaggeration, but perhaps it was nearly true for his first eight years.

There were no paintings at home either, apart from two Alpine scenes in the living room, pencil drawings of him and his sister, and the obligatory print of Jesus on the Mount of Olives, which every good Catholic family owned, and which hung above his parents' bed. You grew up without music as well, Max told Bigsby: 'Nobody had a gramophone; there was scarcely a radio.' His father had one, however – sent by Aunty Anny from New York, of course – and liked to listen to Bavarian folk tunes on it, complete with yodelling, and operettas like the current sentimental favourite, *Christel the Post Girl*. As a result Winfried loathed both Bavarian folk tunes and operettas, and so would Max.

By seven or eight he'd become as bad as Les for his tidy, conventional parents. He and Gertrud played a game of stepping into every cowpat on the road, and when he returned from Willers' farm Rosa would wash him down outside before she let him into the house. And he continued to resist his father in every way he could. The hair-slicking sessions were rarer now, but when they happened, it was war. He scratched the new lederhosen Georg bought him and blackened them with dirt and grease, to make them look like Sepp Willers'. He refused to play with the predictable toys his father gave him – a model railway, a Märklin Meccano set. Above all, he hated the boring jobs he had to do, unless his grandfather did them with him, like cleaning the family's shoes, or sawing wood for the fire.

That was hard work, he wrote about this picture, like the whole of life.[18] He was quite often absent-minded and accident-prone. Once, holding the sieve for his mother, he tipped her freshly made cheese noodles into the dirty water below, like someone in a dream. On another occasion he ran down the stairs so fast that he fell head first into the full bucket that stood by the back door, and nearly drowned. His grandfather told him that you could tell the difference between a cow and a bull by looking underneath them, so he climbed into the field where the Willers kept their bull and looked underneath it – and had to run for his life, tearing one of his ears as he scrambled through the barbed wire. As a small child he swallowed all sorts of forbidden things in order to explore them[19] – sal ammoniac,* for instance, from his grandparents' night table, and polish from the shoe-cleaning table.

Altogether his poor mother must have despaired. Her son admired only the local farmers and wanted to be one himself; all her efforts to teach him better behaviour failed. She loved Wertach, but in town at

*Ammonium chloride, an expectorant used in cough mixture. Probably kept in powder form to be mixed with water. Not dangerous, but hardly salutary.

least there were no muck heaps. That would surely be a factor in her willingness to leave the only home she'd ever known.

It was changing, in any case. When Max spoke later of the good silence of his childhood, before machines and motorcars, he was exaggerating, as usual. The truly silent world of the Allgäu, as of all the rural areas of Germany and Europe, ended with the war. By the early 1950s the hay wagons were still turning in front of Steinlehner's and creaking up the slope to Willers' barn, but they were pulled by a tractor now as often as by horses.[20] And many motorcycles, and even a few cars, were starting to fill the newly paved roads. Nor was this true only of Wertach in general. The flat in which Winfried was born was above Seefelder's workshop and taxi service, which went back to the 1930s. If you examine the photograph of the house in *Vertigo* with a magnifying glass, as he himself might have done, you can see that it says '*Miet-Auto*' and '*Maschinenhandlung*': 'Car Rental' and 'Machine Repairs'.

The Seefelder house in Winfried's early childhood. (Is that Josef looking out of the window on the left, and Rosa on the right?)

Thus Winfried was not only born in a place where there were more and more cars and machines, but on the very spot where those cars and machines were housed and serviced. And so far from loathing them and their noise, as Max would do, he was fascinated by them, and exercised his voracious mind on them as much as he did on words. When later the family sat round the kitchen table at Steinlehner's, he would identify the make of every motorcycle or car that passed outside, just from the sound it made. And when he wasn't at Willers' farm, he was zooming up and down the road on his scooter, being a motorcycle or car himself, varying his *vrrm vrrm* to suit whichever one he was. He did this so often and for so long that Rosa feared his lips would start to fray like the fringes of her rag rugs. Strangely, that didn't happen, but it was from this scooter that (as he would write in *After Nature*) he regularly fell down in the street and tore his hands and knees.

Then, one day, when he was zooming up and down as usual, he disappeared for hours. Finally the mystery was solved: a motorcycle race had come through the village, and Winfried had followed it on his scooter, *vrrm*ing wildly. This time he had got so far away that the police had to bring him home.

Nabokov's chronophobe travelled back only a short time before his birth. Sebald the chronophobe went much further, to barely two weeks after his conception.[21] And then further back still, to the wedding day of his maternal grandparents (though this in the normal way, via family history or legend). The further back he went, the less he knew, and writing to Marie in 2000, he said that he planned to ask his mother more.[22] But time, his enemy and ours, defeated him.

At least the children all knew how their parents had met and married. Their mother had dreamed of emigrating to the United States like her brother and sisters, but her parents had wanted her to stay at home. So pretty young Rosa was still in Wertach when their father, who was already a soldier, came there with his regiment on a skiing holiday. Perhaps Rosa was still dreaming of America; certainly she was dreaming of a handsome young man. Georg was handsome, with his jet-black hair and blue eyes, and though he was only from another part of Bavaria, in 1930s Allgäu that was far away. Marrying Georg was, perhaps, like emigrating without emigrating. He proposed and Rosa accepted. They were married in November 1936, when she was twenty-two and he twenty-five. It was deep winter, there was over half a foot of snow on the ground, and Rosa was driven to the church in Seefelder's taxi, so that at least the bride's feet would be dry.

Wedding day, 17 November 1936.

When Winfried looked at this photo, he saw his parents, but when Max looked at it he saw his father's Nazi uniform. From his mid-teens on, Winfried blamed his father bitterly for his Nazi past, as he saw it. But Gertrud loved her father and tried to understand.[23]

Georg was born in 1911 in Eisenstein, in the poorest part of Bavaria, the Bayerischer Wald or Bavarian Forest, on the border with Czechoslovakia. His father, who was also called Georg, was a stoker on the railway and earned a pittance. His mother, Anna, would cross the border into Bohemia and buy bits of the famous Bohemian glass, then walk around Eisenstein with a basket on her back and sell them. The family was so poor, Georg told his children, that when he was five years old he was too small and weak to climb stairs by himself. At that point his mother, who had his younger sister to feed as well, somehow managed to buy two goats, and at least the children now had goats' milk to drink. Goats' milk is extremely rich, Georg said, and it made all the difference. He loved goats ever after, and would often say to his children, 'The goats saved my life.'

Georg was good at numbers at school; so good that he was sometimes bullied for it, until his fearless sister came to his aid. But the family situation meant that he had to leave at thirteen and learn a trade. He trained as a locksmith, which in those days included general mechanics and metalworking. He qualified in 1927, in the middle of Germany's most desperate period, the Weimar Republic after the First World War. The notorious hyperinflation of the early 1920s was over, but jobs were still scarce to non-existent. Georg managed to get work in the harsh winter of 1927–8, mending frozen taps and pipes. But after that – nothing. In the same year, Rosa's sister Fanny, realising it would take ten years to find a job as a teacher, gave up and left for America. Perhaps Georg too considered emigrating. But for men there was an alternative: from 1921 onwards Germany had been permitted to rebuild a small defence force. Like many poor working-class boys before and after him, in Germany and elsewhere, Georg turned to the army as a source of work, training and a wage. In 1929, at the age of eighteen, he applied, was taken on immediately, and began a career that would last for most of the rest of his working life.[24]

He entered the Reichswehr, as the army was then called, as a driver. Immediately his training started, and his promotion. In 1933 he was made a corporal (approximately – the relation between German ranks and British ones is complicated). In 1935 he was promoted (again approximately) to sergeant. This was the big step, since a sergeant was a junior officer. When he met Rosa Egelhofer a year later, Georg was, accordingly, no longer a private soldier but an officer, with just enough income to marry.

In 1935 Hitler transformed the humiliatingly constrained 'defence force' into the Wehrmacht, the army that would conquer Europe. This was the time when, according to his son, Georg should have understood what kind of state the Wehrmacht was serving, and should have resigned. But it was precisely because it was now Hitler's army that Georg could become an officer and marry a girl like Rosa Egelhofer. Apart from building the *Autobahns*, and generally beginning to restore German prosperity, Hitler did one undeniably progressive thing, which was to democratise the armed forces. In the Prussian Army only Junkers, members of the Prussian aristocracy, could become officers, never in a million years a boy from the Bavarian Forest who'd been so poor he'd only survived thanks to a pair of goats.

He should have left the army now for his immortal soul. But it's easy to see why he didn't.

A year after he married Rosa he was promoted again, and later several times more. In the first part of his war, the invasion of Poland in 1939, he was still probably a driver; in the second part, the invasion of Russia in 1942, a technical inspector; in the third and final part, in France from 1944, the head of the transport unit of his Panzer Division. He was, in other words, never a front-line soldier, but a technical-support officer in charge of vehicles. It is extremely unlikely that he ever killed anyone in the line of duty, and his son never claimed that he did. What he saw is another matter, but that he kept to himself.

In November 1943 his division was sent to the area between Bordeaux and the border with Spain.[25] By now the tide of war had long turned, and, 'Perhaps he saw the end coming,' Gertrud says. He told his children that he tried three times to cross the border near Basel and go home; but each time the Swiss turned him back, and he returned to his regiment and the war.

It's not clear how he got to Basel, which is well over 500 miles away from Bordeaux. In the chaos of the last months his record becomes scrappy and illegible, and it is hard to say where he was between the summer of 1944 and January 1945, when his long war was finally over. All we know is that in mid-May 1944 he was briefly home on leave for the birth of his son;[26] and that in January 1945 he was near Tulle, where he was captured, together with the rest of his regiment. And that in June 1944 a notorious massacre was perpetrated in Tulle by the SS 'Das Reich' Division, members of which also destroyed the village of Oradour-sur-Glane the next day.[27] Georg had nothing to do with that division or those crimes, but it is not impossible that he witnessed something of them. 'I don't know anything about this,' Gertrud says. 'But I think Max may have known something.' He referred to Tulle once, mysteriously, at the end of his life. Perhaps that knowledge was why.

Georg was interned together with his fellow officers in Oflag (Officers' Camp) 163, on the Causse du Larzac, a vast windblown plateau of the Massif Central.[28] For the first year conditions were brutal, and only cooking chestnuts saved them from starvation, as goats' milk had saved

Georg as a child. But in March 1946 a new commandant took over, an ex-*maquisard* (resistance fighter) called René Tabar. Slowly the camp improved, and Commandant Tabar, who was clearly a humorous man, would meet new arrivals at the railway station with hot soup and the words '*Wilkommen im Höhenluftkurort Larzac*' – 'Welcome to Larzac's high-altitude spa.'

The first recorded repatriation transport left Camp 163 in December 1945, the second in March 1946, the third on 15 January 1947. That was almost certainly the one that took Georg home to the little group waiting on Kempten station.

When the Egelhofers had arrived in Wertach in 1912,[29] the family had consisted of Anny, who was eight, Fanny, who was seven, and Josef, who was two. Rosa, the youngest, was born two years later, in 1914, and was thus the only one of the Egelhofer clan to be born and bred in Wertach.

Anny, Josef and Fanny a year after their arrival in Wertach. Sebald used this photo in 'Ambros Adelwarth' in The Emigrants.

Writing in 2000 to Marie about this picture,[30] Max remarked on how pretty Anny was as a child, who grew up shy and awkward. By contrast, Fanny looks as confident as she would always be, with her *Alpenstock* firmly planted in the ground. The dice are cast early for everyone, he said.

Rosa went to the village primary school like the others, and later to a boarding school near Memmingen, since there was no secondary school in Wertach. Secondary schooling was far from standard then, especially for girls, but Theresia was ambitious for her children, and Fanny had gone to Memmingen as well. By the time Rosa started there, both her sisters had already left for America; in her second year her brother followed. She stayed on until she was seventeen, but she was now the Egelhofers' only *Fehl* (the Allgäu word for girl). That meant not leaving them, since girls – especially only ones – were meant to help their parents and prepare for marriage.

Thus Rosa lost not only America but also the chance of a further education. There is no evidence that she regretted it – though her husband would, saying to his children that their mother could have done more with her life than marry him. Anny was a shy girl who became a seamstress and worked all her life in domestic service, Josef a fun-loving, probably dyslexic boy who trained as a tinsmith. It was Fanny and Rosa who had the brains. Fanny trained as a teacher, and only the unemployment of the late 1920s stopped her from having a career. Rosa was a reader and a good writer, when her own children left home and she had to send them letters instead. She was also the mother of W. G. Sebald, who had a brain himself. In another time and place she was just the sort of girl who would have gone on to higher education. Her life would have been very different then, and so would her son's. But the dice are cast for us early, as Max wrote, and not by ourselves.

An education beyond her convent school might also have helped to arm her against Nazi ideology. In 1930 the Bund Deutscher Mädel, the girls' equivalent of the Hitler Youth, was formed, and soon grew popular. At some point in her teens Rosa wanted to join. Her mother stopped her: not on religious grounds, but on social ones. Look at who's joining this lot, Theresia told her, only the riff-raff. You don't want to associate with *them*. So snobbery has its uses too. As did emigration. It was just as well that Fanny left, Max would say: if she'd stayed she'd have been a teacher in the Third Reich, and would have had to go along with things.[31]

The further back he went, as Max wrote to Marie, the less he knew. It's not clear exactly where his maternal grandparents were born: somewhere in the area around Memmingen, just thirty-five miles away from Wertach, but in what was called Upper Swabia, not the Allgäu, which gave their language a slightly different sound. Josef was born in 1872, Theresia in 1880.[32] Both came from families of small farmers. Josef had many brothers and sisters, like most families at the time, Theresia at least seven. Josef's education ended with primary school, and he and his brother Heinrich both trained as blacksmiths. Family history says that Heinrich emigrated too, to Denmark, and that one of his granddaughters became Miss Denmark some time after the First World War. The Egelhofers were a good-looking lot, as Rosa proudly noted.

It was always said in the family that Josef hadn't done military service because of his dicky heart. Gertrud isn't sure if the story was true. And Max cannot have believed it, at least at the end of his life. I don't know when he found it, but in 2000 he sent Marie a photograph of his grandfather in 1893, at the age of twenty-two, and he is in military uniform.[33]

Josef was a soldier in a Pioneer Corps, probably stationed in Munich. Pioneer Corps in the German Army, like those in the British Army, were engineering-support units, charged with building roads and bridges. The Reichsheer, or Imperial Army, as it was then, fought in no wars in the time he served, and the Pioneer Corps were support rather than fighting units, so that Max could preserve the idea of his grandfather as an unmilitary man, a foil to his military father. But there *could* have been a war, and the Pioneer Corps were part of the army, so the difference between Josef in his engineering unit and Georg in his transport one boils down to a matter of timing. On such shifting sands are legends built. And the story of Josef's dicky heart grows more dubious as well. If he had one, it wasn't bad enough to keep him out of military service.

There is no photo of Josef's original family, but there is one of Theresia's. It shows her in the middle of the family group, with a white flower on her lap. She must be about twenty; which means that we are in about 1900.

Theresia's father, Martin Harzenetter, stands behind her, her mother, Genoveva Adelwarth, sits on the right, with her youngest daughter beside her. Behind Genoveva stands Theresia's older brother; on the left her next brother, Ludwig, seems to have claimed the best chair.

Great-Grandmother Adelwarth, with her strong, craggy face, was clearly the head of the family, Max wrote to Marie.[34] He then entertained her with Great-Uncle Ludwig on the left, pointing out that his shoes needed a polish; and with Great-Grandfather Harzenetter, who is sporting a bow tie and watch-chain, and a row of medals from the Franco-Prussian war.

Every Sunday Grandfather Josef would walk the five miles between his workplace and Theresia's, carrying his boots (according to Max) in his hand.[35] Why Josef carried his boots his grandson doesn't explain; perhaps he didn't want to scuff them on the rough roads, like Ludwig's shoes. In any case, he walked barefoot every Sunday to see his beloved in the early years of the last century, and in 1905 they married. Perhaps it was in Obermeitingen, as Max wrote in *After Nature*. Or perhaps he just chose the name for its sound. That was one of the appeals of the past for him: the less that was known, the more room there was for fiction.

Josef and Theresia's wedding day.

The photograph shows that by this time Josef was no longer a blacksmith, but already a policeman, or *gendarme*, as he was called.

Perhaps he and Theresia had to wait until he gained this better position before they could marry. In any case, long after both their deaths, when he was seventeen or eighteen, their grandson Winfried discovered something this photograph doesn't show: when they married in January 1905, their first child was already six months old. Winfried was thrilled to have this proof of his grandparents' humanity. Rosa was predictably furious when he announced his find to the family, and no doubt he enjoyed that too. It probably also increased his sympathy for his Aunt Anny, whom he had always liked. Anny's shyness and awkwardness, above all her solitariness, spoke to him; and perhaps now he'd found part of the reason for them. Illegitimate or *frühgeborene* – 'born early' – children were a disgrace and a shame, whispered about by grown-ups and often bullied by other children. It was probably a relief to Anny and her parents when Josef won his post in Wertach, where no one knew them, or knew how 'early' their eldest daughter had been born. By then, however, Anny was already eight years old, and the damage had been done.

Both paternal grandparents had many sisters and brothers as well: Bavaria was Catholic and large families were the norm. Anna Landgraf, Max's other grandmother, was the eldest of a large brood, and would in normal circumstances have been sent off to a nunnery, but her mother died young, and she had to stay and take care of the younger children instead.

As a railway worker, Georg Sebald Senior (to distinguish him from his son) was a dedicated trade unionist.[36] This meant that he was perhaps a communist and certainly seen as one, as railway workers always were. He was also secular and irreligious, in keeping with his possibly communist views, and he drank a great deal, which Anna probably thought was connected. She, by contrast, was a deeply religious woman who had been prepared for the convent in her youth. One can't imagine that theirs was a peaceful marriage. Anna brought her children up in the strictest Catholic tradition, like Theresia Egelhofer. Both her parents, Gertrud says, had upbringings like those in the famous film *The White Ribbon*: pious, puritanical, repressed. And Georg Senior must have been a frightening figure to his children, with his face and hands blackened from the smoke, his head shaved because of the dust and cinders, his stoker's red scarf always around his neck. And the family was, as we know, dirt poor.

Somehow Georg's younger sister Anni managed to survive all this unharmed and grow into a warm, cheerful, earthy woman. Winfried and his sisters quite often visited this Aunt Anni where she lived in Stein near Nürnberg throughout their childhood, and were fond of her, her husband Toni and their two sons. But these were the only cousins on their father's side they knew; though there were dozens of others, children of Anna and Georg Senior's countless siblings, they never met them. And if this Aunt Anni escaped the more painful effects of her upbringing, their father didn't. His anxiety, his obsessive cleanliness, his dedication to rules and routine, surely had their roots in his hard and insecure childhood. But children aren't interested in their parents' childhood until much later. Max didn't live long enough to think about his father's, or, at any rate, to write about it.

Though there are no pictures of the paternal grandparents when they were young, there are several of them old, when they came to visit their son and daughter-in-law. The best is an early one, which shows all the grandparents together. It was taken in the kitchen of the Seefelder house a year or two before Winfried was born.

Rosa and Gertrud in the middle, Egelhofers on the left, Sebalds on the right.

And there is one more step back before his birth that Max could take on this side of the family: to his great-grandfather, Josef Sebald, born in 1839 in Schwarzenbach in the Bavarian Forest, and his great-grandmother,

Theresia, from Fichtenbach nearby.[37] Josef Sebald was a small farmer, like the Egelhofer and Harzenetter great-grandfathers, but in this poorest of regions he may have owned a cow and a pair of goats. He had fought in the Franco-Prussian war, like Great-Grandfather Harzenetter, and had earned a decoration too, which can be seen in the oldest-looking photograph Max found. It was taken on the golden wedding anniversary of Josef and Theresia Sebald, somewhere between 1910 and 1915. It is blurry and badly faded. But the faces of Winfried's paternal great-grandparents may give some idea, however inadequate, of their lives.

4

Il Ritorno in patria

In November 1987 the narrator of *Vertigo* returns to the village of W. for the first time in over thirty years.

He arrives by bus at the customs post at Oberjoch, where he leaves his bag to be brought after him. He then walks down the mountainside, past the chapel at Krummenbach and the abandoned mill called the Pfeiffermühle, along the long flat stretch called the Enge Plätt to the Starzlachbrücke, the bridge leading into the village: a walk that takes at least three hours, and on a November afternoon would be through growing darkness, cold and snow. In *Vertigo* it becomes a descent into another world, a strange place which is neither past nor present, but somewhere in between. On the bridge into this other world the narrator stops and gazes at the space where the Gypsy camp used to be. Dead tired, he trudges into the village, to the inn where he once lived as a child. There he registers as an English foreign correspondent and is given a room in what was, as far as he can tell, his mother's vaunted living room in those long-lost days. The room has naturally been completely changed and is now a world away from all he remembers. 'I myself, though,' he says, 'was no more than a breath away; and if the living-room clock had started chiming in my sleep, I would not have been in the least surprised.'[1]

Nearly twenty years later, in 2005, Wertach proudly opened the Sebaldweg, the Sebald Way, which follows the descent into the village of Sebald's narrator, with elegant silver stelae along the way showing walkers where they are and quoting the relevant passages from *Vertigo* at each stage. And ten years after that, in 2015, I walked down the Sebald

Way myself, together with Jürgen Kaeser, Max's friend since they were eight years old.

It was a beautiful summer's day in mid-June, and I was exhilarated to be with Jürgen, who is a sweet and funny man, and one of the people closest to Max throughout his life. But everything was so different that I wondered for a while what this walk could really tell me. The chapel at Krummenbach, for instance, which in the narrator's day was mouldering away, had been restored to picture-book perfection, the paintings inside still crudely drawn, but bright and clean.

The sun was warm on our faces, the mountain air cool. Jürgen and I talked of Winfried the whole way, though that only brought home that he wasn't with us. And the stelae reminded me that this was not the narrator's path, but an artfully re-created version of it, as close and yet as far from the original as the narrator's room at the Engelwirt from his mother's living room, and as this account of its author's life from him.

The distance was introduced, of course, by Max himself. Every critic makes this point first and foremost: W. is not Wertach, but an imaginary place that exists only in the narrator's mind.[2] Sebald achieves this distance by stirring inventions into his memories, and by weaving literary echoes into his text.

Compare his description of the first part of his walk, for example, down to the Krummenbach chapel, to the opening lines of Georg Büchner's novella *Lenz*:

> Lenz walked through the mountains. Snow on the peaks and upper
> slopes, gray rock down into the valleys, swatches of green, boulders,
> firs. It was sopping cold, the water trickled down the rocks and
> leapt across the path. The fir boughs sagged in the damp air. Gray
> clouds drifted across the sky, but everything so stifling, and then the
> fog floated up and crept heavy and damp through the bushes, so
> sluggish, so clumsy...[3]

For once Max has stolen no lines (which will become his regular trick), but the echo is unmistakeable.

Büchner was a favourite of his, and Jakob Michael Reinhold Lenz himself was an early Romantic writer, the author of a play the narrator sees in *The Rings of Saturn*. There are, accordingly, not just one but two other writers – both of whom died young, and the second of whom went mad – between Sebald and this descent of his native mountain.

Then the narrator reaches the Starzlachbrücke and pauses on it for a long time, 'looking into the blackness which now enveloped everything'.[4] It is a natural place to stop, and Jürgen and I stopped on it as well. But in *The Castle*, Kafka's hero K. also stops for a long time on the bridge below the castle, 'gazing into the illusory emptiness above him'.[5] Again the echo is clear – especially as K., like the narrator of *Vertigo*, goes on to the village to find a room in an inn.

The whole of 'Il ritorno in patria' is a tissue of such echoes and quotations, from many other Sebald favourites as well: from Thomas Bernhard, Peter Weiss, E. T. A. Hoffmann. And above all from Kafka. Kafka holds the key to Max's literary reconstruction of his childhood memories to such an extent that there is almost as much Kafka in them as Sebald. As the most acute commentator on *Vertigo*, Andreas Isenschmid, puts it: 'He has, as it were, Kafka'ised his autobiography.'[6]

Nonetheless, it is still very much his autobiography: that is his cunning double bluff. Just because a passage echoes – or is even wholly lifted from – another writer doesn't mean that it isn't equally about him, as the narrator's descent into W. shows. It is, for instance, Sebaldianly unclear when Max himself walked down what would become the Sebald Way. According to his appointment calendars[7] he didn't visit Wertach in 1987, as the narrator does; on the other hand, he did visit it in 1980 – in November, like the narrator. And he said over and over again that *Vertigo* in general and 'Ritorno' in particular were self-explorations, and that the events of the narrator's story happened to him.[8] It seems most likely, therefore, that he did the descent the narrator describes in 1980,[9] at the end of his first disturbing journey through northern Italy, and moved it to 1987 in *Vertigo* (adding it to his return to Italy, which *is* in the calendars) in order to fit it into the pattern of repetition and return that underlies the narrative. So the timing may be a literary invention, and the description a literary echo, but the experience of walking down the cold dark mountain into his childhood was Max's own.

What happens next? The narrator goes to the Engelwirt and takes a room where his family's living room used to be, and has his most vertiginous moment, in which remembered time and present time meet nowhere but in himself, and strand him somewhere between them, 'blurred as if he was out in a fog', as his friend Lukas will say.[10]

It is both dramatic and credible that such a moment should occur in
the narrator's old home, which is therefore where Sebald placed it. In
1980, however (or *a fortiori* in 1987), he could not have stayed in the
Weinstube Steinlehner, since that had closed as an inn in 1963, while
he was still at university.[11] In fact he stayed at the Gasthof zum Engel,
which he calls the Engelwirt, and certainly never stayed at Steinlehner's,
which was and still is a private house. Once again, therefore, a tweak, an
adjustment, for literary effect; but whoever has tried to go home again
recognises that orphaning in time, often experienced but never so well
expressed.

The narrator of 'Il Ritorno in patria' thus is and is not Sebald, in
much the way he will remain a literature-ised Sebald, like the Kafka-ised
Sebald; Sebald intensified by literary references and literary techniques,
like a piece of cloth shot through with iridescent thread. But he starts
with himself, and never really leaves himself, in essence and often in
detail. And the same is true for his other characters. They too are shot
through with literature, with echoes and inventions, but they too
remain recognisably themselves, often with painful consequences. So
we have seen with the cast of 'Dr Henry Selwyn', and so it was too with
'Il Ritorno in patria'. Its consequences were much more painful, in fact,
since they came much closer to home. I don't think Sebald ever knew
how Rhoades Buckton's family felt about 'Dr Henry Selwyn'. But he
knew how the people of Wertach felt about 'Il Ritorno in patria'. When
Jürgen and I stopped on the Starzlachbrücke that summer's day, I was
about to find out.

At around three
o'clock we walked
into Wertach, past
the sign for W. G.
Sebald's birthplace to
the Seefelder house
itself, with its small,
discreet plaque saying
that the writer W. G.
Sebald was born here.
'Very Allgäu,' Jürgen
said, squinting to see

it from the road. 'We're not supposed to show off. If you ask us how we are, we say "Not worse", even if we've just won the lottery.' 'Very Max,' I said.

At half past three I had an appointment to meet Inge Speker of the Wertach Tourist Bureau, so Jürgen headed home. Inge has a special interest in Sebald, leading tours to all the places mentioned in 'Ritorno'. She'd promised to search for anyone who remembered him and had emailed the week before to say she'd found three people. In fact she'd found more, but not all had been willing to speak. 'Very Allgäu,' I thought, but it was more than that as well.

When I got to the café Inge was waiting outside. '*Willkommen in Wertach!*' she said, throwing her arms wide. She led me in, and there were the few who'd been willing: three ladies who'd been at the primary school with Winfried. Inge introduced them: Lore, Erni and Irmgard, all of them of a certain age, of course, the same as Max's and mine.

We ordered *Kaffee und Kuchen*. Inge explained about those who had preferred not to come, either because they had no memory of Winfried, or because, in one case, she, well... was still unhappy. 'We were all unhappy!' Irmgard cried, and it soon came tumbling out.

In June 1990 – exactly twenty-five years before – the local paper had begun publishing extracts from a book by a certain W. G. Sebald. No nonsense about imaginary places for them: they called it *Wertach: Il Ritorno in patria*, no doubt hoping to sell hundreds of copies in Wertach alone. The serialisation began on 21 June and ended on 16 July: twenty-one episodes, one every day except Sunday for four weeks. At first it was fine. 'Il Ritorno in patria' starts by being rude about the Tyrol, which was perfectly acceptable, as everyone loves to laugh at their neighbours. Then the narrator's first memory of 'W.' is of a performance of Schiller's *The Robbers*, which the ladies remembered as vividly as Sebald did, and enjoyed being reminded of. They brought out their own photograph – the same as the one in *Vertigo* – and reminisced about Josef Blenk, who played the prodigal Robber and was the handsomest boy in the village. For a few more minutes peace reigned at our table, as it had still reigned in Wertach.

Then, however, the narrator started to recall people – and the trouble began. 'We recognised *everyone*,' Irmgard said. 'Every morning we thought – "What will he say today? And about *whom*?" '

All three shook their heads at the memory – but half-grinning too because, after all, they had lived to tell the tale.

'Most of it wasn't even true,' Lore said.

'What wasn't true, for instance?' I asked.

All three spoke together. 'Lukas did *not* have gouty hands,' Lore said. 'Or crippled ones,' said Erni. Irmgard said something in Allgäuerisch and Inge hid a smile.

'*Bitte*,' I asked Irmgard, 'what did you say?'

'It was about us,' Irmgard replied. 'He said the women of Wertach had skinny braids. How dare he!' And all three ladies burst out laughing.

'What else?' I asked.

'He made the whole village sound horrible and frightening,' Erni said, 'which is ridiculous.' They all nodded.

'It was more about his own feelings than about Wertach, really,' I suggested.

'That's not how it sounded,' Irmgard said firmly, and that was the end of that.

We made small talk about the *Kaffee und Kuchen* for a while. Then I took the plunge.

'What about the true stories?' I asked. The ladies looked at each other.

'Well,' Lore said, 'the Last Battle story – that was true. Those four boys did die in the very last minute.'

'Should he not have told that?' I asked innocently.

'No, that was all right,' Erni said. 'The poor lads.'

I looked at them. I could feel Inge looking too.

Finally Irmgard said, 'The pretty serving girl. That was true.'

Suddenly they were chatting animatedly in Allgäuerisch to each other. Inge did simultaneous translation and I took notes, scrambling to keep up. The serving girl – Romana, Inge put in – was as pretty as Sebald described her. She was called Rosi, and she lived in a hamlet outside the village, just as Winfried wrote. And she did have an affair, but not with a hunter. The person with whom Rosi had an affair was the publican of the Weinstube Steinlehner – the one Sebald calls Sallaba, Inge said. Was he really called Sallaba? I asked. No, the ladies replied, but something similar, like Schigulla, they thought. He really did have only one leg, having lost the other in the war. And he and Rosi had a child. A boy, they thought – yes, a boy. They didn't know what became of him. 'And Rosi?' I asked. Rosi was still alive, they thought, and lived not far away. Inge and I looked at each other in amazement. Was it extraordinary, or utterly normal, that Romana should be alive twenty-five years later and still living nearby? Sebald's vertigo swirled round us.

'Sallaba – I mean Schigulla – ran the Weinstube, but it was owned by Steinlehner, wasn't it?' I asked. They nodded. 'But Steinlehner,' I said, 'surely the story Sebald tells about him isn't true? The wound in his leg that wouldn't close – surely he invented that?' But the ladies were enjoying this now. 'No!' Irmgard said. 'It was quite true.' 'It can't be,' I said. 'It was!' they cried. When he was a boy, Hans Steinlehner was secretly smoking one day when his father appeared, so he hid the cigarette in his pocket, and it burned a hole in his thigh. At the time it healed, but later in life it opened again, and only grew worse. And it was true about his wife too, Frau Steinlehner – she did become strange and take to drink. But that was one of the things Winfried shouldn't have told, they agreed. Poor thing, wouldn't you?

I could see there was more. 'What else?' I asked. But they clearly felt a bit guilty about Frau Steinlehner, and perhaps about Rosi as well. On the other hand, they didn't want to let me down either. Being a biographical interviewee can be morally dangerous too. Finally, Lore said, 'What does he call Dr Dolleschel in the book?'

'Dr Rambousek,' Inge said.

'Well, he did work in the Alpenrose café.'

'Did he really?' I asked. 'And was he a morphine addict?'

For a moment there was silence, but they were too deep in now. 'Yes, he was,' Irmgard said in Allgäuerisch, but that much I understood. Then she added in German, 'He did die, but not here.' The others nodded again, happy to absolve Wertach of being where the poor doctor died.

'What about Lukas?' I asked. 'You called him Lukas too. Did Sebald use his real name?'

Again there was a pause. This time Erni came to the rescue. 'Yes,' she said. 'He was called Lukas.'

'But not Seelos,' Irmgard said. 'His name was Lukas Berger. He died about ten years ago.'

'He did live in the Alpenrose café,' said Lore.

'And his mother and his aunts were just like that!' Erni added. Now they were all laughing and talking in Allgäuerisch again. 'Maria was big and fat. She was beautiful when she was young—' 'And Mathild, in her black coat and hat—' 'And umbrella!' 'We called her Frau Professor—'.

Mathild's family, the Berchtolds, had been rich, they said, and all the daughters were well brought up. But Mathild was especially clever and was sent away to school. They didn't remember Sebald's tale of her briefly becoming a nun, but it was quite possible – Mathild didn't like men, they said, lowering their voices; no one ever spoke of such things in those days, but she was probably a lesbian. And yes, she would often talk with Winfried's grandfather, as he describes. Josef wasn't as educated as Mathild, but he was intelligent, and one of the few people in the village as interested as she was in books and such things. They were great friends.

Maria married Berger, who was a builder, they said, and successful, until the dreadful days after the first war. Then he died young, as Winfried wrote, and the family fell on harder times. Maria ran the Alpenrose café for a while, as did her sisters Resa and Bina, in the 1950s and 1960s, while the ladies were growing up.

'So Lukas's aunts,' I said, 'were Resa and Bina, not Babette and Bina.'

They nodded. 'And they ran the Alpenrose,' I summed up. 'But the story of the apple cake and the *Guglhupf* – that surely wasn't true?'

No, they laughed, that was one of Winfried's jokes. He still had a very Allgäu sense of humour, ironic and deadpan. There were a lot of jokes like that in *Vertigo*. Like the one about Specht the printer, Inge said, the editor of the village news-sheet, who rejected much of his own work as not up to the paper's standards.

'The Bergers weren't happy themselves, were they?' Inge went on.

'I think only Lukas was left,' Lore said.

'Only Lukas in Wertach,' Erni said. 'But Karl was still alive in Oberstdorf.' I made a quick note: *Karl, Oberstdorf.*

'Yes, the policeman,' Lore said. I scrawled *Policeman.*

'And there were some sisters,' Erni said. 'One went to America, I think.'

There was a silence. I remembered Seelos Lena* in 'Ritorno', who emigrates to California after having had an illegitimate child. I could tell from the silence that everyone was remembering Lena.

Finally Irmgard said, 'She did not have a child, however, by a Turk or anyone else.'

---

*It was a traditional Bavarian practice to put people's surnames first.

'Karl and Lukas,' I asked, 'weren't happy?'

It was Inge who answered. 'We don't really know Karl,' she said. 'But Lukas wasn't, was he?'

'No,' said Irmgard. She looked at the others, but the cat was out of the bag. 'It was a sad story,' she said. 'He was a good friend of the Sebalds before.'

'So,' Lore said, 'when Winfried came back to Wertach it was Lukas he talked to. Everyone knew that. So when all those stories came out in Winfried's book, we knew where they came from.'

'And everyone blamed him,' Erni said. 'They were almost angrier at Lukas than at Winfried. I don't know why. Maybe just because he was here.'

'Poor Lukas,' Lore said. 'No one ever forgave him. Right up to the day he died. Even if we tried to, we couldn't forget it.'

'We should just have blamed Winfried,' Erni said.

'Lukas blamed Winfried,' Irmgard said. 'Though he'd been so fond of them all when they were here. So it ended in bitterness all round, just for the sake of a story.'

They looked at me, and I knew what they were thinking: What will she say about us, for the sake of her story? Another return, another repetition.

When I followed up my note – *Karl, Oberstdorf* – I was twenty years too late. But Karl's widow was still alive. She was about to turn ninety but was willing to talk to me. So we fixed a date, and I went to Oberstdorf.

Frau Berger was small and straight-backed and had the patient look of a survivor. Later she told me how she had found her way in 1945 from Silesia to Oberstdorf, and how, when Karl had announced that he was marrying her, one of his aunts said loudly, 'A refugee!' But they had had a good life, and here she still was.

As usually happens, she differed from the Wertach ladies over several things. The aunts Resa and Bina had never run the Alpenrose café. And no, Mathild wasn't a special friend of Winfried's grandfather. Altogether she clearly found Mathild's eccentricities much less touching than Sebald did, no doubt because she had had to deal with them: at the end the old lady became demented, she said, stuffing her room at the Alpenrose with so much junk you couldn't move. I hoped Sebald hadn't known about this sad end, though he wouldn't have minded about the room.

About the main point, however, Frau Berger was in complete agreement with the ladies. Her husband Karl had recognised everyone in the story, including of course his brother, and was furious with Winfried about all of it. He was particularly furious about the photograph. The photograph? I asked. Yes, Frau Berger said, the one of the boy in uniform. I found it, on page 203 of *Vertigo*, and held it out to her. 'That's it,' she said. 'It's of Karl. Lukas should never have given it to him. Winfried never asked us if he could use it, and he never gave it back either. His mother kept saying he'd send it, but he never did.'

I remembered what Sebald wrote about Seelos Benedikt, as he called the boy – that he'd 'always been a timorous child'[12] – and hoped that Frau Berger didn't. She was still cross enough, twenty-five years later. And the anger had clearly spread to Lukas as well. Poor Lukas, as the ladies had said. No wonder his widow had declined to see me (because that is who the absentee was).

Of course I had *Kaffee und Kuchen* with Frau Berger too, and it was then that she told me something else. 'You know,' she said, 'I had a nice neighbour for many years. Just recently I saw in the paper that he had died. And when I saw his name, I realised for the first time who he was. He was Rosi's son, the waitress at Steinlehner's, whom Winfried wrote about. And she's still alive, because her name was on the death notice. Poor Rosi, to live to see the death of her child.'

Finally I took my findings to Gertrud.

Oh, the Bergers! she said. She remembered them all vividly. Especially the two good-looking brothers: Karl, the serious one, and Lukas the joker, as Max had described him. Lukas had a special place in her memory. He was sixteen years older than she was; he taught her to swim, and even, when she was tiny, to walk, standing at the far end of the balcony of the Seefelder house and opening his arms wide. Max too had loved him as a child. There'd been an older brother, Josef, but he had died, probably in the war. And two sisters: the youngest, Rosemarie, who was very beautiful, but died young of cancer, and Resi, the second born, who was a good friend of Rosa's. Max turned Rosemarie into Regina in 'Ritorno', and Resi, of course, into Lena. 'She absolutely did have a child by a handsome Turk called Ekrem,' Gertrud said, 'who made Turkish honey and sold it in the market.'[13] The Wertach ladies were protecting the Berger family's reputation, or perhaps Wertach's, if they denied it, but there were several illegitimate children in the village, as there usually are. 'And,' Gertrud added, 'Resi did emigrate to California,' several years later, in the late 1950s, though she couldn't remember if the child died, nor if Resi herself died later in a car accident, like Lena in *Vertigo*.

She confirmed the other improbable truths as well: Sallaba/Schigulla's single leg, and Steinlehner's unhealing wound, which was probably a cancer, Gertrud said, and certainly ghastly; poor Frau Steinlehner, who dressed it every day, had to drink to face it. Also Dr Dolleschel's morphine habit, and his suicide by morphine, though the narrator's seeing his dead face was surely a fiction. Max's description of Mathild was accurate in every detail, including her communism and her friendship with their grandfather. And when he was old, Lukas *did* have a hand deformed by arthritis – Max dramatised it as usual, but even that was essentially true. Everything in *Vertigo* was based on truth, except the terrifying figure in the attic called the grey *chasseur*. That alone was Max's fantasy.

And now she dropped a bombshell. 'But *chasseur*,' she said, 'means *hunter*. And the other hunter – the one with Romana – wasn't a fantasy. He was real.'

'He *was?*' I said.

Max had said so himself, to two interviewers.[14] But I'd been sure that that was one of his slips between memory and imagination, either a trick or a genuine confusion. When the Wertach ladies hadn't remembered a hunter I'd nodded; of course that was a fiction! But if Gertrud remembered him too… 'I know the sex scene comes from another writer,' she was saying. 'But that's how Max worked. It doesn't mean that the people in it weren't real. Romana was, as everyone told you, and so was the hunter. I don't remember his name. But I used to see him coming into the Weinstube, in his hunter's green jacket. He came from somewhere else, as Max wrote in the book. And he did die, and there were all sorts of rumours about it.'

I stared at her. Max had said that too, but it had only made me more certain that the whole thing was a fiction. Could Gertrud be so close to her brother that she shared even his false memories? It's possible; everything is possible. But I can't believe it. Gertrud is completely sane, and when she's not sure she says so. And that green jacket, which isn't in 'Ritorno', was surely the proof. Perhaps the Wertach ladies were protecting Schigulla's reputation this time, from the implication of murder. Or probably they just didn't know. If Max and Gertrud both say there was a real hunter, there was.

'What were the rumours?' I asked.

She'd been too young to understand them, Gertrud said, and never learned later what they were. Max may have, though – he usually did. Rosi's child was Schigulla's, everyone agreed about that. But the hunter was often in Steinlehner's, and perhaps Schigulla sensed danger from him. And perhaps that did send him into a mad rage. Because Gertrud remembers very vividly the night he destroyed the Weinstube: she and Winfried cowered in their beds, listening to the terrible crashing below. Schigulla often swept the glasses to the floor with one of his crutches when he was drunk, but this utter devastation happened only once. Perhaps it was really connected to the hunter; or perhaps Max just tweaked things to make them fit, as he would say.

There was one thing that Max certainly tweaked, Gertrud said. The diphtheria that nearly kills the narrator after he sees Schlag and Romana making love did not happen to him: 'It happened to me. And he borrowed it for his story.' 'Ah!' I said. Possibly, then, the link between sex and death was not invented for the hunter; but it *was* invented for the narrator. That's where the link mattered most, and that's where it remained.

Rosi, who became Romana, in the Weinstube with Josef Egelhofer (on her left) and another man. As the photo shows, Sebald invented her thick flaxen hair.

But the story is not all apocalyptic – it is also funny, in Sebald's melancholy way. As I'd confirmed with the Wertach ladies, the humour was invented: the two tragicomic sisters in the Alpenrose café, reduced to eating their stale cakes themselves, since no one else ever did… But yet again Gertrud surprised me. 'It was perfectly true,' she said. 'The Alpenrose was a café, but no one ever came.'

'And there really were cakes?' I asked.

'Oh yes,' she said. 'But since no one ever came, they were famously stale, as Max said.'

'But surely there weren't just *two* stale cakes, which the sisters ate themselves every Sunday?'

Gertrud leaned her head back and laughed. 'Probably not,' she said. 'But I'm sure Max didn't make that up. It was a tale people told in the village. Perhaps Lukas told it to him, or, more likely, my mother. I heard it myself, before I read it in *Vertigo*.'

And one other thing was certainly true, Gertrud added, though it might seem as improbable as Resa and Bina's cakes, or Steinlehner's wound. Frau Steinlehner kept her room on the first floor of the Weinstube even after the Sebalds moved in, so that she lived in their flat, and Winfried went in and out of her room, just as he describes in *Vertigo*. Rosa was unhappy about her son visiting a lady in her bedroom, particularly a lady who drank so much that her own children had been taken away. But poor Frau Steinlehner was a gentle soul, Gertrud says, and Winfried already liked strange, sad people as much as Max would. He was very fond of Frau Steinlehner. Perhaps Rosa was even a little jealous.

There was still one awkward subject we hadn't touched on: the story's reception in Max's own family. I knew it was awkward, since Max had told me so, in that long-ago interview: 'I thought I'd done it as discreetly as possible. But my mother was mortified to read details about families in our village. And ever since then she's never gone back.'[15]

Gertrud made a little grimace. '*Vertigo* was a catastrophe for my mother,' she said. 'She thought Max would write a sort of historical description; she was absolutely unprepared for the way he told fictions about some people and revealed secrets about others. She knew how everyone in Wertach would feel, and she agreed – he shouldn't have done it. She was dreadfully upset and angry. She called me every day for ages to complain. I tried to explain to her that he'd written something beautiful, but she wouldn't listen. And I understood how she felt too. Wertach was her home, these people were her friends. And, rightly or wrongly, she'd lost them. She lost the Bergers especially, Lukas and Karl – Karl was a great friend of my parents too, until "the book".'

'And she could never go home,' I said. 'The Wertach ladies confirmed that. 'Poor Rosa could never come back,' they said, 'she knew we'd all rush up to her and say *How could your son do such a thing?*'

'That's right,' Gertrud said. 'And they didn't just blame him – they blamed her.'

'They did?' I asked. Neither Max nor the ladies had mentioned that.

'Well, who do you think told him most of those stories?' Gertrud replied. 'He couldn't have got them all from Lukas. Every time he went home in the 1980s he kept her up till late at night, squeezing the village stories out of her. And when people in Wertach read them, they knew that many must have come from her. That's why she couldn't show her face there again, and that's why she was so angry at Max. He hadn't just betrayed them; he'd betrayed her… That's how she felt, I know. Of course they made it up quite soon, because she didn't want to lose him too, and he didn't want to lose her. But she never forgot, and nor did he.'

I don't know which was worse, this story or my reaction. Art was becoming more costly by the minute, but I still didn't want reading and writing to stop. I tried to say some of this to Gertrud. 'Don't worry,' she said. 'They won't.'

5

Ambros Adelwarth

If we had a keen vision and feeling of all ordinary human life, it
would be like hearing the grass grow and the squirrel's heart beat,
and we should die of that roar which lies on the other side of
silence.

George Eliot, *Middlemarch*

'Il Ritorno in patria' was the first story to come out of the Wertach
years. The second was 'Ambros Adelwarth', inspired by Winfried's
memorable encounter with his Great-Uncle William. That encounter,
and the relationship with his whole foreign family, had awoken in him
the longing for a different life. For the narrator this was for many years
a dream of America, which later turned into 'an aversion to all things
American'.[1] 'Adelwarth' is the story of that reversal, revealing the reality
behind the dream of faraway places.

'Ambros Adelwarth' is the most complex story of *The Emigrants*,
indeed of all Sebald's works. It has five narrators and several times and
spaces, including one long dream.[2] And stylistically it is the freest – the
short, verbless lines of Ambros's diary, for instance, are unlike anything
else Sebald ever wrote.[3] Altogether, 'Adelwarth' is often more surreal
than the rest of Sebald's prose, except for the Vienna pages of *Vertigo*. It
is perhaps no accident that neither the narrator of that part of *Vertigo*
nor Cosmo Solomon, the other hero of this story, is quite sane.

Cosmo is wildly extravagant, brilliant and reckless. He is also
supernaturally sensitive, both physically and mentally: he can hear bats'
cries, and can slip into a trance in which the winning number at roulette
appears to him from out of a mist. He tells Ambros that this is a dangerous

state, during which his friend must watch over him 'as one would over a sleeping child.'[4] This turns out to be true, when during the First World War he is driven mad by visions of the carnage in Europe, even though he is a world away in America; and again in his second and final breakdown, when he enters a hallucination and cannot return from it, but is lost for good.

This vision of a world where time and space are different, or don't exist at all, returns in *Austerlitz*. There it is deeply longed for, because it is inhabited by the lost dead; but again it is dangerous, and can drive you mad.[5] Cosmo is the realisation of this dangerous, longed-for state: the state of the ultimate hypersensitive, who senses the deaths of men halfway around the world, and dies of it. Cosmo Solomon is Sebald's image of what happens when you can hear the grass grow and the squirrel's heart beat, as George Eliot wrote; when you hear the roar on the other side of silence. This will return in Sebald's work; it is at the heart of it.

In sum, 'Ambros Adelwarth' is not just a story of lost love. It is also (for instance) about German poverty in the early twentieth century, and about madness, or what is called madness. But, above all, it is a metaphysical story, using 'metaphysical' in Sebald's sense of going beyond the ordinary space-time structure of our world. Ambros doesn't just love a man. He loves a seer, a Hunter Gracchus, whom Sebald borrowed from Kafka for *Vertigo*: someone living between this world and another. He is like Salvatore ('Saviour') in Kafka's story, sent to welcome Gracchus, but unable to save him from his ceaseless journeying. Sebald's Salvatore, Ambros, cannot save Cosmo, or himself.

Like all Sebald's work, 'Ambros Adelwarth' is a lacework of images so delicate we may not even notice them, but they catch us in their net, so that we feel we are in a world of mysterious, half-caught meaning: that is, in Sebald's world.

Many images connect not just to the other stories ('the butterfly man', Nabokov, for instance), but to the other books. Thus the mysterious countess of the narrator's Deauville dream looks back to Beyle's – that is, Stendhal's – Métilde in *Vertigo*, and forward to *Austerlitz*, and the image of the desert caravan that bears Cosmo away will recur too. There are several nets of such images in 'Adelwarth'. One is the imagery of veils hanging in the air – veils of mist or smoke or dust, which provide the mystery and uncertainty that Sebald's art needs. Another is that of imagined brothers.[6] Here in 'Adelwarth', when Cosmo disappears during his final breakdown, it is in order, he says, 'to see how his brother was',[7] though according to Ambros he never had one; while Austerlitz will be haunted by the image of a twin brother who died on the train, though he never had a twin brother. And Ambros and Cosmo are themselves imagined brothers: as Cosmo tells their hotel in Constantinople, they are the '*Frères Solomon, New York, en route pour la Chine*'.[8] This goes back to *Vertigo* again, in which Abel and Furlan were like brothers to each other,[9] and to Max's first, youthful novel, in which the hero has an older brother – who is homosexual, and whose homosexuality drives his mother to a probable suicide. This net, or knot, of brothers – homosexuality – danger, is clear in the early novel and in *Vertigo*. For Ambros that danger has changed to flourishing, until his love is lost. Thus by 'Adelwarth' homosexuals have become like Jews: victims of the cruel German past, who deserve empathy, not hatred and fear.

The third net of imagery in 'Adelwarth' is made of clothing. Ambros's decline is pictured in his clothes, from the exotic sensuality of his Arab robes in 1913 to the emptiness of his life after Cosmo, during which, as Kasimir says, 'it was as if only his clothes were holding him together'.[10] Theres, by contrast, shows only shyness and sadness, though at her death she leaves (says Fini) a splendid wardrobe of clothes. Ambros hides an inner hollowness, Theres an inner richness, both expressed through their clothes.

It is, I think, Kafka who is once again the source of this imagery. One of Sebald's favourite photos of him showed him in a coat that was (as Sebald said) too big for him.[11]

Kafka with his sister Ottla, 1917.

Now look at the photo of Cosmo in *The Emigrants*. Sebald surely faked it, like much else in 'Adelwarth': the figures clearly come from several different pictures. Especially Cosmo in the middle, who is curiously small, and whose coat is definitely too big.

A few pages later Aunt Fini sees Ambros for the last time, and he is wearing his *paletot* – his overcoat – in which he looks 'very frail and unsteady'.[12] And when the narrator last sees Fini, she too is in a 'dark winter coat that was too heavy for her'. Finally, the photo of the narrator on the New Jersey beach shows him too in a dark winter coat. Judging by the way he has pulled the collar up around his ears, this one may not be heavy enough. But the result is the same: the coat, which is meant to protect, manages only to bring out the vulnerability of its owner. So the narrator, too, belongs to this line of wearers of Kafka's coat. In 'Ambros Adelwarth' Sebald has once again Kafka-ised his biography, and his Aunt Fanny's and Great-Uncle William's as well.

His first step towards his own prose writing was in the early 1980s: quizzing his mother and Lukas Berger about Wertach from 1980 and Fanny about William in 1981.[13] That is, his first literary impulse was autobiographical. It was only when he heard of the death of his one-quarter-Jewish teacher in 1984 that *The Emigrants* was born.[14] It was thus born as a Jewish book; but its first stirrings, in the research for 'Ambros Adelwarth', were German.

Sebald began, then, with his own family. And his portraits of them are as faithful as those of the Bucktons.

Anny, for instance,[15] was as shy as Theres; she wore Theres's white gloves for her eczema and collected Theres's Hummel figurines. She was extremely generous to her whole family, giving her money away, Beate says, and dying a poor woman, as Fini says of Theres. She even spent the first half of her visits home weeping for joy and the second half weeping for sorrow. She was the first profoundly sad person Sebald knew, and the first exile. 'Ambros Adelwarth' is his memorial to her almost as much as to his great-uncle.

In the story Fini says 'Perhaps Theres really was a saint,'[16] and I think Anny *was* one, in Sebald's imagination. She is the patron saint of all his innocents, from Mangold in 'Bereyter' to Stanley Kerry, Michael Parkinson and Janine Dakyns in *The Rings of Saturn*. And not least of the spinster sisters Babette and Bina in *Vertigo*. They, we now see, are the female equivalents of Ambros and Cosmo, with their 'unending dependency on each other',[17] so great that when one dies of a heart attack the other dies of grief on the same day, rather than the years it takes poor Ambros to follow Cosmo. This sheds a new light, too, on the joke of the two cakes, one baked every Sunday to be eaten the next; it now prefigures Theres's weeping-in and weeping-out of W. at the beginning of 'Adelwarth', which in turn prefigures Ambros's dressing and undressing at the end: all on the surface absurd, but in truth tragic.

With the unending loss of her exile, Anny provided the tragicomic image of what 'Adelwarth' and *The Emigrants* as a whole are about. But not for the book's main reason, the persecution of the Jews. Once again, as in 'Dr Henry Selwyn', behind a Jewish theme lies a non-Jewish model. It will happen again in 'Ambros Adelwarth', and later as well.

Anny with her American employer, Mrs Wallerstein.

Fini was similarly close to Fanny.[18] Fanny was a carer for others too – for her family, for Uncle William, for any neighbour in need. When her husband died at only sixty – too soon to have a pension to pass on – her situation was as dire as Fini's. She told her family in Germany that she gave private lessons. Les had a different story: that some rich friends offered her a job running one of their offices. Most likely the lessons were an extra, which she promoted to her main job out of pride.

This is the reality of emigration. Fanny had trained as a teacher, but when she arrived in New York she began as a domestic servant. So Sebald wrote; but he made Fini a governess, in other words still a teacher, whereas in reality Fanny was a maid. Then in the early 1930s she met Joe Stehmer, son of Babette, at a dance. Joe had had a professional training in Germany as well, in his case as an accountant. But since his arrival a year or two before Fanny, he too had been working as a servant to a Jewish family. Later he found the job he would have for the rest of his life, as the superintendent of a suburban apartment block.

Fanny and Joe were typical first-generation immigrants of their time – never losing their foreign accents, never having the careers they'd trained for; educating their American children, and placing their hopes in them. And it *was* a hopeful, ever better life, until Joe died. That was Fanny's tragedy.

The other Joe, Rosa's brother Josef Egelhofer, was luckier.[19] His trade as a tinsmith did not depend on language, as both teaching and accounting do. At one stage he worked in the factory that Sebald gave Kasimir, which made stainless-steel kitchens and large urns for restaurants. After that their ways part. Kasimir spends five years working on the 'dizzy heights'[20] of New York skyscrapers; Josef moved to a job in a brewery, where he stayed until he retired in 1972.

The humour and lightness of Kasimir's part of 'Adelwarth' are a faithful reflection of Josef. He was good-looking, a charmer and a ladies' man, Gertrud says; he would say 'To make a long story short' and then talk for hours, says Beate, and they laugh at the memory. I doubt his daughter Rosemarie learned to belly dance in her fifties, like Sebald's Flossie, but she was a colourful character whose two or three husbands, according to Max, all ran away after a week.[21] Beate remembers visiting Rosemarie later in her life: every room in her house had a theme, such as 'The Environment' or 'The Caribbean'… She can't have been in that house in 1981, or, at any rate, Max can't have seen it. If he had, I can't imagine him not finding a use for a houseful of themed rooms.

The brother and sisters remained close for decades. On retirement all three planned to move to Lakehurst, New Jersey together, to live in bungalows within two streets of each other, Fanny and Anny in one, Josef and his wife Leni in the other. Anny probably helped to buy both houses, Gertrud thinks. But then in 1974 – just before they moved,

Beate recalls – Anny died. She left almost nothing, as we know; but as Fini says in 'Adelwarth', 'Kasimir, and particularly Lina, doubted it'.[22] This was an understatement. Josef and Leni were convinced that Anny had left a great deal and that Fanny was keeping it all for herself. It was a classic family breakdown, never resolved. When Sebald visited eight years after Anny's death, he had to call on Fanny and Josef separately; by the time Beate visited them a few years later, she couldn't even tell one of them she'd seen the other.

Though Anny and Fanny always feared they had inherited their father's weak heart, Anny died of cancer, while Fanny survived three heart attacks before dying of pneumonia in 1998, just before her ninety-third birthday. Josef followed in 2001 at ninety-one.[23] Rosa, the youngest, had to watch them all go a second time.

'Ambros Adelwarth' caused trouble, of course, like everything Sebald wrote. It upset Rosa again, and this time Fanny and Josef as well. Josef, however, shrugged it off; he said, 'I could have something to say, but it's not important,' and sent Max his gold pocket watch, as Kasimir sends his to the narrator. He was always the blithest of the Egelhofers. Fanny minded because of the usual combination of reality and fiction in 'Adelwarth',[24] so that people in Wertach and Kempten could come to believe all sorts of untruths (or even worse, truths) about elegant, distinguished William Schindele. And, no doubt, because of its telling truths about her. Poor, struggling ancestors are a badge of honour after a few generations, but not when they're yourself, and you've left home to seek your fortune.

Sebald first quizzed Fanny about Uncle William on that visit in 1981. Three years later he sent her more questions, and she sent him three long letters in reply.[25] William was born, she wrote, in 1882, in Gopprechts, the youngest of five children; there were also four older half-siblings, which made him the last of nine. His mother died when he was two ('probably of exhaustion', Fanny added). His eldest half-sister took over the care of the children, though she was only seventeen. The family was very poor, and William and his nearest sister Minnie picked nuts and berries and sold them in the market at Immenstadt even before they went to school. At only twelve or fourteen, Fanny wrote, he found work in the kitchen of a Stuttgart hotel, and left Gopprechts for good.

All this Sebald uses for Ambros. He changes the nuts and berries to prickly rosehips, and has the children sell them in Kempten, which is better known than Immenstadt, and he sends Ambros to Lindau, Lausanne and Montreux, with their beautiful lakes and mountains, rather than to plain old Stuttgart.

The next part of the story also comes directly from Fanny, and thus from William himself. At seventeen or eighteen he went to London, where he worked again in a hotel. And here, as a room-service waiter, he met a gentleman from the Japanese diplomatic mission.

Now Sebald starts to fictionalise. He adds the lady from Shanghai and the mysterious incident that begins Ambros's 'career in misfortune'.[26] And Fanny had written that the Japanese diplomat took William to Washington, where no doubt he was posted. There William stayed for perhaps a year or two – with the diplomat's family. So William's Japanese employer was not an 'unmarried gentleman', like Ambros's, and did not take him to Japan, where Ambros is happier than anywhere else in his life: mostly, we guess, because this is the first time he can live in peace with his employer and (probably) lover. That too is Sebald's fiction. And now it grows deeper.

In reality William Schindele worked for two American families after he left the diplomat. He worked for the first until 1915 or 1916, still in Washington; then moved to the other in New York, where he stayed for the rest of his working life.[27] Sebald collapsed the two families into one, making Ambros start and end with the Solomons of New York. In reality 'Cosmo' came from the first family. Which required some rather important adjustments.

Fanny did not tell Max a great deal about the 'Solomons' of New York, just their real name, Meinhard, and the fact that they were 'fabulously wealthy'. She had photographs of Rocky Point, the Meinhards' huge estate on Long Island Sound, where she had often visited William during the 1940s. Sebald put the photos in the story.

Apart from that, he invented the Solomon family: old Samuel the banker, his second wife Margo, and Cosmo. The Meinhards[28] had no children, and Morton Meinhard was a textile manufacturer, not a banker. He didn't retreat from the world like Samuel, and nor did his wife, Carrie, like Margo – these were Sebald's thematic inventions. All that was true of both the Meinhards and the Solomons is that they were Jews, and very rich.

Morton Meinhard died in 1931, but William went on working for Carrie for more than twenty years. When he finally retires, Ambros rapidly declines, falls into his last depression, and dies. In reality William lived on for another decade, and according to Fanny enjoyed his retirement, going often to theatres and concerts and cooking lavish meals for the whole family, serving them clad in his three-piece suit and insisting that they all be properly dressed as well.[29]

This all ended, Fanny wrote, in January 1963, when Joe Stehmer suddenly died, and William fell into Ambros's depression. He couldn't understand, he said, why his nephew had to die at only sixty, when he, William, was over eighty and willing to go in his place. Fanny took him to a psychiatric clinic – clearly in New York, not far away in Ithaca – where he had 'several shock treatments'. She visited him every day, she wrote, and 'sometimes he was like a zombie'. After a few months of this, blood clots formed, and in June he died of a heart attack.

There is (naturally) no mention of a lost lover in Fanny's account. There is only the lost nephew, who seems to have been the closest person in William's life, as far as the family knew.

William and Joe with one of William's many terriers.

If Ambros is mysterious, William is even more mysterious. Why would the death of his nephew, however fond he was of him, plunge him into acute depression?

The only clue may be something that Sebald didn't include in his story: that William had had a nervous breakdown once before, in the early 1930s. So what was happening then?

Morton Meinhard died in April 1931, but there is no evidence that William was intensely attached to this quiet, self-effacing man. Something also happened in the early 1930s, however, in his first employer's family: to the model for Cosmo.

William told Fanny all about him. He *was* a wild young tearaway from a vastly rich family. William did accompany him to casinos in France and America, where he gambled huge fortunes; he did try to ride a horse up the stairs of the Breakers Hotel in Palm Beach,[30] and he did end up in a sanatorium, several times over. In other words, Sebald borrowed a great deal of his story for Cosmo. But that is where the similarities end.

The real Cosmo Solomon was called Ned McLean,[31] or to give him his full name, Edward Beale McLean, son of the owner of the *Washington Post*. Ned was an only child, the possessor of unlimited wealth from the day he was born. He was a sulky boy, both spoiled and neglected in the classic way by his high-society parents. By his late teens he was already drinking so heavily his hands shook when he lifted his glass. So when he was twenty-one or two, his father, at the end of his tether, hired someone to be his valet and minder: William.

Now, first of all: McLean – it's happened again: *the model for Cosmo Solomon wasn't Jewish.* You couldn't find a more thoroughly non-Jewish, establishment Wasp than Ned McLean. Does it matter? Cosmo's role in the story is more other-worldly than this-worldly; his Jewishness sometimes seems almost incidental. And yet it isn't. He takes Ambros to Jerusalem, the emblematic lost home, and the story shows the inability of a German to survive the loss of a Jew... Well, in the end this anomaly makes little difference to the meaning and impact of *The Emigrants*, even now that this book has revealed it. But it does seem quite extraordinary that the key Jewish characters in half its stories were based on non-Jews. It is as though the original source of inspiration for Sebald's writing, the elimination of Jews from Germany, can't be kept out of his work: it's about Jews, but secretly they are still absent.

There is another significant change Sebald made to William's story
as Fanny told it to him. When William was hired, Ned was drinking
especially heavily – partly because the girl to whom he'd been engaged
on and off for years, Evalyn Walsh, had finally broken off their
engagement. And when he went to persuade her to listen to his suit,
William went with him. Ned promised to stop drinking, and in July
1908 they married.[32] In other words, Ned, like the Japanese diplomat,
was unlikely to have been homosexual (there's later evidence to this
effect too); and for all but a year at most of William's employment with
him, he was married.

William's really luxurious time was with the McLeans.[33] Evalyn's
father – an Irish immigrant miner who had discovered a fairy-tale seam
of gold – was even richer than Ned's. During the season they would give
lavish banquets and balls three or four times a week. For one dinner in
1912 they spent $40,000 (almost $1 million today), mostly on orchids
and yellow lilies sent from London. They were both inveterate gamblers
and regularly lost fortunes; after Evalyn had won $70,000 (about
$1,800,000) she bought one of the most famous jewels in history, the
Hope Diamond – which cost more than double her winnings.

This was the occasion that Sebald describes, when Cosmo broke the
bank at Deauville and Ambros spent a whole night packing his winnings
into a steamer trunk: a story William often told, but with Evalyn, not
Ned, as the winner. (In reality this happened not in Deauville but in
Vichy. And Sebald also sends Ambros and Cosmo to Evian – is this a
mineral-water joke?) In any case, there was a basis in Ned McLean's
history for the story of Ambros and Cosmo at Deauville. Was there
some basis for their journey to Jerusalem as well?

Fanny wasn't sure, and Sebald can tease us to his heart's content. He
claimed to have William's diary of the journey, 'in several languages',[34]
but there's no such thing in his 'Adelwarth' files. The photograph of
Ambros in his Arab robes was definitely taken in Jerusalem,[35] but could
also have come from one of William's journeys with the Meinhards.
Perhaps, though, Evalyn can help. In Jerusalem on their honeymoon
trip, she wrote, she went out and bought Arab costumes for herself and
Ned. It would have been very like the McLeans to kit out their servants
in costumes matching their own, and if you look at Ambros's picture in
The Emigrants, it does look much like Ned's.

The McLeans in Jerusalem, 1908.

Even so, the great difference is that neither in Vichy nor in Jerusalem was William alone with Ned McLean, or likely to have been his lover. There's no telling if Sebald picked up any hints (probably from Josef rather than Fanny) about William's private feelings for his wayward young charge. But we can be pretty sure of one thing: the great love affair between Ambros and Cosmo was Sebald's invention. Poor William probably never lived out his homosexual desires, and almost certainly not with Ned McLean.

Naturally, Ned's promise to give up drinking lasted no longer than his allowance. In 1916 his father died and he became the owner of the *Washington Post*.[36] Probably around this time, William's employment ended. John McLean, who'd hired him, was gone, and according to Fanny, Ned went into a sanatorium. Most likely this was an effort to dry out, the first of many; and with Ned away for weeks or months, there was no job for his valet.

After he'd left the McLeans, Fanny wrote, William remained in touch with one of the family. So he would have known of Ned's continuing decline.[37] He was mostly drunk now, and when he was drunk he quarrelled with everyone, especially Evalyn. They had already had such terrible battles in William's time that she had thought of leaving him in 1915; in 1928 she finally did. He immediately installed another woman in his Washington mansion. (This is the confirmation of his sexuality I meant: a wife is one thing, but an illicit liaison is another.) In 1929 he was confined to yet another drying-out institution. In October 1931 Evalyn sued for divorce. His debts were now so huge that the *Washington Post* was put up for forced sale. Finally his behaviour became so erratic that Evalyn filed a lunacy petition, as it was called, against him, arguing that he was incapable of managing his affairs. On 31 October 1933 the *New York Times* reported that the psychiatrists agreed. Ned was declared 'of unsound mind and a lunatic, without lucid intervals', and confined to his last sanatorium, a hospital in Maryland. There he lived on for another eight years 'in a state of mental exile', Evalyn wrote, 'shut off even from himself'. His heart gave out first, before his liver or his brain, which must have been equally ravaged. In July 1941, at the age of fifty-five, he had a heart attack and died.

If Sebald looked into Ned McLean, which is likely, he would have known all this: in particular, that Ned ended up a madman in an asylum. In reality Ned's madness was an extreme case of alcoholic degeneration. That was the ordinary truth out of which Sebald conjured the metaphysical madness of Cosmo Solomon, as he conjured Ambros's desire to die out of William's last depression, and the great love of Ambros and Cosmo out of his great-uncle's service as a gentleman's gentleman.

William would have known about it all too, in detail, and at the time. The worst events – the divorce proceedings, the confinement in an institution – happened between 1930 and 1933, just those years during which he had his first breakdown. Maybe it had something to do with the tragic fate of Ned McLean; and maybe, then, William loved him after all.

Sebald complained often about how hard writing was for him.[38] That could sound like pride or self-pity, but it was the simple truth. Every page he wrote, he said, was boiled down from around twenty.[39] For 'Adelwarth' I counted around 550 pages of drafts for around 120 printed pages of the German text, and the pages of notes and photocopies of sources from which the drafts in turn were distilled were uncountable. No wonder that after eight or nine hours at a stretch Max would emerge pale, 'totally beaten up';[40] that when writing had consumed all his free time to the point of 'monomania' he would ask himself, 'Are you really quite sane?'[41]

It's impossible even to sum up that myriad of sources. To give just one example, Ambros's diary is sewn together from works by Chateaubriand and the Austrian historian Jakob Philipp Fallmerayer (both from the nineteenth century, of course). Chateaubriand alone provides endless details. Ambros and Cosmo resting beneath a laurel tree in a night so bright that Ambros can write by the light of the stars, the sterility of the land around Jerusalem, the promised city as 'a ruined and broken mass of rocks, the Queen of the desert'[42] – all come from him. And much more, including the lovely line about the Moab Mountains of Araby, which dip slightly at points, as though 'the watercolourist's hand had trembled a little'.[43] And almost the same amount comes from Fallmerayer.[44]

One more example: Sebald drew on two sources, an encyclopaedia and a book, for Ambros's shock treatment, which ends in his death. And what the photocopies in his archive show is surprising, and horrifying: he did not invent a single word. Both the German psychiatrist Braunmühl and his 'block or annihilation method', which sounds so Sebaldian, were real, as were the fractures, dislocations and fits that occurred before the advent of sedatives and muscle relaxants. In one draft Sebald gave Ambros himself a broken arm, broken teeth and a bruised heart,[45] but he soon removed them. How to represent violence was always a moral problem for him, and silence his solution.[46]

As for the drafts, they fill two fat files in Sebald's archive.[47] It is no exaggeration to say that he rewrote almost every paragraph of 'Adelwarth' many times. He worked as hard on minor passages as major ones; on the scene of driving beside the black family in New Jersey, for example, which is a bit of light relief. But most of the heavily worked-on sections are the key ones. For Ambros's farewell message, 'Gone to Ithaca', for instance, he tried many different versions; in one Ambros adds that he has taken his dog Toby with him, in another he asks Fini to take care of Toby. (Given that Sebald was devoted to his dogs throughout his life, and that Uncle William was equally devoted to his, these were touching efforts. Look at the photograph of Ambros's living room – that is, William's living room: the object at the foot of the dresser is surely an elegant porcelain dog-bowl.)

The variations are often minute, changing just one word or two, as all writers do. But Sebald alone (as far as I know) rewrites *da capo* every time – from the first word of a line, or the first line of a paragraph, even if the change comes at the end. And of course by hand, and later by typewriter; he would never have anything to do with computers. As a result his drafts convey a sense of obsession – of monomania, to use his own word.

Just one example, this time. As he admitted to me, the bits of Ambros's diary we see were written by him.[48] For this trick he used an old Italian diary for the year 1927 that Gertrud had found in a flea market in Fribourg. (We see that too.) It looked perfect, but there was a hitch: the dates fell differently between 1927 and 1913, when Ambros and Cosmo make their journey to Jerusalem. For instance, Sebald wanted to use All Souls, 2 and 3 November, in the story, as he'd done in *Vertigo*, but All Souls fell on a Wednesday and Thursday in 1927, while in 1913 it fell on a Sunday and Monday. So he cut out '*Domenica*'s and '*Lunedi*'s from five or six other months and tried sticking them over '*Mercoledi*' and '*Giovedi*'. That evidently didn't satisfy him; until he spotted a better solution, cutting '2 Domenica' and '3 Lunedi' out of October, and sticking those in instead. Then he Tippexed and photocopied the result over and over, so that it looked as smooth as possible. (It still didn't quite work, so he drew lines to cover the joins, as the second picture of Ambros's diary shows.)

How much time and fiddly work this took is anybody's guess, and who on earth would have checked on what days 2 and 3 November fell in 1913? If we want an instance of Sebald's mad perfectionism, this is it.

The story leaves us with two questions, I think.

The first is the central one – *are* Ambros and Cosmo lovers? In the published story there are only hints: Kasimir's remark that Ambros 'was of the other persuasion, as anyone could see',[49] and the shared bed at the end. But in one draft Cosmo also takes and presses Ambros's hand; in several, Ambros, disturbed by his vision of home, holds onto Cosmo. And where in the published story the two just lean against a wall on the Mount of Olives, in the drafts they lie with their heads together, or with Cosmo's head on Ambros's breast or shoulder. In other words, Sebald began by describing quite clearly what the relationship is between the two. But bit by bit he cut and refined it, until – typically – all that is left is implication.

The other question concerns Dr Abramsky. He is certainly invented: no doctor can talk about a patient, and everything he tells the narrator about Ambros's torture is in the books Sebald consulted. He is also symbolic: a saint and martyr for the guilt of Samaria, with his fire-red hair like the flames over the heads of the Apostles. But now there's a problem. The horror for which he bears the guilt, though he has deeply repented, is German: the annihilation method, so reminiscent of other German annihilation methods. But Abramsky is a Jewish name, and he grew up in Leopoldstadt, which is the Jewish quarter of Vienna. And Samaria, as Abramsky's sanatorium is called, is Jewish too – Judea and Samaria made up the ancient kingdom of Israel. Sebald certainly knew all these things; yet he chose them.

It is strange enough that the models for Sebald's Jewish characters are so often non-Jews. But that is a hidden strangeness; this one is visible to every reader. Why is Abramsky, the bearer of German guilt, a Jew? His part of 'Adelwarth' is one of the most beautiful, but also the most disturbing.

PART III

Sebe

6

1952–6

In December 1952 Specht's news-sheet[1] carried some important news: retired Gendarme Commissar Josef Egelhofer and his family were leaving Wertach. Specht knew the inside story. For several years now, he reported, the commissar's son-in-law, Herr Georg Sebald, had had a job with the Sonthofen police, 'and had had many difficulties keeping up his connection to the family, especially in winter'. Now, however, he had found a home for them in Sonthofen, and they would all be joining him there.

Specht was not exaggerating the difficulties. Wertach lies nearly 200 metres above Sonthofen, at the end of twenty kilometres of mountain road. Georg had no car, and there was no bus. All he had was a bicycle – and not a modern one with an electric motor, such as everyone in the Allgäu has today, but a heavy old machine. Freewheeling down in the morning was no problem, but pedalling back up again in the evening must have meant a physical effort we can hardly imagine today. And even for Georg, who expected life to be hard, and who had recently been through six years of war, it was too much. He cycled every day only for a short time. After that he rented a room in Sonthofen and stayed in town during the week, coming home only at weekends, as his son told interviewers fifty years later. Every Monday morning, like Leo Lanzberg's mother in 'Max Ferber', Rosa would fill his rucksack with five glass jars, a meal for every night of the week, and he would coast down to Sonthofen with the heavy load on his back; every Saturday afternoon he would labour back up to Wertach, with the jars mercifully empty.

As a civilian worker with the police, he was a public employee and entitled to social housing for his family. As soon as some new blocks had been built, one of the flats was his. On 16 December 1952 he and Rosa and Josef packed everything into Alpenvogel's van[2] and placed a farewell message to the friends of a lifetime in the news-sheet: 'We have moved to Sonthofen!' Winfried's Wertach life was over.

In 'Dr Henry Selwyn', Hersch Seweryn, aged seven, leaves his Lithuanian village on a cart, watching the horse's croup rise and fall and the white geese stretching their necks on the brown land. Winfried gazed out of the window of Alpenvogel's van and saw trees white with frost, looming and passing in the morning mist.[3] The journey took at most an hour, he wrote, but it felt as though he'd travelled halfway across the world (as Hersch Seweryn really would).

But then – Sonthofen! In 'Max Ferber', Luisa Lanzberg, aged sixteen, is thrilled to move to the city of Bad Kissingen, where she imagines a new world will open for her, even more beautiful than her childhood one. Just so was Winfried thrilled, as their van rolled onto Sonthofen's wide, paved streets, with their names on blue plaques, and past the old station building with its round clock. '*Grossstadt!*' he thought – 'The big city!'[4]

Sebald was making fun of himself when he wrote that line. Sonthofen is far from a big city even today, and in 1952 it was a small market town. Over the eleven years he lived there it grew, and in 1963 it officially became a city.[5] But he left in that year, so that the Sonthofen he grew up in was never a city even in name. The grown-up Sebald wouldn't have minded; he never wanted to live in a city, and apart from a few years, never did. But in his teens he chafed at growing up in a small provincial place far from the centres of culture. And as he grew older his view of it darkened, as everything in his mind darkened. He didn't hide this in his writing; on the contrary. Practical Wertach forgave his trespasses and turned him to tourist account. But Sonthofen took another Allgäu route, that of never forgetting a grudge. To this day there is no monument of any kind in the town to its most famous son,[6] and even the latest proud account of itself, published in 2013, doesn't mention his name.

Sonthofen lies in the midst of a glorious landscape of mountains, lakes and forests, in which Winfried and his friends lived a life of splendid freedom. The town itself, however, was a military hub, full of soldiers and barracks. In the 1930s the most important one, the Ordensburg, was built.[7] Hitler ordered its construction himself; during the war it was an elite training school for SS youth and bore his name, the Adolf Hitler Schule. Afterwards it was empty for years. But eventually the new Bundeswehr – the federal defence force – was formed, and in 1956 the German army moved in again. As Winfried learned about his country's recent history, from his mid-teens on, he began to loathe everything military. At home that meant his father; and outside, the vast grey bulk of the Ordensburg, which looms over Sonthofen like a permanent reminder of the Nazis' demonic ambition. In *Austerlitz* Sebald wrote of the appalling will to power expressed by gigantic buildings. The first one he knew was the Ordensburg.

The Ordensburg.

Even today the Ordensburg's past lives on in the town, like an evil spirit under a stone. On one of my visits to Sonthofen, Max's friend Jürgen took me to a flea market where his wife Kristin had a stall. A blue-and-green silk scarf caught my eye, and I asked Kristin if I could see it. She took down the hanger and pulled off the scarf to give it to me. And suddenly no one could look at the beautiful blue-green silk, but only at the naked hanger. Engraved in the pale wood in deep, black, unfaded

letters were the words *Adolf Hitler Schulen*. For a short eternity we stood
in shocked silence. Then Kristin pressed the scarf into my hand, and
held out the hanger. 'I think you should have this too,' she said. 'To
remember how it is with us here.'†

The street where Alpenvogel's van drew up was called Am Alten Bahnhof
(Old Station Road), and had until recently led to the old railway station,
closed since 1948.[8] The house was Number 3a: 3a Am Alten Bahnhof,
Winfried's address for the next eleven years. Today the identical blocks
of social housing stretch along both sides of the street. On that day in
1952, 3a was the second of only two new blocks on the Sebalds' side,
with empty space beyond; and opposite it, where Rosa and Georg
would move in 1964, was a meadow where Winfried would play.

   More than sixty years after that arrival, Jürgen took me to 3a Am Alten
Bahnhof. He pointed to the first floor on the left of the entrance: those
windows were the Sebalds', he said. I looked at the buzzers beside the
front door, wondering which had been theirs. The names were mostly
Turkish and Polish now.

   The building was neat and well-kept, as all German houses are, but secretly
I was shocked. This was where Sebald had grown up, right to the end of his
teens, and it was even more modest than the first block of flats I'd lived in
myself as a child. I thought of his beautiful house in Norfolk, of his love for

even grander houses, where objects can outlive their owners for generations. And for the first time I thought that what Winfred was escaping at nineteen and beyond was not only Germany, but poverty. Not real poverty – he never went hungry, or barefoot, like some of the farm boys at his school. But the genteel poverty of the lower middle class, of his parents.

The first years in Sonthofen were lean ones by any measure. Georg's work[9] was an office job, but also involved fairly menial labour, keeping the police vehicles clean and in good repair. He cannot have earned much, particularly since it seems that he never signed up as a permanent employee. Quite possibly he was waiting for the army to be re-formed; but in the meantime the family had to live on hope. And the memory of that lean time would mark the two children old enough to understand. One day, for instance, a lady called on Rosa unexpectedly. It is inconceivable for an Allgäu *Hausfrau* not to offer *Kaffee und Kuchen* to a guest, but there were no *Kuchen* in the house. So Rosa sent Gertrud and Winfried to Tressel's bakery to buy some. So far, so good; they bought the cakes and ran home. But then – disaster. Somehow on the way they lost the purse their mother had given them. They searched for it in vain, and had to go home and tell her. A scene ensued, but it wasn't really punishment they feared. It was their mother's sorrow at losing the small amount of money the little green purse had held.

In December 1952 Rosa didn't know that there would be several more years before their lives would improve. But though her new home was better than the old one, she had lost her beloved Wertach. She'd pushed hard for this move, but now that it had happened she cried for weeks.

When Winfried began his Sonthofen life he was eight and a half years old. After her first year Gertrud would stop boarding in Immenstadt and live at home, so he would soon have his big sister back; his little sister was still a baby and no trouble to him; and he had his beloved grandfather beside him, in the very next room. All this must have fed his excitement about a new life in the big city. But there was one snag: his father was living with them again. He was there not just every weekend now, but every morning and every evening. And their battles grew.

As before, the worst ones were over his hair. Every two weeks his father marched him to the dreaded barber, Pfrenger. Even worse than Pfrenger, however, were the sessions with Georg himself. These still continued on special occasions, and one day, soon after the move to

Sonthofen, they reached a crisis.
It was the day of Winfried's first
communion: the most special day
of all for a Catholic family. So
that morning his father insisted
on greasing and combing his hair
with special fanaticism. It was more
than he could bear. He twisted and
turned and ducked in his chair,
until Georg too could bear it no
longer. He lost his temper, and gave
his son the hardest slap Gertrud
ever saw.[10]

It must have worked, because in the photograph taken soon after
Winfried still looks stunned, and the grease on his hair has a holy (or
unholy) shine.†

Nearly fifty years later Max described that day to Marie. It was all
absolutely dreadful, he wrote. The only saving grace was the lunch at
the Lion Inn afterwards, when he sat next to his grandfather, and they
had Wiener Schnitzel and ate three different kinds of salad from a plate
divided into sections, a miracle of design he'd never seen before…[11] He
had clearly recovered.

He was his parents' child, in any case, and knew how to present a
good face to the world. In the
photo of the confirmation
procession he stands as straight
and proud as any soldier-father
could wish. He also grasps his
candlestick firmly, and holds
it perfectly vertical, unlike the
boy in front of him (whose
hair leaves something to be
desired as well). The only flaw
in his appearance is that his
confirmation suit is several sizes
too big. That was the need to
scrimp and save again: however

important the day, the suit would have to last for a year or two.

Primary schools in Sonthofen in the 1950s[12] were strictly divided along religious and gender lines: one school for Catholic boys and one for Protestant ones, one each again for Catholic and Protestant girls. At eight and a half, accordingly, Winfried entered Sonthofen's primary school for Catholic boys. It was still in the 400-year-old building – the old town hall – where it had begun in 1919. Today it is a specialist music school, for which it is a good size. As a state primary school in the baby-boom years after the war it was hopelessly inadequate. At its peak more than a thousand boys were somehow crammed into eight classrooms; in Winfried's class in 1952 there were fifty-three.

The building wasn't the only thing that had remained unchanged since 1919.[13] The children still used slates, especially for practising their letters, and writing with the left hand was forbidden. Many of the poorer boys came to school barefoot, wore the same shirt and pair of lederhosen all year, and didn't come at all at harvest time because they were needed in the fields. Then there were the few middle-class boys, better dressed and better off, who were heading for *Gymnasium* or grammar school, while the rest were destined for the ordinary secondary school, or no school at all. Despite the family's financial struggles, Winfried was firmly in the middle-class group. Rosa made all his clothes, very beautifully, and like her mother, she saw education as the route to betterment. Winfried was set for *Gymnasium* from the beginning.

On his first day in Sonthofen, Sebald wrote in 'Paul Bereyter', it began to snow.[14] It snowed all night, and next day the snow was so deep he arrived at his new school in euphoric mood. If that was true, it was lucky, since the boys might easily have turned on a newcomer who showed any fear. Perhaps it was true, because they didn't. We teased him a little, Jürgen says, but not much, because we liked him. And Helmut Bunk, who was a tougher type and might have enjoyed a bit of rough-housing, refrained, because 'our fathers were friends'. That was lucky too. Winfried was accepted, and by the end of his first day he'd made two new friends.

In fact, he met four important people that day: three boys who would become his friends, and his teacher, who would become Paul Bereyter. Helmut and the third boy, Werner Braunmüller, will appear later. The two who were important now, and would remain so, were Jürgen and the teacher.

*Jürgen Kaeser working on his slate,
1952. (His mother had made his
jacket too.)*

The boy Jürgen Kaeser was much the same as the man I met over sixty years later: tall and skinny as a rake, optimistic and open, at home in the world. The opposite, in other words, of his friend Winfried. What Winfried had with Jürgen throughout their childhood and youth was *fun*. From the time they were ten, and going to school by train, Winfried would call Jürgen down at 6.45 every morning with a loud *Kikiriki! – cock-a-doodle-do! –* driving all the neighbours mad, until his voice broke and he couldn't do it any more. They did wild, wicked things together, such as pushing the benches in a local park into the pond, or building a tree house crazily high, or walking across the bridge over the Iller on the handrail instead of the boring old floor. That was their most famous early escapade, which ended with Winfried tumbling into the river, and having to dry out his clothes in the warm shed where Jürgen's father kept his bees, because he didn't dare to go home soaking wet and have to explain.[15]

As this story shows, Jürgen's parents were very different from his own: wonderfully relaxed, even indulgent to their only child. And their house was very different from the Sebalds' modest flat. It was a rambling old place with a big garden, with plenty of room to play table tennis and throw a ball; there was a workshop in which Jürgen's grandfather had had his foundry and cast bells for cows, where the boys cast hundreds of tin soldiers and fought harmless battles for many happy hours. There were bees in the shed and chickens in the yard, and stretching behind the house up to the corner were the beautiful Lerchenmüller market gardens, where Paul Bereyter works in the afternoons, and where in reality the two friends often played. They explored the greenhouses and plantations, and watched Schultz at work – the odd-job man, who was enormous and a bit simple, and could break up plant boxes with one crunch of his hands. Winfried was fascinated by him: the first of many outsiders who would move him over the years. Jürgen's house and garden, and behind them the green Lerchenmüller gardens, became his home away from home. It was as though the fields and freedom of Wertach had come back to life again in the middle of Sonthofen.[16]

Paul Bereyter's real name was Armin Müller.[17] When Winfried joined his class in December 1952, Müller was forty-two years old. He too was tall and very thin, and wore glasses with thick lenses, since his eyesight had been poor since childhood. He had been teaching the third- and fourth-year boys at the school since 1947, and would do so until he retired.

Winfried became very attached to him, and remained attached to his memory for the rest of his life.[18] Müller couldn't be a father figure to him, since that place was already taken; rather, he was like a much-loved and admired older brother. That is how the narrator thinks of him in 'Paul Bereyter', and that, I think, is how Sebald felt about him, looking back: the first of the older brothers he never had.

He wasn't the only one with fond memories of his teacher. Generations of boys loved Armin Müller: everyone says so, and for once it seems to be true.[19] The only exceptions, perhaps, were those whom he gave regular beatings – for though it's hard to believe of Paul Bereyter, Müller did beat his more wayward pupils. All teachers did in those days, at least in the boys' schools. But many beat cruelly, one or two even sadistically, whereas Armin Müller only ever beat fairly, and in proportion to the offence. So his boys of 1952–4 told me, fondly and without a trace of irony. He had two sticks, Helmut said, a light one and a heavy one; with the light one you got smacks on your hand for minor crimes, with the heavy one *Hosenspanner* on your *Hosen* for major ones. He himself received several of both, but Jürgen Kaeser and Winfried Sebald, everyone agreed, never. Clearly they kept their antics for outside school; or else the middle-class boys just got away with everything, as one of the working-class boys said. Certainly it was a working-class boy who got the most beatings of all from Armin Müller: Karl Berchtold, whom Sebald called Fritz Binswanger in his story. Berchtold was the class hooligan, whom Müller couldn't subdue however often he tried; he wore out his sticks on him, then sent him out to cut new ones. Karl was undeterred, and went on to become a high-class chef, as Sebald recounted.

Apart from the beatings, as a teacher Paul Bereyter is a faithful portrait of Armin Müller. Müller was a natural teacher of children – born to teach, as Lucy Landau says of Paul in the story. He explained everything several times, clearly and concisely, so that even the slowest of his fifty-three charges could understand. At the same time he helped the quickest, giving those who would be taking the *Gymnasium* exam extra tutoring after school. And he spotted the quickest everywhere, not just among the 'better-class' boys like Winfried and Jürgen. A few years earlier, for instance, there was a real Fritz: Fritz Ketterle, who came from a modest home, but whose work Müller immediately recognised as out of the ordinary.[20] When Fritz fell ill a few weeks before the exam, Müller went to his house regularly and helped him prepare. Even though he was still unwell, he passed with ease, and got into the *Gymnasium*. When I met him many decades later, he had just retired as chief archivist of Sonthofen.

Müller was staunchly irreligious, as the boys knew, since he was conspicuously absent from the church services at the beginning and end of every year. Of his quarter-Jewish background and its consequences for him twenty years before, they knew nothing, as Sebald recorded. Müller's fellow teachers knew a little, though he almost never spoke of it himself. They also knew that despite it he had served in the artillery throughout the war. And that when he returned in 1945 he was made schools inspector for the whole region, even though he hadn't finished his training; no doubt because he was the only untainted person around. That meant firing many people whose allegiance to the regime had been too enthusiastic, which he did as conscientiously as he did everything, even though he was as sensitive and as deeply German as Paul Bereyter. Those years just after the war cost him as much as the years before it had. They must have cost many parents a great deal too, piling resentment upon guilt; to which their response, like animals caught in a trap, was a paralysed silence.[21]

The boys didn't know any of this either. But they did know that their teacher had served on every front, through all six years of the war.[22] Everyone said so; besides, whenever they grew muzzy from the warmth of the stove, Müller would throw the windows open, even in winter, and make them get up from their desks and do the military exercises he'd learned, as he told them, in the war. Yet there was something strange. He was calm and measured, even when he was angry, but if he caught them playing war games, he changed. Then he lost his temper completely; as Helmut put it to me, he went wild.

Armin Müller with some of his class of 1964. The whole photo shows fifty boys, still much the same as in the 1950s.

Paul Bereyter's special subjects are history and geography, above all *Heimatkunde*, the history and geography of the region. In all these, Paul is an exact portrait of Armin Müller. Winfried had been fascinated by geography ever since he was five or six years old;[23] now, in Müller's class, his lifelong passion for maps and atlases began. They drew endless maps of the land around them, of the Ostrachtal and

Kleinwalsertal, of Sonthofen and Immenstadt, where Müller was born; they wrote about their own mountains, starting with the Grünten, 'the guardian of the Allgäu', and about the Alps beyond; they studied the rocks and trees, the animals, birds and fish of the Allgäu. They listed in alphabetical order the thirty-four town and country districts that made up the Sonthofen region (Wertach coming second to last); they drew the fruit that grew in each season and the grain that was used for each kind of bread. In November 1952, just before Winfried arrived, they drew the plan of their classroom that Sebald would use for 'Paul Bereyter'.[24]

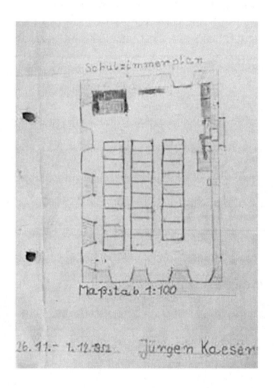

And they didn't learn all this in theory alone. Like Paul Bereyter, Armin Müller was famous for 'marching his troops out of school', as a fellow teacher said,[25] to study the flowers and trees they'd drawn, or on particularly lovely days to do nothing at all.[26] In his story Sebald lists a dozen places that 'Paul' took them to see – Fluhenstein Castle and the Starzlachklamm (a fabulous gorge that would become

Winfried's favourite playground a few years later), the electricity works and wickerwork factory, brewers' cellars, cheesemakers' kitchens and millers' threshing floors; even a gunsmith's workshop, and the collapsed entrance to a long-abandoned mine.

Jürgen and Helmut remember all of these. And as they followed Müller over hill and dale, as Winfried followed his grandfather, he told them old stories – about Leo Dorn of Hinterstein, for instance, the last eagle-hunter of the Allgäu. And he pointed out and named every mountain, so that they soon knew them all.[27]

Apart from the history and geography of the Allgäu, Armin Müller had two favourite subjects. One was cheese, especially Emmental cheese. The reason was clear: Müller's father Magnus owned a famous cheese shop in Sonthofen, which had the concession for selling Emmental in the town. The boys' mothers all knew Magnus Müller, who stood for more than fifty years in his shop, his shirtsleeves held up with armlets, entering their purchases in a vast ledger. Armin taught his pupils every step of the cheese-making process, which they recorded faithfully in their exercise books.

In 1987, when Sebald was sitting down to write 'Paul Bereyter', he asked Jürgen if he still had his *Heimatkunde* exercise books from school; his own must have got lost along the way. Did he have anything on Armin Müller's hobby horse of cheese? Max asked. Or on his other hobby horse, the railways? Could Jürgen send him whatever he could find on either of these?[28]

Jürgen could. His *Heimatkunde* books were full of railway essays and drawings, even more than cheese ones. Max remembered in particular a drawing of signals they'd done in their first year with Müller, but Jürgen couldn't find that straight away. Instead he found his second-year exercise book, from 1953–4. That had quite as many railway pictures as the first one. So he packed it up and sent it to his friend. In it was the plan of the new Sonthofen station that Sebald would put on one of the last pages of 'Paul Bereyter',[29] and several other railway pictures as well: large-scale maps of the whole regional network, and detailed drawings of the routes around Sonthofen. Helmut did the same ones, and so, three years later, did his younger brother Gerhard. The drawings were done with care and are rather beautiful. Müller's boys plainly sensed the importance of this subject to him, though in this case the reason wasn't clear. And the one who became a writer remembered.[30]

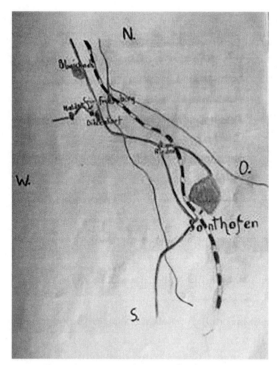

From Jürgen Kaeser's exercise book, 1953–4.

In the autumn of 1954 Beate turned three and started kindergarten.[31] She was a lively, sociable child, but the endless arts and crafts bored her to tears. So she regularly ran away to her little friends' houses. Then Rosa or Winfried would have to fetch her home; and Winfried was also called upon to watch over her as she played outside the house, since she would run off from there too. All this childminding bored him even more than kindergarten bored Beate, and he didn't hide it. Her earliest memory, Beate says, is of putting out a lump of sugar on their bathroom windowsill. Their neighbour called out, 'What are you doing, Beate?' and she gravely explained: she was trying to entice the stork to bring her a little brother or sister. Winfried, aged twelve, was cleaning shoes on the doorstep below. He looked up at her darkly and said, 'If that ever happens, I'll commit suicide.'

The autumn of 1954 brought a change for him as well.[32] He could stay on at the primary school for another year or two, or take the *Gymnasium* exam now, and start at Oberstdorf. With his usual care for his pupils – especially one as bright as Winfried Sebald – Armin Müller called on his parents to make sure they'd put him in for *Gymnasium*. He needn't have worried: they had. So had his friends' parents, the Kaesers and Bunks, and the three boys all took the Oberstdorf entrance exam at ten years old. Winfried was so nervous that he gave the comparatives of 'good' as 'good, gooder, goodest'. Nonetheless, he passed easily, as did the others, and they were all ready for *Gymnasium*.

Now, however, the Kaesers and Sebalds had a further discussion.[33] The Oberstdorf classes would be as big as the primary ones: how about letting their sons start the next stage at St Maria Stern instead, the convent school in Immenstadt, where classes were much smaller? Gertrud was already there; Frau Kaeser had been there herself; and from Rosa's point of view, it was a good Catholic school. They could stay for only three years, after which boys were no longer allowed, but at that point they could move to Oberstdorf. So it was decided. Helmut went straight to Oberstdorf, but Winfried and Jürgen would go to St Maria Stern. The school was private, and neither family was well off. But for their children's education they would manage somehow. So the years of Winfried's driving Blumenstrasse mad with his *Kikiriki* began.

The class he and Jürgen joined was definitely smaller – barely twenty boys, to the primary school's more than fifty. But apart from that, St Maria Stern wasn't a happy choice. In the novel Max wrote at twenty-two he makes it a classically awful boys' boarding school, where it's always freezing cold and the regime is harsh.[34] In reality he wasn't a boarder, and it wasn't a boys' school run by monks, as in the story, but a girls' school run by nuns. But (apart from the usual inventions) his portrait was fairly accurate. Gertrud, who spent six years at St Maria Stern, wasn't unhappy there, since she had good friends, 'But I hated the nuns,' she says. And two of Winfried's later friends agree: the regime was unbelievably strict, the food awful, and the nuns heartless.[35]

These were both girls, one of them a boarder, and things weren't quite so hard for the boys. Still, Jürgen's word for their convent school is a *Kaserne*, an army barracks, or an *Erziehungsheim*, an approved school for delinquents. The nuns could hardly tolerate even small boys among their girls, and policed them with fanatic zeal; once Jürgen was fiercely interrogated for merely looking at a group of girls, long before he had any interest of the kind the nuns feared.

Being Jürgen, he remembers lighter moments as well, such as Winfried's being much amused by the nun who demonstrated running and jumping in her long black habit. And Gertrud remembers that the more they were disciplined, the more mischief they made. On one occasion Winfried set fire to an eraser; the nun followed the strange smell to its origin, and he had to sit on it quickly to douse the flames. (Luckily he was wearing thick lederhosen, and so avoided the fate of poor Hans Steinlehner.) On another occasion he and Jürgen were caught playing with a toy car in a music lesson, and were told to put it down immediately. Jürgen did – but wound it up first, so that when the hapless nun tried to pick it up it sped away from her, to uncontrollable laughter from the class. For such offences Winfried was often made to stand outside in the corridor, where several times he met Gertrud, who'd been similarly banned. Once, she remembers, the head nun saw them, and shook her head sadly. 'But you have such a good father!' she said.

More seriously, not only Winfried and Jürgen but all four Sonthofen boys in their class were repeatedly disciplined for fighting on the train to school. They weren't really fighting, Jürgen says, just messing around, giving each other *Schwitzkasten*, 'sweat boxes' – which he demonstrates with a grin, gripping a phantom boy's head in his armpit. But to the nuns, determined to impose order, this was beyond the pale. They made it clear to the Sebalds and Kaesers that their sons might prefer the *Gymnasium*. And breathed a sigh of relief when after only two years the two bad boys left St Maria Stern for Oberstdorf.

Halfway through Winfried's convent school years something important happened: in November 1955 the German Army was permitted to re-form, and four months later, on 16 March 1956, his father rejoined.[36] His rank at the end of the war had been captain, his job the care of his unit's vehicles and young drivers. Now he took up both once more.

This was the crucial step up that Rosa especially had been waiting for. From now on she would be *Frau Hauptmann*, and eventually *Frau Oberstleutnant* (lieutenant colonel), as she had once been *Kommissars Rosl*, all of which was very important to her. And at last there would be more money, and – more important still – security. That's what counted for Georg, the poor boy from Lower Bavaria. Both his daughters say firmly that he was not a military man by nature, but chose his career now, as he'd done in the 1920s, for financial reasons. And a bit, Gertrud adds, due to pressure from Rosa. Looking back, Max's friends agree: Georg wasn't really a military type at all, but a 'civilian in uniform', more a bureaucrat than a soldier.[37] It was Winfried who saw his father as a soldier (and soon as a Nazi), and convinced them all, through the power of his imagination.

And yet Winfried's imagination wasn't completely wrong. The ability to put a German uniform back on just eleven years after the war showed a certain mindset, and divided one kind of person from another, just as seven years later some of Winfried's friends would do military service, while others, like him, would rather be dead. Gerhard Eschweiler's father, for example, who had been a paratrooper in the war, never returned to what could have been a distinguished career, but remained in the border police for the rest of his working life.[38] And Lotte Küsters' mother, whose husband had died in Hitler's war, was at the other end of the spectrum from Georg altogether. When the Ordensburg was reopened, and the army marched proudly through Sonthofen to reclaim it, she stood by the window watching them pass, the tears streaming down her face, saying, '*Nicht schon wieder!*' (Not again!)

But life in 3a Am Alten Bahnhof now became a little easier, and a little more bourgeois. Back home in Wertach Rosa had spoken pure Wertach Allgäuerisch, and whenever she went back – to tend her mother's grave, for instance – she reverted to her native dialect. In later life Max exaggerated this rustic aspect of his family life, claiming that he only learned *Hochdeutsch*, or proper German, when he went to school.[39] In fact the family never used Allgäuerisch together, since Georg didn't know it; instead they spoke a mix of Allgäu-accented and Bavarian-accented German. In Sonthofen Georg's language remained as it always had been, Bavarian German with a Lower Bavarian accent. But Rosa's German now became more cultivated, and her accent less Allgäuerisch.

For several years now Winfried had had to do something Rosa remembered as a sign of culture from the Berchtolds of Wertach: he took zither lessons. His teacher was Herr Pirner, father of the young piano prodigy Gitti Pirner, whom Winfried knew as the idol of St Maria Stern.[40] He himself, sadly, was no prodigy; Pirner would grimly correct his fingering, while Gitti's perfect crescendos and glissandos poured in from the next room.[41] This was an unhappy experience, especially for a boy with Winfried's need to excel. So, predictably, the awful zither lessons had the opposite effect from the one Rosa had intended, putting him off musical instruments altogether. When he was fourteen or fifteen and listening to jazz, he dreamed about playing the sax, and in Manchester in the sixties he briefly strummed a guitar.[42] But that was just the zeitgeist: there wasn't a boy in the Western world who didn't play the guitar in 1966. Winfried would pick up the zither just once of his own free will; after that, his experience of music, which was intense, was limited to listening. Looking back, he recorded several such experiences from the next few years in Sonthofen: listening from the loft to the organist playing ecstatically in an empty church; peering in at Gogl's music lessons in the old station building, to catch Regina Tobler bending her head over her viola;[43] watching rehearsals for Verdi's *Ernani* from the dim hall of the Ochsenwirt.[44] They all share the same atmosphere: solitude, longing, and looking in from the outside.†

When the family moved to Sonthofen in late 1952 Josef Egelhofer was eighty, and as fit as ever.[45] He continued his daily walks, through the town and out into the woods and mountains all around. Afterwards he would sit in the Lion Inn nursing a small beer, watching the card players and waiting for his grandson to join him. Then he would show him whatever he'd brought back from his walk: a flower or mushroom from the fields, sometimes now a banana or other exotic fruit he'd bought from the shop next door. In the autumn they would gather the nuts that fell from the venerable chestnut tree in the pub garden and take them up into the mountains for the deer.

Josef also continued his games with his grandchildren. He played *Schwarze Peter* with Winfried, a German version of Old Maid, and read Grimms' fairy tales to Beate now. He also teased her mercilessly, sitting her on a table in front of him, poking her tummy so that she looked down, then flicking his finger under her nose. Winfried probably enjoyed this, as he enjoyed his grandfather's little rebellions against Rosa's citified new ways. For instance, in the bathroom to which Beate tried to call the stork there was a fully plumbed bathtub, in which Josef was supposed to take baths like the rest of the family. But he'd never had a bath in his life and he wasn't going to start now. He mounted a quiet resistance, which Rosa eventually accepted, since he was always perfectly clean, washing in the old-fashioned way in a tin tub. And every morning Rosa would make milk-coffee, but Josef couldn't stand the wishy-washy stuff, and as soon as she left the kitchen he'd jump up and pour his away.[46]

There was no sign of change in him, right to the end; at eighty-four he seemed as strong as ever. But even he was declining. As death approaches, old people often fall out of bed: perhaps they've tried to get up and lost their balance, probably they've had small strokes, but it looks like an attempt to escape. So it was with Josef. He fell out of bed a few times in the spring of 1956. Finally it happened again; no one heard him call, and he spent all night on the floor. That brought on pneumonia. He lay in bed for a few weeks, dozing; that is when Winfried picked up his hated zither and played a slow *Ländler* or country air for him. On 14 April he died; and his grandson never touched the zither again.[47]

In his early unpublished novel,[48] Max set his grandfather's death in Wertach, and had the family leave soon after, so that the two great losses – of his grandfather and of his life in nature – coincide. The first person to tell him is Frau Steinlehner, who comes to him immediately. When he has heard her he lies still and smells the lilacs and turned-over earth in the garden. Later he gets up and creeps unseen into his grandfather's room. People are praying, his mother is crying, and incense smoke is rising to the roof. Then the undertaker brings in the coffin and he sees it is full of wood shavings. When his mother comes to tell him in the morning, he already knows; he doesn't reply, and in silence she leaves his room.

This is, of course, fiction, his first (and only) attempt to reimagine one of the most important events in his life. It tells us nothing for certain about what happened, but a great deal about the images of mourning that haunt his work: wood shavings in a coffin, white clouds of incense that will become fog and mist, dust and ashes as well. These all come from the death of his grandfather. Or rather, from his effort to grapple with the death of his grandfather and turn it into literature.

Near the end of his own life he said that Josef's death had made a huge hole in his universe, that he had never got over it, and missed him still. It was, for once, entirely true; he played no games about his grandfather. He kept his moustache brush, his clothes brush and one of his blue-checked handkerchiefs all his life. And on the mantelshelf over the fireplace in Norfolk he placed his photograph and a small shrine of stones.[49]

The loss of his grandfather split apart Winfried's world. Even the return of his father hadn't been able to do that, because his grandfather was there. But now his hypersensitive nature lost its protector, as though he had lost a skin. And his skin reacted: the psoriasis he would have on and off for the rest of his life began. So he said himself, in an interview.[50] That's no proof, of course, and his sisters think it simply started with puberty, as did their own skin problems – since adolescence both Gertrud and Beate have tended to eczema on their hands, like Aunt Anny. On the other hand, there is notoriously a psychological element in most skin diseases; and Max told his friend Marie (whom he didn't tease as he did interviewers) that he was in a bad state after Josef's death, and it was then that his psoriasis started. So he seems to have believed it himself, and it was most likely true.

Yet he did not break then. Perhaps he repressed the trauma, as his characters repress theirs; perhaps it took a long time for its meaning to become clear to him, as often happens to the narrator of his books. But his closest childhood friend, Jürgen, didn't know of his attachment to his grandfather and his grief over his death at the time. Winfried cannot have talked about him, or shown any of that grief, either at twelve or later, during their teens. In fact, the next seven years – the *Gymnasium* years – were lively, engaged ones, among the lightest of his life. That was the first thing everyone who'd known him in his youth wanted to tell me, from his sisters and close friends like Lotte and Jürgen, to other friends like Sigrid Becker and Heidi Böck.[51] When we read his dark, mournful books, they said, we don't recognise the Winfried we knew. He was witty, ironic, but not dark. The words they used were *heiter, lustig, ganz normal* – cheerful, funny, completely normal. They saw no shadow, only the joking, japing boy. Except for a few; and that was later, in his last year or two of school.

One of the best scholars of Sebald, Uwe Schütte, argues that his grief for his grandfather was the real one in his life and work, the one for the victims of the Third Reich a psychic cover.[52] That is going much too far: it is as wrong to say that the Holocaust is not Sebald's subject as to say that it is his only one. His grief over German crimes was what broke him, and what he wrote about. But this grief was the first.†

7

1956–61

In the autumn of 1956 Winfried and Jürgen, as relieved as the nuns, left St Maria Stern behind them and joined Helmut Bunk, Werner Braunmüller and the others in Year 3 of the *Oberrealschule* Oberstdorf.

Oberstdorf was a *Gymnasium*, but was called an *Oberrealschule* (Jürgen explained) because it specialised on the scientific side. There were girls as well as boys now, and Protestants as well as Catholics. The division between the sexes was over because there were too few girls; a mere 15 per cent, since it was still less common to educate one's daughters. But the one between religions continued.[1] The result was that for most of their *Gymnasium* years Winfried and his friends Lotte Küsters and Walter Kalhammer, who were Protestant, were in different classes.

Oberstdorf is high in the Allgäu Alps, almost on the border with Austria. It had always been a popular ski resort, and as a result had had a branch railway line from Sonthofen since the late nineteenth century.[2] Winfried and Jürgen thus remained *Bahnschüler* – commuter pupils – for the rest of their school lives: on the single-track Altstädten line, which ran through a glorious mountain landscape, crossing and recrossing the tumbling Iller and ending at Oberstdorf.

The Sonthofen boys were older now, and the days of the sweat-boxes were over. Instead they chatted, copied each other's homework, and played endless games of cards. Lotte would sometimes play truant and go as far afield as Ulm and Lindau to get away from the Allgäu and see the world. Now and again Jürgen would join her; but never Winfried. If their parents found out they would all be in trouble, but Winfried's trouble would be the worst.[3]

When the *Bahnschüler* arrived in Oberstdorf they found a school very like their old one:[4] 500 children packed into ten classrooms, in a small, old building that had once been the town hall. The overcrowding was so bad that they sometimes had to be taught in shifts, as though they were workers in a factory. A new building would be opened three years later; but from the ages of twelve to fifteen this was Winfried's school.

Life at home went on as before. Gertrud remained at St Maria Stern, taking the other train every morning. After six months of the failed kindergarten attempt, Beate stayed at home, and all too often Winfried remained in charge of her. In the summers he had to take her with him to the swimming pool, where he gave her such thorough lessons that by the age of six she could swim perfectly, and could go alone.

Rosa still had to count the pennies, and their meals remained much the same: cheese noodles, potatoes with Lemburger cheese, pancakes – perhaps there were a few more eggs in the pancakes now. Meat no more than twice a week, and never on Fridays, since they were good Catholics, but not often fish on Fridays either, since fish wasn't easy to get in the Allgäu in the 1950s. But whatever Rosa cooked tasted wonderful; Winfried's friend Lotte has never forgotten her plum dumplings. And Rosa was always health-conscious: they ate lots of vegetables and only wholegrain bread. In Sonthofen there was soon a health-food shop, where she became a regular customer.

The packages from America continued to arrive. In the early Sonthofen years they were still practical – instant coffee for Rosa, Suzanne's shoes and dresses for Gertrud, for Beate lovely fitted knickers with elastic around the legs, unlike the baggy woollen drawers the other little girls had to wear. Later they became presents, like a big panda bear for Beate, or a small box camera for Winfried. Most of the presents came from Aunt Anny, who was godmother to all three children, and who never failed to send them her monthly letters with their dollar bills. Even at university Winfried went on getting Anny's letters, which always began the same way: 'Dear Winfried, How is school?'[5]

Anny herself continued to return, though now that she was coming to Sonthofen rather than Wertach, Beate no longer remembers her weeping. She went on buying her Hummel figurines too. Much as the children loved their aunt, as they grew into their teens they found poor Anny's beloved keepsakes terribly kitsch. It is a measure of Max's lasting love in particular that he never breathed a word against her taste, though he abhorred *Heimat** kitsch above everything, and forgave it in no one else.

Several times during the 1950s and 1960s they visited their Sebald grandparents in Stein near Nürnberg, where they had gone to live with Georg's sister and her family. In old age these grandparents had become slightly strange. Their grandmother had lost all her teeth, so that her nose and chin almost met, like a witch's; she was small and nimble and always busy. Their grandfather, by contrast, was large and almost motionless. He had retired early, at about sixty, and no longer did anything at all. He lay on a couch all day, getting up only for meals, complaining that his feet hurt. (Of course they hurt, since he never used them, says Beate, who was a nurse all her working life.) After some years of this he suddenly became extremely religious, like his wife, which made them even less appealing to Winfried and his sisters. Still, their cousins were nice, their Aunt Anni a dear, their Uncle Toni (Gertrud noticed) a good-looking, witty man; so, despite the grandparents, they went more or less willingly to Stein.

In 1958 Gertrud was seventeen, Winfried fourteen and Beate seven. Gertrud finished the last year at St Maria Stern, but wanted to go on to study for the *Abitur*, the highest qualification, and unlike many fathers, Georg agreed. So that September she started at the Hildisgard Lyzeum in Kempten. Beate started school at the same time. And Winfried began to rebel against his parents.

It was their attitudes – their bourgeois attitudes. Their rigid routines, so that you had to come punctually to every meal, and it was always roast pork on Sunday. Their merciless cleaning, so that Rosa never stopped vacuuming, and when she did, Georg took over. Their neatness, so that everything had its place as though it had never been touched; especially Georg's, who had to have everything in straight lines like his soldiers – the forks on the table, the pencils on his desk. The Kaesers' house wasn't like this, nor was Lotte's, or Babette Aenderl's. Their homes were for

*The untranslatable German word for one's native land or region, carrying a strong emotional charge.

living in, not looking at. None of their parents made the children go to church; Jürgen could even wear jeans on a Sunday if he liked. All Winfried's own parents knew was the Allgäu; for his mother especially, nowhere else could compare. Whereas the Kaesers were always talking of other places and going to see them. Frau Aenderl had no money and couldn't go anywhere, but when she invited him for lunch one day he tasted curry for the first time. Above all, these parents *didn't care what other people thought.* Frau Küsters was sublimely innocent and didn't even know, and the Kaesers didn't care. Frau Kaeser spent every summer at the pool, getting tanned all over; she and her husband had even been seen walking together in the town, *holding hands.*[6]

So Winfried started to dissent and criticise, and arguments began in the family that would last until he left home. Beate was too young to join in at first, and later too practical; she went her own way quietly, without arguing about it. Gertrud agreed with Winfried, and fought particularly with her mother. She agreed with him most of all, in these early days, about religion, and remembers standing with him at the door of their parents' room, laughing at the saccharine image of Jesus on the Mount of Olives on their wall. But though she found their father's mania for order as absurd as he did, she managed to laugh at that as well, and not be driven mad by it, as Winfried was. That would be the difference between them later, too. Gertrud could protect herself and ignore what she wanted to. Winfried could never protect himself from anything.

In 1958 his school life changed too. Something happened now that would be repeated at his first university but not afterwards, and that was key to the difference between these years and later ones: he had a circle of very close friends. They were so close for the next five years that they called themselves the Clique.[7] They were four boys and a girl: Winfried Sebald, Jürgen Kaeser, Werner Braunmüller, Walter Kalhammer and Lotte Küsters. Later there would be a fifth boy, Axel Rühl.

They were from very different backgrounds, says Lotte (who later changed to her middle name, Ursula), but it didn't matter – they hardly noticed. Her own mother was a cultured Berliner who had come to the Allgäu because of her husband's work, then lost him in the war and was left poor. Winfried's and Axel's fathers were in the army, Jürgen's was a bookkeeper and Werner's a railway employee, which put them all in the lower middle class: not poor, but not at all well off. (That lovely old house of Jürgen's had come into the family by sheer luck, when his grandmother came to it as a maid, and ended by inheriting it from her employer.) Walter, by contrast, came from the richest and most cultured family of the Clique. Both his parents had studied music, after which his father became a doctor instead. Walter was the youngest of their five children and lived in the most beautiful house in Sonthofen.

Each of the Clique had their role, and most had a nickname. Winfried now became 'Sebe', and Jürgen 'Kasus', from the Latin for 'case', *Kasus* in German. This was Winfried's idea, and probably a joke, since Jürgen was in the science stream and never studied Latin. But it stuck: some of his friends still call Winfried Sebe, but everyone calls Jürgen Kasus. Walter was 'Waldi' and Axel would become 'Anton'. The other two kept their own names, except when Lotte changed hers to Ursula. This was all a bit complicated for outsiders, who now include us, but that is the point of a clique.

Sebe's role in the early years was to bring to the Clique everything American, which came of course from his Aunt Anny. He was the first teenager in Sonthofen to wear jeans – much envied by the others, who quickly followed. He also introduced them to cornflakes and chewing gum, and later to American writers like Hemingway and Steinbeck. Kasus remembers that he ostentatiously chewed gum even in class, much to the annoyance of the teachers.

Kasus himself was the rascal of the group, and the scientist. It was clear from early on that he would be a chemist; his parents let him build a laboratory in their basement, and the Clique spent many hours there watching him perform pungent experiments. With their famous permissiveness, his parents also allowed him to give Fasching parties – the Bavarian Mardi Gras – in the house; even on one unforgettable occasion clearing out their own bedroom to make room for the friends to dance.

'Waldi' was the second intellectual of the Clique after Sebe, whom he much admired. He was an observer, like Winfried, but without Winfried's wicked and caustic side: 'He smiled and said nothing,' one of the group remembers. He was also an artist and musician, and when Winfried became the literary leader, these became his roles. He was very gifted at both. But Waldi, like Sebe, had father problems. Later they would become even worse than Sebe's; now they were much the same. Dr Kalhammer was older than the other fathers, and even more authoritarian than Georg, while Walter was as sensitive as his friend, but smaller, shyer, even more introverted. He was their classic outsider, more than Winfried. Winfried was too attractive, and too angry.

Walter and his violin, with Helmut Bunk and Winfried, around 1958.

Werner Braunmüller was a good musician too. His father played the violin, so he bought Werner a cello (it cost him a whole month's salary, Werner says), and at school Werner played the cello to Walter's violin. Apart from this, he was Waldi's opposite: tall, blond and handsome, a climber and skier, and soon a great charmer of girls. Winfried enjoyed his company, as he enjoyed that of Kasus; he clearly had an instinct in these years for seeking out friends who brought out his lighter side. As a result, Werner is adamant: 'Sebe was always jolly.'

Lotte Küsters – to come to her last – was similar. She was (and is) *joie de vivre* personified, fearless and independent, ready for any lark and any adventure. At the same time she was critical and rebellious, as opposed as Winfried was to the narrow, small-minded ways she saw around her, if not in her own home. Her role in the Clique was to bring to it her political and historical knowledge. As they grew older, Lotte was the one with whom Winfried could talk about the past, who understood his anguish and shared it. She was the heart of the group; and she and Kasus remained the central friends of Max's youth, which is to say the central friends of his life.

Lotte at about fourteen.

The fourteenth year of Winfried's life brought another vital event as well. In July, France came to Sonthofen.

This came about, like so many good things, through his friends Lotte and Babette.[8] Their mothers, in this time of post-war accord between France and Germany, had heard of an exchange programme for young people. A woman from Sonthofen was teaching German in a lycée in Paris, and two of her girls were eager to partake. One was called Marie, the other Martine. They were both from the best families, Mme Bach assured the Sonthofen mothers, and were two of her top pupils, with a good grounding in German. Frau Küsters and Frau Aenderl both liked the idea, and both needed the money the guests would bring. And so it was arranged. For the next two summers the two *jeunes françaises* came to Sonthofen; after that, Martine came for three summers more.

Marie stayed that first summer of 1958 with Frau Küsters, in her second summer with Frau Aenderl. And if this was an important time for Winfried, for Marie it was a revelation.[9]

She came from a difficult home – indeed from a difficult life, for all her thirteen brief years. She was born in January 1945, four months after her father, a member of the Resistance, was brutally murdered by the retreating Wehrmacht. ('But you never told us that!' Max said, when they re-met decades later. 'Of course I didn't,' Marie replied.) Her mother couldn't manage, and soon took Marie home to her parents.

There she left her; and for the next many years Marie lived with her grandparents, with only lightning visits from her mother.

Marie's grandfather's mill.

Her grandfather owned a beautiful old mill on the river Aisne, which had been destroyed every time the Germans raged through Picardy; the last time, after the First World War, he had rebuilt it himself. There he and her grandmother brought her up together with her five cousins, the children of her mother's brother, without distinction. But Marie felt the distinction every time they called their father Papa and she couldn't. For a long time she thought her grandfather was her father; but when she was seven she was officially made *une pupille de la Nation*, as the child of a fallen hero, and understood that her own father was dead. She still loved her grandfather dearly, but he was extremely strict, and she was a rebellious child, especially after her mother's visits, and he punished her severely, though it never made the slightest difference. One day he punished her cat instead, by killing it. That was the end for Marie; she never forgave him.

When she was nine her mother came to fetch her. She had achieved her aim and married a rich man, who would ensure that she never starved again. Marie was now wrenched from the violent but loving life of the mill, and found herself instead in an elegant flat in the middle of Paris, with a mother who had lost interest in her long ago, and a stepfather who had no idea how to deal with an angry child. And instead of her simple country school, she was now in the Cours Maupré, a lycée for girls, all of them rich and (as Mme Bach had said) from the best families. Fortunately, Marie was very quick and intelligent (though '*orthographe zéro*' – a terrible speller), and her family could more than compete: her grandfather was a *noble vaniteux*, a proud aristocrat, as Marie says, who could trace his ancestry back to Jean Bart, a famous seventeenth-century pirate ennobled by Louis XIV.[10] She was also, despite everything, full of life and fun, with black hair and green eyes, a charming gamine face, and an irresistible gap-toothed smile. She made friends quickly and was soon doing well, at least at school.

Home was another question. When Lotte visited Marie later, she was shocked by the coldness in the perfect flat; by the narcissism of Marie's mother, concerned only with her own beauty; by the whole rigid, formal, snobbish regime.

Furious little Marie, c. 1947. 'We already had the
same attitude to the world,' Max wrote to Marie
about this picture.

That was what Marie came from: first abandonment, now cold control. And suddenly she was in the midst of mountains, which she'd never seen before, with Lotte, who was instantly her friend, and four gorgeous boys, free to roam all day without a grown-up in sight. They rambled through the beautiful green mountains, they lazed in the mountain sun, they leapt off the rocks of the Starzlachklamm into the pool below. And all the while Winfried talked about literature, Walter talked about music and Kasus about chemistry, and Werner flirted with her and Lotte and made them laugh. She couldn't believe how clever they were, but at the same time so friendly, with none of the pretensions of Paris. She fell in

love with them all, and with Sonthofen; for the rest of her life it would
be the place where she'd been happiest and most free.

But most of all she fell in love with Winfried. She was only thirteen,
and fourteen the next summer, but again it would last for the rest of her
life. After 1959 she didn't see him again; but when she got engaged years
later, she told her fiancé she would have to think carefully, because she
was in love with someone else.

She never explained to me why it was Winfried whom she loved,
immediately and for ever. But she didn't have to. He was so intelligent,
so darkly funny, and also so good-looking, with a special, intense appeal.
But he was reserved, in some way unreachable. He was as friendly as
they all were, but that was all. He called her '*freche Kröte*', 'saucy frog',
and somehow she was almost never alone with him, though she longed
to be. So she was very, very careful not to let him see how she felt. She
would rather have died than let anyone see, and no one did. If the
friends thought of her as sweet on anyone, it was Werner.

All the next year at school she thought about coming back to
Sonthofen. At last she was there, and even closer to Lotte this time.
She discovered that Lotte always carried a photograph of her lost father,
just as she did. Their fathers had fought on opposite sides, but that
didn't seem to matter. They had both died; that was enough. The bond
between the two girls was strengthened, and remains to this day.

Marie must have hoped that her friendship with Winfried might
change too, now that she was all of fourteen and he fifteen. And perhaps
they were closer this time, but not in the way she dreamed of. She
went to school with the group and saw that side of his life. He gave her
German lessons, and taught her to roll her 'r's in the Allgäu fashion –
'*Oberrrstdorf!*' He even brought her home, where she met his parents
and sisters, and made a friendship with Gertrud that lasted several years.

These moments were a joy to her, and there were a few others. Once
Winfried showed her a poem he'd written, which she understood was a
gesture of trust, though it showed her too that his mind was on death,
not love – it was all '*Sarg, Sarg, Sarg*,' she remembers, 'Coffin, coffin,
coffin.' And once they were at a concert together in the Ordensburg,
high above Sonthofen; the orchestra played the 'Storm' movement
of Beethoven's *Pastoral* Symphony – and suddenly there was a real
thunderstorm too, they were all astounded and half afraid, and for a
brief moment Winfried put his arm around her.

But that was all. She was still '*freche Kröte*' and he was still unreachable. The summer was over in a moment. The last time she saw him, he rode up to her on his bicycle and gave her a book as a farewell present. She asked him how to say 'Adieu' in German, and he answered '*Lebewohl*'. So she said '*Lebewohl*', which literally means 'live well', 'have a good life'; and he rode off on his bike.

Her mother had never wanted Marie to go to Germany. In 1958 her grandfather had taken her side, but now her mother put her foot down: no more Germany. The next summer she was sent to England to learn English instead. A few years later she managed to get back, though not to Sonthofen: to Lindau, where she re-met Werner by chance at a concert. She asked him about Winfried, and Werner told her that he had become a pastor in Switzerland. Maybe he was joking, or maybe he wanted to make Marie forget his rival. In any case she believed him; perhaps it seemed to her quite likely, remembering the strange, untouchable boy she'd known. She pictured him in black clerical garb with a round white collar, and decided she must forget him. Three years later she married.

Marie at fourteen.

As soon as he could, Kasus's father had taken his family abroad. In 1958 they went to the South of France, in 1959 and 1960 to Italy. And in 1959 they invited Sebe to come along.[11]

His parents were already unhappy that he spent so much time at the Kaesers', with their liberal, permissive ways. And they wouldn't have welcomed this idea – two weeks with them, in Italy, the land of sun and sin for all northerners. There were certainly more arguments. But Winfried won, and at fifteen he left Germany for the first time.

The Kaesers still had no car, so they had to lug all their camping equipment to the Ligurian coast by train. But it was well worth it. They went to see Michelangelo's marble quarries at Carrara; they walked to Marina di Carrara and ate delicious pizza (probably Winfried's first, unless Frau Aenderl had made him pizza too). The two boys spent countless hours floating on their air mattress on the blue-green sea and fishing with the rod that had recently arrived for Winfried from America. Frau Kaeser was in her element, sunbathing and swimming and cooking simple meals on her camping stove (but not fish, since the boys never caught any). She was a little jealous of Winfried, Kasus says, since he was already a big strong boy, while he himself was still a skinny kid. She was right, as this photo shows.

Winfried in Italy, 1959.

A little later that summer the Sebalds joined an exchange programme themselves, with unforeseen consequences.[12]

This had not been Rosa and Georg's idea either, but once again the Kaesers'. On their French holiday in 1958 they'd made friends with a French-speaking Swiss family who had two boys close to Jürgen's age. André wanted to learn German, while Jürgen would soon be studying French at school. So the parents arranged that the next year André would come on exchange to the Kaesers. When the next year came, however, Kasus was smitten with his first girlfriend and didn't want to leave Sonthofen. So the Kaesers conferred with the Sebalds. Perhaps Rosa wasn't ready to let Winfried leave home on his own, or perhaps he wasn't ready himself, despite his longing for faraway places. In any case it was decided: André would come to the Sebalds instead, and a Sebald would replace Kasus in Fribourg. But Gertrud, not Winfried, would go.

The unforeseen consequence rapidly followed, since on this exchange visit Gertrud, aged eighteen, met a tall, dark and handsome young man called Jean-Paul Aebischer and fell in love. She returned to Fribourg again the next year and it hadn't been an illusion. Jean-Paul was everything she longed for, and everything Rosa feared: an artist and singer, a long-haired bohemian, and not from the Allgäu – not even a German. Rosa had dreamed of marrying her to the son of Onkel Hans, the brother of Joe Egelhofer's wife Leni, who was a successful businessman, or at the very least to the son of the pharmacist in Sonthofen. But Gertrud would have none of either. At twenty-three she married Jean-Paul and settled in Fribourg for good. Rosa blamed her ever after for starting the exodus from Germany of all her children, and was never reconciled to Jean-Paul's bohemian ways. Kasus's first girlfriend soon disappeared, never knowing that she was the indirect cause of a mother's sadness and a daughter's happy marriage.

So that summer Winfried gained another foreign friend.[13] André was the closest one this year: he lived with the Sebalds, unlike the *jeunes françaises*. He was also older, and gifted in new and fascinating ways. He was a terrific footballer and an excellent musician. He played the clarinet beautifully and whistled even more beautifully. He whistled Tchaikovsky's Fifth Symphony – every note of it – Brahms's Clarinet Quintet, Bruch's Violin Concerto and many other things, all with a true, pure sound. And, though it was never mentioned, Winfried could not have helped noticing that André had a harelip, so that he made this perfect sound with the damaged part of himself. Winfried must have been moved by this, and André was surely in his mind when he wrote later about the schizophrenic poet Ernst Herbeck, who had a harelip too.

What André remembers of this first summer is what everyone remembers about Sebe: fun. André arrived in a jacket and tie and Winfried made him change into jeans straight away. They laughed and joked and punned in both languages. They went swimming every day, in every lake and river for miles around; Sebe was an excellent swimmer, André remembers, while he was no good at all and sank like a stone. They didn't talk about books or paintings, because André wasn't interested in those yet, only in music. But they did talk about the landscape on their walks. Winfried knew the name of every plant and tree, André says, and adds, 'I heard those conversations again later, in the way he wrote.' This chance meeting was a piece of good luck, as all Winfried's foreign friendships were. '*Nous étions tous les deux fantaisistes* (We were both dreamers),' André says: they both lived in their imaginations. And one day Winfried would also create beauty out of a damaged part of himself.

In September a whole new school life started.[14] Sebe and most of his friends would turn sixteen that year (and Lotte seventeen: she had had TB as a child, and had mostly been taught by her mother at home until she was ten). They were entering Year 6, in which they would be starting to choose the subjects they would do for their final exams. And they were in the big, new, modern building. There was room now for a boarding section, so that there was a leavening of young people from far beyond the Allgäu. Even so, the lower classes had around thirty children instead of fifty; the higher ones, from Year 6 to 9, around twenty, like St Maria Stern.

Compared to today, the regime at ORO (their school had a nickname too) was un-taxing. Classes went till one o'clock; the Sonthofen *Bahnschüler* dashed off their homework on the train (or copied it), and by two they were swimming or skiing, depending on the season. And in the classes themselves the workload was relatively light, the teachers (compared to the past) not strict, and the atmosphere as a whole relaxed. Max remembered that himself, looking back,[15] and so do the girls from St Maria Stern, with amazement and relief. And yet the system worked. 'I thought I learned nothing in chemistry at school,' says Heidi Nowak (née Böck), 'but later, when I had to pass a chemistry exam' – Heidi would become a pharmacist – 'I discovered that I knew a lot after all.'

They all agreed on the reason: their teachers. The scientists fondly remember Herr Weinert, who taught maths and physics, and Herr Zollhoefer, who taught chemistry and biology. Maths and physics were not Winfried's strong points, and at the end of school Weinert's judgement of his performance in the physics lab was recorded: 'Well, Bunk and Sebald, it's a pity about the coal that was burnt for you.'[16] For him and his friends it was the humanities teachers who would be important. Especially three among them: Herr Schmelzer, who taught literature, Herr Meier, who taught art, and Dr Eberhard, who was their class teacher, and taught history and German.

Karl-Heinz Schmelzer,[17] who was young and straight out of training college, brought the latest liberal ideas to the school. Even more importantly, he brought a passionate love of literature, especially for writers who would become Max's own favourites, such as Thomas Bernhard ('I'm a *Bernhardiner*,' he says*), Max Frisch and Jean Paul; it was most likely from Schmelzer that Winfried first heard of them.

He taught Winfried's class post-war German literature: the short stories of Heinrich Böll and Siegfried Lenz, for example ('Marvellous,' he says, 'much better than their novels'), and Günter Grass's *The Tin Drum*, which the parents vetoed as immoral, but he taught it anyway. 'I think I opened a few doors for Sebald,' he says, and for his other famous student, the painter Jan Peter Tripp as well, who would become Max's friend in later years. Both said so; it was Schmelzer, Tripp would say, who inspired his lifelong addiction to literature.[18]

Franz Meier,[19] the art master, was also full of new ideas and enthusiasm for his subject, and a favourite of all Winfried's friends. He laid large sheets of paper on the floor and invited his pupils to paint on them, like a roomful of young Jackson Pollocks; he took them outdoors as often as possible, to paint and draw from nature. Winfried loved this especially, as he'd loved the rambles with Armin Müller. And as he learned from Schmelzer about writers who would become his favourites, so he learned from Meier about a future favourite painter: Matthias Grünewald. They

---

*Which is a nice joke, since a *Bernhardiner* is a St Bernard.

made an intense study of Grünewald; it's likely that Winfried first saw the Isenheim altarpiece in Meier's class at Oberstdorf.[20]

Dr Kurt Eberhard[21] was a different kettle of fish altogether. He was older than Meier and Schmelzer, and firmly old-fashioned: the class had to stand up and say '*Guten Morgen*' when he came in. Yet he wasn't a political conservative, as was almost universal among the senior teaching staff, but a lifelong member of the democratic socialist party, the SPD. He was small and wore thick glasses; if he'd been old enough at the time, the boys thought, he'd have been declared unfit to serve in the war. Despite this, or because of it, he was a severe disciplinarian, and didn't hesitate to slap troublemakers hard. This won him great respect among the more raffish elements, and since he was a first-rate teacher, the others respected him as well. Indeed, they must all have been fond of him, since they gave him a nickname – in fact, two: *Schnautzel*, 'Snout' (because of his moustache) and *Popel* (for which I never got an explanation).

Later on Winfried and his friends would particularly respect Eberhard because, like Schmelzer, he refused to obey the taboo about the past. He pointed out that their history books ended at 1933. Above all, he taught them to be critical, and not to accept without question what people in authority said. Except himself, of course. He was even less consistent outside school, ruling his own sons with a rod of iron. The story went round that when the youngest was asked one day if he knew who God was, he replied 'Dr Eberhard'.

When Winfried was around sixteen his battles with his father changed: they became about the past.[22]

Beate, who was only eight or nine, noticed no difference, and accepted the family story – these were just the usual teenage arguments. But everyone else knew: Gertrud, his friends, his teachers. Meier knew,[23] and so did Schmelzer. 'Winfried suffered from his family,' he told me; when I asked why, he said, 'Because they were German.' It was partly from Schmelzer's classes that Winfried was learning about Germany's hidden history, and partly from his own reading, which was departing further and further from what was prescribed: at one stage, for example, he informed his friends that the nineteenth-century 'Father of Gymnastics', Jahn, who was revered at school, was a racist and proto-Nazi.[24] Altogether, Helmut Bunk remembers, by fifteen or sixteen Winfried was 'already like a '68er', 'a revolutionary' to less-aware boys like himself. And that is what he must have seemed to his father.

Georg refused to talk about the war, apart from jolly stories about his leaves in Berlin and Paris. And the more Winfried attacked him and his generation, the more silent he became – except when he snapped. Then the shouting would start, and Rosa would try desperately to calm them down, because the neighbours would hear. Over the next years this would grow worse, until there was a constant underlying tension in the apartment,[25] and Winfried, and no doubt his father as well, could relax only when they were away from home.

Among his friends' fathers there were a few who had been less involved, and so were less silent.[26] Kasus's father, for instance, having first been exempted from service on health grounds, was drafted like every man and boy at the end of the war, and was just about to be sent to the front when a friend got him out somehow; all sixty of his untrained, over- or underage companions died. He was no friend of the Nazis, Frau Kaeser even less so, and they talked about that terrible time quite openly, so that Kasus was spared this conflict with his parents, like all others. Helmut's father had been in a protected industry and hadn't served either; he was also a religious Catholic, and never joined the Party, so that he was, Helmut felt, quite uninvolved.

Lotte's father[27] had been a soldier, but all men had to be. Something else bothered her more: before the war he had been a sports teacher at the Adolf Hitler Schule. 'How could he have done that?' she asked her mother. 'Was he a Nazi?' 'No,' her mother said firmly. But he was poor, and they couldn't afford to marry – until he was offered that job at the Ordensburg. It was their only chance, and he took it. 'And what did you know?' Lotte persisted. 'When you were in Berlin, and the Jews were being taken away?' 'They did it secretly, at night, so that we wouldn't know,' her mother said. Her mother never lied, and Lotte believed her about both things; but she didn't stop worrying.

Other friends had fathers like Winfried's, or worse. Heidi Böck's, for instance, had been on the Russian front – unimaginably worse than the Western one – and had lost a leg there; from the moment he returned, he immersed himself in Germany's economic miracle and never spoke a word about the war. Eschweiler's father, the paratrooper who became a policeman, almost never spoke a word either. Gundela Enzensberger's father, who'd been a Luftwaffe pilot, had expected to be treated like a hero; when defeat put an end to that, he turned to drink and began abusing his family.

But the worst position was Walter's.[28] During the Third Reich his father, the cultured, respected Dr Kalhammer, had become an early member of the Nazi Party. By 1931 he was the *Kreisleiter* (district leader) of the Sonthofen area, second in command only to the *Gauleiter* of the whole region. This was not simply being a soldier who didn't ask questions: it was a position of power. And Dr Kalhammer had chosen it, proudly and gladly.

When I spoke to Walter's sister Ursula in 2015 she was over eighty and still burdened by sadness. Her father had certainly been a convinced Nazi in the beginning, she said. But by the later years of the war he was no longer a believer. When she asked him afterwards why he hadn't resigned, he answered, 'One doesn't abandon a sinking ship,' and that if he had done so, they would all have been sent to a concentration camp. That, at least, may well have been true.

Ursula didn't claim that her father was a decent man who never pursued anyone denounced to him, but others did. Usually I'd be sceptical, but this time I wasn't, because of the people who said it. Both Ursula (Lotte) and Jürgen, for instance, and above all their friend Peter Schaich, whose own fiercely anti-Nazi father was repeatedly denounced to Kalhammer, but Kalhammer never did anything about it. There was also the grocer Einsiedler, who openly taunted his neighbours with his anti-Nazism; he too was never touched.

I don't know if Walter heard these reports of his father, but if so, he didn't believe them. What he believed was something else. In February 1943 a five-year-old Jewish child, Gabriele Schwartz, was found hidden in the small village of Stiefenhofen, arrested and deported to Auschwitz. Stiefenhofen is part of the district of Sonthofen, and Walter was convinced that his father would have had to give his approval. He was not only a top Nazi official, therefore, but one with blood on his hands.

In fact, this cannot have been true: in February 1943 Dr Kalhammer was thousands of miles away, serving as a medical officer on the Eastern Front. And after the war, like all high-ranking Nazis, he was tried in one of the specially convened *Spruchkammer* courts, which bore out what Max's friends would tell me. He had been an unusually tolerant *Kreisleiter*, the evidence showed, had never approved of violence or used any himself, and – a witness specifically stated – had never been known to send anyone to a concentration camp. Walter's fears were wrong.

Nonetheless, he had wholeheartedly supported a racist, totalitarian and ultimately genocidal ideology. In about 1950 his eldest son Fritz asked him how he could have done such a thing. His father would say only that he couldn't talk about it. Ten years later Walter asked him again and got the same answer. Fritz, who had also seen courage and decency in his father, accepted that it was too painful for him to speak. But Walter belonged to the new generation and could not forgive him. He, Winfried and Lotte were the critical ones; but Walter tormented his father, and himself, most of all.

Compared to this, Winfried had little to complain of. But he treated his father as a Nazi, and spoke of him as a Nazi to his friends.[29] And his father, stubborn and angry, could only live up to his reputation. When he came home to find Rosa entertaining the Clique, he would stalk in, scowling, and the young people would freeze and disappear. Challenged in his own home, he only tried harder to impose order. They were *not* to leave their slippers in the middle of the room, they were *not* to dump their schoolbags wherever they pleased (and when Beate still did so, in her own room, he couldn't resist going in and lining it up with the edge of her bed). All this drove Winfried mad, and he drove his father mad in return. One morning at breakfast he casually cut off a slice of butter crookedly. Georg cut a slice so to leave the edge straight. Immediately Winfried cut another crooked slice, Georg another straight one, and on it went until Georg couldn't eat any more, and realised it was a tease. He let out a furious roar, and Winfried, having achieved his aim, got up and left the room. Georg leapt up after him and gave him a resounding slap. Perhaps it was the last one: at around fifteen or sixteen, Helmut remembers, Winfried told him that he had stopped his father from hitting him any more. At much the same time, Georg tried to stop his Nazi accusations. '*Das sagst Du mir nicht mehr*,' he said: 'You will not say that to me any more.' Winfried turned away, saying, 'But you won't stop me from thinking.'

At school too he showed his new revolutionary side.[30] He refused to come to any of the classes on sex education, saying that they were sheer hypocrisy and only about masturbation. And though he came to the religious education classes, it was mostly to cause trouble. On one memorable occasion he asked the priest about the *Beschneidung*

Christi, Jesus's circumcision: what *was* circumcision, exactly? The priest mumbled something and tried to change the subject, but Winfried wouldn't let him go. He repeated the question until the priest was forced to answer, his face reddening in anger or embarrassment, or both.

And since Dr Eberhard was the strictest of their teachers, Winfried had to resist him too. One day he provoked him so mercilessly that Eberhard gave him the troublemakers' treatment and slapped him hard. After that, however, Helmut remembers Georg coming to school and talking to Eberhard. From their expressions, Helmut is certain that Georg came to object, not apologise ('Unlike my father,' he says, 'who'd have said that the teacher is always right and given me another'). Perhaps Georg felt that only he had the right to hit his son; or else he came at Rosa's bidding, who always protected Winfried like a tigress. In the family Gertrud remembers that Rosa often made their father deliver the reproofs that were really hers, though according to Winfried it was the other way round.[31] In other words, the poor beleaguered Sebalds wanted their children to like them, and each left the dirty work to the other.

Despite all this, at around sixteen Winfried began to stand out at school. He was never *Klassensprecher* (the top student), because of his failures at maths and physics, and because (probably) he preferred attention as a rebel. He was also far too keen on his after-school activities, especially swimming, where he was beginning to excel too, though the serious sportsmen didn't rate him.[32] But his intellect and erudition were becoming unmistakable. He was the most articulate of his class, with wonderfully clear and cultured German (like Uncle Adelwarth). His essays were always the best, original and full of his wide reading; Dr Eberhard would read them aloud to the class, and let Winfried give people notes on their presentations. Franz Meier saw that he was no longer a mere schoolboy, but someone to be taken seriously; the centre point of his class, Meier said.[33]

At home Gertrud noticed how he was overtaking her in reading, in knowledge, in intellectual games; once he challenged her to speak in Alexandrines – rhymed couplets with twelve-syllable lines – for a week, which she managed only twice, while he managed almost every exchange. His friends noticed more and more what a good observer and storyteller he was.[34] He would also entertain them with the books he was reading, for example, Ludwig Thoma's *Filserbriefe* (*Filser's Letters*), a nineteenth-century satire written in thick Bavarian dialect: Winfried read passages aloud and had them all laughing helplessly. He was funny, original and charismatic, and he set the tone. In the *Filserbriefe*, for example, people didn't greet each other with '*Griasdi*' as in the Allgäu, but (archaically) with '*Gott zum Gruße*'. Winfried started saying this, and his friends followed. They'd get off the train in the morning and walk to school calling out '*Gott zum Gruße*' to each other, to the astonishment of passing Oberstdorfers.

As soon as the weather was warm enough the Clique would head for the Starzlachklamm, where they would swim and talk and read. He and Kasus would lie on the tin roof of the bee house and talk about the future in the dreamlike way of the young. And with Lotte he began to talk more and more of the silence around them, like living under a bell jar: the silence of his parents, of her mother, the fear of not knowing what their fathers had done in the war. Lotte told him that she often dreamed of being tortured, asking herself in terror, *How long before I give away the secret?* But what the secret was, she did not know.

By seventeen, Winfried was becoming close to Max. His basic attitudes were set: anti-bourgeois, anti-military, anti-clerical, anti-establishment. He'd found his style, which he kept for the rest of his life: informal and tieless, in jeans and, at most, a jacket. It looked casual, but in fact was carefully chosen: he was already an aesthete too. Not only his clothes but everything around him was selected and placed with care: in his room his favourite books were arranged by author and language; there was a special stone on one shelf and his grandfather's cuckoo-clock on another.[35] His surroundings would always be important to him, and some of his lowest moments would come when he was in ugly places. His room in the family flat in Sonthofen was exactly as he liked it, so he kept low moments away.

Despite the success of these years, he did have such moments, or was about to have them. And not only in the normal adolescent way, but already in the deeper Max way. He managed to hide them from his friends; even from Lotte, despite their grave conversations. But not from his mother. After his death she wrote to Karl-Heinz Schmelzer to thank him for his interest in Winfried all those years ago, even though he'd not been an easy pupil, she wrote, because his pensiveness and melancholy had started early.[36] She was still apologetic now, and had certainly been anxious then. Schmelzer remembers that Georg came more often than any other parent to the parent-teacher evenings, seeking reassurance about his son. Perhaps this was again at Rosa's bidding; more likely it was a shared concern. But while Georg's may have been mixed with anger by now, Rosa's was pure anxiety. Which was, perhaps, part of the problem.

Winfried in his room at around 17, with photos of his younger self behind him.

By the summer of 1961 the other *jeune française* was on her fourth visit to the Allgäu.[37]

Martine came from a strong, stable family, with none of Marie's losses even before she was born. Lotte stayed with them several times, and the contrast to Marie's home could not have been greater. Martine's parents were warm and open and welcomed her like a second daughter. They were both pharmacists, and their pharmacy near Rouen was next to the sea.* Martine's father was also a professor of pharmacology and a man of great culture. There was only one problem for Martine: he was old. Later she would realise how understanding he'd been, but to a young girl growing up, he was a distant figure, reserved and stern. Her

---

*The family moved to Normandy when Martine was fourteen.

convent-school life was one of hard work and discipline, her home life secure but severe; altogether she longed for novelty, fun and, above all, freedom. And like Marie, she found them in Sonthofen.

She spent a month there each time – a different month from Marie, so that they never met in the Allgäu, but only talked about their wonderful summers afterwards. Martine always stayed with Frau Küsters. She became as close to Lotte as Marie had; but while the war orphans shared their grief as well as their summer joys, for Lotte and Martine there were only joys. They were alike – both positive and optimistic, both keen sportswomen – and they loved each other's families. Marie loved Frau Küsters too, with her disregard for material things, so unlike her own mother. Martine loved her for her courage and kindness, though she was, she says, 'très sévère et pas gaie', and very poor. They often had only sausage and brown bread for supper, Martine remembers, and Lotte and her brother Nauke had always been a little hungry throughout their childhood.

Like Marie, Martine had glorious times with the Clique. She went to school with them too, and afterwards to the pool; they hiked through the mountains together and swam in the rivers; they hunted fish in the streams with their bare hands. And, of course, they went together to the Starzlachklamm. But later Martine had only vague memories of the others, apart from Lotte. The one who meant Sonthofen to her, as to Marie, was Winfried.

Her friendship with him was different from Marie's. Marie fell deeply in love with him – she told Martine so, in their eager conversations after the first summer. Martine herself was an innocent convent girl. It didn't occur to her to fall in love with Winfried; what she felt for him was rather a boundless admiration. He was her first *maître de pensée*, she says: a father substitute, as cultured and erudite as her own father, but young and exotic. She always sought such brilliant father substitutes, she realises, and ten years later she married one. But Winfried was the first, and her memories of him remain as strong as they were after each wonderful summer.

Already at fifteen, she says, he was like a prince – intense, handsome, romantic. He would stand on a rock at the Starzlachklamm and read Victor Hugo to them, and recite Goethe's '*Kennst Du das Land wo die Zitronen blühn*' to the sound of the waterfall. He seemed to her the very image of the German Romantic hero, like Goethe's young Werther, or Caspar David Friedrich's Wanderer above the Sea of Fog.

As the summers went by, he became more than an image. He began to teach her about German art and literature and music. He took her to the Alte Pinakothek in Munich to see Altdorfer's *Alexanderschlacht* (*The Battle of Alexander*), which had already seized his imagination, and which he would write about in *After Nature.*† They went to the Neue Pinakothek too, to look at the paintings of Paul Klee and Max Ernst, and Winfried talked about the theory of colours. This, especially, Martine has never forgotten, because she had wanted to study art herself, but her father had ruled that one long-haired artist in the family was enough (one of her brothers was an architect). Winfried gave her Brecht's *Caucasian Chalk Circle* and *Mother Courage*, and many other books she no longer remembers, and many records – works by Tchaikovsky, Bach and Chopin, and her favourite, Mussorgsky's *Pictures at an Exhibition*. And in all this he was never dull or sententious, but fascinating and often funny.

As Martine described this ideal intellectual friendship, I wondered why it had never turned to love. It soon became clear that the reason was not only her own innocence. She felt in Winfried a great moral idealism, and above all a great shyness and reserve. His sensual side, she said, came out in nature: he had a great love of the natural world and took much sensual pleasure from it. But with human beings he was *en retraite* – retiring, in retreat. And always, despite his charisma and romance, set apart and alone. 'He was alone,' Martine repeated. 'I'm sure of that.'

He never spoke to her about his family or hers, only about their shared interests in art and literature and music. That came from his deep reserve, but from something else as well – the silence they kept about what had happened between their countries. It was strange, Martine said, how that silence ruled them all. Sonthofen was full of soldiers and the Ordensburg was always there above them, but she never asked about them and no one mentioned them. Lotte's house was full of photographs of her dead father in German uniform, but she never asked about him either, and neither Lotte nor her mother said a word. They had all drawn a curtain over the past, and no one dared to break the silence.

Martine came to Sonthofen every summer until 1962, and one Easter as well. She and Winfried wrote to each other for another year or two.[38] But after that they lost touch. After school Martine acceded to her father's wishes and studied pharmacology at university. She was about to go on to specialise in biochemistry when she met an extraordinary woman: Maïmé Arnodin, who had created the first *prêt-à-porter* brand in France, Prisunic. Maïmé immediately saw the aesthete in Martine and offered her a summer job. Martine accepted – and knew instantly that this, not biochemistry, was what she wanted to do. That is when her father showed his kindness and care, accepting her choice, saying only, 'Once you've chosen your bed, you must lie on it.' Which she did. She stayed with Maïmé Arnodin for eight or nine years, then went into fashion journalism, and finally founded her own fashion consultancy, which was an astounding success. In 2013, at sixty-seven, she retired. But she still lectures at the famous IFM (l'Institut français de la mode) in Paris, and keeps an eye on her creation.

Winfried never knew any of this, and when he and Marie looked for Martine in 2000 they didn't find her. She, in turn, never knew what happened to Winfried. She never forgot him, but she forgot his surname, and though she had W. G. Sebald high on her list of books to read, she didn't make the connection. Until 2016, when I found her (with absurd ease, unlike Max, by simply putting her name into Google). When she realised that the Winfried of her youth and W. G. Sebald were one and the same, it was the greatest coincidence of her life. She immediately read all his books, one after the other without stopping, and heard his voice again, and relived his brilliance. It was as though of all the lucky chances she has had, the final one had happened, and her life had come full circle.

Martine at the Starzlachklamm in the early 1960s.

8

1961–3

In the summer of 1961 André Brünisholz returned to Sonthofen.[1] Again he and Winfried swam and walked and laughed together, but this visit had a more sombre side. Winfried often talked about the firebombing of Dresden, which he blamed on the Americans; he spoke harshly and with great repulsion, André remembers. His American phase was clearly over.

Other troubling things happened too. One day they went with Georg to visit a friend of his, who had a large map on his wall. The two old friends stood in front of that map for a long time, nostalgically tracing the sweep of the victorious German army across Europe in the early years of the war. And then for several days the boys travelled around southern Germany, paying a visit on the way to Winfried's Onkel Hans in Dachau on the edge of Munich. Dachau was the site of Hitler's first concentration camp, which operated for the whole of the Third Reich,[2] but Onkel Hans always denied having any knowledge of it. Now, when Winfried arrived with his Swiss friend, the conversation got round to the war; and no doubt subtly, and with many disarming smiles, Onkel Hans explained that Germans were not responsible for what had happened to the Jews. And when the boys got away to the guest room they'd been given for the night, André found *Mein Kampf* on his bedside table.

'What on earth did Winfried say?' I asked. 'Nothing,' André replied. He didn't notice *Mein Kampf*, or pretended not to notice it. And they never mentioned the strange conversation with Onkel Hans. It was clear that Winfried wanted to get away as soon as they could, but that was all. He was talking, painfully, to Lotte and Walter – but they were German; they shared the burden. With their foreign friends there was shame, and the constraint that Martine always felt. The silence remained unbroken.

Winfried didn't argue with his father that summer. But what he did was worse. Every time they met Georg in the flat, Winfried would waggle his finger under his nose, in Charlie Chaplin's Hitler parody, and say something in Allgäuerisch. Georg would say something back, but quietly, because their guest – their foreign guest – was there. André saw how hard it was to be a German son, and also a German father.

Though everyone who knew Winfried was aware of this father conflict, they never doubted that between him and his mother there was only love and solidarity, as there'd always been. But that was no longer true either.

Rosa was much closer to him in nature, imaginative and with an eye for beauty.[3] Like him she was a marvellous storyteller, captivating him with the tales that went straight into *Vertigo*. And she adored him, and took his side in everything, as we know. I think there is no doubt that Winfried loved his mother in return, as he could never love his stiff, literal-minded father.

Yet there had always been a problem with Rosa too. In his childhood it had centred on his appearance: he couldn't bear the way she fussed over him, doing up his buttons, brushing invisible dirt from his jacket, making him feel, as he would write to Marie, as pawed about as little Peter Rabbit before he was allowed out of his burrow.[4]

Now that he was older, Georg's control of Winfried's hair had finally stopped, but Rosa's control of his clothes hadn't.[5] It never would. She went on complaining about his wearing jeans on Sunday to the end of his student years; afterwards she fretted about his informal style, so unsuitable for a Herr Professor. Now, when he was in his teens, they fought over the tightness of his jeans. Once he insisted that they be made tighter than she had ordered; once he achieved the same result himself, by sitting in a full bathtub until they had shrunk to his taste. On the first occasion they ended up so tight he couldn't sit down, on the second so tight he couldn't get them off. On both occasions his mother had to undo the seams and re-sew them, and for once she was as cross as his father.

But this was only the outward sign of the problem between them. The real trouble was that he was breaking Rosa's bourgeois code. It was she who cared what the neighbours thought, she who insisted on church-going, and suits on Sunday, and white napkins at table. And as he grew older, this increased rather than diminished. We don't have to rely on memories now, however good his sisters' are: we have his own words. In 1961 Gertrud did her final exams and left school; during the next two years she took *au pair* jobs abroad, and she and Winfried wrote to each other.

In every second letter he aches to be gone, like her. His mother nags him about his clothes, his behaviour, his coming home late and going away at weekends. She watches his every move. When he goes to visit Werner she writes to him several times a week. She harps away on the same few subjects, and all his attempts to make her think about other things fail.[6]

For Rosa's point of view, we have a letter she wrote to Gertrud at the beginning of this time, in November 1961. I can't talk to him, she told her daughter. I hardly say a word, and he starts shouting. Just like his father.

That was the ultimate irony – *just like his father*. If Winfried had ever heard that, it would be hard to imagine his fury.

There was a new element to add to all this, now that he was seventeen and older: sex.[7]

Rosa was very concerned for her children's sexual respectability. Her objection to Jean-Paul was above all this: he was unmistakably a sexy man, and the physical happiness he and Gertrud shared was clear. One day, Gertrud recalls, they were out with her parents in Sonthofen, when Jean-Paul leaned over and kissed her on the neck. She saw her mother notice. Rosa said nothing then, but as soon as the door of the family home closed behind them she turned to Gertrud and slapped her hard across the face. She didn't say why; Gertrud knew.

Similar things happened to Beate. When she was eleven – around now, in 1962 – she had her first innocent childhood love, and she and the boy sat together in the cinema holding hands. She already knew enough to say nothing at home, but wrote about him secretly in her diary. And disaster – someone told Rosa, and Rosa rushed into her room and read her diary. That was the end of her innocence, Beate says, because from that day on her mother watched her like a hawk.

These were her daughters: in the 1960s it was different for sons. But not for Rosa. She fretted intensely if Winfried stayed out late. Once he went to a party and still wasn't home at two, three, four in the morning. Finally Rosa could bear it no more. She got up and hurried to the house where she knew the party was being held. She peered in through a window until she spotted Winfried. He was talking to a girl, but that was all. They were upright; they weren't even kissing. She went home, relieved, but still didn't sleep until she heard the creak of the front door.

The trouble was that she had been brought up by her strictly pious Catholic mother. And already in her mother's teaching there had been that secret element of guilt and fear, as Winfried had discovered, and announced to the family – Theresia had herself transgressed and paid the price, which was poor Anny. It was that guilt and fear that Rosa was passing on. Perhaps even intensified, Gertrud thinks, by her own. For Rosa once told her that she had lost a first daughter five years before Gertrud herself arrived. Five years before her own birth, Gertrud calculated, was 1936. Her parents had married in November of that year. She'd always thought that November was a strange time to marry in the Allgäu, when everything was frozen and deep in snow… Perhaps they had had to marry, and then Rosa had lost the child.

If that did happen, it was another secret, never spoken of. But her children saw Rosa's distress when Theresia's secret was revealed, and realised that their mother would never change. So all three hid their teenage affairs from her. Gertrud lied; Beate told her boyfriend to send his letters *poste restante*; and Winfried kept silent. It was one of his mother's great complaints against him, he wrote to Gertrud in 1962: he wouldn't talk to her. Well, he wouldn't. She wanted to know too much. Better to stay silent.[8]

Both his sisters managed to escape unscathed from this regime, but it was harder for Winfried. He internalised many of his mother's teachings, however much he tried to resist them.[9] And he almost certainly internalised Rosa's sexual guilt and fear as well. This surely contributed to his resistance to *les jeunes françaises* when he was young and to his unshed Catholicism later. Love was not a successful part of his life,[10] and it was not a successful part of his writing either. His mother gave him several precious gifts – her devotion, her aesthetic eye, her storytelling skill. But she may have given him this poisoned one too.

He was now in Year 8, the second to last of school. He worked hard, writing essays, giving lectures, tutoring younger pupils at the school, at one point ten of them a week.[11] He felt overwhelmed with work, as he would often do later, but he was young, and found time for many other things. He read like a madman – new favourites like Tennessee Williams and Truman Capote, old ones like Kleist, Pushkin and Gogol, Hawthorne and Melville, Dickens and Shakespeare; and philosophy now too – Jaspers, Kierkegaard… From Paris Gertrud sent him Camus' *La peste*, and books by Mallarmé, Cioran, Mircea Eliade. He was still swimming, coming fifth in a competition between schools and breaking his own school record for the fifty-metre crawl. He joined the school choir and listened to every kind of music – Joan Baez and Bob Dylan, jazz and classical, Brahms, Bach and many others. He was thoroughly in love with photography now too, and spent many hours in the school darkroom. And his greatest interest of all in Year 8 was the school newspaper, as we'll see. You begin to wonder when he slept.

Sometimes he didn't. Then he drank and smoked and played skat all night with Kasus, Helmut, Esche (as they called Eschweiler) and others at their favourite hangout, a newly opened bar called La Brava, rolling home drunk in the wee hours, waking the outraged burghers of the Grüntenstrasse.[12] It's strange to read W. G. Sebald talking like a teenager about these things – the beer is *sakrisch teuer* (damn expensive), school is *anödend langweilig* (dead boring), and everything is *Essig* (crap – literally 'vinegar').

He and Kasus continued to have fun. For one Fasching party – always a major event of the year – Kasus fixed straps onto a barrel and went as Diogenes. He wore only a pair of swimming trunks, so that he appeared to be naked inside his barrel; when several girls were persuaded to climb in and dance with the nude philosopher, great hilarity ensued. For another Fasching ball he built a cardboard cannon and filled it with thousands of pieces of confetti, produced with a hole punch; he and Winfried lugged it to the hall of the Nebelhorn Hotel in Oberstdorf, and in the midst of the festivities lit the fuse. It made a most satisfying explosion, and rained bright confetti on the revellers.[13]

Fasching, early 1960s. From left, Helmut, Esche, Winfried,
Ilse Hoffmann.

In Year 7 Werner's family had moved away; he came back to see his friends in the Clique now and again, but it wasn't the same. And now came another change. By Year 8 Kasus had chosen his path in science, while Winfried, Walter and Lotte were more devoted than ever to literature, art and politics. They all remained fast friends, but in the last two years of school Kasus drifted away from the Clique as well, to be replaced by a strange and interesting boy, Axel Rühl.[14]

Axel was very thin and suffered from rheumatoid arthritis, so that even as a teenager there was something bent about him: he looked like a figure from Picasso's Blue Period, Kasus says. He was the son of an officer, yet mocked everything his father stood for. Sebe would have liked him for that reason alone; but there were others as well. Axel was close to him in nature: thoughtful, hypersensitive. And he was a painter, like Walter, but far more confident, already seeing himself as an artist, and determined to become a great one. This was probably Winfried's first glimpse of such an ambition in someone of his own age, and I suspect it stirred his own. Teasingly, they addressed their letters to each other to 'Your Majesty'.[15]

Things were beginning to change now. The trial of Adolf Eichmann took place in the spring of 1961 and ended with his execution a year later, both reported in detail around the world. The departure of Kasus and Werner, the two more light-hearted members of the Clique, meant that it consisted now of the burdened ones – Winfried, Walter and Lotte – joined by equally burdened Axel. They still swam at the Starzlachklamm in the summer and skied in the winter, with Kasus and Werner too, and sat up all night at La Brava together, and lived their teenage lives – especially Lotte, who extended her illicit outings as far as Heidelberg and played drums in a band (secretly – her mother would have been horrified).[16] But the core of the group were now all rebels and intellectuals; and Winfried could talk to them all, not only to Lotte, about the past.

Someone else grew closer to Winfried now: his friend from primary school, Helmut Bunk.[17] In Year 8 they worked together on the school newspaper, *Der Wecker* (*The Alarm Clock*); in Year 9, they would become desk partners. In the last two years of school Helmut was one of Winfried's closest friends outside the Clique.

He had a nickname too – 'Birkel'.* Like Kasus, Birkel was an excellent foil for Winfried. He was a robust, humorous boy, who took life as it came, and began his own reckoning with the past only later. Like Kasus, too, he was more inclined to science than Winfried, and became an aeronautical engineer in later life (that failure in physics must have been the result of Winfried's influence). Latin was not his style, and Winfried helped him to get through it. But he was intelligent and politically aware. He played the cello, like Werner, and he and Winfried spent many hours listening to music together, as well as smoking and drinking together – Paulaner Starkbier, a specially strong brand, Helmut remembers. They also worked together on organising their class festivities, the Fasching parties every year, and the balls. (I imagine Helmut was the leader in such practical activities; they weren't Winfried's strong point, then or later.)

Helmut was also a good observer, and many of the sharpest memories of Winfried in these years are his.[18] He especially noticed (and envied) Winfried's religious freedom, as it seemed to him, compared to the piety of his own family. He didn't tell me about Winfried's *Beschneidung Christi* tease; perhaps that was too shocking to remember. But he recalled another example, probably from Year 8. In their Catholic

---

*Birkel was (and is) the biggest manufacturer of noodles in Germany. Thus, in the complimentary way of boys, his name was, in effect, 'Noodle'.

religion class, Winfried raised a question: What was more important, conscience or the Church? They were no longer taught by the priest, but by a lay teacher. He too prevaricated, and Winfried pursued him too like a terrier. For a quarter of an hour he put the question in a dozen different ways, until finally the teacher had to admit: conscience was more important. During their battle Winfried had also brought in the shameful history of the Church itself, which had clearly failed to exercise its own conscience. Game, set and match to Sebe. Years later Helmut drifted away from the Church for much the same reasons, but he never forgot that first introduction to doubt.

He remembered something else as well, for which I was very grateful. People mostly tell biographers only their good memories, because they don't want to sound mean about your subject. But Helmut said that Winfried could also be cruel. He judged quickly, and could speak cuttingly. And he could tease cruelly as well. One day, for instance, someone arrived at school in a black leather jacket, then the absolute height of cool. All the boys gathered round to admire, including Friedemann Reich, who was wearing a cardigan knitted by his mother, with leather patches on the elbows. 'Well, well,' Winfried said, 'a leather jacket! But Friedemann's got one already.' And everyone laughed.[19]

People followed him in this, as in other things, so that he could sometimes incite a bit of bullying. It was minor, and only verbal, but though he must have known it happened, he didn't stop. I thought of his later attacks on writers and critics he disapproved of, which were similar: only verbal, but surprisingly harsh. It was as though he could sometimes cut off his sensitive imagination and become the opposite. That went far back too.

In 1961 a new person joined the school, who would have an entirely new view of Winfried.[20]

This was Rainer Galaske, whose father had come to Sonthofen to head the ABC (Atomic, Biological and Chemical) Defence School. Rainer was born in Potsdam, and had been living in the Rhineland, all of which made him a Prussian to his new Bavarian schoolmates. Prussians are automatically loathed in southern Germany, so this was not a good start. But Rainer was undaunted, and set about making himself accepted. At his previous school he'd been the photographer on the school newspaper. There was no school newspaper at the ORO when he arrived: that was his chance – he'd start one. He picked out Winfried Sebald straight away as extremely intelligent and an independent thinker like himself. He would run it, he promised, and handle the finances – do all the dirty work, in fact; Sebe could be literary editor. What did he say? Sebe said yes, and *Der Wecker* was born. They recruited the rest of the Clique and several others, including a clever young artist from the year below them called Jan Peter Tripp. Rainer was in, and he and Winfried became friends.

Kasus, Werner and Helmut were all opposites for Winfried, but no one was as opposite as Rainer. Winfried was like a lake, full of deep currents, while Rainer was like an arrow, shooting straight at every goal. You might never know what Winfried was thinking; with Rainer every thought was immediately put into action. He was a sprinter and shot-putter, and went climbing with the real alpinists, like Esche; as soon as he finished school he started flying planes and racing fast cars. He would have an extraordinary medical career, including being the head of several large hospitals. When I met him he was seventy-one and had left Germany, where you have to retire at sixty-five, for Switzerland, where you don't, and was still working flat out. He was also still racing cars, flying planes and climbing mountains, had recently remarried and had a six-year-old daughter. I've never met a more confident, risk-taking, life-grabbing man.

It was probably this super-active nature that lay behind his unusual view of Winfried. All the Sonthofen friends insist on Sebe's happy normal teenage life. Not Rainer. He'd never met anyone like him, he said. Winfried was a dreamer, all in his head; a resister but not a fighter; critical and negative, but detached, never betraying any interest in anything. Rainer lived in Fischen, five miles from Sonthofen; they met one or two evenings a week, but Winfried would never come to him, it was always he who leapt on his bike and cycled to Sonthofen… And today Rainer has a theory: 30 per cent of girls and 20 per cent of boys who are extreme dreamers develop depression in later life, he says. When he read W. G. Sebald's dark, despairing books many years later, he saw a confirmation of his idea: Winfried was one of the 20 per cent.

Rainer's theory sounds convincing to me. Others who would sense something else beneath Winfried's 'completely normal' surface had their own theories, as we'll see. That there *was* something else I'm sure was true. Perhaps Walter and Axel, the two friends who shared something of his nature, could have told us more. But – and perhaps it's no coincidence – they are dead too.

Winfried and Rainer would edit *Der Wecker* for a year, from the autumn of 1961 until the autumn of 1962; after that they handed it over to the next generation, in order to prepare for their exams. Rosa thought this was far too late, and fretted about the time her son was spending on the paper.[21] But she needn't have worried, of course. And Rainer's activism was a boon for Winfried, since it gave him his first chance to publish his writing.

In the first issue, as well as an account by Rainer of a trip to Paris, book reviews by Babette Aenderl and two short pieces by Lotte – who'd become Ursula by now – there were three contributions by 'Wise', who was Winfried. ('Wi' from Winfried and 'se' from Sebald, but I'm sure he enjoyed the English pun.)

One was a denunciation of the philistine managers of German theatres, who were refusing to stage Brecht. But this attack is nothing compared to the other, which was Wise's first appearance in *Der Wecker*.[22] It's called '*die situation*', and is about the DDR, the other Germany. What do you know about it? Wise challenges his readers. We have no right to judge others when we lack the courage to face ourselves. We must change, root and branch.

I suppose I would have found anything Wise wrote full of signs of the future, but this surely is. The anger at complacency and hypocrisy, the accusation of guilt (which includes himself), the impossible requirement of radical change – all these will be permanent themes. And not least the challenging, attacking tone, which will persist in his academic writing. The empathetic writer of his literary work would come later. In 1961 there is only the furious adolescent, like the furious three-year-old of 1947.

The second *Wecker* came out in the spring of 1962, and has little by 'Wise' in it. This may have been because Winfried was concentrating on a new experience: acting in a play (though it may have been for another reason as well, as we shall see).

The play was *Antigone* by Jean Anouilh, directed by Herr Schmelzer. Schmelzer had had to justify doing something as modern as Anouilh, but he carried the day.[23] Kasus and another boy did the lighting; Winfried played only a small part, the First Watchman. But it gave him a new identity to play with, which he immediately seized, signing his next letter to Gertrud '*Der Wächter*' (The Watchman). And this first encounter with the theatre clearly impressed him. For weeks he talked in *Antigone* quotations; afterwards he kept photographs of the production on his wall, and later joined theatre groups at two of his universities. And when he began writing, he would turn first to plays.

There was another new activity this year: riding. He didn't carry on with that either. It's not clear why. Marie would say of Max that he needed a dominant position to see things, and Gertrud says that the perfect height for him was on a horse. But he gave it up, and in his work the ability to see near and far at once remains a constant wish.

The third issue of *Der Wecker* appeared in June 1962. In it 'Wise' was back stronger than ever, with several pieces. One is a powerful account of a new hero of his, Camus. This already has the hallmarks of a Sebald literary essay: a focus on the biographical, and a strong identification with its 'religious atheist' subject. Another is a short story: Winfried's first published piece of literary prose.

It's called '*An einem Sommertag*' ('On a Summer's Day'). Ten-year-old Hans Roy, going fishing with his friends, sees Philipp sitting alone. He asks him if he'll come with them next time. But Philipp says no. I have leukaemia, he says, and explains: it's something that kills people. The sky clouds over as he adds that still, he'd have liked to live.

This is plainly a youthful effort, with its obvious pathos, and obvious use of pathetic fallacy. But it too has the hallmarks of the future Sebald – an eye for landscape, an ear for language, and, of course, a deep, death-obsessed gloom. 'On a Summer's Day' shows that this was – *pace* Lotte, Kasus and the others – nothing new, but something that went back to at least his eighteenth year.

For its beginnings we have to go back to several events of a year or two before, when he was sixteen or seventeen.

One happened in the summer of one of those years.[24] Like Kasus and other friends, he took a holiday job in a factory. Kasus worked in the machine shop; Winfried was sent to paint one of the factory's flat tin roofs. He toiled day after day in the broiling sun, and one day in the second week he suddenly became ill with severe sunstroke. He was seen by a doctor and soon recovered. But the examination showed something unexpected: there was something wrong with his heart.

This was a great surprise to everyone. He was such a strong swimmer, famous especially for swimming long distances under water; how was that possible, with a dicky heart? All his friends knew him as strong and healthy, and couldn't believe it was true. Yet so it seemed. It's why the family came to believe that he had inherited his grandfather's weakness – though that was a myth, as we know, or at least exaggerated. And Sebe's heart defect, if it wasn't also a myth, must have been similarly minor. He went on skiing and hiking and setting swimming records, and later would walk long distances for his books. Nonetheless, at sixteen or seventeen he was told that he had a heart defect.[25] At twelve he had almost been felled by the loss of his grandfather, at fifteen he was writing about death (*coffin, coffin, coffin*, as Marie says). Now it had come still closer. Both his life and work would be pervaded by the sense that death is always near. That surely started now; and it surely inspired 'On a Summer's Day'.

The second event involved someone else: Gundela Enzensberger, the daughter of the disappointed Luftwaffe pilot.[26] Gundela was three years younger than Sebe, so not in his circle of friends. But she saw him often and was one of his tutorial students. Like both *jeunes françaises*, she was entranced by his brilliance, and like Marie, at thirteen or fourteen she fell deeply in love with him. But she didn't say a word either. She felt that he was intensely sensitive and shy, even fearful. He built a wall of words around himself, she says, so that no one could get near. And she believed she knew why. She was a hurt person herself, and so was he.

I didn't dare to ask her to explain. But she did so herself. It wasn't only that she had a violent father: she was also sexually abused by an uncle when she was very young. That was what she recognised in Winfried: she was certain that he had a sexual wound, like her.

There is no evidence that he ever suffered abuse of any sort, yet Gundela's insight felt deeply true to me. In just these years his mother was passing on to him her own sexual guilt and fear: perhaps that was enough. But I thought of the question raised in many readers' minds by the dread of sex in Sebald, by his exclusive sympathy with men, by 'Adelwarth', and (as we'll see) by *Vertigo*: was he homosexual? My researches would show that the answer to this question was no. But was he afraid he was? For some time in his life the answer to that would be yes.

Homosexuality was a crime under Paragraph 175 of the criminal code in Germany until 1994.[27] In early 1960s Bavaria it was another taboo, never talked about in Catholic families, as Max would say himself,[28] or at school, as Kasus told me, though the boys would taunt each other with being '175ers'. In Max's early novel the hero is approached by a man on a train. Perhaps that was based, like the rest of the novel, on a real experience. And perhaps it frightened him, especially about himself. Look again at the photograph of him in Italy at fifteen; and at this picture, when he was around seventeen. It's hard to imagine that he didn't attract looks from men as well as women.

But there was another guilt and fear as well. This one came to a head in April 1962,[29] when he was nearly eighteen. Dr Eberhard showed his class Billy Wilder's film about the death camps.[30]

Max always said the same things about this event. He said that he was seventeen or eighteen, and that it was the beginning of his awareness about what the Nazis had done to the Jews. That wasn't true, since it had been the major point of his battles with his father and conversations with his friends for years. Nonetheless, it *was* true: to know about something is one thing, to see it is another. It was a lovely spring day, he always said, and they were expecting some light entertainment as usual. Instead emaciated corpses were piled on their desks. Afterwards nothing was said. No one knew how to react, so they just went off to a football match.

Again I wondered if this was true – wouldn't Dr Eberhard have led a discussion afterwards? But Rainer says there wasn't one, and Helmut says he would have been too shocked to take part in one, so perhaps that is how they all felt, including Eberhard. They did talk among themselves, Rainer says, but only briefly. Maybe then they really went to that football match.

To one interviewer decades later Max would say a bit more: 'I can't exactly remember how I reacted. Naturally, normal life went on, but these experiences lay down a sediment in you, that somehow moves on, pushes itself on, like the moraine in front of a glacier.'[31]

That is: trauma cannot be recognised at the time or remembered afterwards, but grows slowly and inexorably inside you. That is what happened to him with the sight of those mountains of bodies. And that is what he would write about.†

At seventeen too came the final turning point: he left the Church.[32]

This was a long time coming as well; he had been mocking religion for years. But actually leaving the Church was a huge step in his Catholic world, as Uwe Schütte points out. Especially for his mother.

In fact, it was too huge to take officially or openly, and he didn't.[33] Beate offered the solution. She too was losing interest in the faith – this was the 1960s, and it was happening all around them. So she and Winfried made a pact. They still went to church with their parents. But whenever they were able to go on their own, they took turns not to. Afterwards they'd meet, and whoever had gone that week would prepare the other for Rosa's questions.

At any moment someone could have betrayed them. But the plan went off without a hitch. Beate spent her church-free Sundays with her friends and Winfried spent his at Ursula's. Instead of listening to a sermon, he talked to Frau Küsters about literature, politics, the recent past – everything that really mattered. Like Marie, like Martine, he loved Frau Küsters, and these Sunday-morning conversations were an important part of his education. But they had to stop the moment church was over: he had to meet Beate, and be home in time for lunch.

Elizabeth Küsters, Ursula's mother and Winfried's friend.

All these things came together between his sixteenth and eighteenth years: his encounter with mortality, and perhaps with homosexuality, his confrontation with the reality of the Holocaust, and his shutting the door on his faith. And they led to the final event of this time. He had a breakdown.

He spoke of this only once.[34] He said that it happened in the early 1960s, and that it went on for a considerable time. No one noticed; he would always be good at covering up his crises, as he covered up his psoriasis. It was probably a deep depression, with moments of panic and anxiety, such as he would have in Manchester a few years later. He wasn't sure if he was still sane; he was 'close to the edge of my reason'. He only hinted at the things that might have caused it. One was thinking about what had happened in his country; the other was that losing one's reason wasn't rare: '…it happens to many people, when the psychological and social identity they've built up over a decade or two goes up in flames. With creative people, the danger is even greater.'

When the psychological and social identity they've built up goes up in flames. Did he mean his German identity, his Catholic identity, his sexual identity? Perhaps all three. It was soon over, I've guessed. But from then on he was vulnerable, and he knew it; he could always fall into that abyss again.

Life went on regardless.[35] In September Beate started at the ORO, and enjoyed a very cool reputation when her new classmates thought that Sebe was her boyfriend. Gertrud took a new *au pair* job, and during the cold, snowy Christmas of 1962 Winfried met her and Jean-Paul in London. It was his first acquaintance with England, and he liked it immediately. Perhaps that played a role in his choice of Manchester four years later (though it would take some time then for his liking to return).

In February *Wecker* Number 3 won second prize in a Bavaria-wide competition for school newspapers.[36] That was the issue that Winfried had dominated, with his essay on Camus and 'On a Summer's Day'. The first literary writing of his life thus received some official recognition; it would be a long time before that happened again.

Now, however, he had to prepare for the *Abitur*, and for the next two terms he disappears into silence. The only word we hear is a poem he wrote for Gertrud in April 1963, which she treasured and kept. She was home between jobs, and Jean-Paul came all too briefly to see her. Gertrud saw him off at the station, and when she returned she was crying. Half an hour later Winfried pressed the poem into her hand.

It's called '*Entfernung*' (Distance). Its three short verses all begin with the same line, '*In einem gläsernen Spiegel*' ('In a glass mirror'). In a glass mirror the 'I' sees a glass face she no longer recognises, glass eyes shining with a light that no longer exists. In the last verse the mirror is breaking, and it's her whole self she no longer recognises. This is Gertrud, no longer herself when she is far from Jean-Paul, but at the same time Winfried, no longer himself after the traumas of the last year.[37] In it, autobiography and empathy merge, as in all the best writings of W. G. Sebald.

It's the end of June before he emerges again.[38] The exams are over, and he's done well. His best marks were in German and music, with good ones in most other subjects as well. In maths and physics he only scraped through, which certainly surprised neither Herr Weinert nor himself.†

There was one thing left to do: the special *Abitur* newspaper. The one for his class was written almost entirely by him. He composed verses and jokes about their teachers – in Latin – and joke verses in German about his classmates. Ilse Hoffmann contributed several more, about the boys in the class. About Sebe himself she wrote (approximately):

> Our Sebe finds the perfect word,
> and as a man he's not half bad.
> But with our faults he makes so free
> He's not the charmer he could be.[39]

It was a good summary: clever, handsome, but too critical for comfort, especially his own.

As part of the *Abitur* celebrations, some of Sebe's class went on a camping trip for several happy days. He didn't join them; instead he disappeared for a week or so, and never explained where he'd been.[40]

Neither Gertrud nor Beate remembers him disappearing. But by July Gertrud was in Zurich, working as a secretary, and for her birthday Winfried sent her a little book of Rilke poems, saying that he hoped it would be a consolation.[41] He always believed she was perfectly happy, Gertrud says; even then she thought it wasn't herself whom he imagined Rilke consoling. And now she remembers a conversation before she left. Winfried said that he was very happy when his results came – for two days. Then it was over. He realised that it would always be like this: you'd strive for a goal, and reach it – but as soon as you'd reached it, another goal would appear, and you'd have to start all over again. 'I fell on my arse,' he told his sister, 'and as I'm skinny, it hurt like hell.'[42] I suspect that was his way of saying, or rather not saying, that he had had another crisis.

As soon as school was over, the next challenge indeed appeared: how to avoid national service.

You could register as a conscientious objector and do *Zivildienst* (civilian service) instead – work for six months in a hospital or care home, for example.[43] But he didn't want to do that either; he wanted to start university as soon as possible. So he concocted a plan. What really happened is uncertain, since he made it into one of his best stories, which changed with every telling. But the story, at least, went something like this.[44]

He volunteered, rather than waiting to be called up. He told his father it was because that way the army would finance his studies, but really it was because he knew that the medical tests for volunteers were more stringent than for ordinary draftees. Then he stayed up all night the night before the exam, and drank as much coffee, or whisky, or both (depending on the version of the story) as he could on the day. Finally, just before he went into the room, he held his breath until he nearly passed out, and felt himself how madly his heart was racing. The doctor gave him a wise look, he thought, but signed the certificate: *Unfit to serve.*

I'm sure the doctor did give him a wise look. Fake ailments to get out of national service were so common in the post-war years that there was a name for them – '*Volkskrankheiten*' (national illnesses).[45] Kasus faked a back problem;* a friend of mine faked a heart problem, like Sebe. The army doctors knew better than anyone about these tricks. But if the doctor knew, but had to let him go anyway – that just made it more of a victory over his old enemy, the military. I imagine Winfried leaving with a secret smile.

There's a final twist to the story.[46] The next summer Fanny's daughter Suzanne, who'd come to visit the Sebalds, overheard a violent argument between Winfried and his father. Later, Winfried told her that it was about his not doing national service, and of course Suzanne believed him. But according to Gertrud and Beate, Georg was not at all upset that Winfried ducked out of military service. He'd seen too much of war to watch his son prepare for one. Besides, no one knew better than he did that Winfried would make a terrible soldier. No: very likely this was another of their usual clashes, but Sebe would rather his American family not know that he called Georg a Nazi. So he told this tale, which I believed too.

The Clique prepared now to go their own ways.[47] Ursula set off to study French history in Paris, then economics in Munich. Kasus would go to Munich to do chemistry (of course). After his two years

---

*So Kasus, like Sebe, didn't do national service. Nor did Walter or Axel. Helmut and Werner joined the draft and did the obligatory two years; Rainer and Esche did what Sebe pretended to do, and volunteered. Esche served six years, during which he was a paratrooper like his father. Rainer did the two draft years first, then signed on for six more in order to get his medical training. All these choices could have been predicted from their mid-teens.

of national service, Werner would study law. Axel went to art school in Berlin and Walter to Stuttgart to study architecture.

As for Sebe, it had been clear to everyone for at least two years that literature would be his path, even if – characteristically – it had not always been clear to him.[48] What *was* clear to him was that he wanted to get as far away as possible: from his parents, from the Allgäu, from his past, of which the hero of his early novel would feel he had too much,[49] even though he was only nineteen or twenty years old. So he didn't choose his home university, as Kasus would do, but the furthest one his parents would accept. He would go to Freiburg, to do German.

Sebe and three girls: Charlotte Klöne, Babette Aenderl and Ilse Hoffmann.

Gertrud had found her love, and the next summer she would marry. Beate was still a child. What about Winfried?

We know about the block in him with those who loved him. But he was always surrounded by admiring groups of girls at school. With those who didn't get too close, he was a great success.[50]

With Kasus he talked about girls as boys do, discussing which were the '*Pfirsiche*', the peaches.[51] And from around sixteen he had recognised girlfriends. Public pairings were still uncommon, and against the prevailing ethos, especially so early: teachers would disapprove and fellow students tease. That may be one reason why Sebe did it.

The first one was Helga Müller, in Year 6 or 7. She was a lively, tomboyish girl, according to Winfried's classmate Friedemann Reich: an activist like Rainer Galaske, I imagine, who probably made the running in their friendship. By Year 8 she'd gone, and he had another: Madeleine Wenz from the Kleinwalsertal, the remote and beautiful valley beyond Oberstdorf. This relationship lasted all that year and into the next. It was certainly still innocent, and shouldn't have worried Rosa (though it probably did). But at seventeen Sebe counted Madeleine as his first love, telling Gertrud wisely that first love is best, and that he'd be daft to give Madeleine up.[52] A few months later, however, she gave *him* up. He couldn't compete against rivals with Mercedes cars, he told Gertrud – and nor, he added, did he want to. His pride was wounded, but he didn't fight for Madeleine.

Sometime later he had a third, probably brief, friendship with a girl called Sabine Ritter, more intense than the one with Madeleine, according to Kasus, but still innocent.[53] Sabine lived nearby, and regularly joined him and Sebe on their way to and from the station. There were long, impassioned conversations between the two on those walks, until one day Sebe suddenly said to her, 'It's over between us,' and they never spoke again. 'It was cruel,' Kasus agrees, 'to dismiss her in front of me… Winfried *could* be cruel, but usually only when he was angry, and this didn't look like anger.' Perhaps, I thought, Sabine was coming too close now. Or perhaps he'd met someone else, and didn't know how to tell her.

That, indeed, is what had happened.[54]

Like the others, he kept this new girl secret, but Rosa soon knew about her. She was always with him. He brought her to the parties and balls at school, to the evenings at La Brava; most importantly, he brought her to the Clique. The friends were astonished by her. She was so beautiful, and so sophisticated. She wasn't from the Allgäu, or even from Germany; she'd been living in Vienna – *Vienna*, as romantic as Paris! – and she was their age, but already working. She worked in a beauty salon, and knew everything about beauty – her clothes, her hair, her make-up were perfect. But they were also puzzled by her. She was so mysterious, so silent; how could Sebe, who lived through language, have such a silent girlfriend? She never said a word; she just sat beside him as though she belonged to him. Or did he belong to her?

They were either each other's completion or the most improbable pair. Or else they were each other's fate, like Büchner's characters Leonce and Lena, who would soon fascinate Winfried.[55] In any case, she would be his girlfriend for the next five years, then his wife for the rest of his life.

The way they met was already a repetition. The beauty salon in which she worked lay between his house and the station, and he passed it every day on his way to and from school. One day he happened to glance through the window and saw her. The next day he stopped again. At last he stood outside the window and gazed through the glass at her for a long time, as he'd gazed through the glass at Regina Tobler playing her viola. Then he plucked up his courage and went in.

9

Paul Bereyter

Sebald said both publicly and privately that 'Paul Bereyter' closely followed the course of his schoolteacher's life,[1] and it was true. The date of Paul's death he gives on the opening page, 30 December 1983, was the date of Armin Müller's.[2] Paul's teacher training was Armin's, his French exile was Armin's, his return to Berlin and his service in the artilllery throughout the war were both Armin's. The photographs of Paul in all these times are photographs of Armin (except for the picture of Paul's 1934 probation class, which is one of Max's flea-market finds).[3]

Most importantly, Paul's 'quarter-Jewish' origins, the cause of his German tragedy, were Armin's. Müller was a devoted historian: historian of the school whenever one was needed,[4] chronicler of cheese in Sonthofen, above all genealogist of his own family. He traced the Müllers' history back for almost 250 years, writing out each generation's births, marriages and deaths on cards, pasting the cards onto cardboard sheets, and hingeing the sheets together, so that they could be folded up and kept neatly in a box. In early 2016 his niece Ursula Rapp brought them out of their box and spread them out for me to read.

What they showed was that the Müllers had lived in the Allgäu since at least 1692. If Paul Bereyter was 'a German to the marrow, profoundly attached to his native land in the foothills of the Alps',[5] the reason is documented in this extraordinary folded history. There may have been other people in Sonthofen as deeply rooted as Armin Müller, but no one can have been more.

But this was only Armin's father's family. He also preserved his full family tree from the Nazi period, in which everyone was required to show their ancestry going back two generations. And that, of course, shows his mother's side as well.

In 'Paul Bereyter' Paul's father Theo is half Jewish, because his Jewish father married his Christian maid, who was thirty years younger than he was.[6] Armin's mother Babette was half Jewish, because her father, Heinrich Hirsch, was Jewish, while her mother Maria was Catholic. The family tree also shows that Maria was thirty years younger than Heinrich; it doesn't show, but the family knew, that she was Heinrich Hirsch's maid. In other words, Sebald moved Armin Müller's Jewish grandparent from his mother's to his father's side. Otherwise he almost exactly described his family.

And the trouble was that to have one Jewish grandparent was to be a *Mischling* (hybrid, or half-breed) of the second degree, under the Nazis' insanely precise racial laws. It didn't make you a Jew, but it did make you a non-Aryan. That meant there were all sorts of things you couldn't do: for example, marry another *Mischling* of the same degree, or a half-Jew without official permission, though you could marry a full Jew or – oddly – an Aryan German. Presumably the idea was either to keep Jewish blood separate, or breed it out altogether.

The Nürnberg Racial Laws. Person of German blood – Mischling of the second degree – Mischling of the first degree –Jew (three quarters) – Jew (full).[7]

The Nürnberg Laws were passed by the Reichstag on 15 September 1935. That is, no doubt, why Sebald set Paul Bereyter's expulsion from teaching then: at the beginning of the school year 1935, 'before he had had time to do more than remember the children's names'.[8] But the Racial Laws were only the culmination of many anti-Jewish laws that had been passed from the moment Hitler took power, starting with the first one in April 1933, which required civil servants to provide proof of Aryan ancestry or be summarily dismissed. Over the next few years the net expanded to include lawyers, doctors and teachers. From his documents it seems that the non-Aryan student-teacher Armin Müller was caught in this net in early 1934 at the latest, when he was just twenty-three years old, and hadn't even started his career. By 1 March 1934 he had registered in Paris; by 1 March 1935 in Besançon. His exile had begun.

Back home in Sonthofen – or S, as Sebald calls it in 'Paul Bereyter' – things were not quite as bad as Sebald painted them.[9] Armin's father Magnus had been born in Immenstadt; not, like Theo Bereyter, in Gunzenhausen in Franconia, which Sebald chose because of the Palm Sunday pogrom that took place there in 1934, the first communal act of violence against Jews in Germany.[10] So Magnus did not die of 'fury and fear'[11] like Theo, but lived on for over forty years, dying in 1978 at the age of ninety-six. Nor did Armin's mother Babette die now, as Paul's mother Thekla does, but only in 1955, and not of depression, but probably of asthma.[12] The reason for both was that Sonthofen, though no better than anywhere in the Reich for Jews, was not Gunzenhausen. No Jewish shops were looted and no Jews hung from railings, partly because there were no Jewish shops, and after the departure of Dr Weigert no Jews, apart from Magnus Müller's half-Jewish wife. And – perhaps through Dr Kalhammer's influence again – Magnus Müller's cheese shop was never closed down, or sold off for next to nothing to an Aryan, like Theo's emporium. Nor were Magnus, Babette and their other son, Robert, arrested and deported. What happened was small and mean instead. The contract to sell Emmental cheese, which was the main source of Magnus's income, was withdrawn for the six years of the war. And the owner of the Café Köberle (which Max changed only very slightly, to Schöferle) 'begged to request'[13] the Müllers not to enter his establishment any more, in order not to embarrass his clients with the presence of a half-Jew.

Köberle was the most elegant café of Sonthofen, where all the respectable citizens gathered, and the snub could not have been plainer. Nor could Max's anger. As Lucy Landau says to the narrator of 'Paul

Bereyter': 'I do not find it surprising... not in the slightest, that you were unaware of the meanness and treachery that a family like the Bereyters were exposed to in a miserable hole such as S then was, and such as it still is despite all the so-called progress; it does not surprise me at all.'

Apart from the central fact of Armin Müller's quarter-Jewishness, Sebald sticks close to him and to Sonthofen for 'Paul Bereyter' in countless smaller ways. The names of the mountains, the shops (Turra, Einsiedler) and enterprises (Alpenvogel's van) are all – as he would say – authentic;[14] the description of the apple orchard with its starling boxes next to the school, 'Mangold', the idiot savant, the magical case of Gütermann's coloured sewing threads, the narrator's pullover with its image of a leaping stag – these are all authentic too, though 'Mangold' wasn't called Mangold, and naturally no one remembers if Winfried wore that pullover on his first day of school. The small things about Bereyter/Müller are as authentic as the big ones, including his cataracts later on, and the places he lived in, from Blumenstrasse, where he grew up next to Lerchenmüller's nursery (and the Kaesers), to the ugly block of flats he lived in at the end. In fact this was worse than in the story: the block that was built on the grounds of Lerchenmüller's, where Sebald puts Paul, is not as bad as the real block where Armin Müller spent his last years, on a noisy main road.

There are several inventions, such as the Wittelsbacher Hof Hotel, or Theo Bereyter's emporium, which takes the place of Magnus Müller's cheese shop. This latter invention provides the marvellous images of Paul's childhood – as well as the comic pair of clerks, Hermann Müller and Heinrich Müller, like the comic pair of sisters in *Vertigo*. All four are echoed again in the comic pair of religion teachers, Meier-with-an-i and Meyer-with-a-y, whose lessons on the blackboard Paul always rubs out on his return, 'with a conspicuous vigour and thoroughness'.[15] And the best joke of all – Paul's filling the holy water stoup with his garden watering can, which makes Meyer-with-a-y half hope it's a miracle – is most likely also a wicked Sebald invention. Most of Armin Müller's class agree that this never happened.

What about the other big things about Paul Bereyter, apart from his quarter Jewishness? His end, sadly, was equally accurate: Armin Müller sought his death just as Paul does.[16] And Paul's teaching closely mirrored Armin Müller's, we know, apart from beating bad boys like Karl Berchtold. But what about Paul's character – his seeming so cheerful, but being in fact 'desolation itself', his being a most entertaining companion, but 'almost consumed by the loneliness within him'?[17] His being, in sum, a bearer of Sebald's theme, 'the great time lag between the infliction of injustice and when it finally overwhelms you',[18] like the other heroes of *The Emigrants*, like Austerlitz. Was that true of Armin Müller?

Before we can answer this question, we have to go back briefly to Paul as a teacher. Because however close this part of him is to Müller, it is equally close to someone else: Ludwig Wittgenstein.

Sebald made no secret of this, telling both the critic James Wood and me, for instance, that many aspects of Paul Bereyter came from Ludwig Wittgenstein's time as a schoolmaster in several remote Austrian villages.[19] Some of these aspects they actually shared – the passion for outside lessons, for example, and the habit of flinging the windows open even in freezing winter weather – which is surprising enough. But the number of details that Sebald borrowed from Wittgenstein is quite astounding. To give just a few examples: the songs Paul teaches come from Wittgenstein, as does his habit of biting on his handkerchief when frustrated by his pupils' stupidity; and, most memorable of all, boiling the carcase of a fox on his kitchen stove and bringing the skeleton to school for lessons.[20]

And not only these striking details, but several of the key things about Paul Bereyter come from Wittgenstein. Above all, his tormented love/hate for his pupils, for instance, so that though he has always felt affection for them, they can also seem to him 'contemptible and repulsive creatures' who unleash in him 'a groundless violence'.[21] That comes directly from Wittgenstein, while there was no sign of it in Armin Müller's fairly administered beatings. And almost as important, Paul's gifts for music and mathematics. Mathematics was the central interest of Wittgenstein's philosophical life, and like Paul he played the clarinet, and was a remarkable whistler. There is no record of Armin Müller being 'a first-rate mathematician', as Sebald says of Paul.[22] And though he was extremely musical, and played the piano, as everyone recalls, no one remembers a clarinet, or whistling either. Both came instead, I'm sure, from Wittgenstein, and from André Brünisholz.†

What then of my question about Paul's desolation and consuming loneliness: were these Armin Müller's? Was his death an example of the slow emergence of trauma? Or was all this true only of Paul Bereyter, a construction of Sebald's creative imagination?

Paul Bereyter has only two loves in his life: Helen Hollaender in the summer of 1935, and Lucy Landau from 1971, when he is over sixty and retired. Helen is Viennese and (though the word is never mentioned) Jewish; while Paul is serving in the German Army she and her mother are deported, probably to Theresienstadt. Paul never speaks about her, and is 'plagued by a sense of having failed her', Mme Landau tells the narrator.[23] Mme Landau is very likely Jewish herself; again this isn't said, but place names like Landau are typically Jewish, and Lucy's father (an art historian, like Max Ferber's) leaves Frankfurt for Switzerland in 1933, the year of Hitler's accession to power. Between these two loves, one murdered and the other probably driven into exile by the Nazis, Paul spends the thirty-six central years of his life alone, unwilling or unable 'to correct his patchy knowledge of the past'[24] – like Jacques Austerlitz, for whom he is a forerunner.

'Helen Hollaender' was a real person in Armin Müller's youth: the photographs in *The Emigrants* show young Armin together with a girl, and are certainly from his album. That is all we can know, however. Who she was, if she was Jewish, what happened to her – none of this can be told from the photos. We can't even tell if she was important to Müller: he looks happy, but pictures can't show why, and she may have stayed in Sonthofen only very briefly, since she seems to be wearing the same dress in all the photos. The whole story of Helen Hollaender may, therefore, be Sebald's invention. As to Lucy Landau, I could find no evidence that anyone like her existed in Armin Müller's later life, and the scholar Kay Wolfinger – who has also made a close study of the background to 'Paul Bereyter' – has firmly concluded that she is a fiction.[25]

This picture of Paul's two Jewish loves, at the beginning and end of his life, is thus almost certainly Sebald's invention. And so is the great desert of loneliness in between.

Armin Müller spent most of his life married.[26] His first wife died in 1967; in 1972 he married again, and was still married to his second wife when he died. And in the five years between his marriages he wasn't alone either. In fact, as his family says, he was a charmer, a good dancer, and something of a womaniser. Between his marriages he also had an affair, perhaps two. In other words, Paul Bereyter's thirty-six years of solitude are as fictional as the two loves that bracket them.

And his desolation? Was it true of Armin Müller, as of Paul Bereyter, that he would suddenly 'sit down somewhere, alone and apart from us all, as if he, who was always in good spirits and seemed so cheerful, was in fact desolation itself'?[27]

Absolutely not, according to all who knew him (or all who could be found, thirty years after his death). He was cheerful, sociable, a great teller of jokes and composer of humorous verses, which he would recite to loud applause at Fasching celebrations. All this seems far from deeply withdrawn Paul Bereyter. And yet... Paul always seemed cheerful and in good spirits too, Sebald wrote. And people always said the same of him, when he was young, yet underneath it was already untrue. I had to dig deeper about Armin Müller.

When I did so, these are the things that emerged. At school he was a wonderful colleague, friendly with everyone, and '100 per cent reliable',[28] but he had no special friends, no one who was close to him. He did not hide his expulsion from teaching in the Nazi period, but he rarely spoke of it, and of its most traumatic moment, the year in Besançon, he never spoke at all. If he was permanently hurt by the theft of his hopes and identity in 1933 or 1934, he didn't show it; but then he wouldn't, if he could possibly manage. And for most of his life, he did manage.

When Paul meets Lucy Landau in 1971 he tells her lightly, calling it 'an embarrassment of the first order',[29] that he had recently attempted to take his own life. In 1967 Armin Müller's first wife died, and at much the same time, around 1967 or 1968, he was forced by the deterioration in his eyesight to take early retirement. The affair he began during this time also became very fraught. There were, therefore, several sources of stress in his life in the years around 1970. And in just that time he did the same as Paul Bereyter, and made a first attempt at suicide on the railway.

He did not succeed, because he took a large number of sleeping pills as well, and either passed out before he could position himself on the track, or rolled away from it while he was unconscious. He told his colleague Adolf Lipp that he had done it because his doctor had warned him he would become blind; this was the reason everyone at the school believed.

His family thought that it had had more to do with his difficult love affair. Whichever it was, it was an extreme solution. His eyesight would serve him for many more years, and if everyone in a painful love affair turned to that way out, there'd be few of us left. Despite appearances, there was surely something special about Armin Müller.

Actually, several people knew there was. His family knew that he was very sensitive and did not take things lightly. Adolf Lipp saw that he sometimes seemed depressed, when he would express great pessimism; and a few friends knew that he did indeed have depressions 'now and then'.[30] Adolf Lipp was clear that he carried around the failure of his first attempt to die for years. Armin had wanted to get out, he told me, and was not happy to have been saved.

And then there was the second attempt, thirteen or fourteen years later, which was successful. This time everyone believed that it was the fear of blindness, now approaching, that was the reason for his renewed decision to die. They included his family this time,[31] and also his wife, who said that 'He could not imagine a life without books.' She added that an unusually strong *föhn*, or warm, dry wind, had blown that day, which may have triggered his depression – just as Lucy Landau tells the narrator.[32]

Sebald thought that it was something different: that Armin Müller had at last been overwhelmed by the long-delayed effects of an injustice. And there is some evidence for this too.[33] Five years before, in December 1978, Müller had spent ten days in the DLA (the German literary archive) researching the lives of several writers: Kurt Tucholsky, Walter Hasenclever, and Klaus and Erika Mann. All except Erika had died by suicide either definitely or probably. And Müller took extensive notes on two of Kafka's aunts as well, who had also taken their own lives: these are the pages from Paul Bereyter's notebooks that Sebald reproduces in *The Emigrants*. The notebooks were Müller's, and in one of them he also made a long list of writers who had had to flee the Third Reich, mostly because they were Jews. There is no proof that this literary rehearsal of his own exile and its solution was still in his mind five years later. But it is hard to believe that it was without meaning.

There is another piece of evidence as well. Unlike Paul Bereyter, Armin Müller was twice married, and never alone. But his marriages were not all they seemed. His first wife was 'not his ideal woman' (Peter

Schaich says): she had come to his rescue during his difficult days in Berlin, and he had married her out of gratitude and admiration. His second marriage was perhaps more of a love match – but an elderly one, since he was sixty-two and she fifty-nine when they married, and their last years, as Armin's sight worsened and she grew impatient with him, were unhappy.[34] Though he was always married, he may often have felt alone. And from the start he – the devoted teacher – insisted that he didn't want children at any cost. There is no proof – there is never proof in things of the heart. But it seems to me that Sebald's intuition may have been right, and that delightful, cheerful Armin Müller, like Paul Bereyter, had had something in him that stopped like a clock in 1933 or 1934, at the age of twenty-two or -three, and only freed himself by dying fifty years later.

I don't know whether it was a deliberate change or a mistake, but Sebald put Paul's second, successful attempt once more on the Altstädten line. In fact, Armin Müller did not die there, but on the main Immenstadt line, which you have to take every time you travel by train to and from Sonthofen: at the 6.350 kilometre mark, as Müller's death certificate records, where the line crosses the No. 308 road in the suburb of Rieden and runs by the Tannach wood. It was six in the evening, too dark for anyone to see the thin figure walking along the track and lying down.

In Lucy Landau's clearest image of her first days with Paul Bereyter, they are gazing down from the summit of Mont Rond at the countryside around Lake Geneva. The tiny faraway scene, she tells the narrator, 'had for the first time in her life awoken in her a sense of the contrarieties that are in our longings'.[35]

The image of the countryside around Lake Geneva links 'Paul Bereyter' to key moments in both 'Dr Henry Selwyn' and 'Max Ferber', and so signals a locus of connection and meaning. As it is: for the 'contrarieties that are in our longings' are the key to Paul Bereyter's story.

The narrator claims not to understand how Paul could have returned to Germany in 1939 (and served in the German army, as he doesn't add) after the traumatic loss of his German identity. But really the reason is clear: the loss was so important because the identity was. Paul's longing is to be the German he has always thought himself to be, but that longing is now impossible. That is why he knows as a soldier that he is 2,000 kilometres away from home, but not where home is; that is why he becomes increasingly incomprehensible and abstract to himself. He can understand himself only if he is a German, but he cannot be a German. The contrariety in his longings breaks him apart.

This theme of contrariety runs through everything we hear about him: his seeming so cheerful but being 'desolation itself'; his being a most entertaining companion but almost consumed by loneliness; his seeing best when his eyes are covered. It is mirrored in the contradiction Sebald borrowed from Wittgenstein, Paul's love/hate for his pupils, and the one he lent from himself: Paul's love/hate for Sonthofen and Germany. The point of 'Paul Bereyter' is that he hates so much because he loved so much. He is, as Sebald said, in a double bind.[36] The same was true of another of his literary models, Jean Améry, who was as deeply attached to his beautiful *Heimat* in the Austrian Alps as Paul was to his in the Allgäu, and hated it as much, and found the same way out of the contradiction. And also of Paul Bereyter's creator, who found his way out through writing.

And it was surely true of Armin Müller and his whole family, including his half-Jewish mother. Just weeks after Armin's years in limbo ended, when war broke out and he was called up into the army, he came home on a visit. And they must all have been proud and happy, since they went to a photographer to have their portrait taken with their

German soldier. Magnus looks stern. Robert's mild mental handicap –
which stopped him from serving, but not from working in the cheese
shop throughout his life – is clear. Babette, who had been barred from
Köberle, smiles. The most pensive one is Armin.

Paul Bereyter is drawn to his Jewish side through the two loves of his
life, Helen Hollaender and Lucy Landau. Without Müller's photo
album the search for the real Helen Hollaender ends before it begins.
But what about Lucy Landau?

There is a great deal about her that is almost certainly invented. Her
living in Yverdon, for instance. Yverdon was the birthplace of Pestalozzi,
the great liberaliser of children's education, who is clearly Paul's model
as a teacher, and the author of the book Lucy reads to him when he
can no longer read himself, *The Evening Hour of a Hermit* – which
is both genuinely a work by Pestalozzi, and the truth about Paul, the
hermit living his evening hour. This is the sort of perfect coincidence
that signals the working of Sebald's artistic imagination.

On the other hand, Sebald talked to me about Lucy as though she
were real. I know that means less than nothing. But the way he did it
this time was particularly convincing. I'd asked if any of his models
had ever objected to the use he'd made of them. If they were private

people, he replied, he showed them what he'd written, and if anyone objected, he didn't publish. And then he added: 'In the case of the lady at Yverdon, it was more complicated. It took me a long time to convince her that what I was up to was actually all right.'[37]

This still sounds real to me. And obviously he talked to *someone* about Armin Müller, from whom he got the details of Armin's life, and the photographs from his album. Lucy Landau is still mostly fiction. But who could the basis for her have been?

There are two candidates, or perhaps three. One is Armin's widow, Elfriede. Sebald would surely have begun with her, and she is the most likely to have had Müller's album and notebooks, left in their flat at his death. The second is someone who was certainly a friend: her name was Ludmilla Moser, and she ran a bookshop in Immenstadt. The third is the widow of the writer Walter Hasenclever, to whom Müller wrote about his admiration for her husband, and whose name and address he recorded in one of the notebooks that ended in Sebald's possession.

It could have been any of them, or perhaps a mixture of all three. But my best guess is the bookshop owner Ludmilla Moser.[38] She was a close friend, and she lived for books, like Armin. And – perhaps most important – her name Ludmilla was always shortened to Lu. The echo of Lu in Lucy may be a coincidence, but we know what Sebald thought about coincidence.

Lu Moser.

Lu, however, was not Jewish, and neither were the other two. And the writers whom Müller researched in 1978 were often not Jewish, but political exiles like Hasenclever; what interested him was exile and suicide, not Jewishness. As a good historian, he kept the record of his mother's origins. But I suspect that in practice he and his family excised the memory of their Jewish taint as soon as possible after the war, and partook with the rest of Sonthofen in the pact of silence and forgetting. It was Sebald who could not forget, and it was most likely he who added this aspect to his fictional version of Armin Müller.

Even so, Paul Bereyter remains closer to his main model than any of the other heroes of *The Emigrants* to theirs. And though all the portraits of *The Emigrants* are lit up with fondness, the one based on Armin Müller is the fondest. We feel in every word that the narrator loved Paul when he was his teacher, and that Lucy Landau loved him deeply in later life. Lucy's love for Paul is the tenderest love of a woman for a man in all of Sebald; indeed, almost the only one, apart from Charlotte Ives's love for Chateaubriand in *The Rings of Saturn* and Marie de Verneuil's for Austerlitz in *Austerlitz.* In the general desert and darkness of Sebald's treatment of heterosexual love, the love between Paul Bereyter and Lucy Landau is the best exception. It still does not release Paul from his past, or halt his drive towards death. Nonetheless, it lightens the sadness of his life, as the love between Ambros and Cosmo lightens Ambros Adelwarth's, who isn't saved by it either. That seems the greatest hope Max could imagine for love of either kind.

From that height, Lucy Landau says, the country around Lake Geneva looks like the landscape for a model railway. Twelve years later the image returns, in the form of Paul's own model railway, laid out on a table in his flat in S. And we realise that Lucy's vision at the start of their happiness had been a glimpse of Paul's inevitable end. She glimpses it again when Paul tells her of a childhood holiday, when he was so absorbed in watching trains that he never once appeared on time for dinner. His aunt shook her head at his behaviour, Paul had remembered, while his uncle just said that he would end up on the railways. When she first heard this innocent remark, Lucy says, it cannot have had the importance she sees in it now. But it struck her as 'darkly foreboding',[39] as though she had seen an image of death.

That is exactly what she *has* seen, of course. In Sebald's world, past and future are interchangeable, and things can be sensed in both; certainly by Lucy Landau, who had such an uncanny premonition when they arrived in S that she wanted to turn back immediately. And we know something else as well. The image of death she saw was not only of Paul's, and nor was the sense Paul himself had probably always had, that the railways were headed for death.[40] The railways had headed for death for millions of Jews: without the trains that delivered them to the extermination camps, the Holocaust would have been impossible. That meaning of Lucy Landau's vision and Paul's intuition is unstated, but silently, powerfully there, as the Holocaust always is in Sebald's writing. He said so himself: 'The railway played a very, very prominent part, as one knows, in the whole process of deportation… And I do pick that up at one point when I talk about my primary schoolteacher's obsession with the railways.'[41]

He picks it up in these last pages of the story, and almost states it there, when Lucy Landau says that 'Railways had a deeper meaning for Paul', and that his model railway is to her 'the very image and symbol of [his] German tragedy'.[42] The ending of 'Paul Bereyter' thus silently takes us back to the Jewish part of Paul's identity, which he expressed in his two loves, especially the first: Helen Hollaender, who was deported with her mother 'in one of those special trains that left Vienna at dawn'.[43] Paul was plagued, as Lucy Landau says, by a sense of having failed Helen, or let her down: what we now call survivor's guilt, because he escaped her fate when he should have shared it. All those years ago he chose the side of his fellow German soldiers. Now he chooses Helen's side, and the side of all the Jewish victims of the Holocaust, and takes their route to death, on the railways.

It is impossible to say if there was any trace of survivor's guilt in Armin Müller's railway obsession or in his choice of death. All we know is that his obsession with railways was real, since he made his pupils draw the railway lines around Sonthofen, with their signals and stations, over and over again. So, like Lucy Landau with Paul Bereyter, we too have had a prevision of his death. For one of the lines he made his boys copy from the blackboard, year after year, was the one we've already seen three chapters ago. This, once more, is Jürgen Kaeser's version.

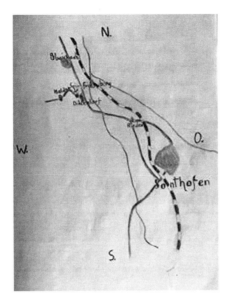

If you look to the north, you'll see that the line crosses a road at the place called Rieden. When I first saw this in Jürgen's exercise book for 1953–4 I had just received Müller's death certificate, and knew the spot where he died – and there it was, carefully copied from his own drawing, thirty years before. I felt how exact Sebald's beautiful ending to his story is: the prevision passed over me like the shadow of a bird in flight.

PART IV

Cocky

10

Freiburg, 1963–5

Bliss was it in that dawn to be alive,
but to be young was very heaven.
William Wordsworth, *The Prelude*, 1799

Winfried Georg Sebald registered with the philology faculty of the Albert-Ludwigs University in Freiburg im Breisgau from 29 October 1963 to 23 July 1965.[1] His major subject was *Germanistik*, German language and literature; his two minors *Anglistik*, English language and literature, and philosophy.

Some time that summer he went to Freiburg to find a room.[2] This was no easy task. The city had been so badly bombed during the war that housing was still scarce; several hundred young people that year had to give up their university places because they couldn't find anywhere to live. Most rooms were unheated, even in winter, and hot baths were a luxury. At the same time landlords imposed all sorts of rules and requirements. No visits from the opposite sex, of course. And often services to be rendered: babysitting or car-washing. Ideally, the students joked, a tenant who was absent seven days a week visiting home.

Winfried was clever, or lucky, and with Georg's help he could evidently pay enough. He found a room on Konradstrasse, about a mile from the university. In late October he packed his bags and left Sonthofen.

On 28 October he wrote to Gertrud from Freiburg. Here he was, he told her. He was alone and didn't know a soul. Not knowing what would happen a few years later, when again he'd be alone in a cold room, Gertrud wasn't alarmed. And as it turned out, she was right. The first thing Winfried had hoped to do at Freiburg was to join a theatre group, and again he was lucky: less than a month after his arrival he was in not just one play, but two.[3] He seemed to have survived his first encounter with loneliness unharmed.

Not easily, however. At the end of November he reported to Gertrud that things were going well – despite occasional bad turns; a few days later he reassured her that his life was calm – as far as possible.[4] And his first published piece of prose at Freiburg would explore a very dark state of mind, which very likely went back to those lonely first weeks.

In his second letter to Gertrud from Freiburg he sounds quite positive about his courses.[5] This wouldn't last: he would soon become disenchanted with the teaching at the university. He was particularly bored by the required courses such as 'Introduction to Middle-High German',[6] not least because they were required. He was also unpleased by his fellow-students. They were mostly, he told Gertrud in his Holden Caulfield voice, a load of phoneys.

In fact Freiburg was not the right place for him. It was still a very conservative Catholic institution, in which the vast majority of students were sons (still largely sons) of the middle classes, right wing in their politics, and members of the traditional drinking and duelling clubs, the notorious *Burschenschaften*.[7] Though 1968 was only five years in the future, there were few centres of liberal resistance that were paving the way. Perhaps, indeed, only one such centre. It would take a miracle for a raw new student to find it.

And then the miracle happened. His name was Dietrich Schwanitz:[8] a brilliant scholar of *Anglistik*, four years older than Winfried, who'd been at the university since 1961 and was tutoring first-year students. Early in the autumn of 1963 he became Winfried's tutor in one of his special subjects, Shakespeare. And with that meeting Winfried's real Freiburg life began.

Schwanitz's great passion was the theatre, and he was directing a play that term: Eugene O'Neill's *In the Zone*, in English. He enrolled Winfried straight away, giving him the part of Cocky the Cockney.[9] That was how Winfried came to be in a theatre group within weeks of arriving in Freiburg, and that was how he acquired his new nickname, Cocky. Just as his Oberstdorf friends almost always called him Sebe, so now his Freiburg friends would call him Cocky. It was only his family who still called him Winfried: one good reason why he would consign the name to the past a few years later. Schwanitz, in turn, was almost never known as 'Dietrich', but only as 'Paolo'. That name came from a play too – Goldoni's madcap comedy *Summer Follies*, in which he'd played the servant Paolo, almost the only sensible person in the story.

And now Paolo did something that was even more vital for Cocky: he got him into the student hostel at No. 15, Maximilianstrasse, the Maximilianstrasse Studentenheim.[10] This was the rare centre of anti-conservative, anti-establishment resistance in the university I meant: a pre-1968 version of 1968. It suited Cocky down to the ground. If he hadn't found the Maximilianstrasse Studentenheim – or if it hadn't found him, through Paolo Schwanitz – I doubt he'd have lasted the two years at Freiburg he did. It, and the friends he made there, were a decisive influence on the rest of his life. When he consigned 'Winfried' to the past and chose 'Maximilian', shortened to 'Max', for his future, it may have been at least partly in memory of Maximilianstrasse:[11] the place in his life after Wertach where he was most at home.

The Maximilianstrasse Studentenheim.

The Maximilianheim had long been considered practically communist by the university authorities.[12] It had been established after 1945 as part of the drive to make Germany a stable democracy, and someone had suggested the model of an Oxbridge college: a small, independent community of scholars. But the Maximilianheim far outdid any Oxbridge college. The students ran it themselves, being responsible not only for its administration but for its admissions policy, choosing their fellow residents when places became free. That is how Paolo could co-opt Cocky, and how several girls managed to live with their boyfriends in the Heim over the years, though of course this was strictly against the rules. The result was a creative disorder. The Heim resounded with discussion and argument from dawn to dusk – or more often from dusk to dawn. On the other hand, no one ever bothered to wash up, so that the kitchen sink almost rivalled the one in *Withnail & I*; some of Cocky's friends occasionally attempted a clean-up, but it was a losing battle. No doubt the authorities thought that this proved their case – these young students were dangerous communists, and the place should be closed down. Sadly it would be, soon after Cocky left.[13] But for many years it fulfilled the hopes of its founders, and was an island of freedom and openness in what was still a reactionary and authoritarian world.

The Maximilianstrasse students didn't just choose their friends as residents.[14] Thomas Bütow, for instance, was elected sight unseen when he became the editor of the liberal, reforming student newspaper. 'That's the kind of person we want,' Paolo said, and the committee unanimously agreed. Much the same will have happened with Winfried Sebald, even though he hadn't had time to prove himself: Paolo must simply have recognised his special qualities. He was elected some time in his first term, and moved into the Heim in the summer semester of 1964. The Maximilianstrasse was a few streets over from the Konradstrasse, so he didn't have far to go. But in reality he'd moved not just streets, but worlds.

The Studentenheim[15] was small, housing (officially) no more than thirty students. But it had an excellent kitchen (despite the sink), its own library and grand piano, and a large and beautiful garden. In the middle of the garden was its most famous feature – a huge old sequoia, the seed of which, according to house mythology, had been brought from the East in a walking stick. The canopy of the sequoia was so thick that you could sit under it even in the regular Freiburg rain without getting wet. And that is where they all gathered, in the afternoons and throughout the mild summer nights, reading, arguing, discussing their work with one another by the light of a few lamps, and drinking endless cups of tea, the Maximilianstrasse trademark.

As part of its mind-opening plan the constitution required that 20 or even 30 per cent of the residents should be foreign students; in Cocky's time there were five, including an Indian and a Korean. And there was always a student or two from the College of Music as well. As a result the house resounded with music – especially jazz, in Cocky's year. That no doubt increased the university's suspicions. So did the fact that the Heim had its own excellent wine cellar and did its full share of student boozing; and that with all these natural advantages – the music, the wine, the glorious garden – it was famous for its wild parties. In early 1965 one was so wild that the organisers were nearly expelled.[16] Their friends signed a letter of defence, including one Winfried Georg Sebald; and they managed to eke out the rest of the term.

The thirty students were a close-knit group, breakfasting together in the kitchen, sipping tea (or something stronger) under the sequoia, and having heady debates on their favourite subjects – art and literature, the state of the university and nation. That, of course, disturbed the authorities even more than the wild parties. But the debates of Cocky and his friends were rarely political, though 1968 was so near. They were anti-fascist and anti-conservative; they mocked the philistine bourgeoisie, as the young had done since the previous century. But essentially they were still well behaved. 'When we wrote to the Rektor we still addressed him as "*Ihre Magnifizenz*",' says one of the friends, Rolf Cyriax. 'Just three years later it was "*Du Schwein*"!'

Nonetheless, the university was right to worry. These young people were the bearers of a new reform spirit, and the flow of history was with them. Their fathers were dead or discredited and it was up to them to start anew. 'There we were,' Michael Sukale told me, 'battling against the nationalists, the Catholic Church, a conservative and highly hierarchical university structure – and loving it.'[17] The world was our oyster, Berndt Ostendorf says, just waiting for us to remake it in our own image. That is what it was like in Cocky's time in Freiburg.

In the Zone portrayed the lives of seamen – with compelling realism, Paolo wrote in his programme note, presenting the characters and their 'rather crude habits of speech' with 'uncompromising fidelity'.[18] I wish I could have heard Cocky cursing in Cockney-accented English years before he heard it. But probably he wasn't too bad: Paolo was brilliant at accents himself, and a hard taskmaster. They rehearsed for over two months; and finally performed the play in the English Studio Theatre during the week of 29 January 1964.

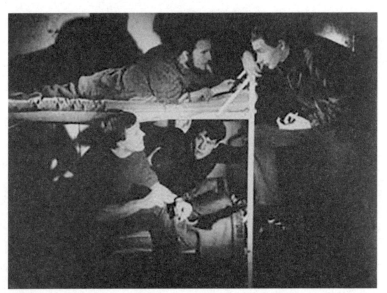

Cocky in rehearsal for In the Zone *(in the centre, on the bottom bunk). Beside him is Bob Barcklow, playing Yank; an American himself, and the only native English speaker in the cast.*

In the end they'd bitten off more than they could chew. O'Neill's use of demotic speech had been daring enough in America, but for a German audience the dialogue was almost completely incomprehensible. They'd foreseen this problem, Paolo wrote,[19] and accompanied their speech with gestures to make it clear. Result? Those who could follow the English thought the play overacted, while those who couldn't weren't enlightened. A total failure, he stoically concluded. But they'd learned from it, and for their next production they would stick with a familiar classic: Shakespeare.

The play they chose was *A Midsummer Night's Dream*. Bob Barcklow directed; Rolf Cyriax played Oberon, Paolo Schwanitz Bottom, and Paolo's girlfriend Etta the First Fairy. Cocky's friend Albert – real name Albrecht Rasche – played Starveling, and Cocky himself the double part of Snug and the Lion.[20]

Though Bob was the director, the moving spirit was once again Paolo. Berndt Ostendorf remembers that their rehearsals were like seminars: 'We learned more from Paolo,' he says, 'than from any of our teachers.' It was a thrilling experience, and the cast must have felt that they were on the right track this time. They were. When the play was staged in the university's Auditorium Maximum on the 1 and 2 of July, the result was a runaway success.

A Midsummer Night's Dream, *Freiburg, July 1964. On the left, Paolo as Bottom, with his foot on Cocky as Lion.*

A Midsummer Night's Dream was the beginning of a string of theatrical successes for Paolo, some of which were lauded far beyond Freiburg.

And theatre remained his great passion throughout his life: as a professor he would found a student theatre, writing and directing dozens of plays for it, and his last years would be spent in a fantastical theatre he would build for himself. It was different for Cocky. He was fascinated by the theatre in his youth, but mostly, I think, because it was the home of role play and shifting identities. He wasn't an actor, as Paolo supremely was. Paolo loved to have all eyes upon him, but not Cocky. To remember their great success in *A Midsummer Night's Dream* they all signed one another's programmes. Paolo signed all his names, *Dietrich Paolo Bottom Schwanitz*. Albert corrected the name beside his part and signed it. Cocky appeared as someone called 'Winfried Tebald', but he didn't correct it. And beside it he signed, not his name, but *Roar*.

Cocky's other activity at Freiburg was his true and lasting one: writing. The first public signs of it appeared in his second year, when he began to publish regularly in the student newspaper. Over the year he would contribute seventeen pieces, which made him the second most prolific writer after Paolo.[21] But again there was a difference between them. While Paolo wrote at least one political article – about the 20 July plot to assassinate Hitler – Cocky's pieces were all literary. W. G. Sebald would be the same: the heart of his work would be about oppression, persecution, war, but he would never write directly about politics.

The first contribution signed 'Winfried Sebald' was a review of György Lukács' latest book on German literature.[22] Lukács' Marxist and anti-Modernist line was fashionable among Germanists of the day – so Cocky attacked it, as W. G. Sebald would attack the fashionable line of Germanists throughout his life. His critical stance (pro-Modernist and pointedly off-piste) is already in place, as is his style (satirical, polemical). They would develop, but never change.

After this first piece his contributions multiplied. In the December 1964 issue alone he had five poems, in the 1965 issues seven more: these would become the first twelve poems in *Across the Land and the Water*, the collection of his poetry published in 2008, in Iain Galbraith's English translation. Many are short and almost haiku-like, like the final poems of his life. Most are allusive, even (as the critic Ruth Franklin says) 'maddeningly cryptic',[23] but with moments of great beauty. This combination of beauty and enigmatic meaning will always characterise Sebald's writing, in both poetry and prose. As Franklin argues, it will work best in his prose. In the poems, where the unexplained allusions crowd together, the effect is 'like reading *The Waste Land* without the notes', she remarks, though she treats his poetry with great respect as well. I agree, and Sebald surely did so himself, or he wouldn't have put the main effort of his mature years into prose. I'll say no more, therefore, about these early poems.

Cocky's first prose piece, *'Jeden Abend'* ('Every Evening'), also appeared in the December 1964 issue of the paper.[24] This is the one that may go back to the first lonely weeks of his first year – or to any time after, since his 'bad turns' almost certainly continued. Some of his school writings had been dark enough. But there'd been nothing as dark as this before.

Every evening, it begins, as night falls, the world outside the narrator's window recedes. Even the trees become inexplicable to him; he thinks only about the past, and his thoughts find no way to escape. This has been going on for two years.

It soon becomes clear that he lives in an Orwellian dystopia, in which all negativity is banned on pain of death. To protect himself, he has pretended to enjoy this world and to fall in love with girls. But now his girlfriend has seen through him and denounced him to the authorities. He has been tried and sentenced. He follows his executioners quietly, as it makes no difference whether he is alive or dead.

This is, of course, a fiction, and recalls both Aldous Huxley and Kafka. Nonetheless, there is another writer it recalls even more: W. G. Sebald. The circling thoughts, the obsession with the past, the importance of trees – all these motifs recur more and more frequently in Cocky's later writing. Only an extreme devotion to the theoretical divide between a writer and his work could stop you from seeing his own cast of mind in all his works, with their notable consistency; including in this story, when he was twenty years old.

When he wrote 'Every Evening' he'd only recently left his teens behind, and his strangely blocked relationships to the girls who loved him: Marie, Martine, Gundela Enzensberger. When the girl in this story gets close to the narrator, she sees that he is not the happy person he is pretending to be, but is hiding a terrible lack of connection to the world, including her. I cannot say: This was Winfried's secret, perhaps even Max's. But somehow, sometimes, the disconnection described in 'Every Evening' would happen. This we know, from witnesses both in his youth and later,[25] and see reflected in much of what he wrote, starting with this little story.

In the summer semester of 1965 – his last Freiburg term – he published three more prose pieces. '*Über den Regen*' ('About the Rain')[26] is a comic monologue written in slang. '*Teegeschichte*' ('Tea Story') is a slice-of-life account of an awkward young couple in a café, each afraid that the other will think him or her a bore. The third and longest piece, '*Erinnern*' ('Remembering'), is the most ambitious: a surreal, stream-of-consciousness story of a journey in which times and places shift, and different voices break in. It ends with the narrator reading a fairy tale called '*Das Geisterschiff*' ('The Ghost Ship'), in which the dead passengers are condemned to sail for ever, coming to life every night and replaying their last hours. (Shades of Gracchus on his boat in *Vertigo*.)

All these pieces sound familiar. The narrator's travel fears in 'Remembering' anticipate the motif of travel 'as a fearful descent into the unknown'[27] in the great prose works of the future. As for 'Tea Story', Marie recounts of Max in his mid-fifties that he often asked her anxiously, 'I hope I'm not boring you?'[28] Everything in Sebald stretches back into the past; everything connects.

The main jokers in the student paper of Cocky's years were Paolo Schwanitz and his friends.

For all his scholarship, at heart Paolo was an entertainer. He wrote many serious pieces too, but the vast majority of his contributions were send-ups, satires and comedies. There were also special Fasching numbers, which were largely given over to jokes. None of them was signed, so we have to guess, but I'm sure that many were by Paolo, and many by Cocky as well.

In the Fasching issue of February 1965, for example – which was a great success, and read all over Freiburg[29] – there was a parody of Gertrude Stein by 'Trudi Stein' ('*Ein Stein... Ein Stein ist ein Einstein*') that was surely by Paolo, the English scholar. In a joke application form for the new student village was the delicious question '*Sind Sie katholisch, wenn ja, wie sehr?*' (Are you Catholic? If so, how very?), which could be any of them, but sounds very Cocky to me.

In the Fasching 1966 issue there were several extended jokes. One was about a mandatory Ability to Think exam before being allowed to vote, for which Catholics were granted exemption on faith grounds; another explained a new law allowing medical students to dig up bodies for dissection, called the *Leichenaushebungsgesetz*, the Corpse Exhumation Law, the licence for which was called the *Leichenaushebungsermächtigungsschein* (there was a lot of linguistic self-mockery). This piece ended with exceptions to the law, of which one was 'Old Nazis should be left in peace at last!'

These could have been by any or all of them, including Cocky (who had by now left Freiburg for Switzerland, but was still sending back material).[30] But there were two joke pieces that I'm certain were by him. They went back to his Wertach childhood, in which the men spent their free time in their garden sheds, making things from scraps of wood or old machinery.[31] The first appeared in the December 1964 issue, only two pages away from the suicidal 'Every Evening'. It gave long, pedantically precise instructions, complete with diagrams, for the construction of a hand-made Christmas crib, called (tellingly) a *Sebakrip*. It ended by suggesting that live white mice could be used for lambs, by fixing their feet to the base with plaster; and that if covered with egg white and baked, the *Sebakrip* would also make a tasty Christmas treat.

That one was definitely by Cocky.[32] A similar send-up appeared in the June 1965 issue. It was signed 'Mechanicus', and was for the construction of a protest flag for an upcoming demonstration. You'll need two components, Mechanicus advises, a protest flag pole and a protest flag flag. There follow similarly solemn instructions (plus diagrams) about the flag, to be cut out of red cloth and sewn onto the pole. When this complex procedure has been followed, then and only then can we go protesting.

It's to the credit of editors Reiner Geulen and Bütow that they were happy to print this mockery of the very serious demo they were planning. And it suggests once again (if my guess is right) that Cocky was not as devoted to political activism as some of his friends.

Cocky had several circles of friends at Freiburg: a theatre one, a newspaper one and a Maximilianheim one. His two most important friends belonged to all three: Paolo and Albert.

He met Paolo first, as we know, in the autumn of 1963. By the next summer at the latest, when he moved into Maximilianstrasse, he'd met Albert as well. By the winter semester of 1964 he and Albert were room-mates[33] and publishing their work in the paper together. And all three had an announcement to make, which appeared in the December 1964 issue.[34]

Group 64[35]

In Maximilianstrasse 15 in Freiburg on 21 November, Group 64 was formed. The aim of the members is to discuss their own literary works together.

If this sounds almost comically self-important, it was. Alone, perhaps they wouldn't have dared to display such self-confidence; certainly Cocky wouldn't. But a group confers power, and the other two members were hugely confident, to say the least. This confidence, even arrogance, became the trademark of Group 64 – and the trademark of part of the work of W. G. Sebald.

Group 64[36] was their own name for themselves; other friends called them the writers' group. They were fiercely intellectual, extravagant in argument, and as a group almost entirely closed. A few friends joined in sometimes, but most just sat and listened. It was like the Oberstdorf Clique, but even more high-powered, and more exclusive.

And that was on general subjects: when it came to their work, it was just the three of them. 'We aimed to be great writers,' Albert told me[37] with a smile (challenging? disarming?), 'and were quite certain we would be; we thought we were special, and were aggressive towards outsiders. We read our work to one another constantly, under the sequoia tree. The moment any of us had something new, we rushed out to hear it. All that mattered was our writing. It was legitimate to use anything or anyone for it – as Paolo would do in his novels, and Max in the one he would soon write about us all.'

And not only in that novel, I thought, but in all his work after – in 'Dr Henry Selwyn', in *Austerlitz*... It felt as though I'd found a key to so much that puzzled me in his work – the aggression of his academic writing, and the unfeeling side of his literary writing, which sat so oddly with its extraordinary empathy. We can thank, or blame, Group 64 for that; thank or blame Paolo Schwanitz and Albert Rasche.

Paolo was the star.[38] He was not only a first-rate actor and director, and an extraordinary talker, delivering mini-lectures on any topic at the drop of a hat. He could draw as well; the only thing he couldn't do was sing, but he did that too.

He was the wittiest of them all, a master of wordplay both in talk and in writing. He was hugely prolific, not only producing dozens of pieces in the paper, but writing a whole detective novel in his Freiburg years. And he was also practical. So, for example, he was careful to provide himself with a teaching qualification as well as his degrees, and when his perfectionist friend Bütow went on researching for years, Paolo said: 'Thomas, you're not meant to be discovering the truth, you're meant to be getting your Ph.D.' Which, Bütow says, he was at last able to do.

But comedy was the heart of Paolo.[39] He was famous for his leg-pulls and teases – an *enfant terrible*, Albert calls him; you never knew when he was being serious and when he was tripping you up with some poker-faced joke. That wouldn't change: his friends at fifty had to watch him as carefully as those at twenty had done. He told marvellous tales, which everyone believed, but which turned out to be elaborate fictions. The most famous one was about his childhood just after the war, in which the seven-year-old Paolo is sent to live in the remote Swiss Jura for three years. By the time he returns to civilisation he is unable to read or write, and speaks nothing but an incomprehensible Swiss dialect: a veritable Kaspar Hauser. One of the teachers recognises the boy's remarkable intelligence, and – just as in the story of Kaspar – takes him under his wing. And the little savage graduates as the top scholar in his class.

Paolo did live for a while in the Jura.[40] But thereafter all ties to truth are cut, and the story lifts off into fantasy. His parents were teachers and his home full of books; by seven he could read and write fluently, and would quickly have regained whatever he'd forgotten, if he forgot anything. The story was wildly dramatised, Etta says with a smile. I believed it implicitly, Thomas Bütow says, until I heard him tell it again and again, and it was different every time. 'Paolo's stories were like plants,' he says, 'they grew and grew. He was always feeding his plants.'[41]

Of course, Paolo was a terrific egotist, and the butts of his jokes and tricks didn't always enjoy them. Certainly his fellow professors in later life, who saw themselves mercilessly satirised in his novels, heartily loathed him. But more people loved him, especially when he was young. And love or hate are not really the point about Paolo, or perhaps about

anyone, at least to a biographer. What I notice about him as trickster
and storyteller is how like Max and W. G. Sebald he was (including in
that literary touch, the weaving of Kaspar Hauser into his fable). Is that
where Max learned it? In his Maximilianheim novel Josef tells fibs and
fantasies very much like Paolo. Did Cocky? None of his male friends
of the time says so – with one exception, as we'll see – and Etta firmly
denies it, as his women friends all do. Perhaps he didn't, yet. But he was
sitting at the feet of a master.

Paolo.

The 1964 group, like the Oberstdorf Clique, included one girl: Paolo's
fiancée, Etta Uphoff.[42]

Etta was a student of literature in her own right, one of the small
minority of girls who made it to university in the mid-1960s. But she
would not have partaken in the ruthless cut and thrust of the group's
debates, as Lotte had taken part in the Clique's. Etta was (and is) a quiet,
contained person. I think she listened, and had her own thoughts; not
in Paolo's shadow, but in his support.

The two of them lived together in the garden house at Maximilianstrasse.
This was a double crime: girls weren't supposed to live anywhere in the
Heim, and no one was supposed to live in the garden house.[43] Paolo
delighted in breaking the rules, of course (another thing in which Max
followed him, though only in writing). Etta calmly broke this rule too,
though she doesn't say so, telling me that she lived nearby. All the friends

I found, however, were quite clear: Etta lived in the garden house with Paolo. It became a centre to rival the kitchen and sequoia: a hub of debates, parties, editorial meetings. And Etta, I imagine, was always there.

She was Paolo's opposite in every way: modest, quiet, leaving all exhibitionism to him. Her childhood story, for instance, was genuinely extraordinary, but she never told it. Her father died when she was small and her mother married one of his brothers; when he too died, she married the third brother. Whereas Paolo changed his name with every part he played, throughout this succession of fathers Etta remained Uphoff. Until she married Paolo and became Schwanitz; and although they later divorced, and she has had another partner for decades, Schwanitz she remains. If Paolo's signature was mercurial change, Etta's is constancy. It was the great sadness of her life, but perhaps not surprising that their marriage did not last.

Apart from literature, she says, the great love of the group was for role play, for all sorts of identity jokes and games, on the stage, on the page ('Mechanicus') and in the garden. She remembered one in particular, and found the photograph. It was planned for the newspaper, she said, but never used.

Cocky, Albert and Paolo with the corpse of higher education.

Beside it was another photo. It wasn't of role play, but of a classic student scene, clearly taken in a small, dark room. I had to have it, and kind Etta gave it to me.

Paolo, Cocky and Etta.

The second man was Albert.[44] He was closer in nature to Cocky than to Paolo, more introverted, not an exhibitionist at all. He was, however, just as powerful a personality, with the most logical and erudite mind of the three. He too was witty, energetic and relentless in argument, determined to win, and usually did; he suffered fools even less gladly than Paolo, and was probably the leader in the aggression he described to me with that ambiguous smile. He was Paolo's age – that is, four years older than Cocky – and had already worked on a national newspaper.

He was studying psychology and working part time as an academic assistant in the Psychological Institute in Freiburg. In the group, and in general in the Heim, he was the psychologist, psychoanalysing his fellow residents, and naturally uncovering the hidden sexual meaning in their dreams. His writings and letters were full of surreal jokes, and in life he seems to have been much the same. In the winter semester of 1964, for example, he brought a hamster called Hugo to the Maximilianheim, and presented the case for a hamster resident to a full plenary session of the admissions committee. Hugo was formally approved. (He didn't last long, however, since he persisted in eating all their cigarette butts and soon died of nicotine poisoning. So, at any rate, Pit Wichmann and Rolf Cyriax told me, though they may have been pulling my leg in their turn.)

When Cocky first joined the Maximilianheim in the summer semester of 1964 he was a shy young student, visibly in awe of Paolo and Albert, rarely speaking, feeling unconfident and a country bumpkin.[45] By the autumn all this had changed. His charisma emerged. His silence and apartness, when they persisted, no longer seemed shyness, but a romantic mysteriousness, 'like a young Hölderlin'.[46] His bad times seemed part of that romantic character too – if they were noticed, which they mostly weren't, just as they hadn't been at school. Above all, he was an equal partner with the other two in Group 64, and their closest friend. And this came from his relationship to Albert even more than to Paolo. It was Albert who was his room-mate; Albert with whom he went on a holiday to Italy in the summer of 1965; Albert with whom he bonded, according to Etta; the friendship with Albert that gave him confidence and brought him out of himself. And their work in the paper displays this bond: echoing, referencing or teasing each other, often appearing on the same page.

In other words, there was more than a friendship, I think, between these two: there was a symbiosis, a deep exchange. The relationship with both his brilliant, slightly older Group 64 friends formed Max as a man, a writer and a critic, confirming for ever his stance as a critical outsider, his aggressive, hyper-intellectual side, his ambition to become not just a writer, but a great writer. But it was dominating, introverted Albert more than Paolo the sociable star who was Cocky's first older brother. Albert, who had no father (like so many, his had died in the war), and who, judging from a piece called 'Background', was cut off from his mother and his roots as well.[47] Albert, who was alone and free.

Group 64 is the proof that Max's claims to have come to writing almost by accident, as a refuge from academic life, were untrue. He'd aimed at becoming a writer before, but now that aim was shared and publicly declared. And put into practice: he started to keep a notebook permanently in his pocket, ready to note down everything (and everyone) for use.[48] He became a writer with Paolo Schwanitz and Albert Rasche around 1964, not alone in England around 1984. That is one of his tallest tales; one of his biggest lies.

It began for all of them now, but then life happened. Paolo and Cocky became academics, Albert a psychoanalyst, and they didn't start writing as they'd imagined until much later: Max and Albert in their forties, Paolo in his fifties. Maybe they started so late because they'd

had such vaulting ambitions in their twenties. Albert, perhaps the most
ambitious of all, has written two novels. They have not yet appeared,
but at the age of eighty he is about to publish a collection of short
stories.[49]

Despite his busy life, Cocky did attend his courses. But he found
the teaching of literature at Freiburg less and less to his taste. It was
entirely formal, in the art-for-art's-sake tradition called in Germany
werkimmanente Kritik, which dismisses as irrelevant the social or
historical background that he was already convinced was the heart
of the matter.[50] Only the works of Benjamin, Adorno and the rest
of the Frankfurt School, he would say, saved them from the 'dismal
and distorted' approach to literature they were fed[51] – and which had
grown up, not by accident, in the Nazi era. And in the same way he
despaired of Freiburg's syllabus: it was finally beginning to stretch as
far as the early twentieth century, but got nowhere near the post-war
literature he had studied with Schmelzer at school. Altogether, he
would write towards the end of his life, German studies at Freiburg in
his day 'were a branch of scholarship stricken with almost premeditated
blindness'.[52]

In his last term, however, the professor of modern German literary
history was briefly replaced by someone from elsewhere: Professor
Ronald Peacock of Bedford College, London, until recently Henry
Simon Professor of German at the University of Manchester.[53] Cocky
took his course on European drama of the 1890s, and instantly found
a style of teaching much more to his liking: less formal, more personal,
and open to the free play of ideas, even from students. He got his best
mark on this course: an A/A+ for 'The Conflict of World-Views in
Shaw's *Man and Superman*'. And a year later he applied to be a *Lektor*
at the University of Manchester. We'll never know all the reasons that
made him think of England and Manchester, but the attraction to
Professor Peacock's Anglo-Saxon style was the most important.[54]

That was still in the future, but he took the first step now. The important
thing in his Freiburg life, his friendship with Paolo and Albert, would
continue wherever he was. There was nothing else to hold him. At the
end of the summer semester of 1965 he left Freiburg. In the autumn of

that year, instead of returning, he went to live with his elder sister in Fribourg in Switzerland and entered the university there.

This was one of the most crucial moves he ever made: the start, in retrospect, of his life of exile. Given the writer he later became – in sum, his country's severest critic – it's an important question. Why did he leave Freiburg?

It was complicated, he said.[55] There was his unhappiness with the way literature was taught. Beyond that, he was unhappy with the whole university. Part of the problem was the ailing state of higher education that he and Paolo and Albert had satirised with their corpse in a coffin. Libraries were poor and buildings crumbling; the number of students was growing, but not the number of professors, so that the classes grew ever bigger and ever more anonymous. On top of this, the system hadn't changed. German universities were still hierarchical institutions. Professors were distant, authoritarian figures, 'demigods', as one of Cocky's fellow students put it; when she went as a graduate student to the US, she couldn't believe how informal and accessible her teachers were. Also, universities in Germany were politically divided: either left or right, and staff had to toe the line. Freiburg was conservative, or what we would now call neoliberal; left-wing professors kept quiet and never felt secure. None of this would Max find in British universities, to his relief. It made his German teachers, he would say, 'monochrome'.

But the overriding factor was of a different kind: money. In an early Freiburg letter[56] he tells Gertrud of his despair at remaining dependent on their parents, and the great thing about Switzerland was that he could finish his degree there in one year, instead of two, as in Germany. In almost every letter after that he mentions a new financial worry. Gertrud helped, sending him parcels of coffee and chocolate, and knitting him a jumper so that he didn't have to buy one. But the problem weighs so heavily on him that already in his first term he's planning to leave.[57] Maybe he'll come to Fribourg for his fifth term, he says, and go to Vienna for his sixth… In the event he would stay in Fribourg for both, where he wouldn't have to pay for housing either, since he could live with Gertrud and Jean-Paul.

At this stage he was still thinking of returning to Freiburg for his final exams.[58] At the end of his Fribourg year, however, he wouldn't return, but went instead to England. Again that was because he found a job and money there – not a lot of money, but a great deal more than he'd had before. But you need a push as well as a pull to head into the unknown. The push came from the last problem.[59]

He had thought that things would be different at university: that here at least the conspiracy of silence would be over. But it wasn't. The recent past was as carefully avoided in the classroom as it had been at home, and at the same time just as present. Many professors were of the generation above or older; they'd got their jobs in the 1930s and 1940s; and almost all had either actively supported the regime, or at best been silent. 'You were surrounded by dissembling old fascists,' Max would say, and 'The ghosts of the Third Reich were still floating through the halls.' He had 'a sense of discomfort there all the time'.

This was how he remembered it, nearly forty years later. But was it true, mostly, in hindsight? His writings at the time show no interest in politics, nor would the novel he would soon write. And he himself occasionally suggested that his unease was only in hindsight.[60] 'I really left Germany for practical reasons in the first instance,' he told Joseph Cuomo, who interviewed him in 2001. 'It's in retrospect that I seem to think – and I'm not entirely sure whether it's true – that I did have a sense of discomfort about the whole thing.'

The trauma of the concentration-camps film was still repressed, and the reason for his unease perhaps not always clear. But he was underestimating his young self with these doubts. He had, after all, been fighting with his father over the past since he was sixteen. And it was while he was at Freiburg that the Auschwitz trials took place, and were reported in detail for many months. 'I read those reports every day,' he told Christopher Bigsby, 'and they suddenly shifted my vision.'[61] The moraine in front of that glacier certainly moved on. The question had become public, the evidence definite and detailed. How could any intelligent person not have known?

Among his professors, Walter Rehm, who died shortly after his arrival, had been an anti-Nazi humanist and above suspicion. But one of his teachers had been close to Heidegger – the famous philosopher who as rector had fervently supported the Nazi regime – and he and the other professor of German both had the reputation among the students of having been Nazis. So did the rector, H.-H. Jeschek. There were rumours about all three, which Cocky would have heard, like everyone else.[62] Combine these with his daily readings about the Auschwitz trials, and it's hard to imagine him *not* feeling some unease about his Freiburg teachers.

Whether the rumours were justified is, of course, another question. There had been resisters among the Freiburg staff, including one of Rehm's assistants, as well as Rehm himself. On the other hand, it is undeniable that all the professions remained stuffed with Nazis after the war. The legal system was particularly notorious, and the universities came a close second. A city history published in 1992 records the early and eager *Gleichstaltung* (conformity to Nazi law) of Freiburg University under Heidegger, and admits that much of the post-war effort to de-Nazify it was unsuccessful. Nazi students were stopped from entering, but Nazi professors stayed in place. 'It thus seems,' the authors conclude, 'that in the following years the University employed stronger measures against its students than against its teachers.'[63]

Freiburg was far from the worst.[64] During Cocky's time there, the universities of Munich, Würzburg and Göttingen still had ex-Nazis teaching law; until the early 1960s Göttingen still required applicants to certify that they were not Jews. But Freiburg wasn't the best either. Around 1964 Paolo and his friend Berndt Ostendorf asked for a course on the Third Reich, but were told it was too soon, while in the same year Tübingen and Marburg were offering lectures on the subject.[65] Heidegger had tried to turn Freiburg into a model Nazi university. He hadn't succeeded, but it took a long time to recover.

In the end, then, the balance sheet of Cocky's Freiburg years comes out even. They were the first great step into freedom and a new world. And they brought him Paolo and Albert, his most important friends since Kasus and Lotte. On the other side of the balance lay the bad times, and the discomfort with his country, stirring whenever he read an Auschwitz report or passed an older professor in the corridor. He'd thought that complicity and silence lived only in the provinces, among the less well educated and well informed, like his father.[66] Now he knew they were everywhere.

Leaving Freiburg would be, as it turned out, leaving Germany. Since he never did return to do the final exams, his fate as an outsider would be sealed. Without a German university degree, a career at a German university would be impossible.[67] He must have known that, or at least suspected it. If not now, then when he left Fribourg a year later, and instead of returning went still further away: like Paul, like Kasimir, a long way away, but from where?

When I tried to pursue Group 64 fifty years later, it was too late to catch Paolo: he had inherited his mother's Parkinson's disease, as he'd always feared he would, and died in 2004, just three years after Cocky.[68] But Etta is alive, still living near Freiburg, still in a house with a beautiful garden.

She was kind and generous, talking about Paolo, though she'd warned me she wouldn't, and helping me to find other Freiburg friends. But about Cocky she would say very little, except that he was closest to Albert, closer than to Paolo. She got out her photos and made copies for me. One was 'an early selfie', she said, taken by Albert on a timed camera.

Cocky, Etta and Albert at the back, Paolo in front.

As we leaned together over this picture she turned to me. 'I know,' she said, 'that it looks as if Albert and I are smiling madly at each other, as though we're in love. But there was never anything like that between us.' She gave me her steady gaze, and I nodded. 'I believe you,' I said, and I did. But at the same time I didn't. Because it doesn't look as if she and Albert are smiling at each other. She is smiling at him; but the two who are smiling at each other, across her, are Albert and Cocky.

So I went to see Albert.

He was Cocky's best man at his wedding two years after Freiburg, he visited Max in Manchester, and he has letters from him from the late 1960s to the early 1970s. But then the letters ended, and for a decade they were out of touch, though after that they reconnected. It's one of the things I asked him: why did their friendship lapse in their thirties?

'Our paths diverged,' he said, 'we simply grew apart.' But I wondered if there hadn't been another reason. The keynote of Group 64 was ambition, and ambition means competition. Albert still competes with his friends fifty years later: 'Paolo's books are brilliant, but not literature,' he said to me, 'and Max wrote great books but was spoiled by success.' I don't think that is at all true. But perhaps Albert already competed in those early years, when Max was too uncertain to bear it.

I felt that competition on my own skin. Albert told me that he plans to write something about Max himself, and would therefore share nothing – not his memories, not his letters, not with me, not with anyone. I tried everything, but nothing worked. He saw every move before I made it. He is one of the most impressive people I've ever met, and perhaps that Max ever met. Maybe that was the matching reason why their friendship had to end for a while. Max was secretly just as competitive himself; in that he was Albert's best pupil.

As I left I said, 'What you didn't say was just as interesting as what you did say.' He cocked his head at me and grinned. 'And you wrote that down too, did you?' he said.

From my notebook, Freiburg, 4 August 2015

He said he wouldn't tell me anything, and I believed him. But actually he told me a lot. That they were determined to write the Great German Novel, that they were convinced they already were great writers. And Max kept their attitudes to the end. So it all went back to their group, he said, everything about Max's writing went back to the group. An exaggeration? Yes, but also right.

He said more about Max then too – about Cocky. That he was mostly quiet, but could also be fun. And sometimes *garstig* – nasty, sarcastic. That he had great unrest inside him. 'We settled,' he said. 'Max never settled.' That's what Gertrud says too: after Wertach, he

never settled. 'He was always searching for his way and his place,'
Albert said, 'not just geographically, but in himself.'

The key question about Max's work, he said, is why he mixes fact
and fiction in the way he does. I told him about Max's mixing them
in interviews too, including with me, at which he laughed heartily.
'I'm not sure if he deliberately misled us, or just mixed things up,'
I said, at which he stopped laughing and gave me a pitying look.
I looked back and said, 'Josef, the hero of his Freiburg novel, is
always lying and telling untrue stories.' 'Yes,' he said, 'I came across
that a lot with Max.' 'You did?' I asked. He was smiling now, so
I went on. 'Why *did* he blur the line between fact and fiction,
then?' 'That is what I shall write about,' he said. 'You'll have to wait
and see.'

His second point came later.

The reactions to Max's work are extreme, he said. Some people
think that he's one of our greatest writers, others that he's a fraud
who steals people's stories and sentimentalises their suffering. That
sort of extreme response means that something is going on, and
we need to ask what. I'd learned now, and stayed silent. And he
said that what was going on was trauma. Max wrote out of trauma,
and passed it on to us – he didn't say this in so many words, but
it's what he meant. Max *had* to write, he said, 'The loneliness and
despair in his work is his.' And: 'When one writes about trauma, it
is always about oneself.' And: 'Being an artist is a way of passing on
the trauma.'

I'm sure this is right – it accounts for the power of art, especially
Sebald's art, better than a million other theories. He wrote out of
trauma, and survived by sharing that trauma with his readers. If
we share it, we survive by sharing it with him; if we don't, or won't
admit it, we call his work a fraud. But the question is, of course,
what was his trauma? That is where Albert stopped. *He* will tell that,
and no one else… He implied that it was a childhood trauma, and
that it had to do with the familiar business of his relationship with
his father.

Of course, it could be that – his father's return was certainly a
trauma. But was that the trauma Albert really meant? Just because
he pointed me in that direction, I doubt it. And he said some other
strange things. For instance: 'Don't think the secret I'm keeping

back is important. It's just on the personal level.' What on earth did he mean by that? To a psychoanalyst the personal *is* important.[69]

My notes ended there. Afterwards I sent him some follow-up questions. He replied that he wouldn't answer them, since, as I knew, he did not intend to help me with my work on Max; I would have to wait until he wrote his own. And that, he repeated, would be 'A personal story between him and me.' I was puzzled all over again. How did that relate to his subject being Max's lying, and to his thesis that Max wrote out of trauma?

I don't know; we'll have to wait until Albert writes his book. But there is surely a story to be told about that friendship. It was early, it was close, it influenced Max for ever. And there is that photograph that Etta showed me. There was something between Albert and Cocky. I doubt it was physical: it was much deeper than that. They wrote for each other and about each other; in their writing they almost became each other. They were as dependent on each other as the pair of murderers in *Vertigo*, who 'were like brothers to each other and had no idea how to free themselves from their innocence'.[70] Behind W. G. Sebald's imagery of brothers, which links love to fear, hover the ghosts of Albert and Cocky.

Cocky, winter semester 1964–5. Photo by Albert.

11

Fribourg, 1965–6

As Cocky travels towards Fribourg in September 1965, I imagine lending him the 1928 Baedeker guide to Switzerland. It would still serve him well today. '*Fribourg*, Ger. *Freiburg*, capital of Canton Fribourg, the ancient *Üechtland*, is most picturesquely situated on a steep peninsula formed by the *Sarine*,' he reads. 'It has retained its medieval features to a remarkable degree: walls and towers, churches and convents, gabled and turreted houses, and numerous fountains of the 16th–17th centuries.'[1]

He steps down from his train (the new station building wasn't quite open yet) and, following Baedeker, turns left towards the 'GRAND' PLACES, a large open space with a fine view of the town and the Sarine valley from the E. side.' He then follows the rue de Romont to the Place St-Pierre, which features in its 'S.E. corner … the cable tramway to the lower town'. He doesn't take the funicular, but sees that he can descend 'by the Route des Alpes or the rue de Lausanne'. The rue de Lausanne is where Gertrud and Jean-Paul live, so he chooses that; at the top, if he looks to his left, he sees the road to the university he'll take most days for the next year. At the bottom of the rue de Lausanne, he reads, is the 'PLACE DU TILLEUL, with a lime tree. According to tradition, it grew out of the twig with which, on the evening after the battle of Morat, a runner brought the news of the Confederates' victory.' But here he is – Number 11, on the left, just before the Place du Tilleul. He closes Baedeker and climbs the stairs, puffing a bit – he's smoking too much – up four floors, to the attic flat. The door opens, and there is Gertrud.

*11 rue de Lausanne in 2017. Their flat
was at the back, above a small garden.*

Fribourg,[2] as he would learn, went back to the twelfth century. During
the Burgundian Wars Fribourg fought with its sister city Bern against
Charles the Bold of Burgundy: this was the war decided by the Battle of
Morat, mentioned by Baedeker. On 22 June 1476 the Swiss descended
on Charles's camp like the wolf on the fold, driving thousands of his
soldiers into the lake below, which in Fribourg legend turned red with
blood. That evening the runner brought the news of victory to the
town, bearing a branch of a lime tree, a *tilleul*, from the battlefield. It
was planted in the square at the bottom of the rue de Lausanne, and
grew into a tree that flowered for nearly 500 years. Byron saw it in
1816, when it was 340 years old, and reported that it was 'a good deal
decayed'; soon after that its branches had to be supported by columns,
as the etching on the next page shows.

But it survived everything, including a fire, and was still there, the
living memory of a bloody battle, in 1965. Winfried – he was Winfried
again now, living with his sister – saw it many times. It finally succumbed
ten or fifteen years later, defeated by the traffic fumes of the twentieth
century. He wouldn't have been surprised.

*The lime tree planted in Fribourg, in commemoration of
the Battle of Morat, 1476. An etching of 1831.*

Fribourg's history is preserved in strata, like those in rock. It starts at
the bottom, in the old town on the peninsula in the river, where most
of the houses were built before the sixteenth century. Then you climb
up through the sixteenth, seventeenth and eighteenth centuries to the
centre, just steps from Gertrud's door. Nestled between its steep hills,
Fribourg is a city of bridges – fourteen in all, from the oldest, built
in wood, through the stone bridges of the eighteenth century to the
concrete ones of today. And, as Baedeker says, it is a city of churches
and monasteries, of medieval walls and towers (there are fourteen of
those too), and of fountains. There are, for instance, the Fontaines de
Samson, de la Samaritaine and de la Vaillance, de Ste Anne, St Pierre and
St Jean, and nearest to the rue de Lausanne, the Fontaine de St Georges
in the Place de l'Hôtel de Ville. Winfried, it seems, could not escape St
George; but in George's Fribourg form, he probably didn't mind.[3]

No one could be more Fribourgeois than Jean-Paul:[4] Aebischer is one
of the commonest surnames in the city. Fribourg's working class lived
in the lowest part, the old town, and that is where he was born, under
the Zähringen bridge, named after the family that founded the city. His
parents came from poor families, with sixteen brothers and sisters on
each side. His father, Étienne, had left school at ten and was a building
worker all his life; his mother, Anna, took in washing from rich people in
the upper town to make a bit more to feed her own large family: one girl

and five boys, of whom Jean-Paul was the youngest. Soon after his birth the family moved to the Place Petit St Jean (home of the Fontaine de Ste Anne), also in the old town, where they lived until he was eight or nine. Then they too moved up the hill to the upper town, where they became neighbours of the Brünisholzes, and where Jean-Paul and Gertrud met in 1959. Now, in 1965, the two were living right in the centre of the city, minutes away from the bridge under which Jean-Paul had been born.

All this – Fribourg's layers of history, Jean-Paul's rootedness – would have pleased Winfried. So would the language all around him. The local German dialect, Senslerdeutsch, is Alemannic, like Allgäuerisch, and Fribourg is even more border country than the Allgäu: it straddles the language line between German and French. You could study in both languages at the university in 1965, and you still can. Winfried wrote his dissertation in German, but spoke mostly French at home, since Jean-Paul belonged firmly on the French side and spoke no German; Max's French retained a Swiss flavour ever after, according to Marie.

In the autumn of 1965 Gertrud and Jean-Paul had their first child, born only weeks before Winfried's arrival.[5] And their attic flat was small for two adults, let alone three. But Winfried, who was baby Solveig's godfather, loved her from the start, and he and Jean-Paul had been fond of each other for years. He fitted in to the little family with ease. 'It was like reliving our childhood,' Gertrud says, and blissful for both of them.

Winfried had the tiniest room in the flat, with just enough room for a bed and a small table and chair. During the day he attended his courses and worked in the university library. In the evening and deep into the night he wrote his dissertation in his room, while in the sitting room next door his brother-in-law rehearsed for his next concert. Jean-Paul had a day job, but his passion, and many years of training, lay in music. He sang the tenor arias from Haydn's *Die Jahreszeiten*, 'Dalla sua pace' from Mozart's *Don Giovanni*, Donizetti's 'Una furtiva lagrima', and much more; and in between penning violent attacks on his subject, Winfried would listen, and smile.†

His pleasure in the baby was less predictable. Visiting Gertrud when she was an *au pair* in Paris, he had eyed her horde of small charges with dismay, and never expressed the smallest tenderness for children since; but clearly Solveig was different. When she was born he wrote a short, lyrical poem for her, called '*Kinderlied*', 'Children's Song'. It is

Sebaldianly mysterious, since it never mentions a child, and is plangent and melancholy (opening with 'The day sinks towards the field'). But it is also Sebaldianly beautiful, with images of stars strewn over the sky and held in a hand like 'a thousand butterflies'. Today Gertrud and Solveig herself cherish it and don't try to explain it, which is the best way to treat a poem, especially one by W. G. Sebald.

The baby was a few weeks old when he arrived and just over a year old when he left. He took care of her when Gertrud accompanied Jean-Paul to his concerts, or when the two went dancing at one of Fribourg's street fairs on the weekend. Because of Winfried's moustache, Jean-Paul took to calling him Eustache, from stories he'd heard in his own childhood: *Les aventures d'Eustache et du Bourdon Bzz*, about a little boy and a bumble-bee.[6] So now Winfried called himself Eustache-Moustache for Solveig, letting her tug at his moustache as he did so. One morning, when she cried for a long time and Gertrud thought she should be left, he went to her and saw that she'd fallen out of her cot. 'So he saved her from some suffering,' Gertrud says, 'which is what he always tried to do for everyone.'

Solveig with Eustache-Moustache, 1966.

He worked hard in his Fribourg year. So he had little spare time, and still less money – his allowance from Georg was reduced now, Gertrud recalls, no doubt because he was living with her. And Jean-Paul was on a starting salary in his job as a designer with a packaging firm. So there was never enough money. The little family was proverbially poor but happy; or – better perhaps – happy but poor.

As a result they couldn't do very much. They went on occasional outings in the Aebischers' tiny Renault to swim in a nearby lake: perhaps Lake Morat, or the Lac de Bienne, which Max said he saw first in September 1965, with the Île St-Pierre 'flooded with a trembling light'[7] in the middle. They strolled the streets together, which was free. And they explored Fribourg's many churches, including the Cathedral of St Nicolas with its famous organ, whose glorious sound made Dorothea sob in *Middlemarch*. They liked the smaller choir organ too; if Winfried had known that it was built by Sebald Manderscheidt of Nürnberg,[8] he might have liked it even more.

With cash so short, they went to no concerts or exhibitions; besides, Gertrud says, 'Fribourg was a very sleepy place in the sixties,' and nothing of great interest was on offer. For music they relied on the radio and on Jean-Paul's sitting-room rehearsals. Their one entertainment was the cinema, which was cheap. Because of baby Solveig, they couldn't go together, but Winfried went alone or with friends whenever he could. Among the films that made it to Fribourg in 1965–6 were the most famous movies of the early 1960s. Max talked about many of them later, and very likely saw them then: Fellini's *Juliet of the Spirits*, Godard's *Pierrot le Fou* and Truffaut's *La peau douce*, for instance; also two of Hitchcock's most terrifying tales, *Psycho* and *The Birds*.[9] 'We both loved Hitchcock,' Gertrud says, and I can't imagine he would have missed them.

Alone he explored the city, taking photos with Jean-Paul's camera, or browsing the junk shops and flea markets for old postcards – the latter a hobby that seems to have started now. Until 1965 only restorations had added to his idea of cities as ruins. The ancient, undisturbed beauty of Fribourg must have seemed like a revelation to him, and so must the peaceful farmland all around, and the snow-capped mountains nearby. The landscapes of Switzerland are among the most beautiful in his work, and the locus of its most transcendent events. This love of Switzerland, especially of the land between Geneva and Bern, had its roots in his Fribourg year.

He'd only recently escaped his own family with relief, but Gertrud's, of course, was different. And Jean-Paul's was a solid working-class clan, with none of the bourgeois pretensions that had driven him mad in his own. He liked them all, especially Jean-Paul's eldest sister Jeanette and his eldest brother Joseph, who was a postman, and their father

Étienne, who was the same type as Winfried's beloved grandfather, spare and quiet.

But the happiest times were spent at home. After his long nights of work, he and Gertrud would have their breakfast of coffee and croissants at ten; on Thursdays it would be earlier, when he had an early-morning class at the university and bought *Silserbrötchen* on the way home – small dark rolls covered with salt, like pretzels. Supper was simple: vegetables from the Market Square at the top of the rue de Lausanne, often trout caught by Jean-Paul at the weekend. Occasionally the brothers-in-law went mushrooming together to add to Gertrud's supplies. Winfried stopped smoking, and instead took to having a small whisky before going to bed. Jean-Paul drank very little, but Gertrud shared Winfried's nightcap. And so they ended the day together, as they began it.

Fribourg in the mid-1960s was still a deeply conservative, Catholic town, even more conservative and Catholic than Freiburg and Sonthofen. But there was one big difference: *it had nothing to do with him.* Sonthofen's Catholicism had dominated him in the shape of his mother; even in the Maximilianheim the authorities had lurked in the wings like Big Brother. In 11 rue de Lausanne they were three young people together, and no one tried to control him. If he had one need that outweighed all others, it was for freedom: freedom from academic rules, from literary rules, from all rules. In the end he couldn't escape them, because no one can. But now was the one time in his life when he was free.

Gertrud and Jean-Paul with Solveig, 1965.

The university suited him too.[10] It was small, with only about 5,000 students: on a human scale, like Fribourg itself. He had to continue with the philology courses that didn't passionately interest him, but those in English literature, and above all those in his major subject, German literature, would have interested him very much. Among the latter there was, for instance, a course on post-Expressionist literature[11] (so he was getting beyond Weimar at last!) and one on the beginnings of the German novel. And there was at least one on the history of German-language drama. This was in effect the history of Austrian drama, since six of the eight playwrights were Austrian.

Winfried seems to have specialised in this area, since it was the subject of his oral examination at the end of the year.[12] Clearly someone had sparked his interest in Austrian theatre. There can be little doubt who that was: his professor of German literature, Ernst Alker.[13]

Unsurprisingly, Alker was Austrian. He was seventy years old in 1965: just the sort of older professor who had made Winfried uneasy in the corridors of Freiburg. But Alker was the opposite of those shadowy figures. He had done his doctorate in Holland. In the early 1930s he worked in Leipzig and Bonn, but soon after Hitler came to power both his institutes were closed down, and he emigrated to Sweden. There he championed the anti-Nazi Norwegian writer Sigrid Undset, and in 1935 published an essay criticising the nationalist *Blut und Boden* (Blood and Soil) literature back home. From now on he was an open enemy of the regime. In 1944 his German citizenship was revoked,* and two years later he became a Swedish citizen. He never returned to either Germany or Austria. In 1946 he moved to Switzerland instead, to the University of Fribourg.

This was the man who was now Winfried's professor and the supervisor of his dissertation: the main teacher of his Fribourg year. And he would have been congenial to Winfried in other ways too – even a kindred spirit, as Max's colleague Richard Sheppard says.[14] As a literary scholar, Alker specialised in the nineteenth century, and above all in Gottfried Keller, Adalbert Stifter and the writers of the declining Habsburg Empire, such as Hugo von Hofmannsthal and Kafka, all to be among Winfried's own favourites. And like Winfried, but unlike most

---

*Austria had been part of Germany since *Anschluss*.

Germanists, certainly of the time, he believed that literature should be studied within its social context, and would accept the biographical approach of his student's thesis (as we'll see) without a murmur.

Alker was a devout Catholic, but liberal-minded and private; he wouldn't have imposed his religion on anyone. In person he was an old-fashioned, courtly and charming Viennese; like so many exiles, like Winfried himself perhaps in the distant future, someone in whom the ways of a lost home were preserved far more than in those who stayed. He had the Viennese sense of humour too – ironic, often mocking. These traits spoke to ones deep in Winfried, and were things his own students and colleagues would see in him years later. If this Austrian professor was a role model to him, as Sheppard acutely suggests, it was because Alker's example brought out what was already in him; that may be all that role models can ever do.

Winfried's other two professors were a Swiss and an Englishman, both equally unlikely to be tainted by fascism, and neither was.

Eduard Studer,[15] who taught philology (that is, medieval language and literature), was the youngest, just made full professor when Winfried arrived. He wrote a book on how to spell the local Sensler dialect, which would certainly have appealed to his young student, who'd been amusing himself by writing Allgäuerisch since school. Studer's usual medieval subjects, however, appealed less. Winfried 'distinguished himself by his active participation in our seminars', Studer's final report says.[16] But neither Winfried nor Max could ever fully apply himself to something that didn't touch his imagination. His marks on the oral exam were only 'Good' and 'Satisfactory', and he ended with only a second in philology.

James Smith, Winfried's professor of English at Fribourg, was probably the first Englishman he met after Ronald Peacock. Winfried didn't talk about him, then or later,[17] so it's hard to say how well he knew him. But in many ways Smith was a kindred spirit too, and it's likely that Winfried responded to that side of him. It was his first encounter with a very English kind of melancholy.[18]

Smith's background was like an English version of Winfried's own.[19] He was a provincial grammar-school boy who won a scholarship to Trinity College, Cambridge, home in his day (he was born in 1904) almost exclusively to the upper classes. As an undergraduate he flourished, graduating with a double first in modern languages.

But then he failed to win a research fellowship at Trinity. 'This was the greatest disappointment of his life,' Edward Wilson, professor of Spanish at Cambridge, would write in his memoir of his friend.[20]

Smith went to Princeton instead, as a visiting fellow. This still looks like the start of a glittering university career, but for some reason it ended there. Instead he taught at a grammar school, publishing half a dozen essays in T. S. Eliot's *Criterion* and F. R. Leavis's *Scrutiny*. He spent the war abroad, as director of the British Institute in Caracas. In 1946 he returned to Cambridge and teaching, but without a regular university job. That was his position in 1947, when the professorship of English at Fribourg was advertised. Leavis and Eliot both sent their high praise to Fribourg, and Smith got the job.

He liked the city and was an excellent teacher. But as the years went on, 'Fribourg,' Wilson wrote, 'brought him little happiness.'[21] His lectures and classes were prepared with such extreme conscientiousness that they left him exhausted, and without time for the writing he'd hoped to do. By the time Winfried met him in the autumn of 1965 he was hollowed out, like Ambros Adelwarth. In 1969 he retired and returned for the last time to Cambridge, dying there just three years later.

It's a strange story, with that bright beginning, then a life of several exiles. Did everything come out of that first blow, never recovered from? Or was Smith a conscientious objector, not only against war but against success, or merely against pleasure, especially for himself? This is the English melancholy I meant – like Shakespeare's Jaques, whom Winfried had written about at Freiburg, or that of Hamlet, with whom he identified for much of his life. Or like Max's own, in later years. If Winfried saw any of this in James Smith, he may have liked him as much as Alker.

He took at least one of Smith's Shakespeare courses, and his course on the nineteenth-century novel. Smith examined him on both and was more than satisfied. 'The candidate gave a highly intelligent account of Melville as novelist and short story writer,' he wrote. 'Some of his judgements were original. So was that on Emily Bronte's *Wuthering Heights*.' He gave Winfried a first.[22]

The major work Winfried did at Fribourg was the dissertation, or *mémoire*, with Alker. It was his first long piece: sixty typewritten pages.

He began it in September or October, and handed it in five or six months later, at the beginning of March.[23]

His subject was, at first sight, surprising. Carl Sternheim[24] was a satirical playwright of the early twentieth century who had died in 1942 and been more or less forgotten ever since. In 1963, however, the first volume of a new edition of his work was published, and something of a Sternheim revival was underway.[25] Winfried no doubt consulted Alker, who would have told him what he said in his book on German literature: Sternheim was no good. His characters were stereotyped, his plots unbelievable, his language artificial and his satire ambiguous. You wonder, then, what can possibly have attracted Winfried. Could it have been that Sternheim was half Jewish, and that the combination of his Jewish origins and his social satire got his work banned during the Third Reich?[26] But Winfried didn't set out to defend Sternheim. On the contrary, he takes Alker's literary dismissal to new levels of destruction – and, adopting the social and psychological approach of Adorno and Benjamin, adds a strong critique of Sternheim's personal morality. So far from defending a victim of the Third Reich, he savagely attacks him. What was going on?

First of all, it was simply what he did. Almost all his early academic writing was critical and attacking, right up to the 1980s; he was carving out a place for himself in opposition to everything. This was partly the legacy of Group 64, but most of all it came from a genuine anger at institutional *Germanistik*, with the 'almost premeditated blindness' of its methods, and the dubious history of many of its older proponents. If a prominent Germanist was touting Sternheim – as Wilhelm Emrich was doing with his new edition – Winfried was automatically on the other side. The first target of his thesis was less Carl Sternheim than the Germanist establishment, as his opening line made clear: 'The aim of this work is to revise the current image of Sternheim as propounded by Germanists.'[27]

The second target was, however, Sternheim himself. Sternheim's comedies satirised the bourgeoisie of the Wilhelmine era, which was the peak of conservativism, militarism and Junker domination in Germany.[28] But his problem, Winfried argued, was that he had not only assimilated into that society, as many Jews were doing at the time: he had radically assimilated, abandoning his Jewish roots, and more than half taking on the flawed value system he was claiming to criticise. As a result his satire is technically adept but deeply ambivalent, and all the other faults identified by Alker follow. Sternheim's plays are built on no real ethical values, and so cannot be true satire, like that of Swift or Karl Kraus, and unlike such true satire, they cannot outlast the era they were written in.

Thus Winfried's attack was on Junker values, and on Sternheim for accepting them. In effect he criticises Sternheim twice, once for abandoning his own Jewish heritage and once for taking on, or wanting to take on, the *ur*-German one of the Prussian nobility. So in effect he is doing what he would always do, which is attacking a German anti-Semite,[29] except that this one happens to be a Jew.

Whether Winfried's assessment of Sternheim was right or wrong is not very important.[30] What is important is how his first major academic work seems to contain his whole future practice.[31] It is polemical and extreme to the point of exaggeration (Group 64 again!), designed to attack and provoke the Germanist establishment; it focuses strongly on the author's biography; and perhaps most important of all, it insists that literature, and literary criticism itself, are ethical activities, and inseparable from questions of moral value. Judging literary works apart from the values they embody is as false as judging them apart from the history and society from which they emerge (and is often the same thing). Moreover, these values can only have been placed there by their authors, and can only be genuine if their authors actually practised them; if they are falsely claimed, the falsity will show up in the writing. (He will argue this again, in one of the biggest controversies of his career.)

All these steps were and still are against all academic rules – identifying the author with the text, and aesthetics with ethics, and using both heresies to put history and biography at the heart of the study of literature. Winfried could not have placed himself any further outside the world of academic criticism, and there he would remain.

He wanted to be outside the German part of it for one main reason, as we know: he thought most of the older members of the profession were tainted by their association with Nazism. And in setting himself against Wilhelm Emrich now, the editor and promoter of Sternheim, he didn't know how right he was.[32] Emrich was an eminent academic with a progressive reputation, but during the Third Reich he had been not just a fellow traveller, but an active Nazi working in Goebbels' propaganda department. He was joined in his revival of Sternheim by another older Germanist, who was calling himself Hans Schwerte, but who, under his real name of Hans Schneider, had been a high-ranking SS officer during the Nazi years.

All this came out only later, but it shows that Winfried's suspicions of the Germanist establishment were far from a fantasy. And it shows something else as well, which illuminates the ambiguous, hall-of-mirrors world of post-war Germany: the devoted revivers of a forgotten Jewish writer were in fact old Nazis trying to cover their tracks, while the young student who so sharply attacked him could do so precisely because he was not an anti-Semite.

Winfried's *Zu Carl Sternheim* broke not only the methodological rules of academic criticism, but the formal ones as well. And in this too it anticipated his later work – though the basics, such as spelling, would improve.

Richard Sheppard sums up its failings from a scholarly point of view: '...careless and inconsistent footnoting, inaccurate, selective and tendentious citation, an inattention to punctuation, orthographic consistency and the strict rules of German grammar, a moralising tone, generalised and unsubstantiated opinion, a refusal to read piles of secondary literature...'[33]

These are rather grave complaints, and would certainly fail most students. But Winfried got away with them, and so would W. G. Sebald. Sheppard argues that they are not simply slapdash, but 'signs of [his] oppositional stance', deliberate assertions of his 'right as a critic to ignore established authority and be thoroughly subjective'.[34] This is surely right – though Max did say that he had had trouble at school learning to spell, so some of it at least might be making a virtue of necessity.[35] But he was lucky in his time: there was more tolerance of quirkiness and rule-breaking in universities in the 1960s and 1970s than today, at any rate in Britain, and evidently in Switzerland. Alker's judgement of *Zu Carl Sternheim* was positive but clear-eyed. It showed, he wrote, 'critical insight and the ability to support it clearly', but in quality it only 'approaches a successful Dissertation'.[36] Nevertheless, he awarded it the highest grade possible, a *summa cum laude*. Much the same would happen in Manchester. Winfried's (and Max's) teachers recognise his scholarly limitations, or resistance, and don't seem to mind. Despite the selective use of evidence, the generalisations, the deliberate and unacknowledged misquotations, they saw greatness in him anyway.

He must have applied for the Lektorship at Manchester – a junior post teaching German language – soon after arriving in Fribourg, perhaps even before. In mid-March[37] the answer arrived: he was accepted. From then on he knew he was going to England. And he prepared for it, like Adelwarth, by making 'certain adjustments ... to his inner self'.[38] Someone who saw him every day on the rue de Lausanne thought that he looked *sehr Englisch*, very English. And by the time he left he had probably decided:[39] he would not go to England with a Nazi name like Winfried. From now on he'd be Max: short for 'Maximilian', which he would later claim – even on official forms – was his third name.[40] It wasn't; he just chose it himself. We know some of the possible reasons – the Maximilianheim, the naughty boys Max and Moritz – and there were probably others. The best explanation is the one he gave to Marie (though it comes from Max the writer more than thirty years later, and sadly, therefore, is probably untrue). He would have wanted to be called Josef, after his grandfather, he told her, but that didn't happen. So he chose Max: *M* as a reversed *W*, *a* for a vowel, and *x* for the big unknown.[41]

Changing his name was a magical but still relatively calm preparation for his next step. But the reality was almost certainly different, and his dissertation gives us the clue. He argued there that if the need to escape one's origins was too strong, it could produce worthless works, like Sternheim's. And wasn't escaping his origins exactly what he himself had done, ever since he left the Allgäu for university? And did he not also aim to do it through writing? So his plan for life was dangerous: perhaps he too would produce only worthless works.[42] As he set off for a higher degree and the novel he was planning, or had even begun,[43] he would not have been calm at all, but anxious and uncertain.

Perhaps he even hesitated when the moment came to board the plane for England. But it was too late. As long ago as July 1964 he had written to Gertrud that when he finished his course he'd like to go to England for a while.[44] So the idea of England went back to the end of his first year in Freiburg, perhaps even to that brief visit to London of Christmas

1962. He was almost certainly worried and divided, but underneath he had decided long ago. In 1967, in his new English life, he would give one of his grandfather's Kempten diaries to a friend, inscribing in it a line that summed up his vision of time. *The future*, he would write, *lies in the past.*[45]

12

The Novel

Max wrote his first prose book between the ages of twenty-two and twenty-three. It would be twenty years before he wrote another.

For his subject he looked back to the halcyon days of the Maximilianheim: to the last two days there, he would tell a friend.[1] And if he had worried about writing it, once it was done, ambition prevailed, and he wanted it published. For at least half a year, perhaps longer, he looked for a publisher – in vain.[2] Later, when he was W. G. Sebald and famous, he made a joke of it: 'When I read it out to my girlfriend,' he said, 'she fell asleep. So I thought I'd better just give it up.'[3]

He didn't take this first failure as lightly at the time. Later, though, he was glad of it, and didn't want this apprentice work to be seen.[4] He was right: it *is* apprentice work, and should remain where it is, in his archive. But for all its immaturity, it has strong signs of the writer he would become, and being almost undiluted autobiography,[5] it's of great interest here.

At first sight this is a standard novel, with lively characters and a good deal of dialogue. But the impression is misleading. By the time we get to the end we realise that there's been much talk, but little action. There is a novel-within-the-novel, of which the hero reports that nothing happens in its thousands of pages, and it always rains. This is clearly a literary device planted by the knowing young author as an image of the book itself; and apart from the joke about the rain, it's pretty accurate. The novel is like a long short story, or a poem (and Max would stick to poetry for many years): a captured moment, like a photograph.

I say 'the novel', but in fact there are two: or rather two versions,[6] containing the same characters and scenes, but in a different order, and differently developed. Version 2, the rewritten version, is richer and more sophisticated – already in the six months or so of writing Max made great strides. He began with the end, then worked back towards it (this was his friend's suggestion, as we'll see). But there are more substantial changes as well. Both versions are written in an experimental, stream-of-consciousness mode, but the second adds another element – short, verbless, often one- or two-word sentences, the diametric opposite of W. G. Sebald's mature work (and one reason, perhaps, why he could write this one so fast). Version 1 is told in a flat, detached style, while the second is more engaged, with the hero Josef's parents, for example, showing ordinary feeling – his mother fussing over him, his father trying to stop her. Version 1 is also more solipsistic, with most of it taking place in the hero's head; the second moves several speeches from Josef to other characters: to his girlfriend Ann, to his friends Paolo and Bernhard.

The language is close to Max's in his letters – peppered with dialect and schoolboy jokes – but far from the beauties of W. G. Sebald's mature prose. And there are, interestingly, few references to either of W. G. Sebald's silences – or just one reference each, when Josef buys Weiss's *The Investigation*, and when he mentions the 50,000 dead of Dresden.[7] There are one or two jokes about Hitler – Paolo sings 'Hitler has only got one ball', for instance – but otherwise no mention of the Third Reich, and Josef's trouble with his father is entirely personal. The glacier of trauma has not yet pushed its way into Max's writing.

Nonetheless, there are signs of what is to come. Josef is as gloomy as any of W. G. Sebald's narrators: Version 1 begins, for instance, with his reflection that all waiting is waiting to be shot. He has *Vertigo*'s moments of sudden absence from himself, and *Saturn*'s circling thoughts (like Max's own, from 'Jeden Abend' to *A Place in the Country*), as well as *The Emigrants*' preoccupation with suicide (one of the possible authors of the novel-within-the-novel kills himself, for example, and when Josef shaves, he thinks of Stifter cutting his throat with a razor).[8] Here too is the gloom about writing of 'Ferber' and *A Place in the Country*. In this novel, written twenty and thirty years earlier, he gives this gloom to Paolo, and that may well be where he first heard it.[9] Paolo compares writers to poor mules, who spend their lives walking in circles, and says of writing that it can only be done about failure or loss: about perfect moments there's nothing to say.

Last but not least, the novel contains one very Sebaldian element: a system of imagery that runs through the story. Here the images are of birds, especially trapped birds: Josef's mother has a blind bird in a cage, there's a swallow trapped in a church, and he recalls an injured bird that he tried to put out of its misery, only for it to fly away. And finally there's a cascade of animal imagery in comic mode, in one of the letters that Albert sends to Josef from America: a long riff about saving creatures from suffering in the rain, for which he will be honoured after the fifth exhumation of his bones. This letter, which ends both versions, is by Albert himself, as he told me; so that Max not only put both his Group 64 friends into his book, but used them for it. As they'd taught him.

The novel plays in three locations: the university; Switzerland and Belgium, where Josef visits Ann; and his parents' provincial home, where he returns before leaving for a job in England. In all three it is almost entirely true to life.

At the university[10] Paolo and Albert appear, very accurately, under their nicknames, though Albert is already in America, as he was when Max was writing, and we meet him only in the three long letters he sends to Josef. The Group's friend Bernhard Holoczek, later to become an art historian, appears under his own name.[11] The Korean student Kim becomes an unnamed Chinese or Korean with an extensive Heideggerian vocabulary but little other German; and several other Maximilianheim residents appear under different names (or, in one case, his own).[12] The unloved Austrian tutor Dr Götz becomes the much-mocked tutor Wondraschek, someone who lived in the attic becomes the Spanish artist Jesus Wperczeck, and a doctoral student who died by suicide becomes the scholar Friedrich Mannersheim, who does the same. Jesus and Mannersheim both become the author of the novel-within-the-novel at different points, as do two other characters, D. H. Atkinson and Ruben Lantmann, but this novel, everyone agrees,[13] is Max's invention. And there is a pair of students, with different names in the two versions, who enact a nasty ritual of bully and victim: these too Max almost certainly invented.[14]

Most interesting of all, of course, is the character of the hero, Josef. And judging from what we know of Max and his narrators later, he too is remarkably true to life. His gloom, his circling thoughts, his moments of absence I've noted. And there's much more. He already has trouble with trains. His health is already poor: his back aches, his skin is given to red spots, probably of nervous origin; he says he has a bad heart and thinks his life will be short. He is afraid of dogs (that *doesn't* fit the later Max!) and loutish soldiers with their Nazi haircuts; his memories of school are anxious ones, and sometimes, says Ann, he still looks anxious. He loves humanity but often can't bear people, especially fat or ugly ones, but sad old ones, like the ex-clown Pachl, move him. He experiences, as we know, a homosexual approach, which is described in detail. He tells the man that it won't work with him, though it might with his father, and that his elder brother was of the man's kind; both are fantasies, of course, one a revenge, and the other perhaps a projection. He also tells the man a pack of lies: that he is a journalist working for an American paper, and that his parents have died in a car crash in the Rocky Mountains.

Here, and also elsewhere, he asks himself why he always tells such tales – to everyone, even to his friends in the Group. His answer may help us with Max as much as Josef. He does it unintentionally, almost unconsciously, he says. He has spent his whole life playing roles. Perhaps lying is the only way of dealing with the world.

This early novel is the only book in which Max wrote about his wife. In the novel's moment she is his girlfriend, and what it shows is a young man in love. Josef is sad when he has to leave Ann even for a night, happy when she takes his arm. He describes her eyes, which are grey but change with the colour of her clothes, and with the light, like her hair. She is braver than he is, a better driver, and more decisive: he loves animals, but she is a vegetarian. We never get inside the head of anyone but Josef, so we can't know directly how she feels, and she never expresses her love to him, as he does in a letter to her. Her gently noticing his anxious face is the only indication we have that she returns his love. It may be determined by the literary form of the 'I' narrator,[15] but the sense we get is La Rochefoucauld's: Josef is the one who loves, Ann the one who lets herself be loved.

The third focus of the story is Josef's family: his Aunt Anny, who sent her letters and dollar bills from America, and of whom he was always fond; his parents and his grandfather.

The death of his grandfather, we know, is the great private trauma of Max's life. He wrote about it only once: here. And even here it is kept at a distance. The main account comes in the first, detached version, and – unlike most other scenes in the novel – is hardly expanded at all in Version 2. Instead it is almost more muted, and the thunder and lightning that rage around the house in Version 1 have retreated to the mountains.

Josef describes facts and people, including himself, only from the outside. The storm has brought down the lilac tree in the garden, so that his room is filled with the smell of lilac, and of the earth turned over the day before. Frau Steinlehner is dressed in black when she comes to tell him. No one hears him when he goes into his grandfather's room, as though he doesn't exist. The room is full of incense smoke and lit only by candles, so that he cannot see his grandfather well, only the shadows over his face. He goes back to bed and sleeps.

When his mother comes to tell him in the morning she doesn't look at him, and he doesn't reply. He eats breakfast alone. Then the coffin is brought in. He sees the wood shavings in it, and watches as his grandfather is laid inside, which doesn't happen easily. Two days later they bury him. At first it rains, then the *föhn* blows away the clouds. His mother and Frau Steinlehner sob and the fire brigade plays. Later he goes with his mother when she tends the grave, around which she has planted fuchsias and juniper. He looks down on the village below, so quiet that you could think no one has ever lived there. His grandfather's absence has become the whole world's.

His parents, it is plain, he cannot love as he loves his gentle aunt and grandfather. His reasons are some of those we know from Winfried: his mother's anxious piety; his father's infuriating neatness, lining up his pencils in rows or right angles, stacking his newspapers in one precise, invariable order. Their house is so appallingly clean, with everything always in the same place, as though it's never been touched... And so, as he says, in his lies he almost always murders them. First, in a lie to Wondraschek, he murders his father; then, in the lie to the man who approaches him on a train, he murders them both.

This wish-fulfilment fantasy – as it clearly is – is the most Sebaldian thing in this not-yet-Sebaldian story. For it seems as though the future really does lie in the past, as Max would write in January 1967, when he was halfway through writing this novel. In Josef's tale to his pursuer, his parents plunge to their mountain deaths because his mother fails to turn the wheel of their car on a curve: perhaps, he says, on a suicidal impulse. And he almost suffers the same fate himself. He is visiting Ann in Belgium, where she is working for an artist and his family.[16] First he plays 'car accident' with the artist's son; then he, Ann and the child set out in his car. Josef, who is driving, turns to smile at Ann, and doesn't see a curve. They don't die, but end up against a wooden fence. All Max's many future accidents seem to be signalled: including the last one, which happened on a curve, near a wooden fence.

PART V

Max, 1966–70

13

Manchester, 1966–8

On 17 March 1966 Max Sebald was appointed to the post of *Lektor* at the University of Manchester for the academic year 1966–7, teaching German language and conversation.[1]

The date is a solid foothold, like the ones that secure the beginning of every Sebald story ('In mid-May of the year 1800...', 'In the second half of the 1960s...').[2] But immediately, as in the stories, all solidity disappears. The start of Max's English life is shrouded in uncertainty. Released from Germany, from all he knew and all who knew him, for months now he lifts off like the little balloonist of *Speak, Memory* 'into an abyss of frost and stars – alone'.[3]

The first thing he tells us in *A Place in the Country* (the collection of essays on his literary favourites) is what books he packed to accompany him: Keller's *Der Grüne Heinrich*, Hebel's *Schatzkästlein des Rheinischen Hausfreunds*, and Walser's *Jakob von Gunten*.[4] We can be sure that his first thought was for books, but did he really take these three? For Paul Bereyter he would borrow the *Hausfreund* from Wittgenstein, who loved Hebel – and now possibly borrowed it for himself as well, as a link to his beloved grandfather. *Der Grüne Heinrich* and *Jakob von Gunten* are alternative versions of himself: the ambitious, self-doubting young man setting out on life. Perhaps he *would* take literary images of himself and his grandfather with him. But all three are so perfect, they are just as likely to be the writer's later inventions as genuine memories.

Next he says that he left from Switzerland, where he'd been living.[5] That was more or less true: his last visit before leaving was very likely to Bern, to see his girlfriend. Before then, though, he must have gone home to see his parents. He'd have said goodbye to them there, then taken the train back to Switzerland. It wouldn't have seemed so momentous to them that way. Besides, he thought that he was leaving for only a year, and so, therefore, did they.

He arrived in Manchester on 15 September: that we know.[6] We have a date to stand on, once again; the rest is fiction.

Once his plane had crossed the Channel, he wrote in 'Max Ferber', he gazed down in wonder at the network of lights that seemed to stretch unbroken from London to the North. Then as they sank towards Manchester, the lights below faded in the dense fog, leaving only 'a faint glimmer, as if from a fire almost suffocated in ash'.[7]

That was his first (fictional) sight of the city. He also describes Ferber's, on his return there after the war: a curiously shaped cloud lit by the last rays of sunlight, and above all thousands of chimneys, belching out a yellow-grey smoke without cease. This too is fiction, covering two realities: Ferber's repressed knowledge of the death camps, and the account of the French critic Hippolyte Taine, who visited Manchester in the 1870s: 'In the copper sky of the sunset, a strangely shaped cloud hangs over the plain; beneath this immobile cover, the high chimneys, like obelisks, bristle in their hundreds…'[8]

Thus the vision of the 22-year-old student fuses with that of the writer twenty years later, and that of another writer a century before.

In the taxi from the airport he asks for a 'not too expensive' hotel, and is dumped in front of a narrow, soot-blackened building in the centre of town. This, he tells us, is the Arosa Hotel. It is still early morning, and for a long time no one answers the bell, until at last the door is opened by a Lorelei-like blonde of about forty. The two gaze at each other in disbelief, and the tragicomedy of his first term begins.

There was an Arosa Hotel in Manchester in 1966, but it wasn't a narrow building in the centre of town, and Max certainly didn't spend a whole term there. Rather it was a long, low building with a gimcrack modern front on Wilmslow Road in Withington, which he would soon pass every day on his way to the university.

The Arosa Hotel, where Max never stayed, and which no longer exists.

Most likely he spent the first night or two in a hotel in the centre.[9] The next day he went to the University Accommodation Service to look for a room; and now his soot-blackened hotel was not the only shock. First of all, beside many of the listings were the words *Europeans Only*.[10] He'd never come across such casual prejudice before, if only because there were no non-Europeans in Sonthofen, and hardly any in Freiburg. It didn't affect him; but I'm sure he noticed.

And then there was the room. He may have had no choice, but was allotted the first on the list;[11] or he may have taken the first available one, since he knew nothing and no one in Manchester. He would also tell a friend that he had been painfully poor in those early weeks, because his father wouldn't send him any more money. More likely he'd told Georg that he didn't need any more, but the result was the same: he had only his *Lektor*'s salary, which hadn't yet begun. So he now had the classic Manchester experience of the 1950s and 1960s – so classic it feels like a myth, but for once the myth was true.

A decade or so before him another writer described his first Manchester room: narrow and dark, with thin, skimpy curtains. There was not even a table, and the window looked out on a brick wall.[12] 'I said to myself as I undressed [on the first night]: "I cannot stay here, I must not stay here, I shall be done for if I stay here."'

This is, I admit, from a novel – *L'Emploi du temps* by Michel Butor, who had been a *Lecteur* at Manchester in the early 1950s. I admit too that Butor was a mythologist *par excellence*, imbuing his version of Manchester with his own existential angst. But he wasn't alone. Max's colleague Rosemary Wallbank Turner had arrived at the university in the early 1950s as well, and followed a route exactly like his, fifteen years later: first a vile hotel, then a vile room, then a slightly less vile room, still not fit for human habitation. It wasn't until her third room that she rejoined civilisation.[13] Rosemary, however, was an active, optimistic person, at home in England. Max was none of these things, and unusually dependent on his surroundings. I don't know if he felt any foreboding; but as he opens the door of his first vile room, I do.

The narrator's room at the Arosa contains a wardrobe, a washstand and an iron bedstead. Perhaps this was a portrait of Max's first room – or perhaps not. All we know is that it was as awful as the fictional Arosa, and that the whole house was kept 'bolted and barred'.[14] That was, at least, how he felt in it; and after a few weeks he'd had enough. He went back to the Accommodation Service and took (probably) the next room on the list.

Like Rosemary's second room, this was only slightly better, if at all. By now it was October, and winter was setting in. The room was dark and freezing cold; so cold that when his girlfriend came on a visit she found him in bed with one of his attacks of kidney colic, and rushed out to buy him a blanket.[15] There was only a bed, table and chair, and at night mice would scurry along the curtain rail. Still worse, for Max, was his landlady. She was intolerably nosy, he told friends; he felt watched, as he used to feel with his mother at home. He was very unhappy, and too embarrassed by the place to invite anyone there. Nonetheless, he stayed in this second room for the rest of the term. Here he read *L'Emploi du temps* and saw his experience reflected. That must have helped, as literature always does.

*25 Stockton Road, Chorlton-cum-
Hardy: Max's second unhappy
Manchester home.*

But it wasn't only his rooms; it was the whole city.

Manchester is a vision of hell in all his work. In *After Nature* it is a wasteland of empty mills and canals, haunted by the souls of industrial slaves so stunted they were rejected even as cannon fodder for the First World War.[16] In 'Max Ferber' it is coal- and time-blackened, the city from which industrialisation once spread across the world, but which is now degraded, 'almost hollow to the core'. Its old Jewish quarter is smashed and deserted, many of its old working-class districts have been reduced to piles of rubble by slum clearance; all that remains are abandoned gasworks, bonemills, slaughterhouses, 'like a necropolis or mausoleum…'.

Mancunians, naturally enough, are less than happy with this portrait of their city.[17] They're unhappy with Butor too, who portrays it as a similar hell of darkness, fog, soot and rain. In his case, though, it was undeniable: Manchester was dark for days on end well into the 1950s,[18] suffering industrial fogs worse even than London's pea-soupers (which

also lasted to the early sixties). And there were still wastelands, where
bomb sites remained from the war.

But by the 1960s this was all over, say loyal Mancunians: Sebald's
portrait is a reflection only of his own state of mind. So it is, but
not only. To anyone who came from elsewhere, Manchester was still a
shock.[19] The nineteenth-century buildings were still soot-covered and
black. The rain never stopped and nor did the fogs; in winter you
could still go for days without seeing the sun. The chimneys went on
smoking, and you went on getting smuts on your clothes, your hair,
your washing if you hung it up outside; when you approached the city
you still smelled coal. You continued to see streets of mean housing,
and wastelands of rubble where slums were being cleared.

Michel Butor had come to Manchester from sun-drenched
Egypt.[20] The Allgäu is hardly sun-drenched, but Max's plunge into
Mancunian darkness was equally extreme. He'd grown up amid
mountains and forests and had just spent a year in small, beautiful
Fribourg. Now he was in this great black city, alone and unprepared.
Apart from his brief visit to London he knew nothing about
England.[21] His English was good enough to get a first-class grade
from James Smith, but bookish and unpractised; being Max, he felt
that he hardly spoke it at all. Term was only just starting, he knew
no one, and if he did meet people, he couldn't speak to them. He sat
in his first hideous room alone, and walked the dark streets alone,
and fell into an acute depression.

It was his most serious crisis so far, so serious that he wrote about it
in 'Max Ferber', and it marked his writing for ever.[22] He was overcome
by feelings of alienation and futility, of hopelessness, of panic; above all,
as he wrote in 'Ferber', by 'a deep sense of isolation in which I might
well have become completely submerged'.[23] He made a Sebaldian joke
of the danger he was in, writing that it often seemed as if it was only
his (fictional) Teasmade, with its phosphorescent glow, 'that kept me
holding on to life'. His only consoling thought was that Wittgenstein
and Elias Canetti had also lived in Manchester – indeed nearby, in
Palatine Road.

12 Ferndene Road, Withington. Max's first Manchester
home, site of his deep depression of autumn 1966.

It may have been in these weeks that someone else had a disturbing experience.[24] Her name was Stevie Davies, and she too would become a writer. In 1966 she was an undergraduate at Manchester. She was hurrying along a corridor when she passed an open office door. After a moment she retraced her steps, and quietly peered in. No, she hadn't dreamed it. A young man sat behind a desk, alone, and on his face was a melancholy beyond imagining.

She drew back, shaken, glancing at the name on the door. She was young, life took over, and after a time she forgot all about it. But such things have a way of returning, as Max would write. It came back to her thirty years later, when she picked up a famous book, and there on the cover was the same name: W. G. Sebald.

The next door along the corridor had another name emblazoned on it: 'R. O. P. Tabbert', one of Max's fellow *Lektors*. 'R. O. P.' – standing for Reinbert Otto Paul[25] – clearly amused Max. In the many letters he would later send him he would never write 'Reinbert', only 'R.O.P.' or 'ROP'. I will follow his example here.

There were, unusually, four young German teachers at Manchester in 1966–7. Two, Wolf Dieter Ortmann and Dietmar Kremser, came from the University of Erlangen, which was the department's usual source.[26] Kremser was a *Lektor*, Ortmann an assistant lecturer, filling in for Martin Durrell for a year. Max, as we know, had applied independently, probably with a recommendation from Ronald Peacock. ROP's arrival was still more unorthodox: he got the job when his fiancée Brigitte was offered a Lektorship in Leeds, and made it a condition of acceptance that her future husband be able to stay in England too. Kremser and Ortmann were thus the normal newcomers for the year, Max and ROP the abnormal ones. That may have been the first thing that drew them together.

They met in early October, at the first staff meeting. And immediately Max's charisma began to work – together with his imagination. 'Herr Sebald,' ROP wrote enthusiastically to Brigitte, 'comes from the Allgäu, but is also at home in Vienna, Baden and Switzerland … He seems the most brilliant of the four of us: he wants to finish a novel here, which apparently Suhrkamp has already accepted, and he talks … about neuroses he's overcome.'[27]

Ten days later he's still Herr Sebald.[28] Two weeks after that he's finally Max, and they're firm friends. Max has read some of his novel to ROP, who thinks it has 'grace and melancholy' and is going to be wonderful. He, ROP, will help with editorial advice 'on style and composition'.

By now Brigitte has arrived on a visit, and she is equally impressed. Max Sebald looks like a young Rilke or Hofmannsthal, she thinks. He keeps notebooks, like a real writer, and makes notes in them every day. There's a special atmosphere around him, as though he's already someone, and behind it a melancholy.[29] He looks very young, and is mortified by his passport picture, taken the year before. He wears a moustache to make him appear older, ROP says. Without it he'd look about fifteen.

Perhaps Max told ROP about the 'neuroses he'd overcome' in order to make light of them, or to add to his aura of the romantic artist, like one of his heroes, poor mad Hölderlin.[30] His worst crisis was indeed over. But in 'Max Ferber' the narrator's disturbance lasts for months, and so did his author's. He told one interviewer in his last years that he had been 'cast into turmoil' for three or four months, another that his 'considerable depression' had lasted until Christmas. He did his teaching and writing, he talked more and more to ROP, and he was no longer prey to the worst feelings of the early weeks. But for the whole of the first term he remained unsettled: near the edge of his reason, as he would say about the earlier breakdown at school. ROP recorded this in early December, towards the end of term. Max was unusually volatile that day, he wrote:

> and suddenly asked me … how I would feel about going crazy. He sometimes feels near the edge, and would happily give into it, if it weren't for three or four people, for whose sake he doesn't. He feels it break out inside him, like Herzog,* and fill him with a whirlpool of ideas and images, and long-forgotten thoughts and imaginings. In that state he can make speeches and write letters like never before....[31]

This sounds like mania, and is the only suggestion I've ever heard that he might have suffered from that as well. I doubt he did, and suspect that he was just identifying with Bellow's Herzog in his usual intense, permeable way. But the line about going crazy, and how he'd let himself go if it weren't for three or four people – that sounds real. Whom was he thinking of? His family, his girlfriend? It was they, not the Teasmade, who kept him holding on to life in the most dangerous times.

Apart from his odd arrival, ROP was an improbable friend for Max.[32] First of all, he was a Prussian. His family had fled from there in 1945 and he mostly grew up near Stuttgart, but to Max he was still a Prussian, and ROP agreed. He was also six years older, old-fashioned in values and law-abiding – he'd taken a teaching degree, for instance, and would follow the standard long and winding route to a German university job. Looking back, he is surprised himself that he and mutinous, half-mad Max became such fast friends, almost instantly, and (with a gap in the 1980s) for ever.

---

*The hero of Saul Bellow's *Herzog*, which the two friends were reading. (See pp. 243–4 below.)

But there were good reasons for it too. ROP was highly intelligent, and as passionate about literature as Max. He was also more willing to step out of line than he seemed. For his doctoral thesis subject he'd chosen ultra-modern Harold Pinter, and now, after many lively tussles, he agreed that traditional *werkimmanente Kritik*, which he'd accepted without question, was inadequate for a true understanding of an author's work, and sociological and psychological analyses were also needed.[33] He admired Max's thesis, he admired his novel, he admired him. That admiration restored Max, I think. Living near the edge, he needed ROP's steadiness and belief in him. He might be the romantic hero of their story, the artist and iconoclast; but he depended on ROP, not the other way around.

And ROP didn't come alone: there was Brigitte too.[34] She visited several times, and at least once the friends went to Leeds together to see her. Like ROP, she had studied *Anglistik* and *Germanistik* at Tübingen, but they'd met as exchange students in Bangor, five years before. They were a happy, solid couple, who would marry at the end of their English year. Together they were perhaps Max's replacement for Gertrud and Jean-Paul. Most of the time, though, he and ROP were on their own – and that was fine too. Max, the boy who had rejected one father and lost another, still needed someone: if not a father, then at least an older brother, like Armin Müller and Albert Rasche. ROP was the last.

Max was meeting his other colleagues, of course, especially the younger ones; but no one apart from ROP has any clear memory of him during his first year.[35] In the first term in particular, I think, he was skulking in his horrible Chorlton room and seeing no one but the Tabberts. Apart from that, what he was doing was writing.

First of all, he was rewriting his Sternheim thesis for a Manchester MA. At the same time he was writing his novel, and poetry as well. By the end of October he'd written enough of the novel to read passages to ROP.[36] He also gave him several poems, including the longest one to date, 'Remembered Triptych of a Journey from Brussels', signing it *W. G. Sebald*, like the someone Brigitte felt him to be. And 'Triptych' impressed his friend as much as the novel: the long poem was the right genre for Max, ROP thought, and Max agreed.[37] Thus encouraged, he began to gather material for a new long poem, and wrote it in January, finishing it on the 26th, as both he and ROP recorded.

It's called 'Bleston', Butor's name for Manchester, and is the main trace of Max's Manchester experience until his mature writing of the 1980s. Unfortunately, the esoteric material he'd gathered remains undigested,[38] and the trace is unclear. But there are a few things that appear here, and again twenty years later in 'Ferber' and *After Nature*, as though they could never be forgotten – the darkness, the flocks of screaming starlings, the Gospel church where the sick are (supposedly) healed.[39] And there are a few lines that sound like the Sebald we know, fully formed:[40]

> Now that death is all of life
> I wish to inquire
> Into the whereabouts of the dead

for instance. Finally, close to the end, he wrote something we recognise, but in a dark key:

> In this cave within a cave
> No glance back to the future survives

The remarkable thing is how much he wrote, and planned to write, in that first term, in which he was either in 'a quasi/ sub-lunary state of deep/ melancholia' (as he wrote in *After Nature*) or near it. But that was how he would always be. His sub-lunary states drove him to write, rather than stopped him from writing. 'Max can't understand Kleist,' ROP wrote in December, 'who in an attack of madness burned his best work. But he understands Hölderlin very well, who was mad for years, but went on writing.'[41]

A large part of the problem was his horrible room – he had to get out of it. He may have given up on the Accommodation Service, or they on him; in any case, the solution arrived from somewhere else.[42] One day a colleague told him that he knew an architect and his art-teacher wife who let rooms to students; they'd recently bought and renovated another house, which was ready to take tenants. Knowing them, it would be beautifully done, and the house was in Didsbury, a leafy suburb straight up Wilmslow Road from the university.

I imagine Max rushing to Kingston Road as soon as he could. Straight away it looked perfect – a quiet street of Victorian houses, and in front of No. 26 a great chestnut tree, bare now, but surely lovely in the spring and summer. Then he stepped inside. The house was clean and light and welcoming. There were only two bathrooms for six tenants,[43] but what was that compared to the darkness of Stockton Road, and mice on the curtain rail? The same day, or same hour, he made ROP come and see it. ROP was already living in Didsbury in a perfectly pleasant room, but this was different. They decided instantly. Next term they would both move into Kingston Road.

On 19 December they cooked a good lunch, walked beside the Mersey, went to an antique shop and a cinema, and at 9.30 that night Max left for the airport to fly home for Christmas.[44]

His season in hell was over.

The new term started on 17 January. On the 14th, they moved in.

26 Kingston Road today.

Their rooms were on the first floor. ROP's was at the back, overlooking the garden and Fletcher Moss Park, Max's at the front, overlooking the chestnut tree and Didsbury Park across the road.[45] It was like his discovery of the Kaesers' house in Sonthofen in 1952 – he was almost back in the countryside. And their rooms themselves were beautiful. Both had warm carpets and sun-coloured curtains, and in their kitchen corners teapots, cups and glasses 'just as you'd have chosen yourself', Brigitte wrote.[46] This was the work of the architect's wife, as the whole light-filled house was his own work. Max knew now that his surroundings were more than important to him: they were crucial to his sanity. Years later he would say that his landlord had saved him from his Manchester melancholia.[47] He was certainly thinking of their conversations, but also of his house.

He carried on now with new heart. His discussions with ROP – about their work, about literature – continued, and could last till late at night.[48] And ROP gave him the editorial notes he'd promised on the novel, which despite his admiration were extensive and often tough. Max made notes in the margins as they talked, at one point scrawling '*Scheisse!*' (Shit!) down one whole side. Then ROP went even further. Maybe, he suggested, it would be better to do what Bellow did in *Herzog*: start with the end of the story, then go back to the beginning, and tell the rest in the normal way. Max was clearly smitten with this idea. He rewrote the entire novel, keeping large parts of it, but switching the end to the beginning as ROP recommended, and adding more and richer detail. He was teaching again, and reading widely for his thesis; but he was young, and writing fast in those days. By March, it was done.

ROP's Kempten Kalender for 16 March 1967: Max's novel finished.

For the rest of the term and long after he tried to find a publisher, but in vain. At least two turned it down.[49] ROP was as disappointed as the author, and perhaps felt rather guilty: the *Herzog* switch was a mistake, he came to think. But that wasn't the problem. The novel is apprentice work in both versions. The important thing was that it got written and rewritten: Max wasn't a good writer yet, but he was a writer.

The two friends spent even more of their free time together now.[50] Unless they were at the university they ate together, joined by Brigitte on her visits. Max was the cook – and a sophisticated one, always using plenty of garlic (learned perhaps from Gertrud, or from Frau Aenderl long ago). Brigitte was impressed: 'I must get the recipe!' she wrote after one particularly delicious Sunday lunch.[51] That evening they read out loud to each other; Max read a story by Ludwig Thoma in Bayerisch. In January they gave a ghost party, under the motto 'There are more things in heaven and earth than are dreamt of in your philosophy.' Several of their students came and told ghost stories; Max told a story by 'a young writer' – probably, said wise Brigitte, himself.

On their own the two friends went to many films and plays, and to watch the strange English sport of greyhound racing; in April they were in Tiffany's Dance Hall, where ROP discovered, like others before him, that Max couldn't dance. And now and again they went to the louchest working-class pubs Max could find, of which his favourite was Liston's Music Hall, recalled in both *After Nature* and 'Max Ferber' twenty years later.[52]

He took his visitors from home to Liston's as well: Kasus, probably Albert, and Sigrid Becker from Oberstdorf, who was also spending a year in England, working at a girls' school.[53] When she and a friend chose Scotland for a holiday, she remembered that Max was in Manchester.

Off they set to see him. They hitch-hiked (this was the 1960s) and on the last leg to Manchester were picked up by an oil tanker. The driver insisted on delivering them right to Max's door – so that one day he would have seen a gigantic tanker squeezing its way up Kingston Road, to spill out two laughing girls. It probably made one of his comical stories for months after.

What else did he do, now that he was settling to this strange English life? He played the guitar sometimes, as we know. He played billiards a lot – it was now his favourite game. And he did a very peculiar job, to make a bit of extra money.[54]

He'd been approached, he said, by a German paper that wanted to find out how ready Britain was to join the Common Market (as it then was), and sent him round the North of England to check menus for any trace of continental cuisine. His answer was always the same: there wasn't any.

He can't have made very much, but he saw a good deal of England. And he told the Tabberts something striking: that the first thing he did in every hotel was to look for the fire escape, because he was afraid of fire. Everyone who grew up in a 1950s German village, with its wooden buildings and long memory, is afraid of fire, Brigitte says; she is afraid of it herself. I remembered the narrator's horror of fire, especially in *The Rings of Saturn*, and thought: it's Wertach again. It's biography.

One day that spring, Max's landlady Dorothy came to Kingston Road on some business and knocked on the door.[55] No one answered, and after a few more tries she turned to go. But as she did so she thought she saw someone at the first-floor window. She looked up just in time to see a white face, before it vanished behind the curtain.

It was a girl's face, and that was Max's room. Dorothy thought she must have been dreaming. People weren't supposed to have another person in a single room. Most of them did anyway, of course – but surely not Max, one of her best tenants, so quiet and well behaved! And a girl… She had never imagined Max with a girl. He was so serious, so absorbed in his work, so separate somehow; he didn't seem to need anyone. And yet she'd seen that white face. Hadn't she?

Max's girlfriend would always be silent and rarely seen. But it was her at his window that day. She was visiting from Switzerland, where she was working.[56] Apart from Dorothy's brief glimpse, no one saw her except the Tabberts, and that was for only a few days. But they were extraordinary days, like all their days with Max. His girlfriend is a lovely girl with red-blond hair, ROP wrote.[57] She's as young as he is, and like him as slender as a sprite; they're both so delicate they seem endangered, and both believe they won't live long. She's quiet, but full of caprice – once she played the clown, for instance, and sat under the table instead of at it. She is cool and elusive, and he is the pursuer. 'I can't imagine a better muse for Max,' ROP said, and Brigitte agreed.

Sometime that spring he and ROP talked about art. Max didn't like the print on ROP's wall – Rembrandt's fleshy wife, raising her skirt as she bathes in a stream. 'What would *you* have?' ROP asked. 'Do you know Ingres' portraits?' Max replied. ROP did – ivory-skinned beauties like statues, often seen from the back. 'One of those,' Max said.[58]

The Max of ROP's memory is already the Max of his mature years.[59] He liked to remember his childhood, and spoke lovingly of his Egelhofer grandfather. He had an ironic, absurdist sense of humour and told wonderful stories. He was thoughtful with people, but could be astoundingly harsh in his judgements, especially of writers. ROP put this down to his most recognisable trait of all: melancholy. Sudden accesses of anger are typical of melancholics, ROP says – look at Hamlet with his mother, with Ophelia, with almost everyone. Altogether, for ROP, Max was a real-life Hamlet. They had the same enormous intelligence and sharp wit, the same father problem and Ophelia problem, the same sense that there are more things than are dreamt of in our philosophy. And, of course, the same melancholy.

ROP also remembers some less well-known things. For instance, that at twenty-three Max wanted to be rich and famous. 'Famous' goes back to Group 64, but 'rich' is new. At the same time he longed not to have to work for the rest of his life. He had various plans for dealing with this dilemma. One was to marry a rich student, which he joked about for months. Another was to go to America and get rich quick, after which he would retire and buy a house on the Mediterranean. 'It's strange,' I said to ROP, 'how hard he worked all his life, when he always longed not to.' 'We always dream of what we don't do,' ROP replied. 'But what's even stranger,' I said, 'is that all those jokes eventually came true. He did become rich and famous – though not quickly – and he did think at the end of buying a house, perhaps on the Mediterranean.'[60] And this time ROP agreed.

The last thing he remembers is the most intriguing of all: the explosion of myth and invention at the start of Max's English life. It didn't happen only when he came to write about it decades later. That was minor – a matter of a few books, probably. By contrast, some of the tales he told at the time were whoppers.

At their first meeting, we know, he told ROP that his novel had already been accepted, and that he was 'at home' in Vienna, when he'd never set foot there.[61] That was only the beginning. Later he said that he'd directed a Pinter play at Freiburg, which wasn't true but could have been, and that he was working as a photo-reporter for an American magazine, which wasn't even possibly true. The arrival of an attractive girl unleashed his most impressive inventions. He told Brigitte that he had six first names (not just three, his usual claim later, which wasn't true either), and that he had ridden to his final exams on a horse.[62]

After a while he calmed down, but never stopped. There was the story of his bizarre job, which I want to believe, but may also have been invented. And he turned his discovery of Kingston Road into a classic Sebaldian fiction for the Tabberts.[63] In fact he'd learned of it quite normally, through that helpful colleague. What he told them instead was that it happened through a chance encounter, when he met Dorothy in a greengrocer's. He told me the same Sebaldian fiction thirty years later, and I believed it too.

Perhaps these were just the tricks of a natural storyteller – like Paolo's, who was probably his model. But surely there was something deeper at work as well, as Albert had hinted. Like the hero of a book he was reading, Max 'needed a certain measure of disguise in order to feel at ease with people'.[64] He wanted to have six names, and in his joke letters to friends he'd invent many more.

They talked most of all about books.

One of their favourites was Adorno's *Minima Moralia*,[65] a work of immediate post-war despair that would inform Max's historical pessimism for ever. The others were all fiction.

Bellow's *Herzog* was one. Herzog despairingly loves his wife, who has betrayed him with his best friend and wants a divorce. He spends the novel writing furious letters, which he never sends – to his psychiatrists, to Nietzsche and Heidegger, to his dead mother, to God. He sets out to kill his wife and/or her lover but can't do it. He retreats to the country where the book began, and at last the madness is over.

Max loved the opening line – 'If I am out of my mind, it's all right with me, thought Moses Herzog.'[66] He loved the maddened unsent letters, and probably also the murderous desire. He was twenty-three and looked fifteen, but he identified completely with middle-aged Jewish Herzog, who when he's not writing crazy letters thinks obsessively about his childhood. ('Depressives cannot surrender childhood,' Bellow wrote, 'not even the pains of childhood … somehow his heart had come open at this chapter of his life and he didn't have the strength to shut it.')

He loved another hero who was 'out of his mind' as well – J. D. Salinger's Catcher in the Rye, Holden Caulfield. Holden is only seventeen, but he's as angry as Herzog. His favourite word is 'phoney', which he applies above all to the lies and meannesses of the bourgeoisie. That appealed to Max, of course, and 'phoney' became his own favourite word that year. In fact, he identified so strongly with Holden Caulfield that *he sometimes wore Holden's red baseball cap*. This may be hard to believe, but ROP took the photograph.

Among ROP's own favourites were two short stories, Johann Peter Hebel's '*Unverhofftes Wiedersehen*' ('Unexpected Reunion') and '*Des Lebens Überfluss*' ('The Superfluities of Life') by Ludwig Tieck, one of the first Romantics. '*Unverhofftes Wiedersehen*' was a lifetime favourite of Max's as well, but what struck ROP was his response to '*Des Lebens Überfluss*'.[67] This is the story of Clara and Heinrich, who marry against her parents' will, and are so poor that they can only survive the winter by burning the wooden steps up to their room – an unforgettable image of the love that unites them, but cuts them off from the rest of the world. All ends happily, however, with Heinrich rich and his book of poems successfully published. Max liked this story very much, no doubt for its ending, but also, I'm sure, for other reasons. In his later writing the narrator's wife appears only two or three times, fleetingly. But she always has the same name: Clara.

Then ROP mentioned perhaps their greatest favourite of all. To my shame it was a book I'd never heard of. I rushed out and bought it, and found a masterpiece.

It's by the Swiss writer Max Frisch, and is called *Stiller*. In English its title is its opening line: *I'm Not Stiller*.

A man arrives in Zurich and is immediately recognised as the sculptor Stiller, who disappeared six years before. He insists, however, that he is not Stiller. He is held in custody, and confronted by Stiller's brother, wife, ex-lover – all of whom identify him as Stiller, which he continues to deny. In the prison notebooks that make up the novel he tells his story, which no one believes. At the same time he is falling in love with Stiller's wife Julika – not *his* wife, he still insists. She was ethereally beautiful, but could bear no close contact. For his part Stiller loved her to distraction but felt gross and guilty every time he touched her. Eventually he withdrew, took a lover, and cruelly neglected Julika when tuberculosis forced her to retire to a clinic in the mountains. In the end he ran away, 'to avoid committing a murder'; 'and now' – the pronoun slips at last – 'I've learnt that my very attempt to run away was the murder'.[68]

His case is heard, and he is formally declared to be Stiller. He and Julika go to live in a chalet on Lake Geneva. Eighteen months later nothing has changed, and both Stiller's despair and Julika's TB have returned. Six months after that, as a last resort Julika has an operation. She survives the night, but in the morning Stiller doesn't come, and she dies.

The play with truth and invention, the fluidity and ambiguity of identity – all this must have seemed very close to Max, as though he could have written it himself. And what people say about Stiller seems very close to Max to me – that he suffers from 'inferiority anxiety' because he makes excessive demands on himself; that he felt a different man, so said he was one, projecting his inner world onto reality, as Max did with his whoppers (and his fiction).

As to Stiller's marriage – what that could have meant to Max at twenty-three, who loved '*Des Lebens Überfluss*', is a mystery. But I think it must have meant something; perhaps a fear. Stiller's lover says, 'He didn't want to be loved. He was afraid of it.' In any case ROP was so struck by his friend's resemblance to Stiller that he told him so. Yes, Max said, he'd identified with Stiller for a long time.[69]

As the end of their contracts approached, the friends drew up a *Festschrift* for their supervisor, Professor Parry.[70] ROP contributed an essay on Pinter's *Birthday Party*, Max four of his poems. He typed out the slender pamphlet, and they presented it to Parry at the end of term.

When they planned this joint farewell, Max must still have been thinking of going home after one English year. But some time after that he changed his mind. Manchester as hell was long over. He liked the department, he loved Kingston Road, and the money was still better than anything he could hope for in Germany. He applied for a second year as *Lektor* and was accepted.[71]

In July ROP returned to Germany and married Brigitte.[72] Max probably went home in the summer as well, but had to tell poor Rosa that he wouldn't be staying. And he also had another piece of news. Recently he and his girlfriend had gone on holiday together, to somewhere with no telephone, no radio, not even a newspaper – just the two of them, like Clara and Heinrich; and like Clara and Heinrich, they were happy. So he had decided. He was getting married.[73]

The wedding took place on 1 September, in Sonthofen.[74] It was a small, family affair – smaller than it should have been, since Jean-Paul had to have an operation, and he and Gertrud couldn't come. On the photographs Albert's tall lanky frame stands out. Everyone looks happy and slightly drunk, as they should. And a week or two later Max returned to Manchester a married man.

Back at Kingston Road he and his wife now moved into a proper flat on the top floor.[75] Their surroundings mattered as much to her as they did to him, and she not only kept the flat neat and clean, but painted a pretty blue design on the kitchen wall. She was a good photographer, and took many pictures around Manchester, which Max helped her to develop. Together they began to explore junk shops, antique shops and auctions, and developed a good eye for furniture and curios of all kinds. On Max's pay, and living in a small furnished flat, this was mostly window shopping at first, but it was the start of a shared hobby.

After that first terrible term he'd begun to socialise a bit more with his colleagues.[76] He'd exchanged witty German banter with Dietmar Kremser and subjected him to Sebaldian teases, which Kremser received with a grin; Kremser and Ortmann had invited him to their parties, and at least once he went. Peter Skrine – the colleague who'd told him about Kingston Road – had invited him to his house, where he heard Bellini's *I Puritani* for the first time, and fell in love with Bellini forever.[77]† And now that he was back for a second year, his friendships in the department grew stronger. But his young wife was still shy. Some of the staff gave each other exuberant dinner parties, but the Sebalds didn't take part; like Clara and Heinrich, they remained enough for each other in the top flat at Kingston Road. Eda Sagarra, who came to know Max well, remembers thinking that his marriage was good for him, but can't recall his wife. He came to her dinner parties alone.[78]

He was working harder than ever, despite his dream of *dolce far niente*. On his own initiative, for example, he expanded his teaching to include lectures on 'contemporary literature and life in Germany'.[79] History does not record if he laid into them as rudely as in his later writings, but his head of department noted that his courses 'were much better attended than voluntary courses normally are'. In any case, he was popular with his students, which should have helped his confidence in this second Manchester year.

His main focus, however, was on his dissertation. He expanded this too, from sixty pages to 226, the bibliography from thirty-seven books and articles to 118.[80] Much of his new reading was of left-wing theorists such as Benjamin, Marcuse and especially Adorno, and as a result his own argument took on a more left-wing and theoretical flavour. His thesis remained the same: that Sternheim's satire of bourgeois society was fatally compromised by his need to join it. But apart from the expansion of his argument via Adorno *et al.*, Max made several substantial additions. For example, he 'somewhat reluctantly added … a perfunctory review of preceding research' (in Richard Sheppard's words).[81] And most importantly, he added a chapter of astoundingly intimate psychological analysis of Sternheim's double bind, the consequences of which were (he argued) profound feelings of anxiety and insecurity and a hyper-normal aggressiveness against society, plus 'schizoid' symptoms such as voyeurism and anti-Semitism.[82] The last two had, for once, nothing to do with himself – unlike the first three, which had everything to do with him.

This, however, is not the only striking aspect of his academic writing that first appears here. In the Foreword, a few pages into the work, he claims that Adorno himself supports his thesis, giving him advice in personal letters; later he quotes from those letters, to show that it's true.[83] The first surprising thing is that it *was* true. Despite his 'profound feelings of anxiety and insecurity' he was also quite fearless, sitting at his desk alone with his thoughts: that is how he could fire off his missiles at the *Germanistik* establishment later, and how he could fire off letters to Adorno now. And it worked: Adorno replied.

But he still hasn't stopped surprising us. Although he quotes from two Adorno letters, Adorno only ever sent him one. The quotation from the 'second' letter comes, like the others, from the first and only one. The solemn footnote referencing the second letter is a fake.[84]

Richard Sheppard, who uncovered this Sebaldian joke, says that it 'is not a case of academic dishonesty', but of 'Max the *Schelm* [trickster] having a … laugh at his examiners' expense'. It's true – Adorno wrote the line, so no evidence was fabricated, and by inserting a fake footnote, Max was certainly having a laugh. But having a laugh in your MA dissertation is unusual, to say the least. And it wouldn't stop with his MA. He would always hate the boring practice of citation, and even as a respected professor would occasionally, after hunting in vain for a forgotten source, throw up his hands in despair and invent it.[85] Later he would say that his academic and literary writing were close in his mind, that as far as he was concerned, he always did much the same thing.[86] And I think that was true. But not sourcing quotes in literary work is called *hommage*; whereas not sourcing them – or even worse, falsely sourcing them – in academic work is trickery, and *pace* Sheppard, dishonesty, at least post-MA, when others may actually read your work and rely on it. As in Frisch's hero Stiller, and his own hero Josef, somewhere in Max Sebald lay (as Albert implied) a deep compulsion to lie. It made him an extraordinary writer of fiction; but also an extraordinary academic writer, on these occasions in a dubious way.

But there is a last surprise, which sheds a very different light on this strange fake footnote. Adorno was a Jewish refugee from Nazism. Max dated the fictional second letter from him to 17 May, which is the date both of Ferber's escape from Germany and of his murdered mother's birthday.[87] And, of course, the day before Max's own birthday. That is, in his dissertation of 1968 he was already making a magical connection between himself and victims of the Holocaust. Thus, what he hid in his fake footnote was not only a lie and laugh, but beneath them the opposite, the catastrophe for which he would spend the rest of his life trying to atone.

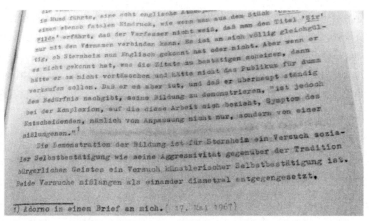

'Adorno in a letter to me': Max's fake Adorno footnote, with the date 17 May.
It looks as though he added it on a different machine, after he'd finished
typing the whole: perhaps when he had moved out of academic mode to
another.

He submitted the dissertation in March and waited to hear its
fate: not too anxiously, I imagine. Professor Parry, his supervisor,[88] had
been minimally critical throughout. He was an extremely kind man,
and more interested in imagination than scholarship in his students.
He kept only the weakest on a tight rein, preferring the *rhaff eira*, the
rope of snow (he was a Welsh speaker) for the brightest, who included
Max. Max knew that he'd been given an easy ride by Parry. Manchester
had an even better choice than he'd hoped.

He now had several weeks of term left, with his main task over. This,
then, was the moment for *Leonce and Lena*.

In fact the first play he'd suggested to the university's German Society
was rather different:[89] a mysterious script he claimed 'had been found
by chance' on a train in Germany. The cast soon guessed who the author
was. They worked on it for a few weeks, then binned it – in other words,
Max binned it – and they turned to *Leonce and Lena* instead.

Leonce is another typical Max hero: not a furious Herzog or rebellious
Holden, but a melancholy Hamlet.[90] Like Hamlet he is a prince, son of
King Peter, ruler of the Kingdom of Popo. He loathes the shallow, venal
world of the court and vows that he will rule the kingdom differently,
but by the end it's plain that nothing will change. He also vows not to

marry the princess chosen for him from the Kingdom of Pipi (Popo and Pipi mean Bum and Pee respectively, which makes Büchner's view of them pretty plain). But he ends up marrying her anyway, after meeting her by chance, and falling in love with her before he realises who she is. At the end Lena says 'Oh chance!' Leonce replies 'Oh providence!' We may think it is chance, but in truth determinism rules.

So here they are again, Max's themes – identity, chance, fate, melancholy – in what was called a comedy, but a very black one. Rulers are stupid, intentions are futile, fate is inescapable. And not even Leonce's love for Lena can mend his deep melancholy. So the programme note for Max's production concluded: 'the final fulfilment…can only stifle, never extinguish, the desolate anguish previously unleashed in him who is incurable, merely because he is'.[91] Max didn't write the note himself. But he asked his Leonce to do so,[92] and we can be sure that Leonce's ideas came at least in part from his director.

Büchner's mix of realism and romanticism could present a problem, said a reviewer, but Herr Sebald solved the problem at a stroke. He took his cue from Leonce's being called a '*Kartenkönig*', a playing-card king, and imbued the whole action with a strong sense of stylisation. This 'not only suggested the "unreal reality" of Büchner's play', the reviewer wrote,[93] it also enabled the actors to 'mime the sense of what they were saying' in a way that perfectly fitted their characters, but at the same time helped the English audience to follow the German lines. So Max had gone one better than Paolo, stealing his idea of mime from *In the Zone*, but making it work.

Leonce and Lena was a triumph. His young cast – though only a few years younger than he was – hugely admired him.[94] He got excellent performances out of them, the reviewer said; and 'How many of that cast,' Swaby asked, 'owe their knowledge of Albinoni's *Adagio* to Max's use of it throughout the production? Melancholic or what?'

The play was such a success that people lined up to congratulate him, from the whole German department to the director of Manchester's Goethe Institute.[95] There was even a rumour that he might be offered a job in the drama department, he wrote to ROP. If one was ever offered, he turned it down. And in this letter to his friend, perhaps for the first time we hear a tone that anyone who knew him in his later years will recognise – comically gloomy, fleeing praise as though pursued by a bear. 'All this praise was a lot of nonsense,' he wrote. He liked English self-deprecation and adopted it. But the English use it to hide self-confidence, while he used it to hide self-doubt. You could hear the difference.†

Now what? He knew that the easy ride he'd had with Parry wouldn't continue beyond MA level, even in England. And the prospect of years following academic rules did not appeal. The academic enforcers would goad him into satire one day, he wrote grimly to ROP, Ph.D.s were lies anyway, and if he ever wrote one it would be to dismantle academe from the inside.[96] Even while he was writing his MA, therefore, he was looking for an alternative. In the first term of this second year he applied to the Goethe Institute in Munich to train as a *Dozent*, or German language teacher.[97]

No one who knew him thought this was a good idea, and his two women colleagues told him so.[98] The Goethe is a bureaucracy, they said, why on earth are you applying there? But 'Max wanted money and freedom,' Eda says, and clearly he wanted to return to Germany as well. His application remained, and Rosa's hope (if he told her) could still live.

He probably didn't hear from them for months. But he needed a job. So now he thought of an old plan: school teaching. His wife's last job had been in St Gallen;[99] perhaps that's what gave him the idea. In any case, he applied to the Institut auf dem Rosenberg, an international boarding school in St Gallen, and was offered a post teaching English and German.[100] It wasn't Germany; but it was a step back to the Continent, and he could look around from there. He accepted.

All that was left now was his dissertation. The fake Adorno letter wasn't its only dubious aspect; many of the scholarly failings of his *mémoire* persisted, and 'A careful examiner,' says Richard Sheppard, 'would have failed it.'[101] But Max's luck held, and on 11 July 1968 he was awarded his MA – with distinction, he told ROP.[102] There is no proof of this last part, since Manchester did not record MA grades. It could be a Max fantasy, but his Fribourg degree was *summa cum laude*, and despite everything, it's likely that this one was too.

In July he and his wife went on holiday to Yugoslavia. On 1 August he wrote to ROP, and his mood had darkened. They'd been in some ghastly dump, he said, packed with tourists, mostly Germans. And the closer September came, the more his doubts grew. He saw himself in front of his class, words jumping out of his mouth like frogs. This won't end well, he wrote. I feel it in my bones.

Max at Kingston Road.

14

St Gallen and Manchester, 1968–70

The Rosenberg-Schule, St Gallen, Switzerland.

On 15 August the Sebalds arrived in St Gallen and moved into a small, pretty flat on Metzgerstrasse (Butcher Street). Max's wife went back to work in a beauty salon. And on 1 September he took a deep breath, and embarked on his life as a schoolteacher.[1]

The Rosenberg-Schule was the most expensive private school in Switzerland[2] (and still is). It was an absurdly rich place, more like a five-star hotel than a school, set amid green lawns and lovely woods. The one thing Max didn't lack at the school was beauty, at least of a certain kind.

He lasted exactly a month. On 2 October he wrote to ROP[3] that the job was a nightmare and he'd have to dump it. He couldn't break his contract, but after a year he was getting out.

He probably knew from the first day that he wouldn't stay.[4] His idea of teaching was already Pestalozzi's, which was as far from the Rosenberg's manicured lawns as it was possible to be. He couldn't stand the authoritarianism of the system, and what the narrator of 'Max Ferber' calls 'the Swiss attitude to life',[5] by which both he and Max meant materialism and petty officiousness, which could be as bad here as in Germany. And his own job was too hard: he'd been hired to teach English and German, but in fact was teaching everything. I'd like to be able to say that at least he liked the students, but he didn't. He disliked their parents even more, who abandoned them to the school and gave them nothing except too much money. That sort of treatment produces not only spoiled brats but unhappy ones, and it's not surprising that he was unhappy too.

We know what he did when he was unhappy: he turned to work. He wrote a comic monologue about a character he'd met on his Yugoslav holiday, an eighty-year-old Viennese who told the most fantastical lies.[6] And he rewrote his Sternheim dissertation one more time, to turn it into a book.[7]

He began by sending the current incarnation to a publisher soon after he arrived.[8] Typically, he chose a distinguished publishing house, Kohlhammer Verlag of Stuttgart, and typically too he enclosed no covering letter, hoping perhaps that this would stand out more than anything he could say. It worked: Kohlhammer responded immediately, remarking that they assumed he had publication in mind. On 6 February 1969 they wrote to say formally that they would publish the work, but it required some rewriting. His citations, they said, didn't follow the usual German rules, and he should avoid using 'I' wherever possible. In fact Max hadn't committed this dreadful solecism in his original *mémoire*; it was a step he'd taken in Manchester, as part of his Adorno-led rebellion. But that would have to wait. Publication was more important. He buckled down, and by April the job was done.

He'd worked hard, cutting the first chapter completely, changing the structure of another, writing a new afterword. But above all he rewrote hundreds of sentences, to make them more strident and attacking. His introduction made his intentions clear: 'The aim of the present study is the revision of the image of Sternheim as propounded by German studies. It goes without saying that this revision will predominantly take the form of destruction.'[9]

He returned the proofs to Kohlhammer in late July[10] and waited for his first book to come out. He was hoping for a furious reaction, I'm sure. That must have been part of the plan – to make an impact, and to give the old Nazis of *Germanistik* a good kicking. But I'm sure too there was more to it than that. Would *Carl Sternheim* have been quite such an intemperate attack if he hadn't been so unhappy in St Gallen? Ever since he was three or four years old, an unhappy Max was an angry one. That's one reason why unhappiness would always drive him to write, rather than stop him from writing. He couldn't have written his great literary books, which are anti-Nazi too, out of sorrow alone; sorrow alone would only have bowed him down. They too contain a core of anger. But now, at twenty-four and wanting to shock, he let the anger show.

There were only a few happy things in St Gallen to keep him going.[11] There was the pretty flat on the Metzgerstrasse, and having his own family life. There was his first animal companion – not a dog, as he would have later, but a cat: a crazy cat, Gertrud remembers, who'd dash around the flat and into a paper bag he was holding open. And there was the beautiful Swiss landscape all around, which he had loved since Fribourg, but probably loved more intensely since his Manchester experience, like the narrator of 'Max Ferber'.[12] At least from the Rosenberg he could see Lake Constance; and nearby was Herisau, where Robert Walser had spent his last twenty-three years in the asylum.

By late 1968 he had decided: school teaching was not for him. And he'd been reading Alfred Döblin, the celebrated author of *Alexanderplatz*, and had found a new icon ripe for destruction. He would do a Ph.D. and dismantle academe from the inside after all. But now, after three years and two degrees away, that could never happen in Germany. So be it. It's what he'd more than half intended all along.

I don't know when he told his poor mother. The person he did tell was his substitute father of those years, Adorno.[13] He wrote to him on 14 December, telling him that he was applying for a junior research fellowship at Sidney Sussex College, Cambridge and asking him to provide a reference. Adorno never replied, and Sidney Sussex turned down his application. The image of himself as a Cambridge don, if he ever had one, drifted away, like the image of himself as a schoolteacher. It was probably just as well. It's hard to imagine him surviving the rituals of Cambridge for very long.

But what now? He fell back, I'm sure with relief, on Manchester. The Jordans welcomed him back warmly, as did Professors Keller and Parry. It was most unusual for *Lektors* to serve more than one year, but 'in the case of Mr Sebald', Keller said, they made an exception 'with great pleasure'. Parry went even further, saying that they gave him 'a second run as a *Lektor* only because we have no permanent post to offer'.[14] On 22 May, four days after his twenty-fifth birthday, Max was reappointed as *Lektor* in the German department at the new rate of £960 for the year – the equivalent of about £12,000 today, a very survivable salary in 1969.[15] In late July he finally withdrew the application that had been languishing at the Goethe Institute in Munich for nearly two years. All his other selves were now in the past. And in the autumn he returned once again to England.

In mid-October he registered to do a part-time Ph.D. on Döblin, once more under Parry,[16] and began what would be his final year as a student. He taught his usual language classes and read for his Ph.D.

Right at the start, however, in early October, came the event he'd been waiting for: the publication of his book.[17] And he got what he'd hoped for – attention and, from Sternheim scholars, fury. Between December 1969 and May 1972 this first work by an unknown student received thirteen reviews in German newspapers and academic journals. And though the papers were often sympathetic, the academics roared their disapproval. They were not only outraged by this young pup's insolence – that chapter accusing Sternheim of all sorts of perversions! – but maddened by his cavalier disregard for their rules. And as we know, he did disregard them. Donald Daviau, soon to be editor of *Modern Austrian Literature*, would sum up their objections unusually fairly.

> Because of his direct attack on literary critics, his arrogant,
> aggressive tone, his many doubtful generalisations, and his
> doctrinaire style, Sebald's own approach will probably evoke as
> much negative reaction amongst *Germanisten* as their aesthetic
> '*werkimmanente*' approach has seemed to arouse contemptuous

feelings within him. Nevertheless, his book does present a consistent (if not consistently argued) point of view that will have to be taken into account by future critics of Sternheim.[18]

Despite everything, part of Max must have been pleased by that last line. But I'm sure that his favourite response was rather the violent drubbing he received from a Soviet scholar in *Die Zeit*.

Sternheim was favoured by the Soviets as a scourge of the bourgeoisie, and the scholar – Valerij Poljudow, of the University of Perm – leapt to his defence.[19] He pointed out that Sternheim had been a pacifist, against the ideology of both Wilhelmine and Nazi Germany, and had suffered for it under both regimes. He accused Max of extreme ahistoricism and of quoting selectively and out of context, and denied absolutely that Sternheim was in any sense a proto-fascist. Maybe it was rather Sebald who was a neo-Nazi, he sneered. His book, Poljudow concluded, was *barer Unsinn*, sheer nonsense, from start to finish.

Max joined battle with a will, publishing his reply in *Die Zeit* two weeks later. Poljudow was so indoctrinated himself, he said, that he couldn't see the flaws in Sternheim's work. To Poljudow's slur that he was probably a neo-Nazi himself, he snapped back that Poljudow was covering up for Soviet anti-Semitism. And – going the whole hog now in Sebaldian hyperbole – he countered that Sternheim not only *was* a proto-Nazi, but an early instigator of the persecution of the Jews.

After this peak of sound and fury the controversy died down.[20] Max wrote one more article on Sternheim in October, and early in the next year took part in a radio discussion of his book with the critics Hellmuth Karasek and Peter von Matt. In both of these he stuck to his thesis, but was much fairer and more balanced, and consequently more convincing. But that was an end, not a beginning. His first book had made the stir he'd hoped for, but had no lasting effect. By the 1990s interest in Sternheim was effectively over, and in the latest survey of scholarly work on him the name W. G. Sebald does not appear.

Finally, then, his four-year-long tussle with Sternheim had led nowhere.

But it was the first step on his journey, and a searchlight into his mind. It shows that by twenty-five – even twenty-two – he was intellectually fully formed. His critical methods would remain as unorthodox all his life: the identification of authors with their texts, and the use of biography and psychology as tools; the privileging of subjective over objective and imagination over facts; a polemical and hyperbolic tone; and a regular flouting of scholarly rules, especially about reading other scholars, crediting them, and quoting them accurately.[21]

If particularly the last part of this list sounds infuriating, it is. As a scholar Sebald could be outrageous. But he was extremely brave, and on the big questions I think he was right. Anyone who writes must realise that they can only express what is in them – their experience, their character, their imagination. We don't put authors' names on their books for decoration, but in recognition of this truth. And almost his most important and challenging critical point, now and later – that aesthetics cannot be separated from ethics, that writers have a duty to portray society truthfully and critically – I also believe is true. That is why he attacked Sternheim, why he would attack other writers in the future, and why he attacked German Germanists and their purely formal approach to literature. For him literary criticism was as much an ethical attempt to live a just life* as the rest of his writing, all the way back to *Carl Sternheim*.

Modern languages at Manchester had been gaining in strength since the war, under its two great professors, Peacock of German and Vinaver of French.[22] By the 1960s they had reached their golden age, which would last to the mid-1980s. During that time German produced at least five graduates who would go on to hold chairs in universities across Britain. Max's Manchester years came at the height of that flourishing.

Ever since his second term he'd been happy there. The department was not only liberal and un-hierarchical,[23] but full of people from unorthodox backgrounds, like him – Parry's father was a postman, Durrell's a salesman and Blamires' a factory worker, and Kerry and Furness were also grammar-school boys. It was full of laughter and scholarly fun, its members writing humorous pieces in their staff magazine and competing to slip the most obscure word they could find into their lectures (David Blamires recalls, for instance, 'anfractuosity').

---

* The words are Uwe Schütte's.

And it was full of eccentrics, always one of Max's favourite features of Britain. Idris Parry was a great joke-teller who deliberately played the Welsh windbag. Peter Skrine's lectures were hugely learned, dotted with Latin words, while Ray Furness was an entertainer, keeping his students in gales of laughter. David Blamires was a keen Labour man, often sporting red socks and a red tie; he was also a devoted Quaker, and openly gay. The two young women, Eda Sagarra and Rosemary Turner, were both formidably intelligent and strong supporters of women's rights, and at the same time the life of the department's parties. Rosemary always sported the latest fashion, especially miniskirts – this being the 1960s – so that students took bets on what she would wear, and how much leg she would show. Anything further from the formality of Freiburg would be hard to imagine.

A staff meeting at Manchester, late 60s. From the left: Max, Rudolf Keller, Stan Kerry, David Blamires, Idris Parry, Peter Skrine.

When Max returned in 1969 these congenial colleagues were already friends.[24] He shared an office now with Martin Durrell, and in the evening he and his wife would often meet Martin and his new young wife for a drink at the Old Cock on Wilmslow Road. With Ray Furness he would go for long walks and talk about literature, preferably anything outside the canon. Among the senior staff, Parry and his wife Eirwen regularly invited him to supper, as did Stan Kerry and his wife Stella; to them, as to his younger colleagues' dinner parties, he almost certainly went alone.

Among those younger colleagues, Peter Skrine[25] was a particularly congenial person – erudite and humorous, and both English and European, with an English Manx father and a German Swiss mother. He spoke six languages, including his mother's Bernese dialect. He also had (his wife says) a happy temperament and a childlike sense of fun. He could have been one of Max's more sunny-natured friends, like a kind of academic Kasus, and to some extent he was.

Closer than the Skrines, however, were the Sagarras, Eda and her husband Albert. Eda was Irish – the daughter of Kevin O'Shiel, a friend of the revolutionary leader Michael Collins and an important player in the founding of modern Ireland. She was a historian, working at the time especially on Bismarck. She would prepare delicious dinner-party meals, at the same time reading Bismarck's letters propped up beside her and talking nineteen-to-the-dozen to their friends. Albert was a Catalan, so she spoke Catalan as well as German. For his part, Albert was, everyone agrees, a remarkable man. He was a petroleum engineer by trade, but immensely learned about all sorts of things, especially art. Albert's quiet humour appealed to Max, and they would exchange droll remarks and mutual teases. Albert would take his pipe out of his mouth and start, Max would riposte, and they were off.

He was wonderful company, Eda says: like the friends of his youth, she doesn't recognise the Max she knew in his books. That is a tribute to how comfortable he must have felt with both Sagarras. It didn't stop him telling Eda a fib or two, though. At one point, for instance, he told her that his mother was Viennese. (Rosa Viennese! – she'd have been mortified.) He'd said that he was as he was because his parents were so different, his father German, his mother Viennese. 'How was he?' I asked. 'Different,' Eda said.[26]

The closest of all among Max's Manchester colleagues, however, were three others: his supervisor Idris Parry, Ray Furness, and Stanley Sephton Kerry, always known as Stan.[27]

Parry[28] was the other professor in the department, alongside its chairman, Rudolf Keller. Parry was the opposite of the old-fashioned, formal Keller – warm, relaxed, and more than maverick as a scholar. His education had been disrupted by the war and he never did a higher degree; Manchester had had to award him an honorary doctorate in order to offer him his chair. He never wrote an orthodox academic book, but published only his successful radio talks on his favourite authors, who included many of Max's (for instance, Kleist, Walser, Kafka, Canetti). His books – such as *Speak Silence*, whose title I've stolen – were beautifully and simply written, and full of emotion and subjectivity, much like Max's later work, for which indeed they may have been a model. And as they show, Parry was a contemplative, even a mystic. He was deeply opposed to rational, dualistic ways of dividing up the world; what was important, he insisted, was imagination, and opening ourselves through art, ritual or coincidence to underlying reality, which is uncertain, fluid – *a flow of connections*, he would always say.

This surely had a lasting influence on Max. But it didn't appeal to everyone. Many young searchers for the Meaning of Life, like Stevie Davies, responded to his passion and poetry, and felt, like her, that in his lectures 'subtle, unlikely, paradoxical and sophisticated truths were being unfolded in that calmly measured North Walian voice'. Others were less on his wavelength: 'Another hour of fluidity', they would grin. Parry wrote the blurbs for his own books, and a student sent one of them to *Private Eye*'s Pseuds' Corner. It got in. Thus Parry set Max yet another example – the tribute of English mockery in *Private Eye*.

Ray Furness[29] was the department's most extravagant character, which was no doubt what drew Max to him. He was an actor to his fingertips, who loved to play the most fantastical and preferably shocking parts, including when he played himself. He was a *Querkopf*, an oddball, Martin Durrell says, and enormous fun; in Eda's words, he was creative, imaginative, gifted and self-absorbed.

He was the opposite of slow, reserved, introverted Max – an extrovert and enthusiast, bursting with energy. He'd been a passionate admirer of Wagner since his teens, and would write several books on him, as well as many more on (for example) Nietzsche, expressionism, and decadence in German literature. When he retired he turned to fiction, as he'd always wanted to do, and at the age of seventy-four published a novel, which, he would stoically report, very few people ever read. Nonetheless, he was a good writer, with a vivid, observant style that no doubt came from his instinct as an actor. This comes out very much in his letters to Richard Sheppard about Max. He liked and admired him enough, he wrote, 'to make fun of this lugubrious German with the Zapata moustache, so very German in his rejection of things German'.

Was he a lugubrious optimist? A hilarious pessimist? He certainly
didn't exude hilarity, but the mournful exterior did conceal an
elusive sense of humour…

…the more I think about Max, the more elusive he becomes
somehow. His stance was oblique, quizzical, bemused. Yet intensely
moral, whatever that means. We talked a huge amount about death,
as you can imagine.[30]

Max saw Ray Furness several times in later years, when Ray became
an external examiner for UEA,[31] and he kept in touch with Parry. Stan
Kerry he probably never saw again. Yet it was Kerry to whom he was
closest in Manchester, and who remained in his mind, that is to say, in
his reality. So much so that Kerry, alone of Max's Manchester friends,
entered his work.

The book he entered was *The Rings of Saturn*. In it he is, as Richard
Sheppard says, 'One of the multitude of innocent, gifted, harmless
victims who are prematurely and unjustly sacrificed on the altar of
history.'[32] *The Rings of Saturn* is the peak of Max's mythology of the
holy innocent, which started in his work with Mangold the idiot
savant in 'Paul Bereyter', and with Paul himself, who 'in the eyes of his
contemporaries … had never really grown up';[33] and in his life with his
Aunt Anny and the gentle giant Schultz in the Lerchenmüller gardens.
The paradigms of the holy innocent in *The Rings of Saturn* are Janine
Dakyns and Michael Parkinson, both of whom die young; and the
paradigm of this paradigm is Stan Kerry.

Kerry had the reputation of an eccentric, the narrator tells us, because
he kept his distance from his colleagues and devoted his spare time to
studying Japanese, 'in [which] he was making astounding progress'.[34]
He has created a Japanese garden at the back of his bungalow in
Wythenshawe, we learn as the two stand there talking. When you talked
to Stan, the narrator says, out of his great courtesy he inclined his whole
body towards you, like a man leaning into the wind, or an angel 'gliding
down from on high'. This, as Sheppard says, makes him not merely a
person, but an avatar of Walter Benjamin's Angel of History,[35] who faces
the past but is constantly blown backwards into the future, while the
debris of history piles up at his feet.

So far, then, Max has made two mythical figures of Stan Kerry, a
holy innocent and the Angel of History. But there's more. He goes on
to describe his friend struggling to speak. Often, he wrote, Kerry's face

contorted with the effort, 'bringing beads of perspiration to his brow, and the words came from him in a spasmodic, precipitate manner that betrayed severe inner turmoil and presaged, even then, that all too soon his heart would cease to beat'.[36]

The narrator does not explain what kind of 'inner turmoil' Kerry was suffering, but clearly it has to do with language and what he cannot express in it, at least in his native tongue. That may be why he is studying the most difficult language he can find, in the hope that it may be adequate to express what he wants to say. This third myth of Kerry makes him into another avatar: of Hofmannsthal's Lord Chandos, who despairs of language, and who would become more and more important to Max. Looking back at Stan Kerry, whom he met thirty years before *The Rings of Saturn*, Max sees the first embodiment of a Chandos-like crisis. *The future lies in the past.*

The last myth about Kerry connects him to the narrator's friend and alter ego Michael Hamburger. Hamburger met him, the narrator tells us, when they were young fellow soldiers; then Kerry was one of the first people the narrator himself met in Manchester. When he thinks back now, he says, 'It seems incomprehensible that the paths of Michael's life and mine should have intersected in the person of that extraordinarily shy man, and that at the time we met him, in 1944 and 1966 respectively, we were both twenty-two.' This makes Stan Kerry a figure of repetition and coincidence, which in Sebald (and Parry) means a locus of insight, an entry point to metaphysical reality. What that reality might be he will never say. But that Kerry embodies a mystery beyond the natural is clear from this link to coincidence, and perhaps too from the fact that he appears to both Hamburger and the narrator on Christian holy days.

These, then, are the four myths of Kerry that Sebald created in two short pages. That is a surprising achievement, even for him, but the most surprising thing of all is that he tweaked the truth only slightly to make his portrait. The character of Kerry in *The Rings of Saturn* is one of the best examples of his genius, which was to see the fiction in facts, and tell the one without (or almost without) departing from the other.

Stan Kerry[37] *was* extraordinarily shy, and did have a reputation as an eccentric. He did study Japanese for years, and did make astounding progress in it – Japanese visitors were amazed. He didn't 'keep his distance' from his younger colleagues, since he was an understanding listener, and he and Stella happily took part in the dinner-party round. But Max was not wrong. Stan was extremely reserved and spoke little.

He did create a Japanese garden behind his bungalow, though it was in Sale rather than Wythenshawe, and was, Rosemary says, so subtly and unpretentiously Japanese that if you weren't told, you mightn't realise what it was. Altogether, she says, the word for Stan was *subtle*: his mind was subtle, his humour was subtle, the expressions he allowed to appear on his face were very subtle. With Stan, she says, 'You had to look and listen.'

Kerry really was, then, the shy, gentle eccentric that Max describes – the portrait in *The Rings of Saturn* is 'spot on' (Durrell), 'marvellous' (Eda), 'rings absolutely true' (Blamires). But surely the Chandos myth, at least, is hardly credible – the image of Kerry struggling so hard to speak that his face would contort and sweat would break out on his brow. Rosemary says tartly that it wasn't true; he only perspired when he drove, she says, because he was a very nervous driver. But Eda disagrees. Stan 'perspired ferociously because he was so shy', she says. He wrote beautifully, but had great difficulty in formulating sentences, and 'spoke in a very convoluted way'. Max dramatised, mythologised; but that Stan Kerry struggled to speak was true.

One reason, at least, was what everyone told me – *he was a Burnley boy*. That is, a working-class or lower-middle-class boy from a provincial town, with a lingering Lancashire accent, who'd moved into an entirely different world. Like Max himself, and like James Smith of Fribourg, who'd travelled the same road before. Max was speaking for all of them, across half a century, when he wrote, 'Whoever … has, as it were, worked his way out of a state of aphasia by his own efforts knows what it means when you can't get your mouth open.'[38]

It is hard to say how much his 'inner turmoil' contributed to Kerry's early death, as Max suggests in *The Rings of Saturn*. But he was a heavy smoker, with an undiagnosed heart condition; and on the night of 16–17 February 1980 he died of a heart attack at only fifty-six.[39]

On his return to Manchester, Max found it changed. 'Buildings are getting face-lifts,' he wrote to ROP. 'Business is thriving.'[40] Mancunians were pleased and proud – but not Max. He was only twenty-five, but his dislike of modernity was already in full flow.

Nonetheless, he still liked the city. This third stint as a *Lektor* was a stopgap, and the future was uncertain. But he was happy enough back in Manchester to help someone else to come there: his sister Beate.[41]

Beate finished school in July 1969 and was due to start her nursing training the next spring. In the meantime she needed experience with children. So as soon as he returned from St Gallen, Max went to his landlords and said, 'I have a little sister who would like to be an *au pair*.' The Jordans had three adopted children: eight-year-old Nick, five-year-old Ben, and two-year-old Sophie. As a result, they were always in need of help. Quiet, serious Max was a good advertisement for Sebalds, and they agreed straight away.

Beate was a great surprise to them, they say, smiling reminiscently at each other. She was completely different from her brother – open, with a smiling, round face, full of laughter and fun. She took to the children straight away, and they took to her, especially Sophie, who wouldn't be parted from her, but held tight to Beate's fur-topped boots and was pulled along behind her like a sleigh. Three children under ten are what nannies call a handful, but Beate coped effortlessly (now it's my turn to think how different she was from Max). She played endless games with them and told them stories of her own childhood escapades. One day, she recounted, she couldn't resist tipping a bit of her sister's perfume out of its blue bottle, to see if it was blue too. She had the answer – it wasn't. But now she also had a problem. The precious fragrance filled the room for hours, and her crime would certainly be discovered… The children were agog.

Beate stayed with the Jordans for five months. They lived not far from Kingston Road, and on Sundays she would go to see Max and his wife, or sometimes just his wife, while Max worked at his desk or in the library. Together they went to a Christmas ball at Dorothy's art school, to an opening at the Goethe Institute, where Max's wife worked, to a formal occasion at the university that ended with the singing of 'God Save the Queen'. Beate was impressed. But the happy, busy interlude was soon over, and in April she returned home to start her training.

Max had known Peter and Dorothy Jordan for several years now. Like all the tenants, his contact was mostly with Dorothy, who handled the houses – three of them by this point, with twenty-six tenants altogether. Clearly she was a woman of great energy, and also of great warmth and charm. She came from a town near Manchester: 'As far away as Munich,' she says, with a wry smile.

Peter left the houses to her for several reasons. First of all because he had no time: he was a dedicated architect, who would help to rebuild the slums of Whalley Range and Moss Side. And secondly because he was

a reserved person, without Dorothy's easy openness to people. She was
the lively, chatty one, with a quick intelligence and wicked green eyes.
He was quiet and thoughtful, a slight, wiry man who hadn't changed
size since his teens, and still climbed the peaks near Manchester in the
shorts and socks he'd worn at school.

Dorothy didn't compare her town to Munich by chance: Peter had come
from there. He'd arrived in England in his teens, had gone to school in
England (hence those shorts), and had become indistinguishably English.
But Peter Jordan was in fact what Dr Selwyn would be in fiction: a Jewish
refugee. He was the first Jewish refugee Max met – indeed the first Jew
Max met, or came to know. Peter Jordan's house saved his life, but Peter
Jordan's friendship – I'm sure Max felt, looking back – saved his soul.

When I interviewed him in 1996, he told me as many fairy tales
about Peter Jordan as about Dr Selwyn. When he met Dorothy in that
mythical greengrocer's, she mythically said, 'You know, D. is actually
from Munich' ('D.' being Max's cover-name for Peter, perhaps borrowed
from Dorothy herself). So in the fairy tale he knew Peter's history from
the start; and yet, in the fairy tale, they never spoke of it. 'There was
a sort of shyness,' he told me, 'a sort of paralysis on both sides. It has
taken all these twenty or thirty years for the paralysis to fade.'[42]

I can't blame myself this time for believing him – that shyness, that
paralysis happens all the time. How *do* you sit down, a German and a
Jew, and talk about the Holocaust? But the tale wasn't true.

His main contact was with Dorothy – that was true enough. But he and
Peter bumped into each other sometimes: perhaps when Max called on him
about some problem, or when Peter came in response to Kingston Road;
perhaps even in that grocery shop. And when they met, Peter says, 'I felt an
immediate connection.' He could have intelligent conversations with this
tenant; he felt that he could talk to him, that he could even be a friend.

They must in fact have 'bumped into each other' often. 'We became
very friendly,' Peter told me, with his gentle smile. 'Max was always very
serious with me,' he said, 'not ironic.' His life 'had no froth in it, no
soft indulgence' as far as either of the Jordans could see. To Dorothy he
felt like the melancholy wanderer of the *Winterreise*; to Peter he was 'a
powerful mind, always focused'. Max talked to him – about his father
who would never speak of the war, about his beloved grandfather, about
thinking that all cities were piles of rubble. And Peter talked to Max.

It was the first time, and he couldn't yet go very far. But he outlined to
Max the story of his family, his leaving Munich in 1939, his never seeing

his parents again. He told Max that his grandfather, aunt and uncle had all written memoirs; Max asked to see them, and Peter gave them to him. He felt listened to and understood as he had never been before by any German, or by any English person either. And Max was deeply moved, and would retell the story of their landlord's life at length to his new housemate.

Perhaps he knew already then that he was on the edge of a revelation. Because this was one of the key moments of his life, as a man and a writer: the moment he saw that historical events had happened not to numbers or even names, but to real people who had lived across the landing. However hard Germans tried, he would say, they never met a Jew, so their victims remained ethical abstracts to them. *Truth can only really be grasped through the encounter with real individual persons,* he said in the last year of his life.[43] That is the key to his reading, which valued first-hand reports and diaries over all but the greatest fictions, and the key to his writing, which relates his personal encounters with real, individual persons. He understood it now, talking to Peter Jordan, who had lived in Munich, and skied on the same hills as he had, and fled at the age of fifteen.

Peter Jordan.

The new housemate was called Peter Jonas.[44] In the autumn of 1966 he came to study singing and musicology at the Royal Northern School of Music, and had his own Manchester experience at the same moment as Max.

Peter lived in Whalley Range, which had once been a fashionable Victorian suburb, but was now bedsit land, and home of the red-light district. His room, like Max's in Chorlton, was freezing cold; the only heating was a small gas fire, and Mancunian moisture dripped down the walls. And like Max's fictional Arosa, Peter soon learned that the lower floors housed a brothel. (In fact this was a consolation, he says, since the girls were very nice to him.)

Like Max, he grew very depressed in his horrible room. Unlike Max, however, he had an irrepressible nature and a busy social life, so he just spent as little time there as he could and stayed on. But he regularly went for long walks through the tree-lined streets of Didsbury to cheer himself up, mostly to the area around Fletcher Moss Park. On one such walk he noticed a brand-new gable on one of the roofs on Kingston Road, and opposite it a glorious chestnut tree. If only he could live in the room behind that gable! He passed it often now, always glancing up. One day someone came out of the house, Peter went up to him – and to his astonishment the room behind the gable was to let. He discovered that the rent was beyond his means and moved in.

The gable room was small but light and airy, with a beautiful view of the chestnut tree, and Peter lived in it very happily for the rest of his Manchester time. Next to him was an attic flat that stretched from the front of the house to the back. That was the Sebalds' home for a year.

In future Peter would be Sir Peter Jonas CBE, with a distinguished career as director of English National Opera for a decade, and of Bavarian State Opera for fourteen years after that: one of the great and good in both Britain and Germany. In 1969, he says, he was a callow boy, interested in nothing but sport, parties and fast cars (apart from music, about which he admits he was always serious). He was only two years younger than Max, but the Sebalds seemed to him much older – a settled, domesticated couple, Max intensely serious and his wife an innocent, deeply shocked when he quoted what a friend had told him about Manchester ('It's so rainy and dark, all you can do is fuck'). Despite this, it was she who seemed to him the free spirit of the two compared to Max, who was quietly melancholy, even a bit morose. Together they were like a home for Peter, which, he says, 'I needed.' He had a clapped-out old Mini, in which he would take them to places round about; in turn they looked after him, and invited him regularly for spaghetti bolognese, which Max's wife would cook while Max and Peter talked.

They would sit together in the Sebalds' living room, its curtains drawn against the Manchester night, Peter on the floor with his long legs crossed, Max in an armchair, 'in father-confessor mode'. To the immature boy he was then, Peter says, Max seemed already old: sedentary, everything about him – his eyes, his 'hangdog moustache' – sloping downwards; when the two re-met decades later, he looked the same. He would tell long, rambling stories, 'like a storyteller of old', mixing together several tales and adding fantasies of his own – just as he would in his books, Peter realised when he read them. And just as much, or even more, he would quiz Peter about his life. He was a listener, Peter says, and, like a psychoanalyst, he could trigger you to talk. When Peter confessed that he was afraid he'd never amount to anything, Max told him not to worry, his fate was probably already decided. My background has always been a handicap, Peter said, and Max replied, No, your background will be your greatest asset. And he would ask Peter to tell him more.

Peter had a lot to tell. Unlike Max, he was a true mixture. His mother came from a powerful Lebanese family in Jamaica, which also produced the notorious socialite Lady Colin Campbell. Most people would have been intrigued by this exotic side of Peter's heritage, but the other side interested Max more. Peter's father Walter had been a German Jew from Hamburg, who came to England in April 1933, almost as soon as Hitler became Chancellor.

Walter was interned, like all 'enemy aliens', in 1940, then entered the intelligence service, from which he was not released until 1953. He wasn't given British citizenship until then either, which meant that when Peter was born in 1946 his father was stateless. At the age of forty-three Walter Jonas finally became a British citizen, but died less than ten years later, when Peter was only sixteen.

Max was riveted. What about the rest of Walter's family? Had they got away as well?

It had been quite enough for Peter, growing up in 1950s England, to have a Lebanese mother and a German-Jewish father, and he hadn't paid much attention to the tragic side of his family history. But he couldn't help hearing the family stories. These recounted that two of his aunts had managed to get to England on Kindertransports, but that their parents had stayed behind. His grandfather Julius Jonas was a famous criminal lawyer, who, like so many of his age, could not contemplate leaving Germany. As the net tightened he was taken in for questioning several times. One of the Gestapo officers (so the story went) recognised him as the lawyer who'd successfully defended him on a rape charge, and got Julius released. But on the third occasion he went to him and said, without explanation: 'You must leave Germany. If you can't leave, it would be better to kill yourself.' No one knows what Julius knew, but he believed him. His wife secretly gathered enough tablets to kill them both, and on 4 March 1939 they took them.[45]

Max listened intensely, and plied Peter with questions, but Peter knew no more. Perhaps it was now that Max said, You know, our landlord's the same as your father. Peter didn't know; he hadn't got close to the Jordans, and hadn't told them his own background. Very likely he hadn't told anyone – except Max Sebald.

Max also asked him about his own life, and listened to his answers with the same attention. His parents' strange match was very stormy, Peter told him, and eventually they gave it up. As a result his mother was first a divorcee, then a widow, and always poor, and he grew up in a very modest home in south London. Fortunately, he won full scholarships to both school and university, or he would have remained entirely uneducated (here he no doubt grinned at Max, as more than five decades later he grins at me). When he was five his Catholic mother sent him to Worth, a Benedictine boarding school, where he remained for the rest of his school life.

Boarding school from the age of five... Such things hardly exist in Germany, and Max was intrigued. How had Peter survived? With difficulty, Peter replied, probably with another grin. He told Max about the violence and abuse that underlie boarding-school life, and that he felt lurking beneath exchanges with his headmaster, some of which he described in vivid detail. Not to mention the attitudes of the other boys. What was he – a Kraut, a Kike, a towel-head? Each was worse than the next. He was an outsider many times over, and the perfect target for bullying of every kind.

But it didn't happen. The reason, he told Max, was that he was good at sport – the one thing boys respect without question. He was on the school's top rugby team, and its next-to-top cricket team, and good at both. As a result his school life was far from the Calvary he could have expected. Worth was giving him an excellent education, he knew; it was quiet and calm, and incomparably more beautiful than Croydon. In fact, he told Max, he was happier there than at home.

When Peter finished his story in the Sebalds' living room in 1969 or 1970, the three friends tucked into their spaghetti bolognese. When he finishes the story of the story in a Munich café in 2016, we look at each other. 'You recognise it, don't you?' Peter asks. And I do. The foreign boy saved from bullying by being good at rugby – his being happier at school than at home – it's Jacques Austerlitz. Even the scene in the headmaster's study has echoes of the ones Peter described to Max all those years ago. 'He wasn't just a listener,' Peter says. 'He was a recording machine.'

And, I think, a camera. Because Peter has told me something else: that in 1969 he had a photograph of himself on the Worth rugby team. Max asked to see it and pored over it for hours. Then when he came to write *Austerlitz* he searched for a photo as like it as possible. Austerlitz, he tells us, is the boy on the far right in the front row. In the Worth School photo Peter Jonas is the third from right in the back row. It's 1963, and he has no idea that nearly forty years later he will become part of a fictional character called Jacques Austerlitz.

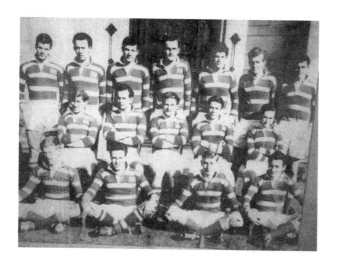

By the spring of 1970 Max had to think of the future. He applied for several jobs, and was offered one in the drama department of Parry's old university, Bangor, to teach German and French drama in English translation. He turned it down,[46] saying 'this would have completely exiled me'. As there was nowhere in Britain for him to be exiled from, he must have meant exile from his language. Whatever he felt about his country, German was his home.

Then in March he saw a new advertisement: for the post of assistant lecturer in German language and literature at the University of East Anglia.[47] On 21 March he applied. He had glowing references. Professor Keller said that he was 'really outstanding as a teacher and in his contact with students'. Parry's words were typically direct: Max was, he said, 'a pleasant, gentle, sincere person, a scholar to the fingertips' and 'a worker [who] gets things done'. Ronald Peacock praised his 'very striking and masterly contribution' to Sternheim studies, which must have helped a great deal. Best and truest of all, perhaps, was his comment that 'Sebald has a genuinely original mind', and also Parry's: '[He] is a man of rare literary perception.'[48]

His interview was at 11.15 on the morning of 26 May, in a beautiful old building, Earlham Hall. He performed brilliantly, and the younger members of the panel argued strongly for him. Two days later the university wrote to offer him the post. His fellow applicants seemed extremely nice, he would say later, and UEA 'a rather pleasant place'.[49] On 1 June he accepted.

In August he was in Sonthofen, and if he hadn't told his parents before that he'd taken a permanent job in England, he told them now. His father would have been impressed by his salary of £1,480 a year – about £22,000 today, and about 12,900 Deutschmarks in 1970.[50] Rosa's response would have been harder to handle. I hope he was kind.

As soon as he knew his future was settled, he and his wife had taken a long three-month holiday in France, in Pont-Aven in Finistère.[51] He had another plan as well: he wanted to see the house in Bordeaux where Hölderlin had been a tutor in 1802. 'Probably will tell me more about him,' he wrote to ROP (in English), 'to look at the facade of this place, than to read the latest news from the intellectual stock-exchange.'[52]

He had felt a strong affinity with Hölderlin, the homeless wanderer, for years.[53] Hölderlin had lost his father at two and his stepfather at nine. From then on, by his own account, he lived with grief and sorrow. He struggled to establish himself as a poet and worked fitfully as a private tutor. In 1789 he broke off his engagement, writing to his fiancée that 'you could never have been happy with your morose, ill-humoured and sickly friend'.[54] Seven years later he fell in love with Susette Gontard, the wife of his employer; she returned his feeling, but when their affair was discovered he was harshly dismissed. By then his melancholy was becoming true mental illness, which worsened after his last secret meeting with Susette in 1800. He left Germany and worked as a tutor in Switzerland; then, at the end of 1801, accepted the post of tutor in the household of the German consul in Bordeaux, a wealthy wine merchant called Daniel Christoph Meyer.

Max's identification with Hölderlin lasted to the end of his life, and one of the last things he wrote contained a tribute to him. Hölderlin walked everywhere, he said – in the Rhône and Harz mountains, from Frankfurt to his home in Nürtingen, near Stuttgart. And in December 1801 he walked almost a thousand kilometres, from his home to Strasbourg, Colmar, Besançon and Lyon, where he registered as an *homme de lettres*, toiling for nineteen days over 'the fearful snowbound heights of the Auvergne, through storms and wilderness, in ice-cold nights, with my loaded pistol beside me in my rough bed';[55] finally entering Bordeaux on 28 January 1802.

The Hôtel Meyer was one of the most distinguished houses in the city. It was opposite the Grand Théâtre on the Allées de Tourny, an elegant street in the heart of the old town. Hölderlin lived there at the beginning of his stay, and sounded like Max at the Rosenberg-Schule: 'I'm living almost too nobly,' he wrote to his mother. 'I'd be happy with a safer simplicity.'[56]

No one knows what happened to Hölderlin in Bordeaux. But after just three months, on 10 May he applied for a pass to return to Germany, and walked the thousand kilometres back again. In July he arrived in Nürtingen in a state of complete mental collapse, 'eyes flickering', Max wrote, 'and dressed like a beggar'.[57] Soon afterwards he learned that Susette Gontard had died of influenza as he was approaching home.

In the years after Bordeaux Hölderlin wrote some of his greatest poetry. But he never regained his sanity, and in 1805 he was committed to a clinic in Tübingen. Three years later he was discharged as incurable. He was taken into a house which had been a tower in the old city wall;

and in this famous *Hölderlinturm*, or Hölderlin's Tower, he lived on for another thirty-six years, writing poetry that would have to wait until the twentieth century to become celebrated.

This was the wanderer fallen into madness and melancholy, his love lost – like Büchner and his hero Lenz, and the hero of the *Winterreise* – who meant so much to Max in 1970 that he sought him in a house he'd stayed in more than a century and a half before. Hölderlin had written one of his most famous poems, 'Remembrance', here, recalling the days of love, and the point where the waters of the Dordogne and Garonne merge and flow as wide as the sea. 'But the ocean,' it ends, 'takes/and gives memory,'

> And Love too labours to capture our eyes,
> But what abides, poets create.[58]

15

Max Ferber

...the memoirs, which at points were truly wonderful, had
seemed to him like one of those evil German fairy tales in which,
once you are under the spell, you have to carry on to the finish,
till your heart breaks, with whatever work you have begun – in
this case, the remembering, writing and reading.

'Max Ferber'[1]

'Max Ferber' – or 'Max Aurach', as it was in the original German –
is the culminating story of *The Emigrants*. We have felt the narrator's
strong sense of brotherhood with all his subjects, but with Ferber there's
more: an identity, signalled by their sharing their first name. Hero and
narrator are of the same dark kind; with 'Max Ferber' biography and
autobiography merge.

The opening lines are laced with warnings. The narrator doesn't
know how he'll manage on his own – his sense of security is false –
Manchester lies below him like that fire suffocated in ash. Then he
descends, and enters a black, blasted world. On his long, lonely walks
the only signs of life are screaming birds, ghostly sighs and small gangs
of children skipping around fires. In the *Walpurgisnacht* of his soul even
the children are frightening.

Halfway through this nightmare comes light relief – the encounter
between the narrator and his landlady, the ex-Salvation Army girl
Gracie Irlam, he on the brink of sleep and she just roused from it,
each astonished by the other. Gracie will remain comically strange and
mysterious, vanishing every Sunday, perhaps still to play her flugelhorn

with the Salvation Army. But the date on her portrait is that 17 May, which to seasoned Sebaldians is a sign of affinity, and Gracie indeed turns out to be the good spirit of Manchester ('Yes, Irlam like Irlam in Manchester,' she says).[2] She is no Lorelei luring this traveller to his death, but a bringer of comfort in the form of her bubbling Teasmade, a mechanical version of herself – absurd, benign and utterly English.

After this interlude of grace the narrator continues his wanderings. On one of these he discovers Ferber and his studio, and over the next sixty pages Ferber's story unfolds.

It unfolds in two stages, like a delayed revelation. At first Ferber says nothing about his early years. When he does recall something – a beautiful day with his father on a mountain above Lake Geneva – he recalls too that when that memory first surfaced, he was overcome by anxiety, nearly leapt off the mountain, to which he'd returned, and was afflicted by a spreading 'lagoon of oblivion'.[3] He offers no explanation for any of this; it remains both precisely detailed and deeply mysterious. The delayed revelation works twice over: it keeps us in suspense, and it enacts the block to memory that the story is about.

After this the narrator leaves Manchester and, as with Dr Henry Selwyn, doesn't think about Ferber for many years. But as with Dr Selwyn, a chance event brings him back to mind. With Ferber it is the sight of one of his paintings, accidentally come across in the Tate, followed again by a newspaper article encountered against the odds, since the narrator (as he remarks) has long avoided reading the Sunday papers. That accidents and improbabilities give us glimpses of profound meanings we cannot rationally reach is Sebald's underlying metaphysic from the start.

What the Sunday paper reveals is that in 1939, at the age of fifteen, Friedrich Maximilian Ferber left Munich for England, and that in 1941 his parents were deported from Munich to Riga and murdered there. For weeks the narrator carries the article around with him like Medusa's head and looks at it over and over again. He feels now that his long-ago failure to ask Ferber what lay behind his hints was unforgiveable, and in the winter of 1989 he returns to Manchester.

They talk for three days, far into the night. Naturally, Ferber says, he tried to keep the thought of his parents' fate at bay; but this avoidance brought only its own suffering, spreading over him 'the poisonous canopy … which has kept me so much in the shade and the dark in recent years'.[4] He chose Manchester to escape the past, but instead the immigrant city with its many Jews constantly reminded him of it, and that is really why he came. With every year, he says, he has realised more clearly that 'I am here, as they used to say, to serve under the chimney.' Finally he allows himself to remember fully, and tells his story to the narrator. When he now recalls his suitcase of 1939, so neatly packed by his mother, he feels 'as if I should never have unpacked it'; and saying this he covers his face with his hands, in the only open gesture of grief made by any of the heroes, apart from their final acts of suicide. Ferber is the only one who doesn't take his own life, though he too is clearly dying at the end. That is surely because he has been serving under the chimney all along, through his painting; and in his last gesture he passes on that saving grace to the narrator, by giving him his mother's memoir, and with it the heartbreaking work of remembering, writing and reading that is the story.

When the narrator first meets Ferber, Sebald gives us two of the most powerful pages about an artist at work I know. They describe the working methods of a real artist, Frank Auerbach, which, without any added fiction, perfectly mirror his own. When he came across the portrait of Auerbach in Robert Hughes' biography, it must have been like finding the report of Johannes Naegeli's body emerging from the ice: the moment that a spark leapt from the page and closed the circuit of his story.

Over and over Ferber lays on paint and scrapes it off, draws with charcoal and rubs it off, so that his studio floor is covered with the rising detritus of his work. Just so does the narrator continually score out what he has written, leaving a debris of hundreds of pages covered with his scribble; and just so did the author cover thousands of pages with notes and drafts and endless corrections. The narrator feels that his portrait of Ferber is a failure, just as Ferber felt his portraits were. But in reality Ferber's desperate works are far from failures. 'Time and again,' the narrator says, 'I marvelled to see that Ferber, with the few lines and shadows that had escaped annihilation, had created a portrait of great vividness.'[5] And though Sebald doubted it as deeply as Ferber, so had he.[6]

As we know, *Austerlitz* will raise the question of true art: is it the evocative sketch of Turner's *Funeral at Lausanne*, or faithfulness to every detail of reality, as in the impossible ideal of Jacques' teacher, André Hilary? 'Max Ferber' answers it (typically) in a dream. In this dream Ferber sees that his own paintings hardly differ from clichéd salon pieces. That is his (and the author's own) first answer: whatever true art is, his work does not attain it. Then he enters another gallery, deserted and full of dust, which he recognises as his parents' drawing room. There a stranger called Frohmann sits, holding on his lap a tiny model of the Temple of Solomon.[7] Look, Frohmann says, you can see every curtain, every sacred vessel. 'And I,' Ferber says, 'bent down over the diminutive temple and realised, for the first time in my life, what a true work of art looks like.'[8]

So Hilary's ideal wins, according to which, properly describing a battle (or, we can add, a genocide) would require 'some inconceivably complex form, recording who had perished, who had survived, and exactly where and how'.[9] That this is Ferber's ideal is clear not only from the Temple of Solomon, but from the copy of a painting that has hung on his studio wall for twenty-five years: Rembrandt's *Man with a Magnifying Glass*. True art requires the detailed vision of a magnifying glass; Frohmann surely used one in building his temple.†

But this ideal is impossible. Ferber's endless struggle shows it, as does the narrator's. And so will Sebald's: *Austerlitz* awaits, his longest and most detailed work, which will also seem to him a failure.[10]

That is the conclusion of the story: art is impossible, and inevitably fails. It replaces reality with a petrified form of itself, like the petrified twigs in the salt frames of Bad Kissingen. Sebald provides a photograph of one such twig – his image for the story, I think, and for 'the entire questionable business of writing'.[11] In this last extraordinary image, art destroys the reality it portrays, as it destroys the artist who devotes his life to its impossible task. For this too Sebald provides an image, this time in the ironic mode, which is, as he said, the other side of melancholy.[12] When Ferber works for endless hours with charcoal, its dust covers his skin as well as his studio floor. Looking at his darkened hands, he tells the story of a photographic assistant in Manchester, whose body had absorbed so much silver 'that he himself had become a kind of photographic plate, which was apparent in the fact (as Ferber solemnly informed me) that the man's face and hands turned blue in strong light, or, as one might say, developed'.[13]

This is wonderfully grotesque and comic, but what it means is that, like the assistant, Ferber is being slowly poisoned by his art. And behind him stands the author.

'Max Ferber' is the culmination too of *The Emigrants'* net of imagery. Nabokov, the hunter of beauty, makes his final appearance, saving Ferber from self-destruction. Cosmo Solomon's desert caravan reappears on the wall of the Wadi Halfa, quivering like a mirage, so that Ferber seems to the narrator to belong to the scene, as Cosmo belonged to it, since he disappeared with it. So Ferber is linked to Cosmo Solomon, another visionary tormented by a far-away massacre, and both are linked to the image of a caravan crossing a desert, like the flight from Egypt of the children of Israel. And the woman in watered silk who haunts the narrator's dream in 'Ambros Adelwarth' reappears in Ferber's vision of a beautiful woman in grey silk who comes to his studio almost every day. She sweeps in, takes off her hat and gloves, and bends down towards him, much as the mysterious Gräfin Dembowski took off her hat, in a gesture deeply significant to the narrator. Is the dream-woman in silk the past, perhaps, or love? All we can guess is that she stands for loss and longing.

And there is, finally, an image that is unique to 'Max Ferber', and that sums up not Ferber's suffering but the narrator's. It comes at the end, when he spends the night in a Manchester hotel. He seems to hear an orchestra tuning up next door, and then 'far off, far, far off'[14] he hears once again the tenor of Liston's Music Hall in the 1960s. The little singer wore a too-long overcoat (like Kafka and Cosmo, Ambros and Fini) and sang popular hits and arias from Wagner. And now the narrator sees, on the flats of the stage that doesn't exist, photos of the wartime ghetto of Łódź, taken by an Austrian accountant called Genewein.[15] There are pictures of the ghetto streets and of laughing German officers; but most are of the workshops and factories where the inhabitants worked, as their only chance of staying alive. One photo transfixes the narrator. In it three young women sit at a loom weaving a carpet that reminds him of the settee in his parents' home. They seem to be staring at him, since looking at the photo puts him exactly in the place of Genewein. The woman on one side holds her head slightly tilted; but the one on the other side looks straight at him, 'with so steady and relentless a gaze that I cannot meet it for long'.[16]

Genewein's photo of the three weavers.

He asks himself what their names were, and answers in his lovely last line: 'Nona, Decuma and Morta, the daughters of night, with spindle, scissors and thread.' They are the Three Fates, who spin the thread of life for all of us. Nona spins, Decuma measures, and Morta – Death with her scissors – cuts us off.[17]

In that line 'Morta' comes last. But if we read Genewein's photograph naturally, from left to right, the young woman whose gaze the narrator cannot meet comes first. So this time Sebald doesn't include the photograph in the text. His words stand alone: the young woman accusing him from the doomed ghetto is Death.

Biographically, 'Max Ferber' is the culmination of something else in *The Emigrants*: the problem of the stories' relation to their models.

It was based, as Sebald often said, on two people, his Manchester landlord and 'a well-known artist'.[18] And unlike the models for his other heroes, both were still alive. This was likely to kick up still more trouble, and so it would prove. But he didn't try to guard against it. On the contrary, he planted clues all over his text, particularly to Auerbach. In the original German edition he even included one of Auerbach's drawings,[19] as if the name 'Aurach' weren't already enough. And still not content, he slipped in a classic Max tease, including in his list of beautiful German-Jewish names both 'Frank' and 'Auerbach' – in the German edition, actually together ('...Arnsberg, Frank, Auerbach, Grunwald...').[20] In the application he made for a grant to finish *The Emigrants*, he didn't even bother to tease, simply calling his hero 'Auerbach'.

He also increased the internal problem of the stories: the doubt about the reliability of photographs. He devotes two pages to Ferber's uncle's claim that, though the book-burning in Würzburg took place, the photograph of it was clearly a fake, and then shows that it was, by including it. As we saw with 'Dr Henry Selwyn', this undermines the whole point of the documentary technique, and quite deliberately. 'I had that picture,' Sebald told Arthur Lubow. 'I thought very consciously that this is a place to make a declaration. It couldn't be more explicit. It acts as a paradigm for the whole enterprise.'[21]

This is where we are brought up short. How could he both want to shock us with the reality of his photos and at the same time remind us that they could be fakes? It's an insoluble question. He gives us the most powerful proof of what we must face and a moment later whips it away. Perhaps because, although he faced it constantly, at the same time he couldn't bear to, as the last lines of 'Max Ferber' reveal, or perhaps just because he was always drawn to trickery. But the second probably derived from the first long ago.

Peter Jordan never saw a notebook in Max's hands during their Manchester conversations.[22] He may have jotted things down afterwards; or he may simply have been a recording machine, as Peter Jonas says. But however he did it, Ferber's history corresponds almost precisely to Peter Jordan's, from his boyhood in Munich to his arrival in Manchester and his war.

Thus (for example) Ferber's father was an art dealer and was interned in Dachau: so was Peter's. The suicide of Ferber's grandmother in 1936 and the death of his grandfather in Theresienstadt both come from Peter. The events of Ferber's escape from Germany and arrival in England are almost exactly as they happened to Peter (including even the boarding school in Margate, to which Sebald added only the comic absurdity). Ferber's letters from home cease at the same time as Peter's, and for the same reason: his parents were deported on one of the first transports from Munich, and murdered at Kaunas near Riga in November 1941.

The fidelity doesn't end with words. Every Ferber photograph comes from Peter Jordan's family album, including the photo of Fritz Ferber on his last skiing holiday, which is of Fritz Jordan on his, and the cameos of Luisa and Fritz Ferber, which are of Paula and Fritz Jordan. After Peter sent them to him, Sebald asked more questions and put the answers in the text: for example, where Fritz had been skiing – on the Brauneck in Lenggries.[23]

There are only two things in Ferber's past history that didn't come from Peter. One is his family's going for their summer holidays to Oberstdorf or the Walsertal;[24] the other is his date of exile: 17 May. That was in fact Peter's mother's birth date, which was coincidence enough. Peter nearly left on that day, and thus nearly began his life of exile on Max's birthday. But not quite. With these 'tiny little rapprochements', as Sebald would say,[25] he secretly slipped his empathising self into the story.

Peter also gave Max something as important as his life: Ferber's mother's memoir of her German-Jewish childhood before the war.

The real memoir was written not by Peter's mother Paula Jordan, but by her sister Thea Gebhardt, who survived the war in Switzerland and wrote it in the 1960s.[26] Peter showed it to Max in the late 1960s, along with the other family memoirs, and Max asked to see them all again in the late 1980s. Paula's brother Julius's was the most factual and clear-eyed, but, 'It left Max cold,' Peter says. Thea's, by contrast, was full of colour and emotion; it moved Max deeply, and his version of it in 'Max Ferber' is deeply moving in turn.

The transformation of the ninety-seven pages of Thea's memoir into the twenty-five pages of Luisa Lanzberg's is an extraordinary work of Sebaldian *bricolage*. To follow the whole process would drive us almost as mad as it drove him. But, for example: the whole of one page of 'Max Ferber' – the approach and entry to Steinach – comes from Thea, including, almost verbatim, Lazarus getting down from his calèche to spare the horses and 'the tip of the church tower and the old castle – Steinach!' Most of the next page comes straight from Thea's loving recollection too, including the telling remark about 'Papa's sister, who people say was the most beautiful girl for miles around, a real Germania'. And so it goes on, in startling detail, both in Steinach and later in Bad Kissingen, from the Sabbath walk to Bad Bocklet to the snowy scene of the goose-feather cutting. And most beautiful of all, the blue-and-white jay's feather that stands for the whole of Luisa's lost childhood, just before the move to Kissingen: 'And who was that strange child, walking home, tired, with a tiny blue and white jay's feather in her hand?'[27] Thea did not write this Sebaldian line, but the image of the jay feather came from her. And, Gertrud remembers, from their grandfather, who wore jay feathers in his hat, which the children would help him to find.

All this raises some hard questions, which would dog Sebald especially after *Austerlitz*, but began here. To what extent is it legitimate to use other people's lives, and even their works, for literature? And what responsibility do you have to them if you do?

Well, to start with Thea's memoir: Sebald plundered it ruthlessly and used most of the best bits. But in this case I think that what he did remains legitimate. He used only a small proportion of the whole; and most of what he used he transformed. The line about the jay feather is a perfect example: in Thea's memoir it is a happy memory; in Sebald it is a haunting image of lost time. This is true of all the people, events and images he lifted from the memoir. There they are recalled in vivid, concrete detail; in 'Max Ferber' they are set in a penumbra of meaning and become more than themselves. The memories are Thea's, but the art is Sebald's.

He achieved this not only by recasting Thea's words in his own, as in the jay-feather line, but by using only her best lines. He also made other important subtractions and additions.

For example: in Thea's memoir, as in reality, the Franks were a large, warm clan. In Luisa's Sebald leaves them all out, apart from her twin, Leo (that is, Paula's twin, Julius). As a result Luisa is a far more isolated figure than either Paula or Thea ever was. And then, since in 'Max Ferber' only Leo survives, Ferber himself is in turn a much more isolated figure than Peter Jordan ever was. For all Paula's siblings survived, as well as most of the rest of the clan.[28] This is not to minimise Peter's loss. It is simply to point out that the sense of isolation around Ferber, which begins in his mother Luisa's isolation in her memoir, is one that Sebald did not find in his models but created.

What did he add? Most importantly, Luisa's two lost loves, Fritz Waldhof the horn player and Friedrich Frohmann the blind lieutenant, both of whom die, and leave her not knowing 'how I got over the terrible pain of parting … or indeed whether I have ever got over it'.[29]

Paula and Thea Frank both worked as nurses during the Great War, and Thea did meet a wounded soldier (though hers was an airman) who proposed to her. Their parents were reluctant for her to marry a non-Jew, as Luisa's are, and their reluctance was overcome in her case too. But Fritz Gebhardt didn't die; he and Thea married and had two daughters, and though the marriage ended unhappily, it was quite a different story from Luisa's.

These, then, are the things that darken Luisa's story, and that were not in Paula's or Thea's: isolation and death, and a sense that her fate has been signalled from the start. For all Luisa's loves are called Fritz ('Friedrich' is the usual origin for 'Fritz'), the last two being echoes of the first, who was her great love. Or: the first two being premonitions of the last, except that this time she will share his untimely death with him.

And Sebald is silently present in Luisa Lanzberg's memoir as well. For Luisa's loss of Steinach mirrors his own loss of Wertach, and Luisa's knowledge, while she writes, that that idyll was a cruel illusion mirrors his own. When he first read Thea's evocation of her seemingly enchanted German childhood, it must have struck a deep chord in him. Together with the revelation of meeting Peter, it was the seed of his identification with Germany's betrayed Jews, and of his desire to write about them.

There remains the question of responsibility to his sources: did Max ask Peter's permission, did he show him what he'd written? Yes – he told him what he was doing, showed him the story and asked for corrections, which Peter made.[30] But also – no. Peter never explicitly gave Max permission. Both were too shy, too afraid to talk openly of what they were doing – the Jew giving his family history to the German, and the German taking it, to transform into his own work of art. As soon as the book was published, Max sent Peter a copy, saying how much it meant to him to include his story, and how much he hoped Peter would approve of the result.[31] Peter did approve, and still does. He is very happy to have his family history preserved in a work of literature he deeply admires. He also knows that he gave his permission implicitly,[32] by co-operating willingly throughout, and doesn't blame Max for his reluctance to confront the question openly, since he shared it. Nonetheless, he does blame him: not about his family history, but about Thea's memoir. Max should not have used that so closely without crediting it, he says: not just in interviews, but in the book itself.

This, then, is the last question: should Sebald have credited Thea Gebhardt in *The Emigrants*? The trouble is that doing so would disturb what he constantly strove for, *l'effet de réel*. If we are reminded that Luisa is not real, but Paula and Thea were, we start thinking about Paula and Thea instead. That is what I want to achieve here. But Sebald didn't; he wanted us to believe in Luisa Lanzberg. He wanted us to believe in her so much that he put her photograph in the story. But now we are back to that dilemma – the photograph itself makes us wonder who was behind Luisa Lanzberg.

So I think in the end he was wrong. It wouldn't destroy the effect of his story to let us know that it is a fiction, *and that real people stand behind it*. He could have put a short note at the beginning of the book, saying that these stories draw on several real lives; and on one real memoir, by Thea Gebhardt, who survived the war, and was a sister of 'Luisa Lanzberg', who did not. He is no longer here to make the decision. But his publishers could.

The brilliant short biography of Auerbach by Robert Hughes came out in 1990. Here was another Jewish refugee story – and this one was about an artist. Max must have recognised it all – the refugee story like Peter's, the artistic struggle like his own. And so Aurach/Ferber must have leapt to life in his mind – half Peter, half Auerbach; and in the Auerbach half, himself.

So he set to work to weave the two stories together. And as he'd done with Thea's memoir, he took a great deal from a small part of Hughes' book. He took Auerbach's dedication, working ten hours a day, seven days a week, for decades. He took the approach to the studio, with its roughly lettered sign TO THE STUDIOS (and added Bonnard's almond tree). He took the studio itself, with its dark corners and gleaming pots of colour. Above all, he took Hughes' striking descriptions of Auerbach's practice: the constant scraping away of paint and rubbing away of charcoal, so that 'one walks, gingerly, on the remains of innumerable pictures'.[33] Auerbach's charcoal portraits, Hughes wrote, constantly rubbed out and restarted, finally retrieve a likeness, but as of ghosts, of 'blackened wraiths of ash'.[34] Ferber's portraits seem to have evolved, Sebald wrote, 'from a long lineage of grey, ancestral faces, rendered unto ash, but still there, as ghostly presences, on the harried paper'.[35]

Not only must he have recognised in Auerbach's long, effortful process his own weeks and months of rewriting. He also recognised several of his own private tics, and took them for Ferber: his aversion to travel – even to leaving his city, not to speak of his country; his 'overriding sense of being alone in the world'.[36] And finally, I think, he took Auerbach's torment. Hughes was careful, talking of the 'absurdity' of interpreting Auerbach's art in the light of the loss of his parents when he was a small child – and then did it anyway. Auerbach 'has transposed the wound of parental loss into … art-making', he wrote.[37] Sebald never says this of Ferber, but it could not be more clearly implied.

Is any of *this* stealing? He certainly took the key points of Hughes' book for his purpose – but that's what any fiction based on a biography must do. And he took no phrases; his imagery of ghosts and ash is close to Hughes' but not the same. Crucially too, Hughes' book was published, unlike Thea's, and published material can be drawn on (as Sebald himself argued).[38] At the very least, Hughes' case for any acknowledgement is far weaker than Thea's, and he never made it.

Nonetheless 'Max Ferber' stirred up big trouble. It came not from Hughes, but from Auerbach himself.

Die Ausgewanderten was published in Germany in 1992.[39] Auerbach had no contact with Germany and knew nothing about it. But four years later, with the English edition already at the printers, the British publishers, Harvill, contacted him. They had checked on the permission for including his drawing, *Head of Catherine Lampert VI*, in the text and discovered to their dismay that it had never been sought.

Auerbach is famous for not mincing his words. He wrote an extremely rude letter to Christopher MacLehose of Harvill, and in some accounts threatened to sue. Max admired Auerbach's toughness as much as his work,[40] and agreed that all overt references to him be removed. The drawing disappeared, as did a photograph of Auerbach's dark eye, and 'Aurach' was changed to 'Ferber'.

Auerbach must have calmed down about Harvill, but not about Max. Some time later he complained furiously about him to his fellow artist Tess Jaray. Tess had been bowled over by *The Emigrants*, and did her best to defend it. The next time they met, Auerbach had clearly read the book himself. To Tess's great relief he said, 'You were right.' She thought then, and for a long time after, that one great artist had recognised another, and Sebald was forgiven.[41]

In 2011 I wrote to Auerbach and asked if I could talk to him about Sebald. I knew it was almost impossible – he sees very few people – and enclosed a few written questions as well. To my amazement, he replied. His answer was generous, explaining the events as I've retold them above. But his anger had returned.

'I only glanced at *The Emigrants*,' he wrote,

> but found the tone of presumptuous / humourless solemnity repellent, and deprecate the use of other people's misunderstood biographies to lend weight to what appeared a narcissistic enterprise.
>
>   I did not have any personal contact with Sebald, and regard the whole business as a boring intrusion.[42]

And he went, I imagine, straight back to work.

In my German paperback of *Die Ausgewanderten*, published in 2003, the hero is still called Aurach, and both Auerbach's drawing and his dark eye are still there. But by the next printing in 2006 they'd gone,[43] and the hero was Max Ferber in German as well. I suppose that is the end of the story. Auerbach has never forgiven Sebald, but the last traces of his offence have disappeared.

So this is Auerbach's accusation: the portrait of Max Ferber is a 'narcissistic enterprise', to which Sebald tries to lend weight with a stolen biography. And though he doesn't say it, the narcissism is a German's, and the stolen biography a Jew's. Quite a few people do say it, about both *The Emigrants* and *Austerlitz*, especially among Germans themselves, who are hypersensitive about any German treatment of Jewish stories. And if you feel this, you are almost bound to feel that his tone is presumptuous and self-advertising, rather than grief-stricken.

I have argued that you can only fail to hear the grief and mourning in Sebald's voice if your ears are blocked by a belief such as this one – that no German can legitimately tell a Jewish story. But Auerbach's ears were blocked by personal anger, which is a great deal more justified. Max did steal his drawing, part of his name and his eye, and though he didn't take his biography – that was Peter's – he took the heart of it, Auerbach's work as a painter.

Was that invasive? Not really – Robert Hughes had already invaded it, with Auerbach's permission. Was it legitimate to use it for a fiction? That is a much harder question, and one I put to Sebald in our interview. He didn't seem to understand it. I thought this was because he simply put his book before his models, and I still think so. But it was also because he saw using other people's work as *hommage*, the tipping of his hat to artists with whom he felt an affinity.

The question remains: was it legitimate to use a living artist in the way he used dead ones, like Kafka and Stendhal? That is surely the key. Writers often spin stories about famous figures across the ages – but they usually wait until their subjects are long dead. Sebald used Auerbach before that. He treated him, in other words, as though he were already dead. That *is* an offence. He should have identified Thea Gebhardt, and he should not have identified Auerbach, certainly not so openly as to use his drawing without his permission. 'Max Ferber' is a great work of art, but to its models Max did wrong.

Finally, though, there is that accusation of narcissism. With all the examples of Sebald filling his subjects with his own pain – especially here in 'Max Ferber' – the charge of narcissism looks hard to escape. And yet I want to say to Frank Auerbach: the charge is unfair. Narcissism is not imagining that you have my pain. It is imagining that only I have pain; that other people's pain is different, unimportant, not pain at all. That is the start of the road to Auschwitz, and the opposite of everything Max Sebald strove for. It is true that he took whatever he needed for his work. But that's not narcissism, it's ruthlessness. And every great writer who has ever lived is ruthless. Even every writer altogether. As Max told his students, it may be necessary in order to write as well as you can.

I said that the last traces of Max's offence have disappeared, but it's not quite true: one remains. It happens when the narrator comes across a Ferber painting by chance and the second part of the story unfolds. The painting, he tells us, is called 'G. I. on Her Blue Candlewick Cover'. This picks up his amusement about candlewick, which is probably what we notice. But two other things lie behind it. One is that 'G. I.' must be Gracie Irlam; and the other is that one of Frank Auerbach's most famous paintings is 'E. O. W. on Her Blue Eiderdown'.

Some striking consequences follow. First, that Gracie Irlam clearly sits for Ferber – so *that* may be where she goes every Sunday. And second, if we know Auerbach's story, we know that 'E. O. W.' was Estella Olive West, not only Auerbach's first model but his lover for twenty-five years. Ferber is desperately alone, his vision of the grey silk lady the closest he ever comes to feminine contact. But 'G. I. on Her Blue Candlewick Cover', with its unmistakable echo of 'E. O.W. on Her Blue Eiderdown', slips a new Sebaldian uncertainty into the story.

And I wonder if it doesn't also tell us something about Gracie Irlam. Perhaps she was based on Stella West, whom Sebald came across in Hughes' biography. There are several connections – Stella was initially Auerbach's landlady, as Gracie is the narrator's; they are both older women;[44] and Gracie is a home for the homeless young narrator, as Stella was a home for the homeless young Auerbach. In reality Stella was an emotional and sexual earth mother for Auerbach, while in Sebald's hands Gracie becomes a distant comic character. Nonetheless, she is the good spirit of Manchester who helps the narrator to survive the first dark days of his English life. And at some point Sebald may well have planned to put Stella West directly into his story: there are many Auerbach heads of E. O. W. in his 'Ferber' papers.[45] In the end he didn't go that far. But he left us the hint of 'G. I. on Her Blue Candlewick Cover'.

Perhaps, then, he not only openly stole from Auerbach the things we already know, but also secretly stole his first model and lover. I fear Auerbach will be even angrier now. But like Tess Jaray, I still hope that he may one day recognise another great artist.†

PART VI

Max, 1970–2001

16

1970–6

On the morning of 26 May 1970[1] there were three jobs to be filled in the German department. Among the candidates waiting to be seen was a tall young man called Gordon Turner, who had dressed with care for his interview, in a dark blue jacket, trousers and tie. In a corner of the room he saw another young man, smoking one cigarette after another and intent on reading a book. He had a fine full moustache like a late-1960s pop star, the top button of his shirt was undone, and his tie was only half knotted. Gordon was intrigued.

Eventually the other candidate looked up from his book. Gordon went over and introduced himself. Now he saw that the young man had alert dark eyes and a serious face that changed when he smiled. He spoke with a strong south German burr, in a humorous, self-deprecating tone. They touched briefly on his MA, and Gordon knew immediately that this was someone of wide reading and powerful intellect. He was captivated – and also worried, since they were applying for the same post.

Gordon came away from his interview feeling that he hadn't made any awful mistakes, but surely couldn't compete with that young man with the original mind and casually knotted tie. He was right: Max got the combined literature and language job. The other candidate that day, Cedric Williams, got the one in literature. But Gordon was offered the third post, in German language. He was delighted, of course, not least because the dark young man with the laugh in his voice would now be a colleague.

Another German sector friend, Richard Sheppard, met the new recruit when the term began.[2] In his recollection Max was shy and reserved at first. But he made a very good impression on them all: at first a serious impression, but soon a humorous one as well. He was not only funny himself but liked to laugh at other people's jokes. 'There was a lot of humour around UEA,' Richard says, 'and Max would get fits of giggles, and laugh fit to burst over a good one-liner.'

Very soon his new colleagues discovered his characteristic attitudes. 'He was very German,' Richard says, 'especially in his criticisms of Germany.' Whenever he visited there he seemed to meet only the most unpleasant people, whereas Richard's own experiences were quite the opposite. 'Bourgeois' was Max's favourite term of opprobrium and 'sinister' one of his favourite words: 'This is all very sinister,' Richard remembers him saying – 'about events that struck me, in my English naiveté, as harmless or unexceptional.' He loved cooking and gardening and furniture restoring, and could even change the tyres on his car. In these early years he was, in Richard's words, 'a jolly bloke'.

Gordon agrees.[3] Max was easy-going and relaxed in the German language classes they taught together, breaking off regularly to tell a funny tale. His German, Gordon noted, was idiosyncratic, flavoured with phrases from French, Dutch or Italian. They spoke German together from the first day to the last, Gordon with the Munich accent he'd learned in his teens, Max in his rich voice with its rolling Allgäu 'r'. Gordon can still do Max's voice today, intoning 'The reverse of melancholy is irony' in such a lifelike way that I find myself looking behind me. And always Max smoked, mostly strong, unfiltered German cigarettes called Roth-Händle. Roth-Händle were made of dark tobacco like Gauloises and were lethal. There were many slang names for them in Germany: '*Lungentorpedo*', for instance, and because of the dark red packet, '*Roter Tod*', the Red Death. Max would have known them all.

In 1970 the University of East Anglia – always known as UEA – was all of seven years old.[4] It had been built on the site of Norwich's golf course, whose bunkers, in those early days, were still visible. The School of European Studies (EUR) had begun in a log cabin (to quote Richard Sheppard) near the Earlham Road, and had moved into the new Arts Block just three years before Max arrived.

When Max joined EUR there were several other native German speakers already there: Franz Kuna in the German sector, for instance, an Austrian who became a friend, but went home in 1976.[5] There were also two German-Jewish refugees: Willi Guttsmann, UEA's first librarian, and Werner Mosse, dean of the school. Max got on very well with quiet, reserved Guttsmann (but probably never knew that he had lost both his parents in the Holocaust, since Guttsmann never spoke of such things). Mosse was another matter – a brilliant but difficult man, who fell out with his department in 1972 and referred to them ever after as 'my former colleagues'. He was also famously paranoid and saw plots everywhere. Max would regale friends with his report of being invited to dinner with Mosse in his newly built house, which still had a sign outside that read 'Plot 75'.

The other important members of EUR for Max were two of his interviewing panel:[6] James MacFarlane, who became his thesis supervisor, and Brian Rowley, the professor of German. MacFarlane – always known as Mac, or Big Mac – was a large, warm and welcoming figure to whom Max grew quite close. Rowley was the kind and liberal head of the German sector. He was a birdwatcher and collector of old postcards, and a most sympathetic character as well. Finally, in the early 1970s there was a small group of Austrian specialists, consisting of Kuna, Keith Pollard, a Stifter expert who'd been appointed in the first year, and now Cedric Williams, who would publish a book on Austrian literature in 1974. Max had grown up closer to Austria than to most of Germany, he often let people think he was Austrian, or even told them he was, and he'd been interested in Austrian writing ever since his work with Ernst Alker at Fribourg. This mini-department of Austrianists was thus a natural home for him, and especially after Williams' departure a few years later, he'd move increasingly into Austrian literature. He found this main focus of his career now, ready and waiting – and quite unique among British universities, which mostly treated Austrian writing as a minor province of German. One more instance (perhaps the last) of his good luck.

But the greatest good luck of all had been finding the university itself. No other place and time could have suited him better.[7] From its founding moment UEA had set out to break the mould – *Do Different* was its motto. It was un-hierarchical, un-bureaucratic and interdisciplinary, with subjects organised into capacious schools rather than individual departments. In those early years its teachers were almost all young. Its students came from every level of society, most of them from Max's own. The basic teaching unit was the seminar rather than the lecture, which meant that staff and students came to know each other well. Professors were supporters, not dictators, and junior staff – even beginners – were free to invent courses, to experiment, to do their own thing. It was an intellectual climate that was, as Richard Sheppard says, 'in the best sense, anarchic ... and unbelievably free'. And all of this in Norwich, the most complete medieval city in Britain, and in Norfolk, a remote rural idyll until the M11 motorway was built and the main roads improved in the 1980s and 1990s. In a piece he published in the travel section of *Die Zeit* in 1974, Max took his German readers on an early *Rings of Saturn* tour through East Anglia, urging them not to miss the beautiful churches, villages and great houses. What first strikes you about Norwich, he wrote, is the presence of its past.[8] That is what he always sought, and he had found it.

As soon as he knew that he'd got the job, he replied to an advertisement he'd seen for a flat in the country, but got no reply. Those were the glory days of flat-hunting, as of job-hunting, and he went off on his summer holiday unconcerned. On his return he looked in earnest for a home. He tried the university lodgings agency and four others, but found nothing to his taste. Then he remembered the advert he'd seen in the summer. He tried it again – and the flat was still available. Thus it was that he found Abbotsford, and in early October he and his wife moved in.

All this he reported gaily to Kasus in broad Allgäuerisch.[9] We live in the servants' quarters, he wrote. But it wasn't bad, since there was a tennis court and two horses they could ride (this seems very unlikely), plus a fine view of the countryside. So things weren't going too badly – even the work wasn't terribly hard, though he'd be happier with no work at all.

As he also explained, there was an auction every Friday, and he'd just bought a spruce-wood cupboard for eight shillings. In 'Dr Henry Selwyn' Elli gives her new tenants permission to make other minor alterations, and they immediately paint the bathroom and its footbridge white. Max almost certainly did the same, and more: he's painting the bedroom Mud Brown, he tells Kasus. Every year he uses at least a hundred litres of paint, and he wonders when it will end. It never would; the Sebalds' houses were always freshly and beautifully painted. (We can be sure, however, that 'Mud Brown' was a joke.)

'Not bad' was an Allgäu joke too. Abbotsford and its garden were quietly beautiful, with just the sense of a peaceful history he needed. And Wymondham was an unchanged village, as picturesque as those he'd recommended to his German readers. It was the home of the grand, half-ruined Wymondham Abbey, which Benedictines had founded eight centuries before. Abbotsford was nearby, and Dr and Mrs Buckton – the real Dr Selwyn and Elli – were much involved with it: especially 'the rather indomitable Mrs B', Gordon Turner says, who 'held the members of Wymondham Abbey parish in her thrall. Not a person to be crossed, I recall, and quite a contrast to the mild-mannered gentleman who was Dr B.'[10] But Dr Buckton too, as Gordon remembers him, was quite the country squire, with his Norfolk tweeds, his church fêtes in the garden, and a county life of hunting and shooting. Rhoades Buckton was a devoted naturalist and a lonely man, and touched Max in a way he never forgot. But the rest, as always with W. G. Sebald, was fiction.

Rosa and Georg were still renting their flat in Sonthofen, and would do so till the end of their lives, like most Germans. But Max had evidently picked up the English wish for a home of his own, and by the end of the first term he and his wife began looking for one.[11] Their first hope – an English idea as well, or just Max's – was to find an old house. But for that, they discovered, the salary of an assistant lecturer would not suffice. Eventually they settled for a new one, on a brand new housing estate near the centre of Wymondham. The Turners were already living there; the Sebalds had seen their comfortable, practical home on several occasions, and around April of 1971 they bought the house a few doors down from their friends.

Now a new marathon of cleaning and painting began. Max drilled holes in the wrong places and hammered nails in crookedly (he claimed), but by early May it was more or less done, and Kasus and his wife Saint Kristina (Max was teasing his friend now) were cordially invited to Number 38 Orchard Way, Wymondham. It would be his home for the next four years.

He was well-tuned to English distinctions by now: 'You can guarantee that a street with a name like that will be full of new houses,' he remarked to one of his classes.[12] Nonetheless, the Sebalds were happy there too. They joined the social round in the estate and made friends with neighbours.[13] They continued to attend the Friday-morning auctions in Wymondham, spreading their net now to other small towns, and to Norwich itself; snapping up old pine pieces, stripping them down or occasionally repainting them, and setting on them a few striking things they'd picked up cheaply in junk shops. Several of their neighbours started to join them on their auction rounds, and before long they found themselves the interior-design gurus of Orchard Way. Max would write his Ph.D. here, and his first (unpublished) poetry collection; here his daughter would be born and his first dog acquired. Being Max, he would have dark times here too. But he was young, and hope would always return. After Kingston Road, Wymondham was his best home.

It had another advantage as well: despite its seclusion, Wymondham was only ten miles or so from Norwich, an easy twenty-five-minute drive to the university. Curiously, though, this wasn't only an advantage. It was also a danger.

Max had got his driving licence in August 1967,[14] a month before he married, no doubt as part of his preparation for grown-up life. At the same time his father gave him a car: a white VW estate, in which he and his new wife drove to England to start their married life. No sooner had they arrived, however, than some time in the autumn of 1967, Max had his first accident. The other car was unscathed, but his own cost £48 to repair – over £800 in today's money, which suggests quite considerable damage.

Apart from 'a crash', he recorded no details of this event. But about a year later came a second. He and his wife had visited the Tabberts in Reutlingen and were driving towards Stuttgart when a car overtook them just as another was hurtling towards them on the other side. Max managed to swerve, and somehow disaster was narrowly avoided. It wasn't his fault. But I think back to Josef's crash in his novel, surely based on a real event as well. In some mysterious way, Max Sebald and car accidents were connected.

Now, in Wymondham, the connection becomes a bit clearer.[15] Max and Gordon took it in turn to drive each other to and from the university when their teaching schedules coincided. Over the four years they were neighbours, Max drove Gordon many times. And Gordon recalls several near misses.

On one occasion, for instance, they ended up half in a ditch or a driveway, facing the wrong way. On another Max was talking volubly – and didn't notice until the last moment that a tractor had turned into the road in front of them. He slammed on the brakes, the car went into a spin, and they ended up in the entrance to the field from which the tractor had emerged seconds before.

The reason, Gordon says, was always the same: Max would get distracted, and take his eyes off the road. He would be telling a story, or pointing out something in the landscape, and forget what he was doing. It was as though the pictures in his mind were all that existed. As they always were.

Alongside preparing his courses, Max's major aim was to finish his Ph.D. He'd begun it the year before in Manchester. Now, on 9 October, he registered it at UEA.[16] He was in a hurry, as usual, and applied for permission to submit his thesis in three years instead of four. He submitted it on the dot in August 1973, was promptly promoted to lecturer, vivaed the next April and awarded the degree in July.

This was quite a remarkable achievement. First of all in its speed, and second because, after only six years in England, he wrote it in English, as was required. That is, he wrote it first in German, and actually seems to have finished the German version by the summer of 1972. He then tried to translate it, together with Gordon, but after a few months of discussing every word they gave up, and Max simply rewrote it anew in English. In clear, lively, vernacular English, according to Richard Sheppard. He asked many people to check it, especially his colleague Cedric Williams, whom he thanked warmly at the start of the thesis. But it was Max who wrote it. His last translator, Anthea Bell, said that he could have written his English translations himself; he'd already proven her right in 1973.

It was also another kind of achievement: like his Sternheim work, his dissertation on Döblin was as unacceptable as he could make it.[17] It too was an aggressive attack, this time on a famous and much-loved author (though Max exempted Döblin's most famous book, *Alexanderplatz*, from the general condemnation). It too took a biographical approach, arguing that Döblin had destroyed his authenticity just as Sternheim had – not only by abandoning his Jewish roots, but by converting to Catholicism (even worse than poor Sternheim, who had stopped at Lutheranism). To these arguments Max added an important new one: that because of his pathologies, Döblin's attempt to warn against violence and horror in his work turned into the opposite, a wallowing in them, even a glorification of them. This was, in fact, the most lasting insight of the thesis, and a major influence on Max's own writing, in which horror is always present, but never presented.

The Ph.D. also continued the sweeping, hyperbolic tone of *Carl Sternheim*. It made little reference to other Döblin scholars, but presented often extreme suggestions, backed by selective and tendentious quotation. The footnotes – always Max's bugbear – were unchecked by his advisors, and according to Richard Sheppard are packed with errors (and probably inventions). Like his MA, in sum, it should have been referred, or even failed. But Max 'got away with blue murder', as Richard says with a grin. Once again his examiners recognised the originality and power of his work, and despite its glaring flaws, passed it.

As soon as the German version was finished he began sending it to publishers; when the English version was done he tried British ones too. By 1974 he had amassed six rejections. Finally, during his study leave in 1978 he rewrote it again, it was accepted by Klett Verlag – another prestigious press – and came out in 1980. Just as with Sternheim, the book was harsher and more extreme than the dissertation. In the meantime he had read Klaus Schröter's notorious 1978 biography of Döblin, which accused him of being a racist and anti-Semite. This was grist to Max's mill. *The Myth of Destruction in the Work of Döblin* accused Döblin of anti-Semitism, fascism, and paving the way for Nazism by glorifying violence, and added an accusation of repressed homosexuality for good measure.

The response was like that to Sternheim, but worse. There were only three reviews, all fairly negative, one excoriating. The excoriating one was written not by an obscure Russian scholar but by a distinguished German professor who was the leading authority on Döblin. He systematically destroyed Max's case. Max did not reply. His book hung on in print for ten years, then disappeared.

What was going on? He was continuing his guerrilla war against *Germanistik*, which universally lauded Döblin. But that can't be all.

Added together, his Sternheim and Döblin campaigns lasted nearly twenty years.[18] There is something obsessive here.

Richard Sheppard identifies it, I think: 'The problem of assimilation long occupied [Max] as the heart of literary failure.'[19] Now, in 1972, he wrote to the Jewish scholar and writer Gershom Scholem, asking for support on an assimilation project he was working on, explaining that he first encountered 'the devastating consequences of this process on a German writer' in Sternheim and continues to see it in Döblin.[20] Now, therefore, he wants to write a series of essays about it – and he adds a wildly ambitious list of names, including Heine, Kraus and Kafka. Nothing, in fact, came of this assimilation project. But it occupied him for several more years.

Why? Why did he blame the literary failure (as he saw it) of his two German-Jewish subjects on their betrayal (again as he saw it) of their Jewish origins, and why did it make him so angry? Was it something to do with his fear of betraying his own origins, as I've suggested before? Was it anger at the Germans who forced them into betrayal if they were to have any chance of success? Whatever it was, it drove him hard throughout his twenties. Only in his thirties would it let him go.

Richard Sheppard points out another feature of Max's attack on Döblin:[21] that it is the reverse of what we find in his literary work. In both the Ph.D. and the book, Max attacks Döblin's irrationalism on the basis of an Enlightenment rationalism; whereas in his literary work he condemns Enlightenment rationalism as the destroyer of nature and our place in it, and is drawn to a form of mystic irrationalism himself.

I think this is right. I think that Max himself was confused during these years, battling his own irrational mind. He could accept it only much later, when he had distinguished it from the darkness of Nazism. He spent his youth confused, in other words, which is how most of us spend it, one way or another. His way was to write two wrong books before he could write the right ones.

The other place in which he waged his one-man war against *Germanistik* was the EUR's *Journal of European Studies*, founded in the spring of 1971. He wrote seventeen aggressive articles and reviews in it over the next years. Finally, by the mid-1980s, his long battle against the tainted Germanist establishment was over, and he began to write quite differently – positive, unacademic essays, almost indistinguishable from his literary work. These he no longer published in the *JES*, but in international journals like the *Modern Language Review.*[22]

As Uwe Schütte says, he could never have published his violent pieces anywhere but in the ultra-liberal pages of the *JES*, in the heady early days of UEA.[23] John Flower, one of its founders and early editors, remembers that he occasionally indulged in his other habit of making up references as well, but the editors turned a blind eye. Sebaldian good luck once again. But I agree with Schütte when he says that 'Sebald's reviews reveal a very angry young man indeed';[24] and when he was angry, I've guessed, he was also unhappy. I think he was often unhappy, even in his first years at UEA: writing his wrong books, fighting his own mind.

As a teacher Max showed none of the aggressiveness of the *JES* pieces he was pouring out at the time.[25] On the contrary, he praised books by Grass, Böll and even Döblin to his students (though they read only *Alexanderplatz*, the one work he unreservedly admired). He required little background reading, except for the occasional unorthodox suggestion, such as Wolfgang Hildesheimer's biography of Mozart. His seminars were more like conversations than lessons, in which he listened as much as he spoke, turning callow questions into intelligent ones and giving thoughtful answers. At the same time he was challenging and subversive. He set an essay on 'Sexuality, Perversion, Violence' and said that it could be any length, 'a book or an aphorism', but if it was an aphorism it had better be a good one. No one remembers him as melancholy, except in what underlay his lugubrious voice and deadpan humour – very like the tone of his writing, as those who read his books later would notice. There was always laughter in his classes. One student, though, having asked why he'd written about Sternheim, whom he clearly detested, recalls Max's reply: 'Because these people are so awful,' followed by a laugh 'which seemed to me at the time like Beckett's authentic laugh at despair'. Another remembers him likening teaching to schizophrenia: we have different masks for different situations, he said, and are consequently different people.

He made, as always, a striking physical impression. 'He was elegant, enigmatic and unattainable, with his horn-rimmed glasses, gaucho moustache and long belted raincoat,' says one early student. Another remembers that he was 'elegantly casual' – almost never in a jacket and never with a tie, mostly in a polo-neck sweater and dark trousers. He was less than a decade older than most of them, but seemed to come from a different, more brilliant age. At the Fasching parties held by the German Society he came in a series of fantastical disguises, partly for fun, and partly to remain unrecognised, because as one undergraduate puts it, 'At the time, by my reckoning, 95 per cent of the female students fancied him something rotten.'

He didn't talk about his family, either past or present, in these early years, and his students knew nothing about him personally. But he said many memorable things. That literature, for example, was the best way to know oneself, and that to write about one's country one needed to be away from it. That it is easier to tell when someone is lying on the telephone. That the Catholic Church was a good opponent of communism, but not of fascism, because it was too like it. That he liked German Chancellor Willy Brandt for kneeling in apology in Poland. That 'the concentration camp is the logical extension of capitalism' and 'a medical rep with his pocket stuffed with biros is like a general with all his medals'. That the survivor is always guilty. That 'Austrians make good anti-Semites but lousy Nazis. In Germany it was the other way around.'

Over the next years he fired off dozens of his comic dialect letters to his friends back home – to ROP in Reutlingen, to Albert in Freiburg, and most often of all to Kasus,[26] who was then in Freising near Munich. He signed them with a wild array of cod-antique names – Sixtus Bonifaz Meir (former Rabbi of Novara), for instance, or Sebaldus Mothamiker, inventor of the telescope. In one he informs Kasus that his new project is on the African Saltpeter Bird, quoting a great work of 1042, and adds a postscript warning his friend that a vast ice block fell on France in 1510, so he'd better be careful where he stands. In another he says he's back in the Bunzrepublik (his debunking version of the Bundesrepublik, i.e. West Germany) and *le cafard* has got hold of him again.

One of the wildest – the one Kasus is most often asked to read to Sebald fans – is the Sauerkraut Letter. In it Max proposes that the two start a small sauerkraut factory together. They'll weave carpets out of sauerkraut, make sauerkraut juice for communion, and construct a whole orchestra (including conductor) out of sauerkraut. Sauerkraut, he pronounces, is good on the head for migraines and somewhere else

for impotence. If things don't work out at the Hunifersity he'll come
back to the Bunzrepublik and open a sauerkraut shop.

When Kasus reads out these letters of the 1970s in his thickest Allgäu
accent, his audiences laugh till they hurt. And the letters are indeed
wonderfully funny. But once again there is surely something different
underneath. The mad riffs really are a little mad, the piling up of comic
names not quite comic ('*died 1043*'). It seems to me that Max Sebald
had a violent need to invent. And until he found a form of writing
that fulfilled that need, he tried to do it in other ways – through his
disobedient academic writing, through his witty letter writing. But
neither sprang him from his trap. That is the feeling I get from these
letters, when I stop laughing. He is in a trap and hasn't found the
way out.

In July 1972 his daughter was born and his life changed. He had an
extra responsibility now. And he wanted to be the perfect father:[27] never
dictate to her, never invade her, as he had felt dictated to and invaded as
a child. Naturally he was bound to fail, and every time he was impatient
or rebuked her, he felt guilty.

A year later he acquired a dog as well:[28] a seven-week-old golden
Labrador, so light gold he looked white. They named him Jodok
(pronounced 'Yodok', which sounded to their English friends like 'Your
dog'). He fitted into the family easily, becoming the first vegetarian dog
anyone had ever met. His doggy ways fascinated Max – the way he peed
twenty times on the same spot, and turned around ten times before he
settled down to sleep. He has a very gentle face, Max told Kasus, he
forgets bad deeds and remembers good ones. No animal is as devoted as
a dog, he wrote. From now on he would never be without one.

He had a complete little family now – a wife, a child and a dog. It's
what he had wanted, and was part of the happiness of those years. But
it was also a burden, on top of his teaching and the thesis he was writing
at breakneck speed. He didn't cope well with burdens, or indeed with
anything. And the wider world around him was starting to go wrong
as well.

The turning point was, I think, 1973: the year of the oil crisis, which
started a downturn for the whole of the West. For Britain it meant
the price of petrol and heating oil shooting up. By early 1974 there
was a miners' strike and a three-day-week ruling to conserve electricity.

English people, Gertrud was informed, were foraging in the woods for camel dung. One could only hope that the university would soon close and he could finish his work on the garden.

The university did not close, but it was not wholly a joke.[29] The visionary new foundations like UEA had hardly begun when student unrest after 1968 made them the object of official odium. And now inflation caused by the oil crisis meant serious financial difficulties as well, and increasing attacks on pure academic study in favour of learning that would lead to jobs. All this impacted more on the humanities than the sciences, and most of all on those pointless subjects, the modern languages. From the start, EUR was the most exposed.

Max's letters to Gertrud and Kasus of late 1973 and early 1974 show the effect on him of these stresses and strains. In all of them he refers to the comet Kohoutek, which appeared close to the earth in December 1973 for the first time in 150,000 years.[30] The German group Kraftwerk sang about it, an American cult said it meant the end of the world. Awaiting it, Max wrote about monstrous planetary alignments, unimaginable geological disasters and an imminent ice age – sounding, despite his droll tone, as apocalyptic as he ever would. In the event the world survived and Kohoutek retired for another 75,000 years. Its disappearance could bring a bad time too, Max told Gertrud.[31]

He told her something else as well: he'd had another accident. This time it was the fault of a pair of pheasants, who were sitting in the middle of the road as he came round a curve, and he'd had to brake violently. When he looked up he was in a ditch, the engine had cut out and the radio was playing Beethoven. As usual (except for once) he escaped without a scratch.

In fact, says Richard Sheppard,[32] his friend had had a melancholy, apocalyptic strain from the moment they met. Several of his early articles were already preoccupied with mortality. He always asked the same question: *Does the world have any meaning? Is there a hidden order in it, or are we in the midst of chaos?* At first he still gave a positive answer, but it was becoming harder.

We have a few more glimpses of him in these years. In 1973, for instance, EUR hosted a German conference which several of his Manchester colleagues attended. Eda found him changed.[33] He was more serious, she says, less approachable: 'He seemed out of sorts, and didn't engage with his old Manchester friends.' And in 1975 he interviewed a visiting poet from East Germany, Reiner Kunze. In the film of the interview that was made for the new Audiovisual Archive he still looks at least a decade younger than his thirty-one years. But he is very quiet and contained, and his eyes are melancholy. His most animated question is about the use of 'I' in poetry. 'Is it a kind of self-therapy?' he asks. 'I wouldn't use that word,' Kunze replies. 'It suggests pathology.' 'Ah,' says Max, and goes still quieter.[34]

Part of the problem was that, despite everything, he wasn't sure he could settle in England.[35] They're so *insular*, he told Kasus. They thought his first name was Winifred and his second name anything but Sebald – Webald, Febald, Ebald or Sebalb. When he stated his destination on the bus or at the railway station they said 'Pardon me?' When the postman knocked with another letter from abroad he swore 'Damn foreigners!' (That was surely paranoia.) When ROP visited them in Wymondham, Max's wife said she was so glad – at last he could talk to someone who understood him. He'd been very down recently.

In October 1974 he wrote his wildest letter of all to Kasus, either using a piece of paper his daughter had scribbled on, or letting her scribble over it afterwards. He never knows which language he's speaking any more, he says – English, German, academic lingo… So he's thinking of returning to the Fatherland. He wants nothing to do with the German Germanists, whose brown shirts are still visible. Instead he's coming to Munich in June, for a week's course in language teaching at the Goethe Institute. Maybe that'll bring great new opportunities.[36]

Just as in Manchester in 1968, his EUR friends advised him against this plan.[37] In vain. In February 1975 he formally applied, and in June attended the selection course. His application was accepted. He applied for a year's leave of absence from UEA – still leaving his options open – and sold the Orchard Way house. Followed by the removal van, he drove the VW (without incident) to Coburg, where his family would live with his wife's parents for the year – including, after some months in quarantine, Jodok.

Having settled them there, he returned alone for the autumn term. For the next eleven weeks he lived on the top floor of the Turners' house in Norwich, where they'd moved from Wymondham the year before. They'd decorated the room with curtains and a desk from his house in Orchard Way so that he'd feel at home, and he did, entertaining the family with his stories and cooking them a vegetarian meal once a week. Nonetheless, he suffered from his old kidney trouble all term. Wheat beer, he told Gordon, was good for the kidneys, and he drank it, only to feel wretched the next day. The pain was sometimes so bad that he may even have spent a few days in hospital. But the decision had been made. When the term ended he packed his bags and left for Munich.

In fact the whole thing almost didn't happen.

Not even the German economic miracle could escape the scythe of the oil crisis. Just six weeks or so before the Goethe course was due to begin, the trainees of 1976 received a letter to say it was cancelled. Several of them, including Max, protested vigorously and with patent justice, and the course was restored. But the uncertainty had decimated it: the class of 1976 would consist of only five people, instead of the usual fifteen to twenty.[38]

This near collapse of his plans was not a good start. Neither were his living conditions – and we know by now how crucial those were to him. He'd found a room in Olympiapark, the 1972 Olympic Village, which had been turned into flats and bungalows.[39] I don't know how close he was to Connollystrasse, where the massacre of the Israeli athletes had taken place only four years before. But he had just one room: probably a small one, probably high in one of the vast tower blocks. That was quite enough to oppress him. And it did.

Things looked up slightly when he met the people he was to work with. He liked the head of the teacher-training programme, Korbinian Braun, who'd once been a carpenter,[40] and Braun's representative, Kristin Völker, even better. He'd met Kristin before, when she was at the Goethe Institute in Manchester. And now here she was in Munich, the organiser and mentor for their group, and spending much of her time with them. That must have been a help when he first arrived, and indeed throughout. He and Kristin became fast friends.

That the group had ended up so small was an advantage as well: they could get to know each other. Sabine Hagemann had been working with the ASA (a German version of VSO – Voluntary Service Overseas) in Ethiopia; Manfried Wüst was an Old Testament scholar from the University of Tübingen; Ulrich Gründler was a student of East Asian politics; and Gabriele Irwin was a beautiful German-American who (it was rumoured) was escaping some love trouble back home. They

were a highly individualistic bunch; and the most individualistic of all
was Max.[41]

1. Ulrich Gründler 2. Max 3. Sabine Hagemann 4. Gabriele Irwin 5. Manfried Wüst.

Ulrich Gründler died some years ago, and Gabriele Irwin disappeared
back to America. But both surviving members of the group have strong
memories of him. Max, says Manfried Wüst,[42] was the most original
among them, who spiced their days with his ironic, biting wit. Manfried
admired Max's brilliant talk and sharp observation, but was never close
to him; there was always, he says, a certain distance between them.
What he didn't know was that Max the lapsed Catholic would have
been wary of a theology student from the start; and I imagine he was
wary of Max the iconoclast as well. He felt his charm, but kept his own
counsel about the Goethe Institute, in which he would go on to have a
long and successful career.

Sabine Hagemann got a bit closer.[43] Max's focus, she says, was on
theatre and film. He didn't talk about writing to her, just about being
a literary academic. But he was clearly a quirky academic, interested
in the 'aesthetic of error' – he was making a collection of linguistic

mistakes, which he showed her. And every Monday morning, before classes started, he would write an impromptu poem on the blackboard about the beauties of the world outside, compared to the grey of the Institute building.

He said almost nothing about his background, except that his father was an old Nazi. By contrast he talked a great deal about his small daughter. He went to Coburg every weekend to see his family, and came back with endless stories about her: how he'd given her a camera, for instance – she was all of four years old at the time – with which she took wonderfully creative photos of feet on stairs. About himself he said so little that he was a mystery. Was 'Max', for instance, really his name? Hadn't he hinted that he had another? The others were so intrigued that one day when he left his jacket in the classroom they went through its pockets and found his passport: 'Winfried Georg', no mention of Max. They speculated for days, but didn't dare to ask him. The mystery remained.

It was Kristin Völker who got closest.[44] Not only did she know that he wrote poems, but he gave her several. And when they got bored in a lecture they would send each other little notes. Once she asked him if he'd read a book that someone had mentioned. Certainly not! Max replied. I never read authors with alliterative names.

Kristin remembers too that the group saw several films together – Wim Wenders' *Kings of the Road* and Joseph Losey's *Accident*, for example, both of which sound like Max choices to me. And Sabine remembers that they went together to a live show: Jérôme Savary's *Grand Magic Circus*, an anarchic drag extravaganza, packed with nudity and surreal satire. That was definitely Max's choice – indeed organised by him, no doubt to shock his colleagues. Sabine wasn't shocked; it was a fabulously weird, poetic show, she says, and in the intermission she and Max acted out one of the scenes together. My mind – like the others' at the time, I imagine – boggled.

So he had some good times in his Goethe year. But almost from the start he began to feel his old unease at living in Germany.[45] And almost from the start, too, he began to chafe under the Goethe regime.

Already at the end of January he was complaining (one hopes with his usual hyperbole) about the 280-page protocol they were required to read.[46] He mocked a professor who made a formal complaint about someone *taking his eraser*, and after only five weeks wanted to leave. On one unforgettable occasion he reverted to his schoolboy self, standing up and challenging a lecturer: What use, he demanded, was an explanation that was twice as long as its subject? Sabine felt that he had really decided for England from the start, and was only giving Germany a last test 'because he didn't want to live without reflection'. Manfried too felt very soon that he wouldn't stay. Yet stay he did, for the whole six months of the course. Despite everything, he hesitated to make a final choice. And his kidney trouble continued, so badly that one day in his horrible room, in pain or despair, he tore a bookshelf off the wall.

The second half of the training was practical: a period spent teaching German to foreign-language speakers in Germany. Sabine was sent to Freiburg, Manfried first to near Kassel, then to Radolfzell on Lake Constance. Perhaps if Max had been sent to one of these, things might even now have turned out differently. But he wasn't. He was sent to Schwäbisch Hall, a sleepy town in the heart of Swabia. Swabia is famous for its ultra-cleanliness and orderliness, the German virtues Max found both actually and metaphorically the most disturbing. Nonetheless, he packed his bags once more and prepared for life in Schwäbisch Hall.

Before that, though, he did something that shows how uncertain (or secretly certain) he was: he bought a house in England.

He was due to start in Schwäbisch Hall at the end of June.[47] In early June he and his wife were back in Norwich. In a nearby village they saw the kind of house they'd always dreamed of: an early-Victorian rectory, with lovely light rooms and a large garden. It had been empty for several years, and was in such a decayed state that they could actually afford it. As his future was still unclear, Max told Kristin Völker, he had made an offer on it; if he decided to stay in Germany, he could withdraw.

It's true that offers can be withdrawn, but I doubt very much that he would have let the Old Rectory slip through his fingers. He knew it would take years of work,[48] but that would bring it even closer to his dream. And the house was mysterious, perhaps even haunted… When he and his wife first saw it, he would say, it was deep in snow.* And in

---

*Not June, then. Perhaps they'd seen it before. Or more likely, of course, this was a Max fiction.

the snow leading to the door were footsteps, which went in but not out. Yet inside there wasn't a living soul.

The teaching practice in Germany varied: Manfried Wüst did two years, Sabine Hagemann did four.[49] Max expected to be in Schwäbisch Hall for two to three years. In the event he lasted seven weeks. On 20 August he wrote to the secretary-general of the Goethe Institute and resigned.

Over the next months he gave contradictory and often rude reasons for his decision. Prime among them was the *Öde* – soullessness – and *spiessige Atmosphäre* – petit-bourgeois atmosphere – of Schwäbisch Hall.[50] To ROP he said the money wasn't enough; to Kasus he said it was the only thing that was better. To Sabine Hagemann he said that he'd hoped to teach at least at intermediate level, but they'd stuck him with the beginners, which he couldn't stand. To her and to Kristin Völker he sent word-paintings of his Schwäbisch Hall colleagues – wicked caricatures, but so accurate that when Sabine went there some time later, she recognised everyone. The secretary-general of the day didn't take offence at his resignation. Dr Sebald had made the right decision, he said (perhaps thinking as much of the Goethe as of Max himself); and he added several kind words about him, Max reported to Kristin.[51]

To her he gave perhaps his truest reason.[52] The Goethe life, he said, was that of a wanderer. But he was already a wanderer, and he wanted to choose his own destinations.

By the start of the academic year 1976–7 he was back where he'd started. They were camping in a friend's house in Norwich while the heavy work was done on the Old Rectory, and he no longer remembered what it was like to live in his own home.[53] They were back in cold, rainy Britain, he wrote to Kasus, and all around were signs of decline.

It was no better at the university. Student numbers were declining, he told Kristin.[54] Some colleagues laboured frantically to devise new and more attractive programmes, while others just waited for UEA to be closed down. He had no more hope than they did, but doing nothing must be avoided, so he joined the frantic labourers. For once, he was not inventing or exaggerating. By late 1976 the threat that UEA might be closed down was real.[55] The glory days were over.

Now he feared that he'd made another mistake, he admitted. Might he not have amounted to something at the Goethe after all, given the nice things the secretary-general had said? Well – who could tell. If it all went down the toilet in England, they'd go back to the Bunzrepublik and open a shop in Coburg.

In *Austerlitz* the narrator gives up a botched attempt to settle in Germany and returns to England in 1976. He knows he should tell Austerlitz of this change of plan, but somehow he doesn't, and they lose touch for twenty years. His failure, he says, may have come from the fact that 'soon after my return I went through a difficult period which dulled my sense of other people's existence, and from which I only very gradually emerged by turning back to the writing I had long neglected'.[56]

That would be the story of Max's next years.

17

1977–88

Nel mezzo del cammin di nostra vita
mi ritrovai per una selva oscura
ché la diritta via era smarrita
Dante, *Divina Commedia*, Canto 1

A year after his return he was still brooding about his decision.[1] And three years later he was still repeating his complaints about the British. In railway stations, he told Gertrud, they look as though they're about to die if you ask for a ticket abroad. A few years after that he made a serious move once more.

In 1982 his old friend Paolo wrote to say that he was coming to England on leave (to the delight of his students and colleagues, he reported).[2] By then Max had been at UEA for twelve years and was still a mere lecturer, with no promotion in sight. He began to discuss with Paolo the possibility of doing a belated *Habilitation*,* in order to be able to work at a German university after all.

For a while he did nothing, and thought about Switzerland instead. But after fifteen years he was *still* a lecturer, and his first academic book was about to be published. So in August 1985 he applied to Paolo's university, Hamburg, for leave to submit a *Habilitation*. Leave was granted. He entered his newborn book, *The Description of Unhappiness*, as his dissertation, and in April 1986 received his *Habilitation*.

---

*A second doctorate after the Ph.D., required to qualify for a chair in a German university.

This whole procedure was slightly strange.[3] Paolo had certainly pushed his friend's application through, and was one of his examiners. It was all very much in the spirit of Group 64 – that is to say, in accordance with no rules but their own. Still, *The Description of Unhappiness* was as good as any normal dissertation, indeed better. And however it had happened, it was official: Max was qualified to teach in the German system at last.

In October he was finally promoted to senior lecturer,[4] no doubt as a result of his book. Still he tried. Germany itself remained difficult, though he'd had hopes of Würzburg, he told Gertrud.[5] In early 1986 he applied to Bern, later that year to Lausanne. Nothing came of these efforts. Then, suddenly, further promotions followed in quick succession – to reader in 1987, to full professor in 1988. And by then he'd found another way out. So once again he stayed.

Ever since Manchester – probably ever since school – he'd dreamed of a life of leisure. But the more you did, he wrote to Gertrud, the more you had to do.[6] And now, from his mid-thirties on, he worked hardest of all, as though he was driven.

One huge job that awaited him in the autumn of 1976 was his house.[7] The technical work required professionals, but his salary wouldn't stretch that far, so one of the first things he did was to take on a translation for the extra money. Then in early 1977 he and the family moved in and took over the rest of the labouring themselves. For the next two years, apart from his teaching and academic writing, Max was roof-tiling, floor-laying and taming the wild garden, while at the same time translating into German a hefty book (by Richard Evans, who would become a friend, and soon one of the most distinguished historians of Germany in Britain). Finally both were done. In 1979 *Sozialdemokratie und Frauenemanzipation im deutschen Kaiserreich (Women and Social Democracy in Imperial Germany)* came out,[8] and the Old Rectory was perfect. It would be so to the end: the image of Max's dream of rest in the peaceful English countryside.

The reality was different. As soon as he'd returned, he'd thrown himself into another strenuous activity – the effort to save the university, and in particular EUR, from financial collapse.[9] That meant everyone's least favourite job: serving on committees. Over the next decade his committee workload alone was quite astounding, from admissions and planning committees to the Working Party on Teaching Rationalisation (how he must have loved that one!). Already in 1979 he dreamed of retirement, or of retreating to an asylum like Walser.

From 1978 on, the effort to increase student numbers in German was (temporarily) successful and his teaching load increased as well.[10] Half his classes were still in German language, and after his Goethe experience he rededicated himself to those. But as always, most of his thought and work went into literature. Between 1976 and 1988 he taught his usual courses on Kafka and post-war German writing, plus five new courses on drama and on German cinema (including *The Student of Prague* and the *Dr Mabuse* films, which would soon play important roles in *Vertigo* and 'Ambros Adelwarth').

He was now in his thirties and early forties; he had a decade of experience behind him and he was not yet a famous writer. So these were his peak teaching years as well.

The first glimpses we have of them were gathered by Gordon Turner for *Saturn's Moons*.[11] As ever, they show someone far outside the ordinary run. He brought everything into the discussion of literature – art and film, politics and philosophy, history and psychology. He talked about his childhood and made British students born long after the war understand the tragedy of his generation of Germans. He was ready, as ever, to break the rules, and dropped heavy hints to at least one student about which texts to prepare for exams. And as ever, again, many fell for him. One would always remember 'his lovely smile and sad eyes'; at the end of a year with him, another wrote to a friend 'A month without Max!' How would she survive?

A few years later Gordon introduced me to four students from the early part of this time. Anne, Ruth, Celia and Joan did German at UEA between 1977 and 1981. They'd arrived at a low point in the department's fortunes; their honours group was only a dozen or fifteen people, and they got to know Max well. They'd kept in touch, but hadn't met all together for years, and the reminiscences came pouring out.[12]

He was a good mimic, Celia remembered, and loved to mock pretension. His teaching was like his writing, going off at tangents, and his essay questions open-ended. With some teachers you knew the question and the answer, but, 'Max,' said Anne, 'only asked the question.' He was naturally 'cool and charismatic' and girls fell for him, but he hardly noticed. And though he told them stories of

Wertach – they remembered tales of laying out the dead, of winter and snow – he remained remote. Even though he was Anne's personal tutor, for instance, he never came to see her when she had to spend her first week in hospital; Gordon came instead. Max wasn't good at dealing with people – he was shy, Joan said – but very helpful with academic problems, Ruth remembered. On one occasion, for instance, their work was wrongly marked, and they complained to Max. 'Clearly the books were cooked,' he said, 'so we've re-cooked them,' and he gave them an average of their term marks instead. He was unconventional in every way. He brought his dog to the university and often to their seminars, where it lay among their feet. He began their first class on post-war German literature by saying that most of it was rubbish. And he didn't like the bare and ugly seminar rooms, so sometimes they met in his office, at his house, or in their study-bedrooms instead. Twice in their last year they met late, once at eleven at night; to make up for the late hour Max brought along a bottle of wine. (All of which would be quite unimaginable, and probably illegal, today.)

He would say, 'I must go home to my scribblings,' and Gordon had told them he wrote poetry, so they knew he was writing, but they didn't take it seriously.[13] Only looking back later did they realise he was working out in his teaching many of the ideas he would explore in his books, so that they were, in effect, his first readers. In his classes on Hans Erich Nossack and Alexander Kluge he said that they were the only ones who wrote adequately of the bombing of the cities, and that their witness-messenger style was the only possible and decent one; in his Kluge class in March 1981 he already asked, 'How to use this material creatively? Stage? Novel? Not film either…' In his classes on Peter Weiss and Jean Améry he said that 'only from these Jewish writers can we get any real insight' into the experience of the victims, and attacked Andersch for writing in bad taste and probably bad conscience. In his Kluge class he said, 'People lose the faculty of remembering. *This* is the function of literature.'

The group didn't feel he was depressed.[14] But they knew from his every word – about his past, about the books they were reading – that 'he was somehow a tortured soul'. He said, 'The disastrous past is still in everybody and still determines our lives to a great extent' – which wasn't true of them, but was clearly true of him. Once, talking of *The Investigation*, Weiss's 1965 play about the Frankfurt Auschwitz trials, he went on so long and obsessively that Anne scribbled in her notes: *This seminar is unbearable.* When I asked if he ever laughed, they all said no. Then they looked at each other, and agreed that he must have laughed – he certainly chuckled. But it's odd, they said, that's not how we remember him. He always had an air of sadness, Joan said, though he was often extremely funny. Anne remembered that when they met in his office he would sit in a low chair, almost hiding behind the coats hanging above him. When he talked about Kafka, Celia said, he was also talking about himself.

There was someone else I should meet, Gordon said. She was called Sarah Cameron, and she'd done German and history at UEA from 1983 to 1987. That was in the better time for EUR, when there were forty students in the German honours programme – more than double the number of the class of 1977.[15] But she'd got to know Max well.

He was right. Sarah remembers Max's dark office, 'The darkest on the dark side.' Like the others, she recalls how everything was connected in his teaching as in his writing, so that he brought in all sorts of things that at first sight had nothing to do with Germany: slavery, for instance, and apartheid. 'He spoke in sentences as long as the ones he would write,' she says, 'so long that you'd forget the subject, but nonetheless be held. His classes on film were as revelatory as those on literature, and on translation he was unforgettable: rigorous, profound, unsparing in the effort to pursue the author's meaning.'

Max was her personal tutor,[16] so she saw another side of him as well. She came from a difficult family background, with an abusive father and divorced parents, and took her troubles to him. For instance, she'd entered UEA under her father's name, but now that she was adult she wanted nothing more to do with him. I'd like to take my mother's name, she told Max. What did he think? 'Be what you want to be,' he replied, and she has had her mother's name ever since. At the end of her four years she went to him for the last time. She could apply to do an MA, she told him. 'What do you want for your life?' he asked. 'To be an academic?' She hadn't thought about her life, only about the next year. But now she knew: 'No,' she said. So she didn't apply for the MA, but to a law course instead, and became a lawyer. She owes that too, she says, to Max Sebald.

He didn't seem a 'tortured soul' to her, she says, 'Maybe because I was more tortured in those days than he was.' Her torture spoke to him, as did her grit and independence; she'd already done several jobs, and at the university she faced her many self-doubts and won through. He recognised her, I think, and felt at ease with her. That wouldn't happen often.

The years from 1976 to the mid-1980s were also a peak time of academic writing for him, when he produced (among others) the essays that went into *The Description of Unhappiness*. He wrote on dozens of writers, from Hofmannsthal to Canetti and Bernhard.[17] And throughout, over and over, on Kafka.

The Description of Unhappiness came out in 1985 and caused as usual quite a stir, mainly in response to its first chapter, a classic Sebald destruction of the famous author Adalbert Stifter as a compulsive eater, fetishist and pederast.[18] As Uwe Schütte says, this 'pathographic portrait' is less fact than fiction, and paves the way for the fictionalised portraits of writers in *Vertigo* and *The Rings of Saturn*. In this sense Max had been paving the way ever since Sternheim. But as Schütte also says, the book contained many remarkable pieces.[19] It got Max his *Habilitation* and probably his promotion, and established him as a scholar. He was proud of it, I suspect, and sent copies to his family and friends.[20]

Before that he had rewritten and finally published his Döblin dissertation, and sent that to family and friends as well.[21] And despite its poor reception, he remained engaged in Döblin scholarship for several years. In December 1981 he went to an international Döblin conference in New York (the trip on which he quizzed Fanny about Uncle William), and in the summer of 1983 to another, this time at his old university of Freiburg. His New York contribution was only minimally offensive. But his Freiburg paper, 'Prussian Perversions', was, as its title suggests, another matter.

It was 'something quite wicked', he told a friend,[22] so wicked it might even get him thrown out of the lecture hall. Clearly he hoped it would. He had devised a final kick in the pants for the ghosts of the old Nazi Germanists he'd fled in 1965: a talk even more scandalous than his destruction of Stifter, in which he accused Döblin of having been a proto-fascist and a necrophiliac. The audience was suitably outraged. But they weren't only academics, whom he was pleased to annoy. Among them was also Claude Döblin, the author's son, in the front row. Max saw his horrified face, so like his father's that Döblin himself seemed to be listening as he tore him to shreds. Another ghost – a real one. As soon as he'd read the last word he left the room without speaking to anyone, and never again returned to Döblin.

He always hid his feelings and turned everything into stories, so it's hard to say what he really felt about this disaster. But he may have sealed himself off from feeling anything. He'd been capable of that, we know, ever since his teens. And now, in the early 1980s, he was sealed off more and more. Something had happened.

He gave a few hints of it to interviewers. In 1992 he said that he had had a 'midlife crisis' at the end of the 1970s.[23] And in 2001 he said: 'The illusion that I had some control over my life goes up to about my thirty-fifth birthday and then it stopped.'[24]

His thirty-fifth birthday came in May 1979. The crisis had probably begun a bit before then, since by early May it was at its height: Kasus saw him in a deep depression only once in their lives, and it was almost certainly then.[25] Gertrud agrees. Until his house was built, she says, Max was just an angry young man. Once he had realised his dream, his real suffering began.

What brought it on, and would deepen it over the coming years? Partly what was happening at work. On 4 May Margaret Thatcher became prime minister, and the 'Stalinisation' of academic life began. The regime of 'value for money' and evaluation exercises that has come to dominate universities was born then, grew harsher by 1981 and became intolerable – not only to Max – by the mid-1980s.[26] It began in the early 1980s with something called the Teaching Quality Assessment, or TQA (the nastiest things always had acronyms). This meant the inspection of classes by teams from the Department of Education. To the amazement and admiration of all, Max refused to take part, and showed the inspectors the door.[27]

But it wasn't only the university. Something was changing within himself, beyond the melancholy that was his old companion. He had had crises of anxiety and depression at least twice before, in his teens and in Manchester. But the one that hit him in 1979 and rippled on through the early 1980s was the worst. I think he feared, as he had the first time, that he might really go mad.

His mother knew and worried intensely about him.[28] Gertrud knew; no doubt his wife knew; his close childhood friends knew. But Rosa is dead, neither Gertrud nor his friends want to speak about it, and his wife is silent, as we know. Of all the hundreds of people I talked to or read on the subject of Max only two are willing to say anything about what went on in that bad time.

One was a graduate student of his from the mid-1980s to the early 1990s. Ralf Jeutter is a sensitive, empathetic man, a German who would settle in England like Max himself. Between him and Max there was a sympathy, like the one I've guessed there was with Sarah Cameron. But Ralf was older, and German, and occasionally Max spoke to him about himself[29] – elusively, evasively, but enough to make it plain to Ralf that he struggled to remain mentally stable. Once Max told him that his hair had turned grey 'overnight, literally, and then he was old'.[30] On another occasion he said that his wife 'had saved him from alcoholism'. That was typical hyperbole, Ralf says. But there was a time when he would go to a wine bar in Norwich and drink himself senseless, until his wife came and fetched him home.

The other person was a young woman called Philippa Comber. She got closer to Max in the early 1980s than anyone but his family, and she kept a diary, in which their meetings were faithfully recorded. In 2014 she published a memoir, *Ariadne's Thread: In Memory of W. G. Sebald*, using her diary entries. It contains a devastating portrait of Max in his darkest time.[31]

Philippa wasn't German, but she'd lived in Germany for a decade, and she and Max spoke and wrote German together as much as English. This always made him feel on some deep level at home. And she was a psychotherapist. Max would never have anything to do with the dark arts of psychiatry and psychoanalysis, especially for himself.[32] But that would be important as well.

Philippa met him in late August 1981. A week later he called on her, bringing courgettes and tomatoes from his garden. After that he called often. They talked endlessly, about literature, film, life. His visits felt like a shy, old-fashioned courtship, and Philippa hoped that they were. But after a few months she realised that Max was in too bad a way for romance. He told her that he was a melancholic and 'tired of life', but it was worse than that. In four months he didn't laugh once. His view of the world was so dark it was almost pathological. He was 'in the grip of a dejection so profound,' she would write, 'that I began to worry for his safety.'[33]

In January 1982 her father died and she turned to Max for consolation. Now she learned another aspect of his dejection: when he was overwhelmed by his own grief, he sealed himself off from others'. And also, she thought, from the erotic charge that death had lit in her, as it often does. He couldn't come over, he said; he had to walk the dog.

So he withdrew, but his own need grew. In March the dam broke. He rang her and said that he had to talk. They met in a soulless modern hotel near the station. He started hesitantly, struggling for words, but soon he was wiping away tears. He talked of bitterness, of self-doubt, of feeling repulsive. All Philippa could do was listen.

After that he retreated. She didn't hear from him until July. Finally, in September – a year after they'd first met – he came out with what he'd really wanted all along: he asked if she would be his therapist.

It was too late. By now they'd been friends for a year, and psychotherapists cannot take friends as clients. Philippa had to say no. Then in early 1983 she took a new job in Cambridge and returned only sporadically to Norwich. In March that year Max called again, said he'd come – then said he couldn't – then came and talked for seven hours. He said that he was interested in people only for what they could give him. That was far from true in his good times, but it was true in the bad ones, as Philippa knew. All he longed for, he told her, was peace.

In July he came to her birthday party and was wonderfully funny and entertaining, then suddenly silent and distracted. After that there was a gap of many months, then of years.

During those years Philippa met the man she was to marry. In 1988 her Cambridge job was over and she returned to Norwich. The friendship with Max resumed, this time including her partner, Barrie Hesketh. By now Max was a published writer and a full professor, but their glimpses behind his façade showed that in bad times nothing had changed. One day he rang in a state of extreme distress. Philippa wasn't home, and he spoke to Barrie instead, pouring out his pain. As Philippa had done years before, Barrie feared for his safety. And as she had done too, all he could do was listen.

After that they saw him only rarely, and knew no more.

Philippa Comber in 1982.

Gordon Turner doesn't like to speak about Max's emotional troubles. At most he'll talk of his *cafards*, his having the blues. If you press him on depressions he'll admit they happened, but insist that they weren't permanent, that they passed.[34] That is true, and they passed especially with people like Gordon. For when Max liked and trusted someone, he could relax and be happy. So he was always happy with his sisters and their families, with Ursula and Kasus, with friends like Gordon and Michael Hamburger. It happened now with Kristin Völker.[35]

In 1985 the Goethe Institute sent Kristin to England for five years. And once a year or so, on Max's rare trips to London, they would meet. He was writing some of his darkest work in that time – *After Nature* and *Vertigo* – and his despairing moments would never leave him now, but Kristin didn't see them. He could always be gloomy, about the university, for instance, which was a madhouse. But mostly he was relaxed and cheerful, and as amusing as ever. They sat in her office, or on the terrace of the Polish Club in Exhibition Road, a few doors down from the Goethe Institute, and chatted and laughed as they'd done in Munich. One of their subjects was painting, Kristin remembers. They talked about Pisanello's extraordinary painting of St George in a straw hat, which Max would put into *Vertigo*, and his perennial favourite, Altdorfer's *Battle of Alexander*, as he'd done with Martine a quarter of a century before. And like Martine, Kristin felt the closeness of his mind, but no more. He never asked her about her own life. And he never touched her, not even to share the usual hug on meeting or parting. That hadn't changed either.

Kristin remembers two other things they talked about, both of them serious, and both full of coincidences, which seem to hover around her like one of his moths, which carry the souls of the dead.

One of those topics was the war. Kristin lived through it as a small child in Hamburg, and Max very much wanted to hear about that. Hamburg was heavily bombed from the start. As a result thousands of children were evacuated, as they were from British cities, and in 1944, after the worst bombing of all, Kristin's mother decided that she should go too. She took her little daughter to the safest place she could think of: Bad Hindelang, near Sonthofen in the Allgäu.

Kristin no longer recalls what Max said when she told him this astonishing coincidence, but being Max, he may not have been astonished at all. And it was not the only one. The terrible bombing that had decided her mother was Operation Gomorrah,[36] the devastating Allied bombing raids of July 1943 described in Nossack's *Der Untergang*,[37] which Max was making his students read. Gomorrah created one of the worst firestorms of the war, killing 42,600 civilians and virtually destroying Hamburg. She would never forget, Kristin told Max, standing on the balcony of their flat and seeing the Katharinenkirche ablaze, its tower like a burning torch, leaning further and further till it fell.

Max must have caught his breath this time. The founding myth of his life was seeing Nürnberg on fire in August 1943 – and here was Kristin remembering how she'd seen Hamburg on fire a month before. And as though to set the seal on the fatedness of their friendship, she was telling him the tale in the club called the Ognisko Polskie, the Polish Hearth: and the central meaning of *Ognisko* is fire.[38]

Their other serious subject came in 1989, when a complete draft of *Schwindel.Gefühle*. was done, and Max sent Kristin a copy. She was deeply impressed – especially by 'Il Ritorno in patria', which she loved – and when they next met she told him so. He must have been pleased; he'd waited anxiously for her judgement.[39] Then they talked about the book in detail. The only thing she wasn't sure she understood, she told him, was the last part, when the narrator doesn't dare to take the final step into the dark Tube station. What did that mean?

She has never forgotten his answer: 'Didn't you realise? It's the suicide motif.' And most of all she remembers her deep shock at those words.

Despite their good times she knew that he wasn't just talking about his book, but about himself. Like Gracchus, he wanted to die. But like Gracchus, he couldn't take the last step.

He was very good at hiding his feelings, and most of his colleagues never guessed at the despair that could take him over. (Or they may just have decided not to tell me.) He could also hide it from his students, yet he said things to them that were secretly revealing. In March 1981, for instance – a few months after the first journey described in *Vertigo*, and a few months before meeting Philippa Comber – he gave a seminar on Handke's *The Goalie's Anxiety at the Penalty Kick*, about a man who loses his job and his marriage, and drifts into paranoid breakdown. How does he move from a mere neurotic state to breakdown? Max asked. It's a gradual process, but there must be a point – a straw that breaks the camel's back. Then he moves from one side to the other. 'It doesn't become manifest to people around you,' Max told them – switching from 'he' to 'you' – 'because so many signs of madness can be accepted as normal', and 'deranged people still have periods of normality, as normal people have mad moments'. But, he said, it is quite clear to you.[40]

He had always been drawn to writers on the edge – Kafka, Walser, Büchner, Hölderlin. Now he added Handke, Herbert Achternbusch, Gerhard Roth. And first of all Ernst Herbeck,[41] who had suffered from schizophrenia from the age of twenty, entered the Gugging psychiatric hospital in Klosterneuburg near Vienna six years later, and remained there for the rest of his life.

Herbeck had begun producing poems in therapy sessions with the psychiatrist Leo Navratil, who would make several of the Gugging patients famous as artists and writers.[42] In 1977 Navratil published *Alexander's Poetic Texts,** which Max acquired in the late 1970s. His fascination with Herbeck's strange, haunting language grew. In October 1980, as part of research into literature and psychopathology, he went to Klosterneuburg to meet him.[43]

In the next years he would write twice about Herbeck, first in an academic essay, then in *Vertigo*; later he would write about him again.

*Herbeck's work was published under the name Alexander during his lifetime.

The first essay, which he wrote in late 1980,[44] was the forerunner of the empathetic portraits of authors he would write from the mid-1980s onward. As for the account in *Vertigo*, it likens Herbeck to Max's grandfather, and includes a photograph of him, which is actually of Robert Walser. Both these links encode a profound sympathy.

Back home in December, Max told Kasus that his visit to Klosterneuburg had had a most positive effect on him. He recommended such holidays for the psyche: far better, he said, than two weeks in the tropics.[45]

He always put on the best face he could with his friends. But in a paper he gave on Herbert Achternbusch the next spring he wrote that 'Not many have yet got as close to the language of schizophrenia without losing their own minds;' and that Achternbusch's work is like 'the tribute of one who has escaped the reservation to his brothers who are sadly still living there'.[46] This surely reflected his own experience with Herbeck in late October 1980. So at least one of his poems of the early 1980s, 'Crossing the Water', suggests. In it the poet, crossing a Viennese bridge in November 1980, feels that he is losing his mind.[47]

A few years later he poached this poem for *After Nature*. He removed the date, and placed it after his mother's vision of Nürnberg on fire and his own sensation of 'having seen all of it before'. So he turned it into an image of historical madness: his sense, like Cosmo Solomon's, of witnessing a catastrophe he cannot rationally have seen. But *Crossing the Water* suggests that it began as a private madness, after communing with Ernst Herbeck, his brother left behind in the reservation.

He spent 23 to 28 October with Herbeck,[48] then left for Venice. By 'early November', therefore, he was no longer in Vienna. The experience of 'nearly going out of his mind' may thus have happened during his time with Herbeck rather than after it – or before it, or not at all. He may never have suffered the hallucinations that the narrator does either. But that *something* happened, sometime in the autumn of 1980 – something that showed him he had crossed over the goalie's line from ordinary neurosis – seems to me inescapable.

We know one thing: the episode in the pizzeria in *Vertigo*, when the narrator sees the name *Cadavero* and is overcome by the terror of death, did happen. Max wrote about it to Kasus a month later,[49] and preserved the bill itself, complete with the name, in his papers. He also had some kind of blackout on the roof of the Milan Duomo, so that he 'nearly fell

into the depths': so he would tell Marie thirty years later.[50] He adjusted
these events for his book – changing the date on the pizza bill, and
setting the Milan episode in 1987, when it almost certainly happened
in 1980. But like almost everything in his work, they had their roots in
real events in his life. He didn't attempt to deny it, but on the contrary
claimed it, as we'll see,[51] and peppered the pages of *Vertigo* with proofs
that its story was his: not just the pizzeria bill, but (for example) his
passport photograph.

What was the truth, then? How close *were* the narrator of *Vertigo* and
its author in the autumn of 1980?

I think we can guess, for a start, that the hallucinations of the
Wertach villagers and Dante weren't real, because they are clearly
artistic devices: the first ties the narrator's two sections together, the
second evokes the main motif of those sections, the darkness *nel mezzo
del cammin* – midway through the journey – of a poet's life.

But what about the other 'mad' things – the maddest of all, for instance,
the narrator's fear that he is being pursued by two young men? He glimpses
them first in a bar in Venice, then several times more, and finally in the
Verona Arena, in which he feels 'entangled in some dark web of intrigue',[52]
and is so paralysed by fear he can hardly move. In the pizzeria he reads
an article about a group called the Organizzazione Ludwig, which has
claimed responsibility for several brutal murders in the last few years. He
unfolds his bill, sees the name *Cadavero* and flees… Seven years later, on
the return journey to probe 'those fraught and hazardous days',[53] he learns
that the murderers have been caught and convicted, and that they are two
young men called Wolfgang Abel and Marco Furlan.

Furlan and Abel were all too real.[54] They began their killings in 1977,
when they were seventeen and eighteen, and first claimed responsibility
for them in a letter to *Il Gazzettino* in November 1980, as *Vertigo* records
(though again Max changed the date to fit his scheme). Their mission
was to cleanse the world of 'deviants' – prostitutes, drug addicts, 'sinful'
priests, viewers of pornographic films. As the swastikas on their letter
show, they acted in the name of Nazism. The final total of their victims
was twenty-eight dead and thirty-nine wounded. They were arrested in
1984, tried in 1987, and sentenced to thirty years, as Max wrote. They
would not be released until long after his own death.

That is the delusion of the narrator: he clearly imagines he is being
marked by Abel and Furlan as their next victim. The death he sees in

Cadavero is not abstract, but immediate and real. He is in the grip of a true paranoia.

And Max?

He talked about it twice in interviews. First to Andreas Isenschmid, one of Germany's best literary critics and his great supporter, and second to Piet de Moor, a sympathetic Belgian journalist.[55] On both occasions he insisted that he really had found himself caught up in the horrific crimes that had been taking place in northern Italy, or so it had seemed to him. He summed it up thus to de Moor:

> As is always the case when you are telling stories, there are
> exaggerations here and there … but remarkably, things happened
> exactly as I narrated them. Even the crime story has a genuine
> background. It is the account of two young male murderers who
> for many years committed the most terrible crimes in northern
> Italy. I felt as if I really had been caught up in their immediate
> environment…

And when Isenschmid couldn't hide his surprise, Max insisted. Later on, he said, he'd read an article about Abel and Furlan, complete with photographs. He was convinced then and remained convinced now that these were the two young men who had followed him.

Some of this simply couldn't be true. The narrator spends several days in Italy, which gives time for the chase, whereas in reality Max seems to have spent barely a day there.[56] And the narrator reads about Organizzazione Ludwig's claim to be the murderers in the *Gazzettino* of 5 November – whereas the claim did not in fact appear until 25 November.[57] So he cannot have believed at the time, as the narrator does, that his pursuers were Abel and Furlan. The likelihood is rather that he read the article about the two when it came out in 1986, and that this gave him the idea for that part of the story.

That is what the Sebald scholar Scott Bartsch argues, in detail,[58] and I'm sure he is right. But all it shows is that Max cannot have believed in 1980 that he was being pursued by Abel and Furlan: it says nothing about whether he believed he was being pursued *tout court*. Even one day could be enough for that – even, indeed, one sighting. In an early draft, that is what happens:[59] he sees the young men only once, in the Verona Arena, but it is already a mysterious and disturbing encounter.

Did he fall, however briefly, into that delusion? Or was he carrying on the fictionalising of his narrator in interviews, as he carried on the fictionalising of his other characters? That is, I think, Isenschmid's view, and it is more than possible.

But it is not the whole truth. That became clearer when I asked Marie. Max told her that he saw the two young men following him, as they follow the narrator in the book.[60] To Andreas Isenschmid he said this with a grin on his face, so that Isenschmid didn't believe him. But he didn't grin as he told Marie; she believed that he believed it, and I think we must too. He did fall into true paranoia in the autumn of 1980.

And when he read the article about the Organizzazione Ludwig six years later, and identified his pursuers as Abel and Furlan? Was *that* just literature?

I fear not; or not entirely. His imagination was so strong that even in good times he hardly distinguished it from reality. And in bad times imagination undistinguished from reality was paranoia. When he told a sane person like Isenschmid that the Organizzazione Ludwig had pursued him, he could see Isenschmid didn't believe him, and of course he knew himself that it was highly improbable. That was surely why he grinned. But he also told Marie that the two young men *were* Abel and Furlan. He knew he could tell her, because whatever she thought would make no difference to her trust in him. What did that release? His deepest feeling, a fantasy, a fear? I think he sometimes believed it, sometimes half believed it, and sometimes knew it was a delusion. The last of these probably most often: as he said to his students, 'Deranged people still have extended periods of normality.'[61] But that – to know he was 'deranged' – was surely the most frightening of all.

And after all, it made sense. The Organizzazione Ludwig's targets were 'a series of social misfits', he told de Moor.[62] Writing to Philippa Comber in the early 1980s, he had repeatedly called himself something similar: the most boorish, uncivilised creature.[63] In his bad times Max Sebald felt a social misfit. Naturally Abel and Furlan would want to murder him.

Still, he wasn't a prostitute, priest or porn watcher, so he should have been in the clear. But they had another target: homosexuals. We don't know this, because he doesn't say in *Vertigo* that their second and third victims were both homosexuals. He did say it in an early draft, but later removed it.[64] To Max, the ex-Catholic, the boy brought up under Section 175, homosexuality was still a dangerous stain. That is the paranoid fear hidden in this first book, which he always said was about love. To Beyle in its first chapter, love was an illusion; to Kafka in its third, it was impossible, because (the narrator suggests) his secret desire was for men. And the narrator himself? Well, there is his mysterious encounter with the Venetian Malachio, met in what all the critics assume is a gay bar.[65] And he first glimpsed the two young men in the same bar… In fact Kafka's problem with love was almost certainly different; and so, as we'll see, was Max's. But in these fraught years, that, I think, was his fear.

Andreas Isenschmid concluded that *Vertigo* was far removed from pure autobiography: 'Through a series of highly refined artistic manoeuvres,' he wrote, '[Sebald] has stylised … the material of his life into a formally conscious and formally perfect book.'[66] That is beautiful and right, but I would reverse the emphasis. Max threaded his experience through with references from his reading, from art and history, and transformed it into literature. But beneath the formal perfection of his prose lay the truth of his suffering.

As soon as he returned home he sat down to write. He wrote his first essay about Ernst Herbeck. And that November, or at the latest by the next summer, when the academic year was over, he began his own literary writing at last.[67]

He'd never stopped writing poetry, as we know. But now he began a new collection, which he would call *Über das Land und das Wasser – Across the Land and the Water.* This one would finally be published (though not all of it, and several years after his death). And large parts of it would go into his first published literary work, the long narrative poem *Nach der Natur – After Nature.*[68]

Max thought of *After Nature* as his first real piece of literary writing.[69] We don't know exactly when the personal parts were first drafted; perhaps early on. The Steller section we can date: a first version was finished in 1983.[70] In October 1984 he published it in the literary magazine *Manuskripte;* and by late 1985 the whole poem was done. Over the next year it was rejected by ten or more German publishers. Finally he approached his friend and fellow writer Christoph Ransmayr for help. Ransmayr showed it to Hans Magnus Enzensberger, who saw its originality and power, and recommended it to the publisher Franz

Greno. In the late summer of 1988 Greno brought it out, and W. G. Sebald's first book was in the world.[71]

After Nature was the beginning, however, only in the sense that it was his first published literary work. In fact he had started with a different kind of writing altogether, and almost certainly earlier: in the turning-point year of 1979.[72] He said so himself, in the first application he made for funding his new 'prose work', in 1987: his literary work had begun, he wrote, with scripts for television.[73]

Television, we might think, *Max Sebald*? But on second thoughts it's not so surprising. He'd been intrigued by drama since *Antigone*, and he'd written several plays in the late 1960s. In any case, over the course of the 1980s he wrote two television scripts and planned a third.[74] And between 1981 and 1985 he tried tirelessly to get the first performed: *Jetzund kömpt die Nacht herbey: Ansichten aus dem Leben und Sterben des Immanuel Kant – Now the Night Descends: Scenes from the Life and Death of Immanuel Kant*, the script he'd begun writing in 1979.[75]

Jan Franksen, his friend at Sender Freies Berlin,* tried as hard as he did, but there were endless delays, mostly over money. Franksen, who was a most congenial, sardonic person, explained that they had to make Kant as easy to understand as Donald Duck; after twenty years in the business, he wrote, he hoped they could get the film made without his ending in a *Nervenklinik*. In the end, sadly, that was exactly what happened: in 1985 Franksen fell into a serious depression. And once he was no longer there to support it, the project collapsed. Like the other script, *Jetzund kömpt die Nacht herbey* was never made, and only Sebald's greatest fans know he ever wrote them.[76]

Over the years he sent *Now the Night Descends* to more than twenty publishers, film producers and television companies, all in vain.[77] The trouble began with its gnomic title, continued with a series of 'boring, formally weak' scenes (as one rejection baldly put it), and culminated in a puzzling failure to mention even a single one of Kant's philosophical ideas. No one knew what to do with it, and it's hard to blame them.

Nonetheless, it was the first step in Max's new literary journey, and sheds light on how it began. Which was very close to how *After Nature*

---

*The West German public radio and television service.

began: with some of the bleakest despair in all his writings. Through the dying Kant, Max explored his profound pessimism about human progress, which in truth is the opposite of progress. In the final scene the narrator speculates about how an alien would see human expansion on earth: as a growing affliction, he says – early villages like measles spots, big cities like boils, huge industrial areas like outbreaks of eczema everywhere.

This image of civilisation as a skin disease is horribly striking – and even more striking when we remember Max's own skin disease, which had begun when his grandfather died. It is as though he is ascribing his secret pathology to the whole globe. And that is indeed one way to look at his writing. Wittgenstein was right: it is not just that a happy man is different from an unhappy one. It is that the world of the happy man is different from the world of the unhappy man. Everything is how you see it – especially if you are Max Sebald.

And what about that title? Its seventeenth-century source is an elegy for lost love.[78] The first line – 'Now the night descends' – fits Max's despairing play well enough, but the rest of the poem doesn't fit it at all. On the other hand, *Vertigo* would be about love too, and half-hid a fear he might be homosexual; and we know from Philippa Comber that he sometimes felt deeply repulsive in just these years. Part of his disturbance, surely, was a pathology about love.

So he started with poetry and plays; it took some time before he found his way to his true medium, prose. That happened six or seven years later, in his favourite part of the world. In July 1986 he travelled to Fribourg, and on the train from Zurich read the newspaper account of Johannes Naegeli's body being released from the ice.[79] And in Fribourg he bought Stendhal's *De l'amour*, which gave him, he told Gertrud a few months later, some wonderful ideas.[80] When he got home at the end of September he sat down and began to write.

Vertigo and *The Emigrants* were thus born together.[81] And they stayed together for at least a year. In his grant application in 1987 he proposed a 'prose work with pictures' that would become *Vertigo* – except that the last part went on to include the stories based on his teacher and his Uncle William.[82] But then, in 1988, *Manuskripte* announced that its one-hundredth-anniversary issue would feature the theme of ageing.[83] So he took the image of the body returning from the ice that he had thought of using for 'Bereyter', turned Rhoades Buckton into Hersch Seweryn, and wrote 'Dr Henry Selwyn' for *Manuskripte*. Now he realised that several other stories of the 'prose work with pictures' were about the emergence of trauma in old age as well: those of Bereyter and Adelwarth, for instance. So was Peter Jordan's story, which he'd also been thinking about since late 1986 or early 1987.[84] Finally he saw his way through. In October 1988 he wrote to Gertrud[85] that 'Dr Selwyn' would be part of a future project about the lives of Jewish people he knew. He has so much good material, he can't wait to begin. The Stendhal and Kafka stories, the third part, in which he is the traveller (as he'd also said to Kristin and the grant agency, the Deutscher Literaturfonds) and the last part, the return to W., belong to another project altogether. At last his first two books were clear.

In the summer of 1989 he visited Corfu, probably still in pursuit of Ambros and Cosmo; and there he wrote 'Il Ritorno in patria', he would tell Richard Sheppard, 'without hesitation, no papers, just pad and pencil'.[86] For this ease of writing (if it was true) 'Ritorno' would always be his favourite among his writings. That autumn he clearly felt the book was done and sent the whole typescript to Kristin.[87] It would be published in the spring.

He always said that he started his literary writing as a way out of the frustrations of academic life.[88] It was his biggest lie. Only once, to an interviewer in faraway Madrid, did he say something closer to the truth: that he began 'Out of fatigue. Out of illness. I don't know how to put it. I went through an important crisis.'[89] With the script of *Now the Night Descends*, the poetry of *After Nature*, and finally the prose of *Vertigo*, he began writing in order to explore and perhaps save himself from the times in which he had crossed the line from melancholy to madness.

18

1989–96

By the late 1980s the crisis in the university had become acute. But Max didn't want to leave the Old Rectory, or indeed UEA. In 1989 he came up with a way of securing his position: he founded the British Centre for Literary Translation at UEA, and became its first director.[1]

Somehow he squeezed support out of the Arts Council, and later out of the EU as well; never enough, but a remarkable feat nonetheless.[2] And he knew where he wanted its home to be: in Earlham Lodge, a centuries-old farmhouse on the edge of the campus, with a beech tree beside it and land sloping down to a river. Sadly, the university refused its permission, and BCLT always had to struggle for space in the crowded Arts Building. Despite this, it was a success from the start, attracting translators from around the world. And today it is a proud feather in UEA's cap, like Max's own fame, though it took the university several years after his death to recognise both.

BCLT brought him several new friends. One was the poet Adam Czerniawski,[3] who became its first translator-in-residence and later its first associate director. With Polish Adam Max let his feelings about his native land rip, saying roundly that he couldn't go home because it was still full of Nazis. 'He was glad to have a Polish friend,' Adam says. Another was the Dutch author and translator Ria Loohuizen, a passionate writer about the natural world. Ria recalls above all Max's deep anxiety about the environment, decades ahead of its time. If they were drinking water, he would worry about water in the future; in the middle of BCLT parties he would brood about how we are destroying our planet. Sometimes he had withdrawn, moody times, she says, but then he would come back to life and be charming and funny. 'He had great charisma,' she remembers. 'Something happened when he walked into a room.'

For Max, however (and not only for him), the most important person at BCLT was its secretary.[4] Beryl Ranwell was immensely energetic, a mother hen to the young translators, and a centre of laughter and homeliness to her colleagues, especially Max. Her office was opposite his, on the light side of the corridor. He would pop across for chats, and join her Friday night 'seshes' (short for 'sessions'), at which sherry and more laughter were served. He never missed the parties she gave in her cottage in Bergh Apton either. Beryl was different from him in every way – as English as he was German, as impulsive as he was intellectual, as emotional as he was reserved. He was fascinated by her, and she was devoted to him – which was just as well, since he drove everyone as hard as he drove himself, and could reduce her to tears with his demands. But she always forgave him.

Beryl got as close to him as anyone, her daughter says, and she would have loved to talk about him. Alas, she died in 2013, before anyone thought to ask her. We'll never know what this shrewd, warm-hearted woman might have told us about the great writer who was her friend. Or might have decided not to tell us, of course.

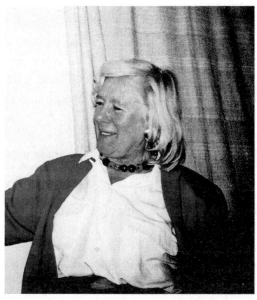

Beryl Ranwell.

Over the months in England Max's longing for the landscape of his youth would grow, but as soon as he returned, reality would descend like a cloud, and he would want to flee once more. It was a problem to have no home, but the real problem was that he had one.

At least, though, he could see his friends. Ursula and Kasus, always; and others as well, such as Heidi Böck, who'd become Heidi Nowak.[5] Heidi had only glimpsed Winfried – in Sonthofen he was still Winfried – over the years, and was very struck now by the change in him. He'd become so serious, so unlike the larky, joking boy she remembered. She won't say 'gloomy', but only 'very, very serious'. As to his feelings about Sonthofen – Heidi hesitates. She knows that it's more complicated than many Sonthofeners feel. 'I don't think he was happy here,' she says. 'But he always returned to his roots in his books.'

I don't know whether he ever went to see his fellow sufferer from father problems, Walter Kalhammer. But I fear not. Walter was in a bad way, and I don't think he could have borne it.[6]

Walter had seemed set for a successful career in architecture. But a successful career was what the world wanted, and so the last thing he wanted. He refused to work for rich capitalist architects (i.e. most architects) and took on only a few social projects for hardly any money at all. Slowly his paintings became smaller; eventually he stopped painting altogether, and made only tiny metal sculptures, mostly of birds. Then he gave up architecture as well and took a job as a night watchman in a psychiatric clinic. There he could play his music in peace, and be useful to the patients, who came down to his basement flat to talk to him all night. He listened to radio lectures on science, philosophy, history, and began to write about them, at the same time as his friend Winfried began to write in England.

That was in the early 1980s. Some time after that he started to break down himself, imagining that someone on a tram was watching him. Eventually he walked up the stairs of the clinic and became a patient, until he felt better and became the night watchman again. That was where he was when Max came to Sonthofen in the 1990s. Walter's sister told him what had happened and gave him Walter's phone number, but she doesn't know if he ever used it. Over the next years Walter's paranoia gradually worsened, until he constantly heard people coming down the stairs to punish him for some awful crime. Finally the inevitable happened, and he took his own life.

That was in 2006, five years after Max had died. The only better ending I could imagine for Walter was his writing: perhaps he'd made something out of his suffering, like his friend. I asked his sister – of course she had kept his notebooks, and she fetched them for me. The first surprise was that there were only two. But I took them gratefully, and read them that evening. When I closed them again I felt a great emptiness. They didn't contain Walter's thoughts. They were a record of the radio lectures he'd heard: a detailed record, but not a single word of his own. Walter, the first artist of the Clique, had vanished.

There was another friend of his youth whom Max sought out when he came home: Gundela Enzensberger, the girl who had secretly loved him when she was thirteen.[7]

Gundela's life had not become easier with the years. She had a daughter out of wedlock and brought her up on her own. She became an artist and ceramicist, selling enough to survive. But her past weighed on her. Finally her resistance broke, as it did in Max's heroes, and memories of her childhood abuse came flooding back. Now, like Austerlitz, she suffered more instead of less. But she sought help, her work began to change, and slowly she healed, as far as possible.

That was her situation in the late 1980s, when one day there was a knock at her door and Winfried Sebald was standing there. She was astounded, and thrilled. He seemed to her as marvellous as ever, as profoundly intelligent, as darkly funny, and they talked for hours. After that it happened every time he was in Sonthofen: the knock on the door, the extraordinary talk. She was, of course, in love with him again. And he? He spoke sometimes of coming to live not far away. But there was still the same block, the same distance in him she had felt when they were young. He was so sensitive, so vulnerable; she couldn't reach across the gap until she was certain that was what he wanted. And she never was.

In March 1990 *Vertigo* was published in Germany. It attracted little attention, though most of it positive. This time one colleague sent him a brief note, others mumbled something; only 'Mac' MacFarlane congratulated him warmly.[8]

In June, however, the book was up for one of the most important German-language awards, the Ingeborg Bachmann Prize, and Max travelled to Klagenfurt for the decision.[9] Andreas Isenschmid and Peter von Matt strongly supported him, but in the final vote the prize went elsewhere. However little Max may have hoped or even wanted to win, after coming so close this was surely a disappointment. At the same time Rosa was at the height of her fury about 'Il Ritorno in patria' and kept ringing his hotel and shouting at him down the phone. His old friend Franz Kuna, at the university in Klagenfurt, tried to cheer him up. Obviously he should have won, Kuna said: 'The gentlemen of the jury are about as comprehensible as the ones for the Eurovision Song Contest.'[10]

That would have made him smile. But the most pleasing response of all, I'm sure, came from his old friend and rival Paolo. It was remarkably warm and generous. He'd read the book in one go, Paolo wrote, and 'apart from occasional attacks of envy', he was gripped from start to finish. 'In sum,' he said, 'I'm impressed;' *Vertigo* was real literature.[11]

Jan Franksen too was full of praise; but he sent Max a warning. 'The spirits you've allowed to possess you are dangerous,' he wrote. 'You won't be able to stop writing now. Take good care of yourself, because no one else can help you.'[12]

Max was longing to get on with *The Emigrants* now, as well as working on a book on post-war German literature, organising a three-year seminar series on Holocaust writing, and doing a week's tour of *Vertigo* around Germany. It was a foretaste of his life for the coming decade, and already it was almost too much. Recently his old friend ROP had got back in touch, and last year, he told Max, he'd had a heart attack.[13] In October Max answered his letter. An early warning may be a good thing, he wrote. Sometimes he felt that a *Herzkasper* was around the corner for him as well.[14] *Herzkasper?* I asked ROP. Slang for 'heart attack', he replied.

Around October too the first journalist came from Germany to interview W. G. Sebald.[15] Like most interviewers from now on, Renate Just was surprised to find nothing visibly depressed or deranged about him. His home was wonderfully English, with tea served in front of the fire, but as Max's black humour grew, she thought of Joseph Losey's film *Accident* – an English idyll with an emotional hell beneath. He described the horrors of life as an 'academic manager'; he took breaks both as a professor and a family man, he said, and travelled alone in Europe. Soon he was making jokes about suicide ('Drowning is not as bad as they say'). 'As with many fundamentally sad people,' Just wrote, 'you never stop laughing with him.'

In 1991 he was still more a professor than a writer. In March he published his second academic book, *Unheimliche Heimat* (*Unhomely Homeland*), with essays on Améry, Handke, the two Roths, Gerhard and Joseph, and many others. In it the new empathetic note was already strong.

Just before, he'd unleashed his old academic persona and penned one of his violent attacks.[16] Once again it was on a Jewish writer: but this time one who had lost his mother in the Holocaust, and had himself survived the Łódź Ghetto and several concentration camps as a child. Jurek Becker's books failed, Max argued, because he could not allow himself any real memory. That was understandable, but the literary result was a lack of authenticity, a fake realism, and an overarching sense of bad faith.

The piece was intended for a book being edited by his friend Irène Heidelberger-Leonard. But Max had gone too far this time, as he'd done with Döblin in 1983. Heidelberger-Leonard declined the essay, and it remained unpublished until nearly a decade after his death.

What was he like to work with, now that he was chafing more and more under the system? Well, he grumbled theatrically, and walked around looking like Pooh Bear under his cloud, but as a colleague he was as affable and helpful as ever.[17] The only thing you couldn't ask of him, one EUR friend recalls, was to make any public pronouncement: he thought he sounded foreign, which he did, and that this would put people off, which it wouldn't. Also, she adds, he hated academic disputes and would stay out of them; he would withdraw from conflict and prefer not to tackle people head-on. On the other hand, he could be dismissive of people if he thought they were fools or, even worse, hypocrites. Another EUR colleague reports,[18] for instance, that he would call those whose work he didn't respect 'dumbos'. As the chairman of committees (according to the same colleague) he made sweeping decisions and left the detail to others… Clearly this colleague was one of Max's 'dumbos', and did not forgive him.

In 1991 a new person joined the German sector: Jean Boase-Beier, who two years later would found and run BCLT's MA programme, and who immediately became a good friend of its director. Hers are some of the most vivid memories of Max in the early 1990s.[19]

He could be very rude, she says, delighted to shock or tease serious people. But really he was extraordinarily kind. Before she began, for instance, he sent her the local newspaper every week so that she and her husband could find a house.

He was extremely amusing, as always. Many of his best stories were about trains: one would be delayed, they'd move you to a second and then a third, which would take you back to where you started. 'This is the British railway system,' he'd intone in his deep, mournful voice. He was amusing even when he wasn't telling stories. For instance, Jean recalls, one colleague of theirs always rolled up his sleeves. Whenever he was in view, Max would roll up his own. In committee meetings he would count the number of times people managed to bring up their subject. 'He was a very funny person,' Jean says, 'really loads of laughs' – and suddenly a quite different Max appears.

Until he became too much in literary demand, he would often meet friends for lunch in the cafeteria. One day, Jean remembers, he arrived a little later than the others, and they watched as he made his way to their table. 'Mr Pastry!' one of them suddenly said, and they all had to laugh. 'Mr Pastry' was a popular slapstick character of the day, whose bumbling antics sent audiences into fits of laughter. His walrus moustache was very like Max's, but it was more than that. There was something clumsy in the way Max moved sometimes. He wasn't a smooth person, Jean says; he was always shy, uncertain, 'not quite in himself'. She remembers, for instance, how she noticed a man with an odd walk on her very first day, on the way to her interview. When they reached the door of the building, he opened it for her, but awkwardly, so that for a moment they got tangled up in each other. It was Max. A little, in fact, like Mr Pastry.†

Jean remembers another event as well. It happened years later, when they were old friends, and were having an argument about something. All of a sudden Max lost his temper, said something seriously hurtful and stalked away. But a few minutes later she saw that he was coming back. She watched him approach, as she'd done in the cafeteria, and he made an extraordinary gesture, such as she's never seen anyone make before or since: a slight bending of one knee, as a sign of apology or subservience.

Her memory seems to me profoundly right. That shyness and uncertainty of his had something permanently guilty about it. It was as though he was always about to apologise for something, always ready to bend a knee.

In the spring of 1992 *The Emigrants* was done.[20] By early May he was in the sort of state that always afflicted him at the end of a book. That is when he was interviewed by Piet de Moor about *Vertigo*; and it was the darkest interview he ever gave. We have destroyed the balance of nature, he said.[21] Kafka experienced his own existence as illegitimate, and so should we. Human beings are supreme parasites, who subjugate other species through sheer power. And our danger is not least to ourselves: 'We have organised our society in such a way that we threaten to burn ourselves.' Even a refrigerator, he said, is constantly burning something. Only two things give us hope of another order: strange coincidences, improbable overlaps with other people's lives; and, if they are successful, works of art.

He spent the summer term in Germany, working on his book on post-war German literature. When he returned, he found himself back under the old pressures. The last time they had grown too great, he had escaped by walking alone in Europe. But he'd only just got back. So in early August he set out to walk alone in England instead.

He did it, he would say, on an impulse.[22] He had no intention of writing a book – so he said, and I think we can believe him this time. He'd only just finished one, which had used up all the stories he'd carried around for years. He would just walk. Nonetheless, new experiences would flow in, and he wasn't one to let a good experience go to waste. He could do something easy (writers always think that at first) – a piece about remote Suffolk for German tourists, like the one he'd written back in the 1970s. He'd propose the idea to the *Frankfurter Allgemeine Zeitung* – ten short pieces for their magazine.[23]

That is not what happened, of course. The easy piece would become one of his most beautiful but most despairing books. He would call it *The Rings of Saturn*, after the fragments of dust and ice spinning in black space around the planet whose name stood for melancholy. It would take him the next three years.

He set out from Lowestoft, and walked down the coast to Southwold and Dunwich: so far, like the narrator of his book.[24] He tended to let people think that he'd done the whole walk exactly as the narrator does in the book – but that was, as usual, a fiction. The Lowestoft he describes was an empty winter one, not the one he saw now, at the height of the summer season. He visited Somerleyton in February rather than now, Alec Gerrard's Moat Farm often, but not now. When he went to Woodbridge, Orford and the rest isn't clear – again most likely often, but not now. And unlike the narrator of *The Rings of Saturn*, he didn't stop at Dunwich, pass the last grave clinging to the cliff, and cross Dunwich Heath. Again, he would often have done that walk; the heath was one of his favourite places. But in August 1992 he carried on down the coast as far as Aldeburgh and turned inland from there, some twenty miles from Middleton. He arrived at the Hamburgers' footsore and weary. They gave him lunch and he stayed for a while, perhaps even till the next day. They then called a taxi for him, as they do in the book. But rather than taking him back to Southwold, after which the narrator carries on for several more days, the taxi almost certainly took Max home.

He felt much better for the walk, as he'd hoped. But after it he began to suffer from back pain, which a year later became a slipped disc, and took him into the hospital where *Saturn* begins. It was caused, he realised, by his walking for so long on the sloping sand near the sea, so that for days on end his left foot was lower than his right.[25] Many readers have followed him since, moved by the haunting descriptions in his book. It's a marvellous walk, past the salt lagoon of Benacre Broad and the cliffs at Covehithe with their sandmartins' holes, just as he described them. On a lovely sunny day the atmosphere doesn't feel haunted at all, and the writer Robert MacFarlane gave up walking after a while, saying that he was having much too good a time. But Benacre Broad is a strange silent place, the coast is being swallowed up just as Max said it was, and if you get tired enough you can feel him near. Just move away from the water's edge now and then.

In September 1992 came the most important event of his writing life: *The Emigrants* was published. The German critics responded to it instantly. *Schwindel.Gefühle.* had passed almost without notice, but *Die Ausgewanderten* got many reviews and great praise.[26] In January it received the ultimate literary tribute in Germany: a discussion on Marcel Reich-Ranicki's famous television programme, *The Literary Quartet*. Reich-Ranicki himself – the *Literaturpapst*, or Pope of Literature, who was notorious for his deadly attacks – dismissed it as mere academic dabbling. Max was furious, but he needn't have bothered. Everyone knew that Reich-Ranicki was suspicious of anything avant-garde, and despite its old-fashioned surface, that is what *The Emigrants* was. And in any case, the *Literaturpapst* was outgunned. Two of the other critics on the programme, Sigrid Löffler and Hellmuth Karasek, both acclaimed the book as a masterpiece. Karasek especially spoke for critics and readers alike. 'I've discovered an important piece of literature,' he said.

Max's feelings were, as ever, uncertain. The writing had almost done him in during the last year, he told Kristin.[27] When Gertrud asked whether he was happy with the result he replied that he'd just 'cooked something up again'. Sending Peter Jordan a copy, he said how much it had meant to him to be able to include his story; writing again five months later, he sounded like his narrator. His book had had good reviews, he said. But he still felt his work was inadequate and botched, above all in relation to the reality.[28]

Some praise, though, he surely enjoyed again; Idris Parry's, for instance. 'It looks as if you have challenged yourself to write the most convoluted adjectival clauses in modern German prose,' Parry wrote. 'But all are so limpid I am not surprised the German critics have greeted your book so warmly.' He ended his letter: 'I hope you can cope with fame and ignore glory.'[29] That was Welsh hyperbole, but prophetic.

In the first few months of 1993 he spent several weeks on tour in Germany and Switzerland. It was all dreadfully tiring, he said, and he felt like an imposter, with audiences disappointed that he wasn't on the verge of suicide.[30] But when an old school friend came to one of his readings, she found him as changed as Heidi Nowak had: grave, gloomy, depressed.

In the spring he published an essay on Alfred Andersch in a Berlin-based magazine.[31] Andersch was one of Germany's favourite post-war authors, whose novel *Sansibar* was read in every school. But for Max, he distilled the worst of the lies and silences of the Third Reich. Andersch claimed, for instance, to have married a half-Jewish woman despite the racial laws. What he did not admit, Max argued, was that he had divorced his wife in 1943 in order to advance his career under the Nazis, then claimed her back as 'my wife' in order to advance it under the Americans. This double betrayal was deplorable in itself, but Max's point was that – like Becker's more forgivable embargo on memory – it infected Andersch's work with an irredeemable falseness. Ethics and aesthetics could not be prised apart, he insisted. When *Sansibar*'s hero saves his Jewish wife's life, every word betrays the emptiness of its author's imagination.

This attack unleashed one of the most violent controversies of Max's life, much worse than the ones about Döblin and Becker. And it still goes on today. Most scholars accept that the facts he unearthed were essentially right, but his judgements are another matter. Was he unfair to Andersch, in a situation that he himself had never experienced? Did moral failure really lead to literary failure in that way? All I can say is that *Sansibar* rings false to me too. But it is still read in German schools.

One of Andersch's defenders was Hans Magnus Enzensberger, Max's publisher and friend.[32] He was upset by Max's harsh attack, and for a time there was a slight distance between them. But HME (as he was universally called) deeply admired his friend's work – 'Max is a remarkable writer, you know,' he told a group of UEA friends, long before they knew it. Now, despite his Andersch reservations, he nominated *The Emigrants* for the European Prize for Literature. It didn't win. Despite the recognition from Germany's leading literary figure, and from key critics like Isenschmid and the others, Max still met with resistance in the German literary world, as people closed ranks around Andersch, and didn't forget Becker either. Truly, Max didn't make it easy for Germans to like him.

That summer he had his awful slipped disc. From early August he had to lie flat until it could be dealt with. On the 20th he had the operation; on the 30th he finally went home.[33] But it would take him many weeks to recover, and he never quite did. His back would bother him for the rest of his life. And something else had happened too: after the operation he was left with a shadow, or veil, over his left eye. (Perhaps that is the net we see over the window of his hospital room in the opening pages of *Saturn*.) He never mentions it again, and when he had similar trouble three years later, it was with the other eye. But whatever lay behind this disturbance of his sight, it had probably begun by now.

In the autumn term he was given sick leave, and spent it working on *The Rings of Saturn* – at first, perhaps, as he'd begun: lying on his stomach on a bed, his papers on the carpet below and his forehead on a chair. For years after he knew the pattern on that carpet by heart, he said.[34] Later he spun a tremendous story out of this for his friends, describing how he'd written the whole of his third book lying on his stomach. It wasn't true, of course, except for its core.

By October he was upright once more, and giving readings of *The Emigrants* in Holland and Germany. In the meantime[35] Adam Czerniawski had recommended it to someone he met at BCLT: Bill Swainson, who was working as an editor for Harvill, a rare publisher of foreign literature in Britain. Swainson sent the original German version to two readers, Michael Hulse and John Hartley Williams. When both more than confirmed Czerniawski's praise – 'this is an important, a great book', Hulse wrote[36] – Harvill decided to publish.

Max was given three anonymous sample translations, including one by Hulse himself. Max preferred the most measured, formal one, but Bill felt 'there was a brightness' about Hulse's that made it the best. He persuaded Max, and in November Hulse was commissioned. *Die Ausgewanderten* began its journey into English.

In the spring term of 1994 Max was on study leave to work on his book on post-war German literature – but worked on *The Rings of Saturn* instead.[37] He never would write that last planned academic text. He'd finally made the move, at least internally, from professor to author.

But he would be a maverick in this new world, as in the old one. In early 1994, for instance, *The Emigrants* won the Berlin Literature Prize, together with six other writers. That summer the six winners competed over two days of readings for the coveted Johannes-Bobrowski medal. Two won: Erica Pedretti and W. G. Sebald. There were, presumably, two medals; his at least, according to Max, of an indescribable ugliness. Early the next morning he took it to the spot on the Wannsee where Kleist had committed suicide and threw it in. It sank, he told his gratifyingly shocked friends, without trace.[38]

The years 1994 and 1995 belonged not to *The Emigrants*, however, but to *The Rings of Saturn*. He got on only at a snail's pace, he told Peter Jordan, because he had to do almost every page over and over again.[39] For the 400 pages of the published book he covered 1,200 pages with drafts, he said – even more than his labours on 'Adelwarth'. He was racked with doubts about the whole enterprise. But he struggled on.

One reason for his trouble was that 1994–5 was a year of deaths. In just over a year, he would tell one interviewer,[40] he lost fourteen people – friends from school and university, UEA colleagues… As far as UEA was concerned, he wasn't wrong; from the mid-1990s on there would be several premature deaths in EUR. In 1994 there were two such deaths, of two of Max's favourite people. He put both of them into his book: Michael Parkinson and Janine Dakyns.[41]

Janine died of breast cancer. Michael was found in his house in the Portersfield Road just as *The Rings of Saturn* describes: lying dead in his bed, with strange red blotches on his face, but no other signs of illness or accident on his body. People thought of a heart attack, but the inquest ruled that out. In fact, it established, Michael had recently been taking an anti-malarial drug, and an overdose of this had killed him. Nonetheless, the coroner returned an open verdict, as Max wrote, since it was impossible to say whether Michael had taken the overdose by accident or on purpose. Neither seemed likely. He did nothing without careful planning, but on the other hand he didn't seem depressed or suicidal, as far as anyone could tell – though no one *could* tell, since Michael never showed any private feeling. So his colleagues always wondered about suicide. And Max himself believed that that is what it was.

Janine's death followed weeks later, he would write, and again that was only a slight exaggeration. Michael died in April, Janine in August. No one knew she was ill, perhaps not even Janine herself till the end, which came very quickly. Her funeral was enormous, with her students making heartfelt speeches. Max didn't attend; he hated funerals, especially the saddest ones.

Janine and Michael had been devoted friends: almost childlike friends, probably not lovers, and very private – you had to pretend not to know how close they were, and never invite them to anything together. So did Janine really die of shock and grief over Michael, as Max suggests? It's an impossible question; both were as private in death as in life. But I trust Max's instinct as a writer.

In June the new book was finished. Max was still very uncertain about it. He would say so again to Peter Jordan, and to Gertrud. From beginning to end, he told her, he was afraid the whole thing was an abject failure.[42]

It was published in October, and of course it wasn't a failure: for the second time he had good reviews in Germany.[43] Gertrud loved it, which almost made him happy. So did the most important person in *The Rings of Saturn* itself, his friend and fellow writer Michael Hamburger. Michael thanked Max for his beautiful book. 'I think,' he wrote, 'you have hit on a most satisfactory form of essayistic semi-fiction, which

gives rope to both observation and imagination.'[44] 'Essayistic semi-
fiction' is the neatest summary of Max's method anyone ever managed,
including himself. He surely grinned in recognition.

Nothing, however, could make much difference to the usual slough
of despond at the end of a book. On tour in Germany in November,
his black mood was clear. He lived from day to day now, he said, just
hoping to avoid catastrophe.[45] His was a *Toten und Trauer* book, a book
of the dead and of mourning, its central theme grief over the downward
plunge of nature and history. Yet even the dissolution of nature was
not entirely negative: it meant that there would be an end. He said this
even more clearly to Renate Just, who'd come to England again as soon
as *Saturn* appeared. He took her to Southwold, to the Sailors' Reading
Room and to the Crown Hotel for breakfast. 'What's so bad about the
end of the human race?' he asked her. At last there'd be silence.[46]

There was another reason for his black mood during *The Rings of Saturn*
and after it. In the spring of 1994 Michael Hulse had begun translating
The Emigrants, and sending his work to Max for his approval. But Max
did not approve. Instead, he was bitterly disappointed.[47]

This is a long and painful story. Hulse would continue to translate
Max's books – first *Saturn* itself, then *Vertigo* – and the problem never got
better. Instead it got worse, until Max ended their collaboration and chose
another translator: the *doyenne* of her profession, Anthea Bell. Anthea
would translate *Austerlitz*, as well as two other books of Max's that were
published after his death. Her work was superb, as always, and pleased
Max incomparably more, so that his last experience of being translated was
a happy one. But in 1994, and for five years after that, it was a nightmare.

Translation is literature, and the judgement of it is just as subjective. So
I can only give my own account of this saga. This is what I think happened.

Michael worked with great dedication and with profound admiration
for Max's art, which he often expressed to him. But he also worked
under pressure, and therefore quickly, which led to errors and delays.
That was bad enough. But the other problem was that Michael was a
poet, with his own strong sense of language. And he was also a youngish
man (he was forty in 1995). Conflict was inevitable.

There are – to simplify horribly – two poles of thought about
translation. One holds that the job is to render the work as beautifully
as possible in the new language. The other holds that the job is rather
to convey the original as closely as possible. (The ideal is to do both, of

course, but like most ideals it's not always achievable.) Max was strongly of the second school, while Michael's gift lay in the first. The result was that Michael wholly Englished – and Hulse'd – Max's language, and Max furiously re-Germanised and re-Sebaldised it again. He worked almost as long and hard on Michael's translations as he'd done on his own originals, rewriting almost every line. And the result of that, to my ear, was remarkable, and the best of both worlds. He had a poet's flowing English version before him, to which he restored his own unique sound, to make a whole new work of art. In my view, in that of everyone at Harvill, and in that of most English reviewers and readers, Max's books as translated by Michael Hulse, then rewritten by Max himself, are great works of English literature, different from but equal to *Austerlitz*.

That was (I think) the literary situation. Then there was the personal one, that had to do with Michael's being a youngish man. It didn't mean that he insisted on his own ideas; in fact he accepted almost all Max's rewritings, and was far more willing to compromise than many others would have been, as Max acknowledged. And Max, as Michael recognised in turn, was always pleasant – thanking him for his work, begging him not to be alarmed at what were really only minor changes... But beneath their mutual courtesies it was war. Max was horrified at what seemed to him a complete failure to capture his voice. And every time Michael's work came back to him almost entirely obliterated and rewritten, he was filled – as he would eventually admit – with fury and despair. On they would go, since Michael knew that Max was a great artist, and perhaps Max knew that Michael was giving him the basis for a new art. But they were both unhappy; and it had to end.

The consequence was one of the least attractive episodes in Max's life. He was often capable of ingratitude when it came to his work, complaining bitterly about Eichborn's meanness with money, for instance, when they had published him beautifully for many years. But this case was worse. He not only underestimated Michael Hulse's role in the success of his first three English translations, so that Hulse has never received proper credit for it. But the nightmare at the time was just as much Hulse's. Max raged about him to everyone he met; he showed his translations to colleagues, to the fledgling translators of BCLT, and asked for improvements; he said in private and also in public that he had written his English versions himself. The only person to whom he said nothing was Hulse himself, who was left to hear of Max's complaints from other people.

This silence began in kindness, but soon became cowardice, and finally betrayal. Max's weaknesses had changed as little as his strengths. It was how he'd behaved to Sabine Ritter when he was eighteen, dismissing her at last in front of a friend.

II

It was on a grey, overcast day in August 1992 that I travelled down to the coast in one of the ~~On a heavily overcast day in August 1992 I travelled down to the coast in the~~ old ~~diesel railcars, grimed so high as the windows with soot and oil, that ran from Norwich to~~ ~~Lowestoft at that time. There were only a few other passengers.~~ They sat in the half-light ~~semi-darkness~~ on the ~~worn purple~~ seats, all of them facing the engine and as far ~~apart~~ *away from each other* as they could ~~sit~~, and ~~so~~ silent, ~~they might never have uttered a word in their entire~~ lives. Most of the time the carriage, pitching about unsteadily on the track, was merely coasting ~~since~~ there is an almost unbroken gentle decline towards the sea; at intervals, though, when the gears engaged with a jolt that rocked the entire ~~shell~~, the grinding of cog wheels could be heard for a while, till the onward roll resumed, ~~accompanied by~~ ~~an even throb~~, past back gardens ~~and~~, allotments, ~~and~~ rubbish dumps and factory yards *to the east* ~~as we travelled~~ out into the ~~fenlands~~ beyond ~~the eastern suburbs. By way of Brundall,~~ ~~Brundall Gardens,~~ Buckenham and Cantley, where ~~the belching smokestack of~~ a sugar beet refinery ~~sits~~ in a field like a steamer at a wharf, the line follows the River Yare ~~till at~~ Reedham ~~it crosses the water, describes a wide curve, and enters flatland that~~ stretches southeast ~~as far as the coast. There is nothing to see but the occasional~~ solitary ~~farm building~~, the grass and the rippling reeds, one or two sunken willows, and some ~~derelict~~ conical brick buildings, like relics of ~~a dead~~ civilization. These are all that remains of the countless wind pumps and windmills whose white sails revolved

Typescript of the opening page of Chapter II of The Rings of Saturn: *Hulse's translation, with Max's corrections. As usual, Bill Swainson and the other Harvill editors would then polish the text even further, for instance changing 'as silent as if not a word had ever passed their lips in the whole of their lives' to 'so silent, that not a word might have passed their lips in the whole of their lives'. Then it went back again to Max for final approval. The whole process of linguistic perfection, from Hulse to Max to Swainson and back to Hulse and to Max again, was painstaking – but also thrilling to watch unfold in their letters and typescripts in the DLA, as the final version slowly takes shape.*

The translation story doesn't end here. Because Max had his own private editor as well: his secretary and friend, Beryl Ranwell.[48]

Beryl often blithely corrected Max's English when she typed his academic work, or his reports for BCLT. As a result he'd known for years what she could do. So 'What generally happens,' he told an audience at

UEA in 1999, 'is that the translator produces a draft, which I then work through in great detail, and then I take what I have been able to add to Beryl Ranwell … and together we comb through the whole thing again because I need somebody with a good English ear, which I have not got.'[49]

Beryl doesn't seem to have worked on 'Dr Henry Selwyn' at the start of Sebald's prose career or on *Austerlitz* at the end. But she helped with all the rest. Max thanked her particularly for her 'patient and invaluable' labours on *Saturn*, as did his publisher, Christopher MacLehose. MacLehose even sent her a cheque for £1,000 – an extraordinary sum for someone not connected in any way with the publishing house. Clearly Beryl contributed a great deal. Max always said she did, and the six bulging folders of typescripts her daughter found after her death prove it. There are hundreds, even thousands of pages with insertions and corrections in her hand, and a notebook full of passages rewritten almost as often as Max himself did.

Typescript of part of p. 36 of The Rings of Saturn, *with changes in Beryl's handwriting, ending in her shorthand. Almost all were incorporated in the published text.*

Alas, though, there is no way of being certain what these typescripts show. Were the entries in Beryl's hand her own suggestions, changes Max dictated to her, or the result of discussions between them? From everything he said, we can be sure that a great many suggestions were hers. But how many, and which ones? With both gone, we'll never know.*

Whatever the precise truth, this was another kick in the teeth for Hulse: someone was trusted more than he was, and who was she, and why? Max never explained and never apologised. In any case it was quite untrue that he lacked a 'good English ear': his UEA colleague and friend Jon Cook says that he spoke it like a native, and knew better than any native speaker how it worked. Beryl agreed. 'Why does he need me? He could do it himself,' she said. What he lacked was confidence, and that, in buckets, was what she supplied.

Beryl had a posh voice and a breezy way of talking – 'Hello, darling!' she'd apostrophise the students. She was also contemptuous of modern PC rules. No one would any longer say, for instance, that someone was 'just a secretary', but Beryl paid no attention. 'Nonsense, darling!' she would exclaim. 'Secretaries don't matter. Have you spoken to the *man*?' All this gave the impression that she was an old-fashioned upper-class person, with an old-fashioned upper-class education. Max may have thought so too, at first.

But she was nothing of the kind. In fact, Beryl was an example of the porousness of the class system in twentieth-century Britain, much as Max himself was in Germany. Her grandfather was a farmer, her father a butcher; Beryl got into grammar school and became the first educated person in her family. After that she went to secretarial college, not university, as people guessed. But she married a university graduate, and loved learning for the rest of her life. Her job was thus perfect for her; and she was perfect for her boss and friend, Max Sebald.

At a symposium on translation in 2001 he drew a portrait of his ideal translator.[50] It would probably *not* be a young man, he said. Rather it would be someone 'who comes to translation by chance, perhaps', and who possessed passion, 'a deep memory for past generations' words', and a good general education. The student who recorded these words

---

*See the Appendix to this chapter for a further puzzling over this question.

guessed that he meant Anthea Bell. But Anthea was a professional and an Oxford graduate. Rather, Max had precisely described Beryl Ranwell.

The kitchen table at which Max and Beryl worked in the mid- to late 1990s.

Max, we can safely say, had never been an optimist. But *The Rings of Saturn* shows how much his state of mind had darkened by the mid-1990s. His close friends noticed it,[51] and he didn't deny it. He joked about it to Renate Just, in their interview in the Crown Hotel. Sometimes, he said, he was subject to objectless panic, to an infinite weariness. The only solution then was a Japanese one – to take a boiling-hot bath. On the neighbouring table a newspaper showed seas of flame: 'Am I not right about constant burning?' he demanded. And he swallowed a strong anti-headache tablet.

This was part of the problem, whether cause or effect it's hard to say: his health declined throughout the 1990s.[52] Already in 1990 he'd felt the *Herzkasper* around the corner, and after 1992 he was never free of back pain. But around 1995 it became more serious. He began to have increasingly bad migraines, like the one he was clearly having in the Crown Hotel. His blood pressure was probably already high. And he started to have what he called an 'allergy' to alcohol. Wine set off a migraine, so he drank only the occasional small beer. But even that could make him grow quite red in the face; then, says Richard Sheppard, 'he would have what he called a "djooce"' instead. He complained about everything else, but not about these ailments, which instead he covered up as much as he could. Only to people far away did he sometimes let on. To Kristin, for instance, who'd moved from London to Tel Aviv, he wrote that he hoped he'd last a few more years.[53] He was, one interviewer reminded him, only fifty-one years old. True, Max replied, but he felt much older. So yes, his English was quite good, but 'for the eight or ten years left' it wasn't worth the effort of writing in English.[54]

At just over fifty, then, he thought he'd have no more than another eight or ten years… He wasn't far wrong. But for once he erred on the side of optimism.

In early 1996 he spent two more weeks touring Germany with *The Rings of Saturn* – including, in March, a reading in Oberstdorf. Then, in May in Britain and August in the US, the English edition of *The Emigrants* came out.

The early reviewers[55] were already bowled over, but at first only a few papers had picked up the book: 'W. G. Sebald' was still an unknown name that no one knew how to pronounce. The first event surrounding Max's arrival in English was private.[56]

He'd sent the German original to Kristin in 1992. She loved the book, and thought immediately that it should be read in Israel. Now that there was an English version, she set to work. She gave a copy to a publisher, and hoped Max would come to Tel Aviv himself when the book came out. What happened then was – nothing. Israeli readers were still not eager to read German books. Kristin went on trying; when she finally gave up, she was embarrassed to have taken so long to tell Max bad news. In the end she never did tell him, and he never asked. It was a sad ending to a marvellous friendship, which she has regretted ever since. But, of course, she thought she had time. Despite the darkness in him, she never thought he would die.

Then the Christmas recommendations appeared, and many writers chose *The Emigrants*, topped off by an extraordinary rave from Susan Sontag in the *Times Literary Supplement*. Sontag was a star, and the *TLS* the most respected literary journal in the English-speaking world. 'W. G. Sebald has written an astonishing masterpiece,' she wrote. 'It seems perfect while being unlike any book one has ever read.'[57]

After that other wonderful reviews followed – from Cynthia Ozick in the US, for instance, and Gabriel Josipovici in England – and Max's fortunes began to change. Within a few months the English *Emigrants* had sold more copies than all his German originals combined, and anglophone readers could pronounce his name. Then four years later, when *Vertigo* came out in English, Sontag would write another remarkable review, again in the *TLS*. 'Is literary greatness still possible?' she would ask. And reply: 'One of the few answers available to English-language readers is the work of W. G. Sebald.'[58] By now the English *Saturn*, too, had appeared to choruses of praise, and Max had a passionate following among literary readers. Sontag tipped him into world fame.

When *The Emigrants* came out in England, she was in London. Max's publisher Christopher MacLehose and his wife Koukla gave a party for *The Emigrants*, which many people remember, not least because of Sontag.[59] She arrived and paused at the door of the packed room, her dark eyes sweeping the crowd. Max's friend Amanda Hopkinson pointed silently to where he was sitting. Koukla came forward to welcome her, but Sontag rushed past her. 'I'm not interested in who you are,' she said, 'I've come to see the author!'

Back in 1990, or possibly 1991, Max had visited the island of Corsica. In September 1995, when *Saturn* was done, he returned there for two weeks. He took copious notes. When he returned – or before he set out – he decided that Corsica would be his next subject.

Korsika is a secret work by W. G. Sebald, since he never finished it. After a year's work he threw most of it on the fire, and put the rest away in a shoebox.[60] Over the next years he published a few small bits out of the shoebox; after his death those bits were published in the collection of essays and unfinished pieces *Campo Santo*, and the rest – about half the planned whole – in a DLA catalogue that has long been out of print.[61] It thus remains unknown, except to enthusiasts who read *Campo Santo*, and scholars who read the catalogue.

It *is* relatively unpolished – but it wouldn't have remained so if he'd gone on working on it. Why didn't he? He gave me one reason at least in our interview: *Korsika* was too close to *Saturn*, in both theme and structure. And it's true – there was the same obsession with death and cruelty, the same imagery of fire, and most of all the same 'essayistic semi-fiction' style. He couldn't go on in the same way for ever, he said, in a voice perfectly pitched between humour and despair. He was becoming a bore.[62]

Austerlitz is different: still packed with essayistic detail about architecture, painting, Terezín, but with one central hero on a quest for his past. It was so much more like a novel that its German publisher was eager to call it one, and tried to persuade Max to accept the term. He refused, of course.[63] But I'm sure that he deliberately tried not to do 'the same kind of thing' again. It's one reason why *Austerlitz* was even harder for him to write than *Korsika*; the hardest of all.

He'd been anxious about his sight for many years, since long before that 'net' over one eye.[64] And now, around the time of giving up *Korsika*, he suddenly went blind in the other eye.

He would give this to his narrator in *Austerlitz* at the same moment, in December 1996. The sudden blindness may have been psychosomatic, as both the narrator and Richard Sheppard suggest. But another likely factor was his mounting blood pressure: whenever Beate checked it in the later 1990s it was extremely high, and high blood pressure can be one cause of eye pathologies. He was as reluctant as his narrator, but there was no way out: he went to an eye surgeon in London. In *Austerlitz* the surgeon diagnoses central serous retinopathy, which mostly affects males between twenty and fifty ('middle-aged writers' is a Sebaldian joke) and is usually temporary. Max's blind spots were indeed temporary, and his own diagnosis was most likely the same. Perhaps in gratitude, he would give the fictional doctor the real one's name.

The year 1996 was the start of his meteoric rise. But *Korsika* had failed, and for many days he thought he was losing his sight. It would have made a good self-mocking tale, but this one was too true to tell.

Appendix

Beryl Ranwell's contribution to
W. G. Sebald's English translations

In January 1984 the news reached me from S. that on the
evening of 30th December, one week after his seventy-
fourth birthday, Paul Bereyter, once my Volksschule
teacher, had put an end to his life. A short distance
from S., where the railway track curves out of a willow
coppice into the open fields, he had laid down in front
of a train. The enclosed obituary in the local paper,
headed "Grief at the Loss of a Popular Schoolmaster", made
no mention of the fact that Paul Bereyter had died of his
own free will, or through a self-destructive compulsion,
and naturally referred to the dead man's services to
education, his dedicated care for his pupils far beyond
the call of duty, his enthusiastic love of music, his
inventiveness, and more of a like kind. Admittedly the
obituary added, without further explanation, that during
the Third Reich Paul Bereyter had been unable to pursue
his chosen profession. This statement, neither context-
ualized nor committal, and the violent manner of his
death, brought my thoughts back to Paul Bereyter with
ever-greater frequency over the next few years, till in
the end I made the attempt to go beyond my own very fond

Beryl's corrections for page 1 of 'Paul Bereyter'.

In January 1984, the news reached me from S. that on the
evening of 30th December, one week after his seventy-
fourth birthday, Paul Bereyter, once my Volksschule
teacher, had put an end to his life. A short distance
from S., where the railway track curves out of a willow
coppice into the open fields, he had lain down in front
of a train. The enclosed obituary in the local paper,
headed "Grief at the Loss of a Popular Fellow-Citizen", made
no mention of the fact that Paul Bereyter had died of his
own free will, or through a self-destructive compulsion.
It spoke merely of the dead man's services to
education, his dedicated care for his pupils, far beyond
the call of duty, his great love of music, his
inventiveness, and more of a like kind. The obituary added, without further explanation, that during
the Third Reich Paul Bereyter had been unable to pursue
his chosen profession. This statement, neither context...
the violent manner of his
death, ... about Paul Bereyter, until, ... over the next few years, till in
the end, I made the attempt to go beyond my own very fond

Max's corrections for page 1 of 'Paul Bereyter'.

Comparing these two versions of the opening part of 'Bereyter' shows great similarities. I counted seven mostly small divergences; otherwise all the extensive changes in Beryl's handwriting are also in Max's, including the break-up of a long sentence at line ten.

The question of whether Beryl's changes are hers, which Max followed, or ones Max dictated to her, or the result of discussion between them, isn't settled by this comparison. But two points in the passage suggest that, at least where they're concerned, Beryl's edits are her own. One is in line eight, where she put 'Fellow Citizen' and he put 'Teacher': she has stuck close to the original meaning and just put it into better English, while he's gone further – as only the author himself can do. And the second point is where she has written 'remark' for 'statement', showing by her question mark that it is only a suggestion, and he doesn't take it up.

I wasn't able to make many other detailed comparisons, but what I could see in the time available suggested the same: that in many cases, at least, Beryl's edits were hers, which Max largely followed. Which is, after all, what he said.

I have only briefly mentioned the contribution of the Harvill editors, Bill Swainson and Ian Pindar; especially Swainson, who was Max's main editor. This was also very great, partly in 'managing the creative tensions between Max and Michael Hulse', as he says, but mostly in helping to produce his ideal: 'brilliant English faithful to the original'.[65] Swainson recalls that Christopher MacLehose also contributed, particularly to *The Rings of Saturn*; MacLehose demurs, saying he always 'scribbles in the margins'[66] of the translations he publishes, but wouldn't dream of taking any credit, which belongs entirely to Hulse, Swainson and Max himself – and in some unknown proportion, to Beryl Ranwell.

19

1997–2001

When Max put *Korsika* away, he told friends that he was about to begin a new book.[1] But he was so afraid of another failure that he put it off for over a year. Instead he retreated to territory he'd occupied for most of his life, literary criticism.

But this was a new kind of literary criticism: literary admiration, even literary love. He turned to writers such as Hebel, Keller and Walser, whose books he had so symbolically placed in his suitcase in 1966, and wrote about them with profound sympathy. It was a unique form of critical writing, which no one else has ever emulated,[2] and Max's last act of academic defiance, since expressing emotion is the last thing scholars are meant to do. In his literary work he hid his emotions behind formal language and multiple narrators, but in his critical writing, against every rule and law, he didn't even try.

The result now was a book he would call *Logis in einem Landhaus* (*A Place in the Country*). He wrote the first essay for it early in the year[3] and finished the last in September. *A Place in the Country* is thus very much the book of 1997. It is written without the fiction of a narrator, in Max's own voice as reader and writer, and it throws a dark light on his mind in that year.

The introduction sums up the main thing he sees in his subjects: that 'There seems to be no remedy for the vice of literature,' though the victims long 'for nothing more than to put a halt to the wheels ceaselessly turning' in their heads.[4] There is something shameful in this compulsion: when at the end of their lives Walser and Eduard Mörike still wrote things down on pieces of paper, if anyone was watching they hid them away.

All his writers are mad or melancholy, except Hebel – whose essay nonetheless ends with his poem 'Transience', a vision of a burnt-out world unique in German literature, as Max says.[5] And Mörike, Keller and Walser are all more than unlucky in love. Mörike, for instance, failed to run off with a mysterious *vagabonde* when he was eighteen, and spent the rest of his life writing the poems of his Peregrina cycle to her. For this sacrifice of love to convention, he paid, Max wrote, by being trapped in an all-female household, surrounded by his mother, sister, wife and daughters.[6]

Despite their suffering, however, his subjects bequeathed to us some of the most beautiful lines ever written: the image of the glass panel in Anna's coffin in *Green Henry*, for instance, or Walser's elegy to ash. So though they themselves might long never to write another word, Max concluded, we must be grateful that they were driven to go on, since just sometimes 'these hapless writers trapped in their web of words … succeed in opening up vistas of such beauty and intensity as life itself is scarcely able to provide'.[7] He despaired of his own botched efforts, but the same was true of him, including in this labour of love.

Much else went on while he wrote *A Place in the Country*. He and Hulse spent 350 hours working on the translation of *Saturn* (they kept a logbook, he said),[8] after which he probably spent as many again working with Beryl. On top of all this he had his teaching, as always; and the possibility of something else as well.

Paolo's first novel, *Campus*, had made him so famous that he had been asked to set up a creative-writing course at his university. And now he invited his old friend to join him.[9] Max considered this for most of the year. It would probably be his last chance to return to Germany, he knew. It would also be a consummation to work with Paolo, as the writers they had always known they would be. He very nearly agreed, but in the end his old reservations were too strong. He didn't want to be nearer his parents, and he couldn't face months on end in Germany, even with regular weekend trips back to Norwich. After nine months he finally said no. Soon afterwards he spent a week in Sonthofen and knew he had made the right decision.

In the spring *The Emigrants* won an English prize – the Wingate – as well as the Mörike Prize in Germany. In November it would win the Heinrich Böll prize, which was not only prestigious, but came with

35,000 Deutschmarks, or around £12,000. His reputation was growing on both sides of the Channel, and so was his income, the latter still largely due (despite the prize) to the English *Emigrants*. Cannily, he registered himself as a company; mockingly, he called it 'Columbus Travel'.[10]

In October he took *The Emigrants* on his first tour of the US. On his return, he found he'd been elected a member of the Deutsche Akademie für Sprache und Dichtung, the German Academy for Language and Literature. His response was classic Max – as soon as the establishment opened its doors to him, he made certain they would shut again. Starting on 30 October, he gave a series of lectures in Zurich on the subject he'd been teaching for years: the failure of German writers to deal with the air war on their cities. And another controversy began.

The lectures contained much of the hyperbole that was part of his attacking mode. And much of the carelessness too: he wrote them 'off the cuff', he told a friend.[11] By the time he published them two years later, under the title *Luftkrieg und Literatur* (*Literature and the Air War*, called *The Natural History of Destruction* in English), he'd done some careful rewriting. It wasn't that no one had written about that apocalyptic time, he said now, but that so few had written adequately about it. Out of shame and horror they had not recorded the *real conditions*, the true physical and moral annihilation of a people who only a few years before had believed they would rule the world.

Today his arguments are accepted as essentially sound. They are, however, just that – arguments. There are no haunting characters in *The Natural History of Destruction*, no landscapes, no fleeting impressions – all the beauties and mysteries of his prose are missing. It is an important part of his work, because it attacks the other silence of his childhood and opens up the other family secret. But we meet only the man in it, not the writer.

In New York Susan Sontag had introduced him to the famous literary agent Andrew Wylie, who represented all the best writers in America.[12] Now, in early 1998, that meeting came to fruition, and Max signed an agreement with Wylie over *Austerlitz*, plus the two non-fiction books *A Place in the Country* and *The Natural History of Destruction*. They would go to the major German publisher Hanser, with its huge promotion budget and first-rate distribution, not to HME's splendid Die Andere

Bibliothek collection within the prestigious, but small and always struggling, Eichborn.

This was practical Max, who longed more and more to escape his double life and concentrate on writing, which required money. On the other hand, there was the responsible, easily agonised Max. HME had given him his chance, and was his friend. He had, he told his novelist friend Wolfgang Schlüter, sold his soul.[13]

And the main book for which he'd sold it wasn't even begun.[14] For months now he lingered in the part of the work he always preferred: research.[15] His first goal, in early January, was the East End. There he met the poet Stephen Watts, who would walk him through the places of Austerlitz's life several times in the next two years – Alderney Road, Spitalfields Market, Whitechapel.[16]

He'd met Stephen at BCLT nearly a decade before, in 1990. But their connection went back further, in a classic Sebaldian way. One evening in 1983 Max was driving home from the university, alone, when a prize-winning poem was read on the radio. *Lord in dream I was lifted out of London*, he heard, and was struck to the heart, down to the last line: *Lord in dream I was lifted off this earth.*[17] He was so amazed that he did it again – he forgot where he was and veered into the oncoming lane. Miraculously, the road was empty, and a few seconds later he was back on the right side.

The poem was Stephen's. Later Max read more, and thought his work possessed a rare beauty. And everything about Stephen himself moved him too. He was (and is) extremely thin: a hunger artist, Max said. His tiny office was so crammed with books and papers that it rivalled Janine Dakyns' room. He was a true ascetic, who would never betray his principles for money, as Max himself had just done… Perhaps some of this went into Jacques Austerlitz; Stephen's friends think so. Certainly Max took several things from him for his book. There are two lines from another of his poems ('And so I long for snow to/ sweep across the low heights of London'). Austerlitz's long walk from Shadwell to the Isle of Dogs and Greenwich was his; so was the rucksack pictured in the early pages. Stephen had quoted Wittgenstein about this rucksack, saying it was the one thing he could rely on. Max used that too.

He told a story about Stephen in those years. He had, he said, not caught the name of the poet, when he was so struck by 'Lord in Dream' that he drove into the wrong lane. Then a few days later a letter arrived, applying for a bursary to BCLT: and in it was the poem, together with Stephen's name. So of course, Max said, he got the bursary straight away.

Turning him into a coincidence was the ultimate proof of his significance. But it wasn't true. Stephen applied to BCLT *seven years* after he read 'Lord in Dream' on the radio... Now I've spoiled Max's story. But what it showed remains the same.

Stephen Watts.

In the summer of 1998 the English *Rings of Saturn* was published in both Britain and the US. By now Max could no longer hide: his colleagues in European Studies, in BCLT, even in other parts of UEA were starting to realise that this gloomy professor of theirs was becoming a famous writer. And now both *Saturn* and *The Emigrants* were being translated into French and Italian as well.[18] In December he went to Paris to meet his French editor, Martina Wachendorff, and the translator of *The Emigrants*, Patrick Charbonneau. The translation was done; the book would appear in early January. By now too Max had broken the barrier and begun *Austerlitz* at last. It was a good moment.

But not for long. His letters echo with the word *grind* – he grinds away from one bad patch to another; he keeps his nose to the grindstone, his only support his faithful dog.[19] Over the next years he repeated the same thing many times:[20] at first writing had been liberating, an escape from the daily problems of university and family life. But now the demands it made were impossible. He travelled a week every month for the books, and received endless letters and requests, sometimes even phone calls. So from liberation it had become another trap, another prison. He often felt now, he told Robert McCrum in June, 'As if I am in two prisons instead of one.'[21]

And by now his health was much worse. Everyone knew about his migraines and that episode of blindness in one eye. Now they began to notice that his face was flushed, and guessed at heart trouble.[22] When his poet friend George Szirtes asked 'How are you, Max?' he'd reply, 'Not so good,' in his best ironic voice. Beate told him more than once that he ought to do something about his blood pressure. But he merely shrugged. He said that he specially loved moths for the way they die: they just sit still, until life leaves them and they fall to the ground. 'Perhaps that is what we should do,' he said, 'instead of bustling about going to see the doctor and causing trouble to everyone around us.'[23]

He slept little and worked long hours, no longer by the window in the big downstairs room, but in a small study like a monk's cell, with his desk facing the wall.[24] It was as though he *chose* to live in a prison – which is, his student and friend Ralf Jeutter felt, exactly what he did. He dreamed of being free, but it was the last thing he could really be. 'He slaved away to the point of ruining his health,' Ralf says, and when he asked him why, he answered, 'What else is there to do?' He said several times that suicide was a rational choice, and that he had never intended to live beyond fifty. 'Maybe,' Ralf thinks, 'he chose to end his life anyway, by simply undermining his health.'

Richard Sheppard's experience of his friend was much the same.[25] Whenever he tried to speak to Max during the last four years, he says, he found it very hard to break through his silences. He visited him last in 1997, and was shocked by how old and tired he looked. After that he rang him, and Max said he wanted to talk but couldn't. He saw no hope anywhere and no exit; he sounded so morose that Richard didn't know what to say.

Gordon doesn't accept this picture of greater despair towards the end. Yes, he noticed that Max looked wearier and more drawn in the last few years, but put it down to the usual burdens of teaching and travel. Only now, watching the videos of Max's readings in his last months, does he hear shortness of breath, and realise that something was wrong. But he doesn't want to talk about that either.

Max was continuing to research *Austerlitz*, going to Prague and Terezín in April, Paris and Marienbad in the summer.[26] But the writing was getting ever harder. 'It's not like being a solicitor or a surgeon,' he said. 'If you have taken out 125 appendixes, then the 126th one you can do in your sleep. With writing it's the other way around.'[27] It was so bad he even thought of trying to write in English. On a good day, he told Joseph Cuomo in 2001, when the book was safely done and he could joke about it: 'I can do three pages handwritten, just about. But this … I had to resort to writing only on every other line so as to get to the bottom of one page.'[28]

An old trouble was stirring now too: translation. He was working on Hulse's drafts of *Vertigo* and growing more unhappy than ever. He must have another translator.

His first choice to translate *Luftkrieg* was his friend and soulmate Michael Hamburger.[29] But they evidently decided to start with poetry, and in mid-March Hamburger began to translate *Nach der Natur* into English.

Max worked intensively with him, as he worked with all his English translators. It would take at least a year and a half because he was struggling with *Austerlitz*, and Michael always had his own mountain of problems, being an even greater gloom artist than his friend. It was part of what Max loved in him, together with his deeply ethical poetic and critical work, and his profound love and knowledge of the natural world.

Nach der Natur was hard to translate, with its obscure references and archaic diction, which Michael managed elegantly, as Max knew he would. But Michael was not at all easy to work with. He was getting old and tired and some of his first drafts were rough.[30] He'd given up typing too, and sent Max handwritten pages, which he himself called 'scrawls'. Max deciphered them – when he could, which wasn't always – and gave them to Beryl's assistant Christine to type up for their next discussion.

The whole business was time-consuming and difficult. It shows again how Max's attitude to his translators was based less on the objective facts of their work than on feeling and the idea of them in his head. Which was, of course, very Max.

Michael Hamburger.

By the summer of 1999 he had decided not to ask Michael to take on *Air War* after all. He still said nothing to Hulse, but began a search, without success.[31] Eventually the solution came from the obvious source. Harvill had recently appointed Barbara Schwepcke as a director, and it was she who found the candidates and arranged another blind test. Of the three anonymous samples, Max immediately chose Anthea Bell's: 'Michael didn't find my voice,' he said to Barbara. 'Anthea has found it.' So it was settled, first for *Air War*, and soon after for *Austerlitz* as well.[32] In January Max finally wrote the letter he had put off for so long. Hulse asked how the decision had been made, and Max replied that it had been his alone. That was the last Hulse heard from him. They never met again.[33]

Georg Sebald had been retired for thirty years and had done nothing since. So Max said a year before his father died.[34] He was unfair to him to the end: in fact Georg had spent most of those thirty years as a Social Democratic member of the local council, fighting his corner and criticising everyone else. He'd read all Max's books, to his son's amazement. In later life he lost his stiff military bearing and became more liberal and relaxed. He told a young fellow councillor to address him as *Du* – unheard of! – and seemed more approachable even to Max's old school friends. When, in his eighties, he refused to go to church any more, Max himself relented. His soldier father was a bit of a rebel after all, he said.[35]

Georg spent his last years, Max told people, 'morbidly depressed'.[36] That wasn't right either: according to Gertrud and Beate, he had two bouts of depression, each connected to illness, which lifted when he got better. But he'd always been anxious, fearful, pedantic ('All that goes together,' Max said),[37] and now his dying was hard. Rosa wanted them to be reconciled, and said that they had been, though Max reverted to his old attacks later. Probably he needed his old enemy. And he admitted once to missing him, despite the bitter conflicts they'd had in life.[38] Knowing Max, or anyone, that was probably true.

Georg died on 18 June – the day, if not the month, of Max's birthday, as he never remarked. The funeral was a few days later.[39] The whole family came, from England and Switzerland. Georg had asked to be cremated – another departure from his Catholic faith, which Rosa had reluctantly agreed to. The cemetery was only a short distance away from their home, at the end of the street. The mourners walked there, held the brief service, and buried Georg's ashes. After a silence they headed back to the flat for *Kaffee und Kuchen*. Max turned to Gertrud and said, 'I will be the next.'

Perhaps there's no bigger change for a man (especially this man) than the death of his father. But there were other great changes this year.

For the beginning of the first we have to go back to March, when Hanser published *Air War*.[40] Barbara Schwepcke argued passionately for it and Christopher MacLehose agreed. Harvill accordingly approached Andrew Wylie for the right to publish it in English.

Susan Sontag had not suggested Wylie to Max for nothing: he was famous for being the toughest agent in the Western world. And now he clearly saw his chance to be tough for Max. If Harvill wanted *Air War*, they could have it, but only as part of a three-book deal: they would have to publish *After Nature* and *Austerlitz* as well. A long epic poem was death to sales, and *Austerlitz* was unfinished and unseen. They were being asked to buy a pig in a poke, and for Wylie's kind of money. But this was W. G. Sebald, whom they couldn't bear to lose. MacLehose dug deep; Peter Strauss joined him, offering to take on the paperbacks at Picador; and they made, Barbara says, 'a sensational offer'. Now Wylie did the sort of thing that has earned him the nickname Jackal. He turned Harvill's offer into the opening bid in an auction and invited the biggest publishers in London and New York to take part.

Harvill was devastated. MacLehose rang Max; Barbara went to Norwich to plead with him. The situation was a repetition of the one with Eichborn the year before. Harvill, too, had taken him on when he was unknown, and had published his difficult books beautifully. He owed them loyalty – and yet… Like Eichborn they were too small.[41] Max replied that he was truly sorry. But he had one more book to write, he wanted to get off the treadmill of academe, and he needed the money.

Maybe the second betrayal was easier than the first. But I doubt it; I expect he blamed himself quite as much as he had over Eichborn.[42] But he had longed to escape academic life for years, in vain – and now Wylie had made the dream come true. Rumour had it that the three-book auction had been won by Penguin in Britain and by Random House in America, with Penguin paying about £175,000 and Random House 'a great deal more'.[43] Max was already contracted in the US for his three earlier books, but Wylie certainly got a hefty sum for *Austerlitz* and the other two, and there were foreign rights too (apart from the German ones, already with Hanser). The total was what one newspaper called a 'telephone-book number': six figures, we can be sure, and quite possibly over half a million dollars. At last Max Sebald was rich. And free.

But he didn't go anywhere. He sat in his office, rebranded now as English and American Studies (he felt a bit displaced, he wrote to Peter Jordan),[44] unable to start *Austerlitz* and grumbling that students didn't even know that Kafka wrote in German. Ralf Jeutter was right: he couldn't be free. He couldn't escape. At least not yet.

The artist Tess Jaray[45] had been blown away by *The Emigrants*, like everyone except her friend Frank Auerbach. She read *Saturn* as soon as it came out and loved that too. So now, in late 1999, she went to hear Max read from *Vertigo*.

She was mesmerised by his voice in life, as in his books, and when she got home she did something she'd never done before: she wrote to an author. To her astonishment, Max replied. He was particularly glad to hear from a reader like her, he said. We can guess why: Tess's family were Jewish refugees from Vienna, and an aunt of hers had died in Terezín. Her letter had actually arrived, Max said, just as he was writing the Terezín pages of *Austerlitz* (which may or may not have been true).

Tess soon told him what had been in her mind ever since she'd read *Saturn*: she would love to make a series of screen prints based on it, and now on *Vertigo* as well. Would he be willing? He liked the light that rose from her abstract designs, he said, and he agreed. Over the next months he visited her studio several times so that she could show him her progress. 'He really *looked* at the prints,' Tess says. He called them 'weightless', which seemed to her thrillingly exact. Soon they were working on another plan as well: a book this time, which would combine English versions of the mini-poems he was writing with Tess's images. They became good friends, and Tess saw more of him than most people in the last two years of his life.

She's known three geniuses, she says, and Max was immediately, obviously one. Everyone fell in love with him and wanted to please him, and so did she. But like most geniuses, he was utterly self-absorbed. 'It was hard for him to get out of his head and join the world,' she says. He never asked about her, but only talked about himself or abstract things. He was 'clearly a depressive', but as witty and entertaining as ever; and still a champion complainer, speaking bitterly about both his parents (so Georg was the enemy again).

And once Tess had a vivid experience of his desolation. He was standing by the window in her studio, she wrote.

> It was morning and the room was flooded with light and the
> reflected colours of the paintings on the walls. I don't know what
> happened – or indeed what I may have said – but I looked at him
> standing there and thought, this man has turned into a block
> of ice.[46]

Later, when she read what Marie says to Austerlitz in Marienbad – 'Why have you been like a pool of frozen water ever since we came here?'[47] – she recognised, she says, 'exactly – exactly – how someone else had seen that in him and that he too must have recognised that truth, and recorded it'.[48]

Max in front of Tess Jaray's work. Photographed by Tess.

In January he had another of his accidents.[49] He hated wearing his seat belt, and a day or two before had been stopped by the police for driving without it. This doesn't seem to have changed his ways: he came away now with a bang on his head. The car, he reported, was pretty much a write-off. It hadn't been his fault (he said), but he was beginning to realise that this was becoming a habit. In the spring he would tell himself that he really must concentrate while driving, and remember he was on a road.

In February Sontag ascribed literary greatness to him[50] and his real fame began. Apart from two more German prizes,[51] another honour arrived as well. The Spanish writer Javier Marías had begun awarding dukedoms in his fictional kingdom of Redonda in 1999, and this year awarded one to Max. Claudio Magris is the Duke of Segunda Mano, for instance; Alice Munro the Duchess of Ontario. Max became the Duke of Vertigo. I suspect that of all the awards he received over the years, becoming a Duke of Redonda was the one he enjoyed most.

In the spring term of 2000 he began a new kind of teaching.[52] The university had realised at last that there was a famous writer in their ranks, and had asked him to join UEA's renowned creative-writing school. He'd been reluctant at first, convinced that writing couldn't be taught, especially by a non-native speaker. But for once he had a pleasant surprise. 'That class worked better than I thought it would,' he said to Clive Scott in this first term, and so would the others.

But he was deeply tired now of his normal undergraduate teaching. He'd been doing it for thirty years, and complained bitterly about the decline in student standards[53] (that not knowing about Kafka, for instance). He'd always been a maverick as an academic anyway, not only in his books and seminars – rarely going to conferences, for instance, and never contributing to edited collections; refusing to wear academic robes or attend graduation ceremonies because (he said) his Catholic childhood had left him with a horror of ritual.[54] The surprise is not that he wanted to escape the university, but that he never did.

What he was mostly doing in the first half of 2000 was finishing *Austerlitz*. He visited his new publisher in London several times, entertaining his editor Simon Prosser with his usual comic versions of the journey – 'leaves on the line, phantom connecting trains', Prosser recalls, made into emblems of doom.[55] Otherwise he worked every possible moment, getting ever more twisted and deformed, he said.[56] One day he woke at five with a bad headache and worked till the afternoon. On another he worked all day until midnight, with Jodok's successor, the black labrador Maurice, lying companionably at his feet. In his next life, he said, he'd be a mole.[57] He hoped to be done in May; when May had passed, by the end of the summer. Then in July he had another accident, and a minor operation.

By early August, however, *Austerlitz* was finished.[58] He must have been exhausted; soon he was in his post-book depression. He told his most trusted friends – Michael Hamburger, Tripp, Marie – that it was *mal réussi, ein absoluter Reinfall*: a complete failure.[59]

By late August he was travelling in northern France for his new book, in September visiting First World War battle scenes for it, together with Tripp.

This was 'The World War Project', as he was calling it.[60] Originally it was going to be about his parents' generation and the *éducation sentimentale* that had left them undefended against Nazism. By now it had gained several other threads – he was reverting, clearly, to the rag-rug structure that was natural to him. It would reach back to the origins of his family in the glass-blowing trades of the Bavarian Forest, and to the grandfather who fought in the First World War. To him would be matched the grandfather of his French friend Marie, who also fought in that war. It would then move to three fathers in the Second World War: his own, who'd fought in the Wehrmacht, Marie's, who'd been murdered by the Wehrmacht, and his school friend Babette Aenderl's, who'd been a fanatical Nazi. Through him, Max said, he wanted to explore how the fascist time was a happy one for many people, since only that way can we understand it.[61]

Sonthofen and the Ordensburg would also play a role;[62] and so would Babette's own life, which fascinated him. In the intervening years she'd become a teacher, but at around forty she took a course for expedition leaders and began to lead treks in wild places around the world. When she was over fifty she achieved her aim of experiencing the polar night, sledging across Spitzbergen in the winter, in part together with a guide, but for two weeks entirely alone.

This was a crazy adventure, which hadn't brought Babette the revelations she'd hoped for. But she had survived, and it served her well. Before she left she'd been treated for cancer, and when she returned it had spread to her bones. But she had been through the polar night; she was prepared.

Once or twice while Babette lay dying Max came to see her in Sonthofen, and they had, she told friends, the most marvellous conversations. He also read her diaries, though he found those sadly dull. Babette had not found a way to put her metaphysical longings into words. But he could, and it is a great pity that her story, and 'The World War Project' itself, never got written.

For a year or more he'd been talking to his old friend Richard Evans about the project, and getting funds for it. Evans advised him to apply for a NESTA fellowship.[63] He did, and in mid-October he heard that he'd been successful.

This was extremely good news. The fellowship was worth £73,000 – over £120,000 in today's money. It would allow him, he told his friends, to teach only one term a year for the next four years, until his retirement in 2004.[64] In fact, Jon Cook says, it could have allowed him to stop teaching altogether. Once again he didn't choose the complete freedom he longed for. But he did choose a half-freedom, and for a time he was thoroughly happy.

Naturally it couldn't last. His health was no better, and all around him UEA colleagues were dying. Roger Fowler had suddenly gone in 1999, in 2000 both Colin Good and Malcolm Bradbury died, in January 2001 Lorna Sage. Max was immensely saddened by these deaths,[65] and took them, as always, personally. When he attended Malcolm Bradbury's huge memorial service in February, he said to the friends around him, 'Don't let them do this for me.'[66] He talked often of his sense that time was running out; and wrote it too, for instance to his ex-student Sarah Cameron.[67] To the friend with whom he felt the deepest bond, Michael Hamburger, he was even clearer. When he visited the Hamburgers about a year before his death, Michael said, he knew he was going to die.[68]

On 5 February came the last great step in his writing life: the publication of *Austerlitz*.

It was so eagerly awaited that the English translation was already halfway to being done.[69] He would be invited to America in March, six months before the English *Austerlitz* was out, and soon after that would take the German original on tour. It was only the beginning; things would become much more hectic after the English *Austerlitz* appeared in the autumn. But already the readings, the interviews, the letters from readers multiplied. He tried to protect himself, declining invitations, begging off the festivals his friend Chris Bigsby invited him to. He told Marie that if somebody rang whom he didn't recognise, he said he was in the middle of committing suicide. If they were readers, maybe they even believed him.

Among the letters, though, were several wonderful ones. Tripp and Michael Hamburger used the same word in theirs: Max, they both said, *Austerlitz* is a masterpiece.[70] And a generous note came from Freiburg again, this time from Hanno Kühnert. 'I faithfully take all the articles about you to our friend Albert,' Hanno wrote, 'who receives them with pleasure, but also a slightly bittersweet smile. You're almost as famous as Paolo Schwanitz now, which is saying something, since Paolo's comedies are hugely successful. You, by contrast, write true literature. *Chapeau.*'

The invitation to America came from Joseph Cuomo, Professor of English at Queens College in New York. Cuomo could offer only a small fee and no travel money at all. Max hesitated, but said yes.[71]

When they met on the steps of the college building, a dog came bounding up to them and Max stooped to play with him. Then the evening began. Susan Sontag introduced him, he read from *The Rings of Saturn*, and he and Cuomo talked for an hour. It was the most powerful interview experience he has ever had, Cuomo says. And afterwards Max said that their conversation had been the best part of New York for him as well.[72]

Once more, I think, he'd found a brief *Wahlverwandtschaft*, an elective affinity, like those with a few students or fellow writers, or the long one with Michael Hamburger. For the main sense that Cuomo got from Max was of something he deeply shared: an intense awareness of human ignorance. 'Max walked around with this awareness always present in him,' Cuomo says; it was the source of his melancholy, even more of his humour, and above all of his writing. Because things could be articulated there that are not demonstrable, but are real. That is what he did in his work, Cuomo concludes: he articulated what is largely inexpressible, always respecting its inexpressibility.

This seems to me profoundly true. It reminds me of Max's admiration for Kafka's *Investigations of a Dog*,[73] in which the poor dog tries to explain his experience without realising the role of his human masters. And that reminds me in turn of the dog on the steps of the Queens building, and of Max's description to Cuomo of his random research method, like a dog running through a field. Their conversation was watched over by dogs, whom Max always loved. That is an explanation too.

Tess Jaray's exhibition 'From *The Rings of Saturn* and *Vertigo*' opened on 26 April. It meant a trip to London, and Max hadn't promised to attend.[74] But he did. From late May to mid-June he was in Germany, doing readings, visiting Sonthofen, and researching his World War Project. By now, though, he was very low.

In July someone saw this.[75] His friend from Manchester days, Peter Jonas, had been the director of the Munich State Opera since 1993. He'd followed Max's lightning rise with unmixed delight – unlike Paolo and Albert, he was in a different trade, and had no cause for jealousy. Each opera season opened with a ceremony that included a speech from a famous guest; and for 2001 Peter Jonas invited W. G. Sebald.

This was a request he couldn't refuse. Peter was part of his past; and the work that would open the season was Bellini's *I Puritani*, which he'd first heard in that same Manchester time. On 7 July he came to Munich and gave his talk.

It was brilliant, Peter Jonas told me loyally – but as idiosyncratic as ever. Instead of the usual encomium, the audience got 'a ramble, like his books', as Peter says, through Max's musical past, culminating in a description of his favourite performance of *I Puritani* – on a battered ship in the middle of the Amazon, in Herzog's *Fitzcarraldo*. People were left puzzled. Just so does W. G. Sebald puzzle his academic readers, and literary readers too, who expect to find normal works between the covers of his books. I don't suppose he regretted bewildering the good burghers of Munich one bit.*

Peter Jonas didn't mind that either. But Max was, he says, morose in a way he hadn't seen before, 'deeply sombre'. He felt great depression in his friend. And he saw too that he was suffering from heart disease. Peter knew about heart trouble – he had an arrhythmia himself, and had had a pacemaker fitted. Max's slowness, his floridness – it was all plain to him. His friend was ill.

In early September Max was back on the Continent: this time in Switzerland, for a party to celebrate a clutch of family birthdays, from Jean-Paul's sixty-fifth to Solveig's thirty-fourth and her brother Valentin's thirtieth.[76] The whole family gathered in Solveig's house near Fribourg. Max brought masses of roses for his niece, to whom he felt as close as ever, as she did to him. Max, she says, was so sensitive that he understood her feelings without her having to say a word. Nonetheless, she meant to talk to him one day, and then, she was sure, all her problems would be resolved. But this was the last time she saw him. She never did talk to him. When she says this to me sixteen years later, she turns away so that I can't see the tears in her eyes.

---

*'*Moments musicaux*', as he called his talk, can be read in *Campo Santo*, pp. 188–205.

I asked Gertrud about Max's health in those September days, which was the last time she saw him as well. She noticed no sign of heart trouble – he leapt around like a goat in the garden, picking tomatoes to make a delicious soup. His problem was stress, she thought. And the burden of responsibility he took, for everyone and everything. She remembers how on one of those days he touched her lightly on the shoulder and said, 'You are the only person who has never asked anything of me.' Maybe it wasn't even true, she says, turning away too. But it is one of her most precious memories.

He must have reached home on 11 September 2001. He was preoccupied by that terrible day for the time left to him.[77] But around the middle of September, the British edition of *Austerlitz* came out,[78] followed by the American. And now he was on a merry-go-round he couldn't stop.

The reviews flowed in on both sides of the Atlantic, almost all of them splendid. In the *New York Times* Richard Eder put the final seal on his fame, writing that 'Sebald stands with Primo Levi as the prime speaker of the Holocaust and, with him, the prime contradiction of Adorno's dictum that after it, there can be no art.'[79] In the Old Rectory the letters and phone calls, the requests for readings and interviews, exploded. We know how he felt about that. And he couldn't always hide his weariness.

On 24 September, for instance, he gave his main British performance for *Austerlitz* in the Royal Festival Hall in London. He read from the book, then took part in a long conversation with Maya Jaggi and Anthea Bell. One of his ex-students went eagerly to hear him.[80] She hadn't seen him for many years, and was shocked to see how much he had aged. He smoked heavily throughout and seemed to stoop under some invisible burden. That was what made him look so much older, she thought: it wasn't so much a physical ageing as an inner one.

A month later he was doing the same thing for his American edition. He travelled for ten days, was wonderfully received everywhere and gave two more long, intensive interviews.[81] His main performance in the US was on 15 October, at the famous 92nd Street Y in New York.

This time he reads strongly, from the Marienbad episode of *Austerlitz*. He looks well, and at the end there is a flash of his twinkling smile. You can't sum anyone up in a sentence, or even a book. Least of all Max Sebald.†

The autumn term of 2001 was his teaching term, under the NESTA arrangement, and his second creative-writing class. It's our last glimpse of him as both teacher and writer.[82]

There were sixteen students, ranging in age from 21-year-olds fresh from their first degrees to a few in their late thirties and early forties. Only the most maturely literary had read him and were thrilled to be taught by him; most hadn't heard of him. One arrived at the initial meeting to find a white-haired man who pointed him to the meeting room 'like an old retainer', then turned out to be one of the tutors. The other was the course director Andrew Motion, who was young, dynamic and famous; this older tutor said not a word, leaning against the whiteboard and looking lugubrious.

In the first week he introduced himself by saying that he was only there by accident, because the university had outed him as a writer. He then followed Wittgenstein, who had begged his students not to become philosophers. Think carefully about going into this writing business, Max said, you'll be miserable if you write and more miserable if you don't. And make sure you have a day job. Being a solicitor is very good, or a doctor – people tell you their stories. Being a dentist is not so good. You see the same holes every day, and your patients can't say a word.

For the second class he told them to bring an extract from their favourite work. Eagerly they brought passages from famous authors, and Max tore them apart. The students were taken aback, but realised why he'd done it. They would make mistakes, but they were in good company.

He taught out of his own practice, telling them what mattered most was 'acute, merciless observation'. For instance, he said, don't describe physical action, since it's almost impossible to get right. 'Go on, walk the way you've written that,' he said to one young writer, and they all had to laugh at the result. Famously, he recommended that they steal ruthlessly for their work.* Read books that have nothing to do with literature, he said; collect oddities, because they're interesting, but don't think that anything is too boring to write about. Never show your work to your parents until it's published. And don't listen to anyone, even us.

He was as droll as ever, saying at the beginning of a session, 'I expect you spent the week in a state of unutterable bliss,' and telling them that

*See his 'Maxims', collected by two of the students: https://fivedials.com/fiction/the-collected-maxims-of-w-g-sebald/.†

when he first came to England in the 1960s there was no difference
between coffee and tea. He didn't speak of his own work, except to
remark that there would be a next book. He rarely spoke personally, just
a bit about growing up in a world of silence that had vanished. He was
friendly, and asked them to call him Max, but there was a distance and
a reserve about him. Often when they knocked on his door he wouldn't
answer, though they knew he was there. He had weary eyes, one of the
older students says. But then there was the amiability, and the humour,
and the vast knowledge and love of literature. He was 'a wise presence',
one sums up, 'a bit removed'.

He managed criticism largely through humour: 'Kill half the Jimmys and
I might be able to follow the story,' he advised one young writer. He praised
one tale for its quirky observation, another for its rendering of dialect. He
was careful not to play favourites, but there were inevitably a few stars. One
of these was a thin young man with dark eyes. 'You look like Kafka,' Max
said to him one day. 'That,' says a classmate, 'was a rave review in itself.'

The few awkward moments were telling, as such moments are.
The most awkward happened early on. A student broke the rule of
fair criticism and violently savaged someone's work, even accusing her
of plagiarism. Max was visibly uncomfortable but said nothing. He
withdrew – he froze, one student says – and just waited for the attack
to end. A young woman said angrily that the plagiarism accusation
was false, but no one dared to point out that the whole rant was out of
order. That was Max's job. But that part of it he couldn't do.

Some of the students formed small groups that met on their own
between classes. One group invited him to dinner near the end of the
term, and were surprised and pleased when he accepted. He told them
several more eccentric tales – one about his boyhood zither lessons 'with
an old Nazi in a closet', for instance – and left around ten, having been
charming and funny, but as private as ever.

By the end of the term everyone knew that the lugubrious German
tutor was in fact a famous writer. The whole creative-writing year wanted
to do an interview with him, and deputed one of Max's students to ask
if he'd be willing. He replied, 'I don't see why not,' and looked at his
diary. 'February fourth would be possible,' he said.

That autumn news leaked from the Nobel committee that he was a
candidate for the Nobel Prize in Literature itself.[83] He heard the

rumour – and was typically unthrilled. He'd been an outsider and a troublemaker all his life. That was what he wanted to remain.

In mid-November he gave what would be his last talk.[84] He'd been asked to speak at the opening of a new Literaturhaus in Stuttgart, and this time, I think, he was happy to agree. Stuttgart was important to him in several ways, he told his audience. It was where he had re-met his old school friend Jan Peter Tripp in 1976, was deeply struck by his art, and thought that he too would like to do something other than academic labour. And it was Hölderlin's *Heimat*, Max said, to which the poet had returned after his disastrous absence in Bordeaux, speaking the line from his great poem to the city: *Receive me kindly, stranger that I am.* He surely meant Hölderlin to speak for him to the people of Stuttgart and of Germany.

In his last two years he aged visibly.[85] In Sonthofen Kasus was sadly struck by it, as were both Max's old teachers, Schmelzer and Meier. In England the Hamburgers noticed it, and so did Tess Jaray. When Ria Loohuizen came to UEA in November, after a gap of five or six years, she was shocked. Max not only looked old, but was very red in the face and clearly unwell. For once she ignored his reserve and asked him gravely how he was. But he just said, 'Fine,' and no more was said.

Friends noticed now that he seemed exhausted and often spoke of death.[86] On 9 December Gordon called on him and they sat talking in his kitchen as usual. The conversation turned to Colin Good, who had died the year before after a long struggle with bone cancer. Max glanced up at the ceiling and said, 'He's better off up there.'

Some time in those last weeks George Szirtes saw a small group of people chatting in a corridor. One of them was Max. When George came up to them Max turned to him and did something extraordinary: he put both hands on George's arms, bent and touched his head to George's shoulder. It was unmistakably, mysteriously, a farewell.

We cannot know what he said to his mother on his last visit to Sonthofen in late October. But Ursula remembers what he said to her. She – the indomitable one – had been gravely ill with cancer the year before. When they parted, Max put his arms around her, in another rare physical gesture. '*Versprich mir dass Du nicht stirbst,*' he said: 'Promise me you won't die.'

20

Marie

'I am as lonely as Franz Kafka,' said Kafka.[1] But Max must have thought that he was even lonelier. For though Kafka could rarely allow any woman to come closer than the letters he wrote to them, something extraordinary happened at the end of his life.[2]

It's a famous story, which Max knew well. When Kafka was forty, and already ill with tuberculosis, he met a young woman called Dora Diamant. Dora came from a devout Hasidic family in Poland. She refused to marry, as Orthodox girls were meant to do, and ran away to Berlin, where she worked in a Jewish orphanage. In the summer of 1923 she was volunteering in a summer camp for Jewish children on the Baltic coast. Kafka, who was holidaying there, visited the camp and saw Dora. They spent the next three weeks together, and made plans to live together in Berlin.

Kafka had made plans before, most famously with Felice Bauer, but he had never carried out any of them. This time was different – miraculously, inexplicably different. Perhaps it was because Dora was profoundly Jewish, and Kafka had been turning to his Jewish roots for over a decade; perhaps it was because he knew he had little time left. But probably it was simply because of Dora. She was strong, vital and entirely devoted to him. He moved to Berlin, and for the last months left to him, he lived with Dora, in great poverty, but also, according to Max Brod, in great happiness. Until early 1924, when Kafka's health worsened. Dora stayed faithfully by his side until his death in June, in a sanatorium near Klosterneuburg.

After his death she defied his wishes and kept all his letters and several of his notebooks. But again she lost him – they were stolen in a Gestapo raid on her flat in 1933 and have never been found. She married, had a daughter, and eventually escaped to London. She died there in 1952, having spoken little and written nothing about Kafka. She had transformed the life of a great artist, but kept almost wholly silent.

Dora.

Marie had wanted to be a doctor ever since she was six or seven years old.[3] Her mother said, 'You'll be a *bas bleu* and never attract a man!' but she wouldn't be deterred. She began her medical studies as soon as she finished her *baccalauréat*. By her mid-twenties she had chosen her speciality: dermatology. The skin is the barrier between inside and outside, she says, so the place where trouble is often expressed. This sense of the meaning of skin disease led her to do a psychiatric training in her forties. She is a scientist, but very much in the human sciences.

Her mother wanted her to marry a *noble*, but that didn't interest her. Instead she married a fellow student who eventually became a professor. She had three children. When they were young, the family moved to the countryside, into part of an old manor house: the perfect place, where the children could have a rural childhood like her own. She was happy, and thought she would spend the rest of her life in the *manoir*.

That was my mistake, she says. Her marriage became more and more strained, and eventually she and her husband separated. The *manoir* was lost and with it the dream of recapturing her childhood. She still had her work, which she loved. But her health was fragile, and her losses had brought back the fears and anguish of her childhood, which often overwhelmed her. At the same time she was as mercurial as ever, filled just as often with pure *joie de vivre*. At fifty-four she was still young, and though she doubted it ('You're no beauty,' her mother had said), still attractive. She was not daunted.

One day in October 1999 she was leafing through the pages of *Le Nouvel Observateur* when something caught her eye. It was the review of a book by an author called W. G. Sebald.

Sebald? How many people could have that name? And there was the *W.* too. Could it be – mustn't it be – her first love, Winfried? She checked the publisher: Actes Sud. Quickly, before her courage failed, she dashed off a letter to him and sent it to Actes Sud's office. She was sure they wouldn't send it on – and if they did, she was sure he wouldn't reply.

But he did reply. Of course he remembered her, he said. In his memory she was always light-hearted. He went back to Sonthofen only rarely these days; he couldn't stand it there for long. But *écoute*, he said, he would be in Paris soon, for a reading. Why didn't she come to it?

The reading was on 8 December, at the Centre National du Livre in St-Germain-des-Prés. Marie knew it well – her mother had worked in the rue de Beaune just around the corner. She didn't tell him she would come, but when the evening arrived she was there.

When Max walked in, time spun backwards. He was dressed all in black with a white collar, exactly like the priest she had imagined a lifetime ago. And he looked – she felt it, like a weight – profoundly sad. He began to read, in that voice she had never forgotten. And all the time he read, his eyes searched the crowd.

Afterwards she went up to him and said her name. 'So it's you!' he said. He put his arm around her and they walked straight out. The Café Flore was full, but they found a small restaurant on the corner of the Place St-Germain. They sat at a tiny table and started to talk. Allgäuerisch words came back to her, she rolled her 'r's as he'd taught her, and soon they were laughing. But then he didn't like the music she did, and she grew nervous – perhaps they wouldn't get on after all.

'*Réaction de sale Boche!*' she said, with her usual spirit. He looked at her quietly and said, 'Now you'll tell me what that means, a dirty Boche.' So she did. 'You destroyed our village four times,' she said. 'You must have liked us, the way you kept coming back.' And it was all right – he leaned back his head and laughed.

When they met, he was in a deep pit. He needed his solitude for writing but, like Austerlitz's, it had gone too far and turned against him. It would take a miracle to bring him out. And that, amazingly, is what happened.

She was a miracle, he told her, as Dora was for Kafka. She rescued and cured him; she was like rain on dry ground. And she saved his book. Since they met, he told her, it had a point again. To his friend Wolfgang Schlüter he said it plainly: without the renewal that meeting Marie had brought him, he could not have finished *Austerlitz*.[4]

She was almost the only person in the world, I think, who could have done it. It had to be someone who knew that language, those landscapes; someone who took him back to his roots, like Kafka's Dora. When he thought of happiness, he told her, he thought of return, and he had always half hoped that his books might make someone like her reappear. So it was possible after all to make appointments in the past, to go back and put right something that had gone wrong.

They were so similar, and always had been, as in those photos when they were just a few years old. Both had a beloved grandfather and a *paradis perdu* of village and countryside. They were linked by their childhood sufferings – hers greater than his, as he recognised, with a father dead before she was born and a mother who abandoned her. And another suffering, even older than childhood, connected them too. His mother's shock at seeing Nürnberg burn, her mother's when her husband died – each believed that these traumas had passed to them in the womb. They talked endlessly about their other bonds, but never about this one. If Max had known that she too felt shaped by the war that happened before they were born, it would have set the seal on their affinity.

And there was a last (or first) thing, the one that had leapt out in their first conversation. She was French, he was German; his country had been ravaging hers for generations. Once he sent her a postcard of a bridge over which the German army had marched towards France in

1914, writing, *So I send you even dearer wishes now.* He had a profound longing for reconciliation, she says. It gave an extra meaning to their relationship, a meaning that was always there, beyond themselves.

They had fun together, Marie says; they were like a pair of kids. He loved her willingness to play games, like talking sternly to Maurice on the phone. He loved her gaiety, her disobedience. Once, he told her, when he'd gone to a bank to withdraw some money, the teller left him alone with a huge pile of banknotes. It was unbelievable – he could easily have whipped a few off the top. 'Why didn't you?' Marie asked. He stared at her for a moment, then burst out laughing.

He loved her not minding all the things he was anxious about – missed trains, spilt coffee, his car left under a tree and covered in bird shit. He could relax with her. He relaxed so much that he even began to drink a little wine again (this was France, after all) and got away with it. He loved her being a doctor and knowing about things he didn't, like molecular biology. Altogether he loved her being different from him, as well as similar. As a scientist she disagreed with his favourite idea, that chance is destiny; chance, she said firmly, is just an event for which we don't yet have an explanation. On the other hand she was irrational and impulsive, while he was careful and logical. And she was still attached to her Catholic faith. He teased her about it, but when she went into every church they passed to light some candles, he came with her and lit them too.

The thing he loved best about her, he said, was that she remained the untameable child she'd been. And underneath that wild child was a sad one, whom he wanted to heal. Perhaps that was even more important.

She went to many places with him – Munich and Mainz, Berlin and Frankfurt, Vienna, Amsterdam and New York – to prizes, speeches and readings. They went to endless museums (and churches). They went to the village where Marie had grown up and to the factory that had made her father's family rich. Max learned ten new French words every day and gave Marie German *dictées* so that they would speak each other's language well.

She came to know him better than anyone in those last two years. She listed his loves for me: trees, especially copper beeches, birds, especially pigeons and including crows, gardens and railway stations, rabbits and hares, dust ('*J'adore la poussière,*' he told her) and dogs. 'I measure my life in dogs,' he said.

'*Il vivait dans son monde à lui*,' Marie says, '*et il te prêtait un moment*' (He lived in his own world and lent you a moment). As a result he was *distrait* and forgot things all the time. As a result too, he sometimes didn't notice where he was and was given to stumbling, falling off a train at Oberstdorf when they were young, for instance, and tripping on the steps of the town hall at Nantes when they went with Patrick Charbonneau to receive his prize for translating *The Emigrants*. When these mishaps occurred he was deeply mortified: he cared too much what people thought, like his mother, and was afraid of not behaving *comme il faut*. He had other fears too. He had a phobia about being boring, Marie says, and another about being noticed: when they went to a bookshop together and she proudly asked for 'A book by W. G. Sebald', he ducked below the counter and told her never to do that again. And he was particularly afraid in cars. One day, for instance, when they were driving to her old *manoir*, such a thick fog descended that for a while they were completely blind. He was terrified and begged her to turn around. She refused, saying that she knew the road so well she didn't need to see it. The fog soon thinned, but it took him a long time to recover.

It was that tendency to be *distrait* that made him such a bad driver himself – not always, Marie says, but often. On the way to St Malo, for example, he drove for a while, but kept weaving wildly from side to side. When she asked him why, he said it was the flowers: there were such *jolies fleurs* bordering the road... His health was as poor as hers. His psoriasis itched much of the time and he had frequent migraines. He was hypersensitive to heat and to noise; as a result, she thought, he seemed to spend most of his time indoors.

But these were the darker sides. Mostly he was a marvellous companion. He was amazingly kind, especially when she was ill, but also in ordinary things, sending her minute instructions for all their journeys. He was a good cook and clever with his hands; he was droll and funny and (with her) a gentle tease. He had a special laugh – holding it in, like an intense inner joy. And that beautiful, rich voice that came not from his throat but also from somewhere deep inside.

But most marvellous of all, of course, was his mind, his exploring, meandering mind – '*le vagabondage de sa tête*', Marie calls it. They talked about everything. About Jean Améry and Armin Müller and Michael Hamburger, about war and the bombing of the cities, about otherness and exile. 'He made me more intelligent,' she says. They talked about his books (except *Austerlitz*, until it was finished) and his book tours: 'I'm like a travelling salesman,' he said. They talked about Germany – all he had left of it, he told her, was the passport. About his father with his ridiculous lederhosen, about his mother, who was not so unlike her mother – rigid, not warm, a slave to bourgeois convention. ('At least you still have yours,' Marie said, 'go and talk to her.' And he did.) About her father, shot in the eye by the Wehrmacht, and about his parents' silence. That was his leitmotif: his parents' silence, and the book he was going to write about it.

She was the inspiration for that book:⁵ at least, for the form it took now. For once they'd met, it was no longer just about his own family, but about hers as well, going back to all four times the Germans so loved France that they'd returned. It would culminate in their fathers' war; but just as important would be the Great War, in which some of the bloodiest battles were fought in Marie's Picardy. The worst of these took place along a road above the River Aisne called the Chemin des Dames.⁶ There the Germans had dug themselves into an old stone quarry they called the *Drachenhöhle*, or Dragon's Cave, because their gunfire would burst out of it like fire from a dragon's jaws. Which, in April 1917, it did, mowing down 40,000 French attackers on the first day, and more than 270,000 by the time it was over. After that the *poilus* – the ordinary French soldiers – mutinied. Max was fascinated by that mutiny, and by what happened after it: the French fought on, and entered parts of the *Drachenhöhle* themselves, where for many months the two armies lived just feet away from each other, divided by a single wall. Max had a photograph of his grandfather Georg Sebald in uniform, sitting outside just such a cave: perhaps it was the *Drachenhöhle* itself, he thought, and perhaps Georg and Marie's grandfather Jean had both fought there, and ended up on opposite sides of that wall.†

For the French side of the story he was reading bits of Jean's journals – twenty-three of them, going from the distant origins of the family in the Middle Ages right through to 1959, when they abruptly stop after the death of his wife. They are remarkable documents: illustrated by Jean with his own watercolour sketches, and full of vivid stories. Her grandfather could have been a writer, Max told Marie, as he'd said about Peter Jordan's aunt. He was most interested in the volumes on the Great War, in which Jean served from the first day to the last, having joined a

cavalry regiment at the age of eighteen. Max made photocopies of them
to take back to England, and promptly left them on a train.

Illustration by Marie's grandfather to his First World War journals: 'Les villages brûlent! La
haine s'accumule.' *(The villages burn! The hatred grows.)*

Because they were mostly apart, he sent her letters – wonderful letters,
composed around images, just like his books. Many relate memories
of his childhood (on which I drew for the early chapters here). One
is about the sad fate of his happy-go-lucky Uncle Josef – his wife and
daughter are still flourishing, while he himself is in a home, depressed
and demented. Several describe Maurice, asleep under Max's table or
walking beside him in the fields, where he picks a small bouquet of
flowers and sends it to her. And many – most – are full of thoughts
and reflections that echo his books. In one he imagines them in a room
where the night enters through an open window; in another, looking
down from a peak into the valley below. When she sends him a picture
of her grandfather's mill he studies it for hours under a magnifying glass
and feels that he lived there long ago. After the Île St-Pierre, he says,
Rousseau went to Britain, which is also an island, but too big. He sends

her a postcard of Blythburgh Church, one of those slowly disappearing places he loves. I think, he says, that the line between our daily life and a miraculous one is very thin and easily crossed.

He's as funny and quirky as ever. He writes one message in cod Italian, another in mock Morse code. Beside the word *Airmail* he draws a little man in a plane; between two stamps featuring eyes, he draws a nose. He thinks of her so often, he says, that when he walks down the street he leans towards France.

For two weeks he sent her two or more tiny little cards almost every day. They were, he said, *Kassiber* – thieves' slang for secret messages to and from prison. On the backs of the tiny envelopes he fixed red stickers saying *Fragile*. The pictures were often of animals – a bear, a cat, a bright green parrot – or of snow; there was a sailing boat, half a ship – because the card was too small for the whole, he explained – and a priest with his head cut off for the same reason.

Kassiber 11 (No. 12 was the back half).

Many of the *Kassiber* feature rabbits, as do several of the postcards. The Île St-Pierre, where they'd been happy, was the *île des lapins*, but there was another, earlier reason. Soon after they met, Max told Marie that he was reading Sartre's memoir of his early years, *Les Mots*. In it Sartre recounts how he was such a precocious child that his fond grandfather insisted he skip the first year of school and start in a higher class. He managed well, until one day they had a dictée. '*Le lapin sauvage aime le thym,*' the teacher read out – 'Wild rabbits love thyme.' Poor little Jean-Paul didn't know how to spell any of these words, but he did his precocious best. '*Le lapin çouvache ême le ten,*' he wrote, and the teacher sent him back to the first year.

From then on Marie, with her *orthographe zéro*, was 'Ten'. He couldn't spell at school either, Max assures her, and regularly asks if his French spelling is right (which it sometimes isn't). Often he signs himself 'Wolpertinger' (the Wolpertinger is a mythical rabbit-like creature that lives in the Bavarian forests). As well as Ten and Marie, he calls her *petite picarde*, *Maria Picarda*, *Sophie* (the name her father had wanted to give her). And he is many things besides the Wolpertinger – Josef, after his grandfather; a butterfly man, a hermit and an avalanche watcher; Stumbler, *ritardato*, *pazzo* and *grand imbécile*.

We know why he's Stumbler; behind *grand imbécile* lies another story. Marie's Picardy grandparents were Philemon and Baucis, she says, touchingly devoted all their lives. Every morning Jean would go to the mill, then return to wake his wife with a cup of coffee and a song to her beautiful brown eyes. And every morning she would say, 'But you know very well my eyes are blue, *grand imbécile!*'

Despite all the fun and loving kindness, however, Max didn't change. His deepest traits, Marie says, remained *tristesse et solitude*. He tried not to depress her with his dark moods, and mostly succeeded. But it cannot have been comforting to hear how, in bed at night, he often thought he was in his coffin. And his expression was almost always gloomy. Once when they were in a café, someone at a nearby table threw Marie a warm smile. 'Why do people always smile at you?' he asked her. 'No one ever smiles at me.' 'You could try smiling at them,' Marie replied.

First they had met too early; now they had met too late. For six months, even a year, the miracle outweighed everything else. But it couldn't last. Every time they parted Marie felt she was being abandoned again. Max understood this very well, and constantly reassured her. But that was afterwards, in letters; in the moment he often couldn't respond. He would go into one of his absences; he would turn away, as he said himself, and seem not to notice. Marie understood that just as well, but she couldn't bear it. She would panic and fall into despair, then into anger. She knows herself too – I'm *colérique*, she says, and when I'm angry I can be *incontrôlable*. That happened several times; once Max even shouted himself, for perhaps the first time in his life. He panicked too, he explained, when he felt powerless. They both felt powerless. They both, he said, bore too much damage. Twice they nearly decided to end things. But that never lasted either.

Perhaps he just wasn't made for happiness, Max said; perhaps he even ran away from it.[7] On some deep level I think he did. He was made for many things, but not to sit still in peace and love.

What would have happened if he had gone on living? Marie knew that he would never leave his family or his solitude. And he knew that she would remain the hurt child he couldn't heal. The only end was Kafka's, whenever it might come.

PART VII

W. G. Sebald

21

To *The Emigrants*

The authentic artists of the present day are those whose works
reverberate with the greatest horror.

Theodor Adorno

The Emigrants was Sebald's breakthrough book, as we know. And
because it's also my own favourite, as I've confessed, I've already dealt
with it in detail, and won't say more here.

This is a biography, not a work of literary criticism. So for the other
books I shall concentrate again on biography: that is, on their origins
and development. But this book exists only because of what, and how,
Sebald wrote, and something must be said about that too. Particularly
how it hangs together as the project of his life, and presents us (to steal
a line from *The Rings of Saturn*) with a cross-section of his brain.

After Nature started, he said, when he read *The Head of Vitus Bering* –
an extraordinary work by the Austrian writer Konrad Bayer – and saw
a passing reference to the German explorer Georg Wilhelm Steller.[1]
Already the great themes of coincidence and connection lit up in his
mind. There was the coincidence of their shared initials, and of Steller's
birth in Windsheim, where Rosa had passed her panic to her son in
the womb; when he moved on to the Grünewald story, he linked that
to Windsheim too, and to himself again, via 18 May, and the artist
Sebald Beham, and Grünewald's face burdened with grief, the eyes
'sliding downwards into loneliness'[2] like his own. (And is it obsessive

to notice that 'Grünewald' also pivots around the letters G and W,[3] and 'Windsheim' around W and S?)

After Nature connects to *Vertigo* through its form: two portraits of others and a self-exploration. But it connects above all to *The Rings of Saturn*, through its pessimism about nature and history, and its concentration on horror and pain. This first work, written out of the crisis of the author's thirty-fifth year, is the most pessimistic and pain-filled of all. Someone who liked and admired him, but saw him clearly, said that he 'mythologised his own private affairs into... the human condition'.[4] That is undoubtedly true. But for all of us some of the time and some of us all of the time, it also *is* the human condition, seen with the clarity of a sufferer.

The next step, *Vertigo*, was a big one. It is orchestrated around the motif of repetition: Kafka repeats Stendhal's Italian journey a century after him; the narrator repeats both nearly seventy years after that, and again seven years later. He begins with a walk into W. and ends with one around London, and in the middle the doublings multiply into dark comedy – the Kafka-like twins, the alliterative sisters Babette and Bina, the two doctors Piazolo and Rambousek; and Piazolo and the priest, who at one point mix up their rucksacks, so that the doctor drives off to his next patient 'equipped for the last rites', while the priest brings medical equipment 'to the next member of his congregation who was about to expire'.[5]

If *The Emigrants* is Sebald's main fact-fiction mix, *Vertigo* is the prime example of his collaging his text from other texts: not only the ones in plain sight, such as Stendhal's *De l'amour* and *Life of Henry Brulard*, Casanova's *Histoire de ma fuite des prisons de la République de Venise*, Grillparzer's *Italian Diary* and Sciascia's *1912 + 1*, but innumerable other hidden ones.[6] The opening of 'All'estero' recalls that of *Death in Venice* and the end of 'Il Ritorno in patria' recalls *The Winter's Tale*; there are bits of Walser, Améry, D. H. Lawrence and Edward Thomas, and echoes of Thomas Bernhard and Hoffmann's *The Sandman*; the key scene of the narrator's childhood, in which the hunter Schlag has sex with the serving girl Romana, is practically lifted from Peter Weiss's *The Shadow of the Body of the Coachman*. But more than anyone else, as Sebald said himself, the text is 'one big homage to Kafka'.[7]

'Dr K. Takes the Waters at Riva', the third chapter of *Vertigo*, is a mass of quotations and half-quotations from Kafka's letters and diaries. But there is a great deal more than that. For example, the central episode of the grey *chasseur* in the attic of the Alpenrose comes almost word for word from a fragment of Kafka's called 'In the Attic'.[8] The fearful stranger Sebald's narrator imagined as a boy, with the curved sabre in his lap, comes from Kafka; and when in his dreams the narrator finally touches the *chasseur*, and sees with horror his hand black with dust, that too comes from Kafka. And most importantly, the figure in Kafka's attic tells the boy his name: Hans Schlag, from Kossgarten on the Neckar. Hans Schlag from Kossgarten on the Neckar is the man in *Vertigo* who copulates with Romana and dies, soon after which the narrator-as-a-boy, who has witnessed their tryst, sickens and nearly dies himself.

The link between sex and death couldn't be clearer. And not only in *Vertigo* – it was already there in Kafka, in the man's sabre and the boy's blackened hand. Was it in particular touching a man that both narrators feared? And their authors as well? We are back to the question of homosexual fear. Both episodes are fictions, in Sebald's case borrowed from Kafka and Weiss. But just because they are borrowed doesn't mean that they aren't crucial to him – on the contrary. Some scholars have argued that the answer in both cases is yes.[9] In *Vertigo* Sebald certainly says yes about 'Dr K.'.[10] This was the time, I have suggested, of his own greatest fear. The identification with Kafka was, perhaps, a consolation.

But there's more. The '*chasseur*' was a Tyrolean soldier, a *Feldjäger*, and the meaning of *Jäger*, as of *chasseur*, is *hunter*. *Vertigo*'s Hans Schlag is a hunter, and that comes from Kafka too.

Hans Schlag in 'In the Attic' is a first sketch for another Kafka character:[11] the Hunter Gracchus, in the story of that name, set in Riva on Lake Garda, where Kafka stayed in 1913. And the Hunter Gracchus is as important to *Vertigo* as Nabokov to *The Emigrants*. He links the four stories of *Vertigo* as Nabokov links those of *The Emigrants*, with a fleeting, enigmatic appearance in each, which at first you hardly notice, but which grows stronger with each repetition, until you realise that the whole delicate lacework of the book is held together by this one unnamed figure.

At the start of Kafka's story a boat enters the harbour of Riva. On it two men 'in dark coats with silver buttons carried a bier, on which, under a large silk cloth with a floral pattern and fringe, a man was plainly lying'.[12] In 1813 Beyle sees this apparition, in 1980 and 1987 the narrator does, in 1913 Dr K. does, and identifies him as Gracchus the huntsman. Finally, in 'Il Ritorno in patria' the bier returns one last time, morphed into a woodcutter's sledge, on which the boy who will become the narrator sees 'what was plainly the body of a man under a wine-coloured horse-blanket'.[13] The man is Schlag, and the autopsy on his body records that a sailing ship was tattooed on his left upper arm. Schlag is thus the Hunter Gracchus, in Sebald as in Kafka.

Who is Gracchus? He is a hunter from the Black Forest who fell from a rock while chasing a chamois and died. But then something irretrievable happened: the boatman to the next world, distracted by his beautiful homeland, took a wrong turn and lost his way. Since then Gracchus has wandered over the waters of the earth, no longer alive, but unable truly to die.

He is thus the ultimate image of the wanderer with no home in this world, either in reality or in metaphor: like all three writers, Stendhal, Kafka and Sebald. Especially, of course, like Sebald: at home but not at home in W., his life already disappearing into his writing. At the same time, Gracchus is Schlag, in whom sex and death meet. And again, in both Kafka and Sebald, Gracchus's fear may be of homosexual love, as he touches the knee of the mayor of Riva.[14]†

Max said repeatedly that *Vertigo* was about love. Or rather, he added, about the problems of love.[15]

More precisely, it is about the impossibility of love. In it, Dr K. runs away from the threat of marriage to Riva, where he enjoys the only kind of love he can bear, a fantasy without a future. The terrors of love, Sebald wrote, 'stood foremost among all the terrors of the earth' for Dr K.[16] That, I think, is the truth about both Dr K and the narrator of *Vertigo*: love itself, including physical intimacy with another human being, either man *or* woman, is terrifying. It hardly happens – and then only disastrously – within the covers of this book or any other by W. G. Sebald.

'Beyle' is explicitly about love – entitled '*Das Merckwürdige Faktum der Liebe*'* in German, in English 'Love is a Madness Most Discreet' (quoting *Romeo and Juliet* – and we all know how that ends). Like *After Nature*, *Vertigo* began from another book: Stendhal's *De l'amour*,[17] the

---

*'The Remarkable Factum of Love'.

story of his great unrequited love for Métilde Dembowski Viscontini. Now Sebald read more Stendhal, evidently including his *Vie de Henri Brulard*, an extraordinary work not unlike Sebald's own, mixing autobiography with fiction and studded with diagrams and drawings. Some of these are reproduced in *Vertigo*, including Stendhal's list of the dozen or so women he loved, whose initials he scratched (he tells us) in the dust above an Italian lake.[18] Few of them returned his love any more than Métilde, and though one or two did, the 'habitual condition of my life', he wrote, 'is that of an unhappy lover'.[19]

In fact Stendhal, who has always been seen as a womaniser, the opposite of Kafka and Sebald, is like them after all: certainly in Sebald's portrait, and probably in reality as well. Love was a chimera for him, something that existed only in art and his imagination. Thus the love duet from Cimarosa's *Il matrimonio segreto*, '*Cara non dubitar*', moves him (in *Vertigo*) more than any actual experience; and the plaster cast of Métilde's hand 'meant almost as much to him', Sebald wrote, 'as Métilde herself could ever have done'.[20] Angela Bereyter, with whom Stendhal lived, took him out of his imagination, and he never loved her;[21] Métilde, who was the most inaccessible of all, he loved most of all.

One of Sebald's gifts is to capture his themes in unforgettable images. So we see the dead return to us when Johann Naegeli's body emerges from the ice; and here we see his picture of Kafka and himself – homeless wanderers, melancholics more dead than alive – in Hunter Gracchus on his bier. And in 'Beyle' he embodies his idea of love in an image taken from *De l'amour*. On their visit to the salt mines near Salzburg, Beyle's companion is presented with a twig brought up from the mine, where it has become encrusted with thousands of glittering crystals. This 'truly miraculous object' seems to him 'an allegory for the growth of love in the salt mines of the soul'.[22] That is: love is a miracle created in our own minds, covering a small and ordinary thing.

Sebald does not, for once, include a picture of the crystallised twig in *Vertigo*. But there is such a picture somewhere else, we know – in 'Max Ferber', when the narrator visits the salt frames at Kissingen. There it is an image of art, and also of the narrator's life, petrified by years of turning it into words. The beginning of that process is here, when he recognises the illusion of love.†

22

The Rings of Saturn

If we start with *Vertigo*, as Sebald did, we can trace five motifs through his prose. First, that of illusory or impossible love, in *Vertigo*. Then that of the first silence, the Holocaust, stretching from *The Emigrants* to *Austerlitz*. Third, returning to the poem *After Nature* and culminating here, in *The Rings of Saturn*, the wider horrors of nature and history. In *The Natural History of Destruction*, the second silence, the bombing of the German cities. And finally, in *A Place in the Country*, the consolations of fellowship across the years.

They are all in *The Rings of Saturn*. Love lost or impossible is in the stories of Edward FitzGerald and William Browne, Chateaubriand and Charlotte Ives, the narrator and Catherine Ashbury, while the dread of physical love first seen in *Vertigo* is in the vision of the 'sea monster' at Covehithe. The Holocaust is in the story of George Wyndham Le Strange, the bombing of the cities in the encounter with William Hazel. The horrors of nature are in the sandstorm of Chapter VIII and the mourning for millions of trees at the end of Chapter IX. The horrors of humanity are everywhere, from the small-scale horrors of the individual to the large one of history, in the stories of Aris Kindt, Casement and the Ashburys, in the rage against our use of fire, in the battle of Sole Bay, the massacre at Shingle Street and the spectre of atomic warfare on Orford Ness, to the baroque cruelties of ancient China and the unceasing sacrifice of the creatures of the earth, sea and sky to our appetites. And despite all this, the consolations of fellowship are also here, in the heartfelt accounts of the writers Browne and Conrad, FitzGerald and Swinburne, of the narrator's friends the Hamburgers, of the true artist Thomas Abrams, and of the innocents Stanley Kerry, Janine Dakyns, Michael Parkinson and Frederick Farrar.

Here too is the delicate binding together of a book with images. In the first two it was Gracchus and Nabokov; in *Saturn* it's the circle.[1] The title tells us so, before we begin. The walk itself is a circle, the trees whose branches touch the ground form circles, the swallows who once held the world together flew in circles, the mazes in which the narrator loses himself are circles. And the last maze, we remember, 'represented a cross-section of [his] brain', in which the thoughts 'went round … incessantly':[2] so that it is really in the circle of his thoughts that he is lost, and the circle of his thoughts that we enter when we read his book.

Just as important is the imagery of silk. It appears first at the end of Chapter I, in the 'purple piece of silk … in the urn of Patroclus'.[3] Later, in a hopeless effort to earn a living, the Ashbury sisters sew linens and dresses they mostly undo soon after:[4] except for a bridal gown made of hundreds of scraps of silk, a work of art so perfect that it almost seems alive. And the last chapter is almost entirely a history of silk, which describes how out of the suffering of weavers and of the silk moth *Bombyx mori* come materials of 'indescribable beauty … like the plumage of birds'.[5] The book ends with a catalogue of silk samples, which seem to the narrator to be 'leaves from the only true book';[6] and, in the last lines, with the silk mourning ribbons with which mirrors and paintings were once covered, in order not to distract the soul on its final journey (as happened, we recall, to the Hunter Gracchus).[7]

Both silk works of art are made not by artists, but by people practising a craft – like Frohmann in *The Emigrants*, whose model of the Temple of Solomon Ferber recognises as the first true work of art he has ever seen. The wretched weavers who yet produce silks of indescribable beauty are like the wretched writers in *A Place in the Country*, who yet open up their vistas of beauty and intensity. And grey silk connects many of the books' lost loves: the Countess Dembowski in 'Adelwarth' – Beyle's impossible love in *Vertigo* – in her grey or brown moiré, the beautiful woman in grey parachute silk who visits Ferber, and Austerlitz's mother, coming to his bedside at last in her grey silk bodice. Finally, silk connects the dead to each other: from the flowered cloth covering Gracchus's body in *Vertigo* to the black veil taken from the passing dead in *Austerlitz*.

What does it mean? the narrator asks about silk's first appearance, in the urn of Patroclus. It means many things,[8] as these instances show: art, which for Sebald is craft; love, which is always lost; and death. Or rather the survival of the soul after death, which is what Gracchus and the small troupes of the dead in *Austerlitz* also symbolise. Thomas Browne the doctor can no longer believe in that survival, but Thomas Browne the Christian still hopes for it.[9] And for Browne we can read Sebald. That is the deepest meaning of the thin scrap of silk, which, Evan the cobbler will tell Austerlitz, is all that separates us from the next world.

For *The Rings of Saturn*, Sebald told Renate Just, he had covered 1,200 pages with his scrawl. Three years later the number had grown to 2,200.[10] For once, what seemed an exaggeration was true: the drafts for *Saturn* in the DLA amount to more than 2,000 pages.[11]

The result is a record of the growth of a book, and a second chance to watch Sebald at work. Once again he redrafts passages over and over, *da capo* – especially, for example, those on Janine Dakyns' room, on fire, on herring, on the episodes of the ghastly fish supper and the monster at Covehithe. There are more than eighty-five pages on Michael Hamburger, forty-six on the Ashburys, twenty-five on FitzGerald. As the labour goes on, his handwriting gets bigger and scrawlier; by the fourth or fifth draft he resorts to abbreviations for half the words. He never wastes an inch of space, writing on the backs of other typed and handwritten pages, often sideways in the margins, or below other efforts, upside down. He began with Chapter VII, the visit to the Hamburgers,[12] and may have begun without the bracketing chapters on Thomas Browne, since there is at least one contents list without them.[13] He played fast and loose with Browne, as always with his sources, bending Browne's words to his own ends, attributing them to the wrong book, even taking them from somewhere else altogether – foxing his translator and infuriating at least one Browne scholar.[14]

He made many changes. To give just a few examples – in early drafts there is no net over his hospital window, he starts the walk on a bright rather than a grey day, and travels all the way to Lowestoft on the diesel train. He moved the story of Roger Casement from after the visit to the Hamburgers in Chapter VII to the beginning of Chapter V. Occasionally he added or expanded lines, and often made them more beautiful or more ironic.[15] But mostly he made cuts. He discarded dozens of details of Lowestoft's glorious past and dismal present, and a whole section on leaving Southwold and being rowed across the

Blyth by a deaf-mute ferryman. He cut back the dream sequence of King Lear, and the encounter with the hare on Orford Ness (he'd first seen the narrator's shoes beside the hare's terrified face – accurate, but distracting).

All these cuts and many more are masterly improvements. One episode especially, which he reworked several times, he finally cut altogether. Thank heaven he did. In it the narrator encounters a bizarre figure on Dunwich Heath: a jogger, variously called Max Feldman (Max again!) or more improbably, Ariel Dorfman.* He is fantastically dressed, in white silk pantaloons and 'self-propelled' running shoes. The narrator learns that he is a chief steward on Virgin Atlantic, and his Virgin Atlantic T-shirt says *Get airborne*. All that matters to him, he says, is to leave tracks that no one can see all around the world. He points to a nearby oak tree, on the other side of which is the road, and runs off so lightly he hardly seems to touch the ground.

Mistakes show you what is essential, Primo Levi said about mountain climbing. So it is here. Sebald's attempt to introduce modern life (T-shirts! Virgin Atlantic!) into his dream-like mental journeys produces absurdity. The sense of another time that pervades the books – through the dated, formal language, the ancient guidebooks, the Renaissance paintings – is no accident, but crucial to their power. Equally, the realism of the jogger's pointing the way out of the heath breaks the spell of the narrator's sudden, inexplicable escape in the final version. Mystery, too, is essential to the 'Sebald effect'. That he cut this embarrassing attempt at realism and modernity shows that he recognised how dangerous they were to his particular art.[16]

The Rings of Saturn is almost as much a collage of other works as *Vertigo*. The disquisition on Rembrandt's *Anatomy Lesson*, for example, is drawn from an extraordinary book by Max's colleague Francis Barker, *The Tremulous Private Body*.[17] Or take the article on the Jasenovac concentration camp,[18] which the narrator says was in the *Independent*: it's in Sebald's archive, and is remarkably close to the version in *Saturn*. He added the line about child survivors ('no one knows what shadowy

---

*The name of the famous Chilean-American playwright and left-wing activist. No doubt a tipping of Sebald's hat, but in the circumstances misplaced.

memories haunt them to this day'),[19] and one or two others, including the last one. Otherwise its author, Robert Fisk, could have sued him for plagiarism if he'd wanted to.

Then there are Thomas Browne's books, Chateaubriand's *Memoirs*, and the biographies from which Sebald took (and adjusted) the stories of Conrad, FitzGerald and Swinburne. And not least the material that came from the Hamburgers. From Michael's autobiography, for example: pages 176–81 of *Saturn*'s rendition of it are remarkably faithful, until the end (as we can guess from the images of grey silk and white vapour). Michael was more than happy with both ways of being treated: 'I'm delighted with your use of the memoirs and the visit – the way that fact and fantasy or dream co-exist in your writing,' he said.[20]

The poet Anne Beresford, Michael's wife, provided as much, or more.[21] The undertaker who always wore mourning, for instance, whom Max melded with the taxi driver Squirrel, then added the joke of a mourner with no memory, and his strange career as an actor in consequence. And two other things: the episode of getting lost on Dunwich Heath, which was a dream of Anne's; and most important of all, the magical-forest dream at the end of Chapter VII, which she recounts to the narrator (though in more than one draft Sebald awarded it to himself). Anne felt less happy than Michael about these borrowings. Max was so charming that you told him everything, she says, and then he went away and wrote it. Mostly she regrets her forest dream, which she can't now use in a poem herself. And he didn't think about the consequences of writing such marvellous things about their house: every summer, several times a week, *Rings of Saturn* pilgrims arrived at their door.

And there is one more example of a borrowing I can't leave out. Sebald introduces his long riff on nineteenth-century China[22] by saying that the small train that once crossed the bridge over the Blyth was originally built for a Chinese emperor, and that the imperial dragon could still be seen beneath the paint of its carriages. This colourful detail he credits in *Saturn* to 'local historians', but no historian said anything of the kind. The only person who delighted in telling this tall tale of emperors and dragons was the wife of Dr Buckton's friend Ted Ellis, Phyllis, who was a famous *raconteuse*. What probably happened, her daughter thinks,[23] is that Sebald heard it from Phyllis at a dinner party at Abbotsford, and squirrelled it away for future use. I'm sure she's right. Both the story itself and its long preservation are very Max.

There are two intriguing biographical puzzles about *The Rings of Saturn*.

The first is about Major George Wyndham Le Strange, who served in the British regiment that liberated Bergen-Belsen in 1945, and afterwards became a recluse, living alone on his neglected estate and sharing suppers with his housekeeper, on condition that she remained silent.

Immediately we smell a fiction. The initials G. W. S., the experience of Belsen, the retreat from the world, the silence – all are obsessive Sebaldian themes. And the archives of the *Eastern Daily Press* contain no article on a George Wyndham Le Strange like the one pictured in *Saturn*.[24]

On the other hand, Max's expert photographic helper Michael Brandon-Jones had nothing to do with faking that newspaper cutting, and doesn't know how Max can have done it himself – it's very good, he says, shaking his head in admiration.[25] And the indefatigable Richard Sheppard discovered in the National Archives at Kew that a Major G. Le Strange was indeed commissioned into the Royal Artillery in 1941, though he found no record of him, he reports, in the 249th Battery that helped to liberate Belsen.[26] *Saturn's* Major seems to hover between reality and fiction, like all Sebald's characters.

Perhaps I should leave him there. But I couldn't help pursuing him through the drafts in the DLA, and there the evidence mounted. Max tried out several names for him, all with the initials G. W. S. – George Wystan Seward and George Wallace Seward, for instance – and several ranks, colonel and captain as well as major. Similarly, he tried out many names for the housekeeper Florence Barnes, all of them rather good – Betty Belmer, June Hargreaves, Frances Ferrier, Mrs Musgrave. The smell of fiction grew. Then some of his scribbles led me to the source of many of Le Strange's traits, such as sitting in caves in his garden, and having in death an 'olive-green complexion' and 'pitch-dark eye': Aubrey's *Life of William Harvey*, a contemporary of Thomas Browne and like him a physician.[27] Finally I realised something else: Bergen-Belsen was liberated on 15 April 1945, but the *EDP* cutting says 14 April. Max's grandfather died on 14 April. That settled it: Major George Wyndham Le Strange was his invention.

As soon as I got home, I dug out the interview I'd done with him in 1998: surely I'd asked him? I had, and he'd answered. He had typed the article himself, he said. He had read a similar story years before, to which he just added the connection to Bergen-Belsen.²⁸ And the name, I thought, and the adjusted date, which are connections to you.

The second biographical puzzle is about Max himself.

The line of lost or impossible love that began in *Vertigo* is picked up here, as I've said. Edward FitzGerald loses William Browne, Chateaubriand loses Charlotte Ives; and the narrator loses Catherine Ashbury, or feels that love with her is impossible.

Why it should be impossible is mysterious, like everything in Sebald. The narrator is clearly deeply drawn to her, and she, we feel, to him – 'Oh, for the countless things one fails to do!'²⁹ she says when he comes to say goodbye. But he never speaks to her until then; and in their only encounters, on his arrival and departure, she looks not at him but through him. There is clearly some block between them – like the block in Winfried when he was young, I can't help thinking. And later as well.

No doubt I'm being crude and simple-minded. Surely Catherine Ashbury is wholly symbolic – one of the Three Fates, together with her sisters, and a fictional saint like Catherine of Siena in Lenz's play, the form in which the narrator thinks he sees her years later. That is how *Saturn* constructs her. But I still feel there is something – or someone – behind her.

And when I start reading Sebald's drafts of Chapter VIII, the feeling is confirmed. He rewrites that farewell meeting often, and for a long time it is different from the austere final version. Catherine says that she has been waiting for the narrator; she looks at him not with empty eyes, but as if through a pane of glass, and he feels his heart beating in his throat. There is no stronger sign of attraction in Sebald – it's what the narrator feels as a boy when his beautiful teacher Fräulein Rauch comes near him, and what Chateaubriand feels in the hours of study with Charlotte Ives.³⁰ Several of the drafts, indeed, are almost absurdly full of conscious or unconscious erotic symbolism. They may, of course, be fantasy. But the feeling of a lived experience that lingers in the published book comes from these abandoned drafts, like the ghostly presence of the erased faces in Ferber's portraits.

I'm not the only person to sense it. Wolfgang Schlüter admitted to Max that the Ashburys seemed so real to him that he wanted to go to the Slieve Bloom Mountains and see if the family still lived there.³¹ Max never answered the implied question. A few years later I asked him outright if the episode with Catherine Ashbury had really happened. He said no, but for a second he had hesitated.[32]

There may be a hint in the story of Chateaubriand and Charlotte Ives, which is a precise parallel. Catherine's mother seems to invite the narrator to stay, as Charlotte's mother invites Chateaubriand, and years later the narrator still regrets his failure to accept, as Chateaubriand regrets his.[33] The block between the narrator and Catherine, then, may be the same as that between Chateaubriand and Charlotte, which he reveals to her mother in his despairing cry – *Arrêtez! Je suis marié!*[34] Perhaps, then, there *was* someone.

Wolfgang Schlüter had a different idea. There is no village called Clarahill in the Slieve Bloom Mountains, or anywhere else in Ireland. Max had invented it. And Schlüter fixed on the name Clara, which Max had given to his wife in the books. Was that, perhaps, behind the episode? he asked – again carefully, diffidently. Again he never had a reply.

SOUTHWOLD RAILWAY. 76
EVENING ON THE BLYTH

23

Austerlitz

The literary world agreed with Tripp and Hamburger: *Austerlitz* was a masterpiece. It won prizes in both Britain and the US, and Anthea Bell won awards for her translation in both countries as well.[1] In 2019 the *Guardian* put *Austerlitz* fifth in its list of the one hundred best books of the twenty-first century.

Despite not being a surgeon, Sebald had by now perfected his unique method of literary collage. The result is his longest and most complex work, which he nonetheless managed to sew together as magically as the Ashbury sisters' wedding gown in *The Rings of Saturn*. A proper account of it, alas, is beyond the scope of this book. Consequently I shall have to leave out so much – the extraordinary section on Terezín, for example, with its eleven-page sentence, and the magical one on Andromeda Lodge; the virtuoso riffs on capitalist architecture, or the feelings of other creatures – not only dogs, but mice and moles (and who knows, Austerlitz says, 'perhaps moths dream as well, perhaps a lettuce in the garden dreams as it looks up at the moon by night').[2]

Much else, too, I can only mention – the return of Wittgenstein, for instance[3] (once identified with Paul Bereyter, now with Austerlitz), of Kafka and Casanova. The reprised images in this book are too many to detail, from the white mist and white tents that go back to *Vertigo* and *Saturn* to the twins who go back again to *Vertigo*, the desert caravan that goes back to 'Max Ferber' and the grey coats that go back, perhaps, to Kafka.[4] And the new image systems that express the deep meaning of *Austerlitz* and all the books – that of Gerald's pigeons, for instance, who, unlike humans, always know the way home, and that of moths, who, like the stag beetles in 'Max

Ferber', seem to return from the dead, and who fly into Austerlitz's house, he thinks, from the Jewish cemetery. The image of squirrels in snow, which embodies Austerlitz's repressed memory – *How do the squirrels know where they've buried their treasure?* he asks, prophetically, as a small boy. The images of silk that go back especially to *Saturn*, from the cobbler's veil between this world and the next to the black silk cravat of Colonel Chabert, who returns from the dead. And not least the images that bind Sebald to the victims, the name '*Max Stern, 18.5.44*' scratched into the wall of Fort IX in Kaunas, and the photograph of the shop window in Terezín, in which the photographer is reflected: Austerlitz in the story, in reality Max himself.

Last, but far from least, I must leave out the story itself: that of a Kindertransport child whose history is deeply hidden from him, first by his adoptive parents and later by himself; so that he only begins to know who he is when he is almost sixty, after a radical loss of language, extreme panic attacks and deep depression, all described in hair-raising detail. I shall also leave out the way it is told – at one remove, or even two ('Vera told me, said Austerlitz')[5] – since that has been discussed before. And something new, and important, as well: the hint of hope at the end, when Austerlitz goes off to learn his father's fate, and to try to find Marie. Instead I shall say something about its deepest meanings, and then concentrate on its biography: who *was* Austerlitz, not in the story, but behind it? The answer is as elusive and challenging as any about W. G. Sebald.

Times often merge in the books: in 'Il Ritorno in patria' in *Vertigo*, in Ferber's visions in *The Emigrants*, in the different centuries that Browne, Conrad and the others bring into *Saturn*. This theme of the simultaneity of times culminates in *Austerlitz*.

It is experienced by Austerlitz in Terezín, for instance,[6] when it seems to him that the wartime prisoners still live there, and by James Mallord Ashman, when he re-enters his childhood nursery after ten years. And for once it is made explicit, by Austerlitz himself, the talker and teacher. Time is artificial, he says, it doesn't exist for the dead or even the sick, and joy or pain changes it completely. He feels more and more that time does not exist at all, but that all moments exist simultaneously (like furniture in a room, Sebald told his students),[7] so that we can go behind time or beyond it, in search of lost places and people.[8]

That is Austerlitz's final wish, as he searches for his mother in the slowed-down film of Terezín, and imagines he may see his father at any moment, sixty years after he vanished. Before this the return of the past was always his greatest fear, against which he defended himself with ignorance and isolation. That defence was bad enough: it made him 'a frightful and hideous creature',[9] and led to his loss of Marie de Verneuil. But when his memory first returns – when he sees himself as a small boy in Liverpool Street Station – his fear is realised: the fathomless anguish he felt as a child engulfs him. Ashman too, back in his childhood room, is overcome by the rage he felt when he was eight years old and being sent away to school.[10] Thus Austerlitz's wish both saves and destroys, as Adelwarth was both saved and destroyed by his memories, two books ago.

Each stage of this double bind is captured in images. Right at the start, Austerlitz the architectural historian presents the narrator with a disquisition on the history of fortifications,[11] which in its obsessive detail, its forgotten names and terms, is itself an image of his thesis: that the whole idea of fortification was insane. The more you entrench yourself, he explains, 'the more you must remain on the defensive', while your agile enemy can attack you from any direction. Despite this, after every defeat the only conclusion drawn was that the defences should be rebuilt even more strongly and pushed even further out, so that for several hundred years the fortresses of Europe grew bigger and bigger, and more and more useless.[12]

This, which Austerlitz understands so well, is a picture of his own insanity, making his defences ever stronger, when all they harm is himself. Then the narrator learns what finally happened to one of these useless forts, Breendonk in Belgium: the Nazis turned it into a concentration camp for their victims, mostly Jews. Terezín and Kaunas were such forts as well, and thus the knowledge Austerlitz has been keeping at bay with his architectural studies is revealed.

Then there is the next stage, when at last the past returns, and he falls into the abyss. And now what happens to his wish that all moments continue to exist? It must mean the prospect not only of joy regained, but also of never-ending anguish.[13] These two prospects are captured in images as well, one early in the book and one later. The first is a painting in which a skater is caught in the moment after she has fallen. The second is a statuette in the antique shop in Terezín, in which, in another preserved moment, a rider rescues a girl. One has always been rescued, one has always fallen. If time is as Austerlitz – as Sebald – desires, you can't have one without the other.

Two more images, one of each stage of Austerlitz's suffering.

First, the extraordinary story of Llanwddyn, his father Emyr Elias's village, under the waters of the Vyrnwy reservoir. Everything Sebald says is true:[14] Llanwddyn did contain nearly forty houses, plus ten farms, a church, two chapels and three public houses. And in the autumn of 1888 the dam built over the previous seven years was indeed finished, and the filling of the lake began. This took almost exactly a year, after which the old village of Llanwddyn was permanently drowned. The villagers were moved (much against their will) to a new site, together with their dead, who were exhumed from the old churchyard and reinterred.

It seems surprising that Sebald didn't include that last, very Sebaldian detail. But the reason he made Llanwddyn Elias's home was to do with the living, not the dead. It symbolises all the lost homes in the books, especially Austerlitz's; and it symbolises above all what Austerlitz has done with that loss, which is to submerge it in the darkness of his subconscious. Like the forts, like the squirrels of Prague, Llanwddyn is an image of most of his life, devoted to keeping the past hidden, underwater.

Postcard of 'A street in Llanwddyn, now submerged'.

The second image is of the second stage: Austerlitz's breakdown. It consists of three long lines of A's, 'like a long-drawn-out scream':

These lines of As recur over and over again, the narrator tells us, in the work of the painter Gastone Novelli, who was tortured by the Nazis in the same way as Jean Améry: by being hanged by his wrists tied behind his back, until 'with a crack and a splintering sound'[16] his arms dislocated from his shoulders.

He came across this terrible event, the narrator says, in Claude Simon's novel *Le Jardin des Plantes.* Simon recalls that Novelli mentioned it only once in their long friendship. It happened in Dachau; and after it Novelli found the sight of any German, indeed of any human being, so intolerable that he retreated to the South American jungle, where for a time he lived with a tribe whose language consisted mostly of vowels, especially the sound 'A'. When he finally returned, he began painting; almost always, in different forms and combinations, the letter A.

There could hardly be a more Sebaldian story than this in its perfect symbolism, and we may guess that it's probably not quite true. Indeed it isn't. The torture took place in Rome, not Dachau;[17] Novelli had been a painter long before, and went to South America to teach painting; and though he did often paint the letter A, he used many letters in his work, and many other images as well. In other words, this seems a classic example of Sebald's bending another text to fit his vision.

For once, it isn't – every detail of the story comes from *Le Jardin des Plantes.* It was almost certainly Simon who moved the torture to Dachau and invented the sequel, as though to answer the need of another artist. Novelli died in 1968. If he was the mover and inventor himself, it's a Sebaldian slip of time as well; in any case, it's a Sebaldian coincidence.

Something else may also be hidden here, in the claim that Novelli's main subject was the letter A. It wasn't. If anyone's, it was Sebald's own. 'A's recur in his work, from Ambros, Adelwarth and Aurach through the Ashburys to this last book, where they are everywhere – in Agáta, Aychenwald, and Ambrosová,[18] in Adela, Alphonso and Ashman, in Andromeda Lodge and Alderney Street, in the Ashkenazi cemetery in London and the Auschowitz Springs in Marienbad, in Novelli's appalling scream. And, of course, in Austerlitz himself, and the title of his book. That may be the clue. 'Austerlitz' is often confused with 'Auschwitz' – even Primo Levi and his companions, when they saw *Auschwitz* scrawled on their train, thought it meant Austerlitz.[19] Could it not be this A that mounts through Sebald's books, to break like a wave in the last one? Perhaps it was even one reason behind the choice of the rare word *Ausgewanderten* for his first book about Europe's Jews.

Sebald talked often about his models for Jacques Austerlitz. Sometimes he mentioned just one; once he said there were three and a half. Mostly he said two, or two and a half, plus 'bits from other lives'.[20]

The half was most probably Stephen Watts: Stephen felt a shock of recognition when Max said, 'Two and a half,'[21] and his intuition was surely right. Several 'bits' are also clear: Peter Jonas for Austerlitz's school, Saul Friedländer's *When Memory Comes* for the encounter with Vera, and in general the Kindertransport stories in Bertha Leverton's *I Came Alone*. That leaves the two main models, and about each of these there is a story.

The first is the culmination of all the stories about Sebald's models, from his mother's fury about *Vertigo* to the annoyance of many Mancunians and East Anglians at his grim portraits of their homes. It is the best-known story, and the saddest.[22]

We've already heard of this model: a Kindertransport *Kind* called Susi, about whom he'd seen the television film in 1991. Her full name was Susi Bechhöfer, and she had arrived in England at the age of only three, together with her twin sister Lotte.* In 1996 she published a book about her experience called *Rosa's Child*, which Sebald also read. It appeared in Germany as *Rosas Tochter* (*Rosa's Daughter*) two years later.

In early 2001 Susi's German publisher rang her up and told her a strange thing: the new book by a famous author called W. G. Sebald told a story very like hers. Susi wrote to Sebald, and he replied, saying that she was indeed one of his models for Jacques Austerlitz.[23] He

---

*Lotte developed a brain tumour at nine years old and died at thirty-five, which is why she doesn't appear in the rest of Susi's story.

probably also promised that she'd receive a complimentary copy of the English translation as soon as it came out.

In late September the copy arrived, and Susi, who knew no German, read *Austerlitz* for the first time. And what her publisher had said was true: *this was her story.* Here was her home in Wales, her minister father, her years in boarding school, her parents' silence. Worst of all, here were the most traumatic moments of her life: when she first discovered, taking an exam at school, that she wasn't who she thought she was, and when she heard people talking about the Kindertransports on the radio decades later, and realised that this had something to do with her. And here was her deepening distress throughout her life, until at last she determined to learn the truth, and slowly did.

A year later Susi published a piece called 'Stripped of my tragic past by a bestselling author'.[24] She had read Sebald's book, she wrote, with mounting anger. She felt that her identity had been stolen and the most important moments of her life taken from her. She determined to ask Sebald to acknowledge his debt to *Rosa's Child*; but before she could do so, he died. Her lawyer then asked his publisher the same thing. She was sure that if he had lived, Sebald would have agreed, but the publisher clearly didn't. No acknowledgement ever appeared.

This account is broadly true, and Susi's faith in Max's response generous. In fact he had put her off, pleading his many burdens, and saying that he wasn't certain 'joint publicity' would work.[25] And earlier, when someone told him of Susi's anger that he'd used her story without permission, his response was 'a bit nonchalant'.[26] As he said to his students: I can only encourage you to steal as much as you can.

Can there be any defence of Sebald here, with his special empathy for Jewish victims, and his special awareness of the moral dangers of a German writing about them? He didn't ask Susi's permission, he didn't warn her he'd done it, and no one thinks he would ever have agreed to disturb his fiction with an acknowledgement. What defence could there be?

There can be a general one, at least. What Susi felt was that she should own her own life at last, which is more than understandable. But as Janet Malcolm wrote, 'We do not "own" the facts of our lives at all. This ownership passes out of our hands at birth, at the moment we are first observed.'[27] We cannot stop people talking about us, or (short of libel) writing about us, especially if we have already done it ourselves.

No one has the right to say, *All writing on this subject stops here.* (And that, incidentally, includes W. G. Sebald.)

There are particular defences as well. Austerlitz's character, his Welsh home, minister father and school years are all very different from Susi's. And Sebald did not steal every aspect of her life that *Rosa's Child* revealed. He left out, for example, one of the worst ones: the fact that her adoptive father sexually abused her from the age of nine. Max used her story – but only what was relevant in it to the experience of Kindertransport children. 'I try to keep at a distance and never invade,' he told Maya Jaggi.[28] He did invade: but only her public privacy, we might say. Her private privacy remained inviolate.

Finally, as one scholar argues,[29] *Austerlitz* goes far beyond the facts that Sebald took from Susi. Its central theme is about time, as I've suggested, and this scholar adds others – memory, melancholia and evanescence, to name just a few. All these have nothing in common with *Rosa's Child*, but everything in common with the other works of W. G. Sebald. Even the facts he takes he develops in quite different ways, into the great motifs of culture and history that animate *Austerlitz*, but do not enter *Rosa's Child*.

On the other hand, he did take those facts without asking or acknowledging their author, just as he did with Peter Jordan's Aunt Thea. Both were wrongs, against just those people with whom he felt more imaginative sympathy than any other German writer... It's a paradox. But the clue lies in the word 'imaginative'. That he lived more in his imagination than in the real world remained true even here. The little girl in *Rosa's Child* came from Munich, she was born on the same day as Peter Jordan's mother – 17 May, the day before his own birthday – and she learned her real name from a teacher at school. These things caught his imagination, and inspired Jacques Austerlitz. The real person disappeared.

That may be bad enough. But there's more. When he was asked whether he had sought permission to use the life stories that went into *Austerlitz*, he answered '*Das mache ich grundsätzlich*': he did so on principle.[30] In the case of Susi Bechhöfer's story, says another scholar – very much the lawyer for the prosecution – 'This must be regarded as a blatant lie.'[31]

It *was* a lie, applied to Susi. Or to Frank Auerbach, or the Buckton family. It was perhaps true of the lady from Yverdon, if she existed, half true of Peter Jordan, and entirely true of Michael Hamburger. Most novelists are worse, never asking anyone permission to borrow bits of them. In this way Sebald was a normal novelist. That is the worst we can say.

Susi Bechhöfer died in 2018, at the age of eighty-one. In our last exchange, several years before, she assured me that she was no longer interested in 'the "stolen" issue', but wanted only to 'extol Sebald's deep deep understanding of the plight of the refugee'.[32] This made me happy, especially for her. But it didn't last. In an interview a year before her death she still spoke of Sebald's 'painful assault on her identity' and his 'appropriating' her story.[33] Her son finds a middle position: 'I think my mother was torn,' he says, 'between feeling proud that her story had been used and aggrieved that her book had not been acknowledged.'[34] That would make Susi's feeling the same as Peter Jordan's. I hope it was.

A year before she died, she published a second book, *Rosa*, about her mother, who had had to put her twin daughters in an orphanage, and who – like Austerlitz's mother, most probably – had been murdered in Auschwitz.[35] That tribute to her mother consoled her. And there were other consolations too, though she probably didn't know them.[36] Rosa had been deported together with the last children from the orphanage and their carers, who had hopefully been able to tell her that her own girls were safe in England. And not only is the orphanage now commemorated in Munich, but so are Rosa and both her daughters, with *Stolpersteine* giving them their true names.[37]

The Stolpersteine *to Rosa, Susi and Lotte, Leopoldstrasse, Munich.*

Sebald spoke most often about the other main model for Austerlitz, which only made him more mysterious.

He was, Sebald said,[38] a colleague and friend, a decade or so older than himself; an architectural historian who worked in London; an eccentric man and gifted teacher, whose story was close to Austerlitz's: late in life he began to look for the first time into his past, and discovered things he had never wanted to know. His story was not as tragic as Austerlitz's, he was not a Kindertransport child (that was the other model, Max said) and he didn't come from Prague; but otherwise many elements of their stories corresponded.

At first the solution seemed easy: he was Stefan Muthesius, an architectural historian and friend of Max's, who also came originally from Germany and taught at UEA from 1968. Everyone at UEA thinks he was Max's model;[39] Stefan himself thinks he was Max's model.[40] He didn't work in London, but that was an easy disguise. Stefan is five years older than Max rather than ten, but at any rate older; he was a gifted teacher (long retired now), and is definitely eccentric – friendly to everyone but detached and other-worldly, famous for his bright braces and for cycling everywhere, his feet turned out in Chaplinesque style. Austerlitz's office in the book is his, like a secret mark of his role; you can see the photo of it on p. 43 of *Austerlitz*.

But there is one big problem: what can Stefan have in common with tragic, tormented Austerlitz? He seems, and is (according to himself and his wife), permanently happy. He has produced a great deal of much-admired work, so clearly has no problems with writing, and he is not Jewish. When he talks of what he contributed to *Austerlitz* he mentions only his conversations with Max about architecture.

I was stumped, and went off in search of Jewish refugee architectural historians of anywhere near the right age. There weren't any. But slowly I grew wiser to Max's tricks, as I've recounted. Probably he was just talking about Austerlitz himself, and making us think he was real, as he'd done with Dr Henry Selwyn. The model – if there was one – could be anyone at all. I gave up.

And just as I gave up, something came in from the wings, as Max would say.[41] I discovered, quite by accident, that Stefan Muthesius had a story that was not as tragic as Austerlitz's, but did in a way correspond to his.

The only thing everyone knows about Stefan is that he is the great-nephew of the famous architect Hermann Muthesius. One of Hermann's nephews was Stefan's father; the other was called Hans.[42]

Hans Muthesius[43] had a meteoric career in social work after the war, ending as the long-serving head of the main German organisation for social welfare, with its headquarters and a top award named after him. He died in 1977, laden with honours. But in the mid-1980s doubts began to grow. Finally, in 1990, a Nazi-hunting journalist published an article in *Die Zeit* entitled 'Crimes against Polish children'. It exposed Hans Muthesius's role as a Party official during the war. He had overseen the establishment of a murderous concentration camp in Łódź, in which 10,000 Jewish and Polish children had been imprisoned, the majority of whom had died. His name was removed from the social welfare building and the award in his name withdrawn.

This was awkward. Stefan had told me about his father, an anti-Nazi who had remained in his job as a journalist during the war. He'd said that he felt lucky in his family, who had been completely clear of any involvement in the Third Reich. Did he not know about this uncle? Or did he know, and was that the story Max meant, that was not unlike Austerlitz's – a secret in Stefan's past, which he'd never wanted to know?

I was terrified of asking him. It would be a cruel shock if he didn't know, and if he did know, I'd be breaking his cover. Or was he, like Austerlitz for so many years, in some kind of denial, and would my question push him into Austerlitz's breakdown? I didn't have the right to do any of this, and for a long time I didn't. But in the end I just had to know. Was his *whole* family clear, I asked, wasn't there someone? ...

He wasn't shocked, and didn't break down. He laughed. 'Oh,' he said, 'you mean Uncle Hans?' He was indeed an exception. But he was much older than Stefan's father, and they hardly knew him. They really had nothing to do with him. 'You must come and tell my wife about this,' he said. So we went straight home for tea, Stefan on his bike, I on a bus. When I got there he was waiting. 'Kasia!' he called out eagerly, as soon as we were in the door. 'She knows about Uncle Hans!'

For the next hour or two we talked, more and more seriously. 'Max and everything he writes about is constantly on one's mind,' Stefan said. 'No German can be free of it.' But he does feel personally free, despite that distant uncle; he made his peace with that long ago. Or perhaps, I said, he represses it? It would only do him credit, to be unable to bear such a connection. Stefan denied this: I don't know what such phrases mean, he said. Kasia smiled at him. 'Stefan represses everything,' she said. Surely he did feel some guilt – why else did he come to Poland, and write about Polish architecture, and even marry a Pole? 'Stefan!' she said suddenly. 'You didn't marry me *because* I'm a Pole, did you?' He took her hand, and soon they were laughing. It was quite clear: these were two happy people.

Later I rang them several times, hoping I hadn't disturbed that happiness. No, Kasia reassured me, on the contrary. 'Don't worry,' she said. 'Stefan is at peace with himself.' 'Or,' she added, 'he pretends to be.'[44]

So nothing can be certain, as nothing ever is, in relation to W. G. Sebald. Did Stefan talk to him about Uncle Hans? He doesn't think so; they talked about architecture. But Max probably knew anyway, I thought: he was a regular reader of *Die Zeit*, and could hardly have missed the name Muthesius. Stefan may, then, be a model for Austerlitz in much more than his profession and his office. He may be a model as Peter Jordan was a model for Ferber. Peter didn't feel suicidal over the loss of his parents, as Max thought he should; and Stefan didn't feel suicidal over Uncle Hans, as (perhaps) Max thought he should. He filled the characters based on both of them with his own grief and horror. So Ferber is Peter, Auerbach and Max; and Austerlitz is Susi, Stefan and Max. (Perhaps.)

That would bring him close to Dr Henry Selwyn in another way as well. For the model for Dr Selwyn – the secretly suffering Jew Hersch Seweryn – was not, as we know, Jewish. And now a main model for Sebald's most suffering Jew of all, Austerlitz, may not be Jewish either, as I had always assumed he was. Rather than a Jew suffering from German crimes, he may be a German, secretly suffering *for* those crimes. Like Max himself. That is terrible, or brilliant. Either way it dissolves the boundary between victims and perpetrators, Germans and Jews.

Austerlitz and 'Dr Henry Selwyn' share yet more: Sebald lied about both of them.

Some of the untrue things he said about his characters may have been genuine slips of his artist's mind. But there are two about whom I simply can't believe this: Dr Selwyn and Austerlitz. Sebald *cannot* have forgotten that Rhoades Buckton was far from Jewish when he told me that his model was. And something similar is true of Austerlitz.

There are only two photographs of Austerlitz in the book: one at around seventeen, in the rugby team at school, and one at four, six months before he left Prague.[45] This is the haunting cover picture, in which, as Vera explains, he is dressed as the Rose Queen's page, in order to accompany Agáta to a masked ball.

About this picture Sebald said several times, very clearly, that it was a childhood photograph of his architectural historian model.[46] But it isn't of Stefan Muthesius, or of any other model for Austerlitz. It isn't even a normal 'childhood photograph'. It is a postcard: an old junk-shop postcard, for which Max paid (as it says on the back) 30p.

This was first discovered by the critic James Wood, who found it in the *Austerlitz* papers in the DLA.[47] He was quite right, I saw when I got there. There was the clear postcard form, with the space left for the address on the back. And there was the '30p', as Wood had said, in the top right-hand corner.

But there was more. On the back of the photo, Vera says, written in Austerlitz's grandfather's hand, are the words (in Czech) *Jacquot Austerlitz, the Rose Queen's page*. And on the back of the postcard, written down the side, also by hand, are very similar words in English: *Jackie Grindrod, Train-bearer to the Rose Queen*.

I stared at the name: Grindrod. What on earth was it? Czech? German? I sat down to pursue Grindrods through the internet, thinking I wouldn't find any. In fact I found dozens, instantly. Most of them around Rochdale, near Manchester. In England.[48]

So that is the truth about the cover picture of *Austerlitz*. The photo dates from the 1920s or 1930s.[49] The child in it is a small English boy, dressed as a page for an English festival: the Rose Queen's Carnival, which still takes place in many northern English towns today. He has nothing to do with any architectural historian model for Austerlitz, whether Stefan Muthesius or anyone else. He is a boy on a postcard no doubt found in Sebald's usual way – in a junk shop, probably in Salford, and probably in the late 1980s, when he was visiting the Jordans. And he cannot have forgotten that either.

Why did he tell this lie? Surely to back up his claim that the art-historian model was real – which, unless it *was* Stefan Muthesius, was probably also a lie. I don't mean either point as a judgement. They just show what a strange person Max Sebald was.†

I'd often wondered: why *Jacques* Austerlitz? It's not a Czech name, or a Jewish one. The postcard of Jackie Grindrod suggested one possible answer. Max often said that he'd had it for a long time;[50] perhaps the name came, at least partly, from there.

In the book Vera tells Jacques that he was named after Offenbach, in whose opera *Tales of Hoffmann* Agáta made her debut as a singer. She played the role of Olympia, the sublimely beautiful girl in Hoffmann's *The Sandman*, for whom the poet Nathaniel abandons his beloved fiancée Clara. But Olympia, it turns out, is only a mechanical doll, and the realisation drives Nathaniel mad. In his final madness he sees Clara as Olympia, tries to kill her, and dies himself. This last appearance of Hoffmann's Gothic tale in Sebald's work is his own explanation of the origin of Jacques' name.[51]

And there may be one more. In the first thing Sebald ever read about the Kindertransports, the *Die Zeit* article of 1988, he would have seen the story of three brothers, aged eleven, nine and four.[52] They lived in Vienna, but were sent to Poland when their Polish father was deported there. From Gdynia on the Baltic coast, they were sent by ship to England, and landed in the Port of London in the summer of 1939, just as Austerlitz arrived at Liverpool Street. Like Austerlitz's, their parents disappeared, their father murdered in Auschwitz like Agáta, their mother's fate unknown. The four-year-old was called Erich, his oldest brother Jacques. It's as though Max remembered that four-year-old, and gave him his brother's name.

Five years after Max's death a statue was erected at Liverpool Street Station to commemorate the Kindertransports. Erich is the small boy in the cap in the statue, and hovering behind him somewhere is Austerlitz.

The Kindertransport memorial
at Liverpool Street Station.

24

An Attempt at Restitution

Anita Albus, The Burning House.[1]

Today W. G. Sebald is the most revered twentieth-century German writer in the world: more revered even than Günter Grass, far more than his own heroes Bernhard, Canetti and Handke, though two of them won the Nobel Prize.

Why?

The most obvious reason is the one that has dominated this book: his unique empathy with the victims of the Holocaust. That is indeed important. But some have claimed that it is the only explanation for his success. That is far from the truth.

The other key reason is the one Susan Sontag gave for her astonishment at *The Emigrants*: it was, she said, 'unlike any book one has ever read'.[2] All Sebald's work is unlike any book one has ever read. It achieves the impossible Romantic ideal: it is original. Its language is unique, its mix of genres and use of photographs uniquely famous and influential. These originalities are well known. But there is another, deeper one: the originality of his underlying vision.

He often alluded to this in interviews.[3] He was most interested, he would say, in metaphysics: the enquiry into the true nature of reality, which lies beyond physics, beyond this world, 'beyond one's ken'.[4] And that, I believe, is his underlying subject – unlike any other literary writer of our time, indeed of all recent times, until we go back to the seventeenth century and writers like Thomas Browne, the hero of Sebald's most metaphysical book, *The Rings of Saturn*.

So *of course* he has nothing to do with the novel, the quintessential literary form of this world, of society. His work is not about society at all, which is another reason why it contains no dialogue. And it is only in part about this world. Instead it is pervaded by the aura of another reality just beyond our grasp, of which we get only hints and glimpses. These glimpses come in moments that make least sense, like Ferber's feeling of brotherhood with Wittgenstein, whom he never knew, and the eccentric movements of the narrator's mind, who never knows why he does things, who decides one thing and does another, or does it only thirty years later. The loveliest images carry the same meaning, of 'the invisibility and intangibility of that which moves us', as Sebald wrote in *Saturn*, again echoing Browne.[5] The most important things are almost invisible, almost inexistent, like the distant depths in the stories of Bereyter, Adelwarth and Ferber, the moths in *Austerlitz*, who appear only as an afterglow in the spot they have already left, or the windmills in *Saturn*, which the narrator sees even though they vanished long ago.

This takes us back to coincidence, the recurring theme in Sebald's life and work. Coincidences, overlaps with other people's lives (Walser's with Kleist's, the narrator's with Michael Hamburger's), experiences of *déjà vu* and *déjà vécu* – already lived through – are all signs we don't know how to read. It is the spell of these signs that pulls us through a book by W. G. Sebald, as plot pulls us through an ordinary story. But like the signs on Dunwich Heath, they point to somewhere we never reach.

This somewhere is the world beyond our ken that is his hidden subject. We feel its nearness in every Sebald book, like the twin brother who Austerlitz feels accompanied him on his forgotten journey, and who still walks beside him in his Welsh childhood. We feel – we *are* – in an in-between world, somewhere between the past and the present, the living and the dead, reality and dream, like the narrator in his parents' living room in *Vertigo*. So Ferber sees the drawing room in his lost home, and out of his Suffolk window Michael Hamburger sees Berlin;[6] so Austerlitz sees the dwarfish figures of the dead, divided from the living only by the scrap of silk seized from their bier. The great image of this in-between state is *Vertigo*'s Hunter Gracchus, who is dead but cannot die, who has left this world but cannot enter the next. He is like the dying soul at the end of *The Rings of Saturn*, whose mirrors and paintings have been covered so that he is not held back by images of this world – but the ruse has failed; he sees himself and the beauties of the earth, and cannot depart. This is the obverse of Sebald's despair about our world: it is also beautiful, and our home, and we cannot bear to leave it.

The main element of this in-betweenness is the presence of the past, the return of the past in the present, of which the great image is the emergence of Johann Naegeli's body from the ice. The wish that drives all Sebald's art is Austerlitz's: that time 'has not passed away', so that 'the living and the dead can move back and forth as they like'.[7] This wish is also a fear, as we know: since if past time never ends, moments of anguish never end either, and madness threatens, as for James Mallord Ashman in his childhood nursery. Nonetheless, it is the underlying wish of all the books: that time stop, as it does in photographs, and the lost return to us.

The other Sebaldian wish is similar – that spaces should also merge, so that the boy born in the peaceful mountains knows the sufferings of the distant war. This too can bring anguish and madness, as it does to Cosmo in 'Ambros Adelwarth'. But it means that the narrator in his Manchester hotel can hear the little singer far away in Liston's Music

Hall, and dream of driving all the way to Jerusalem with Thomas Abrams.

Ultimately even the divisions of identity dissolve, so that the narrator feels he once lived in Michael Hamburger's house, and Sebald thinks that he invented a word of Robert Walser's.[8] This is reflected in the prose, so interwoven with lines from other authors, often changed and made his own by Sebald, and partly told by witnesses whose voices sound like his and meld into his without transition. The aim of the entirety of his work, mirrored in his prose, is the absence of division between times, places and selves: so that all is one, as in the vision of mystics and saints.

Now we know (or at least can guess) the nature of that other underlying reality to which all the signs in the books point: it is *oneness*, the mystical vision that cannot be described. Wisely, Sebald never does describe it. But he embeds it in that most metaphysical book, *The Rings of Saturn*: in the episode of the beetle in the well, beside the Hölderlin pump in the Hamburgers' garden.

It is no coincidence that this key to his deepest meaning should be connected to Hölderlin, one of his best-loved literary forebears and another link to Michael Hamburger, the poet's translator. But it comes not from Hölderlin himself, but from another of Sebald's great ancestors and affinities: Hofmannsthal.

Chapter VII of *Saturn* ends with the other-worldly dream of Michael's wife Anne, in which she floats through an immense sunlit forest. Then they walk out into the garden, and wait for the narrator's taxi beside the Hölderlin pump. In the last line of the chapter he sees, 'with a shudder that went to the roots of my hair, a beetle rowing across the surface of the water, from one dark shore to the other'.[9]

There is no more mysterious image in the whole of Sebald. What does it mean, and why does he shudder?

The line comes from one of Hofmannsthal's most important works, *The Letter of Lord Chandos*. In it a once-famous author writes to his friend and admirer, the seventeenth-century philosopher Francis Bacon, to explain why he has written nothing for two years, and will never write again. It is because his relationship with language has broken down. He can no longer think or speak coherently. Words have fragmented for him, giving him (note the term!) vertigo.[10] All he has left in the world are a few 'good moments'.

Scholars have seen this as a seminal text about the modernist crisis of the early twentieth century, in which old forms of literary writing were breaking down. That is certainly right: writing was Hofmannsthal's (and Sebald's) main activity and concern. But in fact only the first half of the *Letter* is about the breakdown of language and the inability to write. The second half is about those 'good moments', which Chandos struggles to describe.

They come, he says, unpredictably, and mostly from seeing the lowliest things – rats, a crippled apple tree, a peasant's hut. And suddenly he is filled with 'an immense sympathy, a flowing over into these other creatures'. It is a 'divine sensation', a 'mysterious, wordless and boundless ecstasy'. It has nothing to do with pity, he writes,

> when, on another evening, on finding beneath a nut-tree a half-filled pitcher which a gardener boy had left there, and the pitcher and the water in it, darkened by the shadow of the tree, and a beetle swimming on the surface from shore to shore – when this combination of trifles sent through me such a shudder at the presence of the Infinite, a shudder running from the roots of my hair to the marrow of my heels…"

Sebald's shudder may be one of fear, or horror, or anything at all. But it is Chandos's shudder. It is, therefore, 'celestial'. It is a shiver at the presence of the infinite and (as he also says) of love. It is a flowing into other creatures and things that is the ultimate form of Sebald's empathy; it is the oneness of all that is his ultimate aim. It is unattainable through words, which necessarily divide things off from each other. It is, Chandos writes, 'as if we could enter into a new and hopeful relationship with the whole of existence, if only we begin to think with the heart'.

That is why ordinary language has broken down for him. And this is the new, impossible language he envisions, in which he will never be able to write. Sebald cannot write in it either, since no one can. But it is what his mysterious signs, his silent images – Nabokov with his net, Austerlitz's moths and so many more – all point to.

But while we are here, we are separate, in different selves, places and times, some men and some women, some perpetrators and some victims, and we can only try to grasp each other's existence, to understand what happened in other times and places. And here the fundamental Sebaldian principle is that first-person experience is the closest we can get to the truth. So the narrator must always hear directly from the survivor of experience – from Dr Selwyn, Ferber and Austerlitz, from Nossack and Kluge. Or if that is no longer possible, from those closest to them – Lucy Landau, Aunt Fini, Vera. That was an article of faith for Max, and a mark of respect: when his friend Clive Scott said of the film *Shoah* that those who had undergone things were not necessarily the most reliable sources, he was upset, even angry.[12] On the other hand, no one was more aware of the fallibility of memory and the power of trauma to induce forgetting; they were two of his greatest themes. So once more, as in the quest to understand the nature of reality, truth is elusive, a vital but impossible goal.

The most famous Sebaldian originality – the placing of photos and documents in fictional texts – embodies this key point about truth. It produces an unrivalled sense of reality – and a moment later, when we realise the stories are fictions, snatches it away: which makes us *feel* the elusiveness of truth more keenly than any simple fiction or non-fiction could do. Thus a key Sebaldian form mirrors a key Sebaldian theme, as in any great work of art. It sits awkwardly with the subject of the Holocaust, as we explored at the start; but it is a central part of his vision.

So, of course, is his tracing of connections across space and time – of Walser with his grandfather and himself, 'of dates of birth with dates of death', as he wrote,[13] of his own date of birth with the date of death of another Max, in the final image of *Austerlitz*. These connections are the closest we can come to the inexpressible oneness that is his subject. And again a form – this time his collecting, collaging prose – expresses a deep underlying theme.

Another aspect of Sebald's prose does the same. His formal, old-fashioned German is not that of Germany now, his English not that of Britain or America at any time. His is a language of an in-between world, more of the past than the present, and not of anywhere. It is, as his student Luke Williams has said, how the dead would write:[14] a memoir from beyond the grave, like Chateaubriand's. Or one from Gracchus, or *Saturn*'s dead soul, held back by the beauty of the world.

So, as he always said himself, W. G. Sebald is not a novelist. Nor a travel writer, since his journeys and landscapes are more inward than outward. He is a historian, biographer and autobiographer. But beneath these, he is at heart a visionary and a mystic. That is why there is no one like him in modern literature.

And that is why *Austerlitz* is, after all, his masterpiece. For it is not only the peak of his imaginative identification with the victims of the Holocaust and of his psychological investigation of trauma. It is also where the mystical vision he has pursued from the start, then hidden in *Saturn*, is displayed as fully as it can be – in the moths' flight, in Alphonso's watery sketches and Turner's *Funeral at Lausanne*, in the play of light over Barmouth Bay and on the wall in Andromeda Lodge – including an earlier intuition, when Adela leans towards Austerlitz and says, 'Do you see the caravan coming through the dunes over there?' Alphonso puts it, tentatively, as clearly as it can ever be put. 'It was,' he says, 'the sudden incursion of unreality into the real world … that kindled our deepest feelings, or at least what we took for them.'[15]

So Sebald is a mystic and a visionary. And simply a writer. He turns everything – his experience, his reading – into writing. And sometimes – often – like Keller and Walser and all his other great models, into writing so beautiful it breaks your heart. The recurring image of Gracchus on his bier – the ending of every story in *The Emigrants* – in *Saturn* the magical forest of Anne's dream, the fancy that the world is held together by the flight of swallows, the vision of the boy Algernon with his fiery hair – in *Austerlitz* Adela appearing in a watery glow, the snow-white goose listening spellbound to human music – all these passages and so many more open up vistas of such beauty and intensity as life itself is scarcely able to provide.†

Despite all this, Sebald is also the target of much criticism. Or rather, because of this, he is the target of much criticism. For no one expects a book to be about a mystic vision these days. Famous detractors include Günter Grass in Germany and Alan Bennett in England, and critics such as Georg Klein and Iris Radisch in Germany and Michael Hoffmann and Adam Thirlwell in England. Sebald has to accept even violent criticism, since he dished it out so liberally himself. But like his own attacks, not all are justified.

One of the commonest objections made in readers' letters to him,[16] German as well as English, was to his long sentences, and even more to his long paragraphs, great blocks of print that go on and on for page after page. It's unarguably strange (though not unique: Bernhard does it too, for example). But once again it reflects Sebald's vision. Look at those pages and you *see* what they hint at: everything is connected, everything is one.

A second objection is that the books are hyper-literary, stuffed with references to other writers, often difficult ones like Kafka and Borges. Well, Max turned his reading into writing, and that was his reading. But it undoubtedly keeps many readers away, and on the other hand makes him a darling of academics, who have endless fun excavating his sources. He wouldn't have enjoyed either of these consequences. But he just was hyper-literary, and his work isn't for everyone. That objection (if it is one) is valid.

Perhaps, though, style isn't crucial. More important is something so well known that it became the butt of *Private Eye*'s satire: his extreme, unrelieved, and (some would say) ethically and aesthetically damaging gloom.[17] Sebald was perfectly aware that unleavened gloom is not a possible diet.[18] Yet that is what he serves up, these critics would say. His deep despair about nature and history, his concentration on pain and horror, destruction and decline – it's all too much, too unvaried, to be palatable, or even true.

Well, no one can say that W. G. Sebald is the lightest of writers. Moments of beauty lift *The Emigrants* and *Austerlitz*, but are there any moments of happiness or humour in either? There is Luisa's happiness as a child in 'Ferber', and with each of her loves – but these are lost; perhaps Paul's contentment with Lucy in 'Bereyter' (too late) and Adelwarth's with Cosmo in Jerusalem (lost as well). For Austerlitz there is hardly any happiness at all – only at Andromeda Lodge, and one fleeting moment with Marie de Verneuil. As for humour – well, Elaine's trolleys in 'Dr Henry Selwyn' and Gracie Irlam's Teasmade in 'Ferber' make us smile, but nothing in *Austerlitz* does, except perhaps the little bow-legged man of the same name who came to circumcise Kafka's nephew. But *The Emigrants* and (especially) *Austerlitz* are the Holocaust memorial works, as we might say, and humour could feel out of place in them. There *is* humour in the other two – think for instance of the Kafka twins in *Vertigo* and Squirrel in *Saturn*, and the episodes of the two cakes in the first and the frozen fish in the second.[19] They're all surreal, with a dark streak, rather than light relief; but they're breaks in the Sebaldian gloom.

So much for palatable: what about true? This sounds a more objective question, but when it comes to a judgement about the whole past and future of the world, how do we amass, let alone assess, the evidence? I can only give my own view.

Sebald is a double Cassandra – a Cassandra about the past as well as the future. And who believed Cassandra? About the burning forests, the problem of water, the desertification of vast tracts of the world, we know now that he was right.

About pain and suffering we remain constitutionally optimistic, because we have to. If we truly took in all the suffering in the world, and the inevitable end of ourselves and those we love, we could hardly live at all. W. G. Sebald could hardly live at all. Like Cassandra, I think, he paid the price for being right.

Finally, there are some objections that seem to me not even worth dismissing. Let me dismiss them anyway.

Some German critics accused him of sentimentality about his subjects – meaning the subjects of *The Emigrants* and *Austerlitz*, mostly Jews who fled from Germany or Eastern Europe, often (Selwyn, Ferber, Austerlitz) as children. 'Sentimentality' is cheap or excessive emotion. To suggest that any amount of sympathy with persecuted Jews could be excessive is disgraceful, and I can only suppose that those critics (very few) never imagined they'd be read outside Germany.

The worthless English objection is the opposite – that Sebald's restraint, his measured, formal tone on this subject as on others, is cold. Both views can't be right, and this one isn't either. The fact that they can both be taken is proof enough.

Lastly there is a shared objection, which is the most worthless of all. It is that Sebald's portrayal of Germany's victims, and of all the victims, human and animal, of the manifold cruelties of nature and history is exploitative, an appropriation of suffering that is not his in order to lend his work a spurious seriousness. This is not a textual point, but a personal one, about his motivation and sincerity. It is, in other words, a biographical point, made by people who know nothing about Sebald's biography. It would have been better for him if they'd been right. But they're wrong. The unique empathy of his work was genuine.

So literary issues merge with biographical ones, as Max himself knew.
And my first question becomes my last: why was he the one to suffer for
Germany, and beyond Germany for the whole world?

Everyone who knew him well knew how sensitive he was, how hard
life was for him, how he grew more depressive with age.[20] But there was
more. He had so many phobias,[21] some of them strange – about noise,
about heat, about surgery, especially on his eyes; about train journeys;
about being talked about. Once he saw Marie on the other side of a
wire fence and literally ran away;[22] afterwards he explained to her that
her face had seemed to him the face of the Gypsy woman in his father's
photograph, and he couldn't bear it. Strong emotions affected him so
deeply he felt them physically. When they spoke on the phone, he told
her, he felt his whole body electrified; if they talked too long, he said,
he would have a heart attack. And after the weeks and months of stress
at the end, he did have a heart attack.

What *was* all that? It was an absolute inability to protect himself from
experience – all experience, inner and outer, so that everything he saw,
remembered or imagined could overwhelm him. He was born without
a skin,[23] as his mother prophetically said when she first saw him, and as
he said himself fifty years later. The skin is the barrier between inside
and outside, as Marie told me, and in him it was not only physically
troubled, but metaphorically missing.

It's almost as if he had, or at least understood, what is called mirror-
touch synaesthesia:[24] a state in which people experience in themselves
what they see others experiencing. So in *Campo Santo* he recalls being
struck motionless as a boy by the sight of some dead deer, and in
The Rings of Saturn his narrator feels the hare's panic, and in its eyes
sees himself 'become one with it'.[25] In *Saturn* too – again the most
'metaphysical' work – he expresses intense sympathy with the swine
at Covehithe, with the herring killed for food, pheasants for sport and
silkworms for profit, with the trees destroyed in the hurricane of 1987.
And all the books express his profound feeling for the whole of nature,
and for his human subjects, dead and alive.

None of this is pity, as Chandos says. Rather it is identification, like
the narrator's with the hare. So for Chandos there is no distinction
between a woman with a dying child and the beetle in the pitcher: he
flows equally into both. Similarly, Sebald makes no distinction between
the herrings and the victims of Bergen-Belsen who follow a page later.

That has disturbed many of his readers. But it can be explained, I think, by his skinless state: his Chandos-like, mirror-touch-synaesthesia-like penetrability.

His sense of others' suffering, in other words, was acutely real. It was not a searching for pain but an inability to avoid feeling it all around him. As it is around all of us, on the news, in our streets and hospitals and homes, every day. We can forget and ignore it, but he couldn't. Perhaps he didn't actually have mirror-touch synaesthesia. But he was among those whom one writer calls 'altruists': people whose 'moral and emotional sensitivities are so finely tuned, their membranes so thin, that they recognise everything, acutely pick up and even "feel" the agonies of others'.[26] They become, this writer says, artists, doctors, human rights lawyers. Above all, I would add, artists. Artists like Kafka, Rilke and Hofmannsthal; like George Eliot, like Lenz. From childhood on they hear the squirrel's heart beating, the whole world's silent scream.

Scholars like Mark Anderson and Uwe Schütte, friends like Richard Sheppard, all look back to childhood trauma as the source of Sebald's troubles.[27] Their candidates are, as we know, the death of his grandfather and his clashes with his father. But what is more common than the death of grandparents, and – especially in his generation – clashes with one's father? Gertrud is sure that Georg never seriously maltreated her brother, as we also know. But now we have, I think, an explanation: *normal experience was a trauma* to the child Winfried, as to the man Max. His father cutting his hair and scrubbing him, his mother dressing and watching him, anyone photographing him – all were ordinary experiences, but to him traumatic and intolerable. So was the death of his grandfather a trauma beyond normal loss, and so too, therefore, was the experience of the film about the concentration camps, and the dawning knowledge of what had happened. That was not an ordinary experience for anyone. Nonetheless, Gertrud and Beate could survive it, Ursula and Jürgen and the other friends could survive it. But not Walter Kalhammer, and not Max.

So much falls into place now. His hyperbole, for instance, so surprisingly common in his subtle work, and the basis of his melancholy humour – it wasn't really hyperbole at all. He wasn't exaggerating about his awful train journeys, or his encounters with awful people, though he played to his audience's belief that he was: it was his experience that was extreme, not its expression. Or his feeling, from his schooldays on, of being overwhelmed by work and longing for peace. He did vast amounts of work, always. But the feeling of being overwhelmed came from far more than that. It came from his universal penetrability, his artist's disease.

As a man he longed to stop feeling so much, and tried to protect himself by cutting off and being alone, like Austerlitz. It didn't work; instead it made him feel like Chandos – empty, frozen, no longer alive.[28] But as a writer I don't think he wanted to avoid the suffering he shared. He knew that his artist's disease gave him an insight into a deep truth. *While looking*, he wrote, *we sense how things are looking at us, and we understand that we are not here in order to pervade the universe, but to be pervaded by it.*[29] That was why he was here. So his artist's disease was not for nothing. Without it he would not have had his artist's vision, and nor would we.

A month before he died he gave his last talk, in the Literaturhaus in Stuttgart. In it he asked *What is literature good for?* And answered: beyond the recital of facts, and beyond scholarship, literature alone can be an attempt at restitution.

He had just spoken of the men of Tulle, ninety-nine of them hanged by the SS Das Reich Division in June 1944, the rest deported to forced labour and extermination camps where many died. He was certainly also thinking, as always, of the Jews of Europe, murdered in their millions, and the citizens of Germany burned to cinders in their streets; of his new subject, the soldiers of the Great War, including his grandfather and Marie's; of all the creatures hunted and eaten by us, of the burning forests, the drying waterways and spreading deserts – of the whole of nature, his subject from the start. To all these, to whom as he said 'the greatest injustice was done',[30] his own literature was just such an attempt: if not at recompense, as he wrote to Peter Jordan, since that was impossible, at least to show how much he remembered them.[31]

But the word 'restitution' – which he used in German in his talk, *Ein Versuch der Restitution* – goes beyond the idea of recompense. It also means restoration. And that, I think, is what he most meant and hoped that literature could do.

In *The Emigrants* and *Austerlitz* he restored the lives of persecuted Jews, at least in the minds of his readers. And he did more. In *Vertigo* he restored his own life and those of his fellow villagers, in *The Rings of Saturn* and *A Place in the Country* the lives of much-loved writers; in 'The World War Project' he was planning to restore those of his parents, of Marie's family, of Babette.

We can neither restore nor recompense in this world what has been lost, but we can recall and preserve it in art. In literature – and in painting and photography, music and film – we can bring the past into now, all places into here, the dead back among the living. Art is thus a faint copy of that oneness before the division into spaces and times, living and dead, which was W. G. Sebald's ultimate vision. That is why he couldn't give up writing, whatever it cost, any more than Hölderlin in his tower or Rousseau on the Île St-Pierre.†

PART VIII

Endings

25

Unrecounted

Über allen Gipfeln	Over every mountaintop
Ist Ruh,	lies peace
In allen Wipfeln	in every treetop
Spürest du	you hear
Kaum einen Hauch:	hardly a breath
Die Vögelein schweigen im Walde.	Birds are silent in the wood
Warte nur! Balde	Wait a while. Soon
Ruhest du auch.	you will rest too.
Goethe, 'Wandrers Nachtlied'	Goethe, 'Wayfarer's Night Song'[1]

In September 2000 Max was in Alsace, clambering round a First World War battlefield with Tripp for his World War Project.[2] After that, Tripp took a long series of photos of his friend. In the bone-tiredness that followed they talked about the project they'd planned together, based on the micropoems Max had been writing for several years. What do you want to do for your part? he asked. And without thinking Tripp replied, 'Eyes.'

The result was the book they would call *Unerzählt* (*Unrecounted*). It would contain thirty-three poems and pairs of eyes, they decided.[3] Max had already sent Tripp several poems; now he began to write and send many more. No doubt they would have decided together which ones to use. But then Max died. Tripp was left to choose alone, and to decide which engraving of eyes to juxtapose to each poem. In the end, therefore, *Unrecounted* was as much the creation of Max's co-author as *For Years Now*, his book with Tess Jaray, had been.

The poems, however, were very much his. He'd already given Tess those in *For Years Now* in his own English versions.[4] Between *Unrecounted* and *For Years Now* there were forty-one; Tess had one more she didn't use and Tripp eleven more. Max thus wrote at least fifty-three mini-poems in the last years of his life.

They are extremely short – just a few lines each – and probably minor.[5] Max thought so himself.[6] That may be why he combined them with artists' images, feeling that they'd struggle on their own. Most of them, however, would now appear in not just one book but two. He remained as ambitious (and pragmatic) as ever, determined to publish all he wrote.

And despite their radical difference from his prose – their brevity, their lack of narrative[7] – these last poems are classically Sebaldian. They are about eyes, about animals, about journeys, about light and darkness; more than ever about death. The most important, he said, was the one about his grandfather's coffin[8] (in *Unrecounted* it is just *the coffin*, his grandfather left unidentified). Like everything he wrote, they are full of borrowings,[9] unsourced and often adjusted – including some borrowings from himself, equally adjusted.

And like everything he wrote, they are elusive, mysterious: because of their brevity, more mysterious than ever. In his 'Translator's Note' to *Unrecounted* Michael Hamburger attributed this mystery to the 'crisis in Max's life and work' that followed the completion of *Austerlitz*.[10] That must, I think, be right. He was under great private stress in that last time, which he would not want to betray, and yet like Rousseau and the others, he could not stop writing. These tiny poetic riddles were a solution.

But there may have been a literary reason as well – and Max, like Kafka, was made of literature. I'm thinking of his 'metaphysical' wish to reach through to another reality beyond time and space. This was also a goal of both his artist-collaborators, in their different ways, which is no doubt why he wanted to work with them. Tess Jaray's abstracts search for the underlying structures of what we see, and in Tripp's paintings, Max said, 'behind the illusions of the surface' lay 'the metaphysical lining of reality'.[11] But this can only be glimpsed, never directly seen. So, he wrote in *Unrecounted*, a painter's gaze must be 'fixed & almost/ averted':[12] like the dog in Tripp's painting in *A Place in the Country*, who sees through us not with the eye fixed on us, but with the one which looks away. Surely that too made the last poems brief, glancing, enigmatic.

Perhaps this suggests a meaning for the title of the book, which is equally enigmatic. It comes from the penultimate poem,[13] which UEA chose for their memorial to Max:

> Unrecounted
> always it will remain
> the story of the averted
> faces

We can only guess, but one meaning is surely the silence of his parents' generation, averting their faces from the past. But another may be the near silence of the poet and the artist, trying to see through their averted eyes, and to recount what they've glimpsed in Chandos's impossible language. Perhaps it was for this reason too that in the time after *Austerlitz* Max's writing reached the brink of silence.

Over the years he had thought of many escape routes for bad times: to Ireland, like Wolfgang Schlüter, in the 1990s; now to the south of France near Ursula's summer home, to Alsace near Tripp, to Fribourg, where Gertrud had prepared a room for him. To interviewers he joked that he'd like to spend his last days in a Swiss hotel, like Nabokov.[14]

But it was too late.

There were signs enough. Some time in the last weeks he fainted in an airport.[15] A colleague saw him sitting down in a corridor; a student saw him taking the lift to go down two floors. And on that last visit to Sonthofen in October he walked with Ursula in the foothills near her house. The path was slightly steep – though only slightly; they'd done it many times at a good clip. But now Ursula noticed with alarm that Max was struggling. After only ten minutes he said he was sorry, they'd have to turn back. He didn't explain, and she didn't ask. It must be his back, she thought. But it wasn't.

Several friends, as we know, saw that it was his heart. Did he ever seek medical treatment? Gordon Turner may have thought he did.[16] One close friend thought not, and Beate, Max's medical sister, also thinks not. But she had warned him so often about his blood pressure;

and the Sonthofen walk and the other events cannot have been the only ones of their kind. He must have known.

There were signs of that too.[17] Already two years before, at his father's funeral, he'd said that he would be next; a year before, the Hamburgers were sure he knew he was going to die. Now, in late October, he wrote his will, including the wish that his body be buried. He chose the churchyard: St Andrew's in Framingham Earl, which he loved for its peace, and where he had buried Frederick Farrar in *The Rings of Saturn*. He left instructions for the management of his literary estate and for his funeral.

Then the accident happened.

He'd had so many since the first in 1967 – the ones with Gordon Turner in the 1970s, two lucky escapes in the early eighties,[18] two in the year 2000 alone. Fatal accidents and near misses haunt his work – in his novel, in 'Adelwarth', in the poem 'The Year before Last',[19] in an unused draft for *The Rings of Saturn*.[20] Everyone knew what a distracted driver he was. So when it happened many friends thought, *He's done it again* – lost concentration, drifted into the wrong lane. But even more thought, *He's committed suicide*. Marie thought it. The Hamburgers both thought it; Kristin Völker and Tess Jaray thought it; Walter Kalhammer in his night-watchman's flat thought it. And many readers thought it too.[21]

On 13 December, Jon Cook invited Max to supper the next week. On the 14th, Hamish Hamilton sent him the proofs of *After Nature* and Michael Hamburger wrote him a letter he never opened. His horoscope in the *EDP* that day warned that an eclipse of the sun was taking place, visible only in North America but 'challenging' for everyone.[22]

Around noon he left the Old Rectory to drive his daughter to Norwich.[23] Ten minutes later he turned onto the main road near a wide curve. Soon after that his car failed to follow the curve and drove straight into the opposite lane. It might have been empty, or another car might have been coming towards him. Instead it was a thirty-eight-ton lorry. The lorry braked hard, but could do nothing. Max's side of the car hit the front of the lorry's cab, spun around violently and ended up facing the other way. The lorry ended in a ditch. The lorry driver was uninjured, the car's passenger not seriously injured. But the car's driver was dead.

Already a few days later his daughter was said to be 'comfortable', at least physically.[24] But now a period of agonising uncertainty began for the whole family, in England, Germany, Switzerland. *What had happened?* Had he had one of his moments of distraction? He'd had a bad headache that day,[25] as so often – had he taken too many painkillers, and been muddled, half-blinded? Had his heart trouble reached its final conclusion? Or had an aneurysm, of which there had been some question, exploded?

Finally, five months later, three days before what would have been his fifty-eighth birthday, the inquest was held and the results of the post-mortem revealed.[26] There was no trace of drugs or alcohol in his body, and no aneurysm. But his heart disease had been serious: all his arteries were affected, and one was 80 per cent occluded. It was a heart attack waiting to happen. On the balance of probabilities, the Norfolk coroner concluded, that was the cause of the accident. Max would have died instantly, before the impact.

The funeral had to wait too, until the autopsy was done. That took three weeks.[27]

In the days before, everything was frozen. The Hamburgers were afraid that they wouldn't be able to drive; those coming from outside Britain checked anxiously with their airlines. The day of the funeral, 3 January, was still very cold, but the ice had melted.

Rosa couldn't come to see her son buried: she was in her late eighties, prostrated by grief and ailing herself. In her stead she sent masses of white lilies. Max's daughter had recovered sufficiently for her and her husband to join her mother. Gertrud and Beate and their husbands came from Switzerland, Max's mother-in-law and brother-in-law from Germany. The Hamburgers came from Middleton and Stephen Watts from London; since he never bothers to dress for winter, Stephen arrived frozen. Gordon Turner, Clive Scott and Beryl Ranwell came from UEA. Tripp came from France, and so did Marie, accompanied by Patrick Charbonneau, Max's French translator. All Max's publishers came – Michael Kruger from Germany, Scott Moyers from the US, Simon Prosser from London. Perhaps twenty people in all. Max had said he wanted no fuss of the kind that had been made for Malcolm Bradbury, just the closest circle of family and friends. That is what was done.

A simple service was held in the church. Jean-Paul sang '*Das Wirtshaus*' from the *Winterreise* for Max one last time – the traveller who comes to an inn that is really a graveyard but, like Gracchus, is not let in. Jean-Paul's voice started low with sorrow and cold but soon grew warm and strong. Then they all walked out and stood around the open grave. Max's notebook and pencil were in his shirt pocket, where he always kept them. Slowly, now, his coffin was lowered. Gertrud dropped Marie's poem onto it. They stood in silence; it was very cold.†

Suddenly there was a whirring of wings and they all looked up. A robin with its bright red breast swooped down from a tree and landed on the foot of the grave. There it stayed for a few long moments, then flew off. Everyone realised they had held their breath. Beryl's clear voice broke the silence. 'It's Max!' she said.

Soon afterwards Michael Hamburger wrote a poem for dead friends,[28] ending with that memory.

> To the open new grave a robin came down,
> An icy wind blew
> On the bird safe there among the living
> And those more truly levelled
> Than sunlight lets creatures be –
> All reduced, irreducible there
> In one darkness stood and lay.†

So his heart had burst, as the narrator often imagines. From ordinary, terrible disease, not from a weakness inherited from his grandfather, who probably didn't have it either. The myth wasn't true. Yet it was true: that is how death came. In a car, as he'd foreseen in his father's photograph of the young soldier on his bier. On a date that combined the day of his grandfather's death with the month of Walser's. And at a point that, like Beyle, he had almost predicted. When ROP's son was born, he had wished the family long life: especially the child, he wrote, since for himself and his friend it was already half over.[29] He was twenty-nine then, now he was fifty-seven. He was only a year out.

As always with Max Sebald, another truth lay beyond the visible.[30] For years he'd been telling Gertrud that he didn't want to grow old; for years suicide had seemed to him reasonable, even desirable, if only he dared. On some level he wanted to die, to join the dead he had unjustly survived: his grandfather, the victims of his father's generation. He'd wanted this for much of his life, even for most of it. How many times before had he nearly died on the road? And when the same thing had happened to a friend – she lost control of her car and swerved into the wrong lane – he didn't say to her *Don't die*, as he said to Ursula, but *Don't kill yourself.* In the novel he wrote at twenty-three, his mother failed to turn the wheel of a car on a curve and both his parents died. He didn't choose that death, with his daughter beside him. But when it came to him that way, it was what he'd always thought coincidence was: destiny.

Acknowledgements

First, I would like to thank Ute Sebald, who did not wish to speak, but put no obstacles in my way.

The most important witnesses to Sebald's early life were his sisters, Gertrud Aebischer-Sebald and Beate Fuchs-Sebald. I am more grateful to both of them than I can say. I specially thank his elder sister Gertrud, who was close to him in age, and who gave me precious support throughout. Without her this book could not have been written.

Among the friends of Sebald's youth I particularly thank the two closest, Ursula Liebsch (née Lotte Küsters) and Jürgen Kaeser. Jürgen helped me tirelessly, and Ursula not only gave me her vivid memories but hospitality in her house in Sonthofen, where I wrote three chapters over as many months. I also thank Sebald's cousins Les Stehmer and Suzanne Siegler, née Stehmer (though I must thank Les, who died in 2017, posthumously). And here and throughout I specially thank the friend of Sebald's youth and last years, Marie, who came to know him better than almost anyone.

In Sonthofen I also particularly thank Sebald's teacher Karl-Heinz Schmelzer and his wife Doris, for their witness and friendship; also Kay Wolfinger, for all his help, and Fritz Ketterle for his, especially about Armin Müller. Among Sebald's schoolfellows I also specially thank Peter Schaich, Rainer Galaske and Helmut Bunk, though again I must thank Helmut posthumously, since he died in 2016. In Wertach I thank Inge Speker of the Tourist Bureau, who arranged meetings for me with several of Sebald's contemporaries.

For Sebald's Freiburg years I specially thank Thomas Bütow. For his Manchester years I am deeply indebted to Peter and Dorothy Jordan and to Peter Jonas, though sadly all three have died in the last years, Dorothy only recently; and to Reinbert Tabbert and his wife Brigitte, who happily are still with us. Also, for his Manchester photographs and for his Goethe Institute information later, Wolf Dieter Ortmann, and to him and his wife Evi for their hospitality in Munich.

For the UEA years I am especially indebted to Sebald's close UEA friend Gordon Turner; and to Richard Sheppard, whose biographical chapter, Chronology and bibliographical work in *Saturn's Moons*, as well as many scholarly articles, have been an indispensable resource. I also especially thank Sebald's colleague Jean Boase-Beier, his secretary Beryl Ranwell's daughter Sally Humpston and her husband Nick, and all Sebald's students who generously spoke to me, especially those with the longest memories or notes of his classes: Dominic O'Sullivan, Anne Fitzpatrick, Sarah Cameron, Ralf Jeutter, Sarah Emily Miano and David Lambert.

Other close friends of Sebald's whom I specially want to thank are Kristin Völker, from the 1970s to the 1990s; Wolfgang Schlüter, from 1991 on; and in the last years Michael Hamburger and Anne Beresford (Michael again, alas, posthumously), Ria Loohuizen, Tess Jaray, George Szirtes and Stephen Watts. I also want to express my sincere thanks to Stefan Muthesius and his wife Kasia Murawska-Muthesius for allowing me to ask difficult questions.

For Sebald's English translations I want to express my great debt to his first publisher Christopher MacLehose at the Harvill Press, and also to Barbara Schwepke, a director there at the time; to his editor at Harvill, Bill Swainson; and to his two translators, Michael Hulse and Anthea Bell (Anthea again posthumously, as she died in 2018), particularly to Michael Hulse, to whom I hope this book does delayed justice.

For the background to the books I am especially indebted to the Buckton family of Wymondham, the models for 'Dr Henry Selwyn'; the Jordans and Frank Auerbach for 'Max Ferber'; and for *Austerlitz* Susi Bechhöfer (posthumously) and her son Frederick Stocken, as well as Janne Weinzierl of the Munich *Stolpersteine* initiative.

For archival help I thank the staff of the Deutsches Literaturarchiv Marbach and the archivists of the city of Sonthofen and the universities of Freiburg, Fribourg, Manchester and East Anglia. Also the British

Library Humanities Reading Room, and the Taylorian and Bodleian Libraries, Oxford, my favourite places.

As well as Richard Sheppard, for scholarly help I deeply thank Uwe Schütte, who is the prime interpreter of Sebald in both Germany and Britain. I don't always agree with him, but I have relied on his superb work throughout, and am most grateful for it.

For financial support I sincerely thank the Society of Authors, who awarded me an Authors' Foundation grant in 2014, and the Royal Literary Fund, whose pension grant helped me through the whole period of research and writing. And for technical support I thank Zac Manasseh and Paul Cunningham, who saved me from complete computer despair.

On the professional side, I want to thank my agent, David Godwin, and Heather Godwin, of David Godwin Associates; and my editors at Bloomsbury: David Avital, who commissioned the book; Ben Doyle, Jasmine Horsey and Sarah Ruddick, who steered it to publication; and Kate Quarry, who checked it meticulously. Also, for their superb design skills, David Mann and Phillip Beresford. And once more, Bill Swainson, by whom I had the great good fortune to be edited.

I also want to thank the first person I turned to: Thomas Honickel, who made the excellent films *Der Ausgewanderte* (*The Emigrant*) and *Sebald. Orte.* (*Sebald. Places.*) in 2007. Thomas helped me to find people, and gave me transcripts of his interviews with them, when I was just beginning this journey. I thank him for his generosity and friendship.

I must end these acknowledgements with a few personal debts of gratitude. First, for steering me through the dangerous early stages, and nearly to the end, I profoundly thank my remarkable friend and editor of thirty years, Diana Athill. I'm only sorry she couldn't read the end of the story. My novelist friends Elspeth Sandys and Evelyn Toynton accompanied me on this journey from the start, and Evelyn also cast her eagle eye over the text – more than thanks to both. Sincerest thanks too to Ian Collins and Joachim Jacobs for their generous hospitality in Southwold and Berlin. And I thank from the bottom of my heart my two biographer friends, Michael Holroyd and Hilary Spurling. I owe everything to Michael for his support over three decades, while Hilary has been my example and encourager for at least that long, and our conversations over all these years have been a constant enrichment.

Carole Angier, 30 October 2020

Guide to the Companion Page

The author and publisher cannot accept responsibility for content published on external websites. Online content is subject to alteration or removal at any time.

p. 92 The hanger

p. 94 'Vaters Sieg im Haarschnittkrieg' ('Father's Victory in the Haircut War'), a comic poem by Manfred Koch, showing that WGS was not alone (Thanks to Manfred Koch)

p. 106 The final aria from Verdi's Ernani

p. 109 A slow Ländler, such as WGS played for his dying grandfather

p. 134 The Battle of Alexander at Issus by Altdorfer

p. 150 Death Mills (Die Todesmühlen), Billy Wilder's film about the death camps, almost certainly the one shown to WGS's class in 1962

p. 152 Rilke's 'Herbsttag' ('Autumn Day'), WGS's essay topic for his final exam in German

p. 163 Brahms, Clarinet Concerto, 2nd movement, Adagio, one of the pieces Bereyter whistles

p. 206 Jean-Paul singing 'Dalla sua pace' from Don Giovanni

p. 247 Bellini, *I puritani*, 'A te, o cara'

p. 252 Albinoni's *Adagio*

p. 280 Rembrandt's *Man with a Magnifying Glass*

p. 291 Frank Auerbach, *E.O.W. on her Blue Eiderdown*, 1965

p. 341 Mr Pastry

p. 378 WGS reading *Austerlitz* at the 92nd Street Y, New York, October 2001

p. 379 'The Collected 'Maxims' of W. G. Sebald', recorded by David Lambert and Robert McGill, *Five Dials* (the online literary magazine from Hamish Hamilton)

p. 389 The *Chanson de Craonne*, song of the French *poilus*, 1917

p. 400 An English translation of *Der Jäger Gracchus* by Ian Johnston (Thanks to Ian Johnston)

p. 401 'Cara non Dubitar' from *Il Matrimonio Segreto* by Cimarosa

p. 424 The Crowning of the Rose Queen, Salford, 1929 (British Pathé News)

p. 433 Schubert, *Piano Sonata in B flat major, Andante sostenuto*, the piece the circus musicians play in *Austerlitz*, to which the white goose listens

p. 439 Gluck, 'Che puro Ciel', from *Orpheus and Eurydice*, the overcoming of the underworld

p. 448 (1) Jean-Paul singing 'Das Wirtshaus' from the *Winterreise*

p. 448 (2) The robin on the grave (photo by Beate Fuchs-Sebald)

PLUS:

A list of some other favourite pieces of music and favourite films of WGS's

Some of WGS's key interviews:

Audio: Eleanor Wachtel and Michael Silverblatt

Print: Maya Jaggi (2), Maria Alvarez, Arthur Lubow, the author

And Susan Sontag's famous review of *Vertigo*

A contact address for comments and questions to the author

Abbreviations

Works by W. G. Sebald

AN	*After Nature*
V	*Vertigo*
S.G.	*Schwindel. Gefühle.*
E	*The Emigrants*
DA	*Die Ausgewanderten*
Dr HS	*Dr Henry Selwyn*
PB	*Paul Bereyter*
AA	*Ambros Adelwarth*
MF	*Max Ferber*
RS	*The Rings of Saturn*
A	*Austerlitz*
NHD	*On the Natural History of Destruction*
LL	*Luftkrieg und Literatur*
FYN	*For Years Now* (with Tess Jaray)
U	*Unrecounted* (with Jan Peter Tripp)
CS	*Campo Santo*
ALW	*Across the Land and the Water*
PC	*A Place in the Country*

Works by others

SM	*Saturn's Moons: W. G. Sebald, a Handbook*, ed. Jo Catling and Richard Hibbitt, 2011
Schwartz	*the emergence of memory: Conversations with W. G. Sebald*, ed. Lynne Sharon Schwartz, 2007

Hoffmann	*Auf ungeheuer dünnem Eis*, ed. Torsten Hoffmann, 2011
Bigsby	*Writers in Conversation with Christopher Bigsby*, Vol. 2, 2001
Loquai 1997	*Porträt 7: W. G. Sebald*, ed. Franz Loquai, 1997
Loquai 2005	*Sebald. Lektüren.*, ed. Marcel Atze and Franz Loquai, 2005

Works by Richard Sheppard

D-S	'Dexter-Sinister: some observations on decrypting the mors code in the work of W. G. Sebald', *Journal of European Studies*, Vol. 35, No. 4, 2005, pp. 419–63
JES 2009	'Woods, trees and the spaces in between': A Report on Work published on W. G. Sebald, 2005–2008, *Journal of European Studies*, Vol. 39, No. 1, March 2009, pp. 79–128
JES 2011	(ed.) W. G. Sebald Special Issue, *Journal of European Studies*, Vol. 41, Nos 3–4, December 2011
JES 2014	(ed.) 'Three Encounters with W. G. Sebald', *Journal of European Studies*, Vol. 44, No. 4, December 2014
Reception	'W. G. Sebald's Reception of Alfred Döblin' in *Alfred Döblin: Paradigms of Modernism*, ed. Steffan Davies and Ernest Schonfeld, de Gruyter, 2009
Ariadne	Review of Philippa Comber, *Ariadne's Thread: In Memory of W. G. Sebald*, *JES* 16 February 2015

Works by Uwe Schütte

Ein	*Einführung ins Leben und Werk, 2011*
I	*Interventionen, 2014*
F	*Figurationen, 2014*
W & TW	W. G. Sebald in Writers and Their Work series, 2018
ÜS	*Über Sebald*, ed. Schütte, De Gruyter, 2016
Sebaldiana	'On W. G. Sebald's Radicalism', in *Sebaldiana*, 13 April 2015, http//kosmopolis.cccb.org/en/sebaldiana/post/sobre-el-radicalismo-de-w-g-sebald/

| Academia | 'Sebald vs Academia', in *JES* 1–6, 2016 |
| Shadows | 'Out of the Shadows', *TLS* 22 September 2011 |

People

WGS	W. G. Sebald
GAS	Gertrud Aebischer-Sebald
BFS	Beate Fuchs-Sebald
JK	Jürgen Kaeser
UL	Ursula Liebsch (née Lotte Küsters)
HB	Helmut Bunk
M	Marie
JPT	Jan Peter Tripp
ROP	Reinbert Tabbert
WDO	Wolf Dieter Ortmann
GT	Gordon Turner
KV	Kristin Völker
WS	Wolfgang Schlüter
RWS	Richard Sheppard
US	Uwe Schütte
MA	Mark Anderson
AI	Andreas Isenschmid
KW	Kay Wolfinger

Institutions

DLA	Deutsches Literaturarchiv (German Literary Archive, in Marbach, Germany)
DLF	Deutscher Literaturfonds (German Literary Fund)
FSZ	*Freiburger Studentenzeitung* (the Freiburg student newspaper)
UEA	University of East Anglia

Notes

The page numbers of WGS's books in these Notes refer to the first hardback editions, which are the ones the author used.

PREFACE

1 Uwe Schütte (US) teaches at the University of Aston in Birmingham and is the foremost scholar on W. G. Sebald (WGS) in both Britain and Germany. He has written half a dozen books on WGS's work and life, most recently *Annäherungen* (*Approaches*), 2019. I have relied a great deal on his work in this book. He has written an introduction to Sebald in English: *W. G. Sebald*, in the Writers and Their Work series. See Bibliography.

2 The friend, the artist Jan Peter Tripp (JPT), met WGS at school and became an important friend from the mid-1970s onwards. The editor is Simon Prosser of Hamish Hamilton. Prosser published an engaging summary of his impressions of WGS, 'An A–Z of W. G. Sebald', in *Five Dials*, the Hamish Hamilton online magazine (https://fivedials.com/fiction/z-w-g-sebald/). I draw on this in Chapter 19 (see p. 373).

3 So he said In *Patience (After Sebald)*, the 2012 film about *RS* by Grant Gee.

4 He was well aware of the originality of his method. Harvill's author's questionnaire for *E* (like all such questionnaires) asked if he knew of any competing books. He didn't know of any that tried to do anything similar, he replied. (Author's form in the *E* papers, DLA.) As we'll see, Susan Sontag would famously say of *E* that it was 'unlike any book one has ever read' (see Chapter 24, Note 2). Ali Smith, e.g., says that WGS 'found [a] new literary form ... Nobody wrote like him, and he has transformed the literary imagination with the few books he had the time to write and we have had the luck to read.' (Quoted by Simon Prosser in his 'A–Z of W. G. Sebald'.)

5 Fortunately he told the same tale to another interviewer as well – the literary critic James Wood, one of his most influential admirers. So I don't bear the guilt alone.

1 All quotations from GAS come from our conversations and emails over the last five years.

2 Quotations in this paragraph from WGS's interviews with Michael Silverblatt, in Schwartz, p. 85; Jochen Wittmann, *Stuttgarter Zeitung*, 27 June 1997; Bigsby, p. 164, and *AN*, Part 3, 'Dark Night Sallies Forth', verse II, p. 87. (Lynne Sharon Schwartz's *the emergence of memory, Conversations with W. G. Sebald* contains six long interviews and four articles on WGS. See the Bibliography.)

3 He would also use this phrase in relation to the writer Robert Walser (see *PC*, p. 124).

4 Information from Herr Fritz Ketterle, the retired chief archivist of Sonthofen, whom I sincerely thank.

5 Information about Oberstdorf during the war from Angelika Patel and Julia Boyd, authors of *A Village in the Third Reich* (to be published in 2022), the English version of Patel's *Oberstdorf, 1918–1952*. Also from Gabriele Rieber, in whose family home the Löwins had rented a flat. I thank all three sincerely.

6 This paragraph from the *Allgäuer Anzeigeblatt* appears in Patel's *Oberstdorf, 1918–1952*, p. 235. The other Nazi organ in the region was *Schönes Allgäu*, which existed from 1933 to 1945. Its crude anti-Semitic propaganda was shocking – and given that there were no Jews in the area who remotely resembled its caricatured urban pedlars and traders, almost laughable.

7 For never meeting a Jewish person, see Cuomo in Schwartz, p. 105. See also e.g. Bigsby, p. 161 and Maya Jaggi, 'The Last Word', *Guardian*, 21 December 2001.

8 WGS often talked about this film, identifying it as about Bergen-Belsen (see Chapter 8, note 30). See e.g. his *Guardian* interviews with Maya Jaggi, 22 September and 21 December 2001; Doris Stoisser in Hoffmann, pp. 226–7; Burkhard Baltzer in Hoffmann, p. 80. Torsten Hoffmann's *Auf ungeheuer dünnem Eis (On horribly thin ice)* contains twenty of the most important German interviews with WGS between 1971 and 2001. My account draws on these. The school friends I talked to were WGS's close friends JK, UL and HB, and other friends and classmates such as Heidi Nowak (née Böck) and Gabriele Rieber. WGS always said that there was no word of discussion after the film, which seems to have been true. See Chapter 8, p. 15.)

9 WGS, interview with Maya Jaggi, *Guardian*, 22 September 2001.

10 See e.g. his interviews with me (Schwartz, p. 67), Lubow (Schwartz, pp. 161–20), Steve Wasserman (in *SM*, p. 367) and Bigsby (p. 142). Also e.g. those with Marco Poltronieri (Hoffmann, p. 92) and Uwe Pralle (Hoffmann, p. 259), in which he laments the inadequacy of public repentance as well, as he often did.

11 See WGS's interview with the journalist and writer Volker Hage, Hoffmann, p. 188.

12 WGS told Lubow that he went to Munich with both his parents, but gave Volker Hage (Hoffmann, pp. 176–7) this version, of passing through with his father and older sister alone. That this is the right version is confirmed by GAS. WGS also mentioned this trip to Bigsby (p. 142), and referred to it in *NHD*, p. 74. Last but not least, he gave his childhood idea of rubble as natural to his narrator in *V* (p. 187).

13 WGS, interview with Lubow, Schwartz p. 161.

14 For *Speak, Memory* being one of WGS's best-loved books, see e.g. Eleanor Wachtel in Schwartz, p. 52. (Wachtel is a Canadian writer and broadcaster.) I should perhaps confess here that I have half-stolen Nabokov's title for this book, and wholly stolen the title of a collection of essays by WGS's Manchester supervisor, Idris Parry. His *Speak Silence* was published by Carcanet in 1997. No doubt he meant to echo Nabokov too. I send apologies to him, though he died in 2008, and thanks to Carcanet for accepting the reuse of the title..

15 See http://thechaosofdeath.blogspot.co.uk/2009/04/first-paragraph-of-first-chapter-of.html.

16 WGS, letter to M, 27 February 2000.

17 *AN*, p. 84.

18 *AN*, p. 85.

19 For the bombing of Nürnberg, see http://webarchive.nationalarchives.gov.uk/20070706011932/http:/www.raf.mod.uk/bombercommand/aug43.html. Also e.g. the BBC's *The People's War*: http://www.bbc.co.uk/history/ww2peopleswar/stories/08/a2015308.shtml. And http://www.revisionist.net/nuremberg-bombing.html.

20 E.g. WGS, interview with Doris Stoisser, Hoffmann, p. 248.

21 WGS gave the photograph to the American journalist and writer Arthur Lubow, who interviewed him in August 2001 (see Schwartz, pp. 159–73). I thank him very much for sending me a copy.

In 1933 there were 812 Jews in Bamberg, 1.5 per cent of the population. After the persecutions began, most fled; the 300 who remained in late 1941 were deported. Today Bamberg has a Holocaust Monument and a permanent exhibition of Jewish life in the town. See, e.g. http://

germansynagogues.com/index.php/synagogues-and-communities?pid
=70&sid=173:bamberg.Also the International Jewish Cemetery Project,
http://www.iajgs.org/cemetery/bayern-bavaria/bamberg.htmland
Encycopedia Judaica, http://www.jewishvirtuallibrary.org/bamberg.

22 WGS said to James Wood that coincidence 'couldn't mean anything in
    the real sense, but it still does somehow' (*Brick* 59, 1998, p. 29). That
    coincidences show that everything hangs together and we should pay
    attention to them he said to Doris Stoesser (Hoffmann, pp. 232–3).
    Coincidence and his use of it was one of his main themes; he also spoke
    of it to e.g. Piet de Moor (*SM*, 352–3), AI (Hoffmann, p. 61), Jean-Pierre
    Rondas (Hoffmann, p. 213) and Nuria Amat (*ABC Cultural, Madrid*, 30
    September 2000, https://nuriaamat.com/wp-content/uploads/2016/05/
    Sebald.-Entrevista-ABC-Cultural.pdf). See Chapter 24 below.

23 WGS, interview with Ciro Krauthausen, *Babelia*, 14 July 2001.
    https://elpais.com/cultura/2016/10/27/babelia/1477566485_771964.html

24 WGS, interview with Cuomo, Schwartz, p. 97.

25 It was to Maya Jaggi that he spoke of Kafka's sister, and to Bigsby, Marco
    Poltronieri, Ralph Schock and Walther Krause that he spoke of the Jews
    of Corfu, Hungary and the whole of the Mediterranean (Bigsby, p. 144
    and Hoffmann, pp. 88, 101 and 138 respectively). US also argues that
    silence and the '*unverschuldete Schuld*', the unmerited guilt, of his birth
    are main drivers of WGS's work (*Ein*, p. 46).

26 Bigsby, p. 144.

27 WGS, interview with Walther Krause, Hoffman, p. 138.

28 WGS, interview with Maya Jaggi, *Guardian*, 22 September 2001.

29 E.g. Bigsby, p. 142, which also includes WGS's account of his father's late
    return. He told Volker Hage that his father came back in 1948, but this
    was a confusion (or exaggeration; Hoffmann, pp. 176–7).

30 That Georg Sebald lived and worked in Wertach for a year after his return,
    and that WGS rejected his father, come from GAS; see also p. 36 of MA's
    account in *Literaturen* 7/8 February 2006, which is largely based on GAS's
    information. MA puts the problem of WGS's 'two fathers' at the heart of his
    account: see Mark M Anderson, '*Wo die Schrecken der Kindheit verborgen
    sind: W. G. Sebalds Dilemma der zwei Väter*', http://www.wgsebald.de/
    vaeter.html and in *Literaturen* 7/8 February 2006. See also his chapter in
    SM, 'A Childhood in the Allgäu', p. 32; and 'Five Crucial Events in the Life
    of W. G. Sebald', *Kosmopolis* 23 February 2015, http://kosmopolis.cccb.
    org/en/sebaldiana/post/cinc-esdeveniments-a-la-vida-de-w-g-sebald/.

31 WGS, interview with Sarah Kafatou, *Harvard Review* No. 15, Fall
    1998. WGS also said he spent his childhood 'under the tutelage of my
    grandfather' to Bigsby, p. 142.

32 WGS, interview with Maya Jaggi, *Guardian*, 22 September 2001. Also the following two quotations.
33 Maria Alvarez interview, *Telegraph*, 24 September 2001.
34 WGS, interview with Renate Just, *Süddeutsche Zeitung Magazin* No. 40, 5 October 1990, Loquai 1997, p. 29. The friends who report no lurid tales from WGS about his father include UL, JK, HB, Rainer Galaske and M.
35 The person who said this was WGS's Freiburg friend Albrecht Rasche.
36 MA, *Literaturen*, 7/8 February 2006, p. 35.
37 WGS, interview with Lubow, Schwartz, p. 171.

2 DR HENRY SELWYN

1 I have borrowed this phrase from Jochen Wittmann, *Stuttgarter Zeitung*, 27 June 1997. About *E* as WGS's breakthrough book in Germany see also e.g. Hans-Peter Kunisch, *SZ*, 5 April 2001 and US, 'Teaching by Example', *The Essay*, Radio 3, 6 December 2011.
2 *A*, pp. 100–1.
3 *E*, p. 8. The following quotations from *E* come from pp. 9, 12, 16, 18, 21, 23 and 7. I have added the italics to the line 'And so they are ever returning to us, the dead.'
4 See Ralph Schock (Hoffmann, p. 99), Bigsby (p. 154) and James Wood (*Brick*, p. 25), among others. To Schock he said that all the pictures in *MF* '*sind tatsächlich diese Personen*', 'are really these people'; to Wood he explained that by 'authentic' he meant that 'they really did come out of the photo albums of the people described in those texts and are a direct testimony of the fact that these people did exist in that particular shape and form'.
5 In the German he didn't change it at all, calling her Aileen, which is probably how he thought it was spelled. I didn't mention this to Christine.
6 He made both claims, about minor details and major events, in my interview with him, Schwartz, p. 72. Also e.g. to Bigsby (p. 155), Ciro Krauthausen (*Babelia*, 14 July 2001) and Maya Jaggi (*Guardian*, 22 September 2001).
7 The account that follows comes from my interviews with Christine Buckton (28 December 2014, 29 December 2014 and 19 March 2015), Tessa Sinclair (3 February 2015 and email 3 February 2015), and Esther Wright (17 March 2015 and email 31 March 2015). I thank them all most sincerely. Some further details come from my email from GT (WGS's friend and colleague at UEA, who also lived in Wymondham), 14 February 2017.

8 See the interview with Eleanor Wachtel, Schwartz, p. 60. 'You have to be very careful,' he said to Joseph Cuomo (Schwartz, p. 112) and to Uwe Pralle (Hoffmann, p. 257).

9 Schwartz, p. 70.

3 WERTACH, 1944–52

Where not otherwise indicated, the information in this chapter comes from GAS and from MA, 'Wo die Schrecken der Kindheit verborgen sind', Literaturen 7/8 February 2006, and 'A Childhood in the Allgäu', in SM.

1 This story is also told in Renate Just's interview with WGS, 'Stille Katastrophien', *Süddeutsche Zeitung Magazin* No. 40, 5 October 1990 (Loquai 1997, p. 25). GAS told it to me; clearly WGS himself told it to Renate Just.

2 His autobiographical hero, Josef, suggests this in WGS's early unpublished novel. This is in the file *Frühere prosa* (Earlier prose), in the DLA (Version 1, second sheet of paper between pp. 59 and 60).

3 The first part of this paragraph is based on letters WGS wrote to his friend M on 2 March and 6 November 2000; the last part – the three-year-old's refusal to run to his parents – on a passage in his autobiographical early novel, Version 2, p. 41. Just before this passage WGS had switched from 'Josef' to 'I', as (tellingly) he quite often did, and that continued for the rest of the book.

4 *V*, p. 193.

5 *V*, pp. 193–4. GAS confirms that this is an accurate description of their living room at Steinlehner's. She also remembers that her mother didn't hear the mockery in WGS's description, so that this was almost the only page of *V* of which she entirely approved.

6 This was said to me by one of the Wertach ladies I spoke to (see Chapter 4, 'Il Ritorno in patria', below).

7 Apart from GAS and MA, information in this paragraph also from US, *Ein*, p. 17.

8 E.g. to Piet de Moor, *SM*, p. 351; to Walther Krause, Hoffmann, p. 138; to Krauthausen in *Babelia*, 14 July 2001; to Bigsby, p. 140; and to Cuomo, Schwartz, pp. 100–1.

9 See *V*, pp. 240–1.

10 To Eleanor Wachtel, Schwartz, p. 39.

11 To Maya Jaggi, *Guardian*, 22 September 2001 interview. This is something he explored in his unfinished book about Corsica, and which remains in *CS*: see the eponymous essay, p. 29.

12 To Steve Wasserman, *SM*, p. 370.

13 Information from Suzanne Siegler, née Stehmer, whom I sincerely thank for all her help.

14 My conversations with Les Stehmer took place in May and July 2016.

15 The identification of Uncle William and information about him comes from Fanny's letters to WGS in 1984, all held in the DLA in Marbach; from Suzanne Siegler; and from US census immigration, First Word War draft registration and death records, found through FamilySearch.org.

16 *E*, p. 68.

17 This and the following quotations from Bigsby, pp. 140–1.

18 Undated letter to M, from early July 2000.

19 From Renate Just, 'Stille Katastrophien', *Süddeutsche Zeitung Magazin*, 5 October 1990, Loquai 1997, p. 29.

20 See Bigsby, p. 140, where WGS himself says that the first tractors appeared in Wertach in 1948. Also e.g. Lala Aufsberg, *Historische Bilder aus dem Allgäu*, Hephaistos, 2010, pp. 37–43, which dates the change in the Allgäu from horse- and even ox-driven ploughs and carts to tractor-driven ones to the war. Seefelder's taxi service continued to exist until a few years ago (as I was told by a tenant in the house in April 2017). The words 'TAXI Seefelder' have been left on the wall, in tribute to its long service.

21 If you count forty weeks back from 18 May, you arrive at 11 August, and Rosa saw Nürnberg on fire on the night of 27/28 August. Two weeks after conception was early to be certain of a pregnancy, in those days long before over-the-counter tests, but GAS remembers that Rosa had morning sickness with all her pregnancies, and she could have recognised this symptom straight away.

22 WGS, letter to M, 18 July 2000.

23 Georg Sebald's history, which follows, is based as usual on information from GAS and from MA. But WGS also talked about his father's background and army career: see e.g. Bigsby (p. 142), Maya Jaggi (September interview), Maria Alvarez (*Telegraph*, 24 September 2001), James Atlas ('W. G. Sebald: A Profile', *Paris Review* 151, 1999) and Hans-Peter Kunisch (*Süddeutsche Zeitung*, 5 April 2001).

24 The information about Georg's army career, which follows, comes from his military record. The original records are accessible only to family members. But when the US Army entered Germany in 1945, they captured all military documents that hadn't been lost or destroyed in the war and microfilmed them. These microfilms are held in the National Archives in Washington and, like all official records in the United States (and Britain), are open to the public. Mike Constandy of Westmoreland Research undertook research for me and discovered that – miraculously – Georg

Sebald's record was among them. It is in Box No. 786 of 'German Army Officers: Period 1900–1945', which contains 201 files, starting with the surname Schwital. I sincerely thank Mike Constandy for his sleuthing.

25 The date and the area to which Georg was sent comes from the history of Panzer Division 273, into which his division was integrated.

26 This is proved by a family photograph taken on the day of WGS's christening, which shows Georg holding his newborn son on the balcony of the Seefelder house in Wertach. See *SM*, p. 17.

27 See   https://en.wikipedia.org/wiki/Oradour-sur-Glane_massacre   and https://en.wikipedia.org/wiki/Tulle_massacre.

28 There is a large amount of material on Camp 163 on the Internet in both German and French (including a montage of drawings on YouTube). Just put 'Oflag 163' into your browser.

29 This date comes from MA, *SM*, p. 19.

30 Letter of 10 August 2000.

31 Letter to M, 7 August 2000.

32 Josef Egelhofer's birth date comes as usual from MA (*SM*, p. 27), Theresia's from *ibid.*, (p. 19), and from GAS. She found it on her *Ahnenpass*, the document about her ancestors everyone had to have in the Nazi period, to prove their 'Aryan' ancestry. This shows that Theresia was born on 3 October 1880. MA says that the Egelhofers came to Wertach from Binnroth (now spelled Binnrot), which is a part of Kirchdorf, forty-odd miles from Wertach (*SM*, p. 19). He also says that Josef was born in Binnroth, but gives no source for this information. GAS is not sure now where her grandfather was born.

33 Letter of 31 July 2000.

34 Letter of 19 July 2000.

35 Letter of 24 July 2000.

36 Trade unions had been growing in Germany since the 1830s, and especially since the revolutions of 1848. See *Geschichte der Werkschaften* (History of the Trade Unions), https://www.gewerkschaftsgeschichte.de/anfaenge-der-arbeiterbewegung.html.

37 This information comes from WGS's letter to M of 26 July 2000. In the notes for his World War Project (the book he was researching when he died; see pp. 374, 376, 443, below) he included Theresia's surname, Herbrecher. There he recorded the names of one generation earlier as well: Franz Sebald, born c. 1800, and his wife Franziska Peier, parents of Great-Grandfather Josef. See *SM*, p. 260. In a later letter to M (6 August 2001) WGS wrote that his Sebald ancestors had been workers in the glass

factories of the Bavarian Forest. This presumably goes back to still earlier generations.

4 IL RITORNO IN PATRIA

1 *V*, p. 195.

2 See e.g. Bigsby, p. 141; KW, *Oberallgäu Kultur*, 23 May 14; US, *Ein*, p. 76. The best discussion of this point is in AI, 'Melencolia', in Loquai 1997. It is also the argument of Dr Martha Egger-Feichtinger, one of Wertach's own WGS experts.

3 The translation is by Michael Hamburger. Edwin Turner uses it on his Biblioklept website, https://biblioklept.org/2017/03/20/the-never-ending-torture-of-unrest-georg-buchners-lenz-reviewed-2/, in his post of 20 March 2017. Here he very interestingly discusses *Lenz* (and compares it to WGS, as well as to, e.g,, Edgar Allan Poe). Others who point out the echo of *Lenz* in 'Il Ritorno in patria' include e.g. US, *Ein*, p. 77 and Anne Fuchs, *Die Schmerzenspuren der Geschichte: Zur Poetik der Erinnerung in W. G. Sebalds Prosa*, Böhlau, 2004, p. 149. US (*Ein*, p. 77) also points out another echo: of Eduard Mörike's 1827 poem '*Besuch in Urach*', 'Visit to Urach'. For an English translation of the poem, see http://www.cingolani.com/55em.html.

4 *V*, p. 183.

5 Kafka, *The Castle* in *The Complete Novels*, London, Minerva, 1992, p. 277. Again all the critics point out this echo of *The Castle*. Three main loci are US, *Ein*, p. 79, MA, *Literaturen*, p. 34, and Daniel L. Medin, *Three Sons: Franz Kafka and the Fiction of J M Coetzee, Philip Roth, and W. G. Sebald*, Northwestern University Press, 2010, p. 135.

6 AI, 'Melencolia', in Loquai 1997, p. 73.

7 WGS's appointment calendars are in the DLA. The information based on them throughout this book relies on work done by RWS and included in his Chronology in *SM*. Needless to say, I am hugely grateful. For these instances, see *SM*, pp. 634 and 629.

8 See e.g. Piet de Moor, Hoffmann, p. 71; AI, Hoffmann, pp. 52ff., 60, 64 and Loquai, p. 71; Poltronieri, Hoffmann, p. 95; Cuomo, Schwartz, p. 103; Ciro Krauthausen, *Babelia*, 14 July 2001. US also recognises that the last part of *V* in particular is self-exploration. (*Ein*, p.78).

9 From her conversations with him, GAS also thinks that WGS did the descent from Oberjoch in 1980 rather than 1987. They did the walk with their parents several times as children, she recalls, so that the route would have been a familiar one.

10 *V*, p. 215. For the narrator stranded between two times, see pp. 185 and 195.

11 See MA in *SM*, p. 28.

12 *V*, p. 203.

13 In his early novel, WGS mentions Turkish honey being sold in the market, thus supporting GAS's account. (*Frühere Prosa* file in the DLA, Version 2, p. 64.)

14 To AI (Hoffmann, p. 61) and Cuomo (Schwartz, p. 103).

15 Schwartz, p. 68.

5 AMBROS ADELWARTH

1 *E*, pp. 70–1.

2 The narrator's Deauville dream, *E*, pp. 121–6.

3 The critic Anja Johannsen agrees, calling Ambros's account of his time in Jerusalem 'a far more drastic piece of writing than any other passage in his written work' (reported by RWS in *JES* 2009, p. 113). We are counting only WGS's mature work, however; the second version of his early novel was full of short verbless sentences (as noted in Chapter 12.)

4 *E*, p. 91.

5 See *A*, p. 153, where James Mallord Ashman recounts how, when he re-entered his old nursery after ten years, 'the chasm of time [opened] up before him', and 'it wouldn't have taken much … to overset his reason altogether'. Austerlitz himself is the main example of someone whose relationship to time – his desire first to escape the past and then to return to it – takes him close to madness.

6 To give just two instances in *AA*: the clouds of white exhaust that envelop Aunt Fini as the narrator drives away, and the veils of spray that rise from the Falls on his return to Ithaca (*E*, pp. 104, 108.) Imagined brothers: in the drafts for *AA* the twin brothers motif is even clearer. Cosmo's brother is called Damian (DLA, *AA* File 7). Cosmo's name saint, Ambros notes in his diary, is St Cosmas: and Saints Cosmas and Damian were twin brothers, martyred in the late third or early fourth century AD. See the diary for 23 September, on p. 132, 'ss. Cosma e D': you can just make out Ambros's remark '*Heute das Namenfest!*' (Today is [Cosmo's] saint's day!). As a good Catholic, WGS would have known about the twin-brother saints Cosmas and Damian; there is even a church in Munich dedicated to them. He evidently decided that the reference was too obscure for non-Catholics and removed it.

7 *E*, p. 97.

8 *E*, p. 130.

9 See *V*, p. 131.

10 *E*, p. 88.

11 See the interview with Christian Scholz, Hoffmann, p. 174.

12 *E*, p. 104. Next quotation from the same page.

13 Re quizzing Fanny: see *SM*, p. 630.

14 See my interview, Schwartz, pp. 69–70.

15 Unless otherwise indicated, information about Anny and the rest of the family comes from GAS.

16 *E*, p. 73.

17 *V*, p. 216.

18 Information about Fanny and Joe Stehmer from their daughter Suzanne Siegler, whom I sincerely thank.

19 The information about Joe Egelhofer's career comes from Fanny's letters of 1984 to WGS, in the DLA.

20 *E*, p. 86.

21 Information about Joe Egelhofer from GAS and BFS as noted, and from WGS's letter to M, 4 August 2000. Les recounted to me with gusto that one of Rosemarie's marriages had lasted all of nine days.

22 *E*, p. 73.

23 Information on the family deaths from Suzanne Siegler, email of 10 July 2016, and from the US Social Security Death Index. Fanny spoke of her worries in one of her letters to WGS, saying that she didn't dare to have an operation for her neuralgia for fear that her heart wouldn't be strong enough.

24 Information from Suzanne Siegler, same email.

25 All in the *AA* files in the DLA.

26 *E*, p. 79. The following quotation comes from the same page.

27 William wrote on a 1921 passport application that he had resided in Washington from 1906 to 1915. His employer there died in 1916, so that may well have been the more accurate date. His draft registration card in 1917/18 shows that he was certainly in New York by then.

28 Information in this paragraph and the next about Henry Morton Meinhard and his wife Carrie, née Wormser, from U.S. Censuses 1900, 1910 and 1930, and articles from the *New York Times*, 3 May 1928, 16 April 1931, and 25 April 1931, kindly sent me by Nola Taylor of the Greenwich Historical Society, whom I thank. Carrie Wormser came from one of the 'wealthiest of the Jewish banking families in New York', as WGS wrote of the Solomons, putting the Wormsers into his list (*E*, p. 88).

29 This last detail was vividly recalled by Les. Carrie Meinhard gave William the house pictured in *E* (on p. 102.) It was in Purchase, New York, near Mamaroneck, where WGS puts it. The gift was only for William's lifetime;

after Carrie's death it went to her children. (Information from Suzanne Siegler, email of 15 October 2017.)

30 Information to this point from Fanny's letters. That he ended up in several sanatoria comes from *Father Struck It Rich* by Evalyn Walsh McLean, FirstLight Publishing, 1996 (first published 1936).

31 Information about Ned McLean from Fanny's letters, https://en.wikipedia.org/wiki/Edward_Beale_McLean and *Father Struck It Rich*, pp. 41, 64, 102.

32 Information from Fanny's letters and *Father Struck It Rich*, pp. 102, 105, 108. In Evalyn's memoir Ned is invited to Colorado after they're engaged, not before, but clearly William accompanied him there at some stage. Since William arrived in the US around 1906 and spent a year or two with the diplomat, he would have begun his employment with the McLeans in 1907 or 1908: hence, at most a year before Ned married.

33 Information in this paragraph from *Father Struck It Rich*; article on Ned McLean's death, *Los Angeles Times*, 28 July 1941; https://en.wikipedia.org/wiki/Evalyn_Walsh_McLean and www.in2013dollars.com.

34 See my interview, Schwartz, pp. 71–2. Another fib to me, I'm afraid.

35 The copy in WGS's DLA/*AA* files shows that it comes from the studio of Charles Raad in Jerusalem, as Ambros says on p. 140; this is also visible in the German edition of *E* (p. 137). WGS said in a letter to Peter Jordan that 'Ambros' was William, almost all the details about him were accurate, and the photo genuine (letter of 12 February 1993; this and all WGS's letters to Peter Jordan are in the DLA). In a letter to M (3 August 2000) he said that it was an authentic photo of his great-uncle when he travelled the world with his 'employer' before the First World War. That identifies Ned McLean, since William joined Morton Meinhard in 1915 or 1916. (But WGS did – rarely – tell M his fictions as truths, and this could have been one occasion.)

36 Information in this paragraph from https://en.wikipedia.org/wiki/Edward_Beale_McLean and *Father Struck It Rich passim* for Ned's drinking. (On p. 156, incidentally, Evalyn includes a list of servants, in which the first is William Schindele.)

37 Information in this paragraph from Fanny's letters; https://en.wikipedia.org/wiki/Edward_Beale_McLean; *Father Struck It Rich*, pp. 133, 159, 163, 178, 220; *Chicago Tribune*, 8 October 1931, p. 1; *New York Times*, 31 October 1933, p. 4; *Los Angeles Times*, 28 July 1941, p. 1A.

38 He complained to fellow writers, to interviewers (e.g. Bigsby, pp. 145–6, Cuomo, Schwartz p. 112, Krauthausen, *Babelia*, 14 July 2001), to his students. In his 1991 grant application he wrote that writing was always

very laborious for him. (From the '*Kostenbegründung*' (Reasons for Cost) in the 1991 application, *Die Ausgewanderten* File 11 in the DLA.)

39 To Sven Boedeker, Hoffmann, p. 108. They were talking mostly about *E.*

40 To Renate Just, in '*Im Zeichen des Saturn*', 1995, in Loquai 1997, p. 40.

41 To Ralph Schock, Hoffmann, p. 103. See also Bigsby, p. 160 ('Writing difficult, complex sentences takes that sort of attention which makes you appear … like someone who keeps staring in[to] the same hole') and Lubow, Schwartz, p. 169 ('It's … devotional work, obsessive').

42 *E*, p. 136.

43 *E*, p. 145. The photocopied pages 830, 996 and 997 of *Itinéraire de Paris à Jérusalem* (they don't show which edition they come from) are in WGS's DLA/*AA* files.

44 Especially e.g. on pp. 141–2 of *E*, the destruction of Jerusalem and its glories before (taken from Fallmerayer's *Fragmente aus dem Orint*). Chateaubriand will play an important role in *RS;* Fallmerayer has already appeared in *V*, when the narrator signs the register at the Golden Dove in Verona with his name (*V*, p. 117).

45 DLA, *AA* File 7.

46 See e.g. Boedeker in Hoffmann, p. 109: 'To write about shock treatment with high drama isn't art.'

47 DLA, *AA* Files 6 and 7.

48 See my interview, Schwartz, p. 72. All the cutting-out and sticking-on I go on to describe is visible in the drafts.

49 *E*, p. 88.

6 1952–6

Unsourced information from GAS and BFS.

1 Photocopied pages are in WGS's archive in the DLA.

2 WGS wrote in both *PB* (p. 29) and *CS* (p. 191) that they travelled into Sonthofen in Alpenvogel's van. This must have been true, since they had no car. The rest of the information in this paragraph comes from GAS's interview with Ruth Vogel-Klein, 'Ein Fleckerlteppich', in *WGS: Memoires. Transferts. Images. Erinnerung. Übertragungen. Bilder, Recherches Germaniques*, Special Issue No. 2, 2005, as well as from conversations and emails between GAS and me, as throughout. The date comes from RWS's Chronology, *SM*, p. 622. KW tells me that the Alpenvogel bus and van company still exists in Sonthofen.

3 See *E*, p. 29.

4 For the blue plaques, round clock and excitement about the city, see *E*, p. 30. WGS's friends JK and Peter Schaich remember that the Sonthofen street signs were indeed blue enamel in the old days (my interview with them of 13 October 2015).

5 See *Sonthofen: Festbuch zur Stadt Erhebung 1963* by Gerhard Wolfrum and Leonhard Bröll, Verlag J. Eberl, 1963.

6 See KW, *'(Un)heimliches Allgäu: W. G. Sebald und seine Heimat'*, in US ed., *ÜS*, pp. 158–76, on p. 176. In 2019 a Sebald-Gesellschaft (Sebald Society) was formed in Kempten, Sonthofen and Wertach, after much promotion by KW and others. But this is an academic foundation, not a public organisation sponsored by Sonthofen city. (See e.g. the 'Allgäu Kultur' section of the *Allgäuer Zeitung*, 4 December 2019.)

7 Information about the Ordensburg from JK. For a few years after the war it housed an American unit: see the website of the US Constabulary School, Sonthofen, http://www.usarmygermany.com/Sont1.htm. See also e.g. Hage in Hoffmann, p. 185, where WGS calls Sonthofen a *Kasernestadt*, a barracks town.

8 That the old station closed in 1948 comes from my interview with JK and Peter Schaich. The boys in WGS's class learned in 1953 that the new one opened on 4 October 1949, as recorded in the drawing by JK that WGS included in *E*, p, 62.

9 Information from Fritz Ketterle, interview of 24 April 2017, as well as GAS. That Georg never became a permanent employee of the police comes from WGS's friend HB, our interview of 27 February 2016. Helmut understood this from his father, who was a policeman and a friend of Georg's.

10 WGS's haircut horrors were shared by many of his contemporaries. The writer and critic Manfred Koch wrote the perfect poem about this, *'Vaters Sieg im Haarschnittkrieg'* ('Father's Victory in the Haircut War'). (See the companion page.)

11 From an undated letter, sometime in September 2001.

12 Information on the division of Sonthofen schools from JK and BFS; on the history of the Catholic boys' school from JK's essay on it, with accompanying material, in his school exercise book of 1952–3; on the peak number in the school, from Adolf Lipp (who was a teacher there from 1954 and ended as principal), our interview of 15 October 2015; on the fifty-three in WGS's class in 1952, JK. (WGS says fifty-two in *E*, p. 46.) JK's schoolboy essay, clearly dictated by his teacher, concludes that eight classrooms were far too few, and at least double that number were needed. The new Sonthofen primary school was built in 1968.

13 Information about the school and its old-fashioned regime from Adolf Lipp and JK, about the boys and their class differences from JK and Peter Schaich, our interview of 13 October 2015.

14 *E*, p. 30.

15 The *Kikiriki* and Iller bridge events from GAS, BFS and JK, the tree house from JK. The benches event from BFS; she added that WGS managed to keep it secret from their parents for a long time, until he wrote about it in a school composition. Writing is always dangerous.

16 The descriptions of JK's house and garden, and of the Lerchenmüller gardens and the odd-job man Schultz, come from JK, in interviews with me and with Thomas Honickel. The account of their happy hours together casting tin soldiers comes from WGS's letter to M of 9 February 2001. His report of their harmless battles, in which the fallen soldiers could rise up again, recalls many images of death and resurrection in his work, e.g. Luisa Lanzberg's vision of the stag beetles in the Windheim woods.

17 Information about Armin Müller from my interviews with Adolf Lipp, Fritz Ketterle, JK and HB. Müller's age from his death certificate, which shows his birth date as 22 December 1910.

18 As he told e.g. Eleanor Wachtel (Schwartz, p. 43); and as is evident not only from *PB*, written in the late 80s, but from the fact that he talked about him to friends to the end, e.g. to M (information from my conversations with her).

19 Information from HB, JK and Peter Schaich. WGS also wrote in his early novel about Berchtold's cutting the sticks with which he was beaten, leaving him his real name, but moving the scene to another teacher and another school. ('*Frühere Prosa*', in DLA, Version 1, p. 42.)

20 Information from Fritz Ketterle, whom I sincerely thank for all his help. (Our interview of 24 April 2017.)

21 Information from my conversations with HB, JK and Adolf Lipp, and from Thomas Honickel's interview with Herr Wagner, another teacher at the school, who died before I got to Sonthofen. This interview, and the others Honickel did for his 2007 film *Der Ausgewanderte*, are published in Thomas Honickel, *Curriculum Vitae: Die W. G. Sebald-Interviews (Curriculum Vitae: The W. G. Sebald Interviews)*, ed. Uwe Schütte und Kay Wolfinger, Band 1, Deutschen Sebald Gesellschaft Schriftenreihe (Vol. 1 in the German Sebald Society series), Königshausen & Neumann, 2021. Also from an article celebrating Müller's seventieth birthday in the *Allgäuer Anzeigeblatt*, 22 December 1980, which for once spoke about his expulsion from teaching in the mid-1930s, and about his great difficulties when he was given the job of de-Nazifying Sonthofen's schools after the war. See Chapter 9, Note 2.

22 Information in this paragraph from HB.

23 See 'Moments musicaux', *CS*, p. 208. In his first novel WGS moves the
    start of his passion for maps – together with his memory of beatings –
    to his second school, the convent school St Maria Stern (first version,
    pp. 41–2). But it is clear that it started under Armin Müller in the
    Sonthofen primary school.

24 Information in this paragraph and the next from JK's *Heimatkunde*
    exercise books of 1952–3 and 1953–4 and HB's of 1953–4. Müller's Nature
    catechism is on p. 10 in both HB's and JK's 1953–4 books; JK's classroom
    plan is on p. 1 of his 1952–3 one. The class made the list of the Sonthofen
    districts on 4 May 1954.

25 Adolf Lipp, in his interview with me, 15 October 2015. Herr Wagner
    agreed (Thomas Honickel's interview).

26 See *E*, p. 40. The places that follow are in *E*, pp. 38–9.

27 From my conversations with HB and his email of 4 January 2016; also
    from my interviews with his brother Gerhard, who is three years younger
    and remembered many of the same excursions, which Müller clearly
    made with successive waves of boys over the years. WGS's class copied the
    account of Leo Dorn into their schoolbooks (p. 37 in HB's, for example).

28 Information in this paragraph and the next from JK.

29 KW spotted that WGS wrote over JK's plan. He made no changes, just
    made both drawing and writing darker, so that they would be clearer in
    reproduction. See *E*, p. 62.

30 The drawing that follows is from JK's *Heimatkunde* exercise book for
    1953–4. All the boys did it, in later years as well.

31 Information in this paragraph from BFS and GAS.

32 Information in this paragraph from GAS, JK and HB.

33 JK thinks that the two families discussed the move together, but can't be
    certain. I take the liberty of leaving out the 'probably' for once. The rest
    of the information from him, HB and GAS.

34 '*Frühere Prosa*', Version 1 of the novel, p. 89.

35 Heidi Nowak (née Böck), interview with the author, 10 August 2015,
    and Gabriele Rieber, née Ilse Hoffmann, interview with the author, 21
    June 2015.

36 Date from RWS's Chronology in *SM*, p. 622.

37 Information from UL, JK and HB. HB called Georg 'a civilian in
    uniform'.

38 From my interview with Gerhard Eschweiler, 10 August 2015. UL's
    account of her mother at the window from my conversations with her.

39 See his interview with Uwe Pralle in Hoffmann, p. 254. He also has the hero
    of his early novel say that he reverts to dialect at home (Version 1, p. 95).

40 That WGS took zither lessons from Pirner is clear in *CS*, p. 192, and confirmed by GAS, despite some suggestions that he took them from the Oberstdorf music teacher, Gogl. Again, whatever their financial struggles, the Sebalds paid for private lessons. In *CS* WGS calls Pirner 'Kerner', and Gitti 'Kathi' (p. 192). Gitti (Brigitte) Pirner's being the idol of St Maria Stern comes from JK.

41 *CS*, pp. 192–3.

42 Information about the sax from my conversations with M. In *CS* WGS says it was the clarinet he dreamed of playing, but this was part of his story about Paul Bereyter (which was not quite true either). Information about his strumming a guitar in Manchester comes from a photograph taken at the time, which can be seen in Thomas Honickel's film *Der Ausgewanderte*.

43 'Regina Tobler' is probably an invented name, as is 'Zobel' for Gogl ('Zobel' was a real name in Wertach). But the experience WGS describes in *CS* was a real one. In a letter of 20 February 2001 he told M that this girl attracted him very much, but was four years older, so that he didn't dare to speak to her; instead, especially on dark winter evenings, he would gaze into the lighted room and watch her play. He added in this letter that Gogl was a very nice man, to whom he later owed a great deal.

44 'Moments musicaux', *CS*, pp. 194–9. *Ernani* is based on the play *Hernani* by Victor Hugo, who was a favourite of WGS's in his teens. Both play and opera are high romance, with the bandit Ernani challenging the king and the elderly aristocrat Silva for the hand of Elvira. Elvira loves Ernani, and after many operatic reversals they marry, only for Ernani to kill himself, keeping an oath to Silva. (See https://en.wikipedia.org/wiki/Ernani.) The death of Ernani is the scene WGS describes in *CS*.

45 Information about Josef Egelhofer in this and the following paragraphs from GAS, BFS, and WGS's letter to M, 4 January 2001.

46 This last account comes from WGS's early novel, Version 1, p. 31.

47 *CS*, pp. 193–4.

48 The account of the grandfather's death takes up pp. 30–5 of the first version and 64–8 of the second.

49 He spoke about the hole left in his life to, e.g,, Maria Alvarez (*Telegraph*, 24 September 2001), Maya Jaggi (*Guardian*, 22 September 2001) and Arthur Lubow (Schwartz, p. 171). The rest of the information from my conversations with M.

50 To Lubow, see Schwartz, p. 171. He always hid this very cleverly, so that most people never noticed, starting with his Sonthofen friends. JK, for example, had no memory of WGS having a skin problem, until I mentioned his fetish for gloves, which I thought I'd seen in some of the

stories. Then JK suddenly clapped his hands over his eyes and said, 'Wait a minute!' Perhaps WGS had had to wear gloves for a time... There'd been a flash of memory, but then it was gone.

51 The close friends I spoke to were UL, JK, HB, Werner Braunmüller and Rainer Galaske; among the other school friends were Heidi Nowak (then Böck), Gerhard Eschweiler, Sigrid Becker-Neumeier (then Becker), Gabriele Rieber (then Ilse Hoffmann), Gerd Greiner and Friedemann Reich. Also e.g. André Brünisholz's brother Bernard, who visited Sonthofen in the summer of 1960, and says that Winfried was '*un jeune homme toujours de bonne humeur*' (his letter to me of 16 August 2017).

52 See US, *F*, pp. 144–5, and *W & TW*, p. 9. In the former he writes: 'The great burden of mourning that overshadowed [WGS's] life primarily resulted, not from guilt over Nazi crimes, about which he learned ... as a young adult, but from the childhood wound ... of the death of his grandfather.' In the latter he says: 'I would like to suggest that the shocking first encounter with the Holocaust that Sebald experienced as a teenager could have functioned as what Sigmund Freud calls a "screen memory" (*Deckerinnerung*) of the traumatic loss of Egelhofer.' This is US's introduction of WGS in English, and so a key source for English readers. It's unfortunate that such a seriously misleading point should be included in it. See also his conversation with Terry Pitts in 2014: 'Conversation with Uwe Schütte' on the *Vertigo* website, 15 January 2014, http://sebald.wordpress.com/2014/01/15/conversation-with-uwe-schutte/#more-5469: 'This traumatic event, I argue, was the key factor for his melancholic disposition and his obsession with reaching out into the realm of the dead, being far more important than the guilt he felt for the crimes committed by the Nazis.'

7 1956–61

Unsourced information from GAS and BFS.

1 Other divisions were also added, e.g. according to whether you were from Oberstdorf or elsewhere, and whether you chose to study Latin or French in the upper years. The account in this paragraph comes from JK and HB.

2 See https://de.wikipedia.org/wiki/Oberstdorf.

3 The description of the Oberstdorf *Bahnschüler* comes from my interview with Werner Braunmüller, 6 August 2015, and from JK and UL.

4 Information from JK, HB and Gabriele Rieber (Ilse Hoffmann).

5 This is from WGS's early novel (Version 1, p. 13a). It contained little invention anywhere (see Chapter 12), and here he slipped and wrote 'Dear Winfried' instead of 'Josef', the name he gave his hero. GAS confirms

that all three children received regular letters from Aunt Anny, often containing dollar bills.

6 As well as GAS and BFS, information in this paragraph from UL, and from WGS's early novel, e.g. p. 93 of Version 1 and p. 3 of Version 2.

7 Information about the Clique on this and the following pages comes from my conversations with its members about themselves, each other, and WGS. About Walter Kalhammer, who died in 2006, from his sister Ursula Schmid and his eldest brother Fritz Kalhammer.

8 Information in this paragraph from UL.

9 The information about M on this and the next pages comes from my many conversations with her, for which I thank her profoundly. A few details also from GAS and UL.

10 For Jean Bart see http://www.theotherside.co.uk/tm-heritage/background/jean-bart.htm See also https://fr.wikipedia.org/wiki/Jean_Bart. This shows his second marriage to Jacqueline Tugghe, remembered in M's family as Mary Tuggs, and said to be of Irish origin: it was from their one surviving child that her mother's family was descended.

11 Information about the Kaesers and the trip to Italy that follows from JK.

12 The story of GAS meeting Jean-Paul from herself.

13 Information about André Brünisholz and his friendship with WGS comes from André himself, in our interview of 3 June 2017, and from GAS, who has known him for sixty years, ever since that first summer. BFS also remembers André from that time, and how Rosa loved to listen to him playing his clarinet.

14 Information in the next pages about the *Oberrealschule* Oberstdorf from UL, JK, Heidi Nowak (Böck), Gerhard Eschweiler and Gabriele Rieber (Ilse Hoffmann). Also from the Oberstdorf yearbooks, shown to me by UL, JK, HB, Gabriele Rieber and Rainer Galaske. Their art teacher, Franz Meier, shared their memories of the easy-going, friendly regime at Oberstdorf in the early 1960s: 'It was a pleasure to teach there,' he said in his interview with Thomas Honickel.

15 He remembered the relaxed regime at Oberstdorf, from which they'd nonetheless learned well, in a letter to Karl-Heinz Schmelzer of 24 June 1995.

16 From *Sancta Stupiditas*, WGS's class's *Abitur* newspaper, on the last page. I thank Rainer Galaske for sending me copies of this class paper, as well as originals of the school newspaper of 1961–2, on which he worked with WGS.

17 Information about Karl-Heinz Schmelzer from our interview of 15 October 2015 and subsequent conversations; from Thomas Honickel's

interview with him; from WGS's letters to him and Rosa Sebald's letter to him of 15 January 2002; and from the reminiscences of UL, HB and JK.

18 In an interview JPT gave at the Villa Jauss in Oberstdorf in 2007 (CD kindly given me by Karl-Heinz Schmelzer).

19 Information about Franz Meier from my conversations with UL and Heidi Nowak. Also from his interview with Thomas Honickel and from the *Allgäuer Anzeigeblatt*, 7 March 2002, which reports a reading Meier gave in memory of WGS, and contains a brief interview with him.

20 Grunewald's famous Isenheim altarpiece plays an important role in both *After Nature* (in Part I, verse V) and *MF* (see p. 170).

21 Information about Dr Eberhard from JK, HB, Gabriele Rieber, Gerd Greiner, Sigrid Becker-Neumeier and Rainer Galaske. BFS remembers that he also hit a girl who deliberately provoked him. Eberhard (1926–2005) was still at school during the war. (Information from HB.) The story of his son was told me by Karl-Heinz Schmelzer.

22 This information from GAS. WGS himself usually dated the beginning of his historical awareness to seventeen, and the shock of the film Eberhard made his students watch (see the next chapter). But GAS remembers the first stirrings earlier, and in his interview with Christopher Bigsby, WGS says they began at 'around 16, 17'. (Bigsby, p. 142.)

23 Information from his interview with Thomas Honickel.

24 Information from HB.

25 This observation was made by André Brünisholz, who came back to the Sebalds again in the summer of 1961. The rest from GAS.

26 Information about their fathers from JK and HB. HB's father's factory produced optical instruments, including for submarines. There were forced labourers in the factory, and I did wonder what he thought about that. But though HB had become much more critical in later life, I didn't feel I could ask him. Even today it's not easy to bring up the past in Germany. I was unable to get information about the fathers of the other two members of the Clique, Werner Braunmüller and Axel Rühl. Axel died before I began my researches, and Werner had suffered memory loss; we spoke only of his happy memories of the Clique. It's likely, however, that as a railway employee, his father was in a reserved occupation, like HB's, and didn't serve.

27 Information about their fathers from UL, Heidi Nowak, Gerhard Eschweiler, Gundela Enzensberger.

28 Information in this section from Walter Kalhammer's sister Ursula Schmid and brother Fritz Kalhammer, from UL, JK and Peter Schaich, and from the transcript of Dr Kalhammer's *Spruchkammer* trial, held on 24 August

1948. The Spruchkammer courts were local denazification tribunals set up in 1946, run by Germans but with Allied oversight (see Tony Judt, *Postwar*, p. 56). The transcript was obtained by Dr Kalhammer's sons in 2008 and was sent to me by Fritz Kalhammer in 2018. After laying out the evidence, it placed Dr Kalhammer, despite his prominent role, in the category of the *Minderbelasteten*, those guilty of less serious offences. He was held in a de-Nazification camp for five years and put on probation for several more. For the story of Gabriele Schwartz, who was born in Marktoberdorf in 1937, see Allgäu Online for 8 June 2008, https://www.all-in.de/kempten/c-lokales/als-der-holocaust-nach-stiefenhofen-kommt_a433506. A film was made of the story by the Allgäu film-maker Leo Hierner: *Leni… muss fort (Leni must leave)*, 1983. See http://www.hiemerfilm.de/filmografie_leni.html.

29 Information about Georg and the Clique from UL; about Georg and WGS from BFS and GAS.

30 The first two examples of WGS's revolutionary behaviour at school come from JK; the memory of his provoking Dr Eberhard is HB's.

31 GAS's version from our conversations; WGS's from a letter he wrote to her in July 1963.

32 Information from BFS, GAS, UL, JK. The serious sportsmen were Gerhard Eschweiler, Gerd Greiner, Rainer Galaske.

33 The classmates who described WGS at around sixteen to me were JK, HB, Heidi Nowak, Werner Braunmuller, Gabriele Rieber and Gerd Greiner, Friedemann Reich. Another, Konstanze Röhrs, also told the *Augsbürger Allgemeine* (sister paper of the *Allgäuer Anzeigeblatt*) that WGS stood out 'for his independent personality and intellectual interests' (18 December 2001, p. 26). Bernard Brünisholz, André's brother, noticed the same: at school WGS '*s'imposait déjà par son intelligence et son coeur*', he says (letter to me of 16 August 2017). Meier's view from his interview with Thomas Honickel, and from another article on the occasion of Meier's memorial reading on 7 March 2003. (In the Culture section, *Oberallgäu Kultur*, of the *Augsbürger Allgemeine*, copy given to me by Friedemann Reich.)

34 The friends whose memories follow are, as usual, UL, JK and HB. The *Filserbriefe* and '*Gott zum Gruße*' stories come from HB.

35 This memory of WGS's room comes from JK's interview with Thomas Honickel. He also remarked in this interview on the importance to WGS of his clothes and surroundings.

36 Rosa Sebald to Schmelzer, 15 January 2002. Schmelzer's memories of Georg's concern about WGS come from his conversations with me. He taught the middle years, 6 and 7, when WGS was between fifteen and seventeen, so it was those years that both he and Rosa were recalling.

37 The account of Martine comes from my conversations with her in 2016 and 2017, with occasional additions from UL. I'm most grateful to Martine for her insights and her friendship.

38 When Josef, the hero of WGS's early novel, goes home to the Allgäu just before leaving for England, he finds Martine's letters (WGS didn't change her name) in his desk (Version 1, p. 93). These disappeared, along with his primary-school exercise books. Martine kept his letters, together with the books and records he gave her, through the many moves she made, and still has them somewhere. I hope she may find them one day.

8 1961–3

1 André's memories in this paragraph and the rest of this section from his interview with me, 3 June 2017, and his letter of 30 July 2017. I thank him sincerely for his help.

2 See https://en.wikipedia.org/wiki/Dachau_concentration_camp. Information about Onkel Hans from GAS.

3 This description of Rosa comes from everyone I spoke to, especially her daughters. That she was a marvellous storyteller comes from Franz Meier, in his interview with Thomas Honickel: 'It was incredible, the way she told stories; you could listen to her for hours and never get bored, she never repeated herself, but told the story, you could almost say, ready to print. Fully formed, thrilling. I think [WGS] inherited that talent from her.'

4 WGS's letter to M, 3 August 2000.

5 Information in this paragraph and the next from GAS and BFS (the tailor memory from GAS, the bathtub one from BFS). WGS also wrote in a letter to GAS in the autumn of 1962, for instance, that his appearance was constantly commented on.

6 From letters of c. Christmas 1961, early 1962, spring 1962 and autumn 1962. (Then, as later, WGS was bad at dating his letters.) There are twenty-two letters in all, between autumn 1961 and July 1964, when GAS married. After that there are a few letters in the 1970s and 1980s, which, since they fall in the private period of WGS's marriage, GAS did not show me. Later still they telephoned regularly and hardly wrote any more. Re 'She watches his every move,' WGS told M that his mother had always *surveillé*'d him (from my conversations with M).

7 Information that follows from GAS and BFS.

8 From WGS's long letter of 'Friday', autumn 1962.

9 This is GAS's view. Decades later, M also noted his need to behave *comme il faut*. (From her conversations with me.)

10 GAS said this in her interview with Thomas Honickel as well as to me.

11 This information and the following from the letters to GAS in 1962. Also, the books GAS sent come from her interview with Ruth Vogel-Klein, 'Ein Fleckerlteppich', in *WGS: Memoires. Transferts. Images. Erinnerung. Übertragungen. Bilder, Recherches Germaniques*, Special Issue No. 2, 2005, p. 213. For WGS's joining the school choir, see *SM*, p. 45. For the music he listened to: Rainer Galaske spoke about Joan Baez and Bob Dylan (our interview of 26 October 2015); WGS writes about Brahms, Bach and many others in his letters. For his spending many hours in the darkroom, see WGS interview with Maya Jaggi, *Guardian*, 22 September 2001.

12 These are the combined memories of HB, JK and UL. WGS also wrote about such a night in a letter to GAS. The teenage slang is from his letters to her.

13 These *Fasching* memories from JK.

14 The school yearbooks show that Werner left the ORO after Year 7. That he returned only occasionally comes from UL; that JK drifted away from the Clique comes from himself and UL. Information about Axel Rühl from UL, JK, HB and GAS.

   Axel never became the great artist of his teenage dream, instead becoming a teacher of art in a Bremen school. The last time the friends saw him was at Walter Kalhammer's funeral in 2006, when he cried inconsolably for Walter. He died of cancer a few years later.

15 WGS and Axel wrote to each other for a while after they had left school. These letters are lost, but Winfried reported their 'Your Majesty' exchange in a letter to GAS (3 December 1963).

16 From WGS's letter to GAS, dated (for once) 3 December 1963.

17 Information about and from HB from our conversations.

18 E.g. the memories of WGS's provoking Dr Eberhard, his Filser letters reading and '*Gott zum Gruße*' antics in the previous chapter, as well as the ones here.

19 This memory from Friedemann Reich, in a letter to ROP, 24 February 2005, a copy of which Friedemann Reich kindly gave me. I should add that he didn't present it as a cruelty; that is my interpretation.

20 Information about Rainer Galaske from our interview of 26 October 2015. The ABC School became NBC (nuclear, biological and chemical), and is now CBRN (chemical, biological, radiological and nuclear) defence. See https://en.wikipedia.org/wiki/CBRN_defense. The school still exists as the CBRN Defense, Safety and Environmental Protection School in Sonthofen. See http://www.cbrneportal.com/the-german-bundeswehr-cbrn-defense-command-a-traditionally-strong-capability-in-a-new-type-of-organization/

21 As she wrote to GAS, on 13 June 1961.

22 On pp. 8–10. *'Der böse Brecht'* ('Bad Brecht') is on p. 22; the third (a review of Bernhard Wicki's film *The Miracle of Father Malachia*) is on pp. 23–4.

23 'We must engage with this new, sceptical generation,' Schmelzer wrote, 'the times of simply repressing the young are over.' In the ORO yearbook for 1962, p. 38. The rest of the information in this paragraph from JK, GAS and BFS. The letter signed 'The Watchman' is from 13 June 1961. This letter is actually by Rosa (hence the date!), but the rest of the family wrote on it too.

24 No one remembers the precise year. The information that follows comes from GAS, BFS and JK.

25 As he wrote in a letter to GAS a few years later (letter of 'July 1963'; no specific date).

26 Information about Gundela Enzensberger from our interview of 20 February 2016. I thank her sincerely for her help.

27 See: https://en.wikipedia.org/wiki/Paragraph_175#:~:text=Almost%20verbatim %20from%20its%20Prussian,prompt%20loss%20of%20civil%20rights. Homosexuality was decriminalised in the UK in 1967, in the states of the US between 1962 and the early 2000s. See https://en.wikipedia.org/wiki/ Sexual_Offences_Act_1967#:~:text=The%20Sexual%20Offences%20 Act%201967,only%20to%20England%20and%20Wales and https://en. wikipedia.org/wiki/LGBT_history_in_the_United_States.

28 E.g. to me, in Schwartz, p. 71.

29 RWS's Chronology (*SM*, p. 622) and US (*Ein*, p. 21) both give this date.

30 WGS always identified the film he saw in 1962 as one about Bergen-Belsen. But it was almost certainly Billy Wilder's *Death Mills*, which was shown around Germany regularly after the war. In fact *Death Mills* is about all the death camps, rather than just about Belsen. It was a short version of a British documentary film, *German Concentration Camps Factual Survey*, which was shelved in 1945 and not shown until 2014. Belsen, however, was the camp the producer of the original documentary saw, and the one with which it began; so WGS's memory that the film he saw was about Belsen had a coincidental truth, in the Sebaldian way. (See https://en.wikipedia.org/wiki/Death_Mills and https://en.wikipedia.org/ wiki/German_Concentration_Camps_Factual_Survey.) The summary that follows comes from: my interview with WGS in Schwartz, p. 64 and Cuomo's in Schwartz, p. 105; Maya Jaggi's two *Guardian* interviews, 22 September and 21 December 2001; and Löffler, Hage, Stoisser and Pralle in Hoffmann, pp. 82, 178, 226–7 and 252–3 respectively.

31 To Doris Stoisser, in April 2001 (Hoffmann, p. 227).

32 See US, *Ein*, p. 20 and Philippa Comber, *Ariadne's Thread*, Propolis, 2014, p. 178. Both say at seventeen, and both probably got this from WGS himself. US's comment in the next paragraph is in *Ein*, p. 20.

33 The account of WGS and BFS's church (or not-church) pact from BFS; of WGS's Sunday-morning conversations with Frau Küsters from UL, and also from her brother Nauke (Hans Alfred) Küsters, our interview of 7 August 2015.

34 In an interview with the journalist Marco Poltronieri: '*Wie kriegen die Deutschen das auf die Reihe?*' ('How do the Germans do it?'), *Wochenpost*, 17 June 1993, pp. 28–9, in Hoffmann, pp. 87–95. When I consulted http://www.wgsebald.de around 2014, it listed this breakdown, but the reference has since been removed. US includes it in the Life section of *Ein*, on p. 20.

35 Information in this paragraph from BFS and GAS.

36 See *Zerstreute Reminiszenzen: Gedanken zur Eröffnung eines Stuttgarter Hauses*, ed. Florian Höllerer, 2008, p. 31. This is the booklet version of the talk WGS gave on the opening of the Literaturhaus Stuttgart on 17 June 2001, reprinted as 'An Attempt at Restitution' in *CS*, pp. 206–15. See also *SM*, p. 622. Here RWS suggests that the prize was for the newspaper as a whole, but the note on p. 31 of *Zerstreute Reminiszenzen* makes it clear it was for that particular issue. (Unfortunately they call it Issue 4, rather than 3, but this is a confusion. The content described is from the third issue.)

37 I said this to GAS – 'This is about him as much as you, isn't it?' – with some hesitation, thinking it might upset her. But she'd understood it from the start, and felt as much as I did that this other, hidden layer gave the apparently simple poem an extra richness.

38 In the letters to GAS, which give the exam information that follows. For this, see also RWS in *SM*, pp. 42 and 95. GAS remembers that his essay for the German *Abitur* was on Rilke's marvellous poem '*Herbsttag*' ('Autumn Day'). WGS may have chosen it himself. For the poem, see the companion page.

39 Ilse's original was: '*Der Sebe, unser Worteklauber,/ist so als Mannsbild so ganz sauber./Das Kriteln ist ihm angeboren,/an ihm ging ein Charmeur verloren.*'

40 Information from HB.

41 Letter around 31 July 1963, GAS's twenty-second birthday.

42 GAS in conversation with the author.

43 See https://en.wikipedia.org/wiki/Conscription_in_Germany.

44 Information from GAS and BFS. WGS told M the holding-his-breath part, so I've added that for good measure. I'd hoped to see the record of his exemption, but though Fritz Ketterle, the ex-chief archivist of Sonthofen, put in the request himself, it was refused.

45 I owe this rather marvellous information to Fritz Ketterle.

46 Information from my conversations with GAS and BFS, and from Suzanne Siegler, in her emails of 10 and 14 July 2016.

47 Information from UL, JK and Werner Braunmüller.

48 All his school friends said this spontaneously, before I asked. WGS said he didn't know yet what he wanted to study in a letter to GAS in the autumn of 1962, at the beginning of his last year of school. That he wanted to get as far away from home as his parents would accept comes from GAS.

49 See 'Frühere Prosa', Version 1, p. 93.

50 This information from GAS, BFS, UL, André. Franz Meier also told Thomas Honickel that WGS was 'admired and adored by the girls'.

51 A memory of André's, who was still very innocent. That public pairings were still uncommon comes from Friedemann Reich, in a letter to ROP, 24 February 2005, a copy of which Friedemann Reich kindly gave me. He left school after Year 6 (to work in his father's construction company and train as an architect), but kept up with his friends at the ORO. The memory of WGS's first girlfriend comes from him. I thank him sincerely for his help.

52 WGS's letter to GAS, c. Christmas, 1961. He recounts the end of this affair in an undated letter of 1962.

53 Information about Sabine Ritter from JK's conversations with me and his interview with Thomas Honickel.

54 The information that follows comes from GAS, BFS and UL, and from JK, both to me and to Thomas Honickel. It was BFS who remembered how WGS first saw his girlfriend through the window of her salon and gazed a long time before he dared to go in.

55 One of his essays at Freiburg would be about the play *Leonce and Lena* (see *SM*, p 96, Note 14), and at Manchester he would direct a production of it (see Chapter 13, pp. 250–1).

9 PAUL BEREYTER

1 E.g. publicly to Eleanor Wachtel, in Schwartz, p. 38, and privately to his first French translator, Michèle Baudry, in a letter of 25 June 1995 (in DLA).

2 Though for some reason (perhaps just by mistake) *E* says it was 'a week after his seventy-fourth birthday' (p. 27) instead of his seventy-third. In *PB* WGS cites only Armin Müller's obituary, '*Trauer um einen beliebten Mitbürger*' ('Grief at the Loss of a Beloved Fellow-Citizen'), changed by WGS to 'Grief at the Loss of a Beloved Teacher'. In his archive there is also a tribute on Müller's seventieth birthday, 'Ein Ideenreicher Pädagoge' ('An Inventive Teacher'), *Allgäuer Anzeigeblatt*, 22 December 1980, which makes his age clear. (WGS took 'his astonishing inventiveness' from here.) That all the stages of Armin Müller's life match Paul's was confirmed to me by his niece Ursula Rapp and his colleague Adolf Lipp, in our interviews of 29 February 2016 and 15 October 2015 respectively, and subsequent emails (4

April 2016 and 4 June 2015). Herr Lipp added that all teachers in Bavaria in Müller's time were trained at Lauingen. I thank both of them sincerely. Armin Müller's documents also confirm the key events. E.g. the certificate of his first marriage shows that he was in Besançon in 1935. It also shows that he was in Paris in 1934, which WGS leaves out, and that he was in Berlin by October 1937, not in 1939, as WGS says (in *E*, p. 55). This certificate was located for me by Fritz Ketterle, whom I sincerely thank. WGS leaves both these out for literary economy. Finally he leaves out this marriage itself – and Müller's second, as we'll see – for more substantial reasons.

3 See *Wandernde Schatten, W. G. Sebalds Unterwelt*, ed. Ulrich von Bülow, Heike Gfrereis & Ellen Strittmatter, 2008, the catalogue of the 2008 Museum der Moderne exhibition of WGS's archive (*Marbacher Kataloge* 62, 2008).

4 This information from Adolf Lipp. For Müller's interest in cheese, see Chapter 6, p. 101. He wrote a history of Johann Althaus, the bringer of Emmental cheese to the Allgau, and his descendants. This is still in the possession of Peter Schaich, one of those descendants.

5 *E*, p. 57.

6 *E*, pp. 50–1.

7 Table of the Nürnberg Racial Laws from https://de.wikipedia.org/wiki/N%C3%BCrnberger_Gesetze.

8 *E*, p. 48. For the widening net of anti-Jewish laws from 1933 see e.g. https://en.wikipedia.org/wiki/Aryan_certificate and https://en.wikipedia.org/wiki/Ahnenpass, plus a myriad of other sites.

   Müller was still a student-teacher, not yet embarked on his career, because he had taken only the first qualifying exam, and was expelled before he could take the second and final one. (This information from Adolf Lipp, and also from the seventieth-birthday article, which notes that Müller had passed only the first exam before he was expelled, taking the second finally in 1947.) The seventieth-birthday article in the *Allgäuer Anzeigeblatt* of 22 December 1980 says that after Müller's expulsion from teaching, he first worked in his father's cheese shop. The *Anzeigeblatt* reporter probably got this history from Müller himself. The registrations in Paris in 1934 and Besançon in 1935 are shown on Müller's first marriage certificate, as already noted.

9 The information that follows about the Müller family in the war, and the later lives and deaths of Magnus and Babette Müller, comes from Ursula Rapp. Armin also noted the withdrawal of the licence to sell Emmental in his '*Zeittafel für meinen Vater Magnus Müller (1881–1978)*' ('*Curriculum vitae* of my father Magnus Müller (1881–1978)'), kindly given me by Ursula Rapp.

10 See https://de.wikipedia.org/wiki/Blutpalmsonntag. The names of the two victims given now differ very slightly from WGS's versions. In all, thirty-five Jews were attacked and beaten, and around a fifth of the German population was involved. See also Thomas Medicus, *Heimat: Eine Suche* (2014), a book by a contemporary of WGS's from Gunzenhausen, who learned of the role of his home town in the Third Reich only when he read 'Paul Beryeter' in *E*.

11 *E*, p. 53.

12 There's a clue that Sebald invented Thekla: the fact that she'd 'been on the stage for some time'. That would also be the story of Austerlitz's mother Agàta, as though this actress-mother was a figure in Max's mind from the 1980s on.

13 *E*, p. 50. This and the next quotation come from the same page.

14 As KW points out in his '(Un)heimliches Allgäu' in *ÜS*, pp. 171–2. The following points come from JK, Peter Schaich, GAS, Ursula Rapp and KW.

15 *E*, p. 36. Re Meier-with-an-i and Meyer-with-a-y: according to KW (in our conversation of 6 June 2016) there were in reality two religion teachers, but the names that make them absurd are WGS's invention. KW is also the source of the point about the hotel ('(Un)heimliches Allgäu' in *ÜS*, p. 172). About Paul's watering-can trick: Peter Schaich thought he remembered Müller doing this, but no one else I spoke to did, and nor did any of Müller's ex-pupils interviewed by KW. I thank KW sincerely for passing on this information, and for all our most helpful conversations.

16 As proved by his death certificate, No. 3 in the Sonthofen death records for 1984, dated 2 January 1984.

17 These quotations come from *E*, pp. 42 and 44.

18 My interview, Schwartz, p. 70.

19 See my interview, pp. 72–3, and Wood in *Brick* 59, 1998, p. 29. See Ray Monk, *Ludwig Wittgenstein*, Chapter 9, 'An Entirely Rural Affair' for an account of this period. WGS took the details of Wittgenstein's life as a rural schoolteacher not from this definitive biography (which was published in 1990, so probably too late anyway) but from a German book dedicated to Wittgenstein's years as a teacher, published in 1985: *Der Volksschullehrer Ludwig Wittgenstein*, by Konrad Wünsche. This is in WGS's library in the DLA, and shows his markings of all the things he borrowed for Paul Bereyter.

20 To these we can add e.g. Hebel on p. 81, the strange voice 'as though from deep inside' on p. 116, the boy and the cap story on p. 190 and the boy whose playing makes him cry on p. 114. WGS was fascinated by

Wittgenstein's personality, as he told Wood (*Brick* 59, p. 29), a fascination that reappears in *MF* (see *E*, p. 166) and in the opening pages of *A* (the bottom pair of eyes on p. 3 is Wittgenstein's). In around 1986 (see *SM*, p. 332 and Note 74 to Chapter 17 below) he wrote a script for a biographical film about him, conceived entirely in pictures: *Leben Ws, Skizze einer möglichen Szenenreihe für einen nichtrealisierten Film* (*The Life of W: Sketch for a Possible Scenario for an Unmade Film*), published in the *Frankfurter Rundschau*, 22 April 1989, Feuilleton, p. ZB 3, and reprinted in *SM*, pp. 324–33. In WGS's archive in the DLA the original typescript is accompanied by twelve photographs of Wittgenstein photocopied from *Ludwig Wittgenstein: Sein Leben in Bildern und Texten*, edited by Michael Nedo and Michele Ranchetti, published in 1983. When we add the fact that Konrad Wünsche's *Der Volksschullehrer Ludwig Wittgenstein* came out in 1985, we can see a constellation of interest in Wittgenstein in the mid-1980s – just when WGS heard of the death of Armin Müller, and began to think about his old teacher. Clearly he saw parallels between them – 'My schoolteacher did remind me of Wittgenstein,' he said in our interview, 'he had the same moral radicalism' (Schwartz, p. 73) – and on the basis of this resemblance he added Wittgenstein's more dramatic and extreme traits to his memories of Müller, to produce Paul Bereyter. Wittgenstein is thus much more important to the composition of Paul than Jean Améry, who contributed only his suicide. Wittgenstein thought often of suicide, but died of cancer at sixty-two.

21 *E*, pp. 43–4. Re this coming directly from Wittgenstein: both Wünsche and Monk describe Wittgenstein's outbreaks of violence with his children *passim*. Wittgenstein got into trouble with several of the parents over this, particularly in one notorious case of a boy called Haidbauer, whom he hit so hard that the child collapsed (see Monk, *Ludwig Wittgenstein*, pp. 232–3). Re Wittgenstein's playing the clarinet and whistling, see Wünsche, 'Die Klarinette, das Pfeifen und Singen', ('The Clarinet, Whistling and Singing') in *Volksschullehrer Ludwig Wittgenstein*, pp. 111–4, and Monk, *Ludwig Wittgenstein*, p. 213 (the clarinet). *E*, p. 40.

22 *E*, p. 40. Re no one remembering Müller playing the clarinet: two people – GAS and Fritz Ketterle – said the clarinet 'rang a bell', but accepted that they could have been remembering the story. The evidence of Müller's family – Ursula Rapp and her brother Walter Müller – seems to me decisive. WGS told me that he took Paul's whistling from Wittgenstein in our 1996 interview (see Schwartz, p. 73).

23 *E*, p. 49.

24 *E*, p. 54.

25 See KW, '(Un)heimliches Allgäu' in US ed., *ÜS*, p. 171.

26 Müller entered both his marriages with their dates on his family tree. That he was a womaniser and had an affair (or affairs) between his marriages also comes from Ursula Rapp. She would have liked me to change his name, or otherwise disguise this information, and I apologise to her for not doing so. But it's not possible in a work of non-fiction, and I'm sure no one will think less of Armin Müller for having had an affair when he was not married. GAS, who had French lessons from Müller, also remembers him as a charming person as well as a good teacher. When he left at the end of each lesson they would shake hands, and she never felt such warm hands again, she says, until she met Jean-Paul.

27 *E*, p. 42. The descriptions of Müller that follow come from his niece Ursula Rapp, his fellow teachers Lipp and Wagner (Wagner's given to Thomas Honickel), Fritz Ketterle, and KW, as the result of his researches ('(Un)heimliches Allgäu' in US ed., *ÜS*, p. 174). That he never spoke of his time in France in 1935 comes from Lipp, and from Peter Schaich; it is also left out of the *Anzeigeblatt* birthday article (22 December 1980), which was clearly based on information provided by Müller himself.

28 Information in this paragraph from my interview with Müller's colleague Adolf Lipp, 15 October 2015.

29 *E*, p. 44. Information in this paragraph and the next two from Ursula Rapp (for the family) and Adolf Lipp. KW reports Müller's first suicide attempt as well ('(Un)heimliches Allgäu' in US ed., *ÜS*, p. 170), from his own interviews with Adolf Lipp.

30 This information from Peter Schaich, whose father was a friend of Müller's. Even the *Allgaüer Anzeigeblatt* article on Müller's seventieth birthday puts a dark view of things among its first observations about him, and mentions both his expulsion from teaching before the war and the 'difficulties' of his de-Nazification job after it.

31 Ursula Rapp was careful to say that she does not know why her uncle killed himself, but it was clear from our conversation that the family believed it was due to his fear of blindness. His wife Elfriede Müller gives this as the reason, and adds the points about books and the *föhn*, in a letter to Edith Hasenclever (widow of the writer Walter Hasenclever) of 22 February 1984 (in the DLA).

32 *E*, p. 61.

33 The information that follows comes from File 5 of the *E* material in the DLA, which includes Müller's two notebooks; and from Müller's letter of 10 February 1979 to Edith Hasenclever, which gives the date of his DLA research (also in the DLA). On E, p. 58, WGS adds several more writers' names to Müller's list, such as Walter Benjamin, who took his own life as well, and Wittgenstein, who didn't.

34 This information also from Peter Schaich. The information about Müller's not wanting children at any cost from Ursula Rapp.

35 *E*, p. 45. The moments in *Dr HS* and *MF* mentioned in the next paragraph are on pp. 23 and 173–4.

36 To Eleanor Wachtel, in Schwartz, p. 46.

37 Schwartz, p. 74.

38 The information about Lu Moser and the photograph of her both come from Peter Schaich, whom I sincerely thank for this and all his help.

39 *E*, p. 63.

40 *E*, p. 61. The English removes 'always' from Paul's feeling that the railways were headed for death, and substitutes 'perhaps' for 'probably', but both are in the original German: '*Wahrscheinlich schien es ihm immer, als führe sie in den Tod*' ('Probably it always seemed to him that it [the railway] was headed for death'), p. 90.

41 From his interview with Eleanor Wachtel, Schwartz, p. 53–4.

42 *PB*, p. 61. 'Railways had a deeper meaning for Paul' is what Lucy Landau says in the German original. It is more allusive in the English: 'Railways had always meant a great deal to him.' All these changes make the relation of Paul's railway obsession to the Holocaust less clear at the end of the English version than the German. Perhaps eight years or so after he'd first written the story WGS wanted to make his meaning more subtle still.

43 *E*, pp. 49–50.

IO FREIBURG, 1963–5

1 See Marcel Atze, *Sebald in Freiburg*, published as No. 102 in the *Spuren* series by the Deutsche Schillergesellschaft in Marbach, 2014, p. 3; and RWS, 'The Sternheim Years', Chapter 2 of *SM*, p. 45. RWS mentions only the two majors, but WGS's fellow students Berndt Ostendorf and Gudrun Drück told me that a third minor subject was also required then in the universities of Baden-Württemburg. It is clear from WGS's letters to GAS that his third subject was philosophy.

2 In WGS to GAS, 28 October 1963, he says that the room isn't as bad as he remembered, so he'd evidently found it earlier. The Konradstrasse address comes from an undated letter, but early January 1964.

The information about housing in Freiburg at the time comes from the *FSZ*, May 1963, p. 21, December 1964, p. 4 and January 1965, p. 3. The students' joke is in the February 1965 issue, p. 18. Also from my interview with Thomas Bütow, 29 April 2016. The *FSZ* from its post-war re-founding in 1951 to 1972 can be read on a CD produced by the Archiv

Soziale Bewegungen (Archive of Social Movements) together with the Albert-Ludwigs University in 2012.

3 Letters 28 October 1963 and 23 June 1963. The first play was *In the Zone*, discussed below; the second was a reading of Miller's *Death of a Salesman*, which he did together with an American student in the *Amerikahaus* (letter 23 June 1963).

4 Letters 23 June and 3 December 1963.

5 Letter 23 June 1963. A load of 'phoneys' also comes from this letter.

6 That 'Introduction to Middle-High German' was required: see *SM*, p. 51.

7 Information from Michael Sukale (*FSZ* editor before Thomas Bütow), email 30 March 2018; Hans Martin Schmid, '*Meine Freiburger Jahre*' ('My Freiburg Years'), on the *FSZ* CD (Schmid was at Freiburg from 1958 to 1961); Hans Peter Hermann in *Innovation und Modernisierung: Germanistik von 1965 bis 1980*, ed. Bogdal and Müller, 2005, p. 71, quoted in *SM*, p. 55.

8 For Schwanitz's becoming WGS's tutor, see *SM*, pp. 45 and 51. Information on Dietrich Schwanitz in this chapter from my conversations with Etta Schwanitz (5 August, 31 October and 2 December 2015) and with two theatre friends of the time, Pit Wichmann and Rolf Cyriax (7 March 2016).

9 RWS records WGS's appearance in *In the Zone* in *SM*, p. 51, photograph on p. 53. My account (see p. 182) comes from Schwanitz's report on it in the *FSZ*, February 1964, p. 2, and from my conversations with Pit Wichmann and Rolf Cyriax, and another theatre friend, Berndt Ostendorf. Everyone remembered that 'Paolo' came from Goldoni, but thought it was from his most famous play, *The Servant of Two Masters*. As there's no Paolo in that one, however, it's clearly from the less well-known *Summer Follies*. See https://teatrouv2014.wordpress.com/le-smanie-per-la-villeggiatura/.

10 See *SM, p.* 46. All the Maximilianheim friends remember that it was Paolo who got Cocky his room. (Etta says its name was never shortened to the 'Max-heim', as mentioned in *SM*, but at most to the 'Maximilianheim'.)

11 Marcel Atze also suggests this, in his *Sebald in Freiburg*, p. 7, as does RWS in *SM*, Note 29, p. 98.

12 See Schmid, on the *FSZ* CD. The account of the genesis of the Maximilianstrasse Studentenheim that follows comes from Berndt Ostendorf, that of the running of the Heim from Thomas Bütow. See also Bütow's article on its closing in *FSZ* May 1966, p. 7, '*Das Studentenheim Maximilianstrasse ist aufgelöst*' ('The Maximilianstrasse Student Hostel is closed down'), written under the memorable pseudonym of Leander Vierheilig. Re girls at the Heim: for instance, the girlfriend of a Lebanese resident, just before Cocky's time, as recorded by Schmid; and in Cocky's

time, Paolo's fiancée Etta, who lived with him in the garden house, as we'll see. Re the kitchen sink: information from Thomas Bütow. Schmid recounts that it was the same in his time, a few years before.

13 See Leander Vierheilig's article, as noted above. The Heim was closed, at least officially, because of funding cuts by the Ministry of Culture. It was turned into the university's institute for folklore (Atze, *Sebald in Freiburg*, p. 1).

14 This and the following information from Thomas Bütow. Looking for future leaders was part of the Studentenheim's constitution; both Christian and Hans Magnus Enzensberger had been earlier residents, for instance. For the date of WGS's move to the Maximilianheim see Atze, *Sebald in Freiburg*, p. 3. The Freiburg year, then as now, was divided into two terms: the winter semester, running from October to February, and the summer semester, running from April to July.

15 Information from here to the end of the section from my conversations with ex-residents Bütow, Ostendorf, Wichmann and Cyriax; also with Etta Schwanitz and Sigrid Becker-Neumeier, WGS's school friend, who visited the Heim several times in 1965 (our interview of 8 August 2017). Also from Leander Vierheilig's '*Das Studentenheim Maximilianstrasse ist aufgelöst*' and from Schmid, on the *FSZ* CD. RWS quotes from '*Das Studentenheim Maximilianstrasse ist aufgelöst*' in *SM*, pp. 47–8 (but guesses wrongly that 'Leander Vierheilig' was Schwanitz).

16 They were Rolf Cyriax and Albrecht Rasche. (Information from Rolf Cyriax.)

17 Sukale's email to me of 30 March 2018. Berndt Ostendorf's remark from our interview, 4 March 2016.

18 *In the Zone* programme, a copy kindly given me by Rolf Cyriax. All the friends agreed about Paolo and accents. WGS told GAS about the rehearsals in his letters of 23 June 1963, 11 January 1964 and 20 January 1964. The performance dates are given in *SM*, p. 51.

19 In his report in the *FSZ*, February 1964, p. 2. Rolf Cyriax doesn't agree it was a total failure, but thinks the crudeness of the language was the problem. (His letter to me of 3 June 2018.)

20 Information from the programme of *Midsummer Night's Dream*, copies of which were kindly given me by Rolf Cyriax and Pit Wichmann. The following information on the success of *A Midsummer Night's Dream* and Paolo's later successes from Berndt Ostendorf, on his talents from Ostendorf and Etta, and on his later life from his obituaries.

21 This point is made by RWS in *SM*, p. 51. The account of his work here and throughout this section from the *FSZ* CD.

22 In the *FSZ* of November 1964, p. 21.

23 Ruth Franklin, 'The Limits of Feeling', review of *ALW* in *New Republic*, 12 July 2012, https://newrepublic.com/article/104208/wg-sebald-iaian-galbraith-poetry. The following references are to this review.

24 On p. 26, together with his first five poems and Albert's '*Mehl*', 'Flour'.

25 E.g. Martine in his youth and Philippa Comber and Tess Jaray in his later years. For the latter two, see Chapters 22 and 24.

26 *FSZ* June 1965, p. 16. '*Teegeschichte*' is on p. 24 of the same issue. '*Erinnern*' is on p. 24 of the December 1965 issue.

27 RWS in *SM*, p. 56.

28 From my conversations with M.

29 Information from Thomas Bütow, email to me of 6 March 2018.

30 Etta remembers that he did this. His signed material in the December 1965 issue proves it.

31 See Sven Boedeker in Hoffmann, pp. 117–8.

32 Reiner Geulen, who was deputy editor at the time, remembers that it was.

33 Information from Etta Schwanitz, Pit Wichmann and Rolf Cyriax.

34 *FSZ*, December 1964, p. 25..

35 The name was a swipe at the famous Gruppe 47, or Group 47, to which Günter Grass, Heinrich Böll, Alfred Andersch and other early post-war writers belonged. In order to rescue their language from Nazi corruption, they advocated an austere realism and a focus on the present rather than a flight into the past. Sebald's later solution to the same problem involved returning to the nineteenth-century past in both subject and style, and the lingering influence of Gruppe 47 is one of the reasons why his work still meets resistance in Germany. For Gruppe 47, see e.g. https://www.britannica.com/topic/Gruppe-47 and https://de.wikipedia.org/wiki/Gruppe_47.

36 Information about Group 64 (Gruppe 64) from Pit Wichmann and Rolf Cyriax, Berndt Ostendorf, Etta Schwanitz and Sigrid Becker-Neumeier. See also *SM*, p. 48.

37 In his interview with me, 4 August 2015.

38 Information about Paolo's lectures and singing from Etta, about his drawing from Thomas Bütow. In the next paragraph: everyone agrees that he was the wittiest of all of them. Etta told me about the detective novel, and that they did the *Pedagogikum* or teaching qualification together in 1962.

39 That he was famous for his leg-pulls comes from Wichmann and Cyriax. For his friends at fifty see Susanne Mayer, '*Dietrich Schwanitz – ein Professor schreibt eine Hochschulsatire*' ('A Professor writes a University Satire'), *Die Zeit*, January 1998, http://www.zeit.de/1998/06/campus.txt.19980129.xml/komplettansicht. Also Daniel Haas, '*Zum Tod von Dietrich Schwanitz*' ('About the death of Dietrich

Schwanitz'), *Der Spiegel* online, 22 December 2004, http://www.spiegel.de/kultur/literatur/zum-tod-von-dietrich-schwanitz-der-professionelle-besserwisser-a-334073.html. For his most famous story see the obituary above, plus e.g. the *Süddeutsche* Zeitung, http://www.sueddeutsche.de/panorama/dietrich-schwanitz-bestsellerautor-tot-aufgefunden-1.659906, the Hamburger *Abendblatt*, http://www.abendblatt.de/kultur-live/article106941892/Professor-Autor-Uni-Kritiker.html, the Frankfurter Allgemeine, http://www.faz.net/aktuell/feuilleton/literatur-bestsellerautor-dietrich-schwanitz-ist-tot-1195636.html, and *The Scotsman*, http://www.scotsman.com/news/obituaries/dietrich-schwanitzauthor-1-572406. Also his Wikipedia entry, https://de.wikipedia.org/wiki/Dietrich_Schwanitz.

40 Etta says this was in order to escape the starvation in the cities. The information that follows about his background comes from her, and from 'The Next is the Best', about Paolo's theatre-home, the old Zum Salmen (The Salmon) inn in Hartheim, in *Literaturland Baden Württemberg*, http://www.literaturland-bw.de/museum/info/122/.

41 From my conversations with Thomas Bütow.

42 Information about Etta Schwanitz in this section comes from herself (apart from the judgements of her character, which are my own).

43 Information from Berndt Ostendorf.

44 Information about Albert from Berndt Ostendorf, Thomas Bütow, Pit Wichmann, Rolf Cyriax, Gudrun Drück. The points about his work on a national newspaper and in the Psychological Institute come from the letter written in his defence by his fellow residents, 18 February 1965. There is a sample of his letters in WGS's Freiburg novel, and the story of Hugo the hamster comes from Wichmann and Cyriax. WGS told GAS that Hugo also ate his jeans, so he may well have eaten cigarette butts too. On the other hand, he told GAS that Hugo was called Hegel 'because he was so stupid' – a good WGS story, but like so many, not true.

45 WGS wrote to GAS of regaining his confidence in an undated letter around Easter 1964; he said he felt a 'country bumpkin' at Freiburg to Uwe Pralle, in Hoffmann, p. 254. That he was visibly in awe of Paolo and Albert comes from Berndt Ostendorf.

46 On his charisma and apartness, Thomas Bütow. The comparison to the Romantic poet Friedrich Hölderlin comes from Reiner Geulen (his email to me of 16 March 2018). That his depressiveness was not noticed, from Pit Wichmann and Rolf Cyriax; and that he became an equal partner in the Group 64, from my interview with Albert, 4 August 2015. Etta told me that Cocky was closest to Albert; Berndt Ostendorf reported that she had told him the rest in his email to me of 27 March 2016. That Cocky and

Albert went on holiday to Italy together in 1965 is confirmed by RWS, *SM*,
pp. 56 and 623. On their echoing, referencing or teasing each other: e.g.
Albert's piece '*Schnurre purre murre surre*', in the *FSZ* for July 1964, p. 20,
echoes WGS's first piece in the *Wecker;* a poem (probably) by WGS in the
February 1965 issue echoes ones of Albert's in the issue before; and one by
Albert in the February 1966 issue, p. 19, in cod-medieval nonsense mode,
is clearly about WGS. Albert also uses joke names in '*Schnurre purre*' just
like the names WGS would later use in his comic letters.

47 'Background' ('Umstände') was in the *FSZ*, January 1965, p. 24. It is a
fiction, but I'm guessing that it's autobiographical fiction. Albert said to
me that the group didn't talk much about their families to each other,
but learned about them through their writings. He told me himself that
his father had died in the war. As the only son of a fallen soldier, he was
exempt from military service, like UL's brother, Nauke.

48 GAS says that he started keeping notebooks at about twenty. Rasche
remembers this, but JK, for example, doesn't, which again dates the
beginning to Freiburg. Josef, in WGS's novel, says that he started keeping
a notebook at the end of school (Version 1, p. 55).

49 Information from my interview with him, 4 August 2015, and his emails
to me and to Reinbert Tabbert of 29 November 2020.

50 See *SM*, pp. 51–3 and *US, Ein*, p. 20.

51 *PC*, p. 8. See also *SM*, p. 53, and his interview with Toby Green, 'The
Questionable Business of Writing', JES, 44:4, December 2014 (interview of
1999). RWS notes in *SM*, p. 622, that WGS began to buy books by Walter
Benjamin and other members of the Frankfurt School in December 1963,
i.e. in his first term at Freiburg. Berndt Ostendorf remembers that the whole
larger group of Maximilianheim friends were Frankfurt School acolytes. That
the Freiburg syllabus got nowhere near the post-war literature Schmelzer had
taught is pointed out by RWS in *SM*, p. 45 and Note 19, p. 97.

52 *CS*, p. 216.

53 Information about Ronald Peacock from *SM*, p. 55. Etta Schwanitz told
RWS how attracted WGS had been to Peacock's more open and relaxed
teaching style. She told me she found Peacock a wonderful teacher as well.

54 WGS said this himself (Bigsby, p. 149). RWS comes to the same conclusion
in *SM*, p. 55, as does *US* in *Ein*, p. 21 and I, p. 77.

55 To Doris Stoisser, in Hoffmann, p. 224. The rest of this paragraph draws
on his interviews with James Atlas ('WGS: A Profile', *Paris Review* 151,
1999, pp. 278–95, especially pp. 289–90; Bigsby, pp. 146–7; Cuomo in
Schwartz, p. 107; Toby Green, as noted above (Note 51); Robert McCrum,
in the *Observer Review*, 7 June 1998, p. 17; Peter Morgan, 'Living Among
the English', in *Planet 158*, April/May 2003 (interview from 1998),

pp. 13–18, on p. 16; Simon Houpt, *Toronto Globe and Mail*, 17 June 2001; Hans-Peter Kunisch, *Süddeutsche Zeitung*, 5 April 2001. Also: *Geschichte der Stadt Freiburg im Breisgau*, pp. 483–4; '*Student und Politik?*', article by Reiner Geulen in the *FSZ*, November 1965, p. 13; SM, p. 51; and my conversations with Gudrun Drück (12 March 2018) and Thomas Bütow. See also the summary of WGS's reasons for leaving in RWS, *SM*, p. 56, and US, *I*, pp. 68–9. US suggests on p. 69 that WGS's description of the poor conditions in Freiburg was exaggerated. For once, however, he wasn't exaggerating, as the contemporary accounts and that in the official *Geschichte der Stadt Freiburg im Breisgau* make clear.

All this he would recall decades later, when he was being interviewed as W. G. Sebald. At the time he knew that Freiburg was far from the worst case. During the winter term of his second year, for instance, he saw his school-friend Sigrid Becker at an ORO reunion. Sigrid was doing English as part of her degree at Munich, and finding her classes there completely impersonal, her professor impossible to approach. Come to Freiburg, Winfried urged her. We can still get into the seminars, and our professors are quite friendly, they even greet you on the street! Sigrid did, and he was right. (My interview with Sigrid Becker-Neumeier, 8 August 2017.) The fellow student who went to America was Gudrun Drück (our interview of 12 March 2018).

56 Letter of 20 January 1964. RWS notes that he could complete his degree in one year (six semesters) rather than two (eight semesters) in *SM*, p. 56. That GAS sent him parcels comes from my conversations with her.

57 Letter of 3 December 1963. GAS remembers today that WGS's main reason for leaving Freiburg was financial. He said so to Robert McCrum in the *Observer*: 'I came because I had to earn a living… I ran out of money and had to find a job.' And to Bigsby: 'Assistant lecturers [in England] at the time earned the equivalent of one thousand marks per month; as a student I had had one hundred and fifty, so this was nearly six times what I was used to' (p. 150). (This was probably an exaggeration: in his first letter to GAS from Freiburg he said that Georg sent him 220 marks that month. But that may have reduced at some stage.)

58 Letter of 3 December 1963. As noted above, he told Bigsby (p. 150) that he earned more money in England than he had had before.

59 The next paragraph draws on his interviews with Eleanor Wachtel (Schwartz, p. 48), James Wood (*Brick* 59, 1998, pp. 23–9, on p. 29), Atlas, 'W. G. Sebald: A Profile', *Paris Review* 151, 1999, p. 290, Bigsby, p. 147, Green and Houpt. 'Dissembling old fascists' comes from Green, 'ghosts of the Third Reich' from Houpt. That he had 'a sense of discomfort there all the time' comes from Cuomo (Schwartz, p. 106). 'Of course, they had been

reconstructed in the post-war years,' WGS said to Wood (*Brick* 59, p. 29). For some, that was good enough: if people accepted the ways of the new tolerant and open society, they should be accepted by it in turn. But WGS had been uncompromising since the age of sixteen, and he never changed.

60 See his interviews with Walther Krause (Hoffmann, p. 131) and Bigsby, p. 147. The quotation from his interview with Joseph Cuomo comes from Schwartz, pp. 106–7.

61 Bigsby, p. 147.

62 Information about Walter Rehm from *SM*, pp. 45 and 54; Etta Schwanitz and Berndt Ostendorf also vigorously defended him to me. The teacher close to Heidegger was Erich Ruprecht, the professor of German Friedrich Maurer (see *Atze, Sebald in Freiburg*, pp. 9–13). In his interview with me, Berndt Ostendorf said that Ruprecht was the only ex-Nazi in the German department, but Thomas Bütow, who was in the department, said that Maurer had been a Nazi as well, and was said to have come to lectures in his SA uniform. Bütow also said that there were rumours about Jeschek, but they were never proven. Schmid in his 'Meine Freiburger Jahre' says in general that 'We were naturally also cynical and above all rebellious and intolerant towards the old Nazis who filled the public posts, including in the university.' In the next paragraph, the information about resisters comes from Heiko Haumann and Hans Schadek, eds., *Geschichte der Stadt Freiburg im Breisgau*, Vol. 3 (1992), p. 480; for Rehm's assistant, see *SM*, p. 55. That the legal system was notorious is a well-known fact, confirmed to me by Thomas Bütow, Berndt Ostendorf and Gudrun Drück.

63 *Geschichte der Stadt Freiburg im Breisgau*, p. 482.

64 Berndt Ostendorf said in our interview that Freiburg was better than most universities in those days (also in his email of 22 December 2015). Information about the universities of Munich, Würzburg and Göttingen from Hanno Kühnert's article '*Der Führerbefehl und seine Interpreten*' ('Hitler's Order and its Interpreters'), in *FSZ*, July 1964, p. 9; that about Göttingen's policy until the early 1960s from the *AJR* journal (journal of the Association of Jewish Refugees), Vol. 17, No. 1, January 2017, p. 7, letter from Frank Bright, reporting the experience of Professor Paul Glees. The letter adds that in April 2016 Göttingen did not extend the contract of Dr Samuel Salzborn, a prominent expert in German anti-Semitism.

65 Information about Paolo and Berndt Ostendorf from Berndt Ostendorf; about Tübingen and Marburg from '*Universität und Nationalsozialismus*', *FSZ*, November 1964, p. 13; about Heidegger from *Geschichte der Stadt Freiburg im Breisgau*, p. 478. See also Hans Peter Hermann, 'Die Widersprüche waren die Hoffnung' in *Innovation*

und Modernisierung: Germanistik von 1965 bis 1980, ed. Bogdal and Müller, pp. 68 and 71, quoted in US, I, p. 15. US (*I*, p. 92) discusses the cases of Wilhelm Emrich and Hans Schwerte, who had successful academic careers after the war, but had been high-ranking Nazis during it (Schwerte had even changed his name to escape detection). Their cases are good examples to show that WGS's distrust of his professors was well founded. (See also the next chapter, pp. 214–15). US also records that Christian Wirth (who today runs the excellent sebald.de website) was a fellow student of WGS's, and shares his judgement of the tainted Freiburg professors of their time (*I*, p. 15.). For a clear statement of the situation, see Tony Judt, *Postwar*, p. 58: 'Universities and the legal profession were the least affected by denazification, despite their notorious sympathy for Hitler's regime.'

66 Information from GAS.

67 Information from Thomas Bütow, UL and others. See also US, *Ein*, p. 22.

68 See e.g. the obituaries in *Der Spiegel*, 22 December 2004, https://www.focus.de/wissen/mensch/tragisch_aid_89727.html and the *Hamburger Abendblatt*, 23 December 2004, http://www.abendblatt.de/kultur-live/article106941892/Professor-Autor-Uni-Kritiker.html.

69 Albert's idea of literature emerging from trauma was also the theory (without the modern terminology) of Edmund Wilson's classic book *The Wound and the Bow* (1941).

70 *V*, p 131. In a story that Albrecht Rasche wrote in recent years and kindly sent to me, the main character stands for himself and another stands for Max. But the Albert character is Max too.

11 FRIBOURG, 1965–6

1 *SWITZERLAND, together with Chamonix and the Italian Lakes, Handbook for Travellers* by Karl Baedeker, 27th revised edition, 1928, page 278. This guide was lent to me by John Spurling, whom I thank. The rest of the account of Fribourg in the next two paragraphs (including the quotation from Byron) comes from pp. 279–82.

That the route to GAS and Jean-Paul's house on the rue de Lausanne was still the same in 1965 (and is still the same today) can be seen on the city centre map. at http://ontheworldmap.com/switzerland/city/fribourg/. The Grand-Places is called the Square des Places today. That WGS was smoking too much and puffed when he climbed up to their flat from GAS.

2 History of Fribourg from John Spurling's Baedeker, p. 278, and from https://en.wikipedia.org/wiki/Fribourg. Byron's report and the record of a fire (which took place in the nineteenth century) from *Fribourg vu par les écrivains*, ed.

Michel Dousse and Claudio Fedrigo, kindly sent to me by GAS. Today the Place du Tilleul is called the Place Nova-Friburgo, after the town in Brazil founded in the nineteenth century by Fribourgeois. The rue du Tilleul, which flows into the square below the rue de Lausanne, still exists.

That the *tilleul* finally succumbed ten or fifteen years after WGS's stay in Fribourg from GAS. The common lime tree can live for 500 years, and some live far longer than that. A lime tree in Nürnberg was dated back 900 years in 1900, and a Gloucestershire lime tree that grows in Westonbirt Arboretum is thought to be at least 2,000 years old. From: http://www.paviliongardenscafe.co.uk/royal-pavilion-gardens/trees/common-lime_tilia-europaea/.

3 Information in this paragraph from Baedeker and Wikipedia as above, plus 'Layers of History in Fribourg' by Paul Hofmann, *New York Times*, 15 January 1995, https://www.nytimes.com/1995/01/15/travel/layers-of-history-in-fribourg.html and the Fribourg websites, e.g. https://www.myswitzerland.com/en-gb/freiburg.html.

4 Information about Jean-Paul from GAS and himself. Senslerdeutsch is spoken in Fribourg itself and some of the country around it. See https://de.wikipedia.org/wiki/Senslerdeutsch.

5 Information from GAS. The rest of this section is all based on our conversations and emails in 2017 and 2018. Wherever my source is different, I will note it.

Jean-Paul also remembers WGS as happy during his year with them. I have constructed the picture of WGS's listening to Jean-Paul singing from GAS's account of the pleasure he took in his brother-in-law's voice over the years.

6 *Les aventures d'Eustache et du Bourdon Bzz* was a Swiss radio series by William Aguet, broadcast in 1942, when Jean-Paul was six. Aguet died in October 1965; perhaps there were commemorations then that reminded Jean-Paul of the stories. The series was repeated several times in the 70s. See https://www.rts.ch/archives/radio/divers/emission-sans-nom/3584342-aventures-d-eustache.html.

7 *PC*, p. 39. The memory of outings in their Renault comes from Jean-Paul.

8 See https://fr.wikipedia.org/wiki/Cath%C3%A9drale_Saint-Nicolas_de_Fribourg.

9 The list of films comes from the '*Ce soir au cinema*' column in the local paper, *La Liberté*, for 18 January 1966, 10 June 1966, 23 May 1966, 11 December 1965, 15 June 1966, 30 August 1966 and 16 June 1965 respectively. I thank Mme Pauline Voirol of the Bibliothèque cantonale et universitaire of Fribourg for putting me on to the website of Presse Suisse, where

I found this remarkable resource: http://newspaper.archives.rero.ch/Olive/
APA/SNL_FR/default.aspx?action=tab&tab=browse&pub=LLE#panel=b
rowse.

10 Information about the University of Fribourg from RWS, 'The Sternheim
Years', *SM*, pp. 56 and 59, plus the reports on WGS's final exams.

11 Expressionism began in German art and literature in the early twentieth
century and lasted until Hitler's rise in the 1930s. See https://en.wikipedia.
org/wiki/Expressionism.

12 Information from Alker's report of his oral exam in German literature,
dated 29 June 1966.

13 Information about Alker from: the detailed chronology of his life in
Gerd Simon, http://homepages.uni-tuebingen.de/gerd.simon/ChrAlker.pdf;
RWS, pp. 59–60 of *SM*, which he drew from Bruno Stephan Scherer,
'*Selbstgespräch des Leides und der Nacht: Ernst Alker, 1895–1972*' in *Ernst
Alker*, 1974 (he also references *Ernte und Aussat: In Memoriam Ernst
Alker*, ed. Egon H. Rakette, 1973); US, *I*, pp. 69–71 (he also references
Simon, and the entry on Alker in the *Internationales Germanistenlexikon
1800–1950*); https://de.wikipedia.org/wiki/Ernst_Alker; the entry on
Alker by Marianne Rolle in the *Historisches Lexikon der Schweiz*, http://
www.hls-dhs-dss.ch/textes/d/D42795.php; and '*Mort du professeur Alker*',
La Liberté, Fribourg, 8 August 1972, p. 11. (RWS gives 1947 as Alker's
first year in Fribourg, but both the *Historisches Lexikon der Schweiz* and
Wikipedia.de give 1946.)

In *I*, p. 70, drawing on Simon's preface to his chronology, US suggests
some reservations about Alker's anti-Nazi credentials, and therefore about
RWS's laudatory portrait of him in *SM*. US's argument is that Alker's
stance was based on his Catholicism and conservatism, rather than
on a rejection of Nazism as such, and that there is some doubt about
the withdrawal of his German citizenship. The first part seems to me a
pointless cavil: the rejection of Nazism was always based on something,
and what matters is that Alker's religion led him to reject it, which was,
sadly, rare. The second is vague and unsupported (Simon says himself that
he didn't check it); and if indeed Alker chose to become Swedish even
though his German citizenship wasn't withdrawn, that surely shows more
anti-Nazism rather than less. I've gone with Simon's chronology, which
draws on the work of Christof auf der Horst (of Düsseldorf University).
GAS remembers that WGS 'particularly appreciated Alker' (email of 19
May 2018).

14 *SM*, p. 60.

15 Information on Studer from: RWS in *SM*, pages 56 and 59; https://
   de.wikipedia.org/wiki/Eduard_Studer; '*Ein Freund Deutschfreiburgs,
   zum Tode von Prof. Eduard Studer*', *Freiburger Nachrichten* 23 September
   1992, p. 13; the university's condolences, *La Liberté*, 23 September
   1992, p. 27. RWS references Anton Näf, '*Eduard Studer (1919–1992) als
   Wissenschaftshistoriker*' in *Germanistik in Deutschfreiburg oder die Suche
   nach dem Gral: Eduard Studer zum Gedenken*, Deutschfreiburgische
   Arbeitsgemeinschaft, 1994, pp. 23–38.

16 All WGS's final exam reports were made available by the University of
   Fribourg archive. I sincerely thank them, and GAS for obtaining them.
   That WGS ended with a second in philology comes from Studer's report
   on him.

17 I'm guessing he didn't talk about Smith at the time because GAS doesn't
   remember him, though she remembers both Alker and Studer.

18 RWS also suggests that Smith's melancholy may have spoken to WGS
   (*SM*, p. 59).

19 Information about James Smith from: RWS in *SM*, p. 59; the memoir
   of his life by Edward Wilson, in Smith's *Shakespearian and other essays*,
   Cambridge University Press, 1974, pp. 343–51; the summary of his life
   deposited with his papers in the Cambridge University Library, online
   at Archives Hub, https://archiveshub.jisc.ac.uk/search/archives/e17d9faf-
   230b-3c42-b004-a2ed86d5f333; *The Letters of T. S. Eliot: 1923–1925*, ed.
   Valerie Eliot and John Haffenden, Yale University Press, 2011, p. 912; and
   Professor Martin Dodsworth, who spent a year at Fribourg in 1952–3.
   I sincerely thank him for digging out his memories of sixty-five years
   ago in several emails (12, 13 and 14 June 2018), and for toning down my
   romantic portrait of Smith. He also added two further records of him: an
   affectionate mention in D. J. Enright's *Memoirs of a Mendicant Professor*
   and an article on him in a *Contemporary Critics* volume published not
   long after his death.

   WGS had some other teachers at Fribourg as well: GAS remembers one
   called Eisenring, for instance. But the ones with whom he would have
   had the most contact were the three professors.

20 This memoir is in Smith's *Shakespearian and other essays*, pp. 343–51.

21 *Ibid.*, p. 346.

22 From Smith's examination report on WGS, supplied by the university
   archive.

23 See RWS's Chronology in *SM*, p. 623. US, *W & TW*, confirms that the
   mémoire was sixty pages (p. 11). It can be read in *JES 2011*, pp. 209–42.

A copy is kept in the Fribourg University library, the Bibliothèque Cantonale et Universitaire.

24 Information on Sternheim from https://de.wikipedia.org/wiki/Carl_Sternheim and from RWS in *SM*, pp. 61–3.

25 See RWS, *SM*, p. 61. This revival was mildly successful, with several of the plays being performed again in the 1970s. See the Wikipedia entry on Sternheim, as above.

   The summary of Alker's criticisms of Sternheim that follows also comes from RWS, *SM*, p. 61. US points out that WGS's criticisms are close to Alker's, even to the often sarcastic tone (*I*, pp. 71–2 and Note 10, p. 181).

26 See https://de.wikipedia.org/wiki/Carl_Sternheim.

27 From the introduction to WGS's thesis, quoted in US, *SM*, p. 161. (I've adjusted his translation slightly.) This paragraph draws on US, *SM*, pp. 161–4.

28 The Wilhelmine era was the period from 1890 to 1918, the reign of Emperor Wilhelm II, roughly equivalent to the high Victorian and Edwardian eras in Britain. For the summary of WGS's *mémoire* I have drawn on RWS's abstract in *JES* 2011, p. 209, and his account in *SM*, pp. 62–3, and most of all on Alker's report on it, dated 23 April 1966, provided by the University of Fribourg archive.

29 There were real traces of anti-Semitism in Sternheim's work. (See US, *I*, p. 93.) Alker's report also notes that WGS makes this point: e.g. that some of Sternheim's shabbiest characters are given Jewish names.

30 As RWS says, given that 'one is dealing with an ambitious BA dissertation by a 21-year-old-student' (*SM*, p. 63).

31 US also argues this, in *I*, p. 101. He picks out the same characteristics as I do in WGS's academic writing, as first signalled in the Fribourg *mémoire*, apart from the point about literature as inseparable from ethics, which I have added. He rightly notes, however, that WGS's literary criticism was itself an 'ethical attempt to live a right life' (p. 103).

32 Though he guessed it, writing that 'German literary critics are always ready to rehabilitate an author who was discredited by the Hitler regime, probably because they are dogged by a subliminal feeling that their own rehabilitation is not yet complete' (p. 129 of the *mémoire*, quoted by US, *I*, p. 95).

   Information about Emrich and Shwerte/Schneider from US, *I*, pp. 91–2. He makes the point that their attempt to rehabilitate Sternheim was actually an attempt to rehabilitate themselves. (See *I*, e.g. pp. 87 and 97.) He also discusses the case of Emrich in e.g. Academia, p. 3 and in Sebaldiana.

33 RWS, *JES* 2009, p. 86.

34 Quotations from RWS in *JES* 2011, p. 210 and *JES* 2009, p. 86.

35 E.g. in a letter to M, with her *orthographe zéro* (undated, but in February 2000).

36 From Alker's final report, provided by the University of Fribourg archive. Alker's full conclusion is even more clearly balanced: 'From the point of view of quality, the present work approaches a successful dissertation, though very limited in subject. It is without linguistic errors. It merits a Summa cum laude (= 1st Class).'

37 From RWS's Chronology in *SM*, p. 623.

38 The person who thought he looked *sehr Englisch* was a young woman who lived on the rue de Lausanne. (From GAS's email of 31 May 2018.)

39 See RWS's Chronology in *SM*, p. 623. We can't be completely certain when he decided on 'Max'. GAS doesn't remember him talking about it in Fribourg. BFS thinks it happened between Fribourg and Manchester, probably when he came home to Sonthofen before leaving, as she also thinks he did, though she can't be sure of that either. Certainly he was already calling himself Max soon after he arrived in Manchester (he arrived on 15 September and was 'Max' by 6 October; see Chapter 16). US in *W & TW* says that 'It was towards the end of his student years that Sebald began to call himself Max.' (p. 10) As this comes in his account of Freiburg, it implies that it happened then, which isn't right.

40 He claimed 'Maximilian' was his third name to many interviewers, e.g. to Maya Jaggi (September interview), Christopher Bigsby (p. 164), and me again (Schwartz, p. 64) in England, and to several in Germany, e.g. Renate Just (1995, in Loquai, p. 97) and Ralph Schock (Hoffmann, p. 96). He gave his name as 'Winfried Georg Maximilian Sebald' on his 1991 grant application to the DLF, for instance (in the DLA).

41 In a letter of 9 February 2000. WGS's editor Simon Prosser has another explanation for the 'x', writing in his 'A–Z of W. G. Sebald' (https://fivedials.com/fiction/z-w-g-sebald/) that it symbolised for him WGS's central theme of coincidence, 'the point where paths cross'.

42 RWS makes this point as well, in *SM*, p. 78, as does US in *I*, p. 102.

US also quotes WGS comparing 'writing as a means of escaping from social disadvantage' among his post-war Austrian subjects to the Jewish movement towards assimilation in the late nineteenth and early twentieth centuries (in '*Damals vor Graz: Randbemerkungen zum Thema Literatur und Heimat*' in *TRANS-GARDE: Der Literatur der 'Grazer Gruppe'*, ed. Kurt Bartsch and Gerhard Melzer, 1990, p. 149, quoted by US in *SM*,

p. 170). Here WGS argues that both forms of 'self-emancipation' produced works of high quality (thinking of writers like Handke, Herbeck and others). But if it went too far, as (he claimed in his *mémoire*) it did with Sternheim, it could have the opposite effect.

43 I'm guessing that he was thinking about his novel by the time he left Fribourg, or had even started it, since he was already talking about finishing it in October (letter from ROP to his parents, 6 October 1966, in 'Max in Manchester', *Akzente*, February 2003, p. 23). In fact he finished it in March 1967. (From ROP's diary, copy kindly sent me. See Chapter 13.) RWS notes this end date in his chronology in *SM*, p. 624, and adds that the novel was begun in the autumn, referencing the copy in the DLA. If that's right, WGS was talking over-optimistically to ROP in October (and wouldn't be the first writer to do so). The point remains the same: it was surely in his mind by now.

44 From his letter of 1 July 1964.

45 These are not his exact words, as I am not allowed to quote them. But they render his meaning as closely as I can.

12 THE NOVEL

1 See Reinbert Tabbert, '*Erinnerung an W. G. Sebald, einen Ausgewanderten aus dem Allgäu*', in *Literaturblatt für Baden und Württemberg*, 6/2002, p. 11.

2 That he wanted it published comes from my conversations with Etta Schwanitz (5 August, 31 October and 2 December 2015). Re his looking for a publisher: WGS's letter to ROP in October 1967 reports that the novel has been rejected by two publishers and he'll probably have to write something else (Tabbert, *Zur Sebald-Ausstellung*, Reutlingen, 8 June 2004). ROP told Rick Jones that WGS went on trying 'for years' ('Out of the Twilight Zone', *Standpoint*, 24 October 2008).

3 From the interview with Piet de Moor, *SM*, p. 350.

4 That he didn't take this first failure lightly comes from my conversations with ROP (7 June 2015 and 4 June 2016); that he was glad of it later from Etta Schwanitz.

5 That it is almost undiluted autobiography comes from both Etta Schwanitz and Albrecht Rasche (interview of 4 August 2015).

6 Both in the *Frühere Prosa* files in the DLA.

7 ROP points out that these lone references to WGS's two great subjects occur on the same page ('*Zur Sebald-Ausstellung*, Reutlingen, 8 June 2004').

8 About suicide Josef also says that everyone knows someone who chose this exit, and if they don't, they still say they do – perhaps thinking of themselves (Version 1, p. 47).

9   Etta Schwanitz says that Paolo often gave little lectures and disquisitions like the ones he gives in the novel; hence my guess that he may have given this one.

10 Information in this paragraph from Etta Schwanitz, Berndt Ostendorf (our interview of 4 March 2016), Pit Wichmann and Rolf Cyriax (our interview of 7 March 2016).

11 See the list of signatures in Chapter 10, p. 181.

12 Gert Bösselmann (see the list of signatures again).

13 E.g. Etta Schwanitz and Berndt Ostendorf.

14 No one remembers this pair in the real Maximilianheim (e.g. Etta Schwanitz, Pit Wichmann, Rolf Cyriax). They may have come from Pinter (WGS's friend ROP's thesis was on Pinter), or perhaps from Walser's *Jakob von Gunten*, or Robert Musil's *The Confusions of Young Törless*.

    In a prank, Bösselmann (see note 12 above) sells the bully's coat to another student. Coats play a bit of a role in the novel, their long overcoats distinguishing both Holoczek and the old ex-clown Pachl. Perhaps WGS already had Kafka's coat in mind (see Chapter 5). It's possible, as Klaus Wagenbach's *Kafka*, where he almost certainly first saw it, had been published in 1964.

15 This form isn't wholly consistent, but it dominates. Even when the text occasionally switches to the third person, Josef is the centre.

16 As WGS's girlfriend really did. The artist was identified by Marcel Atze (*Sebald in Freiburg*, p. 5) as the Belgian painter and theatre designer Serge Creuz. See https://fr.wikipedia.org/wiki/Serge_Creuz.

13 MANCHESTER, 1966–8

1   See RWS, 'The Sternheim Years', *SM*, p. 64, and his Chronology, p. 623. The appointment was recorded in the Senate minutes for 23 February and 17 March 1966. For the role of *Lektor* as language and conversation teacher, see US, *I*, p. 79.

2   These are the opening lines respectively of *V*, WGS's first published prose work, and *A*, his last. Every section of *V*, every story of *E*, and his remaining prose work, *RS*, all similarly begin with a date. They mark the moorings in fact that he needed (see e.g. Scholz in Hoffmann, p. 181, Rondas in Hoffmann, pp. 212–13).

3   *PC*, p. 154.

4   *PC*, p. 1.

5   *PC*, p. 1. See also *E*, p. 149, and p. 185 in *RS*, where he repeats that he came from Switzerland to England in 1966. As noted in Chapter 11, BFS thinks that her brother came home before leaving for England, but isn't sure.

That he thought he was leaving for a year: see e.g. James Atlas, 'W. G. Sebald: A Profile', *Paris Review* 151, 1999, p. 290. A year was the standard contract for *Lektors* at Manchester (see *SM*, p. 64, from a letter to RWS from Professor Ruedi Keller, 31 March 2005). That WGS's parents therefore believed (or wanted to believe) that it would be only a year is clear from Rosa's letter to Karl-Heinz Schmelzer after WGS's death (15 January 2002): '*Ich hatte so gehofft, dass er nach 3 geplanten Semestern in England zurück kommt*' ('I had so hoped he would come home after the three terms he planned in England').

6 See RWS in *SM*, p. 64, no doubt based on WGS's registration card with the Manchester Police, which is in the DLA. Unfortunately I am not allowed to reproduce that document here. There is a photograph of it in Marcel *Atze, Sebald in Freiburg*, p. 7.

7 *E*, p. 150.

8 From Taine's *Notes sur l'Angleterre*, quoted in 'This New Hades', an edited version of a talk about Manchester given by Catherine Annabel, a graduate student at Sheffield University, at the University of Nottingham on 20 June 2016, https://cathannabel.blog/2016/07/01/this-new-hades/. This is a link from Catherine Annabel's 'Passing Time, an Archive for Michel Butor', posted online on 29 August 2016: https://cathannabel.blog/category/literature/michel-butor/. Together the talk and the Archive are a fascinating source of information on Butor and Manchester in general. I've drawn on both for my account, and sincerely thank Catherine Annabel.

The quote comes from p. 192 of Notes sur l'Angleterre, in the online (1872) edition: 'Dans le ciel cuivré du couchant, un nuage de forme étrange pèse sur la plaine; sous ce couvercle immobile, les cheminées hautes comme les obélisques se hérissent par centaines….' Taine (1828–93) was a literary critic and historian who argued for the determining influence of history and environment on literature: a positivist version of WGS's own view.

9 As RWS also suggests (see *SM* p. 65). It is RWS who established the facts of the real Arosa Hotel, and of WGS's first two rooms in Manchester; I take my account from him. (See *SM*, pp. 65–6.) That WGS found his first room (and his second) through the Accommodation Service is a guess, but an almost certain one, which RWS also makes (*SM*, p. 66). It's the obvious first port of call for any student coming up to university.

10 Student accommodation lists, published in the university's *Staff Comment* magazine, e.g. in the issue of March 1967, six months after WGS's arrival (No. 42, p. 15).

11 This was the practice at the time, as my friends Sue and Fred Steinberg recall, who were at Manchester University between 1963 and 1966.

The friend to whom he said that his father wouldn't send any more money was ROP (my interview with him, 7 June 2015). RWS points out that in those days an 'emergency tax' was levied on new employees and refunded only later, so that even when WGS received his first payment it would have been less than he expected.

12 I've put this description together from pp. 40 and 15 of the English edition of *L'emploi du temps* by Michel Butor, *Passing Time*, translated by Jean Stewart, Pariah Press, 2021. The following quotation comes from p. 15. Butor (or his narrator) feels that the brighter, cleaner room he eventually finds saves his life (p. 116): here he 'could stand up to things' (p. 114). WGS felt the same, I'm sure, about *his* best room, when he finally found it.

13 From my interviews with Rosemary Wallbank Turner, 21 December 2016 and 17 January 2017.

14 See *SM*, p. 66. RWS references 'friends who visited him shortly after his arrival', but doesn't name them.

15 This account from UL. WGS told ROP in early October that he had one of his attacks of *Nierenkolik* when his girlfriend was there. (ROP letter to Brigitte, 6 October 1966.) The description of the room that follows comes from *SM*, p. 66. RWS sources it again to unidentified friends of WGS. The landlady problem, and WGS's unhappiness and embarrassment in this room, from my conversations with ROP. That WGS felt watched, as he had felt with his mother, is my interpretation.

In *AN* he spoke of a Mr Deutsch, who some scholars have assumed was his landlord, perhaps here. But in fact Mr Deutsch was the landlord of WDO and Dietmar Kremser, not WGS. He'd emigrated early from Berlin, having been on the German national table tennis team before 1933. (Information from WDO, emails to me, 6 December 2018 and 3 March 2019. See also RWS, *SM*, Note 67, pp. 100–1.) For WGS reading *L'Emploi du temps*, see *SM*, p. 66. RWS puts this in November, but ROP's letter of 17 October shows that WGS already knew Butor's novel then.

16 See *AN*, pp. 95–6. The next two quotations come from *E*, p. 151.

17 See e.g. Janet Wolff, 'Max Ferber and the persistence of pre-memory in Mancunian exile', in *Memory, Traces and the Holocaust in the Writings of W. G. Sebald*, *Melilah* (Manchester Journal of Jewish Studies), Supplementary Vol. No. 2, 2012, pp. 47–56, on pp. 48–9.

18 Information from https://cathannabel.blog/2016/07/01/this-new-hades/. WGS's later colleague at UEA, Ken Lodge, who was born near Manchester and grew up there in the 1940s and 1950s, confirms that Manchester then was 'a black place with bomb sites'. In an echo of WGS's own childhood experience, he adds, 'I thought that buildings were meant to be black.' He also agrees with the descriptions that follow: that in his student years – which were exactly WGS's – the city was starting to change, but the buildings were still black with soot. He remembers a wag who climbed up the Arts

Building and wiped away a patch, revealing bright clean stone beneath, to everyone's amazement. (Interview with Ken Lodge, 18 January 2019.)

19 Descriptions of Manchester in the mid-1960s from WGS's housemate Peter Jonas, Sue Steinberg, and WGS's medievalist colleague David Blamires. 'Manchester must have been a terrible shock for Max,' he says. 'It was a very industrial city. All the nineteenth-century buildings were soot-covered and black. There were bad fogs. You couldn't hang the washing outside because it would get covered with smuts... You couldn't see the Pennines, ever.' Didsbury and Chorlton were the cleanest areas; but in the south and east 'there was very mean-looking housing'. (Our interview, 6 December 2016.)

20 Information from https://cathannabel.blog/2016/07/01/this-new-hades/. Catherine Annabel says that Butor 'plunged into Mancunian darkness'.

21 As he said e.g. to Bigsby (p. 149), James Wood (*Brick* 59, 1998, p. 29) and James Atlas ('W. G. Sebald: A Profile', *Paris Review* 151, 1999, p. 290). And as the narrator of *MF* also says (see p. 149).

He told many of his anglophone interviewers – e.g. Bigsby, James Wood, James Atlas, Maya Jaggi, myself – that he had hardly any English when he first arrived. RWS is sure that he had a great deal more than he admitted (see *JES* 2009, p. 96); and by his second term, when Peter and Dorothy Jordan met him, his English was certainly good (interview of 4 October 2011). Nonetheless I'm sure that perfectionist WGS would feel he could hardly speak it at all. Later he would say that he never spoke English really well, which was quite false. But that he *felt* he didn't, I also believe. See e.g. his interview with Robert McCrum, 'Characters, plot, dialogue ... that's not really my style,' *Observer*, 7 June 1998: 'You never entirely find your feet in your second language.' Also e.g. Cook, *SM*, p. 361, Wasserman, *SM*, p. 371, and Krause in Hoffman, p. 127 ('I'm not a gifted linguist').

22 As Sigrid Löffler, a literary critic and admirer of WGS, wrote in one of her articles about him ('*Kopfreisen in die Ferne*', *Süddeutsche Zeitung*, 4–5 February 1995, in Loquai 1997). WGS spoke of this crisis to ROP at the time (see pp. 15–16), and to several interviewers later (e.g. Bigsby, p. 149 and James Wood, *Brick* 59, p. 15 and Note 51). His family also knew about it, though only later. He wrote about his sense of alienation in a letter to Albrecht Rasche at the time (information from ROP, from his '*Zur Sebald-Ausstellung*', Reutlingen, 8 June 2004). Löffler speaks in her article of WGS's feelings of hopelessness and panic, as well as aimlessness and futility. She quotes *E* for the last two. The first two aren't mentioned there, but as she clearly visited WGS in Norfolk for the piece, she may have got them straight from him. His bad times later included objectless panics (see Renate Just, '*Im Zeichen des Saturn*', *Die Zeit* Magazin, 13 October 1995, in Loquai 1997, p. 40), so it's likely they also happened now.

23 This and the following quotation from *E*, pp. 154–5. That the Teasmade was probably fictional comes from my interview with Tessa Sinclair (3 February 2015): she told me that there was one in the kitchen of WGS's flat in Abbotsford. He clearly imported it into the Arosa. For the consoling thought of Wittgenstein and Canetti, see his interview with James Wood, *Brick* 59, p. 29. He lends the consolation of Wittgenstein in Palatine Road to Ferber (*E*, p. 166), and mentions it again in *CS* (p. 201).

24 Stevie Davies told me about the following event in an email of 14 December 2016. I thank her sincerely for all her help.

25 This explanation of 'ROP' from my conversations with ROP and his email to me, 23 June 2015.

26 See *SM*, p. 64. The following information from my conversations with WDO and his emails of 6 and 9 December 2018. WDO was an Old and Middle German specialist; Kremser was working on Old English. WDO went on to a career with the Goethe Institute. Kremser became a *Gymnasium* teacher in Bavaria, and died young, a few years after WGS. (Information from WDO and from ROP, email of 10 January 2017). The information about ROP from my conversations with him and his wife Brigitte.

27 From his letter of 6 October 1966, quoted in 'Max in Manchester' by ROP, *Akzente* 50(1), February 2003, p. 23.

28 Letter of 17 October 1966, quoted in 'Max in Manchester' by ROP, *Akzente* 50(1). The following quotations are from a letter of 31 October 1966, also in 'Max in Manchester'.

29 From Brigitte's letter to her parents, Hans and Paula Wittmann, 30 October 1966, kindly given me by the Tabberts; and from my interview with them, 7 June 2015. That WGS was mortified by his passport picture comes from his novel, Version 1, p. 69. 'Without it he'd look about fifteen' comes from ROP's letter to Brigitte's parents, 25 March 1967, kindly given me by the Tabberts.

30 ROP remembers that WGS strongly identified with Hölderlin the homeless wanderer at the time (see 'Max in Manchester', p. 25). For WGS's depression lasting months, see *E* p. 153: 'The day of my arrival at the Arosa, like most of the days, weeks and months that followed, was a time of remarkable silence and emptiness.' The following quotations come from Wood, *Brick* 59, p. 29 and Bigsby, p. 149.

31 Letter of 5 December 1966, quoted by ROP, 'Max in Manchester', p. 25.

32 This account of ROP is put together from his interview with me, 7 June 2015, and the CV he kindly gave me. He remarked in our interview on

his more old-fashioned views both morally and intellectually, and alludes to the 'Prussian' problem in his '*Tanti cordiali saluti, Max*', *Literaturen* 05, 2004: 'Though my Prussian background wasn't much to his taste' (p. 46).

33 See ROP, 'Max in Manchester', p. 22. Also ROP's letter of 27 January 1967, which he kindly gave me, and which clearly demonstrates WGS's influence: 'Literary criticism fails to understand that an author like Sternheim cannot be grasped by literary-critical techniques alone. It needs to add psychological and sociological methods, and that's just what Max is good at, I think. I'm learning a lot in this area from him.'

34 Information in this paragraph from my interviews with the Tabberts, 7 June 2015 and 4 June 2016; from ROP's and Brigitte's letters to her parents, 1966/7; and from ROP's CV.

35 So RWS reports from his interviews with them (*SM*, p. 72). In 2005, when RWS did his research, everyone except Stan Kerry was still alive.

36 See ROP, letter of 31 October 1966, in 'Max in Manchester', p. 23. RWS says in his Chronology that WGS began the novel that autumn (*SM*, p. 624). It's possible, since he was writing fast at this stage (see p. 239 below). But his reference to it in early October, and his already reading from it now, suggest that he may well have started it earlier, perhaps in the summer. (As suggested at the end of Chapter 12.)

37 See ROP, letter to Brigitte's parents, 27 January 1967. The other poems WGS gave him were 'Albumverse', like 'Triptych', written at Freiburg and published in the *FSZ*; '*Kinderlied*', the poem he'd written for Solveig's birth in August 1965 (see his letter of 31 October 1966 in 'Max in Manchester'); and 'Bleston', which he wrote now (letter of 27 January 1967.)

The following information about the composition of 'Bleston' comes from ROP in a letter of 27 January 1967 and WGS in a letter to Albert (see *ALW*, p. 177). He began gathering material for it in November (the same letter by ROP).

38 As even Iain Galbraith, the editor and translator of *ALW*, admits: 'The poem presents a labyrinth of allusions, and the reader who attempts to follow them risks becoming … lost' (p. 177). ROP, who is a passionate admirer of WGS's prose but no longer of his poetry, says, 'He was trying to be modern.' I think that he was suffering from the problem he diagnosed in Sternheim: the outsider's need to impress the world he was trying to enter.

39 These images are in 'Bleston', *ALW*, pp. 18 and 20, in *AN*, p. 98 (the Gospel church) and *E*, p. 157 (the darkness and the starlings).

40 The lines from 'Bleston' that follow are from *ALW*, pp. 18 and 22.

41 ROP, letter of 5 December 1966, in 'Max in Manchester', p. 25.

42 The following account comes from Dorothy Jordan, in both my interviews with the Jordans, 4 October 2011 and 6 October 2014.

43 The description of 26 Kingston Road from Peter Jordan, in our interview of 4 October 2011, and from Brigitte's letter to her parents, 17 January 1967. That ROP was living in a pleasant room in Didsbury from my interview with the Tabberts, 4 June 2016.

That WGS and ROP decided to move together comes from Brigitte's letter to her parents, 30 October 1966. It's not clear if this was a decision in principle, or if WGS had already found Kingston Road, so I leave the timing open. That he was the one who found it comes from my interview with the Tabberts of 4 June 2016. Peter Jonas, WGS's housemate after ROP, confirms their portrait of Kingston Road, saying that it had been renovated 'with great imagination and inventiveness'. (His Introduction to WGS's July 2001 lecture, a copy of which he kindly gave me.)

44 From ROP's letter of 19 December 1966, 'Max in Manchester', p. 25.

45 Information from ROP. RWS gets this slightly wrong in *SM* (pp. 69–70), putting them in a flat on the ground floor, and Didsbury Park at the back. In fact it was across the road, as I note. Today it's built over, but Fletcher Moss Park at the back remains.

46 From Brigitte's letter of 17 January 1967. The rest of the description of their rooms from ROP's letter of 27 January 1967 as well.

47 WGS, interview with Bigsby, p. 161.

48 As documented e.g. in ROP's letter of 27 January 1967 and Brigitte's of 2 February 1967. Information in the rest of this paragraph from the same interview, 4 June 2016. ROP records that the margin notes are by WGS himself in '*Erinnnerung an WGS, einen Ausgewanderten aus dem Allgäu*', *Literaturblatt für Baden und Württemberg* 6, 2002, pp. 10–11, on p. 11. He confirmed this to me in our interview of 4 June 2016, and added that it was after their discussions. The word '*Scheisse!*' is scrawled on p. 92 of Version 1, beside a line about sadness that WGS evidently judged a cliché.

49 ROP, '*Zur Sebald-Ausstellung*, Reutlingen, 8 June 2004', p. 2. At one point, ROP told me, the poet Erich Fried tried to help, also in vain. That ROP was disappointed comes from 'Max in Manchester', p. 21. That he came to think the switch was a mistake comes from our interview of 4 June 2016.

50 Information in this paragraph from ROP's Kempten Kalender; ROP, 'Max in Manchester', p. 25, letter of 19 December 1966, and p. 26; ROP's letter of 27 January 1967; Brigitte letters of 17 January 1967 and 2 February 1967; and my interviews with them.

51 This and 'probably himself' from Brigitte's letter of 17 January 1967.

52 Information in this paragraph from ROP's Kempten Kalender; ROP, '*Zur Sebald-Ausstellung*, Reutlingen, 8 June 2004'; and my conversations with him. Re WGS and dancing, the Jordans, for example, also knew that WGS 'wouldn't go to any of the dances at the university' (interview 6 October 2014).

53 The story of Sigrid Becker's descent on WGS from an oil tanker comes from my interview with her, 8 August 2017.

54 This bizarre story comes from the Tabberts, in our interview of 7 June 2015, and from Richard Cocke, a colleague of WGS's at UEA (our interview of 16 December 2013). Perhaps it was one of WGS's inventions, but I'm inclined to believe it, though not all of it. ROP thinks that this experience may have given WGS the idea of travel writing as early as 1967. I wonder whether it might have been the other way around – that he already had that idea, and applied to several German papers as a writer, one of which came up with this job instead. It seems most improbable that he was 'approached', as he told Richard Cocke, and probably the Tabberts as well.

55 The story in this paragraph and the next from Dorothy Jordan, in our conversations of 4 October 2011 and 6 October 2014.

56 This is clear from ROP's letter of 27 January 1967, in which he says that WGS sent a book to his girlfriend 'in St Gallen'.

57 This and the rest of this paragraph from ROP's letter of 25 March 1967, apart from the clown-under-the-table moment, which he and Brigitte described in our interview of 7 June 2015. The Jordans also remember WGS then as 'slight', 'slender' and 'not robust' – as the photograph on p. 253 confirms (interview 6 October 2011).

58 From my interview with ROP, 7 June 2015.

59 From my conversations with ROP, his email to me of 20 June 2016, 'Max in Manchester', pp. 21 and 27, and '*Tanti cordiali saluti*', p. 46.

60 One of the places where WGS thought of buying a house in his last year was Nice (information from UL).

61 His girlfriend grew up there, as we know, and he no doubt borrowed Vienna from her. Etta confirmed to me that he hadn't directed a Pinter play at Freiburg. Someone else had, however: Walter Asman, who became famous as an interpreter and friend of Beckett, had directed Pinter's *Caretaker* at Freiburg while WGS was there. That surely inspired his story. (Information from Dagmar Neis, a fellow student and friend of the Maximilianstrasse group at the time, from our phone call of 19 August 2017.)

Re working as a photo-reporter: ROP may have believed this tale until he read WGS's novel, in which Josef the hero tells the same story, but lets the reader know it's a fib. Josef tells many fibs, as we know, which probably warned ROP about the author. In fact most of the real whoppers WGS told the Tabberts were in the early weeks of their friendship. All these come from my interview with ROP of 7 June 2015.

62 From Brigitte's letter of 30 October 1966.

63 Our interview of 4 June 2016. That he told it to me, see Schwartz, p. 65.

64 Max Frisch, *I'm Not Stiller*, Penguin Modern Classics, 1983, p. 345.

65 This and all the other information about WGS's favourite books of 1966/7 from my conversations with ROP.

66 Saul Bellow, *Herzog*, Penguin Books, 1965, p. 7. The following quotation from p. 149.

67 He wrote about this in his letter of 27 January 1967.

68 Frisch, *I'm Not Stiller*, pp. 51–2.

69 From my interview with ROP, 7 June 2015.

70 From my interview with ROP, 4 June 2016 and his email to me, 23 June 2015. A *Festschrift* is a collection of writings in honour of a scholar, usually on their retirement, but presented to Parry by WGS and ROP on their own (planned) departure. Iain Galbraith says in *ALW*, p. 180, that WGS's poems for Parry included 'Didsbury', 'Giulietta's Birthday' and 'Time Signal at Twelve' (see *ALW*, pp. 22–5).

71 See RWS's Chronology, p. 624.

72 From ROP's CV. (Also in RWS's Chronology, p. 624.)

73 Information about WGS's decision to marry from UL. The date of the wedding comes from RWS's Chronology, p. 624. That GAS and Jean-Paul couldn't come from GAS.

74 Winfried Georg Sebald married Ute Rosenbauer on 1 September 1967. https://www.deutsche-biographie.de/pnd119310007.html.

75 Information in this paragraph from RWS in *SM*, pp. 72–3 and *JES* 2011, Note 43, and my interviews with Dorothy Jordan and ROP.

76 Information from my interviews with Eda Sagarra and ROP.

77 See *CS*, p. 201.

78 From my interview with Eda Sagarra, 15 December 2016.

79 From Professor Keller's letter of recommendation to UEA, *SM*, p. 87. The following quotation from the same letter. That he was a popular teacher comes from Professor Parry's letter *SM*, p. 87

80 See *SM*, p. 75. That much of the reading was of left-wing theorists, pp. 75–6.

81 *SM*, p. 77.

82 *SM*, pp. 77–8. The 'schizoid' and other symptoms: see the copy of the dissertation in the University of Manchester archive: *Carl Sternheim und Sein Werk in Verhältnis zur Ideologie der Spätbürgerlichen Zeit* (*Carl Sternheim and his Work in Relation to the Ideology of the Late-Bourgeois Era*), p. 226.

Both RWS and US point out that anxiety, insecurity and aggression related to WGS himself. See *SM*, p. 78, and also the last part of Note 94, on p. 103: 'he [WGS], like Sternheim, could be regarded as a case of "failed assimilation" into German – or any other – culture'. US makes the same point most notably in *W & T W*, pp. 14–15. But he adds, quite rightly, that WGS's response to his outsider status was the opposite of Sternheim's – not to adapt in order to be accepted, but to stay outside and attack.

83 On pp. 5–6 of the Foreword and pp. 6, 133 and 219 respectively.

84 See *SM*, Note 94, p. 102. The next quotation is from the same Note.

85 From my interview with John Flower, professor of French and founding editor of the *JES*, 18 January 2017.

86 E.g. to me in our 1996 interview, though I didn't include it in the published version.

87 See *E*, p. 187. 17 May was in fact the birthday of Peter Jordan's mother, the model for Ferber's mother. (From my interviews with Peter Jordan.)

88 Information about Parry from Eda Sagarra, our interview of 15 December 2016, and Stevie Davies, email of 14 June 2016. The line about the rope of snow comes from Eda's obituary of Parry in *German Life and Letters* 61:3, July 2008, p. 295. (She used the Irish Gaelic version, *súgán sneachta*.)

89 This account is in *SM*, Note 105, p. 103. It comes from Stephen Swaby, who played Leonce, and was interviewed by RWS in 2005. Sadly, Swaby has since died.

ROP read this play of WGS's – possibly the first he ever wrote – and helped to correct it, like the novel, but it has since disappeared, perhaps into that Manchester bin. (*SM*, Note 95.) RWS speculates that it might have been a 'Viennese-style comedy' he wrote for Eda Sagarra. This in turn may have been a version of the one-acter that WGS wrote in St Gallen. (See Chapter 14.)

90 The following account of Leonce and the play was put together with the help of *SM*, p. 80; the Wikipedia entry on *Leonce and Lena*, https:// en.wikipedia.org/wiki//Leonce_and_Lena; 'Escaping Fate is Futile: Georg Büchner's Leonce and Lena', posted on 27 March 2013 by skadoosh, https://my.vanderbilt.edu/almosthuman/2013/03/escaping-fate-is-futile-georg-buchners-leonce-and-lena/; and last but far from least, the programme note for WGS's production.

91 From the programme note by 'St S.', i.e. Stephen Swaby. The last five words ('incurable merely because he is') are a quotation from the play. The programme is preserved in the Manchester University archive.

92 Swaby told RWS that WGS asked him to write it (see *SM*, p. 80).

93 This and the following quotation from the review by John Prudhoe of the drama department in *Staff Comment*, No. 46, March 1968, pp. 18–19, on p. 18.

94 This point and the following quotation both come from Stephen Swaby's letter of 28 May 2005 to RWS, quoted in *SM*, p. 80.

95 See *SM*, p. 79. That there was a rumour he might be offered a job in the drama department comes from WGS's letter to ROP of 12 March 1968, in ROP, '*Tanti cordiali saluti*', p. 47, also quoted in *SM*, p. 81. The next quotation comes from the same letter, also quoted in *SM*, p. 81.

96 From his letter to ROP of 8 May 1968, quoted in '*Tanti cordiali saluti*', p. 48.

97 See *SM*, p. 82 and RWS's Chronology, p. 625.

98 Information from my interview with Eda Sagarra.

99 See Note 56 above.

100 See *SM*, p. 81 and *I*, p. 79. WGS said he could look around from there to Walther Krause (Hoffmann, p. 146).

101 In his interview with me, 12 October 2016. See his Chronology, *SM*, p. 625, for the date of WGS's MA.

102 See his letter to ROP, 1 August 1968, quoted in '*Tanti cordiali saluti*', p. 48. The next paragraph draws on the same letter. In it WGS says that the frog imagery came from a fairy tale. (The full letter is in the DLA.)

14 ST GALLEN AND MANCHESTER, 1968–70

1 For the dates of arrival and the start of teaching, see WGS's letter to ROP, 1 August 1968, quoted in '*Tanti cordiali saluti Max*', *Literaturen* 05, 2004, p. 48. Information about the flat and WGS's wife working in a beauty salon from GAS.

2 See www.wgsebald.de, under the heading 'Rosenberg' (retrieved in 2020).

3 Letter of 2 October 1968, quoted in '*Tanti cordiali saluti*', p. 46.

4 So he said to Wachtel, Schwartz, p. 49. The following information comes from his letter to the writer Gershom Sholem of 11 June 1972, in the DLA, also quoted in US, *I*, p. 79; my conversations with Peter and Dorothy Jordan and with M; his interviews with Eleanor Wachtel (Schwartz, pp. 49–50) and Walther Krause (Hoffmann, p. 146). That he had to teach everything comes from *SM*, p. 81, that he didn't like his rich-kid students from GAS.

5 *MF, E,* p. 177.

6 See letters to ROP, 1 August 1968 and 2 October 1968, quoted in '*Tanti cordiali saluti*', pp. 46–8. He sent the play to Helmut Qualtinger, the famous Viennese comedian. Qualtinger never replied (see *SM,* p. 82).

7 See *SM,* p. 82. My account of this version is based on RWS's account in *SM,* pp. 82–5 and US's in *I,* pp. 79–80.

8 The publisher's letter saying they'd received the manuscript is dated 29 October 1968 (DLA). RWS's Chronology in *SM* (p. 624) notes the date. The following information about WGS's letter and the publisher's letter of 6 February 1969 from US, *I,* pp. 67–8 and Note 1. US also notes that the 'I' problem did not exist in the *mémoire* version (US, *I,* p. 73). The point that this part of WGS's rebellion was led by Adorno is one he made himself: see his interview with Uwe Pralle in Hoffmann, p. 255. *SM,* p. 82 and Chronology, pp. 624–5 date the end of the rewriting work to April.

9 *Carl Sternheim: Kritiker und Opfer der Wilhelminischen Ära,* Kohlhammer, 1969, p. 7, quoted in US, Academia, p. 2. See *SM,* p. 84 for the detail of the changes WGS made.

10 Chronology, *SM,* p. 625. US also argues in *I* and elsewhere that WGS's main aim in his polemics was to make an impact on the *Germanistik* establishment, which is always hard to do, but hardest of all for someone outside Germany. (See e.g. *I,* p. 96.)

11 Following information from GAS.

12 See *E,* p. 176.

13 Following information from *SM,* p. 82, also US, *W & TW,* p. 15.

14 The quotations from Professors Keller and Parry come from their letters in support of WGS's application to UEA in 1970, quoted in *SM,* p. 87.

15 The information about WGS's Manchester reappointment and withdrawal of his Goethe application from *SM,* pp. 82 and 625. The current value of £960 in 1969 from https://www.moneysorter.co.uk/calculator_inflation2.html#calculator.

16 From RWS's Chronology in *SM,* p. 625. His title at this stage was *Über zentrale Motive im Werk Döblins* (*Central Themes in the Work of Döblin*). (See RWS, Reception, p. 351. Also US, *I,* Note 136, p. 190.)

17 The account in this paragraph is based on *I,* pp. 96–7. *Carl Sternheim: Kritiker und Opfer der Wilhelminischen Ära* came out on 3 October 1969 with a print run of 2,000 copies (*SM,* p. 83).

18 From the review in *Germanic Review* 47 (1972), pp. 234–6, quoted in US, *I,* p. 96.

19 Poljudow's review appeared in *Die Zeit* for 14 August 1970, in the 'Feuilleton' section, p. 15 and is reproduced in Loquai 2005, pp. 56–8.

WGS's reply appeared in *Die Zeit* for 28 August 1970, in the '*Modernes Leben*' section, p. 46, reproduced in Loquai 2005, pp. 59–60. My account of this exchange is based on RWS's in *SM*, pp. 85–6 and US's in *I*, pp. 97–9.

20 This paragraph is also based on RWS's and US's accounts, in SM, p. 86 and *I*, pp. 99–101. US found one last Sternheim-related appearance of WGS's, in an interview on German television in November 1976 (see *I*, Note 85, p. 186). The academic survey in which WGS's name does not appear came out in 2007.

21 US also makes most of these points about WGS's critical methods (see *I*, p. 84).

22 Information about Manchester's golden years from Eda Sagarra, Rosemary Wallbank Turner, David Blamires, Martin Durrell, Sue Steinberg, and Stephen Swaby in a letter to RWS of 28 May 2005 (*SM*, p. 71 and Note 70). Martin Durrell's obituary of Keller, referenced in the German Wikipedia entry on him, https://de.wikipedia.org/wiki/Rudolf_Ernst_Keller, notes that in the mid-1980s five Manchester colleagues held British chairs in German. In her obituary for Peter Skrine in 2017 (see https://onlinelibrary.wiley.com/doi/full/10.1111/glal.12179), Eda Sagarra adds that eight of Manchester's lecturers of the 1960s went on to hold chairs in British, German and Irish universities (including Skrine at Bristol, Furness at St Andrews and herself at Trinity College Dublin).

23 As WGS told Bigsby: 'At the university there wasn't anything that resembled an authoritarian structure. For someone who had grown up in a system of this sort … this really felt like freedom' (p. 150). The following information from Martin Durrell, David Blamires, Eda Sagarra, Rosemary Wallbank Turner, Peter Skrine's widow Celia (email of 16 October 2018) and Ray Furness's widow Janice (email of 15 February 2016). Peter Skrine, Ray Furness and Rosemary Wallbank Turner all wrote satirical pieces in *Staff Comment*.

24 Following information from Eda Sagarra, Martin Durrell, David Blamires and (about WGS and Ray Furness) *SM*, p. 83.

25 I was unable to speak to Peter Skrine myself, as sadly his health was too poor by the time I began my Manchester research, and he died in May 2017. The information about him here comes from his widow Celia (email of 16 October 2018) and the following obituaries: by Celia Skrine, in the *Guardian*'s 'Other Lives', 2 August 2017, https://www.theguardian.com/world/2017/aug/02/peter-skrine-obituary, by Eda Sagarra in *German Life and Letters*, 71(1):1–3, January 2018, https://onlinelibrary.wiley.com/doi/full/10.1111/glal.12179 and in *Bristol University News*, 12 September 2017, http://www.bristol.ac.uk/news/2017/september/peter-skrine.html. The information

about Eda and Albert Sagarra comes from Eda herself, plus details from Martin Durrell, David Blamires and Rosemary Wallbank Turner.

Eda published a biography of her father in 2013: *Kevin O'Shiel: Northern Nationalist and Irish-State Builder*. See e.g. 'O'Shiel daughter sets the record straight', *The Irish Times*, 20 June 2013, http://www.irishnews.com/lifestyle/2013/06/20/news/o-shiel-s-daughter-sets-record-straight-62818/.

26 From my interview with Eda Sagarra, 15 December 2016.

27 Everyone agreed that these three were the closest to WGS, especially Stan Kerry. (Everyone also insisted that Kerry was never called 'Stanley', as WGS formally calls him in *RS*, but only ever 'Stan'.)

28 Information about Parry from Eda Sagarra, Rosemary Wallbank Turner, David Blamires and Martin Durrell, including Durrell's obituary of Parry in the *Independent*, 26 March 2008. GT also told me that there'd been a rapport between WGS and Idris Parry, which he must have gathered from WGS himself. (Our interview of 22 February 2017.)

My summary of Parry's complex ideas is largely based on Stevie Davies's 'Notes on Idris Parry in the late 1960s and early 70s', kindly sent to me in an email of 29 January 2017. I am most grateful for this and for all her help and advice about Parry. Her 'Notes' are the source of the quotation on p. 14.

29 Information about Ray Furness from Eda Sagarra, Martin Durrell, David Blamires and Rosemary Wallbank Turner, plus:
The account of his novel, *On Heligoland*, in *Fife Today*, 13 June 2008, https://www.fifetoday.co.uk/news/from-facts-to-fiction-for-retired-st-andrews-academic-1-151063; a review of his last book on Wagner in *The Wagnerian*, http://www.the-wagnerian.com/2013/07/mini-review-raymond-furness-richard.html; and Ray Furness's own account of himself to the Wagner Society of Scotland, on the occasion of his giving a talk there in April 2014, https://www.wagnerscotland.net/event/27-april-2014-730pm. RWS confirms that WGS 'greatly appreciated Ray's eccentricity' (email of 8 June 2018). Sadly his situation was the same as Peter Skrine's: by the time I began my research into WGS's Manchester period, his health was poor. We exchanged a few notes, but to my regret I never met him. He died on 30 September 2018.

30 From Ray Furness's letters to RWS of 21 February, 26 February and 11 April 2005, quoted in *SM*, pp. 82–3. In *SM* (Note 118, pp. 104–5) RWS writes that 'Furness particularly remembers a strange nursery rhyme that he would recite to Max, for whom it held a special fascination.' This was 'There Was a Man of Double Deed':

There was a man of double deed,
Who sowed his garden full of seed;
When the seed began to grow,
'Twas like a garden full of snow;
When the snow began to melt,
'Twas like a ship without a belt;
When the ship began to sail,
'Twas like a bird without a tail;
When the bird began to fly,
'Twas like an eagle in the sky;
When the sky began to roar,
'Twas like a lion at my door;
When my door began to crack,
'Twas like a stick across my back;
When my back began to smart,
'Twas like a penknife in my heart;
And when my heart began to bleed,
'Twas death, and death, and death indeed.

There is a great deal about 'There Was a Man of Double Deed' on the internet, including its identification as a children's song in Northern Ireland (see https://www.mamalisa.com/?t=es&p=4254) and a podcast about it by the poet Alice Oswald: https://www.theguardian.com/books/audio/2013/feb/22/alice-oswald-poem-man-double-deed-podcast.

31 From Ray Furness, his note to me, undated but from mid-December 2015. There are five letters from Parry in WGS's archive, dated between 1978 and 1995. Both Martin Durrell and David Blamires remembered that WGS was closest to Stan Kerry.

32 *SM*, p. 75.

33 See *PB*, *E*, p. 28. For Mangold, see p. 40.

34 *RS*, p. 186. The complete description of Stan Kerry, from which I go on to quote, is on pp. 185–7.

35 *Angelus Novus* was a painting by Paul Klee. Benjamin interpreted its subject as an angel who sees history as 'one single catastrophe' – which was exactly WGS's view. (See https://en.wikipedia.org/wiki/Angelus_Novus.)

36 *RS*, p. 187. The next quotation from *RS* is from p. 187.

37 Information about Stan Kerry from my interviews with Rosemary Wallbank Turner, Eda Sagarra, Martin Durrell and David Blamires, and from *SM*, pp. 73–5.

38 Quoted by US in *SM*, p. 171.

39 See *SM*, pp. 74 and 628. That Kerry was a heavy smoker comes from Martin Durrell.

40 From his letter to ROP, 7 April 1970, in 'Max in Manchester' p. 29. He expresses his displeasure in this letter.

41 Information about BFS's time in Manchester from my conversations with her, her email of 12 June 2018, and my conversations with Dorothy and Peter Jordan. Information about the Jordans here and in the next section from my interviews with them of 4 October 2011 and 6 October 2014, and from my interview with Peter Jonas, 26–7 July 2016.

42 Schwartz, p. 65.

43 To Doris Stoisser (see Hoffmann, p. 242). The other points in this paragraph come from his interviews with Maya Jaggi ('The Last Word', *Guardian*, 21 December 2001), Sven Boedeker (Schwartz, p. 107), Stoisser again (Hoffmann, pp. 241 and 244), and Joseph Cuomo (Schwartz, p. 106).

44 Information about and from Peter Jonas in this section from my interview with him, 26–7 July 2016, and his answers to my follow-up questions; three texts by him that he kindly gave me: his introduction to WGS's lecture on the opening of the Munich State Opera production of *I puritani*, July 2001, his article on WGS in the *Frankfuter Allegemeine Zeitung*, 21 January 2002, and his introduction to a reading of WGS's work in the Literaturhaus, Munich, 2001/2; also his Wikipedia entry, https://en.wikipedia.org/wiki/Peter_Jonas_(director).

45 This is the story Peter told WGS in 1969, and it was substantially true. Julius Jonas was wealthy, and used his money to help his children emigrate: his younger daughters Elizabeth and Margarethe came to England; his eldest Annemarie managed to get to Peru and thence to America; his other son, Jens Peter, went to Palestine; and Walter, as we know, to England. Julius and his wife Julie (his second wife, so not strictly Peter's grandmother) had in fact made provision to leave as well, but in the last minute changed their minds and took the other way out. See the website Stolpersteine Hamburg, http://www.stolpersteine-hamburg.de/?MAIN_ID=7&BIO_ID=2338. The website also records that in November 1938, when after years of restrictions Jews were banned from practising law, Julius Jonas suffered a breakdown. Nothing is recorded (naturally enough) about the Gestapo officer. But in war, as in peace, such personal connections often play a crucial role.

46 *SM*, p. 87. The quotation is from WGS to ROP, 7 April 1970, in '*Tanti cordiali saluti*', p. 47, and quoted in *SM*, p. 87.

47 This and the rest of the information about WGS's UEA application from RWS, *SM*, pp. 87–8 and Chronology, and from our conversations. That two other people were applying at the same time comes from one of them, GT, and from the interview with Bigsby. The other person was Cedric Williams (see Chapter 16).

48 Quotations from Keller's, Parry's and Peacock's references from *SM*, pp. 87–8.

49 Bigsby, p. 151.

50 The conversion to Deutschmarks is complicated, since the Mark hasn't existed since 2015. But this seems the best estimate. See http://www.historicalstatistics.org/Currencyconverter.html.

51 See *SM*, p. 86 and Chronology, p. 625.

52 Letter of 7 April 1970 in 'Max in Manchester', *Akzente* 50(1), Feb 2003, p. 29.

53 See *SM*, p. 68. Information about Hölderlin from: WGS'S 'An Attempt at Restitution', *CS*, pp. 212–5; Ronald Peacock, *Hölderlin*, pp. 171–2; Ulrich Häussermann, *Friedrich Hölderlin in Selbstzeugnissen und Bilddokumenten*, pp. 136–9; Thomas Knubben, *Hölderlin: Eine Winterreise* (2011), Chapter 21; and the Wikipedia entries on Hölderlin, https://de.wikipedia.org/wiki/Friedrich_H%C3%B6lderlin and https://en.wikipedia.org/wiki/Friedrich_H%C3%B6lderlin.

54 See the English Wikipedia entry on Hölderlin, in the second section, 'Education'.

55 Quoted in Ulrich Häussermann, *Friedrich Hölderlin in Selbstzeugnissen und Bilddokumenten*, Rowohlt, 1961, p. 136.

56 Häussermann, *Friedrich Hölderlin*, p. 137.

57 *CS*, p. 213.

58 These are the last lines of Hölderlin's *Andenken*, The translation is my own. In (Hölderlin's eighteenth-century) German they are: '...*Es nehmet aber/ Und giebt Gedächtniß die See,/ Und die Lieb' auch heftet fleißig die Augen,/ Was bleibet aber, stiften die Dichter.*'

15 MAX FERBER

1 *MF*, *E*, *193*.

2 *E*, p. 152.

3 *E*, p. 174.

4 *E*, p. 191. The following quotations come from pp. 192 and 188.

5 *E*, p. 162.

6 He would feel that both *RS* and *A* were failures, as we'll see. In general GAS hoped he would feel that his writing made his life worthwhile, but when she asked him, he said no.

7 Frohmann and his model temple come from Joseph Roth's *The Wandering Jews*, published in 1927. See http://www.berlin.ucla.edu/research/1920_people/texts/Roth.pd.

8 *E*, p. 176.

9 *A*, pp. 100–1.

10 He had great doubts while writing it, which nearly stopped him, just as he describes in *E*; he spoke about these to several interviewers (e.g. Bigsby, Cuomo in Schwartz, Ciro Krauthausen in *Babelia*, 14 July 2001). When the book was finally done, he told his closest friends that it was a failure. See Chapter 19.

11 *E*, p. 230.

12 See Michael Zeeman, in '*Kamer mit Uitsicht*', *VPRO Nederlands*, 12 July 1998: 'the reverse of melancholy is always irony'. Melancholics, WGS said, need irony to survive.

13 *E*, p. 165.

14 *E*, p. 234.

15 Walter Genewein was the chief accountant of the Łódź ghetto, renamed Litzmannstadt by the Germans. Five hundred of his photographs (actually colour slides) were found in a Viennese shop in 1987, as WGS wrote. They were exhibited in the Jewish Museum of Frankfurt in 1990, and (if I read its website rightly) are still held there. Two boxes are also now held in the United States Holocaust Memorial Museum in Washington (see https://collections.ushmm.org/search/catalog/irn522966). Genewein was convicted in 1947 for having profited from Jewish deaths, but was released after only a month, and died in Salzburg in 1974 at the age of seventy-three. See e.g. http://www.centrumdialogu.com/en/archive/galleries/photo-galleries/77-objects-from-the-ghetto; Nick Fraser, 'Cold Gaze of A Nazi Camera', *Telegraph*, 14 August 1999, http://www.telegraph.co.uk/culture/4718162/Cold-gaze-of-a-Nazi-camera.html; and Kevin Thomas, *LA Times*, 25 June 1999, http://articles.latimes.com/1999/jun/25/entertainment/ca-49886. Dariusz Jablonski's 1998 film *The Photographer* can be seen on YouTube: https://www.youtube.com/watch?v=k4YKbQSSvU0;126 of the colour slides were published in the catalogue to the Frankfurt exhibition ('*Unser einziger Weg ist Arbeit*'. *Das Getto in Lodz 1940–1944*. Vienna, Löcker, 1990). See https://www.juedischesmuseum.de/en/explore/documents-and-photos/detail/colour-slides-from-the-german-ghetto-administration-in-lodz/.

'Our only way is work' ('*Unser einziger Weg is Arbeit*') was said by Chaim Rumkowski, the ambiguous Jewish head of the ghetto (about whom Primo Levi wrote an extraordinary essay in *The Drowned and the Saved*). But even work did not save them for long: only 5 per cent of the Jews of Łódź survived the Holocaust.

16 *E*, p. 237. The last line is on the same page.

17 *E*, p. 237, Nona, Decuma and Morta are the Roman equivalents of the Greek Fates, Clotho, Lachesis and Atropos. The Latin names are resonant – '*nine, ten, death*' – in a way the Greek ones are not, which is no doubt why WGS chose them. (Nona, who begins the thread of life, derives her name from the nine months of pregnancy.)

18 E.g. to me, to Eleanor Wachtel and Joseph Cuomo (Schwartz, pp. 73, 38 and 104).

19 See p. 288 of this chapter.

20 *E*, German edition, p. 335. This trick has never been removed by the German publishers. It is still in the most recent (sixteenth) paperback edition of 2017, as well as in the bound Hanser edition of 2013. This information from my friend Marko Cevid, whom I sincerely thank for all his help.

Frank was the family name of Peter Jordan's mother, which is why it is in this list of surnames (along with Hamburger, in tribute to WGS's friend Michael). But it also allowed him to perform his Auerbach tease. For the list in the English edition, see p. 224. For the grant application see *Bewerbung um ein Werkstipendium des Deutschen Literaturfonds* (*Application to the DLF*, 1991, *DA* File 11 in the DLA).

21 Schwartz, p. 163. He also made the point e.g. to James Wood (*Brick* 59, p. 27).

22 In either the 1960s or the 1980s. 'Max must have had a phenomenal memory,' he said. (Our interview of 4 October 2011.) The facts of his history that follow come from that interview; and from his memoir, *Time of Songs*, and his grandfather Lazarus Frank's memoir *Meine Lieben Kinder*, copies of which he kindly gave me.

WGS changed the headmaster's name from Leach Lewis to Lynch Lewis, presumably in a (token) gesture to protect his identity.The facts about Peter Jordan's family photos come from a list that Dorothy gave me.

23 From Peter's letter to WGS, 4 April 1991, in the DLA, *MF* File 14.

24 *E*, p. 183.

25 See my interview, Schwartz, p. 71. Peter actually arrived in England on 9 May 1939 (from his passport, a copy kindly given me by the Jordans).

26 Information about Thea Gebhardt's memoir from my conversations with Peter Jordan. An independent German scholar, Klaus Gasseleder, has made a close study of the relationship between Luisa's memoir in *E* and

Thea Gebhardt's memoir: Klaus Gasseleder, '*Erkundungen zum Prätext der Luisa-Lanzberg Geschichte aus W.G.Sebald: Die Ausgewanderten: Ein Bericht*' ('Explorations of the Pre-text of the Luisa Lanzberg Story in W. G. Sebald's *Emigrants*: A Report'). It was published in Loquai 2005, pp. 157–75. I made my own study, but agree with almost all Gasseleder's conclusions, and acknowledge his work gratefully here. WGS's photocopies of all three memoirs – Thea Gebhardt's *Meine Kindheit*, Julius Frank's *Reminiscences* (written in English) and Lazarus Frank's *Meine Lieben Kinder* – are in the MF files in the DLA.

27 *E*, p. 207. Other examples are: Franz the albino stable boy; Kathinka Strauss with the seagull's wing on her bonnet, and 'Frau Adelinde, may I have a ball' on p. 196; Regina Zufrass, her husband Jofferle and the 'golden ringlets round the pebbles on the riverbed' on p. 197; and the storm that Papa says cannot make it over the Windheim woods on p. 199. The Beins and Mandels in Steinach and Herr Weintraub and his little boy in Bad Kissingen come from Thea, and so do several other lovely images, such as Aline Feldhahn as Queen of the Night, in her 'dark dress bestrewn with stars' (*E*, p. 202).

28 Apart from his parents and grandparents, Peter recalls only two other family members who died in the Holocaust. (He mentioned the first in a letter to WGS, 11 February 1987, and the second in a letter to me, 24 July 2011.)

29 *E*, p. 215. The information that follows comes from Peter Jordan.

30 For instance, WGS had set Ferber's father's exhibition in 1938. Peter told him that this wasn't possible, since Jews had been banned from the art business before that, so WGS moved it back to 1936 (p. 172).

31 In his card of 17 September 1992.

32 Klaus Gasseleder records that the rest of the Frank family also have the greatest respect for WGS's work, and approve his use of Thea's text in *The Emigrants*. They told Gasseleder that he had asked permission to use it. They must have understood this from Peter Jordan, which shows again that he realised he had given it, however tacitly.

33 Robert Hughes, *Frank Auerbach*, Thames & Hudson, 1990, p. 13.

34 Hughes, *Frank Auerbach*, p. 18. The comparison to ghosts is on p. 14.

35 *E*, p. 162.

36 Hughes, *Frank Auerbach*, p. 29. Hughes mentions several other traits in Auerbach which WGS shared as well: an aversion to superficial social life and the 'international circuit', for instance, and to modern technology (Auerbach hates TV and even the telephone); his dislike of interviews is also well known. Recently Catherine Lampert (*Frank Auerbach: Speaking and Painting*, Thames & Hudson, 2015) added several more: his not liking

'crowds or appointments' (p. 164), his feeling that 'I was born old' (p. 46), his combination of 'surface modesty and extreme internal pride' (p. 117). ('Surface' may not mean 'for show' here, and didn't for WGS: it was a genuine top layer of feeling, under which lay an absolute self-reliance.) Some of this is probably shared by all artists, but WGS and Auerbach do seem to have belonged to the same subspecies.

37 *Ibid.*, p. 9. He speaks of the absurdity of interpreting Auerbach's art in relation to the loss of his parents on p. 18.

38 To me in our interview (Schwartz, p. 75). Also to Maya Jaggi in their interview of September 2001.

39 My account of the Auerbach saga is based on Frank Auerbach's letter to me (see Note 42 below) and my interview with Christopher MacLehose of 27 March 2020. In (undated) 'Notes on Aurach' in the DLA, Bill Swainson asks WGS if he has permission to reproduce Auerbach's drawing and WGS replies that permission was not sought for the German edition. That Auerbach threatened to sue comes from Jan Ceuppens in his chapter on *DA* in the recent (2017) German Handbook on WGS, ed. Claudia Öhlschläger and Michael Niehaus, p. 34: 'Via a legal writ [Auerbach] obtained the change of the hero's all-too-obvious name to Max Ferber, as well as the withdrawal of two images that could be directly connected to him.' (Information from Marko Cevid.)

40 Letter to Tess Jaray, 14 December 1999.

41 This account from my conversations with Tess Jaray.

42 Frank Auerbach, handwritten letter to me, undated, but from December 2011.

43 That the changes were made in the German edition by 2006 I base on a footnote on page 221 of *Literatur als Philosophie – Philosophie als Literatur*, ed. Eva Horn, Bettina Menke and Christoph Menke, 2005. Certainly the latest edition, published in 2017, incorporates all the changes. (Information from Marko Cevid.) In his bibliography in *SM* RWS cryptically notes that 'When overseeing the production of [the German paperback] Max made small but significant changes to the form and deployment of the visual material' (p. 454). Actually he made the changes only to the English version; they were made in the German one after his death.

44 Auerbach was seventeen and Stella West thirty-two when they met; in *MF* the narrator is twenty-two and Gracie Irlam nearly forty (*E*, p. 152).

45 In *MF*, File 16 in the DLA.

16 1970–6

1 The following account comes from my conversations with GT, especially our interview of 22 February 2017 and his emails of 14 February 2017, 8 June 2018 and 10 June 2018. He answered my endless questions with great patience, as will continue to be evident in what follows. He is one of the best sources on WGS's time at UEA, and I am more grateful to him than I can say.

2 RWS's description of WGS comes from his interview with Thomas Honickel for *Der Ausgewanderte*; from my own interview with RWS on 12 October 2016 and his emails to me of 1 July 2016 and 20 June 2016; from JES 2009 and *D-S*. I thank RWS enormously for all his help.

3 Same sources as Note 1.

4 The detailed history in Wikipedia gives 1963 as the year the first students were admitted: https://en.wikipedia.org/wiki/University_of_East_Anglia.

5 See the obituaries of Franz Kuna in *Australian Studies*, http://www.easa-australianstudies.net/node/194 and on the Klagenfurt University website, https://www.aau.at/blog/uninews_40779/

There are two letters from Kuna in WGS's archive in the DLA, from 1978 and 1990. For Willi Guttsmann, see e.g. the obituary of him by Peter Lasko in *The Independent*, 25 March 1998. Guttsman had himself been arrested and sent to a concentration camp on Kristallnacht, 9 November 1938. For Werner Mosse: that Mosse fell out with the department comes from the obituary by Richard Evans in *The Guardian*, 27 July 2001, https://www.theguardian.com/news/2001/jul/27/guardianobituaries.humanities. The 'Plot 75' story from RWS's email to me, 29/30 July 2016.

6 Information about James MacFarlane and Brian Rowley from RWS in *SM*, pp. 89 and 91, and Janet Garton, our conversation of 21 January 2019. Information about the Austrian group from RWS, *SM*, p. 180, Note 19, about Keith Pollard from himself (our interview of 18 March 2015).

7 Information about UEA from RWS, in *SM*, pp. 88–9 and 94–6, in *JES* 2011, in his interview with Thomas Honickel, and on his page on the Magdalen College website; from GT, in *SM*, p. 109, in his interview with Honickel, and in his email to me of 22 February 2017; and from Janet Garton, in our conversation of 21 January 2019.

8 From '*Die hölzernen Engel von East Anglia*' ('The Wooden Angels of East Anglia'), *SM*, p. 320.

9 The letters to JK I've drawn on in this section are in the DLA. This paragraph and the next are based on one that clearly comes from WGS's earliest Norfolk days, but is undated, as usual.

JK remarked in our first interview how the Sebalds were always painting and redecorating, especially their last beautiful house, and almost everyone noticed not just its spotlessness but the freshness of its paint.

10 GT's memories in this paragraph from his emails to me of 2017 and 2018.

11 From WGS's letter to ROP, 8 December 1970, described to me in an email of 10 January 2019. ROP's report shows the desire to find an old house as well: 'He plans to buy a house, unfortunately hasn't found an old one.' Information about the Turners from GT's emails to me of 2017 and 2018. Information in the next paragraph from WGS's letter to JK, c. April 1971.

12 From 'Remembering Max'. This is an unpublished reminiscence, kindly written and sent to me by Dominic O'Sullivan. Dominic, a writer of short stories, plays and poems today, was WGS's student between 1974 and 1978. He was deeply impressed and influenced by WGS, and remembers a great number of the things he said, as will be clear in what follows. I thank him most sincerely for all his help.

13 This and the following information from GT. The detail about other small towns comes from RWS, *JES* 2011, Note 43. For WGS's writing his Ph.D. in this period, see RWS's Chronology, *SM*, p. 626.

14 This information, and that about the two accidents that follows, from WGS's letters to ROP, as reported to me in ROP's email of 10 January 2019. That Georg gave WGS a white VW estate comes from GAS.

15 The following information from GT's interview of 22 February 2017 and email of 8 June 2018.

16 The dates come from RWS's Chronology in *SM*, p. 625. WGS's colleague Ken Lodge told me that Manchester required Ph.D. candidates to be present at the university, so WGS had to re-register at UEA. Ken had to do the same. The information in the next paragraph comes from RWS, Reception, p. 352 and *SM*, p. 626. WGS told Gershom Scholem that he had finished his dissertation in a letter of 11 June 1972 (in the DLA). The information about WGS and GT's attempt to translate the thesis from GT's email of 14 February 2017. The point about Cedric Williams from RWS's email of 29 August 2016 and GT in *SM*, p. 120. RWS's point about WGS's English in Reception, p. 361, Anthea Bell's in 'Translating W. G. Sebald – With and Without the Author', in *SM*, pp. 209–15, on p. 211.

17 I have relied in this summary of WGS's Ph.D., its transition to a book and the book's reception on RWS's Reception and his emails to me of 29 August and 12 October 2016, and on US's accounts in *Ein, I* and Academia. US says (in *W & TW*) that a pdf of the dissertation can be downloaded from http://ethos.bl.uk.

18 The Sternheim campaign started in Fribourg in 1965, while the Döblin one lasted till 1983, as we'll see.

19 RWS, Reception, p. 366.

20 Letter to Gershom Scholem, 11 June 1972, in the DLA.

21 RWS, Reception, p. 366

22 This information from RWS and US as usual. I'm afraid I have lost the record of exactly where.

23 US, *SM*, p. 179, Note 2. The information from John Flower comes from our conversation of 18 January 2017.

24 US, Academia, p. 5.

25 Information on WGS as a teacher in the 1970s from my conversation with Dominic O'Sullivan of 6–7 February 2019, on his emails to me of 9 and 13 February 2019 and his summary 'Remembering Max'; and on the reminiscences of WGS's students of the 1970s gathered by GT in 'At the University: W. G. Sebald in the Classroom', in *SM*, pp. 109–27. The point about laughter in his classes comes from Christopher Smith's monograph, *'Max': W. G. Sebald as I Saw Him*. The memorable things WGS said come from Dominic O'Sullivan's conversations with me and from his 'Remembering Max'.

26 In this paragraph I've drawn on two undated letters to JK, headed 'Montag' and *'Mikde in am verbieslade Sommer'* (Allgäuerish for 'Wednesday in a pissing-down summer'), plus the one from around April 1971 and the one of 29 December 1980 for the joke medieval names. The next paragraph is based on the famous Sauerkraut letter, again undated, headed only *'Im November'*.

27 Information from GAS, and from WGS's letter to her, undated but probably from Christmas 1973.

28 Information about Jodok from WGS's letter to GAS as above, his letter to JK of January 1974, and GT's email to me of 10 June 2018. The letter to JK is again undated, but January 1974 from internal evidence (e.g. reference to the comet Kohoutek).

29 *The History of the University of East Anglia, Norwich* by Michael Sanderson, Hambledon Continuum, 2002 is the authoritative source on all matters UEA. I have relied for my brief summary of this period on RWS's summary of Sanderson's account in Reception (see pp. 373–4).

30 Information from https://en.wikipedia.org/wiki/Comet_Kohoutek.

31 In WGS's undated letter to GAS, probably Christmas 1973.

32 Information from RWS from his interview with Thomas Honickel and *SM*, p. 92.

33 My interview with Eda Sagarra, 15 December 2016.

34 *'Reiner Kunze spricht mit Max Sebald'* (Reiner Kunze Speaks to Max Sebald), video recording 1975, Audiovisual Archive, UEA.

35 Information in this paragraph from WGS's letter to JK, c. October 1974 and the Sauerkraut letter, dated only '*Im November*'.

WGS complains (satirically) of being called Winifred e.g. to Maria Alvarez in her interview (*Telegraph*, 24 September 2001), and to Walther Krause in his of 1 December 1996 (Hoffmann, p. 144.) The list of wrong forms of 'Sebald' comes from WGS's letter to M, 3 August 2000. He made a hilarious collage of these names, cut out from the envelopes of letters addressed to him over the years. The report of ROP's visit to Wymondham from his email to me of 10 January 2017.

36 Letter to JK of c. October 1974.

37 Information in the next two paragraphs from GT's interview and emails, from *SM*, p. 627, and from ROP.

WGS also wrote to Jan Franksen (with whom he would work while he was in Munich) that he was suffering from kidney colic (letter of 10 June 1975, in DLA). That he may have had to go briefly to hospital comes from a letter to ROP from WGS's colleague and friend Walter Bachem, reporting that his colic was so bad that 'it might force him into hospital again for a few days' (7 June 1975, sent to me by ROP on 23 June 2015). GT also told me that his colleagues had persuaded WGS to ask for leave of absence for the year, rather than just resigning. Cautious WGS would normally have decided this for himself; but it's possible that he could only make such a radical move under emotional pressure, and so needed reminding not to burn his bridges.

38 Information from my conversations with WGS's fellow trainees Sabine Hagemann-Ünlüsoy and Manfried Wüst, and from their Goethe Institute mentor and course organiser KV. I thank them all most sincerely. WDO confirmed in an email to me (23 March 2019) that the Institute was in a crisis at this stage and would have preferred to cancel the 1976 course. (His whole career was with the Goethe and he is, according to colleagues, its memory.)

39 See *CS*, p. 156, where WGS says that he had a one-room flat in Olympiapark in 1976. US writes in *Ein*, p. 24 that 'he found the restrictive conditions of living in the Olympic Village unbearable'. US gives no reference for this, and was probably told it by WGS himself.

40 After he left he told KV in a letter (27 December 1976) that he particularly regretted no longer being a colleague of Braun's. That Braun had been a carpenter comes from Sabine Hagemann-Ünlüsoy, email to me of 28 May 2019. The information about KV from herself.

41 Information from Sabine Hagemann-Ünlüsoy and Manfried Wüst. Ulrich Gründler died some years ago and Gabriele Irwin has disappeared, so information about them comes from Sabine Hagemann-Ünlüsoy and

Manfried Wüst as well. That they were an individualistic bunch comes from KV.

Ulrich Gründler went on to head the German Cultural Centre in Taipei. Sabine Hagemann-Ünlüsoy and Manfried Wüst both had distinguished Goethe careers, Sabine Hagemann-Ünlüsoy eventually becoming director in Addis Ababa, Taipei and Ankara, and Manfried Wüst in Bucharest, Ramallah, Damascus and Puna (India). After brief postings to Beijing in 1976 and 1977, KV remained at the Munich Centre until 1985, then went to London for five years, ending as director in Zagreb, Tel Aviv and Ankara.

42 In his email to me, 6 February 2019.

43 Sabine Hagemann-Ünlüsoy's memories in this and the next paragraph from our conversation of 2 February 2019 and her emails of 21 February and 28 May 2019. Later on WGS would tell friends that what had most attracted him to the Goethe was the idea of teaching abroad (see RWS, Reception, Note 18, on the plan being 'to teach in a developing country', and US, *Ein*, p. 24, on WGS's inability to teach for years in Germany before being able to do so abroad). In fact, WDO and the others tell me that this was wrong: Germans only go abroad on the cultural side, with the language teaching done by local employees. But directors have to manage the teaching side as well, and so are required to have practical experience.

44 KV's memories in this paragraph and the next from our conversations of 9 and 15 March 2019. On the Grand Magic Circus see for instance https://www.flickr.com/photos/khiltscher/sets/72157617917859090/.

45 GT knew this from WGS at the time, seeing him on a visit to Munich (from his conversations with me). RWS heard it from him later (see RWS, review of Philippa Comber, Ariadne, p. 85: 'He had tried to return to Germany in the mid-1970s but failed to make his peace with what, for him, was a deeply tainted country with a deeply guilty population').

46 This, and his desire to return after only five weeks, from his letter to Jan Franksen, 27 January 1976 (in the DLA). The other memories come from Sabine Hagemann-Ünlüsoy and Manfried Wüst, except for the one of WGS's kidney pain in Munich making him tear a bookshelf off the wall, which comes from BFS (her emails to me, 2017).

47 See *SM*, p. 627. RWS dates the purchase of the Old Rectory to Pentecost, no doubt from WGS's calendars; in 1976 Pentecost fell on 6 June. The rest of the paragraph from WGS's letter to KV, 13 July 1976. He later told his student Ralf Jeutter that because of its parlous state, the house had been extremely cheap.

48 In a letter to ROP, 8 October 1976, he estimates it will take two years (quoted in ROP's email to me, 10 January 2019). The tale of the Old Rectory perhaps being haunted was told to the Jordans, who repeated it to me in our interview of 14 October 2011.

49 Information from them. That WGS expected to do two to three years he seems to have told RWS (see Reception, Note 18). US says it too (*Ein*, p. 24), possibly because WGS told him the same thing. That he resigned on 20 August comes from *SM*, p. 627.

50 These were to GT and KV respectively. The explanation to ROP came in the letter of 8 October 1976, that to JK in an undated postcard. That to Sabine Hagemann-Ünlüsoy comes from our conversations.

51 Letter of 27 December 1976. I asked to see WGS's resignation letter, which is still held in the Goethe Institute files, but data protection would not allow it.

52 KV reported this reason to WDO in an email of 16 February 2019.

53 Letter to KV of 27 December 1976. The line to JK comes from an undated postcard, evidently from December 1976.

54 This paragraph and the next from the same letter to KV of 27 December 1976.

55 See RWS, Reception, p. 374, quoting Sanderson's history of UEA, p. 245.

56 *A*, p. 46.

17 1977–88

1 See his letter to KV, 25 June 1977. The quip to GAS is in his letter to her of 22 April 1979.

2 Dietrich Schwanitz to WGS, letter in DLA, dated only '1982'. For discussing the possibility of a *Habilitation*, see Dietrich Schwanitz to WGS, letter in DLA, 11 May 1983. I'm guessing that this discussion began during Paolo's leave in England. For thinking about Switzerland, see WGS's letter to Jan Franksen in DLA, 14 October 1983. For the *Habilitation* dates see *SM*, pp. 632–3.

3 It was dubious not only in a general way but in a particular one, since the *Habilitation* was in *Germanistik*, and Paolo was an *Anglist*. (ROP made this point in our interview of 4 June 2016.) In his account, RWS notes that all documentation relating to WGS's application has been lost (*SM*, p. 632). This may be a cover story, given the controversial nature of the process.

4 Information on this and the other promotions from *SM*, pp. 632–5.

5 This and applying in Switzerland from letters to GAS, 22 February and 27 October 1986.

6 Letter to GAS, 22 April 1979.

7 Information in this paragraph from WGS's letters to KV, 27 December 1976 and 25 June 1977; and Richard Evans, our interview of 9 June 2016 and his emails to me, 17 June 2016 and 25 January 2021. The book, which came out of Evans' work for his Ph.D., was never published in English, but several chapters appeared in his essay volumes (*Comrades and Sisters*, 1987 and *Proletarians and Politics*, 1990). *SM*, pp. 496 and 627 also record WGS's translation.

8 *Sozialdemokratie und Frauenemanzipation im deutschen Kaiserreich*, translated by W. G. Sebald (Berlin-Bonn, Verlag J.H.W Dietz Nachfolger, Internationale Bibliothek, Vol. 119, October 1979); https://sebald. wordpress.com/2007/06/06/wg-sebald-as-translator/.

9 Information in this paragraph from *SM*, pp. 628–33; WGS's letter to KV, 25 June 1977 and to GAS, 22 February 1986 and 22 April 1979.

10 See RWS, Reception, Note 77. For his renewed German teaching, GT in *SM*, p. 116; for his courses, *SM*, Appendix 3.3, 'Summary of courses taught by WGS at UEA, 1970–2001', pp. 130–4. He taught the German cinema course together with Dr Thomas Elsaesser, who had established a Film Studies Centre at UEA, and would become a leading international expert on film. Elsaesser left for the University of Amsterdam in 1991. (See https://en.wikipedia.org/wiki/Thomas_Elsaesser.)

11 See *SM*, pp. 110–23.

12 The meeting was on 1 October 2016. The four students were Anne Fitzpatrick, Ruth Guy, Celia Turner and Joan Wickham. I am most grateful to all of them. Sadly, Joan died in 2019. The information in the next paragraph comes from that meeting, except for the details at the end about their third-year late-night sessions, which come from Anne's notes made at the time.

13 From Anne's email to GT, 14 January 2008. The rest of the information in this paragraph comes from Anne's notes of their Post-war German Literature II course, spring term 1981. These are a precious source, and I'm most grateful to her for showing them to me, and for making them in the first place.

14 Information in this paragraph comes from Anne's notes of their Kluge and Weiss classes in 1981, from our meeting of 1 October 2016, from Joan's email to me, 16 October 2016, and from Anne's emails to GT, 14 January 2008, and to me, 10 October 2016.

15 Information from Sarah Cameron, in our interview of 5 June 2016. The following section is based on that interview and our subsequent exchanges. I thank her sincerely for all her help.

16 Strictly speaking, she had been allocated another, but after a short time 'adopted Max' (email, 27 June 2020).

17 See *SM*, pp. 462–7.

18 I've borrowed this summary from US, *W & TW*, p. 21. For the quotation, see p. 20. GAS recalls that Rosa was outraged at WGS's treatment of Stifter, one of her favourite authors.

19 *W & T W*, p. 21.

20 He had all his books, academic and literary, sent directly from the publisher to his parents and sisters (GAS email and text, 24 and 30 April 2019). He sent copies of this one to KV and his film-maker friend Jan Franksen, for instance (see Franksen's letter to him of 22 December 1985 in the DLA), and very likely to others as well.

21 E.g. to ROP (see ROP's letter to him of 11 May 1980 in the DLA) and to Philippa Comber (see *Ariadne's Thread*, Propolis, 2014, p. 45). For the New York and Freiburg conferences, see *SM*, p. 630.

22 The friend was Philippa Comber, a psychotherapist he met in 1981. Her memoir, *Ariadne's Thread*, is an invaluable source of information and insights about WGS in the early 1980s, and will reappear both in these notes and in the text. He says that his Freiburg paper is so wicked it might get him thrown out of the lecture hall on p. 118.

   US suggests a similar motive to the one I do in his account of the event in *I*, pp. 126–7. My account draws on his, both there and in his *W & T W* portrait, p. 17. He recalls WGS telling him of seeing Döblin's son's horrified face, so like Döblin's own, in Note 166, p. 192 of *I*.

23 To Piet de Moor, *SM*, p. 350.

24 To Joseph Cuomo, Schwartz, p. 117. De Moor is Belgian and Cuomo American, and both interviews took place abroad: that is, in neither of WGS's homes, England or Germany.

25 JK couldn't date this more precisely than 1979, but WGS's appointment calendars show that he was in Germany that year in early May. (See *SM*, p. 628.) That it had started some time before his birthday is also suggested by a cryptic remark in a letter to GAS in April (22 April 1979): he's all right, apart from the big things it's better not to talk about. GAS's judgement from her email to me of 3 April 2019 and our conversations.

26 Dates from RWS's interview with Thomas Honickel. The point about government requiring more and more 'value for money' comes from a most helpful account by Tony Flack, EUR administrator during all the crucial years (though he would never use the term 'Stalinisation', which comes from WGS). The account was written on 29 January 2013 in answer to a query by the scholar Scott Bartsch and kindly sent to me by Tony Flack.

27 All WGS's colleagues remembered this vividly. It was dated to the early 1980s by Professor Rudiger Görner, in our interview of 30 September 2015. He was teaching at Aston University, Birmingham, at the time, where a TQA team was due to arrive after UEA. He rang WGS to ask about the experience. WGS reported that he'd chucked the inspectors out, saying 'There's the door.'

   Everyone remembered the 1980s as a terrible time for university teachers (e.g. Richard Evans, in our interview of 9 June 2016). In 2001 WGS spoke of his dismay at the 'Thatcherite so-called education reforms of the early 1980s' to Maya Jaggi (*Guardian*, 22 September 2001), and explained to Maria Alvarez (*Telegraph*, 24 September 2001): 'They come and measure how much you've written each week, all these assessments and various other Stalinist stupidities.'

28 Information from my conversations with JK's wife Kristin. After the Kaesers moved back to Sonthofen in the 1980s, Kristin would often meet Rosa in shops or on the street, and Rosa would pour out her worries about her son.

29 Following information from Ralf Jeutter, 'Some Memories and Reflections: W. G. 'Max' Sebald, Man and Writer', in US ed., *ÜS*, pp. 303–7, our conversation of 5 February 2019 and his email answering questions, 2 May 2019.

30 Ralf Jeutter in *ÜS*, p. 303.

31 The following account is drawn from *Ariadne's Thread*.

32 See e.g. WGS, interviews with Renate Just, 'Stille Katastrophien', *Süddeutsche Zeitung Magazin*, 5 October 1990, Loquai, p. 29, and 'Im Zeichen des Saturn', *Die Zeit* Magazin, 13 October 1995, Loquai, p. 41, with Sarah Kafatou, *Harvard Review* No. 15, Fall 1998 (p. 32), with Jean-Pierre Rondas (Hoffmann, p. 218), with Eleanor Wachtel (Schwartz, p. 60), with Steve Wasserman (*SM*, p. 368).

33 *Ariadne's Thread*, p. 44.

34 To me in our conversations, and also e.g. to Thomas Honickel in their interview.

35 The following account comes from my conversations and email exchanges
    with KV from February 2019 onwards, for which I'm deeply grateful.

36 Seehttps://en.wikipedia.org/wiki/Bombing_of_Hamburg_in_World_WarII,
    and   https://www.historynet.com/allied-aerial-destruction-of-hamburg-
    during-world-war-ii.htm. The raid that set the Katharinenkirche (St
    Catherine's Church) on fire took place on 30 July 1943. It left only the
    outer walls and the base of the spire standing. See https://en.wikipedia.
    org/wiki/St._Catherine%27s_Church,_Hamburg.

37 Hans Erich Nossack, *The End: Hamburg 1943*, translated and with a
    foreword by Joel Agee (Chicago: Chicago University Press, 2003).

38 WGS may not have been aware of this last coincidence, that the name of
    the Polish Club meant 'fire'. But it chimes too much with the others to
    leave out.

39 So he wrote in the covering note he sent with the typescript. When he sent
    her the published book a year or so later, he dedicated it to 'A treasured
    reader'.

40 From Anne's notes of the seminar, held in Week 8 of the spring term in
    Ruth's room. To Sarah Cameron a few years later he spoke of sanity and
    madness too. There's no clear divide, he said: 'There's a spectrum and
    things can flip you over.' (My conversation with Sarah of 5 June 2016.)

41 See https://de.wikipedia.org/wiki/Ernst_Herbeck and the entry on him
    in the Biographisches Archiv der Psychiatrie, by Robin Pape and Burkhart
    Brückner, https://biapsy.de/index.php/de/9-biographien-a-z/50-herbeck-
    ernst. In 1980, after thirty-four years in the hospital, Herbeck was allowed
    to move into a retirement home in Klosterneuburg, as WGS wrote in
    Vertigo (p. 39). A year later, however, he returned, and spent the rest
    of his life in the 'Artists' House' created by Navratil at Gugging. In his
    early committals in the 1940s Herbeck had received both insulin and
    electroshock treatments. That may have been where WGS first heard of
    these horrors. Altogether Herbeck wrote some 1,200 poems and prose
    texts. WGS isn't the only writer to admire his work; so too, for example,
    do Elfriede Jelinek and Gerhard Roth.

42 See https://de.wikipedia.org/wiki/Leo_Navratil. WGS's copy of *Alexanders
    poetische Texte*, together with Navratil's *Gespräche mit Schizophrenen*
    (*Conversations with Schizophrenics*) is in the DLA.

43 See *SM*, p. 629.

44 *SM*, p. 629. This was presumably the paper he gave about Herbeck at
    a conference of Swiss psychiatrists in April 1981. It was published in
    Manuskripte that year, and included in *The Description of Unhappiness* in
    1985. (See *SM*, p. 462.) The conference was held in the Waldau asylum

near Bern, which as US points out (*Ein*, p. 26) is where Walser had first been committed. US also notes how WGS's early essay on Herbeck 'simply ignored the usual scholarly claim to objectivity' and was instead 'a labour of love and the result of a deeply felt psychological affinity'. (*SM*, pp. 167 and 175.) He points out that the photo of Herbeck in *V* is actually of Walser (*SM*, p. 176). The account in *V*, and the photograph, are on p. 39.

45 WGS to JK, 29 December 1980.

46 From '*Die Weisse Adlerfeder am Kopf: Versuch über Herbert Achternbusch*' ('The White Feather on His Head: An Essay on Herbert Achternbusch'), paper given at the meeting of British and German Germanists in Berlin, 12–18 April 1982 and published in *Manuskripte* the next year (No. 23, 1983). Quoted in US, *SM*, p. 169.

47 'Crossing the Water', *ALW*, p. 77.

48 See *SM*, p. 629.

49 In his letter of 29 December 1980. Venice's lack of trees seemed very strange to him, he wrote; and in a pizzeria he nearly hid under the table when he saw the owner's name was Carlo Cadavero.

50 Letter of 3 March 2000. This letter clearly implies that the event happened on the 1980 journey. See also WGS's reference in a piece written in 1995 to 'some strange adventures' in Milan 'fifteen years ago' (*CS*, p. 142).

51 Apart from his claim that the pursuit by two young men really happened, which I go on to discuss, he often said that *V* was autobiographical: e.g. to Cuomo (Schwartz, p. 103), de Moor (*SM*, pp. 350, 353), Poltronieri (Hoffmann, p. 95), and AI (Hoffmann, pp. 50–70 *passim*). In his 1987 application to the DLF for support for a 'prose work with pictures' that includes the *V* material, he openly identifies the narrator with himself. This application, like the 1991 one, is in *DA* File 11 in the DLA. Sometime in 1987 he also sent KV the 'Beyle' and 'Dr K' parts of *S.G.*, telling her that in the next part (they were evidently in a different order then) he was the traveller. 'Were anyone in any doubt as to the real-life identity of the narrator in *Vertigo*,' Philippa Comber says, he used exactly the same phrase about himself in a letter to her in 1984 as he would use about the narrator a few years later (*Ariadne's Thread*, p. 138).

52 *V*, p. 71. After the first glimpse of the two young men in the Riva bar, the narrator sees them again in the buffet in Venice station, where he recalls having seen them cross his path 'more than once' since his arrival, then in the Giardino Giusti in Verona, and finally in the Arena: making a total of four located sightings and 'more than one' other.

53 *V*, p. 81.

54 See https://en.wikipedia.org/wiki/Wolfgang_Abel_and_Marco_Furlan.
   Furlan was released in 2010, Abel (after some years of house arrest) in 2016.

55 See *'Die Natur des Zufalls'* ('The Nature of Coincidence'), interview
   with AI, broadcast on *Beste Bücher* (*Best Books*), Swiss Radio DRS 2, 4
   May 1990, republished in Hoffmann, pp. 50–70; and 'Echoes from the
   Past: a Conversation with Piet de Moor', published in Dutch in *Knack*
   magazine, Brussels, 6 May 1992, republished in Hoffmann (*'Echos aus der
   Vergangenheit'*, pp. 71–8, translated by Marlene Müller-Haas) and in *SM*,
   pp. 350–4, translated by Reinier van Straten. I have slightly adjusted the
   translation on the basis of the German version (Hoffmann, pp. 76–7).
   The discussion of the 1980 journey is on *SM*, p. 353. The quotation from
   de Moor comes from *SM*, same page.

56 This has been established by the scholar Scott Bartsch, who has done an
   intensive study of the composition of *V* ('W. G. Sebald's Prose Project',
   in *ÜS*, pp. 99–134). From WGS's day planners, Bartsch reports that he
   was in 'Ve' (probably Verona) on 29 October, and took the night train to
   Innsbruck that night (p. 107). This corrects RWS's Chronology in *SM*,
   p. 629, which puts WGS in Venice from 29 to 31 October, and was most
   likely based on the diary we see on p. 60 of *V* – which like so many
   documents in the books is probably faked. But *SM*, p. 629 goes on to
   confirm that WGS was in Sonthofen and Wertach in early November.

57 See *V*, p. 63–4 and https://en.wikipedia.org/wiki/Wolfgang_Abel_and_
   Marco_Furlan. That is why WGS changed the date of the pizza bill (i.e.
   the experience in the pizzeria) from 29 October – the original – first
   to 4 November and then to 5 November, the one he uses on p. 79 of
   V: because he wrongly believed the Organizzazione Ludwig's first claim
   of responsibility for the killings was in the *Gazzettino* of 4 November. See
   Bartsch in *ÜS*, pp. 99–134., p. 108.

58 See Bartsch, *ÜS*, pp. 99–134, page 106.

59 Draft of Part 2 of *S.G.* sent to KV, p. 24.

60 M, email to me, 26 May 2019. She also confirms in this email that WGS
   identified the two pursuers as Abel and Furlan.

61 From Anne Fitzpatrick's notes of their seminar on *The Goalie's Anxiety at
   the Penalty Kick*.

62 See SM, p. 353.

63 See Comber, *Ariadne's Thread*, p. 137.

64 KV's draft, p. 28.

65 E.g. AI, Eric Santner, Helen Finch, Scott Bartsch. See Bartsch, *ÜS*, p. 110
   and footnote 24.

66 AI, 'Melencolia', In *Die Zeit*, 21 September 1990, reprinted in Loquai 1997, pp. 70–4, on p. 72.

67 For the dating of the start of WGS's literary writing to November 1980 or at the latest summer 1981, see *SM*, p. 629. Also e.g. RWS, Ariadne, p. 85 and Bartsch, *ÜS*, p. 105.

68 The last section of *ALW*, for instance, would become the middle part of *AN*, on the eighteenth-century naturalist Georg Wilhelm Steller; and eighteen poems from *ALW* would go into the final autobiographical part of *AN*. (See *ALW*, Ian Galbraith's Introduction, p. xv.) The German version was published in 2008, the English in 2011. US says in his book on WGS's poetry that the autobiographical poems of *ALW* went into verses II, IV and VI of the last part of *AN* (*F*, p. 9). And at least one, as we know – 'Crossing the Water' – went into verse I.

69 See his 1987 application to the DLF, in which he says that *AN* was his first literary work.

70 *SM*, p. 630 records that he was working on the Steller section in the spring of 1983. He gave Philippa Comber an early version of it in May (see *Ariadne's Thread*, pp. 115, 119 and 225), and *Akzente* turned it down that year (see US, *F*, p. 58). See also Michael D. Hutchins, *Tikkun: WGS's Melancholy Messianism*, Ph.D. submitted to the University of Cincinnati, 2011, which concludes from a close study of WGS's papers in the DLA that he began submitting the Steller section to publishers in late 1983: https://etd.ohiolink.edu/!etd.send_file?accession=ucin1307321149&disposition=inline. The date of publication of the Steller section in *Manuskripte* comes from *ALW*, Galbraith's Introduction, p. xiv. That the whole poem (or at least a version of it) was finished by late 1985 is clear from WGS's list of publisher's rejections, which starts with a letter from the Residenz Verlag in November 1985 (*AN* files in the DLA). The list of rejections contains ten publishers.

71 For Enzensberger recommending it to Greno, see *SM*, p. 634. WGS spun a story involving his beloved coincidence about how it got to Ransmayr (see his interview with Sven Boedeker in Hoffmann, p. 105). In fact WGS simply wrote to Ransmayr on 10 June 1987, asking if he would take *Nach der Natur* to Enzensberger. (Letter in the DLA. I thank Professor Kurt Forster for alerting me to this letter, and for all his help.)

72 I take this dating from two letters in the DLA. They are from the publisher Suhrkamp, one dated 17 January 1980 and the other 6 January 1983. The first acknowledges receipt of an unnamed manuscript; the second apologises for not having responded to WGS's Kant script for a very long

time. The two letters surely refer to the same thing, which dates the first submission of the script to January 1980, and its writing therefore to some time before, i.e. 1979. This is also the reasoning of Michael Hutchins in *Tikkun*, pp. 149–51.

It thus seems that though WGS conceived of his work on Kant as a play from the start, he first tried to publish it on the page, and sent it to his friend Jan Franksen at Sender Freies Berlin to make as a television film only two years later (Franksen mentions receiving it in a letter of 24 September 1981). He went on trying all forms of publication, sending it to eight book publishers, eight television companies, three theatre companies and both the UK and German representatives of the German Film Board (*Tikkun*, p. 154).He never lost his interest in drama, and in the late 1980s organised a conference and edited the resulting book on German documentary theatre of the 1960s (*A Radical Stage: Theatre in Germany in the 1970s and 1980s*; see *SM*, p. 449). It's not so surprising, therefore (as I go on to argue) that when he turned seriously to literary writing in 1979–80, it should first have been in dramatic form.

73 In '*Kostenbegründung*' (Reasons for Cost) in the 1987 DLF application.

74 In 1985 he would plan but not actually write one about Schumann, and in 1986 he would write one about Wittgenstein, *Leben Ws*. Jan Franksen refers to WGS's Schumann project in a letter of 3 June 1985, in the DLA. For the dating of *Leben Ws*, see *SM*, p. 332. The whole of *Leben Ws* is in *SM*, pp. 324–32. See also e.g. US, *W & T W*, p. 23.

75 The dating of the effort to make the film, and the information on Franksen in the next paragraph, come from his letters to WGS in the DLA, especially those of 6 December 1981, 13 December 1982 and 5 January 1988. WGS's three drafts and *Exposé* (summary) of the project are in his *Jetzund kömpt die Nacht herbey* papers in the DLA.

76 The other, *Leben Ws*, was a life of Wittgenstein. WGS at least saw the script of *Leben Ws* published in the *Frankfurter Rundschau* in 1989. US finally persuaded WDR3 in Cologne to broadcast a radio version of Kant in 2015. For *Leben Ws*, see *SM* p. 332, for the 2015 radio performance of Kant see https://sebald.wordpress.com/2015/05/20/sebalds-screenplay-on-kant-heads-to-radio/.

77 This comes from Hutchins, *Tikkun* (p. 154), like the detailing of how many of each in Note 72. So does the quotation from the rejection letter (from Fischer, on 7 May 1982) and the point about ignoring Kant's philosophy, from the same letter.

78 The whole poem (Martin Opitz's Ode IV), goes as follows (translation from the old German by Michael Hutchins in *Tikkun*):

Jetzund kömpt die Nacht herbey / Now the night descends,
Vieh vnd Menschen werden frey / Beast and men become free,
Die gewüntschte Ruh geht an; / The wished-for rest has come;
Meine Sorge kömpt heran. / My sorrow closes in.
Schöne gläntzt der Mondenschein; / Prettily shines the moonlight,
Vnd die güldnen Sternelein; / And the little golden stars;
Froh ist alles weit vnd breit / Everything far and wide is joyous,
Ich nur bin in Trawrigkeit. / Only I am in sadness.
Zweene mangeln vberall / Everywhere two are missing
An der schönen Sternen Zahl; / Among the number of the pretty stars;
Diese Sternen die ich meyn' / These stars I have in mind,
Ist der Liebsten Augenschein. / [Are] the glow of my beloved's eyes.
Nach dem Monden frag' ich nicht / I do not ask after the moon;
Tunckel ist der Sternen Liecht; / The starlight is dark,
Weil sich von mir weggewendt / Because she has turned from me,
Asteris mein Firmament. / Asteris, my firmament.
Wann sich aber neigt zu mir / But when she bends to me,
Dieser meiner Sonnen Ziehr / The ornament of my sun,
Acht' ich es das beste seyn / Then it seems best to me
Das kein Stern noch Monde schein. That neither star nor moon appear.

79 See the article on p. 22 of *Dr HS*. In *Dr HS* the narrator reads the newspaper article on a train between Zurich and Lausanne, and in his interview with Piet de Moor WGS said he'd bought *De l'amour* in Lausanne (*SM*, p. 350). But his letter to GAS of 27 October 1986 connects both events to Fribourg.

80 Letter to GAS of 27 October 1986.

81 A detailed account of the slow division of WGS's prose work into *V* and *E* is in Scott Bartsch's 'W. G. Sebald's Prose Project' in *ÜS*, pp. 99–134. I have drawn on this for my (very abbreviated) version, and am most grateful for it. As noted, the 1987 grant application is in *DA* File 11 in the DLA.

82 At this stage Uncle William is called William Seelos. Eventually Max would remove the name from his fictional family and give it to the clan he based on the Berchtolds. Their 'Uncle Peter' would prefigure William's decline and disappearance, which Max thus wrote about twice.

83 He told GAS that he'd written *Dr HS* for *Manuskripte* in a letter of 2 June 1988. That he'd thought of using the image of the body returning from the ice for *PB* comes from Bartsch.

84 Peter sent him the memoirs he'd asked to see in February 1987, apologising for a delay. (Letter of 17 February 1987, in the DLA.)

85 WGS to GAS, same letter.

86 RWS's Introduction and Note 6 to *JES* 2014. In fact WGS rewrote it, or wrote it anew; he'd already done a draft the summer before (letter to GAS, 2 June 1988). That 'Ritorno' was his favourite among his writings comes from his answers to questions after his 2001 reading at the 92nd Street Y (in 'Three Encounters with W G Sebald', *JES* 2014. The pages are unnumbered in the online edition I consulted, but this was the last question).

87 The card to KV that accompanied the complete typescript of *S.G.* is dated only 1989, but must come from after the summer, since he says it had been done in the summer; I've guessed, accordingly, the autumn.
Eichborn published *S.G.* in March 1990. (See *SM*, p. 452.)

88 E.g. to Joseph Cuomo, James Wood and Robert McCrum among his UK/US interviewers, and Sven Boedeker, Martin Oehlen and Hans-Peter Kunisch among his German ones. To his friend and colleague Christopher Bigsby he added the pressures of family life (Bigsby, p. 151–2).

89 Nuria Amat, 'W. G. Sebald: Un Encuentro', *ABC Cultural*, Madrid, 30 September 2000, https://nuriaamat.com/wp-content/uploads/2016/05/ Sebald.-Entrevista-ABC-Cultural.pdf.

18   1989–96

1 The date from RWS's Chronology in *SM*. Unless otherwise indicated, all the dating and description of events in this chapter comes from RWS's Chronology.

2 Information from GT, *SM*, p. 121, RWS, interview with Thomas Honickel, and my conversations with both; Jo Catling, Introduction to 'Among Translators: W. G. Sebald and translation' in W. G. Sebald Memorial Issue, *In Other Words*, No. 21, 2003, p. 112; US, *W & TW*, p. 267; Anthony Vivis, in 'Notes on the early years of BCLT' in *In Other Words*, p. 114.

The information about Earlham Lodge comes from my interview with Clive Scott (29 April 2014), Christine Wilson, 'Working with Max at BCLT', in *In Other Words*, pp. 117–18, and Boyd Tonkin's interview with WGS, 'Swimming in the Seas of Silence', *Independent*, 18 February 1998. That it took the university several years to recognise WGS's achievements: US makes this point repeatedly, e.g. in 'Shadows' and in *W & TW*, which notes that the 2002 history of the university still didn't mention him (p. 27). Today he is proudly acknowledged.

3 Information about Adam Czerniawski from 'In memoriam Max Sebald (1944–2001)' in his *The Invention of Poetry*, Salt Publishing, 2005, pp. 110–12, and my interview with him of 16 May 2019. Information about Ria Loohuizen from Dutch magazine *Avondlog*, http://www.avondlog.nl/ tags/wgsebald, our interview of 8 January 2019 and later conversations.

4 Information about Beryl Ranwell from: my conversations with Sally and Nick Humpston (daughter and son-in-law), 23 August 2014 and 13 December 2019; and my conversations with Ria Loohuizen, Christine Wilson, WGS's colleague and friend at BCLT, Jean Boase-Beier, GT and RWS. Also GT's obituary of Beryl, *Guardian*, 1 July 2013.

5 Information in this paragraph from my conversations with Heidi Nowak and Thomas Honickel's interview with her.

6 Following information about Walter Kalhammer from my conversations with Ursula Schmid (née Kalhammer) and Fritz Kalhammer.

7 Information about Gundela Enzensberger from my interview with her, 20 February 2016.

8 Information about colleagues' responses from Christopher Smith, ' "Max": W. G. Sebald as I knew him', in *JES* 2011 also published by Solen Press, Norwich, 2007, pp. vii–viii; about 'Mac' MacFarlane's response from my interview with Janet Garton, 21 January 2019. About the reception of *V* in Germany, see e.g US, *W & T W*, p 23.

9 Information about the Ingeborg Bachmann Prize events from my conversations with AI and GAS. See also Daniel Kehlmann, '*Der Betriebsschaden*', *Frankfurter Allgemeine Zeitung Sonntag*, 15/16 October 2005.

10 Franz Kuna to WGS, 8 July 1990, DLA.

11 Dietrich Schwanitz to WGS, 8 October 1990, DLA.

12 Jan Franksen to WGS, 15 July 1990, DLA.

13 Information about ROP from my conversations with him.

14 WGS to ROP, 16 October 1990.

15 Information from Renate Just, '*Stille Katastrophien*', *Süddeutsche Zeitung Magazin*, 15 October 1990, pp. 28–9, in Loquai 1997.

16 Information on WGS's attack on Jurek Becker from US, *SM*, p. 164 and RWS's Chronology, *SM* 637; see also https://en.wikipedia.org/wiki/Jurek_Becker and http://www.wgsebald.de/becker/becker.html.

17 This and the following information from Janet Garton, our interview of 21 January 2019.

18 See Christopher Smith, ' "Max": W. G. Sebald as I knew him', pp. ix–x and xii–xiii.

19 Jean Boase-Beier information from our conversations of 21 March 2017 and 11 January 2019. I sincerely thank her for them and all her help. The friend who said 'Mr Pastry!' was Ken Lodge, who taught linguistics and phonetics. That WGS could be physically awkward would also be noticed by his friend M. He would sign some of his letters to her '*Stolperer*', 'Stumbler'.

20 So he told Ria Loohuizen, letter of 30 June 1992.

21 For this and the other quotations from WGS's interview with Piet de Moor, see *SM*, pp. 350–4.

22 See his interviews with Sven Boedeker (1995), Hoffmann, pp. 112–13; Sven Siedenberg, Hoffmann, p. 122; Renate Just, '*Im Zeichen des Saturn*', *Die Zeit Magazin*, 13 October 1995, in Loquai 1997, p. 40; Peter Morgan, 'Living Among the English', *Planet*, April/May 2003, p. 14; and Bigsby, p. 162.

23 See US, *Ein*, p. 123 and *W & TW*, p. 72.

24 WGS's letter to Peter Jordan, 20 August 1992, describes his real itinerary. The visits to Lowestoft in January and Somerleyton in February come from RWS, his Chronology in *SM* and Note 45 in *JES* 2011 (on Lowestoft). The information about WGS's call on the Hamburgers from my conversations with Anne Beresford. That he felt better after the walk comes from his letter to Peter Jordan.

25 See his interview with Maya Jaggi, *Guardian*, 22 September 2001. Robert MacFarlane's remark about giving up the walk was told me by a friend.

26 See e.g. Jochen Wittmann, *Stuttgarter Zeitung*, 27 November 1997; Hans-Peter Kunisch, *Süddeutsche Zeitung*, 5 April 2001; US, *W & TW*, pp. 23–4. Details of the Literary Quartet programme from my own viewing. It can be seen on YouTube: https://www.youtube.com/watch?v=Ip-oefN1dB0 (46:20–58:45).

27 WGS to KV, 12 October 1992. GAS's report from her interview with Ruth Vogel-Klein, '*Ein Fleckerlteppich*', in '*WGS: Memoires. Transferts. Images. Erinnerung. Übertragungen. Bilder*', *Recherches Germaniques*, Special Issue No. 2, 2005, pp. 211–20, and to me in conversation.

28 WGS to Peter Jordan, 17 September 1992 and 12 February 1993.

29 Letter from Idris Parry to WGS, 15 March 1993, DLA.

30 See his interviews with Ralph Schock and Sven Boedeker (1993 and 1995) in Hoffmann, pp. 103, 109, 112; with Sven Boedeker, '*Mit dem Vokabular im Gepäck*', *Der Tagespiel*, 11 March 93; and his letter to Peter Jordan, 12 February 1993. The old friend who came to his reading was Sigrid Becker-Neumann (from my interview with her, 8 August 2017).

31 Information about the Andersch controversy from US, *Ein*, p. 28 and *ÜS*, pp. 234–40 (in Markus Joch, '*4:2 für die Literaturpfaffen: W G Sebalds Angriffe auf Alfred Andersch und Jurek Becker*' ('4:2 for the Priests of Literature: W G Sebald's Attacks on Alfred Andersch and Jurek Becker'), pp. 227–49). See also http://www.wgsebald.de/andersch/andersch.html.

32 For Enzensberger's being upset, see US, *F*, Note 29. The rest of the information in this paragraph from *SM*, p. 640 and my interviews with Jon Cook and AI. Enzensberger's remark to WGS's colleagues comes from my interview with Jon Cook, 26 September 2014.

33 The dates and the information that follows about WGS's left eye from his letter to WS, 4 September 1993. The correspondence between WGS and

WS is all in the DLA. That his later problem was with the right eye comes from RWS, *D-S*, p. 432.

34 In his 1995 interview with Renate Just in Loquai 1997, p. 40. Information about the story he spun later from my conversations with UL.

35 Information in this paragraph and the next from Bill Swainson, our interview of 20 January 2020 and following emails.

36 In his reader's report to Harvill, quoted to me by Bill Swainson.

37 See *SM*, p. 641.

38 The story of the prize medal (the Johannes-Bobrowski medal) from RWS in *SM*, pp. 641–2 and GT in *SM*, p. 121; also e.g. Philippa Comber, *Ariadne's Thread*, Propolis, 2014, p. 170.

39 WGS to Peter Jordan, 18 December 1994. Following information from WGS's letter to KV, 5 June 1994 and Renate Just, 1995 interview in Loquai 1997, p. 40.

40 Sven Boedeker, in the 1995 interview (Hoffmann, p. 113). To Renate Just he gave the tally as ten (1995 interview, Loquai 1997, p. 40). The following information about several premature deaths from my interview with Ralph Yarrow, 21 February 2017. By now the EUR had become the School of Modern Languages and European Studies, in one of its periodic efforts to save itself. (See *SM*, p. 642.)

41 Information about Janine Dakyns and Michael Parkinson from my conversations with RWS, Clive Scott, Ralph Yarrow and Ria Loohuizen. Also Michael Parkinson's death certificate. GRO (General Registry Office) reference: DOR Q2/1994, District Norwich (6391D), Reg. D8B, Entry No. 266. The verdict recorded is 'open verdict' and the cause of death is given as 'overdose of drugs (chloroquine)'.

42 WGS to WS, 8 June 1995; WGS to Peter Jordan, 26 September 1995; WGS to GAS, 26 June 1995.

43 See US, *W & TW*, p 24. That GAS loved it: see WGS's letter to her of 26 June 1995.

44 Michael Hamburger to WGS, 29 September 1995 (in the DLA).

45 This and the following points from his Boedeker interview 1995, in Hoffmann.

46 Renate Just, 1995 interview in Loquai 1997, p. 42.

47 The account of WGS's translation troubles with Michael Hulse is my interpretation, from: Michael Hulse, 'Englishing Max', *SM*, pp. 195–208, my interview with him, 27 May 2004, and the key letters of his correspondence with WGS, 1994–2000; Anthea Bell, 'Translating WGS – With and Without the Author', *SM*, pp. 209–15 and my interview with her, 24 May 2004; my interviews with Jean Boase-Beier, 21 March 2017, Barbara Schwepke (then of Harvill), 16 July 2019, Bill Swainson, 20 January

2020 and Christopher MacLehose, 27 March 2020. I particularly thank Bill Swainson and Jean Boase-Beier for our conversations about translation.

Michael Hulse gave me copies of several of his typescripts with WGS's corrections, plus the key exchanges of their correspondence, for which I sincerely thank him. Full copies are deposited in the Houghton Library at Harvard. See https://hollisarchives.lib.harvard.edu/search?utf8=%E2%9 C%93&op%5B%5D=&q%5B%5D=W+G+Sebald&field%5B%5D=&com mit=Search++&limit=&from_year%5B%5D=&to_year%5B%5D=.

The DLA also holds much of the correspondence between WGS, Hulse and Bill Swainson on the translation of *V, E* and *RS* (as well as that between WGS and Anthea Bell on *A*). These are in the files named *Manuskripte Anderer* (Others' Manuscripts).

I have also drawn on WGS's own accounts in his interviews with e.g. Boyd Tonkin, Jon Cook, Maya Jaggi, Sven Boedeker (1995) and Nuria Amat, and the conclusions of e.g. Ulrich von Bülow (in *SM*, p. 255) and James Wood (in 'Reveries of a Solitary Walker', *Guardian* 20 April 2013) that WGS was effectively Hulse's co-translator.

That WGS showed his translations to the BCLT students comes from the poet Will Stone, who took the course in 1998. He reported it in his contribution to the tenth anniversary celebrations of WGS's death, held at Wilton's Music Hall in the East End of London on 14 December 2011, which I attended. Adam Czerniawski found a written version of Stone's talk in his archive and kindly sent it to me. No source is given.

Among the many people to whom WGS complained about Hulse's translations – apart from those I mention in the text – were WS (e.g. in a letter of 8 June 1995), M, the Hamburgers, Tess Jaray, Christine Wilson (of BCLT), Richard Evans, and writer friends such as Clive Sinclair, Tony Rudolf and Ann and Anthony Thwaite. The leading Germanist professor Ritchie Robertson knew of his complaints too; probably the whole Germanist world did.

48 For the account of Beryl Ranwell's translation work with WGS I have drawn first and foremost on my meetings with Sally and Nick Humpston (6 December 2014 and 13 December 2019), whom I sincerely thank for all their help. Also on my conversations with GT and his obituary of Beryl (*Guardian* 1 July 2013), and on those with Jean Boase-Beier and with Clare Savory, a student of WGS's, 1983–7.

The typescripts that Beryl left at her death were *PB, AA* and 'Max Aurach' (as he was still called) from *E*, 'Il Ritorno in patria' from *V*, and two folders of *RS*. These typescripts are now among the material on WGS in UEA's British Archive for Contemporary Writing. Her daughter Sally is certain that she kept all her work for WGS together (email 30 March 2020); hence my conclusion that she didn't work on *Dr HS* or *A*.

WGS thanked her for her patient work in a postcard of 28 June 1995. Her daughter holds this, Christopher MacLehose's letter, and others to and about Beryl. That this invaluable work was editorial rather than simply typing, for instance, is proven at many points. In a letter of 3 March 1995, e.g. Bill Swainson refers to it as 'going through and revising Michael Hulse's translation' (in this case, of *E*). On the cover sheet for the English translation of *RS* WGS wrote that it was by Michael Hulse, with amendments by Beryl Ranwell and himself, in that order (*Manuskripte Anderer*, DLA).

That WGS never explained or apologised to Michael Hulse over trusting Beryl more than him comes from my interview with Hulse.

Jon Cook made his remark about WGS's command of English in our interview of 26 September 2014. Other people who noted the excellence of WGS's English include Paul Bailey, in his interview with him, *Daily Telegraph*, 6 June 1998 (in three hours of conversation, Bailey noted not a single error); Tess Jaray, Barbara Schwepke and Anthea Bell herself (*SM*, pp. 211 and 212, and 'A Translator's View', *Five Dials* magazine, https://fivedials.com/fiction/a-translators-view/). WGS's last editor agreed, saying that he could easily have written his books in English (see Simon Prosser, 'A–Z of W. G. Sebald', https://fivedials.com/fiction/z-w-g-sebald/).WGS told his last creative-writing class that he could write in English (my interview with Jo Wroe, 27 February 2019).

49 WGS interview with Jon Cook, *SM*, p. 359.

50 See Stefan Tobler, 'The portrait of the Sebaldian translator, preferably not a young man', in W. G. Sebald Memorial Issue, *In Other Words*, No. 21, 2003, p. 119. The quotations are from this piece.

51 See e.g. RWS: *D-S*, pp. 432–4 and 449; his Preface to *JES* 2011, p. 201: '… the darkening of his mood and "take" on life that had been happening throughout the 1990s'; and Ariadne, p. 85: 'Max's sense of alienation and awareness of his own mortality were becoming ever more insuperable and beginning to have … [an] effect on his relationships with other friends.' RWS was also very clear in his interviews with me (12 October 2016) and with Thomas Honickel about the darkening of WGS's mood in his last four or five years. US (*Ein*, p. 13, *W & TW*, pp. 2–3) confirms that WGS's vision darkened by the mid-1990s at the latest.

The remarks reported by Renate Just come from her 1995 interview with WGS in Loquai 1997, pp. 39–41.

52 See e.g. RWS, *D-S*, p. 420: 'his health, about which he would rarely speak, got worse and his state of mind grew darker' in the 1990s; also *JES* 2009, Note 34: especially after 1995. Information about WGS's migraines from RWS (e.g. *D-S*, p. 424 and my interview with him) and from GAS and

BFS; about his blood pressure from BFS; about his alcohol 'allergy' from almost all his UEA friends, and from GAS and BFS. The 'djooce' detail and the point about his covering up his health problems from RWS.

In 1998, when he was fifty-four, he already spoke of entering old age (see '*Ausgrabung der Vergangenheit*' ('Excavating the Past'), a piece written in honour of Michael Hamburger, *SM*, p. 344).

53 WGS to KV, 19 January 1996.

54 Sven Boedeker, 1995 interview (Hoffman, p. 121).

55 Information about the reception of *E* on this page and the next from my conversations with Bill Swainson and his email of 31 March 2020.

56 The following information from my conversations with KV and her email of 21 February 2019. WGS's last letter to her is dated 19 January 1996.

57 *TLS*, 29 June 1996, quoted by US, *Ein*, p. 29. He makes the following points about WGS's fortunes changing and the sales of *E* in *W & T W*, p. 25. Cynthia Ozick's review was in *The New Republic*, 16 December 1996, Gabriel Josipovici's in *The Jewish Quarterly*, Winter 1996/7.

58 *TLS*, 25 February 2000. See https://www.the-tls.co.uk/articles/public/mourning-sickness/.

59 The account of Susan Sontag at the MacLehoses' party comes from my interview with Christopher MacLehose, 27 March 2020, and from Amanda Hopkinson's radio essay on WGS, 'A History of Memory or a Memory of History?', Radio 3, 9 December 2011, which can still be heard (along with the other four programmes in the series): https://www.bbc.co.uk/programmes/b0180hh4. Robert McCrum, for example, vividly remembers this event (our interview of 9 December 2019).

60 See his letters to WS and Karl-Heinz Schmelzer, both of 12 December 1996. US recalls WGS describing his *auto da fés* (e.g. in *W & T W*, p. 24 and his radio essay; also in his interview with me). WGS also told Michael Hulse that after a year's struggle he'd put *Korsika* away in a shoebox (WGS to Hulse, 2 February 1997, in the DLA).

61 See Ulrich von Bülow, '*Sebalds Korsika-Projekt*' in *Wandernde Schatten*, ed. von Bülow, Heike Gfrereis and Ellen Strittmatter, pp. 210–24. This was the catalogue to the exhibition of the DLA's WGS materials in the Museum der Moderne in 2008.

62 From my 1996 interview with him; I didn't include it in the published version. WGS had just decided to give up *Korsika* when we met. US suggests this reason too, in *W & T W*, p. 24 and his radio essay on WGS, 'Teaching by Example', Radio 3, 6 December 2011.

63 Information from WGS's editor at Hanser, Wolfgang Matz, whom I sincerely thank (email 9 December 2020). WGS turned this into another

of his dramatic tales, in which Hanser had actually put *Roman* (novel) on the cover, until he objected and it was removed.

64 See *Ariadne's Thread*, pp. 168–9. For going blind in his right eye in December 1996, see RWS, *D-S*, p. 432. RWS suggests here that the cause may have been psychosomatic. Information about WGS's mounting blood pressure in the 1990s from BFS. For the role of hypertension in central serous retinopathy, and the other facts about it, see https://en.wikipedia. org/wiki/Central_serous_retinopathy. For the role of hypertension in eye pathologies in general, see https://www.heart.org/en/health-topics/ high-blood-pressure/health-threats-from-high-blood-pressure/how-high-blood-pressure-can-lead-to-vision-loss. For WGS's fear of eye surgery, see e.g. the interview with Piet de Moor, *SM*, p. 351.

The eye surgeon in *A* and in reality was Zdenek Gregor, who did indeed have a Harley Street surgery. According to Lynn Wolff (*Sebald's Hybrid Poetics*, p. 134, Note 38), Gregor retired in 2013.

65 From our interview, 20 January 2020.
66 From our interview, 27 March 2020.

19 1997–2001

Dating and events are again taken from RWS's Chronology in SM.

1 Letters to WS and Karl-Heinz Schmelzer, both 12 December 1996.
2 As US also says: see *W & T W*, p. 25.
3 The first he wrote was on Mörike, for the Mörike Prize, which he would receive in April. Very likely that gave him the idea. See *SM*, p. 471, and Jo Catling's introduction to *PC*, p. xvii, which also gives the dates of the rest. In a letter to WS of 10 February 1997 WGS said that the Mörike was finished, in another of 13 September 1997 that the whole book was done, apart from the introduction. Catling says that that was added in early 1998 (*PC*, p. xvii). The last essay in the book, on his friend JPT, was written a few years earlier (*PC*, p. xvi.) The title was a homage to Walser, whose short story *Kleist in Thun* was one of WGS's touchstones.
4 *PC*, p. 2.
5 *PC*, p. 30.
6 *PC.*, pp. 82–3.
7 *PC*, p. 3.
8 Interview with Jon Cook, *SM*, p. 360.
9 As well as RWS's Chronology (*SM*, p. 644), see US, *Ein*, p. 29. His reservations come from GAS. He told WS that he'd made the right decision in a letter of 13 September 1997.

10 The name was later changed to Sebald Ltd. See http://www.bizdb.co.uk/company/sebald-limited-03346713/.

11 Professor Rudiger Görner (from our interview of 30 September 2015).

12 See the interview with Maria Alvarez, *Telegraph Magazine*, 24 September 2001. This was not the least thing Sontag did for WGS in these years. Wylie was Sontag's own agent – as well as e.g. Philip Roth's, Salman Rushdie's, Martin Amis's, Saul Bellow's, Norman Mailer's. (See Emma Brockes' interview with Wylie, *Guardian*, 24 June 2003.)

13 Letter to WS, 15 June 1998.

14 He doesn't start talking about it in his letters until September. See p. 366 of this chapter and Note 19 below.

15 In 1998 he went to the East End of London twice, to Antwerp, Breendonk and Paris. Apart from RWS's Chronology, his research journeys are also dated by the photos he took during them. The photos were on display in the exhibition at the Sainsbury Centre at UEA, 'Far Away – But From Where?', from 11 May 2018 August 2019.

16 Information about Stephen Watts from my interviews with him, 16 October 2014 and 19 September 2017; from his 'Max Sebald: a Reminiscence', in *SM*, pp. 299–307; from Rachel Lichtenstein, *On Brick Lane*, Hamish Hamilton, 2007, Chapter 8, 'The Whitechapel Poet', pp. 118–30; and from 'Stephen Watts, Poet' in *Spitalfields Life* by 'the gentle author', 30 June 2010, https://spitalfieldslife.com/2010/11/30/stephen-watts-poet. In *The Last London* (2017) Iain Sinclair also writes extensively about Stephen, including about his relationship with WGS.

In fact the two had been talking about the East End since the early 1990s (Stephen's email to me, 10 June 2020). The lines by Stephen quoted in *A* and here are from his poems 'Lord in dream' and 'Fragment', both in his 2004 collection *The Blue Bag*.

WGS called Stephen a hunger artist in a letter to M of June 2000, and said in that letter that his work had a rare beauty. The coincidence story about Stephen was told me by Ralf Jeutter.

17 Soon after, WGS began the last verse of *After Nature* with an echo: *Lord, I dreamed/ that to see Alexander's battle/ I flew all the way to/ Munich...* (see *AN*, p. 109).

18 They had already appeared in Dutch – the Dutch were the first to translate every book of WGS's until *A* – and there were also a Spanish and a Danish *E*. See *SM*, pp. 454–5.

19 WGS letters to the writer Clive Sinclair, 5 September 1998 and to Peter Jordan, 30 September 1998.

20 E.g. in his interviews with Toby Green (November 1999), Bigsby (12 January 2001), Maya Jaggi (*Guardian*, 22 September 2001) and Maria Alvarez (*Telegraph Magazine*, 24 September 2001) as well as the Robert McCrum interview quoted, which was in the *Observer*, 7 June 1998. In German e.g. Martin Öhlen, *Kölner Stadt-Anzeiger*, 13 June 1997, Julia Kospach, '*Der Spurensucher*', *Profil*, 19 February 2001, p. 122. He told Maya Jaggi that he had to read a hundred letters about *LL* at breakfast (interview of 22 September 2001). Travelling a week every month comes from Bigsby, requests and phone calls from Kospach. He also spoke to Ralf Jeutter of writing as a 'second jail' (*France Culture* radio documentary on WGS by Thomas Sipp, 22 June 2006) and would write it to Sarah Cameron (letter of 1 February 2000).

21 WGS, interview with Robert McCrum, 'Characters, Plot, Dialogue? That's Not Really My Style', *Observer*, 7 June 1998.

22 Migraines and episode of blindness from RWS, our interview of 12 October 2016; his flushed face from e.g. Jean Boase-Beier (our interview of 11 January 2019) and Ralf Jeutter (our interview of 5 February 2019). The rest of the paragraph from the sources named.

23 In Sarah Kafatou, 'An interview with W. G. Sebald', *Harvard Review*, No. 15, Fall 1998.

24 In 1995 Renate Just ('*Im Zeichen des Saturn*', *Die Zeit Magazin*, 13 October 1995, in Loquai 1997, p. 40) described his study as like a monk's cell, with an iron camp-bed and no papers or library; GAS told me that it was upstairs. WGS sent a photograph of it to M, saying that it measured just six square metres. A photograph of his earlier worktable downstairs is in *SM*, p. 274.

Ralf Jeutter information from his interview with me and his essay on WGS in *ÜS*, pp. 303–7. GAS, UL, Tess Jaray and Jeutter all say that WGS slept little; his student Sarah Emily Miano says that his usual time to wake was 4 a.m. ('Hands in Pockets', *Grand Street* 72, Fall 2003, p. 172). US remarks in *F* that sleepless nights are a theme in the poetry (p. 42). He also suggests (p. 127) that WGS may at least sometimes have suffered from tinnitus (with reference to *RS*, p. 5, 'the never entirely ceasing murmur in my own ears' and the title poem in *FYN*, which refers to a whistling sound in the poet's ears).

25 RWS information from our interview of 12 October 2016 and his interview with Thomas Honickel; his *D-S*, e.g. pp. 422, 424, 438, 442 and Ariadne, p. 86. GT information from our conversations.

26 Dating of these research visits comes from WGS's photographs in the 'Far Away – But From Where?' exhibition, UEA, 2019.

27 From the interview with Cuomo, Schwartz, p. 112. To me (1996 interview, unpublished part) he said he could do ten pages on a rare good day, but mostly no more than two. WGS also spoke of writing getting harder and harder to e.g. me (both 1996 and 1998 interviews); Robert McCrum; Kenneth Baker, in 'Up against historical amnesia', *San Francisco Chronicle*, 7 October 2001; Sebastian Shakespeare, *Literary Review*, October 2001, p. 50; and Ciro Krauthausen, *Babelia*, 14 July 2001. He told Bigsby that it had got so hard with *A* that he thought he might have to switch to English, but it was too late (p. 148).

28 Cuomo, p. 109.

29 Information from Steven Spier, our interview of 26 January 2016. RWS dates Hamburger's beginning the translation to February 2000, perhaps from an official contract. But Michael Hamburger's first letter to WGS about translating *AN* is from 19 March 1999 (in DLA).

30 This is my own judgement. Information about Hamburger's 'scrawls' from his correspondence with WGS (especially e.g. letters of 4 September 1999, 9 September 1999, 26 February 2000, 2 March 2000, 8 March 2000).

31 Information from Steven Spier, interview of 26 January 2016.

32 See Anthea Bell, 'Translating WGS', *SM*, p. 210.

33 Information from WGS to Hulse 22 January 2000, Hulse to WGS 1 February 2000, WGS to Hulse 4 February 2000; and Hulse, 'Englishing Max', *SM*, p. 208.

34 In his interview with James Atlas, 'WGS: A Profile', *Paris Review* 151, 1999, p. 289. *SM*, p. 646 shows that the interview was conducted in February 1998. The information that follows about Georg Sebald from GAS, BFS, Fritz Ketterle (our interview of 24 April 2017), Nauke (Hans Alfred) Küsters and UL.

35 From my 1996 interview with him, unpublished part.

36 See e.g. the interview with Arthur Lubow, Schwartz, p. 170. Several UEA colleagues heard this from WGS too. GAS and BFS information from our conversations. WGS spoke of his father's anxiety to me in our unpublished interview of 27 April 1998. That Rosa said WGS and Georg were reconciled comes from GAS.

37 WGS to WS, 17 June 1999.

38 From Christopher Bigsby, *Remembering and Imagining the Holocaust*, Cambridge University Press, 2006, p. 31.

39 The account of Georg's funeral is from GAS.

40 The following account comes from Barbara Schwepcke and Christopher MacLehose.

41 E.g. WGS to M, 20 April 2000.

42 Typically, he would tell it as a funny story (see Stefan Tobler, 'The portrait of the Sebaldian translator, preferably not a young man', in W. G. Sebald Memorial Issue, *In Other Words*, No. 21, 2003, p. 119), and as one about a death, saying that it had all begun with 'the mysterious suicide of his German publisher', who had climbed a mountain outside Frankfurt and lain down to die in the snow. (See the interview with Lubow, Schwartz, p. 171.) Uwe Gruhle of Eichborn did kill himself this way – but nine months after WGS had left there, and with no conceivable connection to his US–UK deal. See http://www.spiegel.de/spiegel/print/d-8608261.html and https://de.wikipedia.org/wiki/Die_andere_Bibliothek.

43 Maria Alvarez, *Telegraph* 24 September 2001. The fact that WGS was contracted in the US (to New Directions) comes from Christopher MacLehose (our interview of 27 March 2020). That New Directions continues to publish WGS's books up to *A* in the US is clear in *SM* (see its Primary Bibliography, pp. 452–7). The newspaper that spoke of 'a telephone-book number' was the *Observer*, in its literary gossip column 'The Browser'.

44 Letter of 2 December 1999. His grumble about students was remembered by Barbara Schwepcke.

45 Information about Tess Jaray from my conversations with her of 18 June 2011, 2 January 2016 and 11 January 2016; her 'Two Pieces' in *After Sebald*, ed. Jon Cook, Full Circle Editions with UEA, 2014; and WGS's letters to her, 14 December 1999, 6 January 2000, 11 April 2000 and 28 April 2000.

46 Tess Jaray, 'Two Pieces', in *After Sebald*, p. 143.

47 *A*, p. 303.

48 'Two Pieces', p. 143.

49 Information in this paragraph from WGS's letters to M, 25 January 2000 and 22 April 2000 and to Tess Jaray, 28 January 2000.

50 Susan Sontag, 'A Mind in Mourning', *TLS*, 25 February 2000, https://www.the-tls.co.uk/articles/public/mourning-sickness/.

51 The prizes were the Joseph-Breitbach and the Heinrich Heine. For the information about Redonda, see https://es.wikipedia.org/wiki/Reino_de_Redonda and https://en.wikipedia.org/wiki/Javier_Mar%C3%ADas.

52 Information on WGS and creative-writing teaching from my interview with Clive Scott, 24 September 2014.

53 To almost everyone, interviewers and friends. His maverick behaviour as an academic is detailed by US, *I*, p. 37; see also his Radio 3 essay, 'Teaching by Example', *The Essay*, Radio 3, 6 December 2011.

54 See Christopher Smith, ' "Max": W. G. Sebald as I knew him', p. xvi. See also Peter Morgan, 'Living Among the English', *Planet*, April/May 2003.

55 See Prosser, 'An A–Z of W. G. Sebald' in *Five Dials*, https://fivedials.com/
    fiction/z-w-g-sebald/.

56 This, waking at five, and working till midnight from WGS letters to M, 9
    January, 29 January and 26 February 2000.

57 This and the next line from WGS to Ria Loohuizen, 17 June 2000. That
    he had another accident in July comes from WGS to Michael Hamburger,
    4 July 2000; that he had a minor operation from the same letter and from
    WGS to M, 30 June 2000.

58 I date the finishing of *A* to early August because WGS applied for a grant
    for his next project on 2 August, and later that month began research for
    it. (See RWS's Chronology, p. 650.) RWS notes that Anthea Bell received
    the MS 'in the summer' (p. 649).

59 Michael Hamburger to WGS, 26 February 2001 (WGS had expressed his
    doubts to Hamburger on the phone); JPT in his interview with Thomas
    Honickel; letter to M, undated.

60 The *Weltkriegsprojekt* file in the DLA was closed in 2008 and no scholars
    have seen it (information from staff of the manuscript section, DLA). The
    information about it here comes from WGS's application to NESTA in
    early 2000, quoted by Ulrich von Bülow in *SM*, p. 257; WGS's interview
    with Arthur Lubow, Schwartz, pp. 163–5 and my interview with Lubow of
    19 April 2016; WGS's interview with Jean-Pierre Rondas, Hoffmann, p. 219;
    WGS's interview with Ciro Krauthausen; KW, '(Un)heimliche Heimat' in
    ÜS, p. 163; WGS to M, 6 August 2001 (going back to the glassblowers of
    the Bavarian Forest); RWS's interview with Thomas Honickel. NESTA
    is the National Endowment for Science, Technology and the Arts. For
    NESTA Fellowships, see www.nesta.org.uk.

61 WGS, interview with Hans-Peter Kunisch, *Süddeutsche Zeitung*, 5
    April 2001.

62 Franz Meier's interview with Thomas Honickel; my interview with
    Richard Evans, 9 June 2016. The information about Babette Aenderl from
    my conversations with Heidi Nowak and UL, and WGS's interview with
    Hans-Peter Kunisch, *Süddeutsche Zeitung*, 5 April 2001.

63 From my interview with Richard Evans, 9 June 2016.

64 E.g. to Peter Jordan (undated postcard). Information from Jon Cook from
    my interview with him, 26 September 2014. That this made him happy
    from Ria Loohuizen, *Avondlog*, http://www.avondlog.nl/tags/wgsebald.

65 Information from Jean Boase-Beier. WGS's graduate student Florian
    Radvan recalls that WGS mentioned the deaths of Bradbury and Good
    in his letters (*SM*, p. 156).

66 See GT, 'At the University: WGS in the Classroom', *SM*, p. 127, Note 5.

67 For his talking often of time running out, see US, *Ein*, p. 31. He'd already written it in a letter to WS two years before (letter of 17 June 1999). The letter to Sarah Cameron is from 1 February 2000. He would also say it to e.g. Susi Bechhöfer, who had written to him about *A* (Chapter 23). (WGS to Susi Bechhöfer, 27 September 2001, in the possession of Susi's son, Frederick Stocken.)

68 Michael Hamburger said this on the *France Culture* radio documentary on WGS by Thomas Sipp, 22 June 2006.

69 Anthea Bell was commissioned to translate *A* and *LL* in December 1999 and started work on *A* in the summer of 2000 (see *SM*, p. 649). WGS's begging off festivals comes from Christopher Bigsby (our interview of 23 September 2014). The information from M from my conversations with her.

70 Information on the JPT and Hamburger letters from JPT's interview with Thomas Honickel and Hamburger's letter to WGS, 26 February 2001 (DLA). The Hanno Kühnert letter to WGS is from 18 April 2001 (also in the DLA).

71 Information about the Cuomo interview from my interview with Joe Cuomo, 7 May 2016; Margo Nash, 'The Write Stuff', Queens College Readings http://www.qcreadings.org/images/QMagSpr07EXC.pdf
and Joseph Cuomo, 'Queens College Evening Readings at 36', *The Knight News* (Queens College newspaper), 20 April 2012 http://www.theknightnews.com/2012/04/20/queens-college-evening-readings-at-36/

72 It can be read in Schwartz, pp. 93–117.

73 Celia Turner remembered this in our meeting of 1 October 2016. For WGS's comparison of his research method to a dog running through a field, see Cuomo in Schwartz, p. 94. He made the same comparison to Sven Boedeker (see Hoffman, p. 118) and to Jean-Pierre Rondas, who used it for the title of his interview, '*So wie ein Hund einen Löffel findet*', 'As a Dog Finds a Spoon' (Hoffmann, p 214).

74 He told Tess he would try to attend in a letter of 15 February 2001.

75 Information about the Munich State Opera event from my interview with Sir Peter Jonas, 26–7 July 2016.

76 Information about the family gathering in September 2001 from my conversations with GAS and Solveig.

77 Information from Ria Loohuizen, in the *France Culture* radio programme by Thomas Sipp, 2006. She last saw WGS in November, but his concern wouldn't have stopped then.

78 RWS puts the publication of the British edition in October (*SM*, p. 457), but some people had certainly read it before the 24 September reading. See e.g. Michelle Lovric, 'WGS's Pockets', http://the-history-girls.blogspot.

com/2016/03/wg-sebalds-pockets-michelle-lovric.html. Diana Athill, e.g., wrote to him on 26 September about how much she admired it (DLA).

79 See https://www.nytimes.com/2001/10/28/books/excavating-a-life.html.

80 Celia Turner, from our meeting of 1 October 2016.

81 To Steve Wasserman (Los Angeles Public Library, 17 October 2001, in *SM*, pp. 364–75) and Michael Silverblatt, *Bookworm* radio interview, KCRW, Santa Monica, CA, 6 December 2001, in Schwartz, pp. 77–86, and https://www.youtube.com/watch?v=lVssOL6olQ4.

82 Information about the last creative-writing class from its members (with the exception of Joanna Minshew, whom I couldn't find, and one other, who left the course): Oliver Emanuel, Kate Grunstein, Lucy Hannah, Sara Heitlinger, Andy Knight, David Lambert, Zoe Lambert, Robert McGill, Sarah Emily Miano, Dave Paul, Sarah Ridgard, Natasha Soobramanien, Luke Williams, Jo Wroe. Sincere thanks to all of them.

Special thanks to David Lambert and Robert McGill for their 'Maxims', https://fivedials.com/fiction/the-collected-maxims-of-w-g-sebald/. And special thanks to David Lambert again, who kept detailed notes and shared them with me. Information also from the interview 'The Permanent Exile of W. G. Sebald' by Jens Mühling, an MA student in comparative literature at UEA, who conducted the interview in 2000. It was originally published in *Pretext 7* (Spring/Summer 2003) and posted in three parts by the Vertigo website on 19, 20 and 21 February 2008. See https://sebald.wordpress.com/category/jens-muhling/. The section 'On teaching creative writing at UEA' is in the third part.

83 All his friends knew of the Nobel Prize rumour. It was reported in the *Eastern Daily Press* and the Norwich *Evening News* items on WGS's death (both 17 December 2001) and is recorded e.g. in US, *W & T W* p. 27. US notes in *I*, p. 50 that WGS heard the rumour himself; that he was unthrilled comes from *I*, Note 124, p. 62. US also makes the point in *W & T W* (p. 12) that WGS would have preferred to be remembered as a 'controversial misfit' than to be adored. WGS himself said something similar to Boyd Tonkin in their 1998 interview: 'I would rather be a recluse than someone on a public cultural stage.'

84 See 'An Attempt at Restitution', *CS*, pp. 206–15.

85 Information in this paragraph from the named persons: in the case of Franz Meier, from his interview with Thomas Honickel; otherwise in conversations with me.

86 See US, *W & T W*, p. 29. GT's memory of their last conversation five days before WGS's death comes from the *France Culture* radio programme by

Thomas Sipp. and in conversation with me. George Szirtes's memory from our interview of 17 September 2014. UL's from several of our conversations.

20 MARIE

1 From Gustav Janouch, *Conversations with Kafka*. Originally published by Fischer in 1961 as *Gespräche mit Kafka: Aufzeichnungen und Erinnerungen*. The latest English edition was published by New Directions in 2012.

2 The information about Kafka and Dora Diamant that follows can be found in all the many Kafka biographies and in detail in *Kafka's Last Love* by Kathi Diamant, published in 2003. It is summarised online in (for instance) https://kafkamuseum.cz/en/franz-kafka/women/dora-diamant/ (the photograph of Dora is on this site); https://en.wikipedia.org/wiki/Dora_Diamant. I have also drawn on an interview with Kathi Diamant in 2013: https://www.radio.cz/en/section/arts/dora-diamant-kafkas-last-love. WGS told the story of Dora in his Kafka course, saying it was the happiest time in Kafka's life (Anne Fitzpatrick's notes, taken between 1977 and 1981).

And he told it to M, explicitly making the parallel to themselves (undated letter, but probably from April 2000).

3 The information about M in this chapter comes from our many conversations since 2016, and from WGS's letters to her, which she allowed me to read. I cannot adequately express my gratitude for her trust and generosity in sharing her memories of WGS not only with me but with everyone who reads this book.

Other occasional sources are signalled in the text. One, for example, is Albrecht Rasche, to whom WGS also mentioned his idea that his grandfather and Marie's might have faced each other in the First World War (see p. 389 of this chapter). (Rasche to ROP, 21 November 2020, letter sent to me by ROP in an email of 23 November 2020.)

4 WGS to WS, 11 April 2001.

5 So Arthur Lubow understood from him, in their conversations of August 2001. Lubow did not include this in his published interview, but told me of it in our own interview of 19 April 2016. WGS spoke extensively of M to Lubow, some of which he did include (see Schwartz, pp. 164–5).

6 This was the notorious Second Battle of the Aisne, sometimes called the Battle of the Chemin des Dames. My brief summary of it, and the story of the *Drachenhöhle* that follows, are based on the accounts on the internet. Put 'Drachenhöhle Chemin des Dames' into your browser and they will come up in German, French and English.

WGS wanted to visit the *Drachenhöhle* with Marie, but couldn't find it. The plethora of information on the internet shows once again that he would surely have come to appreciate it if he'd lived.

7 WGS to WS, 22 June 2000.

21 TO *THE EMIGRANTS*

1 See e.g. Cuomo, Schwartz, p. 99. *The Head of Vitus Bering* had much to appeal to WGS – an experimental style and a dark vision of a mechanical universe. Konrad Bayer died by suicide at the age of thirty-two.

2 *AN*, p. 6. Grünewald hears the news of the terrible battle of Frankenheim on 18 May (*AN*, p. 34). KW also points out the use of 18 May and Windsheim as connecting threads in *AN* (*ÜS*, p. 160).

   WGS spoke of the coincidences that inspired *AN* and held it together to Cuomo in 2001 (Schwartz, p. 99). He already wrote about this at the time, to the photographer who provided images for the first edition, Thomas Beckermann (his letter of 6 September 1987, DLA). Also in his 1987 application to the DLF, very clearly: coincidence was the structural principle of his project, he said ('*Projektbeschreibung*' (Project Description), 1987 application, in *DA*, File 11 in the DLA). In other words, his use of coincidence as connection was conscious and deliberate from the start.

3 'Grünewald' also includes the word 'Wald', i.e. wood, which is a favourite of WGS's for his good characters: think of the loyal dog Waldemann in *Vertigo*, Luisa's love Fritz Waldhof in 'Ferber', and Maximilian Aychenwald (Oakwood), Jacques' father in *A*. Again, I'm sure that WGS the lover of trees did this quite consciously. It may be even more obsessive to note that the initials of the girl with whom Kafka had a brief encounter in Riva (explored in the third part of *V*) were G.W. (biographers soon identified her as Gerti Wasner).

4 Ralf Jeutter, in *ÜS*, p. 304. In his covering letter to his publisher about *AN*, WGS summarises its pessimistic message in his own voice. Together nature and mankind make a self-destructive system, he says, and the world would be better off without humans. (*AN* file, DLA.)

5 *V*, p. 230.

6 For the opening of 'All'estero' and the ending of 'Il Ritorno in patria', see RWS in *JES* 2009, pp. 83 and 97. RWS notes that the opening of Chapter II of *RS* echoes that of *Death in Venice* as well (p. 83). For Walser

see the interview with Piet de Moor, *SM*, p. 353, for Améry see Scott Bartsch in *ÜS*, p. 11. The bits of D. H. Lawrence come from 'The Return Journey' in *Twilight in Italy*, in which Lawrence recounts his similar journey across northern Italy in the key year for *Vertigo*, 1913; there are many photocopied pages of this remarkable essay in the *S.G.* files in the DLA. Edward Thomas's 'Adlestrop' is echoed on p. 259 ('no one ever embarked or alighted'). US (*Ein*, p. 81) points out the echo of Bernhard, and John Zilcosky the one about Hoffmann (in *W. G. Sebald: A Critical Companion*, ed. J. J. Long and Anne Whitehead, Edinburgh University Press. 2004, p. 108). The closeness of the Schlag-Romana scene to one in Weiss's *Coachman* is noted by many scholars, e.g. Peter Schmucker in *Grenzübertretungen: Intertextualität im Werk von W. G. Sebald*, De Gruyter, 2012, p. 73, Greg Bond in *W. G. Sebald: A Critical Companion*, p. 37, and US, *Ein*, p. 83.

7 In the interview with Piet de Moor, *SM*, p. 353.
8 Several critics draw attention to this borrowing from Kafka's 'In the Attic', e.g. Schmucker in *Grenzübertretungen*, p. 73ff and Daniel Medin, *Three Sons, Franz Kafka and the Fiction of J. M. Coetzee, Philip Roth, and W. G. Sebald*, Northwestern University Press, 2010, p. 121 and p. 141. It is in *Abandoned Fragments: Unedited Works 1897–1917* (Sun Vision Press, 2012). The original manuscript, '*Auf dem Dachboden*', is held in the Bodleian Library, Oxford.
9 E.g. Saul Friedlander in *Franz Kafka: the Poet of Shame and Guilt* (Yale University Press, 2013) argues carefully and calmly for the thesis of Kafka's homoerotic longings. (He agrees, however, with MA that it is highly improbable that Kafka ever put those longings into practice.) And e.g. Helen Finch in *Sebald's Bachelors* (Legenda, 2013) enlists both Kafka and WGS on the 'queer' side, though Daniel Medin argues that this is a misreading of Kafka's diaries and letters (Medin, *Three Sons*, p. 131).
10 See *V*, pp. 165–7.
11 As e.g. both Schmucker and Medin note. Medin says that 'In the Attic' was written shortly before 'The Hunter Gracchus', in a different notebook (*Three Sons*, p. 121).
12 The lines I quote are in my own translation. The original German lines are: '*Zwei andere Männer in dunklen Röcken mit Silberknöpfen trugen hinter dem Bootsmann eine Bahre, auf der unter einem großen blumengemusterten, gefransten Seidentuch offenbar ein Mensch lag.*'
13 *V*, pp. 246–7. The previous appearances – in almost the same words – occur on pp. 24–5 of 'Beyle', p. 125 of 'All'estero', and pp. 163–5 of 'Dr K.'.
   When Walser died on a walk on Christmas Day, 1956, his body was brought back to the asylum on a sledge (see *PC*, p. 127). WGS identified his grandfather with Walser in death as well as in life: when he thought

of his death, he said, he always saw him lying on Walser's sledge (see *PC*, p. 127). The parallel between this double image and that in Kafka's story of Gracchus made one of WGS's most inspiring coincidences.

Walser was as much WGS's model of the homeless wanderer as Kafka, if not more. And of Gracchus. Walser once said that one day everything in him would break, and then he would be dead: 'Not really dead, just dead in a certain way, then I'll live my life away like that for perhaps sixty years and so drift into death.' (Quoted in Idris Parry, *Speak Silence*, Carcanet, 1990, p. 129.)

14 See *V*, p. 167. Several critics point out that the line WGS renders as 'confined to bed in our sickness' has a slightly clearer implication in Kafka: '*Der Gedanke, mir helfen zu wollen, ist eine Krankheit und muß im Bett geheilt werden*': 'The idea of helping me is a sickness and must be cured in bed.' Critics also point out that 'Gracchus' means 'jackdaw', and that *kavka* in Czech also means jackdaw.

15 See Maya Jaggi, *Guardian*, 22 September 2001. He also said 'its main theme is love' to e.g. Ciro Krauthausen, in *Babelia*, 14 July 2001. He told M it was about love in two undated letters in March 2000.

16 *V*, p. 167.

17 See the interview with Piet de Moor, *SM*, p. 350.

18 See *V*, p. 27.

19 Quoted in the Wikipedia entry on *The Life of Henry Brulard*, https://en.wikipedia.org/wiki/The_Life_of_Henry_Brulard.

20 *V*, p. 21. This, however, is WGS's image. The plaster cast, which can be seen on that page, is indeed of Métilde's hand; but since it was made after her death in 1825, Stendhal, who never returned to Italy after that date, couldn't have had it on his desk. (I thank Marta Boneschi, author of *La donna segreta: Storia di Métilde Viscontini Dembowski*, Marsilio Editori, 2010, for this insight.) It's a classic WGS invention – collapsing time, bringing together the living and the dead.

21 Stendhal said that she '*m'a oté de mon imagination*' (took him out of his imagination) in his *Journals*, p. 720, and wrote '*qui je n'ai jamais aimée*' (whom I never loved) beside her initials in *De l'amour* (see *V*, p. 27).

22 *V*, p. 26.

22 *THE RINGS OF SATURN*

1 See Ruth Franklin's excellent essay 'Rings of Smoke', in Schwartz (p. 125). See also Renate Just, '*Im Zeichen des Saturn*', Loquai 1997, p. 38.

2 He says this about the bit of the heath on which he walked round in circles, but the picture is of the Somerleyton maze. The trees spreading

their circles are on p. 37, the swallows on p. 67, the mazes on pp. 38 and 171, with the picture on p. 173. The quotations are from pp. 173 and 171 respectively.

In *PC* WGS wrote repeatedly of the thoughts going round in writers' heads, including his own. And he said once to M that he dreamed of someone singing to him '*Meunier tu dors, ton moulin va trop fort*' ('Miller, you're sleeping/ Your mill-wheel turns too fast'); letter of 19 May 2000. '*Meunier tu dors*' is a traditional French children's song.

The trees with their circles exist. I've seen them – not in Somerleyton, but beside the A12 near Wrentham, in the park of Benacre Hall. I believe this is the house that WGS gives to George Wyndham Le Strange: he says it's in Henstead, but Henstead is inland, whereas Benacre Hall (as its name indicates) is near Benacre Broad, where WGS locates it (see *RS*, p. 59). It was a grand house belonging to the Gooch family for generations, but was sold in 2000 and converted into flats. (See https://en.wikipedia.org/wiki/Benacre_Hall).

3 *RS*, p. 26.

4 The three sisters sewing for their lives echo the three weavers at the end of *MF*, who in turn recall the Three Fates. They also recall Penelope in *The Odyssey*; and not least the Seamstress of Krems in the German children's song, who undoes every afternoon what she's done in the morning. WGS compared himself to her while writing this book. (Letter to KV, 5 June 1994.)

5 *RS*, p. 283.

6 *RS*, p. 286.

7 *RS*, p. 296. The English translation has the objects draped with 'black mourning ribbons', but the German original is '*mit seidenem Trauerflor*', with silk mourning ribbons. Apart from losing the silk connection, 'black mourning ribbons' is tautologous, since black is almost always the colour of mourning in the West. I'm not sure how WGS missed this change to his imagery.

8 The 'purple piece of silk in the urn of Patroclus' also contains a trace of the question of homosexuality, since Patroclus was the much-loved friend, and possibly lover, of Achilles.

9 See *RS*, p. 26.

10 In my interview with him of 27 April 1998. He told Renate Just 1,200 pages in her interview of 1995 (Loquai, p. 40).

11 There are nine *RS* files in the DLA. Files I and II contain fair copies, III contains source materials, IV–VI photographs, and VII–IX drafts. My account of the composition of *RS* is thus based on Files I, II, VII, VIII

and IX, the account of its sources on File III. The pages are all loose and (apart from the fair copies) unnumbered, so can't be specified further.

12 He told me this in our interview of 27 April 1998.

13 My notes record two such lists, but in the plethora of pages it's possible both that I counted the same one twice and that there were others I missed.

14 See Verena Lobsien in *JES* 2011. For foxing his translator, see e.g. Hulse to WGS, 5 November 1996, in which Hulse says that he has 'adopted many ways, including despair' to deal with WGS's use of Browne. He asks for WGS's sources, e.g. in letters of 5 April 1997 and 16 May 1997; WGS admits in his reply of 1 May 1997 that he made deliberate changes to Browne's lines and even invented many. (All in the Houghton Library, Harvard; all Hulse's also in the DLA.) WGS told me in our interview of 27 April 1998 that some of the quotes he attributed to Browne came from one of his favourites, the German Romantic writer Jean Paul (Johann Paul Friedrich Richter, 1783–1825).

15 For instance, the line about the swallows and their courses (p. 67) was at first looser, the lines about Kurt Waldheim less sharp (p. 99).

16 There is another similar example in the *RS* drafts, in which he mentioned Gatwick and the M25. He cut this too.

17 See its second essay, 'Into the Vault', especially the first part (*The Tremulous Private Body*, *Essays on Subjection*, Methuen, 1984, pp. 71–85). WGS told me in our interview of 27 April 1998 that he had based his *Anatomy Lesson* section on Barker's book.

18 In File III of the *RS* files, DLA. The real article was in the issue of Saturday 15 August 1992, rather than a Sunday one, as WGS wrote (*RS*, p. 96).

19 *RS*, p. 98.

20 Michael Hamburger to WGS, 28 July 1994 (DLA). In a letter to Bill Swainson during the translation of *RS*, WGS wrote that he would never have published the section on Michael Hamburger if he hadn't been assured of Hamburger's approval (WGS to Swainson, 21 July 1997, in the DLA).

21 Information from Anne Beresford from our meetings of 12 May 2004 and 23 September 2014 and our phone call of 13 October 2014, and in Jonathan Watts, 'Unreal Estate', in *Irish Pages*, Vol. 7, No. 1, p. 74.

22 See *RS*, p. 138.

23 From my conversations with Suzie Hanna, née Ellis, and her email to me of 31 January 2019.

24 This was established years ago by the scholar Adrian Daub, who got it from the *Eastern Daily Press* (*EDP*) librarian. See Adrian Daub, 'Donner à

Voir', in *Searching for Sebald: Photography after W. G. Sebald*, ed. Lise Patt with Christel Dillbohner, Institute of Cultural Enquiry, 2007.

25 From my conversations with Michael Brandon-Jones, 19 September 2014 and 22 February 2017.

26 In fact three other batteries, the 250th, 251st and 252nd, were part of the 63rd Anti-Tank Regiment which, as the (apparent) *EDP* article rightly notes, liberated Belsen. See https://www.google.com/search?q=british+r oyal+artillery+63rd+anti-tank+regiment&oq=63rd+anti-tank+regimen t&aqs=chrome.4.0j69i57j0l6.16604j0j8&sourceid=chrome&ie=UTF-8 ('63rd (Oxfordshire Yeomanry) Anti-Tank Regiment, Royal Artillery was a second line Territorial Army unit formed as duplicate of 53rd Anti-Tank Regiment. It had its HQ at Oxford and was made up of 249th Battery and 250th Battery at Oxford, 251st Battery and 252nd Battery at Banbury.') So the real Major Le Strange may conceivably have been in one of the other batteries. Since, as I go on to show, WGS invented his major, that would be a startling Sebaldian coincidence, rather than any proof of identity. I haven't, therefore, made the trek to Kew, but if anyone else would like to do it, I'd be intrigued to hear the result.

27 For Le Strange see *RS*, pp. 62–4. Aubrey describes Harvey as having an 'olivaster complexion' and 'dark black eye' – though in life rather than death. WGS changes Aubrey's description of Harvey – 'his haire was black as a raven, but quite white 20 yeares before he dyed'– into its opposite when Le Strange dies: 'his snow-white hair had turned to raven-black' (*RS*, p. 64). Was death a return to youth, perhaps? I wish I had asked him. (The quotations from Aubrey come from pp. 298–300 of the oldest edition of *Brief Lives* I could find, in honour of WGS: one published by the Clarendon Press in 1898.) WGS was alerted to Aubrey by his friend WS, who translated *Brief Lives* into German.

When I began looking into the *EDP* clipping I came across someone who thought she remembered the story. Perhaps that was the original article that WGS claimed to have read.

28 He confirmed this in a letter of 8 May 1998, after I'd sent him some follow-up questions.

29 *RS*, p. 221.

30 See *V*, p. 241 and *RS*, p. 251.

31 WS to WGS, 7 October (no year given, but clearly 1995). The later question from WS is from the same letter.

32 In my interview with WGS of 27 April 1998. I'd read (in his interview with Krause, Hoffmann, p. 135) that he'd visited a remote house in Northern Ireland around the mid-1980s, and (somewhere I no longer recall) that

at one stage he'd been an external examiner in Ireland. Either of these, I thought, might have been the occasion. But once he'd said no, the question was closed.

33 For the narrator's invitation see *RS*, p. 220, for Chateaubriand's, pp. 252–4.
34 *RS*, p. 253.

23 *AUSTERLITZ*

1 The British prizes were the 2002 Independent Foreign Fiction Prize and the 2002 Jewish Quarterly-Wingate Literary Prize, the US ones the 2001 National Book Critics Circle Award for fiction and the 2001 Salon Book Award. Anthea Bell won the Schlegel-Tieck Prize in the UK and the Helen and Kurt Wolff Translator's Prize in the US, both for 2002. See https://en. wikipedia.org/wiki/Austerlitz(novel) and https://en.wikipedia.org/wiki/ Anthea_Bell#Notable_awards. The Wikipedia.de entry lists all these, but no prizes in Germany. WGS was still not as lauded at home as abroad.

2 *A*, pp. 133–4.

3 Austerlitz is compared to Wittgenstein on pp. 55–6, and Wittgenstein's eyes (along with JPT's) open the book (p. 3). The Kafka references are on p. 250 (the 'messengers' who bring the orders to Agáta for deportation wear the sinister clothes of the messengers to K. in *The Trial*) and on p. 289 (in Marienbad in 1938 Austerlitz's family stays in a boarding house behind the Palace Hotel, as Kafka had done with Felice). Casanova appears on p. 284.

4 The white mist is on p. 86–7, in Gwendolyn's death room, on p. 192, in the church at Salle, and on p. 305, just before Austerlitz and Marie see the little troupe of the dead (see *RS*, p. 17 on the white mist that according to Browne emanates from dead bodies; and perhaps the original of all these mists, the white cloud of incense in Josef's grandfather's room after his death, in the early novel, p 30 of Version 1, p. 64 of Version 2).

For the white tents see p. 166, and the Israelites' camp in the desert in Austerlitz's Welsh children's Bible, which he knows to be his proper place (p. 77, picture on pp. 78–9). These white tents are later taken over by the Germans, who see themselves as the new chosen people (pp. 239–40, also p. 248. This later scene comes from Leni Riefenstahl's Nazi film *Triumph of the Will*). WGS had always been fascinated by tents, he told KV (letter of 19 January 1996); this may even go back to the little 'tents' he built under the kitchen table in Wertach when he was two or three. The first white ones probably go back to his favourite painting, the *Alexanderschlacht*.

The imagery of twins is on pp. 76, 298 and 316–17, all evidently representing Austerlitz's lost real self. This goes back to the Kafka twins, Balduin and his doppelganger, and Babette and Bina in *V*. The caravan is on p. 159. The troupes of the dead (on pp. 75 and 305) wear grey cloaks and 'raincoats of thin blue–grey Perlon'; and the archive staff in Prague and hotel staff in Marienbad (both places where Austerlitz's dead come nearer) wear long grey coats (pp. 293, 297). For Kafka and his long coat see Chapter 5, pp. 73–4.

For the images particular to *A*: Gerald's pigeons are on pp. 109–10 and 160–1. The horror of the pigeon loft on pp. 301–2 no doubt comes from his love – and Austerlitz's, and the author's – for these creatures, with their mysterious ability to find their way home no matter how far away they are. For the parallel between Austerlitz's moths and Luisa Lanzberg's stag beetles, see *A*, p. 130 and *MF*, p. 207. For Austerlitz's belief that they come from the Jewish cemetery, see p. 408. See also p. 233, where the narrator finds the remains of a moth in a jar on Austerlitz's mantelpiece: it shows no sign of decay, and seems made of 'some immaterial fabric'. That is, it has crossed the veil between life and death, and become like that veil itself: an image, surely, of the immortal soul. (Like the purple silk in *Saturn*: see Chapter 22 above, p. 404.) Austerlitz's question about the squirrels in the snow is on p. 287. Evan the cobbler's veil is on pp. 75–6, Colonel Chabert on pp. 393–4. '*Max Stern 18.5.44*' is on the last page (415). When he wrote *A*, WGS knew that Peter Jordan's parents had died in Kaunas. (Information from the Jordans.) The photograph with its reflection is on p. 276. WGS took all the Terezín photos; and RWS confirms that the part-reflected face is WGS's.

5 E.g. on pp. 216, 220, 226 and increasingly throughout the Prague section.
6 See *A*, p. 281 and pp. 252–3 respectively. Also e.g on Austerlitz's return journey, which repeats the one he made as a child, so that he no longer knows what period of his life he is in (*A*, p. 318).
7 Quoted by Sarah Emily Miano in 'Hands in Pockets', *Grand Street*, No. 72, p. 166.
8 Thesis put together from Austerlitz's three disquisitions on time, on pp. 141–44, 261 and 359–60. The last occasion is in a bar near the Glacière Métro station in Paris, where he is looking for his father, and it is surely no accident that the spot is marked by a glacier.
9 *A*, p. 304.
10 See *A*, p. 153.
11 See *A*, pp. 17–23.
12 *A*, pp. 19–20. That Breendonk, Terezín and Kaunas were all useless fortresses (see the following paragraph) is true. An official pamphlet about Terezín says: 'The interesting thing about this former fortress is that though at the time it was ingeniously built as an unconquerable defence system it was never used for military purposes. Already in the nineteenth

century the whole fortress complex showed itself to be quite senseless'
(p. 118). It became a barracks and then a town, from which the residents
were removed in 1942 to make room for the concentration camp.

13   As Austerlitz says: see *A*, p. 144. The images that follow are on pp. 15–16
and 276. It is in the photograph of the rescue that Austerlitz/WGS's face
is reflected. Perhaps this could be added to the hints of optimism at the
end, when Austerlitz goes off in search of his father and of Marie.

14   The Lake Vyrnwy Visitor Centre is full of information about Llanwddyn's
sad history. This paragraph draws on several of the pamphlets on sale
there: *Llanwddyn and Lake Vyrnwy* and *The Policeman's Story*, both by
David W. L. Rowlands, and *Lake Vyrnwy*, produced by Severn Trent
Water. The postcard of 'A street in Llanwddyn, now submerged' comes
from *24 Picture Postcards of Old Llanwyddyn and the Building of the Vyrnwy
Dam*, also from the museum. It contains the picture on p. 72 of *A* as well.
(I wonder what WGS would have made of the curiously leaning tree in
the postcard here, if he saw it: a presage of the fate awaiting the village?)

15   *A*, p. 34.

16   *A*, p. 36. The story of Gastone Novelli is on pp. 34–6. There are regular
references to Novelli and his works throughout *Le Jardin des Plantes*. The
story of his torture and its sequels as repeated by WGS is on pp. 19–20,
120, 235–6 and 243–5.

Curiously, there was a long interview with Novelli in the *FSZ* in 1964
(No. 4, June 1964, p. 5). WGS very likely saw this interview, and possibly
even the exhibition in Freiburg that occasioned it, so he may well have
recognised Novelli's name when he came across his story in Claude Simon.

17   The information about Novelli's real torture location and career
comes from Italian Wikipedia, https://it.wikipedia.org/wiki/Gastone_
Novelli_(artista).

Terry Pitts says on his Vertigo website that Simon prints Novelli's As
in a block, while WGS draws them out into long lines, thus introducing
the sense of a scream himself. That is true on pages 27 and 85–6, but not
on p. 245, where they are exactly as WGS reproduces them (even to the
number of As, which is thirty-one), and where Simon himself says that
they are '*ondulant comme un cri*'.

See 'Sebald, Simon, Novelli and the Long–Drawn–Out Scream', of 9 April
2011. https://sebald.wordpress.com/2011/04/09/sebald-simon-novelli-
and-the-long-drawn-out-scream/. For a Novelli work that features long
lines of As, see http://www.guggenheim-venice.it/inglese/collections/
artisti/dettagli/pop_up_opera2.php?id_opera=706&page=.

Like WGS himself, I accidentally came across another possible connection: that 'Schumann heard a persistent A-note at the end of his life' (https://en.wikipedia.org/wiki/Robert_Schumann). *A* doesn't mention this, and WGS may not have known it. But it's one of his coincidences.

18 Tereza Ambrosová, the archivist in Prague. When Sebald tried out names for her, they all began with A – Ambrosová, Asdimanová and Ajšman. He tried them out on a letter from Monika Loderová of the Goethe Institute, Prague, who helped him with his Czech research (in *A* File 14 in the DLA). Note that 'Ajšman' is a version of 'Ashman'.

19 See Gabriella Poli and Giorgio Calcagno, *Echoes of a Lost Voice: Encounters with Primo Levi*, Vallentine Mitchell, 2018, p. 140.

20 Cuomo interview, in Schwartz, p. 110. WGS gives one of his fullest answers here, and in the interview with Steve Wasserman (*SM*, p. 372) and *Der Spiegel* ('*Ich fürchte das Melodramatische*', *Spiegel* 11/2001, in Hoffmann, pp. 196–7). He also talked about his model or models to Maya Jaggi (*Guardian*, 22 September 2001), Christopher Bigsby (p. 162), Julia Kospach (*Profil*, 19 February 2001), Jean-Pierre Rondas (in Hoffmann, p. 212) and Sebastian Shakespeare (*Literary Review*, October 2001, p. 50). The first reference I found was in a summary to his publishers, in which he mentions only one model, whom he doesn't identify. (In his *A* papers in the DLA.)

The occasion on which he mentioned three and a half models was in his St Jerome lecture in October 2001. This was told me by Stephen Watts, whose reaction I go on to describe.

21 From our interview of 16 October 2014. Peter Jonas information from himself, as discussed in Chapter 14. WGS cited Friedländer and Leverton as sources to Wasserman, *SM*, p. 172.

22 The information about Susi Bechhöfer comes largely from Susi herself: from my email exchanges with her in 2011 and my meeting with her on 28 July 2011; her article 'Stripped of my tragic past by a bestselling author', *Sunday Times*, 30 June 2002; and her books *Rosa's Child* (with Jeremy Josephs), 1996 and *Rosa*, 2017. Other sources will be signalled in the text.

23 This is Susi's account, given to me in our 2011 meeting, and also e.g. to the journalist Hugo Duncan in 2002. See his article in the Liverpool *Daily Post* of 8 August 2002: http://www.thefreelibrary.com/Susi%3A+P ay+a+final+debt+to+my+past%3B+It+wasn't+until+she+was+50+that...-a090233192. WGS doesn't say explicitly that she was a model in any of his letters found in her papers (see Note 25, below), but it's implied, and he said it clearly to e.g. the *Spiegel* (Hoffmann, p. 197), Steve Wasserman (*SM*, p. 372) and Maya Jaggi (*Guardian*, 22 September 2001).

24 'Stripped of my tragic past by a bestselling author', *Sunday Times*, 30 June 2002.

25 WGS to Susi Bechhöfer, 30 September 2001. She evidently still sent a friendly reply, enclosing a CD of her son's *Lament for Bosnia* (her son Frederick Stocken is a composer). On 27 October 2001 WGS continued to fend her off, repeating the theme of his burdens. Three letters from WGS to Susi (from 27 September 2001, 30 September 2001 and 27 October 2001) are in the possession of Frederick Stocken, who kindly sent me copies. I sincerely thank him for this and for all his help.

26 Information from Janne Weinzierl, in our conversation of 11 January 2019. She heard of Susi's upset from Brigitte Schmidt of the City Archives in Munich, who had helped Susi with her research for *Rosa's Child* (Janne's email to me, 28 January 2019). Janne spoke to WGS about it at his reading in Munich of 5 April 2001. Janne is a Munich city councillor and a member of the *Stolpersteine* initiative. I thank her sincerely for all her help.

27 Janet Malcolm, *The Silent Woman*, Picador, 1994, p. 8.

28 Maya Jaggi, *Guardian*, 22 September 2001. WGS made the point himself in this interview that he had not used the most private events of Susi's life.

29 See Elizabeth Baer, 'W. G. Sebald's *Austerlitz*: Re-mediation as Restitution', in *Reworking the German Past: Adaptations in Film, the Arts and Popular Culture*, ed. Susan Figge and Jenifer Ward, Boydell & Brewer, 2010, pp. 181–99. I thank Elizabeth for our stimulating conversations.

30 *Spiegel* interview, Hoffmann, p. 198.

31 Martin Modlinger, 'You can't change names and feel the same: the Kindertransport experience of Susi Bechhöfer in W. G. Sebald's *Austerlitz*', in *Yearbook of the Research Centre for German and Austrian Exile Studies*, 2012, Vol. 13, pp. 219–32.

   Other scholars who have entered this fray are e.g. Rebekkah Göpfert, '*Susi Bechhöfer Fragt Zurück*' (Susi Bechhöfer Asks Back'), *Frankfurter Rundschau*, 15 March 2003, and Stephen Clingman, *The Grammar of Identity: Transnational Fiction and the Nature of the Boundary*, Oxford University Press, 2009.

32 Susi Bechhöfer, email to me, 13 July 2011.

33 'Susi Bechhöfer: Finding her own history' by Jenni Frazer, *Jewish Chronicle*, 21 August 2017, https://www.thejc.com/susi-bechhofer-1.443118.

34 Frederick Stocken, email to me, 9 June 2018. Frederick also told me that writing *Rosa* consoled his mother.

35 WGS never names the place of Agáta's death, writing only that she was 'sent east' from Terezín in September 1944 (*A*, p. 287). People were sent

to many of the extermination camps from Terezín, but Auschwitz was the main destination.

36 Following information from Janne Weinzierl, email to me, 28 January 2019. The orphanage on Antonienstrasse is commemorated by a stela showing two of the girls at a window: Judith Hirsch, now Judith Rosenberg and living in Montreal, Canada, and Merry Gaber, who was on the last transport from the orphanage, together with Rosa Bechhöfer, and died in Auschwitz. The carers, who also died, were Alice Bendix and Hedwig Jakobi. (Janne's email of 17 February 2019.)

37 The idea for *Stolpersteine* came from the artist Gunter Demnig in 1992. They are made in brass and set in the pavement outside the last homes of victims of the Nazi extermination programmes – mostly Jews, but also Roma and others. By December 2019, 75,000 Stolpersteine had been laid in Germany and the Nazi-occupied countries. The city council of Munich has so far voted against *Stolpersteine*, partly due to the opposition of the head of the Jewish community, who objects to the memorials being placed where people can step on them. But by 2020 about a hundred *Stolpersteine* had been installed on private property in Munich, including those to Susi, Lotte and Rosa Bechhöfer. See https://en.wikipedia.org/wiki/Stolperstein.

A stele (standing memorial) has been erected for Peter Jordan's parents, Paula and Fritz, outside the block of flats they lived in, at Mauerkircherstrasse 13, in Bogenhausen, Munich. See: http://www.nordostkultur-muenchen.de/architektur/mauerkircherstraße_13. Thomas Mann and his family lived there 1910–14, the Jordans 1925–40. Paula and Fritz Jordan's Stolpersteine are currently in the Museum für deutsche Geschichte (Museum of German History) in Bonn. (Information from the Jordans and Janne Weinzierl.)

38 See the *Spiegel* interview in Hoffmann, pp. 196–7, and interviews with Wasserman in *SM* (p. 372), Cuomo in Schwartz (pp. 110–11), Jean-Pierre Rondas in Hoffmann (p. 212). WGS also mentioned this model to Maya Jaggi.

39 Information from WGS's colleague Richard Cocke (our meeting of 16 December 2013). RWS certainly thought so, at least 'to a very great extent' (RWS email to me, 29 or 30 July 2016).

40 From our meetings, 4 March 2014 and 19 September 2014; also e.g. to Sarah Cocke, wife of his colleague Richard Cocke, laughing heartily when she told him that I had guessed someone else (Sarah Cocke email to me, 8 February 2014).

Information about Stefan Muthesius and his family here and later from my meeting with him, 4 March 2014, and with him and his wife, the art historian Katarzyna (Kasia) Murawska-Muthesius, 19 September 2014. Also our email exchanges of 2014 and 2015. I thank both Stefan and Kasia most sincerely for their help.

41 See Cuomo, Schwartz, p. 96.

42 See *Deutsche Biographie* on Hermann Muthesius, https://www.deutsche-biographie.de/gnd118585983.html#ndbcontent. This lists Stefan as his great-nephew ('Gr-N → Stefan (*1939), Dr., Kunsthistoriker in Norwich (Norfolk)').

43 Information from the *Deutsche Biographie* entry on Hans Muthesius, https://www.deutsche-biographie.de/pnd118735403.html#ndbcontent. Ernst Klee's article appeared in *Die Zeit*, 14 September 1990. See *Die Zeit* online, http://www.zeit.de/1990/38/idee-ein-kz/seite-1. Its statistics differ slightly from the *Deutsche Biographie* ones, probably because his were the first researches. I've followed the current *Deutsche Biographie* numbers, as they are likely to be more accurate. Klee published a book uniting all his researches in 2003 (Fischer, 2003): *Das Personenlexikon zum Dritten Reich. Wer war was vor und nach 1945?* (*Who's Who of the Third Reich: Who was what before and after 1945*).

44 Kasia Murawska-Muthesius to me in a phone conversation, 19 February 2015.

45 *A*, pp. 106 and 258 respectively. Vera dates the childhood photo and explains its background on p. 259.

46 To the *Spiegel* (Hoffmann, p. 198), to Maya Jaggi and to Maria Alvarez.

47 See Wood's Introduction to the 2011 edition of *A*, p. xxi.

48 See also Patrick Hanks, ed., *Dictionary of American Family Names*, Oxford University Press, 2003, p. 86: 'habitational name from a minor place in the parish of Rochdale, Lancashire', first recorded in Rochdale in 1541 and deriving from *grene* (green) and *rod* (a clearing). See https://books.google.co.uk/books?id=FJoDDAAAQBAJ&pg=RA1-PA86&redir_esc=y#v=onepage&q&f=false. There is similar information on the website SurnameDB: http://www.surnamedb.com/Surname/Grindrod#ixzz3Q4K1WuaD. In the UK Registry I found ten Jack Grindrods born in Lancashire, of whom four lived in Rochdale, between 1900 and 1937; and fourteen Johns, five in Rochdale, born between 1904 and 1924.

49 Because the photographer credited, Allen Nield Successors, operated from 1923 to 1938. (I made a note of this, unfortunately without a reference, and cannot now re-find the source.) The card locates Nield Successors in Salford, which is why I guess that that is where WGS found it.

50 See e.g. his interview with Susan Sontag in *JES* 2014, p. 397, and the one with Kenneth Baker, 'Up against historical amnesia', in the *San Francisco Chronicle*, 7 October 2001.

51 This paragraph is drawn from *A*, pp. 218, 226 and 228–9. For Hoffmann's *Sandman*, see e.g. Penguin Classics No. 108, *The Sandman* by E. T. A. Hoffmann, translated by Peter Wortsman (2016). For its earlier appearance, see Chapter 21, p. 398. I was referring there to the scene in *V*, p. 250, in which the narrator remembers plunging his hand into a barrel and encountering not eggs, as he expects, but gouged-out eyes. The Sandman in Hoffmann's Gothic fable steals children's eyes.

52 The information that follows comes from Erich Reich and Jacques, now Rich, in phone calls and emails in the first week of March 2020. Oswald, the middle brother, died of cancer at only twenty-seven. Jacques and Erich are now ninety-three and eighty-six. Jacques has lived in Australia since 1950; he was a successful businessman, quite unlike Austerlitz. Erich, who remained in England, was also a successful entrepreneur and a charity fundraiser. Now Sir Erich, he is head of the Kindertransport section of the Association of Jewish Refugees. He published a memoir, *The Boy in the Statue*, in 2017 (i2i Publishing).

Between them the three brothers have produced a total of fifteen children and (so far) twenty-nine grandchildren and seventeen great-grandchildren, in a fine response to the Nazis' attempt to wipe out their family.

24 AN ATTEMPT AT RESTITUTION

1 WGS much admired the paintings of Anita Albus. About this painting he wrote that the reflection of the house being spared from the flames expresses 'the wish that in art things may be restored to what they were before their destruction'. ('*Kleine Vorrede zur Salzburger Ausstellung*', Introduction to the catalogue of an Anita Albus exhibition, Salzburg, 1990, ed. Tugomir Luksic.)

2 See https://www.wwnorton.co.uk/books/9780811226141-the-emigrants. The whole paragraph reads: 'W.G. Sebald has written an astonishing masterpiece: it seems perfect while being unlike any book one has ever read. Bewitching in its subtlety, sublime in its directness and in the grandeur of its subject. *The Emigrants* is an irresistible book.' It is in a list of extracts from laudatory reviews, including e.g. from Cynthia Ozick, Robert Eder and James Wood.

3 See e.g. Piet de Moor, *SM*, p. 352, Bigsby, p. 159, Cuomo in Schwartz pp. 115–16, Lubow in Schwartz, p. 165.

4 From Cuomo in Schwartz, p. 115. As we've seen, this sense of the 'imponderables that govern our life' is also Joseph Cuomo's main idea of WGS. (See Chapter 19, p. 376 above.) Michael Hamburger too noted his 'almost occult, transcendental or even chiliastic proclivities' ('Translator's Note', *U*, p. 8), and Andrew Motion said (in our interview of 12 September 2014), 'Everything to do with Max accelerates away from reality to a mythical structure.'

5 *RS*, p. 18.

6 See *RS*, pp. 179–80. Apart from the fantasy at the end, this is, significantly, the one thing WGS added to Hamburger's story; the rest comes from Hamburger's autobiography, *String of Beginnings*. (Anne Beresford confirmed this to Jonathan Watts, in *Irish Pages*, Vol. 7 No. 1, 'Unreal Estate', pp. 67–77, on p. 75.)

7 *A*, pp. 144 and 261. WGS reprises these thoughts on time on pp. 359–60, where he writes the line I have quoted before, that we may 'also have appointments to keep in the past … and must go there in search of places and people who have some connection with us on the far side of time' (p. 360).

8 See *PC*, p. 128.

9 *RS*, p. 190.

10 The original German is '*Wirbel sind sie, in die hinabzusehen mich schwindelt*'. Austerlitz's loss of language and the ability to write at the height of his breakdown (see *A*, pp. 172–6) is a clear echo of Hofmannsthal's Lord Chandos, as many critics point out. Chandos's own identification across time is with the Roman orator Crassus, who wept over the death of a fish. Perhaps WGS's choice of herrings as a main focus of compassion in *RS* comes at least partly from this.

11 This and the other lines on this page and the next from *The Letter of Lord Chandos*, translated by Tania and James Stern, http://www.jubilat.org/jubilat/archive/vol11/poem_10/.

12 From my interview with Clive Scott, 24 September 2014.

13 In his essay on Walser in *PC*, p. 149.

14 See Luke Williams, 'A Watch on Each Wrist', *SM*, p. 150.

15 *A*, pp. 131–2. Adela's line on the caravan in the dunes is from pp. 158–9. The image of the desert caravan, which began in *MF*, ends when Vera calls the line of Prague's Jews ordered to gather for deportation a caravan (p. 252). Thus the journey of the Chosen People to the Promised Land ends in Terezín and Auschwitz.

16 As he said in a letter to Peter Jordan, 14 September 2001.

17 One person who got fed up with WGS's gloom, for instance, was the writer Jenny Diski. In a review of *V* she wrote: 'After a while this super-sensitised melancholy becomes comic. One's patience is tried as it is with

those tormented heroes of Dostoevsky, if you read them after adolescence. For God's sake, Raskolnikov, get a hold on yourself, pull yourself together.' (*London Reviews of Books*, 3 February 2000.) Nonetheless, Diski ended her review positively.

18 See e.g. his interview with Michael Zeeman, '*Kamer mit Uitsicht*', VPRO Nederlands, 12 July 1998, transcribed by Gordon Taylor, in Denham and McCulloh, *W. G. Sebald: History – Memory – Trauma*, De Gruyter, 2006, pp. 21–9. This interview was played on a loop in the *RS* exhibition in the Norwich Castle Gallery, 2019.

19 Both food again, as in Elaine's trolley and the Teasmade… It's strange that Sebald's humour should break out over food, which is otherwise a locus of unease and fear for him, like our other appetites (e.g. the old woman devouring a piece of meat in *Vertigo*, and the narrator's inability ever to choose a restaurant). But then one of the functions of laughter is to defuse fear.

20 His mother and sisters knew, of course. Also close friends, from M, UL and JK to KV and Tess Jaray, and close colleagues like RWS, Jean Boase-Beier and Ralf Jeutter.

21 In 'being talked about' I'm thinking of the bizarre episode of his ducking beneath the bookshop counter when M said his name, and e.g. of his complaining to Karl-Heinz Schmelzer that his parents told people in Sonthofen his news (letter of 12 December 1996). M and GAS both remember that he was always afraid of being recognised in Sonthofen, another reason why he disliked being there.

   Jon Cook was another friend aware of WGS's extreme sensitivity, both psychological and sensory, e.g. his noise phobia. (Our interview of 26 September 2014.)

22 This and the following information from my conversations with M and from WGS's letters to her of 23 April 2000 and 17 January 2000.

23 What his mother said, according to GAS, was that he 'looked like a skinned rabbit'. He told Renate Just in 1995 ('*Im Zeichen des Saturn*', *Die Zeit Magazin*, 13 October 1995, Loquai 1997, p. 40) that he didn't know where his being so thin-skinned came from. See also his interview with Annette de Jong, 'W. G. Sebald over joden, Duitsers en migranten', in *NRC Handelsblad*, 2 July 1993: 'I experience memories so intensely that I can no longer separate the past and the present. It is abnormal to have such an aptitude, it prevents you from participating in life.'

   As GAS put it in an email to me of 8 June 2017: '*Je crois que mon frère souffrait beaucoup ou souvent. Tout le touchait, les petites et les grandes souffrances*' (I think that my brother suffered a great deal or often. Everything touched him, both large and small sufferings).

24 See https://en.wikipedia.org/wiki/Mirror-touch_synesthesia.

25 *RS*, page 235. The episode of the dead deer is in *CS*, p. 43.

26 Stanley Cohen, *States of Denial: Knowing About Atrocities and Suffering*, Polity Press, 2001. I thank Jean Boase-Beier for introducing me to this classic book. Many people have described this special sensitivity in artists. About Kafka, for instance, Elias Canetti wrote that most people notice life's horror only rarely, 'but a few whom inner forces appoint to bear witness are always conscious of it' (*Kafka's Other Trial: The Letters to Felice*, Penguin Classics, 2012). And Milena Jesenská, Kafka's love after Felice, put it clearly: 'We all seem able to live because we have at one time or another taken refuge in a lie, in blindness, enthusiasm, or optimism, in a belief, in pessimism, or whatever. But he has never fled to a protective refuge, nowhere … He has no refuge, no home. That is why he is exposed to everything from which we are protected. He is like a naked man.' (Quoted in Jeremy Adler, *Franz Kafka*, Penguin Illustrated Lives, 2001, p. 122.)

27 For MA, see e.g. '*Wo die Schrecken der Kindheit verbogen sind: W. G. Sebalds Dilemma der zwei Väter*', *Literaturen* 7/8, 2006; US *passim*, on the death of WGS's grandfather; RWS in *D-S*, pp. 432, 434. WGS himself spoke of childhood traumas to M, e.g in his letters of 2 April 2000 and 18 July 2000.

28 His narrator says this of himself in *RS*, in a passage that Philippa Comber picks out as revelatory: 'I wonder now whether inner coldness and desolation may not be the pre-condition for making the world believe, by a kind of fraudulent showmanship, that one's own wretched heart is still aglow' (p. 86). This takes us back to his first piece of published prose at Freiburg, '*Jeden Abend*'. (See Chapter 10.) In his copy of the *Chandos-Brief*, RWS tells us, he circled the words *Leere*, emptiness, and *Starre*, frozenness (*D-S*, Note 14, p. 453).

29 From WGS's essay on Gerhard Roth's *Landlaufiger Tod*, quoted by US in *SM*, p. 173.

30 *CS*, p. 215.

31 From his wonderful letter to Peter Jordan of 22 February 1987, which I only wish I could quote fully in his own words.

25 UNRECOUNTED

1 My translation.

2 From RWS's Chronology, p. 650 and US, *F*, Note 7. The rest is JPT's account in his interview with Thomas Honickel.

   US says that WGS wrote the micropoems before, during and after *A* (*F*, p. 112), and Michael Brandon-Jones recalls that some of the images for

U had already been prepared by late 1997 (our interview of 19 September 2014). Very likely the ideas went back and forth, with the final decision being made – at least in JPT's mind – in that September 2000 visit. US also places it there (*F*, Note 7).

Eyes and sight are constant themes in WGS's own work, as many critics have noticed. (See e.g. Andrea Kohler in *U*, pp. 96–7.)

3   WGS told this to M in his letter of 27 June 2001. US points out that thirty-three was a number JPT often used in his own work (*F*, Note 7). That Max had already sent JPT several poems comes from JPT's interview with Honickel. That WGS turned increasingly to the micropoems from 2000 comes from US, *F*, p. 128. JPT spoke of having to make the decisions alone to Honickel, and US notes it in *F*, p. 113.

4   That WGS wrote his own English versions of the mini-poems in *FYN* comes from Michael Hamburger's 'Translator's Note', p. 2 of *U*, and US, *F*, p. 112. Some of the *FYN* poems were WGS's translations from his German originals; some (according to US) he may have written in English, since there are no existing German versions. The point that Tess had one unused poem and JPT eleven comes from Hamburger's 'Translator's Note', pp. 4–5. The total of forty-one comes from *F*, p. 113. The twelve unpublished micropoems are in the DLA (*F*, p. 113).

5   *U* was not often reviewed, and then mostly unfavourably: US quotes e.g. J. M. Coetzee ('A work of no great ambition', *F*, Note 13), and *Village Voice* in the US ('an elliptical, ultimately unsatisfying curtain call', *F*, Note 30). *FYN* was not reviewed at all (*F*, p. 111). It was difficult to get these tiny poems to be taken seriously, as US remarks (*F*, p. 113). He himself is critical of *U*, though more of the 'static' combination of texts and images than of the poems themselves. He is much more enthusiastic about *FYN*. (See e.g. *F*, pp. 137–8.)

Typically, perhaps, WGS seems to have told neither of his artist friends that he was giving poems to the other – in thirteen cases, the same poems. Tess told US that she didn't know of JPT's role (*F*, p. 113), and Michael Hamburger thought JPT didn't know of hers either. WGS could compartmentalise his friends, Michael said (phone call, 8 July 2004).

6   Michael Hamburger told me that WGS was 'very disparaging' about the mini-poems (phone call, 8 July 2004). Of course he was always disparaging, and genuinely doubtful, about his work.

7   Michael Hamburger points this out (*U*, p. 7). He also suggests that the shadow hanging over the micropoems 'could have been that of death, his knowledge, kept to himself outside those poems, of a threatening illness' ('Translator's Note' to WGS's 'Marienbad Elegy', *Irish Pages*, Vol. 1, No. 2,

Autumn/Winter 2002/3, p. 130). US agrees that 'death is very prominent' in the mini-poems (*F*, p. 132).

8   He said this to Tess, who told both US (*F*, pp. 144–5) and me. It was still his grandfather's coffin in *FYN*. See *FYN*, p. 42 and *U*, p. 69.

9   US points out borrowings from Paracelsus, Merleau-Ponty, the Bible and other more obscure sources. He says that between a third and a half of the lines are drawn from elsewhere (*F*, pp. 114–15). M told me of another source, the French poet Jean de la Ville de Mirmont, whom WGS encountered through her.

WGS excavated many of his own earlier poems for *AN*, as we know, and he does the same here. A prime example is the opening lines of 'Poetry for an Album', written in the 1980s, which become a free-standing micropoem in both *U* and *FYN*. (Intriguingly, WGS made small changes each time. See *ALW*, p. 81, *U*, p. 23, and *FYN*, p. 48.)

10   *U*, p. 1.

11   'As Day and Night, Chalk and Cheese: On the Pictures of Jan Peter Tripp', in *U*, pp. 86 and 88.

12   *U*, p. 51. The final passage of 'As Day and Night', about the dog's eyes, is on p. 94. The JPT painting referred to is on p. 92, and on p. 171 of *PC*.

13   *U*, *p*. 75.

14   See e.g. Maya Jaggi, *Guardian*, 22 September 2001. Information about WGS's ideas for escape routes from UL (Ireland and France), BFS (Alsace) and GAS (Fribourg).

15   This and sitting down in the corridor from Jon Cook, our interview of 26 September 2014; taking the lift to go down just two floors from Sarah Emily Miano, 'Hands in Pockets', *Grand Street* 72, Fall 2003, p. 167. The rest from UL.

16   One of the UEA German-department students thought she remembered GT saying that WGS had gone to a hospital, but he says now he doesn't know. The information about the close friend comes from RWS, *D-S*, p. 438: 'Someone who knew him particularly well suspected that he realised there was something seriously wrong with his heart but chose not to speak about it or seek treatment.' BFS information from herself.

17   The first sign was noted in Chapter 19, p. 366. Both Hamburgers told me the second in one of our early conversations, on 12 May 2004. Michael Hamburger also saw signs in the late micropoems of a 'knowledge, kept to himself outside those poems, of a threatening illness', as I've noted.

WGS's will, like all probated wills in the UK, is publicly available. See https://www.gov.uk/search-will-probate. It notes that he left £823,124 net. That he loved St Andrew's churchyard from GT. That he left instructions for the management of his literary estate from my meeting with Andrew Wylie, 10 November 2003. That he left instructions for his funeral from my interviews with e.g. the Hamburgers, Tess Jaray, Sally Humpston (i.e. WGS told Beryl). Michael Hamburger also noted this, and the instructions about his works and papers, in *Irish Pages*, p. 131.

18 These were a very serious one, with Solveig in the car, in 1982, and the one listening to Stephen Watts' poem in 1983. The one with Solveig happened much like the last, when WGS turned onto the main A46 road. Solveig told me that they were both sick with shock after it; WGS told Philippa Comber that he'd escaped with his life by seconds (*Ariadne's Thread*, Propolis, 2014, pp. 88–9).

19 See *ALW* p. 106: 'On the journey home/ fantasies of a fatal accident'.

20 The only part of this draft he kept was a passage about Leonardo's burnished green, which he used in the description of Anne's forest (p. 190). Originally the narrator saw a hill of this colour in the distance, which reminded him of a similar hill he'd once seen, driving on the M25 near Gatwick: he'd gazed so raptly at it that he nearly drove off the road. (*RS* files, DLA.)

21 Those who knew what a distracted driver he was include GAS, BFS, M, UL and JK, GT and RWS, the Jordans, Beryl Ranwell, Adam Czerniawski and Ria Loohuizen, to mention only a few. WGS knew it himself: '*Ich bin ein sehr erratischer Autofahrer,*' (I'm a very erratic driver) he told Renate Just in 1990 (*Süddeutsche Zeitung Magazin* No. 40, 5 October 1990, Loquai 1997, p. 30).

   Those who thought he'd lost concentration include GT, RWS and Ria, who told me so in our interviews; also e.g. WGS's student Sarah Emily Miano (see her *Grand Street* essay, p. 166).

   Those whose first thought was suicide also told me so in our interviews. The exception is Walter Kalhammer, who was no longer alive when I began research; I learned of his reaction from my interviews with his brother Fritz Kalhammer and his sister Ursula Schmid.

22 Jon Cook's note, the *AN* proofs and Michael Hamburger's letter are in the DLA. Michael saw it on WGS's desk, unopened, after the funeral (*Irish Pages*, p. 130).

   For WGS's horoscope (Taurus, April 21–May 21), see 'Your horoscope', *EDP*, Friday 14 December 2001. All the other horoscopes apart from one also mention the eclipse. It was annular and took place during the day in North America, the evening and night UK time. (See https://en.wikipedia.org/wiki/Solar_eclipse_of_December_14_2001 and http://www.timeanddate.com/eclipse/solar/2001-december-14.)

23 Information in this paragraph from the inquest report, dated 15 May 2002. I thank the Norfolk coroner for making this available. The accident was accurately reported in the *EDP*, p. 1 and *Evening News*, p. 7, both Monday 17 December 2001. Mitchell Gaze, a director of M. Gaze, the company that owned the lorry, was also helpful.

24 In both the *EDP*, p. 1, and the *Evening News*, p. 7, Monday 17 December 2001.

25 Information from GAS and M.

26 Information from the inquest report. Like the accident, the inquest was correctly reported in the *EDP*, 16 May 2002, p. 49.
   The Norfolk coroner at the time, William Armstrong, and the pathologist who did the autopsy, Dr Danielle Peat, kindly answered my queries. Not surprisingly after nearly twenty years, neither remembered any details. But both recalled finding that the cardiac problem had caused the accident. (Dr Peat's email of 4 February 2020, Mr Armstrong's phone call of 6 February 2020.) I thank them both. Though the cardiac problem caused the accident, the coroner's certificate gave WGS's injuries as the cause of death and listed it as accidental death. These also appear on his death certificate (QJ/2002, District Norwich (639/1D), Reg. D33B, Entry No. 267). Already two days later Clive Scott, for example, thought it had been a heart attack (see Philippa Comber, *Ariadne's Thread*, Propolis, 2014, p. 189). But in his preface to the WGS Special Issue of *JES* 2011 (p. 201), RWS still mentioned the aneurysm idea, which was therefore repeated for some time. US also concludes (*E*, p. 33) that the heart attack occurred before the impact.

27 Information about WGS's funeral from my conversations with GAS, M, the Hamburgers and Stephen Watts. Also GT in the *France Culture* radio programme by Thomas Sipp, and Sarah Emily Miano, who visited the grave a few days later (*Grand Street, p.* 172).

28 Michael Hamburger, 'Redundant Epitaphs', *SM*, pp. 312–14.

29 WGS to ROP, 4 October 1973, in '*Tanti cordiali saluti, Max*', *Literaturen* 05, 2004, p. 49.

30 This paragraph is based on my conversations with GAS; and for WGS's attitude to suicide, on those with KV and Ralf Jeutter, and on JPT's interview with Thomas Honickel.
   Gundela Enzensberger (our interview of 20 February 2016) told me of her similar accident and what WGS had said.
   Peter Jordan also says that for WGS chance events were not coincidence but fate. (In his unpublished memoir, *An Afternoon at Fort IX*, p. 4.) So does US, in his radio essay, 'Teaching by Example', *The Essay*, Radio 3, 6 December 2011.

Select Bibliography

WORKS BY W. G. SEBALD

LITERARY

In German

Nach der Natur, Greno, 1988, Eichborn, 1989, Fischer paperback, 1995
Schwindel.Gefühle., Eichborn, 1990, Fischer paperback, 1994
Die Ausgewanderten, Eichborn, 1992, Fischer paperback, 1994
Die Ringe des Saturn, Eichborn, 1995, Fischer paperback, 1997
Logis in einem Landhaus, Hanser, 1998, Fischer paperback, 2000
Luftkrieg und Literatur, Hanser, 1999, Fischer paperback, 2001
Austerlitz, Hanser, 2001, Fischer paperback, 2003
Unerzählt, with Jan Peter Tripp, Hanser, 2003
Campo Santo, Hanser, 2003, Fischer paperback, 2006
Über das Land und das Wasser, ed. Sven Meyer, Hanser, 2008, Fischer
    paperback, 2012
'*Die hölzernen Engel von East Anglia*', *Die Zeit*, 26 July 1974, in *Saturn's
    Moons*, pp. 319–23
'*Leben Ws, Skizze einer möglichen Szenenreihe für einen nichtrealisierten Film*',
    Frankfurter Rundschau, Feuilleton, p. ZB 3, 22 April 1989, in *Saturn's
    Moons*, pp. 324–33
'*Jetzund kommt die Nacht herbey*,' W. G. Sebald Archive, Deutsches
    Literaturarchiv, Marbach
Zerstreute Reminiszenzen, Gedanken zur Eröffnung eines Stuttgarter Hauses, ed.
    Florian Höllerer, Ulrich Keicher, 2008

In English

The Emigrants, tr. Michael Hulse, Harvill, 1996, Vintage paperback, 2002
The Rings of Saturn, tr. Michael Hulse, Harvill, 1998, Vintage
    paperback, 2002
Vertigo, tr. Michael Hulse, Harvill, 1999, Vintage paperback, 2000
Austerlitz, tr. Anthea Bell, Hamish Hamilton, 2001, Penguin
    paperback, 2002
For Years Now, with Tess Jaray, Short Books, 2001
After Nature, tr. Michael Hamburger, Hamish Hamilton, 2002, Penguin
    paperback, 2003
On The Natural History of Destruction, tr. Anthea Bell, Hamish Hamilton,
    2003, Penguin paperback, 2004
Unrecounted, with Jan Peter Tripp, tr. Michael Hamburger, Hamish
    Hamilton 2004, Penguin paperback, 2005
Campo Santo, tr. Anthea Bell, Hamish Hamilton, 2005, Penguin
    paperback, 2006
Across the Land and the Water, tr. Iain Galbraith, Hamish Hamilton, 2011,
    Penguin paperback, 2012
A Place in the Country, tr. Jo Catling, Hamish Hamilton, 2013, Penguin
    paperback, 2014

ACADEMIC

In German

*Zu Carl Sternheim: Kritischer Versuch einer Orientierung über einen
    umstrittenen Autor* (*A critical attempt at an approach to a controversial
    author*), licence (BA) dissertation, University of Fribourg
*Carl Sternheim und Sein Werk in Verhältnis zur Ideologie der Spätbürgerlichen
    Zeit* (*Carl Sternheim and his Work in Relation to the Ideology of the Late-
    Bourgeois Era*), MA dissertation, University of Manchester
Carl Sternheim: Kritiker und Opfer der Wilhelminischen Ära (*Critic and Victim
    of the Wilhelmine Era*), Kohlhammer, 1969
Der Mythus der Zerstörung im Werk Döblins (*The Myth of Destruction in
    Döblin's Work*), Klett, 1980
Die Beschreibung des Unglücks (*The Description of Unhappiness*), Residenz
    Verlag, 1985, Fischer paperback, 1994
Unheimliche Heimat (*Unhomely Homeland*), Residenz Verlag, 1991, Fischer
    paperback, 1995

In English

'The Revival of Myth: A Study of Alfred Döblin's Novels', Ph.D. dissertation,
University of East Anglia

A Radical Stage: Theatre in Germany in the 1970s and 1980s (ed.), Berg, 1988

ARTICLES BY W. G. SEBALD

In German

'*Kleine Traverse: Über das poetische Werk des Alexander Hebrich*', *Manuskripte*
21, 1974; in *Beschreibung des Unglücks*, Residenz Verlag, 1985, Fischer
paperback, 1994

'*Die weisse Adlerfeder am Kopf: Versuch über Herbert Achternbusch*',
Manuskripte 23, 1983, pp. 75–9

'*Summa scientiae: System und Systemkritik bei Elias Canetti*', *Literatur und
Kritik*, 18, September–October 1983; in *Beschreibung des Unglücks*

'*Preussische Perversionen: Anmerkungen zum Thema Literatur und Gewalt,
ausgehend vom Frühwerk Alfred Döblins*', paper given at the international
Döblin colloquium, Freiburg, 1983 in Werner Stauffacher, ed.,
Internationale Alfred Döblin–Colloquien, Peter Lang, 1986, pp. 231–8

'*Mit den Augen des Nachtvogels: Über Jean Améry*', *Frankfurter Rundschau*,
2–3 January 1987; as 'Against the Irreversible: On Jean Améry' in *On the
Natural History of Destruction*, tr. Anthea Bell, Hamish Hamilton, 2003,
Penguin paperback, 2004

Kleine Vorrede zur Salzburger Ausstellung, Introduction to the catalogue of
an Anita Albus exhibition, Salzburg, 2 August–30 September 1990, ed.
Tugomir Luksic

'*Ich möchte zu ihnen hinabsteigen und finde den Weg nicht: zu den Romanen
Jurek Beckers*', *Sinn und Form*, 62.2, March 2010, pp. 226–34

'*Das Häschens Kind, der kleine Has: Über das Totemtier des Lyrikers Ernst
Herbeck*', *Frankfurter Allgemeine Zeitung*, 8 December 1992; in English
in *Campo Santo*, tr. Anthea Bell, Hamish Hamilton, 2005, Penguin
paperback, 2006, pp. 130–9

'Between the Devil and the Deep Blue Sea: Alfred Andersch', *Lettre
International* No. 20, Spring 1993; in English in *On The Natural History of
Destruction*, pp. 107–45

'*Ausgrabung der Vergangenheit*', a piece written in honour of Michael
Hamburger, in *Saturn's Moons*, p. 344

TRANSLATION BY W. G. SEBALD

Evans, Richard, *Sozialdemokratie und Frauenemanzipation im deutschen Kaiserreich*, J. H. W. Dietz Nachfolger, 1979, translated by W. G. Sebald

BOOKS ABOUT W. G. SEBALD

In German

Atze, Marcel, *Sebald in Freiburg*, No. 102 in the *Spuren* series, Deutsche Schillergesellschaft in Marbach, 2014

von Bülow, Ulrich, Heike Gfrereis and Ellen Strittmatter eds., *Wandernde Schatten, W. G. Sebalds Unterwelt*, Marbacher Kataloge 62, 2008

Fischer, Gerhard, ed., *W. G. Sebald: Schreiben ex-patria – Expatriate Writing*, Rodopi, 2009

Fuchs, Anne, *Die Schmerzenspuren der Geschichte: Zur Poetik der Erinnerung in W. G. Sebalds Prosa*, Böhlau, 2004

Gotterbarm, Mario, *Die Gewalt des Moralismus: Zum Verhältnis von Ethik und Ästhetik bei W. G. Sebald*, Wilhelm Fink, 2016

Heidelberger-Leonard, Irene and Tabah, Mireille, eds., *W. G. Sebald, Intertextualität und Topographie*, LIT Verlag Dr W. Hopf, 2008

Honickel, Thomas, *Curriculum Vitae: Die W. G. Sebald-Interviews (Curriculum Vitae: The W. G. Sebald Interviews)*, ed. Uwe Schütte und Kay Wolfinger, Band 1, Deutschen Sebald Gesellschaft Schriftenreihe (Vol. 1 in the German Sebald Society series), Königshausen & Neumann, 2021

Horn, Eva, Menke, Bettina and Menke, Christoph, eds., *Literatur als Philosophie – Philosophie als Literatur*, Wilhelm Fink paperback, 2005

Hutchinson, Ben, *W. G. Sebald: Die dialektische Imagination*, De Gruyter, 2009

Köpf, Gerhard, ed., *Mitteilungen über Max*, Verlag Karl Maria Laufen, 1998

Loquai, Franz, ed., *Porträt 7, W. G. Sebald*, Edition Isele, 1997

—, and Atze, Marcel, eds., *Sebald. Lektüren.*, Edition Isele, 2005

Öhlschläger, Claudia and Niehaus, Michael, eds., *W. G. Sebald: Politische Archäologie und melancholische Bastelei*, Erich Schmidt, 2006

—, *W.G. Sebald-Handbuch: Leben – Werk – Wirkung*, J. B. Metzler, 2017

Schley, Fridolin, *Kataloge der Wahrheit: zur Inszenierung von Autorschaft bei W. G. Sebald*, Wallstein, 2012

Schmucker, Peter, *Grenzübertretungen: Intertextualität im Werk von W. G. Sebald*, De Gruyter, 2012

Schütte, Uwe, *W. G. Sebald: Einführung ins Leben und Werk*, Vandenhoeck & Ruprecht, 2011

—, *Figurationen*, Edition Isele, 2014

—, *Interventionen*, Editionen Text + Kritik, 2014

—, ed. *Über Sebald*, De Gruyter, 2017

In English

Blackler, Deane, *Reading W. G. Sebald: Adventure and Disobedience*, Camden House, 2007

Catling, Jo and Hibbitt, Richard, *Saturn's Moons: W. G. Sebald – A Handbook*, Legenda, 2011

Clingman, Stephen, *The Grammar of Identity: Transnational Fiction and the Nature of the Boundary*, Oxford University Press, 2009

Comber, Philippa, *Ariadne's Thread: In Memory of W. G. Sebald*, Propolis, 2014

Cook, Jon, ed., *After Sebald*, Full Circle Editions with UEA, 2014

Denham, Scott and McCulloh, Mark, eds., *W. G. Sebald: History, Memory, Trauma*, De Gruyter, 2006

Finch, Helen, *Sebald's Bachelors*, Legenda, 2013

— and Wolff, Lynn L., *Witnessing, Memory, Poetics: H. G. Adler and W. G. Sebald*, Camden House, 2014

Fuchs, Anne and Long, J. J., eds., *W. G. Sebald and the Writing of History*, Königshausen & Neumann, 2007

Görner, Rudiger, ed., *The Anatomist of Melancholy*, Iudicum Verlag, 2003

Hutchins, Michael D., *Tikkun: W. G. Sebald's Melancholy Messianism*, Ph.D. submitted to the University of Cincinnati, 2011 https://etd.ohiolink.edu/!etd.send_file?accession=ucin1307321149&disposition=inline

Long, J. J., *W. G. Sebald: Image, Archive, Modernity*, Edinburgh University Press, 2007

— and Whitehead, Anne eds., *W. G. Sebald: A Critical Companion*, Edinburgh University Press, 2004

McCulloh, Mark, *Understanding W. G. Sebald*, University of South Carolina Press, 2003

Medin, Daniel, *Three Sons: Franz Kafka and the Fiction of J. M. Coetzee, Philip Roth, and W. G. Sebald*, Northwestern University Press, 2010

Patt, Lise with Dillbohner, Christel, eds., *Searching for Sebald, Photography after W. G. Sebald*, Institute of Cultural Enquiry, 2007

Santner, Eric, *On Creaturely Life: Rilke – Benjamin – Sebald*, University of Chicago Press, 2006

Schmitz, Helmut, *On Their Own Terms: the Legacy of National Socialism in post-1990 German Fiction*, University of Birmingham Press, 2004

Schütte, Uwe, *W. G. Sebald*, Writers and Their Work series, Northcote, 2018

Smith, Christopher, '*Max*': *W. G. Sebald as I Saw Him*, Solen Press, Norwich, 2007 (also in W. G. Sebald Special Issue, *Journal of European Studies*, Vol. 41, Nos 3–4, December 2011)

Wolff, Lynn L., *W. G. Sebald's Hybrid Poetics*, De Gruyter, 2014

Zisselsberger, Markus ed., *The Undiscover'd Country: W. G. Sebald and the Poetics of Travel*, Camden House, 2010

JOURNAL ISSUES ABOUT W. G. SEBALD

In German

Arnold, Heinz Ludwig, ed., *W. G. Sebald, Text + Kritik* 158, 2003

Krüger, Michael, ed., *W. G. Sebald zum Gedächtnis*, *Akzente* 50 (1), 2003

Vogel-Klein, Ruth, ed., '*W. G. Sebald: Memoires. Transferts. Images. Erinnerung. Übertragungen. Bilder*', *Recherches Germaniques*, Special Issue No. 2, 2005

Europe, revue littéraire mensuelle, No. 1009, May 2013: W. G. Sebald and Tomas Tranströmer

In English

Bush, Peter, ed., W. G. Sebald Memorial Issue, *In Other Words* 21, 2003

Dreyfus, Jean-Marc and Wolff, Janet, eds., *Traces, Memory and the Holocaust in the Writings of W. G. Sebald, Melilah, Manchester Journal of Jewish Studies*, Supplementary Vol. No. 2, Gorgias Press, 2012

Sheppard, Richard, ed., W. G. Sebald Special Issue, *Journal of European Studies*, Vol. 41, Nos 3–4, December 2011

ARTICLES ABOUT W. G. SEBALD

In German

Anderson, Mark, '*Wo die Schrecken der Kindheit verborgen sind: W. G. Sebalds Dilemma der zwei Väter*', *Literaturen* 7/8, 2006, pp. 32–9, http://www.wgsebald.de/vaeter.html

Bahners, Patrick, '*Magisch zieht des Dichters Grab Gedenkartikel an*', *Frankfurter Allgemeine Zeitung*, 26 September 2008

Gasseleder, Klaus, '*Erkundungen zum Prätext der Luisa-Lanzberg Geschichte aus W. G. Sebald: Die Ausgewanderten: Ein Bericht*', in Marcel Atze and Franz Loquai, eds., *Sebald.Lekturen*, 2005, pp. 157–75

Göpfert, Rebekkah, '*Susi Bechhöfer Fragt Zurück*', *Frankfurter Rundschau*, 15 March 2003

Isenschmid, Andreas, 'Melencolia', *Die Zeit*, 21 September 1990, in Franz Loquai, ed., *Porträt 7, W. G. Sebald*, 1997, pp. 70–4

Joch, Markus, '*4:2 für die Literaturpfaffen: W G Sebald's Angriffe auf Alfred Andersch und Jurek Becker*', in *Über Sebald*, ed. Schütte, pp. 227–49

Kehlmann, Daniel, '*Der Betriebsschaden*', *Frankfurter Allgemeine Zeitung Sonntag*, 15/16 October 2005

Radvan, Florian, '*Unterricht mit Zweifel*', in *Über Sebald*, ed. Schütte, De Gruyter, 2017, pp. 299–302

Schütte, Uwe, '*Mit dem Bulldozer durch die Literaturgeschichte: W. G. Sebald als Literaturkritiker und Germanist*', *Volltext* 4/2014, pp. 4–5

Stahlhut, Marco, '*Ist das jetzt eine zynische Bemerkung?*', *Frankfurter Allgemeine Zeitung*, 12 December 2016

Tabbert, Reinbert, '*Erinnerung an W. G. Sebald, einen Ausgewanderten aus dem Allgäu*', in *Literaturblatt für Baden und Württemberg*, 6/2002

—, 'Max in Manchester', *Akzente* 50 (1), February 2003; in Krüger, ed., *Akzente* 50 (1), 2003, *W. G. Sebald zum Gedächtnis*, pp. 21–30

—, '*Tanti cordiali saluti, Max*', *Literaturen* 05, 2004

—, '*Zur Sebald-Ausstellung*', Reutlingen, 8 June 2004

Vogel-Klein, Ruth, '*Ein Fleckerlteppich*', in *W. G. Sebald: Mémoire, Transferts, Images. Erinnerung. Übertragungen. Bilder.*, *Recherches Germaniques*, Special Issue No. 2, 2005

In English

Anderson, Mark, 'A Childhood in the Allgäu: Wertach, 1944–1952', Part I, Chapter 1 of *Saturn's Moons*, pp. 16–37

— 'Five Crucial Events in the Life of W. G. Sebald', *Kosmopolis*, 23 February 2015, http://kosmopolis.cccb.org/en/sebaldiana/post/cinc-esdeveniments-a-la-vida-de-w-g-sebald/

Baer, Elizabeth, 'W. G. Sebald's *Austerlitz*: Re-mediation as Restitution', in *Reworking the German Past: Adaptations in Film, the Arts and Popular Culture*, eds Susan Figge and Jenifer Ward, Boydell & Brewer, 2010, pp. 181–99

Bartsch, Scott, 'W. G. Sebald's "Prose Project": A Glimpse into the Potting Shed', in *Über Sebald*, ed. Schütte, pp. 99–134

Bechhöfer, Susi, 'Stripped of my tragic past by a bestselling author', *Sunday Times*, 30 June 2002

Bell, Anthea, 'Translating W. G. Sebald – With and Without the Author', in *Saturn's Moons*, Part I, Chapter 8, pp. 209–15

—, 'A Translator's View', *Five Dials* magazine, https://fivedials.com/fiction/a-translators-view/

Czerniawski, Adam, 'In memoriam Max Sebald (1944–2001)', in
    Czerniawski, Adam, *The Invention of Poetry*, Salt Publishing, 2005
Diski, Jenny, review of *Vertigo*, *London Review of Books*, 3 February 2000
Eder, Richard, 'Excavating a Life', *New York Times Book Review*, 28 October
    2001, https://www.nytimes.com/2001/10/28/books/excavating-a-life.html
Forster, Kurt W., 'Sebald's Burning Train Stations and Monstrous
    Courthouses', *Log*, Fall 2014, pp. 10–23
Franklin, Ruth, 'The Limits of Feeling', review of *Across the Land and
    the Water* in *New Republic*, 12 July 2012, https://newrepublic.com/
    article/104208/wg-sebald-iaian-galbraith-poetry
Frazer, Jenni, 'Susi Bechhöfer: Finding her own history', *Jewish Chronicle*, 21
    August 2017, https://www.thejc.com/susi-bechhofer-1.443118
Hamburger, Michael, 'Translator's Note' in *Unrecounted*, Hamish Hamilton,
    2004, pp. 1–9
Hulse, Michael, 'Englishing Max', in *Saturn's Moons*, Part I, Chapter 7,
    pp. 195–208
Jaray, Tess, 'A Mystery and a Confession', *Irish Pages*, 1.2, 2002–3, pp. 137–9
—, 'Two Pieces', in *After Sebald*, ed. Jon Cook, 2014
Jeutter, Ralf, 'Some Memories and Reflections: W. G. "Max" Sebald, Man
    and Writer', in *Über Sebald*, ed. Schütte, pp. 303–8
Jones, Rick, 'Out of the Twilight Zone', *Standpoint*, 24 October 2008,
    pp. 46–7, https://standpointmag.co.uk/issues/november-2008/
    out-of-the-twilight-zone-november/
Josipovici, Gabriel, review of *The Emigrants*, *The Jewish Quarterly*,
    Winter 1996/7
Modlinger, Martin, 'You can't change names and feel the same: The
    Kindertransport experience of Susi Bechhöfer in W. G. Sebald's
    Austerlitz', in *Yearbook of the Research Centre for German and Austrian
    Exile Studies*, 2012, Vol. 13, pp. 219–32
Mount, Ferdinand, 'A Master Shrouded by Mist', *Spectator*, 26 February
    2005, pp. 40–2
Ozick, Cynthia, review of *The Emigrants*, *The New Republic*, 16
    December 1996
Radvan, Florian, 'The Crystal Mountain of Memory: W. G. Sebald as
    University Teacher', in *Saturn's Moons*, Part I, Chapter 5, pp. 154–9
Schütte, Uwe, 'Against Germanistik: W. G. Sebald's Critical Essays', Part I,
    Chapter 6 of *Saturn's Moons*, pp. 161–82
—, 'Sebald vs Academia', *Journal of European Studies* 1–6, 2016, pp. 2–5
—, 'On W. G. Sebald's Radicalism', in *Sebaldiana*, 13 April
    2015 http://kosmopolis.cccb.org/en/sebaldiana/post/
    sobre-el-radicalismo-de-w-g-sebald/

Sheppard, Richard, 'Dexter-Sinister: some observations on decrypting the mors code in the work of W. G. Sebald', *Journal of European Studies*, Vol. 35, No. 4, 2005

—, 'Woods, trees and the spaces in between': A Report on Work published on W. G. Sebald, 2005–8, *Journal of European Studies*, Vol. 39, No. 1, March 2009

—, 'W. G. Sebald's Reception of Alfred Döblin' in *Alfred Döblin: Paradigms of Modernism*, ed. Steffan Davies and Ernest Schonfeld, De Gruyter, 2009

—, ed., W. G. Sebald Special Issue, *Journal of European Studies*, Vol. 41, Nos 3–4, December 2011

—, 'The Sternheim Years', Part I, Chapter 2 of *Saturn's Moons*, 2011

—, ed., 'Three Encounters with W. G. Sebald', *Journal of European Studies*, Vol. 44, No. 4, December 2014

—, Review of Philippa Comber, *Ariadne's Thread: In Memory of W. G. Sebald, Journal of European Studies*, 16 February 2015

Sontag, Susan, *Times Literary Supplement*, 29 November 1996

—, 'A Mind in Mourning', *Times Literary Supplement*, 15 February 2000, pp. 3–4 https://www.the-tls.co.uk/articles/public/mourning-sickness/

Stone, Will, talk given at 'Max: A Celebration', Wilton's Music Hall, 14 December 2011, unsourced copy

Strawson, Galen, 'Elias's Alias Implausible', *Financial Times*, 6 October 2001

Swainson, Bill, 'On editing translations', *In Other Words*, No. 48, November 2016

—, 'Excitement and Possibility' in *My BCLT: A celebration of 30 years of the British Centre for Literary Translation*, 30th Anniversary edition, edited by Duncan Large, Anna Goode and Johanne Elster Hanson (Norwich: BCLT, 2019)

Thirlwell, Adam, 'Kitsch and W. G. Sebald', *Areté*, No. 12, 2003, pp. 27–54

Tobler, Stefan, 'The portrait of the Sebaldian translator, preferably not a young man', in W. G. Sebald Memorial Issue, *In Other Words*, No. 21, 2003

Turner, Gordon, 'At the University: W. G. Sebald in the Classroom', Part I, Chapter 3 of *Saturn's Moons*

—, Obituary of Beryl Ranwell, *Guardian*, 1 July 2013

Watts, Jonathan P., 'Unreal Estate', *Irish Pages*, Vol. 7, No. 1, pp. 67–77

Watts, Stephen, 'Max Sebald: A Reminiscence', in *Saturn's Moons*, pp. 299–307

Williams, Luke, 'A Watch on Each Wrist: Twelve Seminars with W. G. Sebald', in Part I, Chapter 4 of *Saturn's Moons*

Wood, James, Introduction to *Austerlitz* by W. G. Sebald, Penguin
    Essentials, 2011
—, 'Reveries of a Solitary Walker', *Guardian*, 20 April 2013

COLLECTED INTERVIEWS WITH W. G. SEBALD

In German

Hoffmann, Torsten, ed., *Auf ungeheuer dünnem Eis*, Fischer paperback, 2015

In English

Schwartz, Lynne Sharon (ed.), *the emergence of memory, Conversations with
    W. G. SEBALD*, Seven Stories Press, 2007

OTHER INTERVIEWS

In German

I thank Torsten Hoffmann for sending me these.

Baltzer, Burkhard, '*Wir sprechen mit Winfried G. Sebald*', *Schwäbisches
    Tagblatt*, 15 November 1990
Boedeker, Sven, '*Mit dem Vokabular im Gepäck*', *Tagesspiel Berlin*, 11
    March 1993
Just, Renate, '*Stille Katastrophien*', *Süddeutsche Zeitung Magazin*, 5 October
    1990 (in Franz Loquai, *Porträt 7: W. G. Sebald*, 1997, pp. 25–31)
—, '*Im Zeichen des Saturn*', *Die Zeit Magazin*, 13 October 1995 (in *Ibid.*, pp.
    37–42)
Kospach, Julia, '*Der Spurensucher*', *Profil*, 19 February 2001
Kunisch, Hans-Peter, '*Die Melancholie des Widerstands*', *Süddeutsche Zeitung*,
    5 April 2001
Löffler, Sigrid, '*Kopfreisen in die Ferne*', *Süddeutsche Zeitung*, 4–5 February
    1995 (in Franz Loquai, ed., *Porträt 7, W. G. Sebald*, 1997, pp. 135–7)
Öhlen, Martin, '*Die Weltsicht ist verhangen*', *Kölner Stadt-Anzeiger*, 13 June 1997
Scheck, Denis, '*Ein Interview mit W. G. Sebald über Luftkrieg und Literatur*',
    Deutschland Radio Berlin, 26 January 1998 and *Basler Zeitung*, 6
    February 1998
Schröder, Lothar, '*Mitteilungen über Max*', *Rheinische Post*, 13 December 2000
Wittmann, Jochen, '*Ein Besuch bei W. G. Sebald*', *Stuttgarter Zeitung*, 27
    November 1997

In English

Alvarez, Maria, 'The Significant Mr Sebald', *Telegraph*, 24 September 2001

Atlas, James, 'W. G. Sebald: A Profile', *Paris Review* 151, Summer 1999, pp. 278–95

Bailey, Paul, 'Old Order Overthrown', *Daily Telegraph*, 6 June 1998

Baker, Kenneth, 'Up against historical amnesia', *San Francisco Chronicle*, 7 October 2001

Bigsby, Christopher, *Writers in Conversation with Christopher Bigsby*, Vol. 2, EAS Publishing, 2001, pp. 140–65

Cook, Jon, 'Lost in Translation?', 9 February 1999, in *Saturn's Moons*, pp. 356–63

Green, Toby, 'The Questionable Business of Writing', late 1999, in 'Three Encounters with W. G. Sebald', *Journal of European Studies*, Vol. 44, No. 4, December 2014

Houpt, Simon, 'Past Imperfect', *Toronto Globe and Mail*, 17 November 2001

Jaggi, Maya, 'Recovered Memories', *Guardian*, 22 September 2001

—, 'The Last Word', *Guardian*, 21 December 2001

Kafatou, Sarah, 'An Interview with W. G. Sebald', *Harvard Review*, No. 15, Fall 1998

McCrum, Robert, 'Characters, Plot, Dialogue? That's not really my style', *Observer Review*, 7 June 1998

de Moor, Piet, 'Echoes from the Past', *Knack* magazine, Brussels, 6 May 1992, in *Saturn's Moons*, pp. 350–4, tr. Reinier van Straten

Morgan, Peter, 'Living Among the English', 10 July 1998, *Planet* No. 158, pp. 13–18

Mühling, Jens, 'The Permanent Exile of W. G. Sebald', April 2000, *Pretext* 7, Spring–Summer 2003, p. 15–26 (on Terry Pitts' *Vertigo* website, https://sebald.wordpress.com/category/jens-muhling/)

Reynolds, Susan Salter, 'A Writer Who Challenges Traditional Storytelling', *Los Angeles Times*, 24 October 2001

Shakespeare, Sebastian, 'Sebastian Shakespeare Talks to W. G. Sebald', *Literary Review*, October 2001

Tonkin, Boyd, 'Swimming the Seas of Silence', *Independent*, 18 February 1998

Wasserman, Steve, 'In This Distant Place', 17 October 2001, in *Saturn's Moons*, pp. 364–75

Wood, James, 'An Interview with W. G. Sebald', *Brick* 59, 1998, pp. 23–9

Zeeman, Michael, '*Kamer met Uitsicht*', VPRO Netherlands, 12 July 1998, transcribed by Gordon Taylor, in Denham and McCulloh, *W. G. Sebald: History – Memory – Trauma*, De Gruyter 2006, pp. 21–9

In French

Devarrieux, Claire, '*Qu'est devenu Ernest?*', *Libération*, 7 January 1999
de Cortanze, Gérard, '*Le passé repoussé de l'Allemagne*', *Le Figaro Littéraire*, 14
    January 1999

In Dutch

Annette de Jong, 'W. *G. Sebald over joden, Duitsers en migranten*', *NRC
    Handelsblad*, 2 July 1993

In Spanish

Amat, Nuria, '*W. G. Sebald: Un Encuentro*', *ABC Cultural*, Madrid, No. 453,
    30 September 2000, https://nuriaamat.com/wp-content/uploads/2016/05/
    Sebald.-Entrevista-ABC-Cultural.pdf
Krauthausen, Ciro, '*Crecí in una familia postfascista alemana*', *Babelia*,
    suplemento del diario *El País*, 14 July 2001, https://elpais.com/
    cultura/2016/10/27/babelia/1477566485_771964.html

AUDIOVISUAL MATERIAL ON W. G. SEBALD

Audio material

Bookworm interview with Michael Silverblatt (in Schwartz, pp. 77–86)
    https://www.youtube.com/watch?v=lVssOL6olQ4
W. G. Sebald in conversation with Eleanor Wachtel', on CBC (Canada)
    https://www.cbc.ca/player/play/1809173571889
'Looking and Looking Away', *The Essay*, BBC Radio 3, 2011
1. 5 December 2011, Christopher Bigsby, 'Not Responsibility: Shame',
    https://www.bbc.co.uk/programmes/b017ssr3
2. 6 December 2011, Uwe Schütte, 'Teaching by Example', https://www.bbc.
    co.uk/programmes/b017t0t0
3. 7 December 2011, Anthea Bell, 'A Translator's View', https://www.bbc.
    co.uk/programmes/b017t1j6
4. 8 December 2011, George Szirtes, 'Sebald the Poet', https://www.bbc.
    co.uk/programmes/b017t2q9
5. 9 December 2011, Amanda Hopkinson, 'A History of Memory or a
    Memory of History?', https://www.bbc.co.uk/programmes/b017t37y
'W. G. Sebald', by Thomas Sipp, with Anthea Bell, Anne Beresford, Michael
    Hamburger, Ralf Jeutter, Ria Loohuizen and Gordon Turner, Radio
    France Culture, 22 June 2006 (CD in the UEA Audiovisual Archive,
    transcript kindly sent to me by Thomas Sipp)

'*Une vie, une oeuvre: W. G. Sebald*', Radio France Culture, 29 September 2009, http://www.franceculture.fr/emissions/une-vie-une-oeuvre/wg-seb ald-1944-2001-2012-09-29

Visual material

Freiburger Studentenzeitung, 1951–1972, CD produced by the Archiv Soziale Bewegungen (Archive of Social Movements) together with the Albert-Ludwigs University, 2012

W. G. Sebald at the 92nd Street Y, 15 October 2001, https://www.youtube.com/watch?v=ccMCGjWLlhY

J.J. Long, 'Austerlitz', SOURCE Photographic Review, https://www.youtube.com/watch?v=9mooMoJecKg

UEA AUDIOVISUAL ARCHIVE

There is a thorough bibliography of the material on and about WGS in the UEA Audiovisual Archive, compiled by Gordon Turner, in *Saturn's Moons*, pp. 581–90. Gordon Turner has brought this up to date (2019), and the result can be seen in the Audiovisual Archive, UEA. I have drawn mainly on the following:

Audio material

'*Carl Sternheim: Versuch eines Porträts*' ('Carl Sternheim: Attempt at a Portrait'): Discussion between Hellmuth Karasek, Jakob Knauss, Peter von Matt and WGS on Swiss Radio DRS II (Zurich), 11 February 1971

Jon Cook, Discussion with WGS, UEA 9 February 1999 (See 'Other Interviews', p. 591)

Christopher Bigsby, Conversation with WGS, UEA, 12 January 2001 (See 'Other Interviews', p. 591)

Will Self, 'Absent Jews and Invisible Executioners: W. G. Sebald and the Holocaust', recording of the Sebald Lecture 2010

Visual material

'Reiner Kunze spricht mit Max Sebald' ('Reiner Kunze speaks to Max Sebald'), VHS cassette, 1975

Literarisches Quartett, discussion of *Die Ausgewanderten* with Marcel Reich-Ranicki, Hellmuth Karasek, Sigrid Löffler and Barbara Sichtermann, 14 January 1993

Der Ausgewanderte, film written and directed by Thomas Honickel, 2007

The Emigrant, English version (subtitles by Gordon Turner)

Sebald. Orte., film written and directed by Thomas Honickel, 2007
Sebald. Places., English version (subtitles by Gordon Turner)
Patience (After Sebald), film by Grant Gee, 2012

OTHER BOOKS

In German

Andersch, Alfred, *Sansibar*, Fischer paperback, 1960
Aufsberg, Lala, *Historische Bilder aus dem Allgäu*, Hephaistos, 2010
Becker, Jurek, *Jakob der Lügner*, Suhrkamp paperback, 2002
Bogdal, Klaus-Michael and Müller, Oliver, eds., *Innovation und Modernisierung: Germanistik von 1965 bis 1980*, Synchron, 2005
Bröll, Leonhard and Wolfrum, Gerhard, *Sonthofen: Festbuch zur Stadt Erhebung*, Verlag J. Eberl, 1963
Fallmerayer, Jakob Philipp, *Fragmente aus dem Orient*, Bruckmann, 1963
Gebhardt, Thea, *Meine Kindheit*, unpublished memoir, in Sebald's archive, DLA
Haumann, Heiko and Schadek, Hans, eds., *Geschichte der Stadt Freiburg im Breisgau*, Vol. 3, Konrad Theiss, 1992
Häussermann, Ulrich, *Friedrich Hölderlin in Selbstzeugnissen und Bilddokumenten*, Rowohlt, 1961
Herbeck, Ernst, *Alexanders poetische Texte*, Deutscher Taschenbuch-Verlag, 1977
Klee, Ernst, *Das Personenlexikon zum Dritten Reich. Wer war was vor und nach 1945?*, Fischer, 2003
Knubben, Thomas, *Hölderlin: Eine Winterreise*, Klöpfer & Meyer Verlag, 2011
Medicus, Thomas, *Heimat: Eine Suche*, Rowohlt, 2014
Navratil, Leo, *Gespräche mit Schizophrenen*, Deutscher Taschenbuch-Verlag, 1983
Nedo, Michael and Ranchetti, Michele, *Ludwig Wittgenstein: Sein Leben in Bildern und Texten*, Suhrkamp, 1983
Nerlich, Michael, *Stendhal in Selbstzeugnissen und Bildokumenten*, Rowohlt, 1993
Patel, Angelika, *Geschichte des Marktes Oberstdorf, Band 5: Ein Dorf im Spiegel seiner Zeit, 1918–1952*, 2010
Schwanitz, Dietrich, *Der Campus*, Eichborn, 1995
Wagenbach, Kurt, *Franz Kafka in Selbstzeugnissen und Bilddokumenten*, Rowohlt, 1964 (English version *Kafka: A Life in Prague*, tr. Ewald Osers with Peter Lewis, Haus, 2011)

Walser, Robert, *Jakob von Gunten*, Suhrkamp paperback, 1985
—, *Der Räuber*, Suhrkamp paperback, 1986
Wünsche, Konrad, *Der Volksschullehrer Ludwig Wittgenstein*, Suhrkamp paperback, 1985

In English

Adler, Jeremy, *Franz Kafka*, Penguin Illustrated Lives, 2001
Adorno, Theodor, *Minima Moralia*, tr. E. F. N. Jephcott, Verso, 2005
Améry, Jean, *At the Mind's Limits*, tr. Sidney and Stella Rosenfeld, Schocken Books, 1986
Aubrey, John, *Brief Lives*, Clarendon Press, 1898
Baedeker, Karl, *SWITZERLAND, together with Chamonix and the Italian Lakes, Handbook for Travellers*, 27th revised edition, 1928
Barker, Francis, *The Tremulous Private Body, Essays on Subjection*, Methuen, 1984
Bartsch, Kurt and Melzer, Gerhard, eds., *TRANS-GARDE: Der Literatur der 'Grazer Gruppe'*, Literaturverlag Droschl, 1990
Bechhöfer, Susi, with Jeremy Josephs, *Rosa's Child*, I. B. Tauris, 1996
—, *Rosa*, Christians Aware, 2016
Bellow, Saul, *Herzog*, Penguin, 1965
Benjamin, Walter, *Illuminations*, Vintage paperback, 2015
—, *Reflections*, Schocken Books paperback, 2000
Bigsby, Christopher, *Remembering and Imagining the Holocaust*, Cambridge University Press, 2006
Büchner, Georg, *Lenz*, tr. Richard Sieburth, Archipelago Books, 2004
Butor, Michel, *Passing Time*, tr. Jean Stewart, Pariah Press, 2021
Canetti, Elias, *Kafka's Other Trial: The Letters to Felice*, Penguin Classics, 2012
Cohen, Stanley, *States of Denial: Knowing About Atrocities and Suffering*, Polity Press, 2001
Eliot, Valerie and Haffenden, John, eds., *The Letters of T. S. Eliot, Vol. 2: 1923–1925*, Yale University Press, 2011
Enright, D. J., *Memoirs of a Mendicant Professor*, Chatto & Windus, 1969
Friedländer, Saul, *Franz Kafka: The Poet of Shame and Guilt*, Yale University Press, 2013
—, *When Memory Comes*, Farrar, Straus & Giroux, 1979
Frisch, Max, *I'm Not Stiller*, Penguin Modern Classics, 1983
Hamburger, Michael, *String of Beginnings*, Skoob Seriph, 1991
—, tr., *Hölderlin, Poems and Fragments*, Carcanet paperback, 2004
Handke, Peter, *Repetition*, tr. Ralph Manheim, Minerva paperback, 1989

—, *The Goalie's Anxiety at the Penalty Kick*, tr. Michael Roloff, Farrar, Straus and Giroux paperback, 2007

Hanks, Patrick, ed., *Dictionary of American Family Names*, Oxford University Press, 2003

Hoffmann, E.T. A., *The Sandman*, tr. Peter Wortsmann, Penguin, 2016

Hofmannsthal, Hugo von, *Andreas*, tr. Marie D. Hottinger, Pushkin Press, 1998

—, *The Lord Chandos Letter*, NYRB Classics, 2005, http://www.jubilat.org/jubilat/archive/vol11/poem_10/

Hughes, Robert, *Frank Auerbach*, Thames & Hudson, 1990

Illies, Florian, *1913*

Jaray, Tess, *The Blue Cupboard*, Royal Academy of Arts, 2014

Jordan, Peter, *Time of Songs*, unpublished memoir

—, *An Afternoon at Fort IX*, 20 January 2006, unpublished memoir

Judt, Tony, *Postwar*, Heinemann, 2005

Kafka, Franz, *The Castle*, Penguin Classics, 2019

—, *The Hunter Gracchus*, https://www.kafka-online.info/the-hunter-gracchus.html

—, *Investigations of a Dog*, Penguin Classics, 2018

—, *Josephine the Singer*, https://www.kafka-online.info/josephine-the-songstress-or-the-mouse-folk.html

—, 'In the Attic', in *Abandoned Fragments: Unedited Works 1897–1917*, Sun Vision Press, 2012

Keller, Gottfried, *Green Henry*, tr. A. M. Holt, John Calder paperback, 1985

Lampert, Catherine, *Frank Auerbach: Speaking and Painting*, Thames & Hudson, 2015

Leverton, Bertha, ed., *I Came Alone, The Stories of the Kindertransport*, Book Guild, 1990

Lichtenstein, Rachel, *On Brick Lane*, Hamish Hamilton, 2007

Malcolm, Janet, *The Silent Woman*, Picador, 1994

McLean, Evalyn Walsh, *Father Struck It Rich*, FirstLight Publishing, 1966

Monk, Ray, *Wittgenstein*, Vintage paperback, 1991

Musil, Robert, *Young Törless*, Penguin Modern Classics, 2001

Nabokov, Vladimir, *Speak, Memory*, Penguin Modern Classics, 2000

Nossack, Hans Erich, *The End: Hamburg 1943*, tr. Joel Agee, Chicago University Press, 2003

Parry, Idris, *Speak Silence*, Carcanet, 1990

Patel, Angelika and Boyd, Julia, *A Village in the Third Reich*, Elliott and Thompson, to be published in 2022

Peacock, Ronald, *Hölderlin*, Methuen, 1938

Perec, Georges, *W or the Memory of Childhood*, tr. David Bellos, Harvill, 1996

Poli, Gabriella and Calcagno, Giorgio, *Echoes of a Lost Voice: Encounters with Primo Levi*, Vallentine Mitchell, 2018

Reich, Erich, *The Boy in the Statue*, i2i Publishing, 2017

Rowlands, David W. L., *Llanwddyn and Lake Vyrnwy*, Lake Vyrnwy Visitors' Centre

—, *The Policeman's Story*, St Wddyn's Parochial Church Council *Lake Vyrnwy*, Severn Trent Water

—, *24 Picture Postcards of Old Llanwddyn and the Building of the Vyrnwy Dam*, Proceeds to St Wddyn's Church

Sanderson, Michael, *The History of the University of East Anglia, Norwich*, Hambledon Continuum, 2002

Sciascia, Leonardo, *1912 + 1*, Carcanet, 1989

Sinclair, Iain, *The Last London*, Oneworld, 2017

Smith, James, *Shakespearian and other essays*, Cambridge University Press, 1974

Stendhal, *The Life of Henry Brulard*, tr. Jean Stewart and C. J. G. Knight, Penguin Classics, 1973

—, *Love*, tr. Gilbert and Suzanne Sale, Penguin Classics, 1975

Styron, William, *Darkness Visible*, Vintage paperback, 1992

Uffindell, Andrew, *The Nivelle Offensive and the Battle of the Aisne, 1917*, Pen & Sword Military, 2015

Watts, Stephen, *The Blue Bag*, Aark Arts, 2004

In French

Chateaubriand, François-René, *Itinéraire de Paris à Jérusalem*, 1811

—, *Mémoires d'Outre-Tombe*, 1848–50, https://www.ebooksgratuits.com/ ebooksfrance/chateaubriand_memoires_outre-tombe.pdf

Dousse, Michel and Fedrigo, Claudio, *Fribourg vu par les écrivains*, Bibliothèque cantonale et universitaire de Fribourg, 2015

Taine, Hippolyte, *Notes sur l'Angleterre*, Hachette, 1872, online edition https://archive.org/stream/notessurlangleto3taingoog?ref=ol#page/n15/ mode/2up

In Italian

Boneschi, Marta, *La donna segreta: Metilde Viscontini Dembowski*, Marsilio
    Editori, 2010

INTERNET SITES

In German

Christian Wirth's Sebald site: http://www.wgsebald.de
Deutsche Biographie: https://www.deutsche-biographie.de
Ernst Alker: http://homepages.uni-tuebingen.de/gerd.simon/ChrAlker.pdf
http://www.hls-dhs-dss.ch/textes/d/D42795.php *(Historisches Lexikon der
    Schweiz)*
Ernst Herbeck: https://biapsy.de/index.php/de/9-biographien-a-z/50-
    herbeck-ernst (*Biographisches Archiv der Psychiatrie*, by Robin Pape and
    Burkhart Brückner)
Literarisches Quartett: https://www.youtube.com/watch?v=Ip-oefN1dBo

In English

Terry Pitts' *Vertigo* site: https://sebald.wordpress.com/
Edwin Turner's biblioklept website (on *Lenz*): http://biblioklept.
    org/2013/06/13/the-never-ending-torture-of-unrest-georg-
    buchners-lenz-reviewed/
About Fribourg: https://www.myswitzerland.com/en-gb/freiburg.html,
    https://www.nytimes.com/1995/01/15/travel/layers-of-history-in-fribourg.
    html
James Smith: https://archiveshub.jisc.ac.uk/search/archives/e17d9faf-230b-
    3c42-b004-a2ed86d5f333 (Archives Hub)
Michel Butor: Catherine Annabel, 'Passing Time, an Archive for Michel
    Butor', https://cathannabel.blog/category/literature/michel-butor/ and
    https://cathannabel.blog/2016/07/01/this-new-hades/
W. G. Sebald: The Collected 'Maxims', collected by David Lambert and
    Robert McGill, *Five Dials*, 13 February 2009: https://fivedials.com/
    fiction/the-collected-maxims-of-w-g-sebald/
W. W. Norton, publisher of *The Emigrants*: https://www.wwnorton.co.uk/
    books/9780811226141-the-emigrants
Stephen Watts: The Gentle Author, https://spitalfieldslife.com/2010/11/30/
    stephen-watts-poet/

Simon Prosser, 'Compendium: An A to Z of W. G. Sebald', *Five Dials* 5, 2009: https://fivedials.com/fiction/z-w-g-sebald/

First paragraph of *Speak, Memory* by Vladimir Nabokov: http://thechaosofdeath.blogspot.co.uk/2009/04/first-paragraph-of-first-chapter-of.html

The Jewish Museum, Frankfurt, Genewein photographs exhibition: https://www.juedischesmuseum.de/en/explore/documents-and-photos/detail/colour-slides-from-the-german-ghetto-administration-in-lodz/

Sebald Ltd.: http://www.bizdb.co.uk/company/sebald-limited-03346713/

Wills registry: https://www.gov.uk/search-will-probate

In Dutch

Ria Loohuizen: http://www.avondlog.nl/tags/wgsebald

Picture Credits

Every effort has been made to trace copyright holders and to obtain their permission for the use of copyright material. The publisher would be glad, if notified, to rectify any errors or omissions in future editions of this book.

Part I, Chapter 1: W. G. Sebald
4 'One Jew fewer!' from *Geschichte des Marktes Oberstdorf, Band 5: Ein Dorf im Spiegel seiner Zeit 1918–1952*, 2010, courtesy Angelika Patel, © Gabriele Rieber
9 Georg and Rosa, Bamberg 1943, courtesy GAS
11 The family, 1947, courtesy GAS
13 Winfried with his grandfather, 1947/8, courtesy GAS

Part I, Chapter 2: Dr Henry Selwyn
23 Rhoades Buckton in Crete, 1970, courtesy Tessa Sinclair

Part II, Chapter 3: Wertach, 1944–52
31 Winfried on a hated Sunday walk, aged three, courtesy GAS
32 Perfect children, 1947/48, courtesy GAS
34 First day of school, courtesy GAS
34 First-year class, courtesy Irmgard (see Part II, Chapter 4)
38 The American visit, 1951, courtesy Suzanne Siegler
40 Les and Winfried, 1951, courtesy GAS

Part III, Chapter 7: 1956–61

116 Walter, Helmut and Winfried, c. 1958, © Rainer Galaske
117 Lotte at about fourteen, courtesy UL
118 Marie's grandfather's mill, courtesy M
119 Furious little Marie, courtesy M
121 Marie at fourteen, courtesy M
122 Winfried in Italy, 1959, courtesy JK
132 Winfried at around 17, © Rainer Galaske
135 Martine in the early 1960s, courtesy GAS

Part III, Chapter 8 1961–3

142 Helmut, Esche, Winfried, Ilse Hoffmann, early 1960s, © Rainer Galaske
147 Winfried riding, courtesy GAS
149 Winfried at around 17, courtesy GAS
151 Elizabeth Küsters, courtesy UL
155 Sebe and three girls, © Rainer Galaske

Part III, Chapter 9: Paul Bereyter

160 Nürnberg Racial Laws, courtesy Wikipedia
167 Sonthofen railway line, near Rieden, © the author
169 The Müller family, courtesy Ursula Rapp
170 Lu Moser, courtesy Peter Schaich
173 Jürgen Kaeser's railway drawing, 1953/4, courtesy JK, © the author

Part IV, Chapter 10: Freiburg, 1963–5

179 The Maximilianstrasse Studentenheim, courtesy of the Archiv Soziale Bewegungen, Freiburg im Breisgau
181 Maximilianheim signatures, 1965, courtesy Rolf Cyriax
182 *In the Zone*, 1964, courtesy Rolf Cyriax
183 *A Midsummer Night's Dream*, July 1964, courtesy Rolf Cyriax
190 Paolo, © Detlef von Berg, courtesy Thomas Bütow
191 Cocky, Albert and Paolo, © Etta Schwanitz
192 Paolo, Cocky and Etta, © Albrecht Rasche

198 Cocky, Etta, Albert and Paolo, © Albrecht Rasche
201 Cocky, 1964/5, © Albrecht Rasche

Part IV, Chapter 11: Fribourg, 1965–6
204 11, rue de Lausanne in 2017, © the author
205 Fribourg's lime tree, 1831, copyright © reserved
207 Solveig with Eustache-Moustache, 1966, courtesy GAS
209 Gertrud and Jean-Paul with Solveig, 1965, courtesy GAS

Part V, Chapter 13: Manchester, 1966–8
229 The Arosa Hotel, courtesy Richard Sheppard
231 25 Stockton Road, © Richard Hibbitt
233 12 Ferndene Road, © Richard Sheppard
238 26 Kingston Road today, © the author
239 ROP's Kempten Kalender for March 1967, © Reinbert Tabbert
240 Liston's Music Hall, © Reinbert Tabbert
244 Max as Holden Caulfield, © Reinbert Tabbert
246 Max, © Reinbert Tabbert
250 Max's fake Adorno footnote, © the author
253 Max at Kingston Road, © Reinbert Tabbert

Part V, Chapter 14 St Gallen and Manchester, 1968–70
255 The Rosenberg-Schule, St Gallen, courtesy Wikimedia CC
    BY-SA 3.0
260 German department meeting, University of Manchester, late
    1960s, © Wolf Dieter Ortmann
269 Peter Jordan, © Sophie Jordan, courtesy Dorothy Jordan
273 Worth School rugby team, 1963, courtesy Worth Society

Part V, Chapter 15: Max Ferber
282 Genewein's photo of the three weavers, courtesy of the US
    Holocaust Memorial Museum

Part VI, Chapter 16: 1970–6
310 The Goethe group, 1976, courtesy Wolf Dieter Ortmann
313 Max, 1976, © Manfried Wüst

Part VI, Chapter 17: 1977–88
324 Philippa Comber in Berlin, April 1982,
    courtesy Philippa Comber, © Irene Leverenz

Part VI, Chapter 18: 1989–96
336 Beryl Ranwell, © Ria Loohuizen
350 Typescript of the opening page of *The Rings of Saturn*, with
    Max's corrections, © the author
351 Typescript of *The Rings of Saturn*, with Beryl's corrections,
    © the author
353 Beryl's kitchen table, © Sally Humpston
357 Typescript of page 1 of 'Paul Bereyter', with Beryl's corrections,
    © the author
358 Typescript of page 1 of 'Paul Beryeter', with Max's corrections,
    © the author

Part VI, Chapter 19: 1997–2001
365 Stephen Watts, © the author
368 Michael Hamburger, Sueddeutsche Zeitung Photo / Alamy
    Stock Photo
372 Max in front of Tess Jaray's work, © Tess Jaray

Part VI, Chapter 20: Marie
384 Dora, © akg-images / Archiv K. Wagenbach
390 'Les villages brûlent!', illustration by Marie's grandfather,
    courtesy M, © the author
391 Kassiber 11, courtesy M, © the author

Part VII, Chapter 22: *The Rings of Saturn*
410 Bridge over the River Blythe, old postcard

Part VII, Chapter 23: *Austerlitz*
414 'A street in Llanwddyn, now submerged': old postcard, from the
    album 'Lake Vyrnwy Photographs' / Fishing Street, Llanwddyn
    631961: © Edward Hubbard Collection / Coflein.gov.uk
419 The *Stolpersteine* to Rosa, Susi and Lotte, © Janne Weinzierl
425 The Kindertransport memorial at Liverpool Street Station,
    courtesy Wjh31/ Wikimedia CC BY 3.0

Part VII, Chapter 24: An Attempt at Restitution
427 *The Burning House*, courtesy Anita Albus

Index

A Note on the Author

Carole Angier is the author of *Jean Rhys* (Lives of Modern Women series), *Jean Rhys: Life & Work*, which won the Writer's Guild Award for Non-Fiction and was shortlisted for the Whitbread Prize, and *The Double Bond: Primo Levi, a Biography*. She is a Fellow of the Royal Society of Literature.

A Note on the Type

The text of this book is set in Adobe Garamond. It is one of several versions of Garamond based on the designs of Claude Garamond. It is thought that Garamond based his font on Bembo, cut in 1495 by Francesco Griffo in collaboration with the Italian printer Aldus Manutius. Garamond types were first used in books printed in Paris around 1532. Many of the present-day versions of this type are based on the *Typi Academiae* of Jean Jannon cut in Sedan in 1615.

Claude Garamond was born in Paris in 1480. He learned how to cut type from his father and by the age of fifteen he was able to fashion steel punches the size of a pica with great precision. At the age of sixty he was commissioned by King Francis I to design a Greek alphabet, and for this he was given the honourable title of royal type founder. He died in 1561.